We ain't what we ought to be,
We ain't what we want to be,
But thank God Almighty, we ain't
  what we used to be

  —An old slave's prayer
    often quoted by black protest leaders

We Ain't What We Ought To Be

THE BLACK FREEDOM STRUGGLE
FROM EMANCIPATION TO OBAMA

STEPHEN TUCK

The Belknap Press of Harvard University Press
Cambridge, Massachusetts
London, England
2010

Library of Congress Cataloging-in-Publication Data
Tuck, Stephen G. N.
We ain't what we ought to be : the black freedom struggle from emancipation to
Obama / Stephen Tuck.
    p.   cm.
Includes bibliographical references and index.
ISBN 978-0-674-03626-0 (alk. paper)
1. African Americans—Civil rights—History.   2. Social justice—United States—
History.   3. Civil rights movements—United States—History.   4. African
Americans—History—1863–1877.   5. African Americans—History—1877–1964.
6. African Americans—History—1964–   7. United States—Race relations.
I. Title.
E185.T797   2010
323.1196′073—dc22   2009035237TTo

For Molly, Anna, Sam, and Amy

Contents

"If there is no struggle, there is no progress . . . Power concedes nothing without a demand. It never did and it never will."

> —Frederick Douglass, runaway slave and
> leading nineteenth-century black spokesman

"We need power in order to demand respect."

> —Marcus Garvey, post–World War I
> black nationalist leader

"The first duty of any Negro leader is to give what direction he can by means of mobilizing the total power of the Negro in order that he may effectively wage war for complete economic, social and political equality and for first-class citizenship. I say power because in our American system power is the only thing that is respected."

> —A. Philip Randolph, New Deal and
> World War II–era labor leader

"When a people are mired in oppression . . . they realize deliverance only when they have accumulated the power to enforce change . . . The plantation and the ghetto were created by those who had power both to confine those who had no power and to perpetuate their powerlessness."

> —The Reverend Martin Luther King Jr., Civil Rights
> Movement leader

"White people will always take back a part of what is ours as long as they are strong enough to do it. When they are weakest, we suffer least."

> —Hannah Nelson, elderly piano teacher and
> former domestic worker, 1970s Harlem

Prologue

Think of the Civil Rights Movement, and we might think of great men, great marches, and great speeches. Take, for example, the well-publicized speech of a dynamic young minister and brilliant orator to a cheering crowd on a hot August day in a big northern city. He declared, "Liberty in this land must be more than a name." Then he outlined his dream: "I see the schools thrown open for the black child as for the white . . . I see everywhere respect for brains and worth, moral and material. I see everywhere the recognition of the . . . principle 'man is man and no man is more.'" And he was "full of hope" because "real freedom must come. No man or men can rewrite the decrees of God."[1]

The speaker was the Reverend William Howard Day, a prominent advocate of equal rights. The occasion was an Emancipation Day celebration in New York City, in 1865. Almost a hundred years later, on another balmy August day, to a larger crowd, the Reverend Martin Luther King Jr. delivered a rather better-known speech. "I have a dream that one day this nation will rise up and live out the true meaning of its creed . . . [that] little black boys and black girls will be able to join hands with little white boys and white girls as sisters and brothers . . . that one day 'the glory of the Lord shall be revealed' . . . This is our hope, and this is the faith that I go back to the South with."[2]

Two speeches, delivered a century apart, one by a northerner, the other by a southerner, expressing strikingly similar hopes. They remind us that the struggle of black Americans for meaningful freedom was not confined to the world-famous southern Civil Rights Movement of the 1960s. Indeed, that movement was not the climax of protest, nor even the prototype of African American protest in the United States. Rather, the struggle for full racial equality was fought—and needed to be fought—in many different ways and in all regions and in every generation from emancipation. In 1926 A. Philip Randolph wrote of the "unfinished task of emancipation."[3] That, in short, is what this book is about.

This book is intended to be an introduction for the general reader as well as an interpretation for the specialist. Even the most general of general readers might not be surprised by the idea of a "long" Civil Rights Movement. But what may surprise is just how deep the roots of the movement were, and how enduring the subsequent protests. Measured by the size and influence of protest organizations, the 1960s was not the pinnacle "protest generation." The civil rights and Black Power organizations of that decade are more than matched in size and scope by the Union Leagues of freed slaves in the late 1860s, the Colored Farmers' Alliance of the 1880s, black women's clubs at the turn of the twentieth century, the black nationalist movement after World War I, the National Negro Congress for economic justice during the New Deal, the National Association for the Advancement of Colored People during World War II, and a host of race and human rights organizations at the end of the twentieth century. And these protest organizations were only one form of protest. Measured by the actions of individuals, it is impossible to pick a particular protest generation at all.

James Forman, a 1960s militant activist and one of the most thoughtful students of protest, believed that "our basic history is one of resistance."[4] There is a danger of romanticism here. There was no single river of protest, flowing ever more strongly toward triumph. Not all people resisted. Only some followed Forman's example of dedicating a whole life to the pursuit of racial justice. Still, Forman was right. There was resistance in each generation, through all the twists and turns of America's often tortured history of race relations.

Everyday people resisted as much as celebrated leaders. They did so in diverse ways: from a slave girl defiantly wearing her mistress's makeup on the eve of freedom to a grandmother in the 1990s who traveled to Japan to persuade directors of a multinational company to stop dumping toxic waste near her Louisiana home (they did). There was simply no such thing as a single black protest agenda. As the black anthropologist and novelist Zora Neale Hurston put it in her 1924 autobiography, *Dust Tracks on a Road,* "Anyone who purports to plead for 'what the Negro wants' is a liar and knows it. Negroes want a variety of things, and many of them diametrically opposed."[5] Different people gave freedom different meanings. So this book traces many human stories from across the country, and at times around the world. The picture that emerges is sometimes more of a vibrant collage than a neatly woven tapestry, because that is how it was. To illustrate the point, each chapter starts with a handful of diverse stories that introduce some of the key themes of protest for that period.

There was no such thing as a single black protest agenda because there was no such thing as a single black experience. African Americans had multiple identities: they were also men and women, young and old, healthy and ill, comfortable and poor, educated and illiterate, Christians and agnostics, urban and rural, light-skinned and dark-skinned, to name but a few. There was no such thing as a single black culture either, constructed as it was by many different people for different purposes. To be sure, white American thought often lumped black culture into a single dark form. But in so doing, it missed what the novelist Ralph Ellison called the "beautiful and confounding complexities of Afro-American culture," complexities that were present even at the seemingly blackest moments of black nationalism and black power.

Yet for all the diversity of protest, it makes sense to write a history of the black freedom struggle—not least because of discrimination and racism. In her 1956 autobiography, the race activist, feminist, and scholar Pauli Murray recalled movingly, "Race was the atmosphere one breathed from day to day, the pervasive irritant, the chronic allergy, the vague apprehension which made one uncomfortable and jumpy. We knew the race problem was like a deadly snake coiled and ready to strike, and one avoided its dangers only by never ending watchfulness." Of course, racism is based on false assumptions about racial characteristics. But it still mattered, and it matters today. As the oft-told, still painful joke puts it, the Ivy League black scholar who delivers an evening lecture on the social construction of race will nevertheless find it hard to get a cab driver to pick her up afterward. Every black American, wrote the great intellectual W. E. B. Du Bois in 1915, had to deal with the question, "How does it feel to be a problem?"[6] Even in the modern era, the legacies of slavery and segregation gave black families a shared history and shared experiences. This overwhelming sense, in each generation, of continued disadvantage is the reason for the title We Ain't What We Ought to Be—part of a former slave's prayer, repeated down the generations. The prayer ends, "But thank God Almighty, we ain't what we used to be," which also rightly conveys pride in progress.

The job of an interpretation is to draw out general themes from individual stories. As for what black Americans wanted, the most common call in every generation was for the full rights of manhood. Northern "free blacks" during the Civil War said not having the vote "insults our manhood";[7] the firebrand post–Civil War minister Henry McNeal Turner vowed to "hurl thunderbolts at [opponents] who would dare to cross the threshold of my manhood"; the last black congressman of the nineteenth century, George White, pleaded for "the same chance for" the Negro for "raising himself in the scales of manhood and womanhood";[8] one of the first four students who sat-in at a lunch counter in Greensboro in 1960 said, "I felt as though I had gained my manhood, [and] had developed quite a lot of respect for it";[9] the militant leader of 1960s protest in Cambridge, Maryland, Gloria Richardson, said, "We have nothing to gain from a peace with a system that makes us less than men."[10] Wrapped up in talk of manhood was the issue of men's rights as well as race rights. But as George White's inclusion of "and womanhood" suggests—as does the fact that Gloria Richardson spoke of manhood—it was also a more general call for full freedom of action regardless of color. It was a call for self-mastery, and, to quote White again, the "full exercise of citizenship."

Activists used a vast range of tactics to demand full exercise of citizenship. It is tempting to shoehorn these tactics into neat typologies, such as accommodation vs. confrontation, separation vs. integration, violence vs. nonviolence, race rights vs. human rights, reordering society vs. reconstructing it altogether. Such categorizations are useful, but in a long and broad overview they are too narrow. Local activists often favored armed self-defense *and* peaceful protest; they built up separate black institutions *in order to* force integration of the public sphere. Even the same tactic held different meanings in different contexts. A black voter in 1877 South Carolina took his life in his hands when he went to the polls. A century later, it involved no risk at all. Due to the diversity of protest, this book takes a broad definition of black activism; it explores the many ways black Americans sought to build their own world and resist those who interfered. It is a suitably capacious definition, since people can build, and resist, in different ways. Indeed, in times of harsh white supremacy, simply building families and communities was a form of resistance. Seeing protest as building as well as resisting is a reminder, too, that African American lives were defined not only in response to white supremacy. To quote Ralph Ellison again, "Can a people . . . live and develop for over three hundred years simply by *reacting*?"[11]

Still, looking at diverse protest in the long, broad view reveals connecting patterns and themes. And the major themes that emerge do far more than complicate the popular image of protest associated with the Civil Rights Movement. They flatly contradict it. Consider, for example, the following major themes.

Local, not just national. "The colored people have no national leaders," wrote a "Colored Man" to a Nashville paper in response to the National Conference of Colored Men in the city in 1879. Real leaders "are those who are directly located and associated with the colored people . . . All those fellows that lay around Washington . . . are frauds and false."[12]

Nearly a hundred years later, protest leaders in some cities—such as Savannah and Philadelphia—tried to prevent Martin Luther King Jr. from coming to speak and stealing their thunder. More often than not, activists' goals were entirely local.

The key to the story is how local struggles influenced, and were influenced by, broader changes. Local activists connected with the region, the nation, and abroad—through organizations, through news, through family networks. Local activists, from runaway slaves to anti-apartheid campaigners, forced national leaders to act. In turn, the action of national protest leaders and the federal government affected what local activists were able to do—at times constraining them, at times empowering them.

American, not just southern. Race discrimination and segregation in the North and West was as far-reaching, state-sanctioned, and at times as brutal as that in the South. After emancipation, former slaves in the South were able to vote before most black men in the free states could; at the turn of the twentieth century, black Americans were more likely to be lynched in Illinois than in South Carolina; at the end of the twentieth century, black children in northern cities were more likely to be in all-black schools than their southern counterparts.

As a result, protest movements in the North and West were as far-reaching as those in the South, too. To take but one example: when the glossy black magazine *Ebony* (which rarely did more than state the obvious in its brief news section) rounded up news stories for 1957, it paired the world-famous Little Rock, Arkansas, struggle to end school segregation in a joint article with the Levittown, Pennsylvania, struggle to end housing segregation. Pairing the protests in one story was entirely appropriate. Not only were there protests North and South, they were intertwined.

Violence, not just nonviolence. The history of American race relations is remarkably bloody—many thousands of black Americans have been murdered since emancipation because of their race. Black Americans often fought back—soldiers in the army, men and women on streets, youths in night clubs, workers during strikes, and families defending homes. The young Martin Luther King kept a gun in his house. What is striking, too, is the effectiveness of violence in the black community. Race riots forced concessions from the state at least as often as did nonviolent demonstrations. In 1967 the Black Power militant Lemuel Chester was accused of starting a fire that destroyed two blocks of downtown Cambridge, Maryland. The following year, city officials appointed him director of an expensive new community project.

Wartime, not just peacetime. The heyday of the Civil Rights Movement came in a time of prosperity and peace (or at least a cold rather than a hot war). But black activists found most opportunities, and made most progress, in times of war mobilization. The first presidential executive order in favor of African Americans—the Emancipation Proclamation— was issued in the midst of the Civil War. The second such order, which opened up the defense industry to black workers, was issued early in World War II.

In part, this came about because black American leaders used wartime service to cloak their demands in patriotism. But it would be wrong to overstate patriotism. Government intelligence surveys in Harlem during World War II suggested that only a minority of residents wanted America to beat Japan. As the writer J. Saunders Redding explained, "War had no heroic traditions for me. Wars were for white folks."[13] Rather, black Americans used their wartime power to demand progress. Their support was vital for the Union effort during the Civil War, and their potential to disrupt the war effort was vital during World War II. The longer term impact of war is another matter entirely, though. Wartime advances invariably met postwar backlash.

Secular, not just religious. Civil rights activists developed a powerful theology of liberation. Slaves understood freedom in millennial terms. The black church was the major institution free from white control, and churchwomen led reform programs. King was a committed Christian, while Malcolm X's worldview was shaped by Islam. The renowned Mississippi freedom fighter Fannie Lou Hamer told northern student activists, "Don't talk to me about atheism."[14] But there were plenty of nonbelievers on the side of civil rights (hence Hamer's rebuke to the students). The famous Freedom Ride of 1961 started with a moment of quiet reflection, not prayer. Many of the most prominent leaders of the early twentieth century were agnostics—often the only agnostic in their family. Their skepticism reflected their wider questioning of dominant forms of belief, including Christianity, which they believed held black Americans back from realizing their own identity.

Meanwhile, white supremacists also used theology and the church to aid their cause. To be sure, some changed their stance on race on account of their faith—and, significantly, when they did so, they always edged away from white supremacy. But if we listen to the voices of activists in moments of crisis, it sounded as though God was on both sides at the same time. (A personal aside here. When, as a naive young researcher I interviewed the former head of Georgia's Ku Klux Klan, I was surprised to meet not the ranting racist of stereotype but a reasoned segregationist who took his Bible seriously—seriously enough to refuse to sanction Klan violence, for which he had to leave the organization.)

Global, not just national. Imprisoned in South Africa's notorious Robben Island jail, Nelson Mandela heard reports of black American protests against apartheid. My "spirits were lifted," he explained later. "It was an impressive role for Black Americans to choose arrest."[15] Mandela's words are a reminder that struggles for racial justice were not bounded by national boundaries, not even by prison walls. Domestic struggles for meaningful freedom connected with anti-imperial, anti-racist, and human rights struggles abroad.

For people who were denied full citizenship, looking beyond the American nation made sense. Some connected the American struggle with the global human rights struggle; others used the global gaze to pressure American politicians to act. Some (especially in earlier times) believed black Americans would lead the redemption of colored peoples throughout the world. Others (especially in the 1960s) hoped black Americans could ride the coattails of anti-colonial struggles elsewhere. White politicians and business elites felt global pressures too—be it the insatiable demands of international cotton houses at the end of nineteenth century or the judgments of nonwhite nations, fanned by Soviet propaganda, at the height of the Cold War.

Economic rights, not just civil rights. When Civil War General William Sherman marched through Georgia, he heard former slaves call for forty acres and a mule long before he heard the call for a vote. When a World War II survey of African Americans in Memphis asked, "What do you feel worst about right now?" almost two thirds said low wages and employment discrimination; fewer than one in ten mentioned segregation or disfranchisement.[16] Of course seeking better jobs or civil rights was not a zero-sum game. Black voters could demand new labor laws; striking black workers could demand voting rights. Even so, for much of American history, the primary, everyday struggle for black Americans was for a decent livelihood.

Separation, as much as integration. One frustrated black activist told journalists that the Civil Rights Movement was not about wanting to hug a white person. (White supremacists worried they wanted rather more than a hug: as the black writer Sterling Brown put it after touring the World War II South, whites feared "the black herring of intermarriage.")[17] While some black Americans put social interaction high on their list of desirable outcomes, most did not. After freedom, former slaves chose black churches and black schools. Black nationalism resonated throughout American history, and many who weren't nationalists still accepted, or advocated, separate black institutions and community life.

Yet most activists wanted the right to integrate or intermarry, and they consistently opposed segregation. When NAACP leaders pushed to integrate education, they knew they were touching on the rawest nerve: mixing black boys and white girls. Integration, just for the sake of it, was rarely their prime goal. Rather, integration was a way to get equal resources and equal status in a society where forced segregation would always mean unequal.

Plenty of other patterns of protest emerge from a long, broad view of the U.S. struggle for racial equality. For example, activists were women, and workers, not just elite men; protest occurred for representation in popular culture, not just politics. What these patterns reveal is that the Civil Rights Movement of the King era was not the normative style of protest. There was a long freedom struggle, not a long Civil Rights Movement. The short Civil Rights Movement of the early 1960s was a distinctive, even exceptional, moment. But it was not "better" than what had preceded it, or what would follow.

Thus, a key question to ask about the Civil Rights Movement is why did it emerge in the unusual way that it did? Why was it seemingly so religious, so southern, and so nonviolent? Why did it stress civil and political rights above material or human rights? Why did the protest center on rights to consumption (at lunch counters, in schools, and on buses) rather than rights to production (in the workplace)? Why were its values so rooted in the American dream rather than international justice? Why were so many men rather than women at the forefront of protest, and why were they wearing suits rather than overalls? The answers to those questions reveal the limits of, and constraints upon, the Civil Rights Movement as much as its very real successes. The answers also lie, in part, on the media's rather one-dimensional portrayal of 1960s protest.

Looking at protest in the broader sweep also explains why particular types of protest prospered when they did. Black activists protested at particular times and in particular ways not just because they suddenly wanted to, but because they suddenly could—or at least had good reason to think they could. New tactics, new ideas, new outrages, and news of victories elsewhere all affected mobilization. But what mattered most at any given moment was not a fresh hankering for freedom—the hankering was always there—but a newfound power on the part of activists to demand it. Power prompted louder talk of freedom and allowed protest to grow and develop. For example, the two main moments of positive government intervention on behalf of black Americans—Reconstruction after the Civil War and the civil rights legislation in the 1960s—prompted a proliferation of local campaigns for racial equality. In turn, it was the new power that black Americans earned during the Civil War and World War II which enabled them to force the government to intervene in the first place.

Thus, the long history of the struggles of black Americans for meaningful freedom is a story of competing forces—between those seeking social justice and those defending white supremacy. The relative strength of these competing forces is the central organizing tension of this book. It was not a simple black vs. white story—plenty of dissenters can be found on both sides. And just as there was no single black community or activist agenda or community, there was no single white society or segregationist agenda, either. In the U.S. South at the end of the nineteenth century, white supremacy was about keeping African Americans in their subordinate place in society. In the big cities from the mid-twentieth century, the defense of white privilege was conducted in spatial terms, as ghettos became associated with crime and unemployment.[18] Whether the color line was a matter of place or space or both, different groups had different vested interests in preserving it.

Tracing the rise and fall of white supremacy and black activism shows that power (or weakness) was to be found in very many things other than just attitudes toward race. The list is virtually endless: the scope and outlook of the federal government, the union movement, or the women's movement; changes in partisan and municipal politics; the size of the federal bureaucracy; global pressures and global networks; wartime service and wartime needs; land ownership, employment, and consumer income; migration; theological, intellectual, and popular cultural ideas about race; education and literacy levels; urbanization and suburbanization; taxpayers' revolts; technological changes; and gun ownership, to name but a few. These interrelated shifts in power offered opportunities for activists on either side to take their stand.

In the case of the Civil Rights Movement, a focus on the increasing power of black activists goes against popular memory of brutal sheriffs attacking vulnerable protesters. But by this time, for a host of reasons, southern white segregationists had never been weaker, and in fact brutal sheriffs were thin on the ground. Meanwhile, local civil rights campaigns tended to flourish in those cities where large black communities had already built up economic strength and had elected more moderate officials. The black journalist Louis Martin rightly commented when covering the seminal Montgomery bus boycott: "The fact that the Reverend King preached non-violence and rightly warned against hating the white folks had nothing to do with the essential truth that the boycott was a power play. It forced the transit company to its knees."[19] But other forms of race privilege soon took on new power—such as calls for neighborhood schools in white suburbs.

Long after the Civil Rights Movement, and even longer after emancipation, the struggle for freedom and equality continues. The devastation of Hurricane Katrina and the election of Barack Obama signified the continued problems and promise for black Americans at the start of the twenty-first century. What is striking about recent protest is the extent to which hitherto muted (or rather, un-listened-to) African American groups have been able to make their voices heard—groups such as black feminists, black welfare recipients, black lesbian and gay groups, and black environmental activists. That they are still fighting for justice shows the very real problems they face today. That they are able to organize shows the very real gains won by others who went before them.

CHAPTER ONE

The Freedom War, 1861–1865

After the outbreak of the Civil War, Ellen, a house slave in Atlanta, began to use her mistress's toiletries. She continued to do so even after her owner, Samuel Richards, whipped her. Exasperated, Richards wrote in his diary, "I am disgusted with Negroes and feel inclined to sell what I have. I wish they were all back in Africa—or Yankee Land."[1]

Before sunrise in Charleston Harbor on May 13, 1862, Robert Smalls stoked the engine of the cotton steamer *The Planter*. The ship was part of the Confederate navy. Smalls, a 23-year-old father of two, was the slave assistant to the captain. He routinely woke early to prepare the ship. But this morning Smalls and his family sailed while the captain slumbered on shore. Smalls prayed for his nervous crew, "Like thou didst for the Israelites in Egypt, please stand guard over us and guide us to our promised land of freedom." Standing behind the wheel, Smalls dressed up as the captain, wore a large straw hat to hide his face, and answered Confederate checkpoints with the required steam whistle. Then he raised a white flag and headed toward the blockading Union fleet. "I don't know exactly what you are now," said an astonished Union captain, "but you're certainly not slaves, not after what you have gone through tonight for your freedom."[2]

Early in the war, the celebrated runaway slave Sojourner Truth addressed a pro-union meeting at a courthouse in Indiana. She dressed patriotically for the occasion, wearing a "red, white, and blue shawl, a sash and apron to match, a cap on my head with a star in front, and a star on each shoulder." She called on the federal government to arm black men, and said that if she were ten years younger than her sixty or so years, she would head to the battlefield herself. An antiwar mob then stormed the meeting. Truth was arrested for breaking an Indiana law that barred people of African descent from entering the state.[3]

"Mr. president . . . please let me know if we are free, and what I can do." Letter from Annie Davis, a slave, to President Abraham Lincoln, August 25, 1864[4]

During the summer of 1864, 144 delegates gathered in Syracuse, New York, for a national convention of "colored men." Fearful that Lincoln might not pursue permanent abolition, they warned the president, "You are sure of the enmity of the masters—make sure of the friendship of the slaves; for depend upon it, your Government cannot afford the enmity of both."[5]

On January 1, 1863, in the middle of the Civil War, President Abraham Lincoln issued an Emancipation Proclamation ordering that all slaves in the rebellious Confederate states "henceforward shall be free." At Tremont Temple Baptist Church in Boston, the internationally renowned runaway slave, orator, and abolitionist Frederick Douglass joined an all-day vigil waiting for news of the proclamation. Although Lincoln had promised to proclaim freedom on New Year's Day, some feared that he might make a last-minute deal with the southern states in return for peace. Six feet tall with flowing hair, the distinguished Douglass urged the nervous crowd to keep the faith. He saw God's hand behind the war as punishment for America's sin of slavery. Late in the evening, messengers arrived with the good news. "I never saw Joy before," Douglass remembered later. "Men, women, young and old, were up; hats and bonnets were in the air." After the initial tears and shouting, Douglass led the crowd in singing "Blow Ye the Trumpet Blow." At midnight, it was time to close Tremont Temple. Black members of the crowd headed on to Twelfth Baptist Church, the main black church in the city. Many were still singing and rejoicing when dawn broke.[6]

Right across the country, black Americans celebrated. In Washington, D.C., the Reverend Henry McNeal Turner, a dynamic young black pastor, waited eagerly at the telegraph exchange for a copy of the proclamation. Descended (some said) from an African king, Turner had spent the years before the Civil War preparing for missionary work in Africa. But with the coming of war, Turner saw exciting possibilities for black Americans. In 1862 he accepted the pastorate of Washington's largest black church. Waiting at the exchange that New Year's evening, Turner felt vindicated in his decision to stay in America. He grabbed the third copy of the Emancipation Proclamation off the press (the first two had ripped in the rush) and raced to his church. Out of breath, he handed his copy to a colleague to read out. "Men squealed, women fainted, dogs barked . . . cannons began to fire in the navy yard," Turner recalled later. "It was indeed a time of times, and a half time, nothing like it will ever be seen again in this life."[7]

Out West, the renowned black poet James Madison Bell, who had previously urged armed insurrection, wrote "A Fitting Time to Celebrate."[8] The most fitting place was the slave South. For many slaves, January 1 was usually a fraught time of the year, when brief Christmas festivities gave way to a new season of labor and perhaps separation from loved ones. Now, in the few areas where the Union army had gained a foothold, former slaves acclaimed the proclamation. In the Carolina Sea Islands, wrote one reporter, they celebrated "with all the zeal and animation which bright promises of freedom could inspire."

From the outset, though, bright promises of freedom ran up against dark realities of oppression. During celebrations in Union-occupied Key West, Florida, black men marched carrying the Stars and Stripes, women flanked them "dressed in their best attire," and children danced "in advance of and following the procession." But they were "pelted with stones on several parts of the route; basins of dirty water were emptied on their devoted heads; several were knocked down." The Union provost guard had to step in.[9] That summer in New York, white dockers lashed out against black workers after a new conscription law threatened to force them to fight in a war to free black slaves—at just the moment that shipping companies had used black laborers to undercut the dockers' strike. To cries of "No nigger at the North," mobs burned down a "colored orphanage," attacked white prostitutes who took in black men, and tortured and then hanged a black coachman called Abraham Franklin from a lamppost. Crowds applauded a sixteen-year-old white boy—too young to be conscripted—as he dragged Franklin's corpse by the genitals through the streets. "I'm glad I'm a widow," cried one black laundress. "Thank God my husband's dead. They cannot kill him."[10]

Even the proclamation had a worrying subtext. Lincoln made it clear —not once but twice—that he was proclaiming freedom only because of "military necessity." Two years into the war, Union troops were locked in stalemate with dogged Confederate armies. The proclamation was designed to tip the balance. As William Wells Brown, the foremost black historian of his day, wryly pointed out, "The advantages we have so far received have come as much through [Confederate President] Jeff Davis as through Abraham Lincoln."[11] Freedom was dependent on military victory. Yet there was no guarantee the proclamation would stand once "military necessity" was over. And even if emancipation did outlast the war, the proclamation offered the most limited view of freedom. It merely spoke of the end of slavery, not the introduction of positive rights.

Moreover, only a few thousand of America's four million slaves actually gained their freedom on January 1. The proclamation exempted the four loyal slaveholding states of Kentucky, Maryland, Missouri, and

Delaware and applied to only some Union-occupied parts of the Confederacy. Though the Union army was now—as worried Confederates put it—a "negro freeing machine," the proclamation bolstered the resolve of Confederate troops. Thus, most black Americans who joined proclamation parties had already gained their own freedom before January 1. Some were free before the Civil War—5 percent of black Americans lived outside the slave South, and a further 5 percent were "free blacks" living in the South. During the first two years of the war, thousands more slaves escaped to Union lines.

Thus those celebrating knew that the proclamation was not the end of the struggle for freedom. But if final freedom hadn't arrived, it seemed the clearest sign yet that freedom was coming. Black Christians had long anticipated God's deliverance from slavery at some time. The tide of events suggested that the time was at hand: the early nineteenth century had seen the end of the European slave trade, and the middle of the century saw revolution in Europe and emancipation in many countries in the Western Hemisphere.

Before the war, many black leaders had judged the Constitution inherently racist and had advocated emigration. Now, most saw a better future within America. The Civil War raised the prospect of a new social order, as it dramatically changed the balance of power between those seeking freedom and those who would deny it. Slaveowners were literally under attack. The travails of the Union army—"military necessity"—gave black Americans, even slaves, leverage over public opinion, the Union army, and the federal government as never before. The proclamation even called on former slaves to join the armed forces and navy. In doing so, the proclamation gave black Americans across the country new power, not just to demand a permanent freedom but to shape its meaning.

A Longer History of Struggle and White Supremacy

Black Americans' wartime struggle for freedom built on a long tradition of resistance to white supremacy. In the South, a few slaves fought, some ran away, many challenged their owners' dominance through subterfuge, and most sought to carve out as much space for their own lives as possible. How slaves responded to slavery varied from region to region, from master to master, and from year to year. But across the South, slaves developed networks of kin and a culture of survival. In the free states of the North, some aided runaway slaves, some black leaders joined the abolitionist cause, while others promoted emigration. In everyday life, black northerners appealed for their own civil rights, searched for a half-decent living, built community institutions, and defended themselves against attacks.

Free blacks also challenged presumptions of black inferiority. Sojourner Truth circulated photographic portraits of herself sitting in a dignified pose wearing fashionable clothes. Lecturers traced black culture to the glories of ancient Egypt. Black writers speculated on the links between the cruel behavior of white Americans and the barbarism of their Anglo-Saxon forbears. In inimitable style, Frederick Douglass lambasted white Americans to their faces. At one Independence Day gathering in 1852, Douglass thundered, "Your celebration is a sham; . . . your shout of liberty and equality . . . a thin veil to cover up crimes which would disgrace a nation of savages."[12] As for the idea of black inferiority, it was an "old dodge" that was simply "the needed apology for such enslavement."[13]

During the 1850s, though, freedom and equal rights seemed a distant dream. When the zeitgeist of revolution and emancipation raced across the world, it seemed to forget about the United States. Southern intellectuals and theologians mounted a forceful defense of slavery. To be sure, slaveowners in the Deep South (home to the majority of slaves) worried about the long-term future of slavery in the Upper South. But within the Deep South, slaveowners grew rich on a cotton boom. In Congress, southern politicians (partly out of their concern about the Upper South) forced through legislation providing for the return of runaway slaves and fought to reopen the slave trade and expand the reach of slavery out West. Meanwhile, in the *Dred Scott* decision of 1857, the Supreme Court permitted the spread of slavery and ruled that all people of African descent were not American citizens because the framers of the Constitution believed that blacks "had no rights which the white man was bound to respect."

For black Americans in the North, *Dred Scott* merely confirmed their own bitter experiences. As one black writer put it, "The slave bears the irons of slavery; the [free black] has been relieved from them, but, enclosed in the same dark dungeon . . . they are both prisoners."[14] Out West, the myth of the rugged individual finding his own way on the frontier might have suggested more fluid race relations. When California became a state in 1850, slavery was prohibited. But the four thousand black men and women who first settled there experienced a curious definition of freedom. The state legislature barred them from voting, serving on juries, testifying in court, homesteading, or marrying across the color line.[15]

In fact, the status of free blacks in the North deteriorated in the generation before the war. Consider the experience of black Philadelphians, the largest black community outside the South. In 1838 a group of "concerned" white Democrat voters launched an anti-black campaign after a closely contested election in which black voters almost swung the election. Propagandists screamed that Pennsylvania was fast becoming a "negro paradise." Runaways would come and take white men's jobs and marry white men's daughters. Such claims would remain the staple of anti-black campaigns for generations. In fact, white working-men's groups already excluded black rivals, and intermarriage in Pennsylvania was illegal. So campaigners pointed to "the high handed measure of negroes going to the election ARMED WITH LOADED GUNS . . . [we must] guard against a negro revolution."[16]

Black Philadelphians did indeed defend the right to vote with guns. But a revolution was hardly in the cards. In a published "Appeal of Forty Thousand" citizens, black leaders pointed out that "we are in too feeble a minority to cherish a mischievous ambition." They appealed to the American democratic principle "that all men are born equally free," and reminded Pennsylvanians that they too shed blood "to unite . . . TAXATION and REPRESENTATION." The problem was, though, that a mere forty thousand citizens were indeed too feeble a minority—barely 3 percent of the state—to stem the racist surge.[17] Pennsylvania disfranchised black voters, and by the time of war only one in fifteen black men in the North lived in a state where they could vote.

Faced by slavery in the South and legal discrimination elsewhere, black Americans lacked the resources to force change. Hence the importance of war to alter the balance of power. They did, though, have some significant allies, even at the height of slave power. Religious-based abolitionists raged against slavery. Many leaders of the early women's movement supported emancipation and welcomed black women, such as Sojourner Truth, into their ranks. Strident as they were, however, abolitionists and women activists were at the margins of political power in the early 1850s. Political developments changed that. The Republican Party emerged in and after 1854 in the North, in support of free labor and opposed to the expansion of slavery.

To the horror of proslavery Democrats, the Republican Abraham Lincoln, who personally opposed slavery, won the 1860 presidential election. In a series of famous debates with Democrat Stephen Douglas across Illinois in 1858, he called slavery a "monstrous injustice" and defended the "common right of humanity" as set out in the Declaration of Independence. He mocked Douglas's accusation that "because I do not want a negro woman for a slave I must necessarily want her for a wife. My understanding is that I can just let her alone. I am now in my fiftieth year, and I certainly never have had a black woman for either a slave or a wife." But faced with Douglas's charges of being an abolitionist, Lincoln insisted that he only stood against the expansion of slavery—a far cry from standing for freedom, let alone equality. Innate differences between the races were such that "there must be the position of superior and inferior, and I as much as any other man am in favor of having the superior position assigned to the white race." It was a point he made to a delegation of black leaders soon afterward.[18] It would take a war, and the initiative of many thousands of slaves, to challenge his outlook and embolden his politics.

The Coming of War, and the Coming of Freedom

In March 1861, as the clouds of war gathered, eight slaves escaped to Fort Pickens, a federal stronghold in Florida. According to the fort's commander, they presented themselves "entertaining the idea" that the troops "were placed here to protect them and grant them their freedom."[19] They were wrong: the commander turned them over to the local sheriff. But within two years, they would be proved right.

At 4:30 a.m. on April 12, a single mortar exploded above Fort Sumter in South Carolina, signaling the start of the Confederate bombardment of the federal garrison. Lincoln called for volunteers to put down the insurrection in order to save the Union of the South and North. But black Americans supported the war—as the Florida runaways showed—to dissolve the Union of slaves and masters. In normal circumstances—as the Florida runaways found out—what black Americans thought mattered little to the powers that be. But it soon became clear these weren't normal circumstances. Lincoln's promised quick war dragged on into the winter, with no end in sight. It would become the bloodiest war since the time of Napoleon. It would also become a war about the very idea of America.

Black Americans seized the moment. Runaway slaves offered northern troops their support, and in return demanded that the war for the Union become a war against slavery. As the most famous runaway of all, Robert Smalls, put it in a letter to the *Washington Republican,* "We wish to serve till the rebellion and slavery are alike crushed out forever."[20] Thus, runaways forced the question of freedom onto the agenda of Union officers and politicians. To a large extent, therefore, the Emancipation Proclamation did not initiate black freedom but responded to it.

At the start of the war, Union policy toward the "devilish nigger problem"—as one official put it—was to return all runaways. Lincoln needed to keep the loyal slave states loyal, and he clung to the belief that many southern slaveowners might switch to the Union cause. Many Union soldiers, imbued with notions of black inferiority, were only too happy to obey orders. Slaves shared horror stories of Union soldiers forcing runaways to dance at gunpoint, and of so-called liberators raping women in slave cabins, even in the presence of their families. (By contrast, there were very few reported rapes of southern white women.) One white soldier in South Carolina admitted, "I witnessed misdeeds that made me ashamed of America."[21] Yet slaves near the battlefront continued to run to freedom. In King William County, Virginia, nearly half the able-bodied male slaves escaped before emancipation was declared.

Runaways presented Union armies with a practical problem, but as the Union armies struggled, runaways also presented them with practical help. For one thing, they passed on local knowledge. Navy commanders prized the information that Robert Smalls gave them even more than the steamship that he delivered. Vincent Colyer, the superintendent of Negro affairs in New Bern, South Carolina, reckoned his "spies, scouts and guides . . . were invaluable and almost indispensable."[22] In June 1863 the former slave Harriet Tubman helped guide a raid along the Combahee River that freed over 750 slaves—no woman, black or white, had been so involved in army planning before. Tubman did not need Lincoln's Emancipation Proclamation to inspire her. Before the war, the gun-carrying, meticulously organized Tubman had rescued at least seventy friends and family. She remained skeptical of Lincoln throughout. But she was eager to take advantage of the fire power that the enemy of her enemy now provided.

Runaways also helped soldiers with the menial, yet essential tasks of war, such as cleaning camps, cooking, and finding firewood. In Richmond, one slave woman smuggled bread to Union prisoners of war: "She got in . . . through a hole under the jail-yard fence; knowing all the while she'd be shot, if caught at it."[23] Such actions did not suddenly transform soldiers into romantic dreamers of interracial harmony. But they did make some soldiers uncomfortable about returning runaways, to be beaten and put to work for the Confederate cause. In a sense, runaways forced northern soldiers to either oppose slavery or actively support it— just as civil rights demonstrations that provoked a violent backlash would later force white northerners to take sides on the question of southern segregation. "I don't care a damn for the darkies," said one soldier early in 1862, but "I'm blamed if I could . . . send a runaway back."[24]

News of slave support challenged public perceptions of slaves too. Robert Smalls' derring-do became something of a national sensation. The *New York Commercial Advertiser* made the obvious pun, "In spite of his name, he is no small man."[25] Many of the illustrated national papers carried pictures of him. (Later pictures suggest he soon became no small man in terms of his girth, too, no doubt due to the numerous banquets in his honor.) The widely circulated *Harper's Weekly* carried his picture alongside a report on "plucky Africans." One *New York Times* reporter thought Smalls a "fine looking negro," who "spoke with ease and self-possession."[26] Even across the Atlantic, the *London Times* reported that Smalls' expert analysis of Confederate defenses allowed the Union army to mount an assault on Charleston harbor.[27]

Such praise mattered because slaves were not supposed to be plucky, self-possessed, or intelligent. Scientists studied the evolutionary origins of the inferior "Negro." Popular entertainers simply mocked him. Crowds packed theaters to enjoy comedians in black face drink too much whiskey, talk like buffoons, steal compulsively, and sing merrily. Little wonder that proud black northerners were quick to acclaim Smalls' heroics. At one mass gathering, a skeptical onlooker told one of Smalls' admirers, "Smalls ain't God." "That's true," replied the admirer, "but Smalls's young yet."[28] Indeed, during the war, some Republican newspapers began to speak of Confederate prisoners, rather than former slaves, as "deplorably ignorant," and hailed the potential of slaves.[29] The same week that Smalls escaped, the abolitionist journal *The Liberator* told the story of one runaway who, when given money for supper by an officer, skipped the meal and bought a spelling book. One week later, "He is now master of his letters."[30]

Slave support for the war mattered, too, because Union policymakers acknowledged the runaways' demands. Most Union generals had little interest in delivering freedom. But where the army went was where the slaves freed themselves. So most generals calculated that declaring runaways as contraband of war—no longer the possession of their former masters—would aid the fight. Meanwhile in Congress, radical Republicans who advocated emancipation trumpeted the sacrifice of former slaves. Less than a week after Smalls' escape, the Senate passed a bill awarding him half the value of his ship, *The Planter*. The Senate immediately went on to discuss a controversial Confiscation Act that would grant freedom to all runaway slaves of rebels. With the example of Smalls fresh in their minds, senators supported the bill.[31]

The turn of events also enabled Lincoln to declare emancipation. In private he became committed to abolition—as early as September 1862 he told his Cabinet that he had made a pact with God to pursue emancipation, because "God has decided this question in favor of the slaves."[32] But in public, the politician in him initially urged caution. When his first secretary of war suggested arming runaways at the end of 1861, Lincoln dispatched him to Russia as his minister there. He revoked most of his generals' declarations of freedom, out of fear of provoking northern opinion as well as loyal slaveholders. He also recognized that the Supreme Court would be all too likely to invalidate a sweeping Emancipation Proclamation. Like most Republicans, Lincoln's answer to the slave problem was voluntary emancipation, with compensation for former masters and the colonization of former slaves abroad. His first draft of the proclamation, and his December 1862 message to Congress on the matter, spoke of both.

The patriotism of slaves, the actions of his officers, and the course of the war convinced Lincoln that it was time to act. As he famously put it, "I claim not to have controlled events, but confess plainly that events have controlled me." (Even this supposed confession was classic Lincoln political spin. Lincoln hid behind the surging tide of events to undercut opposition from loyal slaveholders.) Perhaps he worried, too, that unless he offered runaways their freedom, they might choose violence. In a global context, Lincoln hoped that anti-slavery sentiment in Britain would counteract the pro-Confederate cotton lobby there. (In fact, the proclamation stirred support for the South, but not enough to provoke British intervention.)[33]

Two weeks after Smalls' escape, Lincoln signed the Confiscation Act. By the summer, he had begun drafting the Emancipation Proclamation. In a nod to the Supreme Court, the proclamation applied only to areas in rebellion and—to reassure loyal slaveholders (and, maybe, himself)—urged free slaves to abstain from violence. Despite the proclamation's caveats and qualifications, Smalls must have been delighted. The final draft made no mention of colonization or compensation for slaveowners, and it authorized former slaves to join the war effort.

Winning the Fight and the Right to Fight as Equals

Lincoln presumed runaway slaves would join the war as laborers. But runaway slaves demanded that they join as soldiers. All sides recognized that putting black men in blue uniforms would be the most radical act of what was fast becoming a race revolution. Northern state militias had been lily-white since the end of the eighteenth century. But the runaway who had so recently suffered a whip on his back was keen to get a bayonet in his hands. Runaways behind Union lines in North Carolina started drilling early in 1862. Black leaders in the North called for black enlistment, fully aware of the wider implications for the freedom struggle. As Frederick Douglass put it, let a black man "get an eagle on his button and a musket on his shoulders . . . and there is no power on earth which can deny that he has earned the right to citizenship."[34]

It was precisely such logic that worried some Republicans almost as much as Confederates. Many Union generals also assumed that black men would lack the courage and discipline to fight, and that white soldiers would refuse to fight with them. But the needs of war allowed black Americans to force their case. Some officers armed former slaves to defend contraband camps before the Emancipation Proclamation. At the request of two generals, Robert Smalls visited Abraham Lincoln on August 20, 1862, to press for runaway recruitment in the Carolinas. Shortly afterward, Lincoln agreed. Mounting white casualties on the battlefield alleviated northern concerns about black enlistment. After the passage of the unpopular Conscription Act early in 1863, many white northerners reckoned that black bodies could take Confederate bullets just as well as white bodies—especially now that the war was about slavery as well as the Union. Recruitment of black troops followed soon after.

For many black leaders, the invitation to fight was as important as the Emancipation Proclamation. Douglass and Turner started recruiting, but no one was more eager than Martin Delany, a rival to Frederick Douglass in his influence on midcentury black Americans. Like Douglass, Delany was a man of diverse talents—an African explorer, inventor, and physician, as well as a prominent orator, novelist, and political organizer. Unlike Douglass, Delany had seen no future for black Americans in the United States before the war. In 1854, the so-called "father of black nationalism" organized the first National Emigration Convention—the main antebellum challenge to black abolitionists. Now, he called on black men to stay and to fight. In February 1865 he even visited Lincoln to propose the formation of a black regiment led by black officers to march into the southern interior. According to Delany, Lincoln liked the idea, though it was too late in the war to be put into action, and handed him a card to present to the secretary of war: "Do not fail to have an interview with this most extraordinary and intelligent black man."[35]

Extraordinary and intelligent maybe, but Lincoln and his generals welcomed black men into the army as second-class soldiers only. They were paid barely half-wages, barred from being officers, and not recognized as prisoners of war. In April 1864 Confederate forces captured, then massacred, black soldiers at Fort Pillow in Tennessee. This was all the more shocking because the war, for the most part, was notable for the civility soldiers showed to white prisoners of war. Black soldiers demanded first-class status, on the grounds that the "ball does not miss the black man and strike the white."[36]

Again, the turmoil of war gave black Americans unprecedented power to press their case. When a northern recruiting agent, Edward Kinsley, headed to New Bern, North Carolina, in 1863, he expected hundreds of runaways—desperately poor, eager for revenge, wary of a Confederate fightback—to sign up. He was in for a shock. On the instruction of local black leader Abraham Galloway, virtually all runaways ignored him. Just twenty-six years old, Galloway was already a veteran of resistance. Born the son of a slave mother and wealthy white father, Galloway escaped bondage in 1857 by hiding among turpentine barrels on a cargo ship. He headed to Philadelphia, joined the abolitionist movement, and traveled to Canada and across the northern states before returning South during the war as a Union spy. With square shoulders, long wavy hair, and a gun at his hip, the swashbuckling Galloway probably swaggered through the contraband camps as he organized militias. Not a man prone to doubt, Galloway judged that he held the upper hand against Kinsley. He was right.

Galloway summoned Kinsley to a midnight meeting. When the recruiter arrived, someone blindfolded him and led him up some stairs. When the blindfold was taken off, Kinsley found himself in an attic room, "nearly filled with blacks . . . armed with revolvers." Galloway suggested to Kinsley that if he wanted black recruits, he should promise equal pay, equal provisions, and, if captured, recognition as prisoners of war. To help Kinsley make up his mind, Galloway held a revolver to his head. Kinsley agreed. Galloway then forced Kinsley to swear an oath. The next day, said Kinsley, "Blacks came to the recruiting station by [the] hundreds and a brigade was soon formed." More than five thousand runaways joined up at New Bern and became the core of the so-called African Brigade—the 35th, 36th, and 37th Regiments, United States Colored Troops.[37] Later that year, a grateful Union general, Edward Wild, helped Galloway smuggle his mother out of slavery to start a new life in Boston.

That a former slave had such influence over a Union official shows just how much leverage the war had given black soldiers. Galloway's bravado was part of a nationwide campaign for equal treatment. Many soldiers refused pay until they received equal compensation from the federal government. The 54th Massachusetts Volunteer Infantry, one of the first black units, even refused their governor's offer to top off their pay from state funds. Some threatened to mutiny. Douglass stopped recruiting.

In 1864, soon after Fort Pillow, Lincoln bowed to the pressure, by equalizing pay and vowing that Union troops would kill one Confederate prisoner of war for each black prisoner killed in the South. The army even appointed a handful of black officers. Henry Turner became the first black chaplain, and Martin Delany became the first black field officer. The secretary of war hinted to Frederick Douglass that he, too, would get a commission. (It never came.) Delany's appointment turned out to be the exception to the rule—virtually all black officers were chaplains. Still, Douglass resumed his recruiting. Black soldiers enlisted with gusto. Two of Frederick Douglass's sons signed up, as did Sojourner Truth's grandson. So did three quarters of eligible black men in the free states. As Union armies penetrated further south, runaway slaves soon outnumbered northern recruits. In total, some 185,000 black men fought in the Union army, and some 29,000 served in the navy.

Many former slaves signed up with a distinctly personal agenda. In the loyal slave states, military service was a way to win freedom—nearly one third of Kentucky's 100,000 slaves enlisted.[38] Some hoped to rescue loved ones. Others sought revenge. Black soldiers shouted "Remember Fort Pillow!" in the heat of battle. In the Carolinas, General Wild handed three former slave women their old master and a whip and allowed them to settle the score. More generally, though, black Americans signed up to defeat the system of slavery. Though black soldiers were not involved in combat during most of the decisive military battles of 1863, the 54th Massachusetts led a valiant, if vain, attempt to storm Fort Wagner, South Carolina, in July, and black troops fought in the decisive breakthrough at Petersburg, Virginia, the following year. By the end of the war, black men in blue battled defenders of slavery in fifty-two military engagements. They paid in blood for the privilege. Three thousand black soldiers died from battlefield wounds, while 33,000 more died from disease.

As Union armies pushed further south in 1864, more slaves than ever ran behind Union lines. Even Jefferson Davis lost a butler and a coachman (who passed on information about war plans). By this time, whole families were escaping together. In the rural South, the well-established slave "grapevine" passed word when Union armies were nearby. Slaves understood full well what a seemingly loyal black pastor meant if he prayed that God would drive back the approaching Union forces. Slave flight dealt a double blow to the southern war effort. As they crossed Union lines, perhaps half a million former slaves stopped working for the Confederacy and started working for a Union victory. This forced Confederates to waste valuable time and resources moving slaves to the interior, away from places where they were most useful. Some lost peace of mind, too. The South Carolina planter Augustin Taveau had once believed that slaves were "content, happy, and attached to their masters." But "the conduct of the Negro in the late crisis of our affairs convinced me that we have all been laboring under a delusion."[39]

Whether black soldiers and runaway slaves decisively swung the war to the Union is impossible to judge. But they made victory sure, and they made it swifter. As the war turned against them, even Confederates recognized the fighting potential of their slaves. In March 1865 the Confederate Congress decided to arm slaves, offering them freedom for service. Abolitionists chuckled at the image of Jefferson Davis "kneeling at the feet of the Negro." One official noted in his private diary, it was a "desperate remedy" for a "very desperate case."[40] It was also too late. Between April and June, as the various Confederate armies surrendered to the Union and as black soldiers marched into Confederate cities, it was clear that the Confederacy had also surrendered the system of slavery. In Charleston, black women "mourners" followed behind a coffin bearing the motto "Slavery Is Dead" in a mock funeral procession.[41] Henry Turner thought white southerners were uncertain "as to whether they are actually in another world, or whether this one is turned wrong side out."[42] Black soldiers clarified matters by ransacking the homes of notoriously brutal masters, or occasionally tying a master backwards on a horse as part of the liberation celebrations.

Seeking Rights as Well as Freedom

Victory set the stage for freedom. As one runaway put it, "I knew we could never be free if the Confederates were victorious."[43] But long before the end of the war, black Americans, North and South, recognized that freedom alone would not be enough. From the outset, they sought to shape the meaning of freedom. Ironically, they were better placed to do so in the South, where they were still slaves, than in the North and West, where they were already free.

The war in the South opened up few opportunities for free blacks in the Union states. Runaways to the North found that racial discrimination remained rife. In 1864 Robert Smalls moved to Philadelphia while *The Planter* underwent repairs there. One day, he took a streetcar to the docks, and since it was raining, he tried to sit in the carriage. Following local segregation laws, the conductor forced him to stand outside on the platform. Smalls' companion, a white sailor, explained that Smalls was a war hero. "Company regulations," said the conductor. "We don't allow niggers to ride!"[44] Smalls walked the rest of the way.

If anything, the onset of war fanned racial prejudice. Word spread of a "black tide [of runaways] heading up the Mississippi."[45] Democrat Congressman Samuel "Sunset" Cox asked in 1862, "Is Ohio to be Africanized?" The specter of a black tide held real menace for white workers struggling to make a living during an economic downturn. In a well-circulated inflammatory address, Cox warned that returning white soldiers would find "negroes . . . filling their places, felling timber, plow-ing land." Little surprise, then, that white workers attacked their black rivals on Lake Erie and Ohio River docks soon afterward—as they did in New York, Detroit, Chicago, and Boston.[46] Northern Democrats played on racial fears, gaining congressional seats at the end of 1862 after Lincoln announced his intention to proclaim emancipation.

As the war progressed, the bravery of black soldiers—publicized widely by black speakers—challenged northern attitudes. Following one of the first black military engagements, Major General Nathaniel Banks—a Massachusetts Republican but no friend of radical abolitionists before the war—judged that "whatever doubt may have existed as to the efficiency" of black troops had been answered. "Their conduct was heroic. No troops could be more determined or more daring."[47] After Petersburg, Secretary of War Stanton agreed. "The forts they stormed were the worst of all." Attitudes mattered. In the American republican tradition, winning respect as men was a vital prerequisite to winning rights as citizens. But many attitudes didn't change. Union General Jacob Cox reckoned that "blacks make excellent troops [because] they are most easily ruled."[48] Meanwhile, condescending news stories—often from abolitionists—reported freed slaves childishly giggling when looking in a mirror for the first time, or of destitute runaways wandering aimlessly through contraband camps.[49]

Moreover, even the positive reports on black soldiers fueled white supremacist scaremongering. The cry of "intermixture" had long been a favored weapon in the Democratic arsenal. But as black men proved their manhood under fire, Democratic Party propagandists deployed "intermixture" as never before. They even coined a new word to describe interracial sex—a word that would be at the heart of supremacist rhetoric for generations to come: "miscegenation." At the end of 1863, two Democrat journalists published a sensational spoof consisting of a Republican tract that promoted miscegenation to erase the color line and bring "perfect peace."[50] By the time the tract was unveiled as a hoax nearly a year later, the damage was done. At a stroke, Democrats had encouraged white voters in the North to focus less on rebellious slaveowners and more on their own innocent daughters. By printing pamphlets with graphic images of white abolitionist women fawning over male former slaves, Democrats also played on male fears of women suffragists. The idea of forced miscegenation spoke to latent concerns about the centralizing power of the federal government, too. The election of 1864 seemed very much up for grabs.

The Democrat offensive over jobs and families showed that war strengthened northern white supremacists more than black activists.

Where they could, free blacks turned to the law. Early in 1865 the elderly Sojourner Truth had a Washington, D.C., streetcar conductor convicted of assault for pushing her onto the road. (Her shoulder would give her great pain throughout the winter.)[51] But as a tiny, relatively poor, discriminated-against minority (less than 2 percent of the northern population), free blacks had little power to do anything other than appeal for change.

Still, they appealed as never before. On the West Coast, black Californians organized a series of statewide Colored Conventions that called for legal and political equality, black rights to homesteading, and the hiring of forty thousand black workers to lay the transcontinental railroad. Some black leaders, including Frederick Douglass and Sojourner Truth, even gained a hearing with the president.

Black Americans deployed a wide range of arguments. The California Convention made an international appeal, flagging the prospect of trade with the "copper-colored nations of China and Japan" and expressing solidarity for the "oppressed of all nations" (including those, such as the Irish, who just happened to have major immigrant communities in America).[52] They trumpeted the patriotic contribution of black men and women. As a delegation from the Michigan State Equal Rights League asked their state legislature in 1865, "Are we good enough to use bullets, and not good enough to use ballots?" Some resorted to flattery. Truth publicly praised Lincoln for standing up to meet her and shaking her hand. "I never was treated with more kindness and cordiality than I was by that great man, Abraham Lincoln." According to her account, she praised him as "the best President ever," and he replied modestly that others, particularly George Washington, were just as good. According to Truth's white companion, however, the meeting was entirely different. Lincoln kept Truth waiting for more than three hours and called her "'Aunty' . . . as he would his washerwoman"; Truth did not praise him, and Lincoln mostly ignored her.[53]

In the face of Democratic propaganda and widespread prejudice, progress was anything but spectacular. No state introduced black voting during the war. But local agitation did win support from abolitionist allies in the Republican Party. State Senator Morrow Lowry of Pennsylvania sponsored a challenge to streetcar segregation. The ejection of Smalls was a timely gift for his argument. "I would rise," he told fellow senators, "and relinquish my seat in favor of him who performed so daring a deed for my country." Soon after the Emancipation Proclamation, California allowed black Americans to testify in court. San Francisco, New York City, and even the major Ohio cities desegregated their streetcars. Philadelphia followed suit a couple of years after the war. By war's end, only Indiana still barred black in-migration. Small as they were, these gains represented a significant change in direction after the increased repression of the previous decades. These gains also emboldened black Americans to push for more rights when the war was over.

While they struggled to win their own rights, black northerners also sought to provide resources for black southerners. Many runaways' first experience of freedom was hunger and disease in squalid contraband camps. Some runaways who worked as military laborers were still waiting for wages when the war ended. In his first tour of the North, Smalls raised money for former slaves back home. Black women in particular sought to meet the needs of runaway families and black soldiers. Sojourner Truth went from door to door in her Michigan hometown, raising money. In one oft-told incident, a white neighbor refused to donate and was rude about slaves. Truth asked his name. The neighbor was evasive: "I am the only son of my mother." Truth replied, "I am glad there are no more."[54]

The work of relief showed that even in an age when only men could vote, and even during a war that prized male heroism, black women also took a lead in organizing for the war effort, and black women helped to make freedom work. The national scope of the relief work is a reminder, too, that at the dawn of freedom the very different lives of southern slaves and free northerners became connected through organizations as well as sentiment and kin. Some organizations would be overtly political. Others, such as aid agencies, church outreach programs, women's clubs, and education societies, were not directly involved with voting and civil rights, but they provided the institutional base for black progress and politics through the Civil War and beyond.

Black women's relief associations often kept their distance from those organized by middle-class white women. Their work heralded the importance black Americans would attach to building their own separate institutions at the end of the war and for generations to come. To be sure, the opportunities of the war marked the end of the call for emigration and a separate black nation, at least for the time being. But many black leaders who now saw hope in America did not envisage a world of social integration. Far from it. Even Delany's commitment to the Union cause did not soften his distrust of white people. One anxious Union officer reckoned Delany was a "thorough hater of the white race."[55]

The relief effort also highlighted divisions among black Americans. When Truth scolded a group of former slaves in Virginia for living "off the government," they quickly threw her out of the building.[56] Not all relief work led to conflict. Many relief groups in the rural South resembled mutual aid societies among kinship networks. More generally, the Civil War saw a far more united approach—to use the war to win freedom and full rights—than the prewar decades. Nevertheless, disagreements between free blacks and newly escaped slaves were common. In Union army–occupied southern cities, the so-called "better classes" often recoiled in horror at the arrival of thousands of "riffraff" runaways. Such clashes set the stage for a long struggle within the black community over who had the right to speak for the race.

In any case, southern slaves did not need to be spoken for. To be sure, many runaways simply tried to survive—begging, sharing, foraging, or stealing as necessary. But slaves had developed a vision of freedom long before emancipation was in sight. And in the contraband camps, and on military bases, they swapped ideas and expanded their vision further. What they wanted was an end to the restrictions of slavery, full rights as citizens, and the means to build their lives and communities. And above all, they wanted land of their own. As Merrimon Howard, a former Mississippi slave put it, land would allow "the poor class to enjoy the sweet boon of freedom."[57]

Lincoln and his generals were willing to give slaves their freedom but were reluctant to let them enjoy the sweet boon. Liberated early in the war, with by far the highest proportion of black residents in America, the Carolina Sea Islands provided the best opportunity for wartime land redistribution. Former slaves quickly settled on the property their masters had abandoned. At the end of 1863, when Lincoln agreed that they could apply for forty-acre tracts, they applied "in mass." But then Lincoln revoked his decision, and only some slaves got land. Others were moved between islands or put to work with the army. One local official reported "almost unbearable" disappointment.[58] In December 1863, in a Proclamation of Amnesty and Reconstruction, Lincoln also promised the return of land to any white southerner who returned to the Union. The following year in Georgia, General Sherman cut a pontoon bridge and left a massive contraband camp of former slaves that was following him at the mercy of Confederate troops. Some runaways drowned as they tried to swim across the river.

On the Atlantic coast, as runaways continued to fill the contraband camps to overflowing, federal officers had to think again—even Sherman. After dark on Thursday, January 12, 1865, in Savannah, he met with a group of black men led by Garrison Frazier, an elderly Baptist minister. Desperate to be rid of his regiment's ever-lengthening black shadow, Sherman, a barnstorming Union general, sought advice from Frazier, a former slave in failing health. Frazier's solution lay in an expansive vision of freedom: "Placing us where we could reap the fruit of our own labor [and] take care of ourselves." A canny spokesman well abreast of national affairs, Frazier stressed that former slaves wanted to have land to assist the Union cause. Four days later, Sherman issued Special Field Order No. 15, setting apart coastal land from the Carolinas to Florida exclusively for former slaves. Sherman saw it as a temporary measure. Former slaves did not, with good reason. On February 2, in a packed black Baptist church in Savannah, the officer in charge of the land program, Major-General Rufus Saxton, interpreted Sherman's order to mean "all these beautiful, fruitful islands spoken of are yours." (Saxon even urged his hearers to take steps when marking out their tracts, to be sure to get more than forty acres.) By the end of the war, some twenty thousand of them—mostly women, children, and older men—had settled on a hundred thousand acres of former plantation land.

The Atlantic coast was a unique case because of the huge contraband camps there and the negligible number of remaining white planters. Elsewhere, Lincoln's officers leased occupied land to northern Republicans, or more often returned it to Confederates who swore an oath of loyalty. They urged former slaves to return to work as free men and women. Early in 1864, in Union-occupied Louisiana, Major General Nathaniel Banks ordered former slaves to take on binding annual contracts. Planters were to provide "just compensation to the Negroes." But Banks did not expect it to be "onerous," and he promised that "perfect subordination shall be enforced . . . by the officers of the government." Northern Democrats applauded. Radical Republicans complained. Black Americans despaired. Douglass reckoned the government was "practically re-establishing that hateful system in Louisiana."[59]

In due course, Douglass's fears would prove to be justified. But the limited nature of wartime reconstruction did not, in fact, doom postwar Reconstruction before it even started. Neither Sherman nor Banks were in the business of setting precedents for peacetime. Their policies were simply designed to win the war. And for the most part the new cash system, however flawed, was better than the old lash system.

The resulting struggle over wage work provided a first glimpse of the labor tensions that would last for generations in the rural South. Former slaves drew on old traditions of resistance as they exploited new opportunities of freedom. They sought good pay and working conditions. Where they received bad treatment, they performed poorly. One Union officer recognized it would be pointless trying to restore the old way of things, since there would be "trouble immediately—and the negroes band together, and lay down their own rules."[60] Former slaves appealed to Union troops, too. In response, early in 1864 the government promulgated clearer rules to protect black laborers.

Government officials expected clashes between former slaves and masters. What surprised them, however, were the clashes between former slaves and well-intentioned abolitionist overseers. Republicans cherished the idea of free labor—the right to earn reward for work (or face poverty for idleness). But former slaves saw freedom in terms of the right to grow the crops they wanted and the right to control their own time. When northern abolitionists first headed to the Carolina Sea Islands, bearing gifts, the freed slaves welcomed them. But when the black farmers refused to pick cotton, preferring to grow edible crops, the superintendent denied them rations. In some instances, slaves even returned across Union lines to their old masters.

As they sought land, former slaves also sought a voice in politics. Early in the war, runaways had engaged in the informal politics of slave days—sharing news, speaking to Union officers. With the coming of freedom, they were able to make their case more formally, and more powerfully. Garrison Frazier's delegation to General Sherman was a case in point. Some threw themselves into embryonic southern Republican politics. In May 1864 a South Carolina Union Convention "without distinction of race" chose Robert Smalls to be the first black Republican delegate to the upcoming national convention (though when the time came, he was too busy to go). Some wrote to the president. Self-assured as ever, Abraham Galloway challenged Lincoln in person. As part of a delegation of former slaves to the White House in the spring of 1864, Galloway urged the president to grant suffrage to all black Americans. Meanwhile, in Louisiana, leaders of the large free black community echoed their northern counterparts in appealing for the rights of citizenship on account of their loyalty.

Lincoln, and most Republicans, avoided the subject for the rest of the election year. Galloway publicly condemned him for it.[61] But black assertiveness in Republican affairs was a foretaste of postwar southern politics, and Lincoln's gradual acceptance of the inexorable logic of black suffrage—at least for black veterans and free blacks—was a foretaste of the postwar Republican response.

Well over three million slaves did not gain their freedom during the war. In many ways, their situation became harder. After the Emancipation Proclamation, slaveowners moved many slaves far away from the battlefront. Urban slaves—accustomed to some freedom of movement—faced curfews and travel restrictions. Paranoid southerners spread rumors of an impending slave rebellion. Southern men who were too old to fight Yankees trained their guns instead on potential troublemakers on the plantations. There was also the issue of protecting their women. With the young men away, said one Georgia slave mistress, "we fear the negroes now more than anything else."[62]

As the rumors suggest, though, slaves turned wartime turmoil to their advantage. One slave mistress in Savannah complained that the slaves "show a very different face from what they have heretofore." The issues might seem petty. "I was sorely tried with Fanny my cook," said one exasperated Georgian; "I make our coffee every morning and then find great difficulty in getting her to get our simple breakfast." But both slaves and their owners knew that authority, and ultimately loyalty, were at stake. Looking back on the war, one Atlanta slave mistress remembered Mary, a "faithful girl" who helped her board a carriage to escape the approaching Union troops. "To her surprise, [Mary] held back & said I am not going—an officer will come to take me; after awhile & he did."[63] Even on plantations deep in the Confederate heartland, slaveowners complained more than normal about insolence and indolence. The South Carolina planter John Henry Hammond thought "the roar of a single cannon of the Federals would make them frantic-savage cutthroats." The mutiny never came. It didn't need to. The fear of mutiny, and a slowdown in production, were sufficient to hinder the Confederate war effort.

Finalizing Freedom

On August 4, 1864, a group of anxious black leaders met in Boston's Twelfth Baptist Church. Their gloomy mood was a far cry from the celebrations in the very same church a year and a half earlier. Before, they had celebrated the coming of freedom; now, they wondered whether emancipation would outlast the war. Before, they had savored the prospect of black men joining the war effort; now, they bemoaned the awful casualties. Before, they had hailed Lincoln as the Great Emancipator; now, they deplored his hesitancy. William Wells Brown (a long-term critic of Lincoln) complained: "We have an imbecile administration." Before, they had faith in God's deliverance; now, some doubted whether God was on their side. If "God is managing the affairs of this nation," Brown continued, "he is making a miserable failure." One leader compared the plight of black Americans to that of Jacob in the Bible, who worked for seven years to win the hand of Laban's younger daughter Rachel, only to be tricked on the wedding night and end up with her older sister.[64]

Black leaders had good grounds to worry. During 1863, abolitionists had called on the federal government to pass a constitutional amendment to secure emancipation. That summer, the Women's National Loyal League had gathered nearly half a million signatures (the largest petition to date in American history) in support. At Lincoln's insistence, the Republican Party platform for the 1864 election had included an explicit call for an emancipation amendment. But as the election swung into view, a Republican retreat on the issue threatened to become a stampede. In July, Lincoln responded to a half-hearted Confederate peace initiative by writing an open letter welcoming "any proposition which embraces . . . the integrity of the whole Union, and the abandonment of slavery." Lincoln hoped the letter would call the Confederates' bluff and bolster Union support at a time when its armies were bogged down. It did the opposite. Lincoln's inclusion of emancipation as a precondition for peace set off an avalanche of criticism. The *Cincinnati Daily Enquirer* complained that "every soldier . . . that is killed, will lose his life not for the Union . . . but for the negro." Northern Democrats made hay out of the furor.

Thus, Republican politicians in the North quickly uncoupled the issues of peace and emancipation. Douglass complained that Republican orators treated "the Negro [as] the deformed child, which is put out of the room when company comes."[65] Some black leaders feared that Republicans might renege on their promise of freedom altogether. Secretary of State Seward declared the question of emancipation irrelevant to the question of peace, because at the end of the war slavery would "pass over to the . . . courts of law." With *Dred Scott* fresh in memory, this was a grave prospect indeed.

Hence the meeting in Boston's Twelfth Baptist Church. There, black leaders decided to call a national convention of "colored men"—the first such convention in nine years. One hundred and forty-four delegates from eighteen states (half from Pennsylvania and New York) gathered at Syracuse, New York, early in October. They discussed their hopes and fears, and issued a "Declaration of Wrongs and Rights." They called for decent wages, a "fair share" of lands for freed slaves, and the "full measure of citizenship." They called on black Americans to embrace unity and "sound morality." They endorsed Lincoln as the only remaining candidate who supported abolition. And they formed a National Equal Rights League to press their claims in the future. But their main purpose was to influence wavering Republican allies in the present—which partly explains the very public emphasis on black morality. The convention printed ten thousand copies of Frederick Douglass's closing "Address to the People of the United States."

Everything was at stake, Douglass explained. "Our possible future . . . may bring to us all the blessings of equal liberty, or all the woes of slavery

and continued social degradation." Douglass insisted, "We shall speak
. . . for our race . . . but we speak not the less for our country" (a tactic
that Martin Luther King Jr. would later follow when he said the Civil
Rights Movement sought to "redeem the soul of America"). He pleaded
with sympathetic Republicans to stand firm, because "our cause may suffer even more from the injudicious concessions and weakness of our
friends, than from the machinations and power of our enemies." He
pointed unsympathetic Republicans to the shared enemy, the despicable
Democrats. He also called for the vote. Black men deserved it for their
military service, and they needed it to protect their freedom. "We don't
want to be mobbed from our work, or insulted with impunity at every
corner. We are men, and want to be as free . . . as other men."[66]

Douglass and his followers then backed out of the election to deprive
Democrats of the charge that the Republicans were the "nigger party."
Even so, black men remained central to the campaign, since Democrats
charged job rivalries and miscegenation instead. Ironically, some Republican supporters of an amendment invoked the same fears, arguing
that emancipation would keep former slaves from fleeing the South and
would stop slaveowners from taking slave mistresses. But in the run-up
to the election, Republicans talked much of peace and very little of emancipation. Lincoln's silence on the subject was deafening.

In the end, military victories swung the election decisively to the Republicans. Atlanta fell, at long last, on September 2. So too did the Democrats' best chance of victory. Even then, there was the danger of a final
twist. As Sherman marched across Georgia, the end of the war was in
sight. And if the end was in sight, Lincoln's justification for emancipation—"military necessity"—would soon be a thing of the past.

As it turned out, Lincoln stuck to his principles, as he promised. He
proclaimed, disingenuously, the election result as "the voice of the people
now, for the first time, heard upon the question" of abolition. He called
for Congress to approve a Thirteenth Amendment that prohibited slavery
and granted Congress the power to enforce it. This was a radical proposal in more ways than one. It would be the first constitutional amendment of any kind in over sixty years, requiring legislators to see the
document as organic rather than fixed and infallible. It would also dramatically expand the reach of Congress and weaken the autonomy of individual states. (This was the first of many occasions that black actions
would ultimately lead to a rearrangement of governing authority.)

On January 31, 1865, Congress approved the Thirteenth Amendment
by the required two thirds majority with just two votes to spare and sent
it to the states for ratification. It was ratified at the end of the year. In the
House chamber galleries there was silence—then pandemonium. Black

observers were stunned by the excitement of white supporters. On March 3, Congress gave black Americans more good news—creating a Freedmen's Bureau within the War Department. Building on the work of freedmen's aid societies, the bureau promised to aid slaves in the transition to freedom. Black Americans fully expected to help run the bureau and use it to champion their demands for land. Douglass half-expected to be put in charge of it. The same day, Congress incorporated a Freedman's Bank to enable black veterans and former slaves to build their savings. A month later, there was still more good news—this time, from the battlefront. On April 9, General Robert E. Lee surrendered the Confederate Army of Northern Virginia to Union Lieutenant General Ulysses S. Grant. By June 23, every Confederate army had surrendered.

In one sense the passage of the Thirteenth Amendment, the establishment of the Freedmen's Bureau and Bank, and the Union victory provided a triumphant end to a fraught wartime struggle for freedom. But even at freedom's triumph, there were plenty of warning signs for the future. The Republican silence on emancipation late in 1864 meant that the election had been anything but a referendum on the issue. During the ratification process in the northern states, Republican legislators insisted that the amendment would not interfere with each state's power to regulate black rights. They certainly did not expect it to confer citizenship. Even Lincoln imagined only that "intelligent men" of the race (meaning formerly free blacks) and "those who serve our cause as soldiers" would gain the right to vote. As for the Freedmen's Bureau, many Republicans hoped it would keep freedmen working on the plantations.

Yet the final months of the wartime struggle for freedom also provided hope. Emancipation was secured, the Confederacy was defeated, and black Americans had proved adept in seizing the moment. Responding to the call of the Colored Convention, black leaders across the country organized local and state Equal Rights Leagues. In North Carolina, Abraham Galloway (who had attended the Syracuse meeting) organized a state chapter and five local chapters by January 1865. From Detroit to New Bern, local leagues petitioned their wartime state legislatures for civil and political rights.

In one sense this was the continuation of an old story. The local leagues were based on long-standing black institutions and community networks. In North Carolina, for example, Bishop J. J. Clinton headed a new league and presided over the state conference of the all-black African Methodist Episcopal Zion Church.[67] The war did not awaken black Americans to the idea of freedom or create in them the desire for freedom—it simply gave them new opportunities to demand it. The leagues also showed that radicalism on race was counterbalanced by conservatism in other areas—

the men who led them were often relatively prosperous former "free blacks" in the South or former abolitionist leaders in the North.

But the formation of these leagues represented a new story, too. They showed a new level of national connections among black Americans— only possible after the liberation of the South. They showed a new level of unity—gone were the rancorous antebellum splits between emigrationists and abolitionists. Now, leaders from Galloway to Douglass sought to force Republicans to follow through on the promise of war. As they did so, they faced a delicate problem—how hard to push their Republican allies and how conciliatory to be to their racist enemies. Even Martin Delany, denouncer in chief of white hypocrisy, cautioned former slaves to moderate their demands.

It would prove a hard argument to make. Black soldiers in particular felt entitled to be treated as equal citizens. As one black soldier put it, "I felt like a man with a uniform on and a gun in my hand."[68] This sense of entitlement fueled demands for meaningful freedom throughout the postwar Reconstruction period and beyond. It also led black veterans to embrace a version of freedom with men as head of the household, the spokesmen for (and voters from) the community. In some ways this might seem inevitable. It was, after all, the male-dominated version of freedom on offer in wartime. But it marked a departure from black women's centrality to slave resistance. Toward the end of the century, it would be challenged by black women in earnest after black men lost many of their rights in a white supremacist onslaught. That, though, was for the future. First was the pressing matter of the postwar Reconstruction.

Shortly before the war, during a speech in New York, Frederick Douglass had famously condemned reformers who urged persuasion rather than confrontation. "This struggle may be a moral one, or it may be a physical one, and it may be both moral and physical, but it must be a struggle. Power concedes nothing without a demand. It never did and it never will."[69] The war had proved him right. Emancipation was a moral issue. But freedom came because black Americans gained power as never before to demand freedom, while defenders of slavery had never been weaker. Moral arguments were one component of black power. But physical confrontations proved to be far more important—the massive numbers of slaves willing to run away, the contribution of black soldiers, and the defeat of the Confederacy.

Thus, the Civil War revealed, rather than created, the desire of slaves and free blacks for meaningful freedom. And the war gave them the power to help win freedom. Whether they would still have the power to win their expansive view of freedom during the postwar peace was another matter entirely. Douglass warned fellow abolitionists that "the work does not end with the abolition of slavery, but only begins." He wondered "what new form this old monster will assume, in what new skin this old snake will come forth."[70] Black leaders were not the only ones to hold their breath at the end of the war.[71] White men and women in the former slave states also worried what freedom might bring. One anxious white writer to the *Baltimore Gazette* complained that the federal government "armed negroes to the teeth" and warned, "If some steps are not taken to check [them], God only knows what will come next."[72]

ROBERT SMALLS, CAPTAIN OF THE GUN-BOAT "PLANTER."   THE GUN-BOAT "PLANTER," RUN OUT OF CHARLESTON, S. C., BY ROBERT SMALLS, MAY, 1862.

1. Many northern journals celebrated Robert Smalls' escape from Charleston by stealing the Confederate ship *The Planter*. (*Harper's Weekly*, June 14, 1862; Library of Congress)

2. As well as joining the army and acting as spies, African Americans—such as this African American cook with the Army of the Potomac—made a vital contribution to the war effort by performing numerous menial jobs. (Ohio Historical Society)

3. During the New York draft riots of 1863, at the height of the Civil War, northern mobs attacked African Americans. (*Illustrated London News*, August 8, 1863)

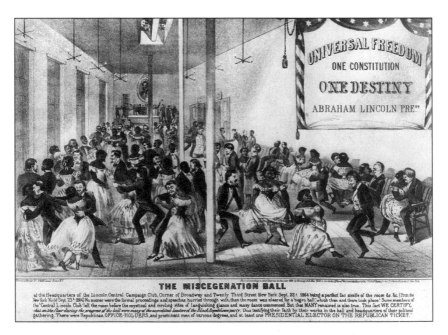

THE MISCEGENATION BALL

at the Headquarters of the Lincoln Central Campaign Club, Corner of Broadway and Twenty Third Street New York Sept. 22d 1864 being a perfect fac simile of the room &c. &c. (From the New York World Sept. 23d 1864) No sooner were the formal proceedings and speeches hurried through with, than the room was cleared for a 'negro ball', which then and there took place? Some members of the 'Central Lincoln Club' left the room before the mystical and circling rites of languishing glance and many dance commenced. But that MANY remained is also true. This fact WE CERTIFY, that on the floor during the progress of the ball were many of the accredited leaders of the Black Republican party, thus testifying their faith by their works in the hall and headquarters of their political gathering. There were Republican OFFICE-HOLDERS, and prominent men of various degrees, and at least one PRESIDENTIAL ELECTOR ON THE REPUBLICAN TICKET."

4. This caricature of 1864 shows Republican leaders dancing and carousing with black women at the headquarters of Lincoln's Campaign Club in New York. (Library of Congress)

5. During Reconstruction, African Americans were the key voting bloc in support of southern Republicans. The professions represented in this picture ("The First Vote") furnished many of the early elected black leaders. (*Harper's Weekly*, November 16, 1867; Library of Congress)

6. For a series of photographs that she sold to raise funds, Sojourner Truth dressed in smart attire to convey a respectable image of black women. (Library of Congress)

CHAPTER TWO

Freedom Is Not Enough, 1865–1877

When the war was over, the former master of escaped Tennessee slave Jourdon Anderson invited him back to work as a free man. Anderson's letter of reply fairly dripped with sarcasm. "Although you shot at me twice," Anderson began, "[I] am glad you are still living." As for returning to work, he and his wife "Mandy (the folks here call her Mrs. Anderson)" would need compensation "for faithful labors in the past" so that they could have "faith in your promises in the future." That compensation amounted to $11,680 (minus the costs incurred by the master for their clothing, three visits to the doctor, and one tooth extraction). They wanted assurance, too, that their daughters would have decent schooling and would not be raped by his former master's sons. Anderson concluded: "We trust the good Maker has opened your eyes to the wrongs which you and your fathers have done. P.S.—Say howdy to George Carter, and thank him for taking the pistol from you when you were shooting at me." The letter was widely republished in northern newspapers.[1]

"When we got freed we was going to get forty acres and a mule. Stead of that we didn't get nothing." Sally Dixon, a former slave.[2]

Seldon Clark, a worried Freedmen's Bureau official, warned his superiors in 1865 that "unless some means is devised to secure simple justice from the planters . . . [former slaves] will take the law into their own hands."[3]

On February 25, 1870, Hiram Revels became the first black man to take a seat in the U.S. Senate. Born to free parents in a slave state, Revels trained as a minister, went to war as a Union chaplain, and settled in Mississippi as an educator before heading to the Senate. Revels completed the term of former Confederate President Jefferson Davis.

On July 14, 1873, the Jubilee Singers sang the grace at a party hosted by British Prime Minister William Gladstone in London. The singers were a group of nine former slaves and children of slaves. The Prince of Wales asked them to sing the John Brown slave song—his favorite. Gladstone was so impressed he invited the group to breakfast the following week. "If the Premier of the United Kingdom can invite 'niggers' to sit and eat with him," wrote one American journalist, "cannot the common folk of America . . . ask if their prejudices are not foolish?"[4]

On Good Friday, April 14, 1865, a Union soldier raised the Stars and Stripes over Fort Sumter—four years and a day after its fall had triggered the Civil War. Union forces held a victory celebration in nearby Charleston. Robert Smalls piloted *The Planter* past the island fort and back into familiar waters. Back in 1862, Smalls had sneaked the Confederate ship out of Charleston harbor before dawn. Now he returned in broad daylight, as a hero. The harbor teemed with ships. Crowds cheered from the land. One admirer wrote that Smalls stood "a prince among them, self-possessed, prompt and proud." (In the mayhem, *The Planter* ran aground, then bumped into a steamer.)[5]

Back in 1862, Smalls had smuggled fifteen slaves to freedom. Now, said one report, *The Planter* was "crowded almost to suffocation." One passenger was Robert Vesey, whose father, Denmark, had been executed in 1822 for plotting a slave rebellion in Charleston. White vigilantes burned down the church that Denmark Vesey had founded. With the coming of freedom, black Charlestonians had started to rebuild the church. Robert Vesey was the architect.[6] Next to Vesey stood Martin Delany—antebellum advocate of emigration, now an army officer returning to live in South Carolina. The South—so long the region of despair—held the prospect of hope.

Freedmen and women celebrating on the shore shared the hope. One group was "arrayed in silks and satins of all the colors of the rainbow."[7] Thus the very bodies of former slaves—many so recently semi-naked on an auction block—were symbols of a new order. Symbolic, too, was the absence of white faces from city streets. One northern visitor "asked Smalls where all the grand dames—the wives and daughters of the leading men, were." Smalls replied, "I hope they are all in their graves."[8] On southern streets, the leading men were now Union soldiers—including eighty thousand black soldiers.

White residents of Charleston, wrote one reporter, "wisely swallowed objections" to the new order of things. They could hardly do otherwise. Northern reporters were shocked by the desolation of Charleston. "Pompeii is not more awful in its ruins," wrote one. A visiting abolitionist crowed that Smalls "is able to give bread to half the bank-presidents and brokers of [Charleston's] Broad Street."[9] The ravages of war had left the southern economy in disarray. Emancipation meant that planters lost nearly half of their capital at a stroke, while the disruption of trade blocked the global flow of cotton out of the South and the flow of money back in. Nearly one quarter of young white men in the Confederacy had died during the war, and thousands of others came home wounded. Mississippi spent one fifth of its revenue in 1865 buying artificial limbs.[10]

The evening of the Charleston celebration, Lincoln went to the theater in Washington, D.C. John Wilkes Booth, a notable Shakespearean actor, lurked outside the president's box, waiting for the play's funniest line. As the audience laughed, he shot Lincoln in the head. Booth hoped to throw the Union government into chaos and revive the Confederate war effort, but to his dismay, Lincoln's death brought about just the opposite in the short term. Union officials united in outrage, Confederate leaders feared a backlash, and a couple of weeks later, Union troops tracked Booth down and shot him dead.

Nonetheless, Booth's defiance would prove to be as much a foretaste of postwar politics as the heady celebrations at Charleston. Just as black Americans planned to redeem the promise of freedom, many Confederates were determined to fight back, by any means necessary. Lincoln's death also gave warning of problems ahead for black Americans in the former free states. The New York City Council voted to exclude black mourners from Lincoln's funeral procession. Frederick Douglass condemned their decision as "the most disgraceful . . . proceeding ever exhibited by people calling themselves civilized."[11] Lincoln's embarrassed widow later sent Douglass her husband's walking stick.

Little surprise, then, that the postwar period known as Reconstruction (1865–1877) was anything but peaceful. At its heart, Reconstruction was a power struggle between competing ideas of freedom—ideas that predated the Civil War. With the coming of peace, former slaves had—to quote one disgruntled planter—"extravagant expectations" of freedom. They wanted the resources to build and defend their own communities. In the North and West, former free blacks wanted full rights of citizenship, and right across the country black Americans wanted a say in the Reconstruction process. By contrast, former masters sought to return to a system as close to slavery as possible. Even southern Unionists had a narrow view of black freedom. To quote one South Carolina Unionist, "We don't believe that because the nigger is free he ought to be saucy."[12]

As for white northerners, they held a wide range of views on freedom—views that would change over time. Northern congressmen ranged from Democratic proslavery sympathizers to Radical Republican advocates of black equality. At the beginning of the peace, many northern Republicans agreed that freedom meant "free labor"—the right to choose a contract. General Howard, head of the Freedmen's Bureau, insisted, "Freedom means work." Most agreed, too, that freedom should mean basic civil rights. But free blacks knew just how basic those rights might be. The *Nation* explained that what "[we] seek for the negro is equality before the law, such as prevails between . . . a London cabman and the earl of Derby."[13]

The course of Reconstruction reflected the interwoven power battles between those holding these diverse views of freedom. The battles over freedom would follow a dizzying number of interconnected twists and turns—reaching from disputes on the ground to debates in national politics to the demands of the international cotton market. The battles over freedom ranged across economics, politics, culture, and everyday institutions. They intersected with wider questions of citizenship, manhood, religion, immigration, and the future of the American nation.

Ultimately, Booth's vision of a resurgent white South would prevail. In 1877 the new Republican president, Rutherford B. Hayes, withdrew the final federal troops from the South. By this time, northern white sympathies had transferred from former slaves to former Confederates, and every single southern state had been "redeemed" from Republicans by white Democrats. Black Americans continued to build their communities as best they could, but by the end of Reconstruction—the so-called period of "Redemption"—their "extravagant expectations" of freedom had been shot down as surely as Booth had shot down the president.

First Freedoms

That, though, was for the future. Many months before politicians returned to Washington after the Civil War to ponder the question of freedom, former slaves and slaveowners grappled with its reality in everyday life. These were very much local battles about community and work. But they would soon push the Congress to intervene in the South—and expand the benefits of freedom for black Americans across the country.

When the war was over, South Carolina rice planter Charles Manigault despaired of the assertiveness of his former slave, Peggy. She took his wife's "Mahogany Bedstead & Mattrass & arranged it in her own Negro House." She also took some "Pink Ribands" and "tied in a dozen bows the woolly head of her Daughter." When Manigault tried to evict her, Peggy blocked him, "her arms akimbo," and "said she would go off to the Provost Marshal." Feeling helpless, Manigault chafed at the thought of Peggy reclining on his wife's mattress, enjoying "her Sweet Dreams of freedom."[14]

For many rural freedmen and women, their first steps toward their sweet freedom dreams were along dusty roads in the direction of the nearest town. For Confederate soldiers staggering home in the opposite direction, the sight of the exodus added insult to defeat. In Arkansas, a white man called Mr. Powell said the customary "Howdy Uncle" to a passing former slave. The freedman replied, "Call me Mister." "How long," Powell asked his companion, "before my ass will be kicked by every negro that meets me?"[15] In a foretaste of terror to come, roadside fights were common. Still, former slaves continued to move. By 1870 the black population of some southern cities more than doubled. One rural freedwoman, Julie Tillory, turned up ragged, with two young children, at Atlanta's Freedmen's Bureau. A white missionary asked Tillory why she had walked so far. Tillory explained, "To 'joy my freedom."[16]

What freedom's former slaves first hoped to enjoy by moving varied from person to person. Some sought to flee the lash, or sexual abuse. Many sought to reunite families. After all, family life had been one of the greatest casualties of the slave system, and the wartime relocation of slaves into the interior had made matters even worse. The search could be bittersweet. One freedman, when contacted by his long-lost love, Laura, replied, "I love you just as well as I did the last day I saw you," but "I am married . . . and if you and I meets it would make a very dissatisfied family." One freedwoman, when faced with the problem of two former partners, seemed less distraught. She gave each man a two-week trial.[17]

Under slavery, marriage had been informal and temporary at best—as one Kentucky preacher put it, "until death or distance do us part." Freedom gave people the chance to make relationships formal and permanent. Not all were in a hurry to do so, especially some black women. But many were. One elderly man registered his marriage even though his wife had been dead seven years. These were emotional scenes to be sure. But marriage had wider implications for citizenship, too. One black corporal commented, "The Marriage Covenant is at the foundation of all our rights . . . now we have it . . . we shall be established as a people."[18]

Individuals rebuilt families. In turn, families built communities on firm foundations laid during slavery. In cities especially, African Americans formed many separate communities, not a single community; emancipation freed people who had experienced very different lives under slavery, and some had never been slaves at all. The church became the institutional heartbeat of black community life. For hard-pressed ministers, freedom seemed to be, literally, a godsend. During a postwar revival, tens of thousands professed faith, and black Baptists formed the largest African American organization in the nation's history. Revival in the churches was matched by the growth of black schools—many people wanted to learn to read in order to read the Bible. Slaves had been banned from learning to read, though perhaps one in ten slaves did so. But within a year of freedom, according to one Freedmen's Bureau estimate, some 150,000 former slaves were studying at school.[19] In the cities, former free blacks and industrial slaves formed fraternal societies and workingmen's groups.

Black southerners built community institutions apart from well-meaning white northerners almost as much as from Confederates. Virtually all black Christians switched to all-black denominations. In the schools, black teachers outnumbered white northern missionary teachers by 1869. Black leaders in Savannah, Georgia, rejected an offer of white teachers from the American Missionary Association. Instead, they raised $800 to found all-black schools of their own.[20] This separatism was a reflection of long-established kinship networks, a distinct theology, and distrust of white paternalism. Separatism also sustained the survival culture of slave times, forging a world hidden from white eyes. Separate institutions provided the basis for black politics and labor organizing, for community meetings and welfare provision, and would be a source of strength for black activists for generations to come.

Yet from the outset, separation from white society was not the same as withdrawal. Former slaves—indeed black Americans across the country—claimed America's democratic ideals for their own. They celebrated Independence Day every bit as much as Emancipation Day. They mourned Abraham Lincoln as the Great Emancipator and read out the Declaration of Independence at community meetings.[21] In antebellum days, black leaders had condemned the U.S. Constitution for supporting slavery. Now, calls for white Americans to live up to their creed carried rhetorical power. It was a strategy that black Americans would adopt time and again—a century later, Martin Luther King's most famous speech would be "deeply rooted in the American dream."

On this foundation of separate communities, black southerners claimed the spoils of freedom. They gathered in mass meetings, and they lobbied Freedmen's Bureau officials and army officers. Some petitioned the president. In other words, they pursued a freedom agenda before one was handed to them by the powers that be. In the towns, former free blacks claimed full citizenship rights and equal access to public spaces. In the countryside, former slaves claimed a fair wage at work and protection from violence, and some called for the vote. Along the Atlantic coast, freedmen and women spread word that the government would give them land, as Sherman had—forty acres and a mule at Christmas.

They believed it would be just compensation for their slave labor and wartime service and that it would enable them to take their place as independent citizens. They firmly believed, too, that God's deliverance was at hand. Many were so confident that they refused to sign labor contracts with planters for the following year.

As they sought new freedoms, black southerners came hurtling into collision with those who sought to restore the status quo ante. For many white southerners, the inclusion of former slaves as equals in any aspect of life signaled the end of white control over their whole way of life. After former slaves—a "disorderly . . . contemptible set of beings"—joined Fourth of July celebrations in Richmond, Virginia, white residents called for the abolition of the festival. They were horrified when black revelers placed wreaths on the statue of Thomas Jefferson.[22] There was irony aplenty here. Before the war Frederick Douglass had told white Americans, "This Fourth of July is *yours*, not *mine*. *You* may rejoice, I must mourn."[23] Now former slaves claimed the festival and led the rejoicing, while white southerners mourned. (One further irony—Jefferson had been a slaveowner.)

As they mourned the loss of their past, former slaveowners feared for the future, stoked by news from abroad. In October 1865 the governor of Jamaica killed four hundred supposed rebels. An attempted revolt by former slaves (black Jamaicans had been emancipated in 1838) was alarming enough. But what made the reports particularly troubling for southern planters were the all-too-familiar accounts of unrest in the run-up to revolt: secret societies that met in black churches, and devious white men (the Jamaican version of Yankee meddlers) who manipulated the "simple-hearted race" into "demons." All it needed was "a mixture of rum and gunpowder" to tip black Jamaicans into "madness." One white clergyman feared that "we are sleeping upon a volcano." Former Confederates must have shuddered in sympathy.[24]

Further reports suggested that the governor had got lucky. The rather minor October revolt had been a mistake. The real revolution—an "indiscriminate slaughter of the white population"—had been planned for Christmas. Christmas! Weren't southern freedmen acting suspiciously in the run-up to Christmas, by refusing to sign labor contracts? Just as southern freedmen spread rumors of forty acres and a mule, apoplectic planters spread rumors of imminent apocalypse. In South Carolina, reports flooded in to the army that freedmen were "arming themselves . . . preparatory to a general revolt on or about the first of January."[25] The slightest challenge to white dominance bespoke insurrection. Elizabeth Meriwether, of distinguished Memphis stock, was so "distressed" by the "swaggering" of black soldiers that she believed "any stranger . . . would have supposed the Blacks not the Whites, were masters in the South."[26]

The problem for "the Blacks," though, was that they weren't. "The Master he says we are all free," complained freedman George King, "but it don't mean we is white. And it don't mean we is equal."[27] Most slaves entered freedom impoverished, illiterate, and with nothing to sell but their labor. Many women carried the added burden of caring for children who were deemed to be illegitimate (often because the father was the former master). Those who moved to towns found a freedom of disease and destitution. One census in Mobile, Alabama, revealed that two thirds of black residents were "literally worthless" with no "fixed place" to live.[28] Some returned to the countryside, where for all their assertiveness, rural people were at the mercy of former owners. And mercy was in short supply, especially as planters blamed the freedmen for a poor cotton harvest in 1865. Ironically, emancipation also freed former masters from the paternalistic duties of slavery. "When I owned niggers," explained one Louisiana planter, "I used to pay medical bills and take care of them . . . I do not think I shall trouble myself much now."[29]

To make matters worse, Lincoln's new successor, Andrew Johnson, wanted to be rid of supporting freedmen too. The practical problem for all northern politicians was that, ultimately, southern states had to embrace the restored Union. Johnson calculated that a lenient peace was the best way to regain southern loyalty. A former slaveowner and former governor of the slave state of Tennessee, Johnson also believed that African Americans were best suited "to undergo drudgery." As for the principle of "all men created equal," Johnson (rightly) insisted that "Mr. Jefferson meant the white race."[30] With Congress out of session until December 1865, Johnson was free to direct Reconstruction as he chose. He quickly pardoned all nonranking Confederates who swore allegiance to the Union, restored land to its original owners, and only required Confederate states to write new constitutions that accepted the Thirteenth Amendment and met with voter approval. A delegation of black spokesmen, led by Douglass, warned Johnson that his polices would "cast down the defenseless." Johnson replied that freedmen could emigrate if they were unhappy.[31]

Thus unexpectedly, just a few months after Union troops had celebrated victory over Fort Sumter, former Confederates had presidential backing to turn the South whiteside up. They wasted little time. Democrats took control of all southern states save Tennessee. New state constitutions duly affirmed the Thirteenth Amendment but also introduced so-called Black Codes. These codes rarely mentioned black people explicitly, but they took aim at the freedoms of freedmen and women. Most states required laborers to sign a binding annual contract or face prison. Some states introduced a convict-leasing system. In Mississippi, freedmen were explicitly banned from "renting land," from committing "affrays, trespasses, malicious mischief, cruel treatment to animals," or—just in case the legislators had missed anything in the rush—"any other misdemeanor."[32]

While southern planters used the Black Codes to restore their control of the economy, white southern men of lower economic status used violence to restore their honor. Ben Griffith, a 27-year-old son of a slave-owning father, was a former Confederate sergeant—except in Griffith's mind, there was nothing former about it. His war was very much still on. Freed blacks were the obvious target, and far easier to hit than Union soldiers. Griffith hid in the woods of Arkansas, from which he would emerge clean-shaven, in federal uniform, to get close to his victims. Then, it was said, he shot freedmen unless they performed like animals. Griffith was a particularly notorious rebel—federal officials called him "a terror," and supporters mythologized him as the "Swamp Fox."[33] But he was only one of many who turned their fire on former slaves. One Texas sheriff shot a black man for whistling "Yankee Doodle."[34]

Bureau officials and Union soldiers provided black southerners with some protection, but they did not share their freedom agenda. Johnson quickly replaced the more radical officers and officials. In some cities, soldiers shipped migrants back to the plantations. Outraged black soldiers in Wilmington, North Carolina, mutinied in protest. Bureau officials urged freed slaves to sign annual contracts, as a first step toward free labor, not as a first step back toward quasi-slavery. Even so, in practice the bureau prodded freedmen in precisely the same direction that planters were trying to force them to go. "If you call this freedom," complained one black veteran, "what do you call slavery?"[35] Christmas 1865 came and went with no land distribution. There was no revolt, either.

Freedmen and women tried to hold their ground. Along the Atlantic coast, Johnson's edicts required freed people to give up the land they had started to cultivate during the war. Some refused. In March 1866 Francis Parker Jr. and a brutal overseer, Denis Hazel, sought to reclaim the Parker plantation in South Carolina. Former slaves with "axes, hatchets, hoes, and poles" turned them away. Parker and Hazel returned with two soldiers. According to Hazel and Parker, a dozen "infuriated women" attacked Hazel. Parker told the freedmen to stop the "maddened women." They refused. The group turned on Parker. One woman, Sukey, hit him with a hickory stick. Parker jumped into a river and swam away "under a shower of missiles." Hazel followed him into the water.[36] The soldiers made their own way home.

Such a standoff was unusual. But right across the South, freedmen resisted a return to slave work. For all its disappointments, freedom gave them some leverage. Planters were now landlords, not laborlords. At the end of each year, families could move from one plantation to the next in search of better terms. Inadvertently, the Christmas rumors of land redistribution helped. By refusing to sign annual contracts in December, workers got slightly better deals in January. Once they had signed deals, workers could always fall back on such slave-time tactics as sabotage and goslows. In March 1866 Malachi Timmerman, an overseer in Georgia, took it personally. "The Negroes . . . don't like me at all," he told the planter, especially the "old man Ben [who] is a contrary old buger."[37] Unlike slave days, Timmerman felt his hands were tied. One planter complained, "There is no power to make the negroes work and we know that without that they will not work."[38]

Meanwhile, black women withdrew from full-time field labor. Planters grumbled that they were just trying to "play the lady" of leisure. In reality, they were busy with household tasks such as weaving, and many returned to the cotton fields at harvest—as long as the price was right. Because men were tied to annual contracts, much of the conflict in the countryside was over short-term women's work. One South Carolina landlord ordered his workers' wives to help out with wool production, as they had in slave days. They refused. Instead, they killed the sheep and ate them.[39] Judging by the number of complaints to the Freedmen's Bureau, what one official called the "evil of female loaferism" increased during 1866.[40] And the harvest failed again.

By digging in for freedom, former slaves provoked an overreaction. Pent-up tensions in anticipation of a Christmas shootout were released through a series of massacres in the New Year. Perhaps the worst was in Memphis in May. After fights between black veterans and local police, white mobs murdered at least forty black men, raped black women, and destroyed black churches and schools.[41] The total number of murders during presidential Reconstruction will never be known, but bureau reports suggest that many thousands were killed.

Far from restoring order, Johnson's policies produced chaos. When Congress convened in December 1865, most Republicans had expected to find common ground with the president. But in response to news from the South, lobbying from black spokesmen, and some well-publicized freedmen's petitions, Congress refused to seat southern delegates pending an investigation. Southern supremacist violence appalled northern public opinion (as it would a century later). Congressmen also worried about slaves taking matters into their own hands (fear of black violence, rather than news of white violence, would often prompt ameliorative action in the future, too). Congress established a Joint Committee on Reconstruction which heard from bureau officials, army officers, and some freedmen. All witnesses said the same thing: presidential Reconstruction would allow former rebels to take control and leave former slaves exposed.

Thus in barely half a year, black demands on southern streets and in southern fields had found their way to the corridors of power in Washington. The committee on Reconstruction proposed a constitutional amendment to confer citizenship regardless of color (overturning *Dred Scott*) and to require states to respect citizenship rights (overturning the Black Codes). Thus, as in the Civil War, the question of black freedom inadvertently led to a questioning of American governance—in this case, the autonomy of states. Initially, Congress shied away from such a radical reduction of state autonomy. Instead, Congress passed legislation to extend the Freedmen's Bureau and to protect civil rights. But Johnson vetoed both acts. Republicans grasped the constitutional nettle. In April, Congress overrode Johnson's veto of the civil rights act—the first time Congress had ever done so. In June Congress sent the Fourteenth Amendment out to the states for ratification. Congress also passed a Homestead Act which gave poor farmers first option to buy uncultivated land. (It was uncultivated for a reason, though: the land was poor.)

In a further twist, southern state legislatures—aghast at Yankee interference and encouraged by Johnson—refused to ratify the amendment. Only Tennessee complied. (The federal government's intrusion into southern state politics would be a recurring flashpoint in American race relations.) Republicans now needed a radical solution even to achieve moderate goals. They opted to create a strong southern Republican party and a free labor economy. Thus, in peace even more than war, northern Republicans needed the help of black southerners to achieve victory, this time as voters and contract farmers.

African Americans tried to ram the message home. An 1866 Convention of Colored Men in Washington established the first paid black congressional lobby to represent "the best interests of the recently emancipated." The "recently emancipated" presented their case directly, too. For example, in March 1868 the foremost Radical Republican senator, Charles Sumner, received a letter detailing the sufferings of Georgia freedmen. Sumner read of a white mob that had evicted two hundred black workers at a federal war cemetery, nailing shut the front doors of their houses from the inside, then exiting the houses by smashing the roofs. That evening, the worst storm in memory had rained down on the homeless. The freedmen pleaded for "the Government to protect us."[42] Their pleas grew louder with every passing month. Starting in 1867—after yet another bad harvest, and after black men began to vote—the Ku Klux Klan mobilized, with murderous intent.

Their pleas were answered. On March 2, 1867, Congress passed—over Johnson's veto—the first of a series of Reconstruction acts that marked the start of so-called Congressional or Radical Reconstruction. The acts put the South under military rule, enfranchised black voters, disfranchised ranking Confederates, and made readmittance to Congress dependent on each state's creation of yet another new constitution that ratified the Fourteenth Amendment and universal male suffrage (as they had with emancipation, though, some Republicans supported southern black voting as a way to stop black southerners heading north). In 1868 Republican war hero Ulysses S. Grant won the presidential election. Grant was no Radical, but he was no Johnson either. The year 1870 saw the ratification of a Fifteenth Amendment that prohibited states from denying citizens the vote "on account of race, color, or previous conditions of servitude."

Thus, the first postwar steps to freedom along southern roads had become giant strides toward liberty on the statute books in Washington. For black Americans, however, Congressional Reconstruction was still far short of what they wanted. The various pieces of legislation were typically messy compromises between congressional factions. The question of enforcement was not settled. Above all, Reconstruction did not make provision for meaningful land redistribution. Even in this radical moment, few Republicans could countenance the thought of abandoning the principle of the right to private property. Most believed that male suffrage and free labor were quite radical enough. Time would prove them wrong. Ultimate power in the South also lay in the ownership of land and guns. Still, Congressional Reconstruction gave black Americans unprecedented power to pursue their visions of freedom. Across the country, they did.

Reconstruction in the Former Union States

On October 1, 1865, in Baltimore, Frederick Douglass gave the inaugural address at a new institute named in his honor. Funded by forty African American donors, the institute's mission was to "promote the intellectual advancement of the colored portion of the community." For Douglass, this was a noble task, full of promise. He anticipated evenings of high culture, with his "soul thrilled with heavenly music, lifted to the skies on the wings of poetry and song." Such events would change Baltimore, and America. With a conviction that many future black leaders would share, Douglass argued, "When prejudice cannot deny the black man's ability, it . . . claims him as a white man." It was also an urgent task. Racial prejudice had survived the war intact. People of color were "pronounced by American learning as incapable of anything higher than the dull round of merely animal life." High achievers like Robert Smalls and himself were still "treated as exceptions."[43]

Trouble at Baltimore's docks later that month showed just how urgent the task was. A group of white caulkers and joiners went on strike to force the firing of the seventy-five black workers in their shipyard. Trouble had been brewing. As former slaves crowded the city's alleys, white workers saw rivals ready to undercut their wages. Black workers had written to a local newspaper in "apprehension of an antagonism on the part of white working men." When the shipyard owners gave in to the strike, black workers from every trade marched to complain. They protested in vain. In the end, about a thousand black men lost their jobs.[44] Even though Maryland had been a (loyal) slave state, virtually all black men in Baltimore had been free before the war. In the antebellum shipyards, their local knowledge of Baltimore's bay and oyster beds had helped them retain their jobs against white immigrant competitors. Paradoxically, it was the coming of freedom that led to their dismissal. (A century later, minimum wage and integration measures would inadvertently lead to black unemployment, too.)

One skilled black caulker, Isaac Myers, proposed the creation of a black-run cooperative. Born free to poor parents, Myers had served an apprenticeship under a black caulker. He then went into the grocery business before returning to caulking. By the end of the war, Myers was the leading man in the black community. Pale skinned, straight-haired, with a light-colored, bushy moustache, Myers could almost have passed for white if he had not been so well known. He was a pillar of Baltimore's largest black church—he ran what one admirer called the country's "banner Sunday-school," a weekly theology class for seven hundred adults. Well-connected and respected, the confident entrepreneur moved fast to get his cooperative up and running. Douglass and others bought stock worth $10,000. Just four months later Myers' cooperative bought its own shipyard.[45]

The first black workers at Myers' shipyard were "mobbed and beaten" by white rivals. Black men fought back. Veterans were not allowed to join the state militia, so they formed their own—starting with the Lincoln Zouaves, Corps d'Afrique. By 1867 some two thousand black men in Baltimore had joined militias. During a parade in October, one militiaman shot a white heckler dead. The city government banned all parades, and police tried to confiscate weapons. By this time, Myers' cooperative employed some three hundred black men. Two years later, Myers founded a Colored National Labor Union, which petitioned Congress and elected a delegate to the upcoming World Labor Congress in France.[46]

Events in Baltimore showed that "free blacks" in the former Union States fought white supremacy every bit as much as freed blacks in the former Confederacy—and that they needed to. From California to Connecticut, second-class black citizens sought first-class status. The events in Baltimore pointed to the wide range of strategies they used: education, challenging stereotypes, marching for jobs, forming cooperatives, fighting back, and seeking allies abroad.

The postwar years held out real promise of change. The northern economy boomed, the Republican Party dominated northern politics, and many state governments embarked on social reforms. During 1865–1867, the New York legislature introduced minimum housing standards and public education.[47] Wartime civil rights gains in some states, however tentative, gave grounds for hope, and the sacrifice of northern black soldiers gave activists a powerful argument. But the trouble in Baltimore warned that peace might not bring first-class status—it might even bring new danger. In 1865 the Republican nominee for Ohio governor, Jacob Cox, said that emancipation meant blacks should be sent back South. Cox won the election. Out West, the Choctaw and Chickasaw Indians enacted Black Codes.[48]

African Americans in the North and West hoped to ride the coattails of southern Reconstruction in order to radically reconstruct their own status. But their struggle was not just a sideshow to the main story. It was very much part of the drama. For the half million black men and women who lived beyond the South, the course of northern Reconstruction was important in its own right. It would set the pattern for race relations there for future generations. Northern Reconstruction had critical implications for southern Reconstruction too. As Myers' union showed, black leaders North and South shared ideas and resources (so too did defenders of white supremacy). And as the Douglass Institute recognized, public opinion mattered. When northern congressmen considered the South, their views were shaped by their experience of race at home.

For Douglass, the main issue was the vote. Without it, he said, "my citizenship is but an empty name." When the war was over, African Americans in the North and West deluged politicians with petitions for black suffrage.[49] But during presidential Reconstruction, every loyal state that considered the issue rejected black voting. So too did voters in Colorado territory, by a margin of almost ten to one. Mexican settlers there were particularly hostile. Led by a lecturer on Touissant L'Ouverture—the iconic Haitian freedom fighter—Denver's tiny African American population petitioned Congress directly, since it had authority to legislate on voting in the territories.[50] In 1867 Congress duly extended the franchise to all adult men in the territories except Indians, at the same moment that it enfranchised black men in the South. Northern black leaders seized upon the precedents and sent out a new round of petitions. But of the several states that considered black voting from 1867 to 1869, only two— Minnesota and Iowa—voted in favor.

The problem for black petitioners was that their opponents were strong and their allies were few—and, ironically, emancipation and Congressional Reconstruction had made the situation worse. Republicans had been united on the question of slavery, but they were divided over the meaning of freedom. Many abolitionists felt their work was done with emancipation. Leading white women reformers—formerly allies in the abolitionist cause—opposed black voting. Or as one put it, "Sambo must wait a while for Sarah." Sojourner Truth tried to straddle the divide, and, at age seventy, toured the North calling for both female and black suffrage. But when black southern men started voting, the divide became a chasm. Leading women's suffragist Elizabeth Cady Stanton warned that "this incoming tide of ignorance . . . and vice" must not vote.[51] Douglass, a friend of Stanton, shot back that women could claim precedence as and when their skulls were smashed on account of being women. Black women campaigners, faced with a choice between supporting their sex or race, chose their race. They would face this invidious choice for generations to come.

Meanwhile, Democratic publicists made Republican support for black voting in the South a top electoral issue in the North. In state elections in the fall of 1867, Democrats reduced Republican majorities by three quarters.[52] The following year Grant won the presidential election with a mere 52.7 percent of the vote, despite the inclusion of black southerners and exclusion of ranking Confederates. His opponent, Horatio Seymour, had called for a white man's government during his tenure as governor of New York State. Little wonder that Republicans played down the issue of black voting in the North, dropping it from their 1868 platform.

This steadfast northern opposition to black voting at the moment of freedom prompts the question, Why? After all, black Americans never numbered more than 3 percent of the population of any former free state. The reason was that black voting—as Douglass pointed out—was a foundation for citizenship. As an 1867 Colored Convention told Illinois legislators, not having the vote "insults our manhood."[53] That was precisely the point. Having exclusive possession of the vote reassured those white men who feared for their own status in the tumultuous aftermath of war.

Many white workers, such as the Baltimore dockers, also feared for their livelihoods. Even in New England, rumors spread of plans to import thousands of freedmen to bring down salaries. Immigrant workers sought job security by asserting the superiority of whiteness. The specter of black sexuality haunted northern households, too. The bravado of returning black soldiers inflamed these fears, while white women sometimes fanned the fires for their own ends. During the 1867 elections in Ohio, Democratic women paraded with banners calling on "Fathers! Husbands! Save us from Negro Equality! White Husbands or none!" Democrats won control of both houses.[54]

Powerless to secure the suffrage through local agitation, African Americans beyond the South were every bit as dependent on federal intervention as were former slaves. In January 1869, in Washington, D.C., more than two hundred delegates to the National Convention of Colored Men called on Congress to act and sent a delegation to the President. Little surprise, then, that the proclamation of the Fifteenth Amendment on March 30, 1870, prompted celebrations that matched those for emancipation. In Detroit, George DeBaptiste, a barber, attached a sign to his building, "OFFICE OF THE UNDERGROUND RAILWAY. This office permanently closed. Hereafter Stockholders will receive dividends according to their desserts."[55] Black voters received a few minor dividends. A few black candidates won elections in northern cities such as Cleveland, Boston, and Chicago. In Ohio, where the parties ran neck and neck, the Democrats briefly reined in their racist rhetoric. Out West, the Denver delegation to the National Republican Convention included a few black men. By 1875, the 42-member Seminole National General Council included six freedmen.[56]

Yet winning the right to vote, and the odd minor election, did not usher in genuine political influence, let alone a better world. American party politics was about building majorities, and black voters in the North and West were far too small a bloc to matter. Republicans rarely courted the black vote with enthusiasm; black voters responded in kind. When Rochester Republicans called a "grand demonstration" of colored men in 1871, six people turned up.[57] Worse still, black voting prompted a backlash in many states. New York police reacted to the Fifteenth Amendment with a reign of terror. Some Democratic legislatures tried to whittle down the black vote within the constraints of the amendments.

The struggle for the vote—eventual gains on paper but little benefit in practice—told the wider story of the northern struggle for equality. Black groups petitioned for new civil rights laws, and some towns and states duly passed them. But most acts lacked enforcement powers. A New York civil rights bill of 1873 was so meaningless that the Democratic leader in the state assembly unwittingly voted for it. Only laughter, wrote one reporter, "aroused the gentleman to inquire what bill he had voted for."[58] Four of the six petitions sent to Congress calling for a civil rights act came from groups in states that had already passed a civil rights law.[59]

Local civil rights legislation put the burden on the victim to sue for damages. And sue they did, with some success. But formal victories did not easily translate into meaningful gains. In 1867, following a thirty-year campaign for equal resources for black schools, black parents in Detroit sued the Board of Education to integrate schools. Because of a new state civil rights law, the board gave in—then segregated children into separate classrooms. When black parents protested, the board integrated classrooms but replaced double desks with single ones.[60] In one school, a single black child was screened off from white classmates so that only the teacher could see him.

For black workers, the battle for decent jobs was the most important struggle of all. As Isaac Myers explained: "If citizenship is worth anything . . . it means the freedom of labor . . . as universal as the freedom of the ballot." Black men worked in the most dangerous and poorly paid jobs, while black women worked mostly in domestic service. Fighting for a job was an old battle in the free states, and it would remain at the heart of the struggle for black equality into the twenty-first century. But the postwar era was particularly significant, because it was the moment when white workers first began to unionize in force.

Myers ran a twofold strategy—to build up the independent strength of black workers and seek alliances with white workers. Myers lobbied the new (white) National Labor Union for a chance to present the case for partnership. At the union's 1869 convention he was granted his wish. By all accounts, he gave a dazzling speech. Choosing his words sensitively, he said black workers wanted nothing more than the right to earn a fair wage and "set aside a few dollars for a rainy day." He pointed out that his Baltimore cooperative employed some white men who had previously attacked black caulkers.[61]

Unbeknown to Myers, he had Karl Marx on his side. In 1867 Marx wrote in *Das Kapital* that American "labor cannot emancipate itself in the white skin where in the black it is branded." *Das Kapital* would not be available in English for another twenty years, but some American labor publicists had already grasped the point. In 1866 a leading labor newspaper, the *Boston Daily Evening Voice*, asked, "Can white working-men [afford to] ignore colored ones?"[62] For the *Voice* the answer was no. For most local unions, however, the answer was yes. Black exclusion at the birth of the union movement was one of the most important legacies of Reconstruction—one that would hamper the labor movement, weaken the hand of black workers, and lead many future black spokesmen to ally with employers.

Thus, Myers was left with his community-building strategy. In 1869 he called a first National Colored Labor Union convention. Douglass chaired the meeting, and Myers was elected the first president. With over two hundred delegates from twenty-three states (including over fifty delegates from the South), this was the first black convention to be truly national in scope. It was also the first truly inclusive workers' convention. Unlike its white counterpart, it positively welcomed workers of any color, and it welcomed women—a reflection of women's vital contribution to black household income.

Shut out from the white national union, the Colored Union looked abroad, to the forthcoming World Labor Congress in Paris, for support. At the local level, the convention called for black cooperatives "as a remedy against [our] exclusion on account of color . . . as well as protection from the aggression of capital." Thus, the union recognized the double burden of race and class carried by black working men; black working women, of course, carried a triple burden. The convention also called on Congress to give forty acres each to southern freedmen. Myers resolved to go South to mobilize a workers' movement. Yet when he got there, he would find southern workers already organized, with some power. In the South, the labor struggle was at the center of postwar politics even more than it was in the North.

Radical Reconstruction in the South

In March 1868 the Reverend Henry Turner gave up his pastorate in Macon, Georgia. The well-traveled minister had become something of a weathervane of the era as regards opportunities for African Americans. He had an unerring sense of which way the political wind was blowing, and he was bold enough to change course as new possibilities arose. Before the war, he had planned to serve God in Africa. With the coming of war, he decided to stay in America. During the war, he joined the army as a chaplain. With the onset of peace, he headed to Macon to save souls in Georgia, and presided over an unprecedented revival. When black south-

ern men gained the vote, he turned to politics. The step from serving the
elect to serving an electorate was actually quite small. Turner reckoned
that every minister in his denomination worked part-time for the Republican Party. In 1868 Turner became one of the first twenty-nine black men
to be elected to the Georgia legislature.[63]

Turner seemed well suited for the rough and tumble of southern politics. This round-faced, broad-shouldered man of God had the physique
of a prizefighter, and a silver tongue, too. Yet his initial approach was
what modern experts might call triangulation—a pragmatic attempt to
find a middle ground between former Confederates and expectant freedmen. His self-proclaimed motto was "Anything to please the white
man." He only stood for office after it became clear that not enough
white men would stand as Republican candidates. He supported the right
of former Confederates to hold office. He even called for a full pardon for
Jefferson Davis.

Turner hoped his conciliatory stance would encourage white colleagues to return the favor. For once, he guessed wrong. The very men
that Turner helped return to the legislature led the charge against him.
Georgia's new constitution gave black men the vote, but it did not explicitly say they could hold office. When Turner had suggested clarifying the
matter during the drafting process, Republicans had reassured him that
there was no need. But when Georgia's legislature assembled in September 1868, Democrats proposed that black representatives be expelled because they had not been granted the right to hold office.

Turner could no longer "fawn nor cringe." His opponents were behaving like a "man who should go into my house, take possession of my wife
and children, and then tell me to walk out." He confronted his colleagues: "Am I not a man?" Turner recounted his wartime service. He
appealed to the liberty promised by classical law and the Founding Fathers. He compared himself to the persecuted Luther and Galileo. And he
warned of the "All-seeing Eye [who] never fails to vindicate the cause of
Justice." With that, he walked out. At the door, Turner scraped the dirt
off his shoes—the biblical sign of condemnation for hard-hearted hypocrites. The House voted 83–23 for expulsion. A few days later in south
Georgia, a white posse (led by the local sheriff) killed nine black men
who were on their way to a political meeting.

With the zeal of a convert, Turner denounced Democrat brutes and
faint-hearted Republicans with equal vehemence. The Klan took note.
You are "being closely watched by the owls of the night," they wrote;
you may "be aroused from slumber ere long by a boo hoo, boo hoo." A
few months later, the Klan assassinated two white Republican legislators.

Turner published the letter and added a defiant pledge: "If this Ku Klux don't like it, let him bring on his owls." But from then on he hid at night when traveling. Embattled in Georgia, he appealed to Washington. Grant appointed him to the plum position of Macon postmaster. Congress re-seated Georgia's black legislators in 1870, and Turner prepared for the fall re-election. So too did his opponents. Allegations linked Turner to counterfeit money and visits to prostitutes.[64] Vigilantes attacked black voters on the way to the polls. Even so, Turner may well have won the most votes. We shall never know, because the votes were counted in a private house, and Turner was declared defeated.

In many ways, the rise, radicalization, and fall of Henry Turner epito-mized the efforts of black southerners during Congressional Reconstruc-tion (although in other southern states black politicians rose further and stayed in power much longer). With the passage of the Reconstruction acts, the South seemed full of promise. In an international context, the fact that former slaves were voting, and even holding office, so soon into freedom was unique among nineteenth-century emancipations. In an American context, few northern Republicans had started the war seeking emancipation, let alone black suffrage. In the South, virtually no white Republicans desired black suffrage for its own sake. But all white Repub-licans needed black voters to win elections in the South. In 1867 eligible black voters outnumbered white voters in five states. Little wonder that black leaders from around the country, like Turner, headed South (or that some pessimistic planters left for Mexico and Brazil).

Former slaves embraced the new politics with millennial zeal. Indeed, black politics coincided with revival and was partly organized through the churches. The timing of Congressional Reconstruction, early in 1867, helps explain why. After the war, planters tried to act as if they were still slaveowners, but freedmen refused to work as if they were still slaves. The resulting stalemate devastated cotton harvests—which were made even worse by untimely rains, poor stock, and the armyworm blight. Some planters feared bankruptcy. Many freedmen faced ruin. Congress enfranchised black voters just as catastrophe loomed. Politics offered freedmen a way to push back. But the politicization of freedmen only led to renewed battles in the countryside.

Across the rural South, former slaves formed Union Leagues—oath-bound, often armed political organizations based on long-standing kin-ship networks. Rural life changed fast. Just one month after the Recon-struction Act, a bureau agent in Hale County, Alabama, reported that freedmen had already visited him "in squads, platoons & companies" to ask about their new rights. They raised funds to send delegates to a state convention of freedmen. In May some four thousand former slaves turned out to hear their report. They adopted resolutions and elected delegates to a statewide Republican convention. A month later, a local black registrar was shot dead by a white man. When the police let the murderer escape, a posse of freedmen tried to hunt him down. They couldn't find him. But they formed a five-hundred-man militia to prevent future trouble.[65]

The Union Leagues channeled this fevered rural politics into support for the Republican Party. As in the Civil War, then, black southerners exploited Republican needs for their own purposes. New members read a model dialogue (written by Turner) between a white Republican and a freedman which explained the need to vote President Johnson out of office. Despite intimidation, over three quarters of eligible black voters in most Deep South states took their first opportunity to vote. One Louisiana planter worried that "they seem to be proud of it [going] in large gangs some with guns."[66] By voting publicly, even carrying guns, freedmen answered Turner's rhetorical question, "Am I not a man?" In aggregate, their votes turned the elections of 1867–68. More than a quarter of the state constitutional convention delegates were black men, all ten reconstructed states authorized new constitutions, and Republicans dominated the new legislatures. And with black support—he only won a minority of white votes—Grant became president.

At the first state constitutional conventions, black delegates, like Turner, were cautious. They deferred to white leadership and mostly stayed silent on the question of land. They calculated that freedmen had to cultivate the goodwill of planters to have any chance of farming land of their own. At work, though, former slaves were emboldened by the new turn in politics to be anything but cautious. During 1867, black longshoremen struck in the docks of Savannah, Charleston, Mobile, and New Orleans, black coopers struck in Richmond, and black restaurant workers struck in Selma. In the cities, black men and women sat in white-only streetcars too. In the countryside, new rumors spread that Congress planned to redistribute land.

In the meantime, black farmers threatened to turn the rural economy upside down by themselves. Back in Hale County, cotton planter Henry Watson was buffeted by the swirls of local politics and global capital. While former slaves pressured planters from below, European financiers pressured planters from above—urging them to get cotton production back on track as quickly as possible, by any means possible. At first Watson tried to maintain a system in the manner of slave times—despite a run of poor harvests, the refusal of workers' wives to help, and the loss of his workforce at the end of each year. With the coming of the Union Leagues, the system collapsed. Watson's brother-in-law reckoned that every man within ten miles had joined a league, which told them to "set up for themselves."[67] Watson gave up trying to contract work and moved toward a system where families rented small plots of land.

Even so, Watson's brother-in-law thought that "*War* between the races" was likely. He was right. The white supremacist counterrevolution got under way before the black farmers' revolution had barely begun. As so often happened in the rural South, power was ultimately settled down the barrel of a gun. White vigilantes assaulted at least one in ten black delegates to the constitutional conventions. Jack Dupree, an outspoken black Republican in Mississippi, had his throat cut out while his wife was forced to watch. She had recently given birth to twins. Deploying their usual rhetoric, Klan spokesmen claimed they were merely "securing the safety of their wives and children." Democratic leaders approved, and conservative army officers kept their troops in their barracks.[68]

In black majority areas, black militias fought back against the Klan. In coastal Wilmington—the wartime home of armed black militancy—black militias took back the streets. But where they were outnumbered, former slaves were outgunned. Many thousands died. Ironically, the very success of black families in renting separate plots of land—and moving out of centralized slave quarters—made them vulnerable. Ironically, too, the readmission of reconstructed states to the Union meant the end of military rule and federal protection.

In a further irony, Klan violence turned out to be counterproductive for the Democrats. To be sure, the violence and Democratic race-baiting struck a blow against Republican attempts to win support from both freedmen and poorer white farmers. In reconstructed Alabama, Republicans lost two thirds of their white voters within a year. But the terror was not strong enough—not yet—to wipe out the power of the black vote in black-majority areas. Yet it was ugly enough to help the Republican campaign in the North and may well have handed victory to Grant. Democratic leaders pulled their support, and President Grant—appalled by the violence—sent in troops to arrest hundreds of Klansmen in South Carolina and Alabama. The formal Klan began to decline. But in the countryside, terror had done its work in restoring the balance of fear.

Violence on the plantations meant that state politics seemed the best hope for black southerners—at least to restrain the backlash. In black-majority states, "New Departure" Democrats sought to find common ground with Republicans. Better harvests, along with rising cotton and sugar prices, calmed rural tensions. Republican governments put in ambitious (as it turned out, too ambitious) plans for railroad expansion, and

Republicans even staged something of a comeback, winning governorships in Alabama and North Carolina in 1872.

This, then, was the most radical moment of black political influence during Reconstruction. In the secure Republican states, the drift of white Republicans from the fold actually increased the power of black voters in the secure Republican states. Between 1869 and 1877, sixteen black congressmen and two black senators went to Washington. Robert Smalls, so recently stoking the engine of a Confederate ship, became a congressman. More than seven hundred black men—most were former slaves—served in state legislatures. The proportion of black officials still fell far short of the proportion of black voters—only South Carolina had a majority-black legislature. But the rise of black political leaders gave black southerners unexpected new power. Over a thousand black men held local posts, and in day to day life, local officials mattered most of all.[69] A black sheriff, for example, gave black workers the protection to protest for better wages. In rural Mississippi, more than one in three freedmen and women lived in a county with a black sheriff.[70]

As they grew in influence, freedmen upped their demands. This, in turn, strengthened the hand of Radical factions within state Republican parties. In some respects this development proved counterproductive. Conservative Republicans in some states moved toward the Democrats. Republican factionalism also accentuated divisions within many black communities. For example, in Mobile, former urban slaves and free blacks (mostly educated and often light-skinned) tended to be cautious, while migrants from the countryside fought—sometimes literally—for better wages and against white vigilantes. Conservative Republicans turned to the established black leadership, while their white Radical rivals played to the demands of the newcomers. The split let the Democrats sweep back into power in Mobile in 1870.[71] Such factionalism was an ominous portent of problems ahead across the South.

Yet in states where Republicans retained control, the rise of Radical factions led to favorable legislation. Republican legislatures passed laws requiring equal access to transport and public facilities. They raised taxes—fourfold in the case of land taxes—and funded public education. They appointed black veterans to state militias and outlawed forced apprenticeship of children. Republican city governments appointed black police and provided poor relief. Republican judges ruled in favor of freedmen over important issues like hunting rights, while state militias restrained planter violence. The British-educated black South Carolina congressman Robert Elliott chortled that his state constitution was "made for the negro by the negro."[72]

Republican state governments did not redistribute land. Only South

Carolina considered the issue in a meaningful way. There, a Land Commission sold small plots of available land to roughly one sixth of the state's black population. By the end of Reconstruction, only about one in twenty black farmers in the other cotton states owned their own land.[73] Even so, Republican legislatures tilted the bargaining power in the countryside away from the planters, giving black freedmen first lien on crops. This meant that money from crop sales went first toward paying black workers' wages; under the Black Codes, planters had received first lien. The sharecropping system that emerged across the cotton South was a compromise. Planters rented out plots of land in return for a share of the crop. Workers used their first lien as collateral to borrow money at the start of the year to buy tools and seed. This was still scratching a living from the earth, to be sure—but it wasn't slavery. Buoyant cotton prices after 1868 helped, as did extra income from women's work.[74] In Hale County, Henry Watson was impressed by the industry of his black tenants and settled for a decentralized system of work.

In the cities, Republican governments provided some patronage for educated black leaders and employment for black artisans. Consequently, blacks in towns—mostly former free blacks—acquired property more than three times as rapidly as their rural counterparts. Thanks to black colleges, the larger cities were home to a small but growing number of doctors and lawyers. Apart from in Washington and New Orleans, though, black professionals remained a minuscule group even at the height of Reconstruction. Meanwhile, craftsmen—perhaps a quarter of employed black men in southern towns—struggled in the face of cheap northern imports and lack of credit. By the end of Reconstruction, these black artisans were considerably older on average than their white counterparts, suggesting that young black men found it hard to break into skilled work. The majority of black city dwellers were migrants who worked in unskilled manual jobs or domestic service, if they had a job at all.

Best estimates suggest that, overall, black southerners—one third of the region's population—gained possession of 1.3 percent of the South's real and personal wealth during Reconstruction.[75] It was not much, but after slavery it was a start. Black families used their resources to build up community institutions. Although federal support for black education stopped in 1870, Republican state governments introduced public schools, and in most states about half the school-age children—black and white—attended school. Many sharecroppers and domestic workers insisted on access to school as part of their contract. Schools were mostly segregated, and often primitive. But by the end of Reconstruction, black literacy had doubled from slave days to 20 percent. It was higher among the younger generation, and among girls higher still. Through a combination of public funding, black donations, and northern philanthropy, Reconstruction also saw the foundation of black colleges such as Atlanta University, Howard (in Washington, D.C.), and Fisk (in Nashville). In the short term, colleges helped meet the demand for black teachers. In generations to come they would provide many race leaders.

Black community institutions provided the basis for black politics. Indeed, there was not really a division between the two. Together, the black church and black schools furnished more than a quarter of all black officials. Black preachers mixed the gospel of salvation with news of political organization. Black teachers acted as voter registrars and supervisors, taught black Republican Club members about elections, and passed on the news from Republican dailies. A high black voter turnout was in the teachers' interest, because it secured public funding for education. White supremacists understood the threat all too well. After Mississippi passed a public school law in 1870, Klansmen destroyed twenty-five schools and killed some fifty teachers. "The people," said one Klansman, as he whipped a teacher, would not pay taxes to keep "lazy niggers at school."[76] The tenacity of freedmen and women, along with protection from planters keen to placate their workers and intervention from Republican governments, kept the education revolution intact. Black education, like the black church, would be an enduring achievement of Reconstruction.

While Congressional Reconstruction bolstered the position of freed people in general, it seemed to elevate the position of freedmen in particular. Reconstruction legislation assumed female dependency on male heads of household. Men voted, and men signed annual labor contracts. Yet in practice, formal politics and economics were never divorced from everyday life. Women were at the center of kinship networks, church life, and education—the old building blocks of the new black politics. They voted at mass meetings. In Richmond, they formed a ceremonial black militia. And in an era of open polling, many women claimed shared ownership of the vote.[77] One black woman attacked her husband with an axe when she heard that he had sold his vote.[78] Other women refused to have sex unless their menfolk cast their ballots for the Republicans. As for the signing of contracts, one Georgia landowner reckoned his greatest problem in coming to terms was "disagreements between husbands and wives."[79]

Black women even found ways to turn their formal dependent status to their advantage. Some used the law to demand protection from errant husbands. In Texas, Emma Hartsfield complained to the Freedmen's Bureau that a white man called Lacy McKenzie persuaded her to live with him on the promise of providing a house. After Hartsfield became pregnant, McKenzie tried to force her to have an abortion. The bureau agreed that McKenzie should provide for her.[80] Some single mothers claimed rights as independent heads of household, demanding the return of their children from forced apprenticeships.[81] On balance, though, Reconstruction politics did more to promote male headship than to preserve the egalitarian structure found within slave communities.

The more pressing issue for both black men and women, however, was their tenuous hold on their newfound freedoms. Henry Turner's travails showed just how unstable it could be. Even in Republican states, Reconstruction was only a start, not a secure settlement. Wealthy, well-armed opponents still longed for a restoration of the old order, and former slaves, who still lacked the resources to defend their freedoms by themselves, remained dependent on Republican allies. This dependency worked both ways, but for most white Republicans, their alliance with freedmen was a marriage of convenience rather than conviction. Factions within the party showed just how rocky that marriage actually was. What black southerners desperately needed were a few more years of good harvests and continued northern support. They got neither.

The Last Days of Reconstruction

Perhaps Radical Reconstruction was doomed from the outset. It quickly alienated most white southern Republicans, yet it failed to give black southerners the power they needed. But what made the end of Reconstruction a certainty was a series of calamitous events starting in 1873. That September, a major lender for a railroad company went bankrupt. A financial panic followed. The New York stock exchange closed for ten days. Then an economic depression set in. A quarter of America's railroad companies folded within two years. By 1876, unemployment had reached 14 percent. Strikes turned violent.

For black Americans, the depression was an economic catastrophe. The price of cotton fell by one third in four years. Renters and sharecroppers faced ruin. In 1874 the Freedman's Bank collapsed, causing thousands of black families to lose their hard-earned nickels and dimes. Myers' embryonic union folded. The depression was a political disaster too. In 1874 northern voters punished the party in power for their economic woes, as voters usually do during a depression. Democrats won control of the House and the Senate. Southern Democrats chaired half the committees. It was the greatest peacetime swing in party power in American history up until that date. The outgoing Congress passed a civil rights act at the start of 1875, but it was not so much a final hurrah as a final whimper. It failed to include schools, cemeteries, and churches, and it placed the burden of enforcement on the backs of black litigants. Even so, Democrats exploited the act to good effect. The Nashville *Banner* chuckled: "Whom the Gods destroy, they first make mad." Congress would not pass further civil rights legislation for nearly a century.

In fact, momentum in Washington had begun to shift even before the panic. Congressional Republicans decided against removing Reconstruction from the oversight of the Supreme Court, in the full knowledge that the Court was likely to take a narrow view of federal enforcement. (In 1883 the justices would duly rule the civil rights act unconstitutional.) Congress cut funding for the Freedmen's Bureau. President Grant fell out with Radical Republican leaders over his proposal to annex Santo Domingo (he thought that freedmen might want to emigrate there). Northern public opinion began to swing against former slaves, too, as commentators blamed lazy freedmen for the failures of southern agriculture, inveighed against black corruption for southern states' default on payments to railroad companies, and held "black barbarian" legislators responsible for the factionalism of southern Republican politics.[82] With worker unrest threatening northern society, Republican leaders concluded that "free" labor of any color was rather too free. In 1874 the Republican lawyer George Templeton Strong compared the nuisance of New York's "Celtocracy" of Irish immigrants with the South's burden of "niggerocracy."[83]

Little surprise, then, that African Americans in the former Union states struggled to make progress during the last days of Reconstruction. The overall picture was of dreams deferred at best, and dreams dashed at worst. In June 1873 news of the appointment of twenty-five black men to patrol the streets of New York caused an outcry—until officials clarified that the men were street-sweepers.[84] That same month, in Charleston, West Virginia, the first black policeman, Ernest Porterfield, was appointed. On a good day for burglars, perhaps, the entire police force resigned.[85] Northern white supremacy hastened the fall of southern Reconstruction, while racism in northern workplaces effectively imprisoned freedmen in southern agriculture. By closing off their escape route, northern white supremacists took away some of black southerners' bargaining power.

In the South, straight-out Democrats—those who wanted no compromise with Republicans—flexed their new muscle. Violence in Louisiana in 1873 provided the model. Following a disputed election, two rival governments set up camp in the Pelican State. In April, fearing a Democratic takeover, black militias in Colfax dug in. They held the town for two weeks. On Easter Sunday, armed white men turned up with a cannon. They reclaimed the town in two hours, then executed at least fifty men. Federal troops secured the state government for the Republicans, but armed White Leagues—basically the Klan without the white sheets—sprung up across the state. The Democratic platform for the 1874 state elections started with "We, the white people." In September, some seven thousand armed white men overpowered half as many black militiamen and police in New Orleans. Again, federal troops restored order, but they didn't crush the mob. Northern Democrats, pointing to southern violence as a reason to vote down the Republican experiment, took back control of the House of Representatives after the 1874 elections.

Straight-out vigilantes across the South took their cue from these events. Four states remained staunchly Republican on account of their large black populations—Louisiana, Florida, South Carolina, and Mississippi. Only Mississippi held elections in 1875. Mobs timed their attacks for maximum effect, and hundreds of freedmen were killed. Governor Ames appealed to the president for help, but Grant—who was so shocked by Klan violence just a few years before—did not send troops. "The whole public are tired out with these annual, autumnal outbreaks," he explained. Ames urged black voters to stay home. The stage was set for an assault on the remaining Republican states. As a sign of intent, Confederate war heroes stood for office in the 1876 elections. Louisiana Democrats nominated for governor "all that was left" of General Francis Nicholls (he had lost his left foot and arm during the war).

The irony was that in these last days of Reconstruction black Republicans had more influence in the remaining Republican states than ever before. The majority of black congressmen went to Washington after 1873. There were more local black officials, and more officials were freedmen, after 1873 than before. More black South Carolinians voted in 1876 than in 1868. Ditching any attempts at conciliation, freedmen and women called aggressively on Republican leaders to address their concerns—and turned against those who did not.

The blackening face of southern Republicanism played into the hands of straight-out Democrats and drove white Republicans from the party. But black political assertiveness was not a naive pursuit of unrealistic dreams—it was a rational response to the imminent demise of Republican state government. In the South Carolina coastal lowlands—a rice-growing region with a large black majority—the depression left freedmen and women facing starvation. In May 1876 they struck for better wages. As so often happened, a group of women workers on day contracts started the confrontation by refusing to accept a pay cut. Planters refused to budge. As kinship networks passed the word, the strike spread. One astounded bureau agent felt the workers were "communicating like magic." After armed black enforcers faced down would-be strikebreakers, the planters gave in.

In the state capital, however, white Republican leaders sought to mollify white voters. Governor Daniel Chamberlain came down strongly against the strike enforcers. Planters murmured their approval. More generally, Chamberlain opposed the "excesses" of his party. In the aftermath of the recent Mississippi massacres, he feared the looming vigilante menace. He feared a taxpayer revolt, too, by planters angry that state relief for the poor helped the very people who were so disruptive at work. In an act of appeasement, Chamberlain reduced the tax burden—which in turn left destitute farmers with less state support.

Chamberlain's concessions had all the effect of throwing a single bucket of water on a brush fire. In 1876 straight-out Democrats sought control of the black-majority state. Their candidate for governor, Lieutenant General Wade Hampton, mouthed conciliatory platitudes, while—in a classic good cop/bad cop routine—former Confederate General Martin Gary did the campaign's dirty work. Gary mobilized over two hundred rifle clubs across the state and arranged for armed supporters—known as Red Shirts—to harangue Republican rallies. In Edgefield County, the self-styled "county that had never been reconstructed" (over a hundred miles from the coast), Gary told his supporters, "If [a black man] deserves to be threatened . . . he *should die.*" In nearby Hamburg in July, Red Shirts shot five black militiamen dead.

Back on the coast, freedmen and women looked on with alarm. Desperate to stiffen the spine of the Republican Party, they confronted Chamberlain. When he ventured to the low country, "colored republicans . . . would not allow him to speak." (When Chamberlain went inland, Hampton's Red Shirts shouted him down, too.) Sensing that time was against them, black workers launched a new round of strikes. But this time, low country planters stood firm. They joined the straight-out ticket and prepared for war.[86]

Black Republican officials—many of whom had never been slaves—now faced hard choices. Some went over to the Democrats. Congressman Robert Smalls, chair of the state Republican convention, denounced Chamberlain for doing nothing "when colored men are murdered" in Hamburg. Even so, Smalls urged strikers not to attack strikebreakers.

The strikers were not impressed. They reportedly warned Smalls to stay away or else "they would tie him up and give him 150 lashes on his big, fat ass." Under pressure from congressional Republicans, Smalls eventually stumped for Chamberlain. No doubt he figured that a conservative Republican was better than a straight-out Democrat. Smalls accompanied Chamberlain to Edgefield County to drum up support. Red Shirts mounted the stage and heckled the governor, threatening to shoot his bald head off. The rally descended into chaos. Smalls felt the political middle ground give way beneath him. And with so many people on stage, so too did the platform. In the melee that followed, Red Shirts shouted "Kill the damn nigger." Smalls got the first train out of town—his second escape from armed Confederates in just over a decade. But this time, Smalls feared there would soon be no Union troops to escape to.

Back in Washington, D.C., Smalls proposed an amendment to an army bill that would leave some troops in South Carolina "so long as the militia of that State [is] massacred in cold blood." He worried that General Custer's recent defeat at Little Big Horn would lead the federal government to remove its remaining troops from the South and send them West. He was right: with Democrats charging black corruption, his amendment was dismissed. Meanwhile, Frederick Douglass called a Colored Convention to shore up black support for the Republicans. To vote Democratic, he thundered, was like "supporting the devil against God." South Carolina freedmen agreed about the devil bit. But they did not look to Douglass for guidance. His world was far removed from theirs, as he well knew. When Douglass was reunited with his brother Perry, a slave for fifty-five years, he felt it was "as if he had lived on another planet."[87]

Down in the low country, black workers made their own last stand. The 1876 state election turned out to be the bloodiest in American history. Black Republican enforcers—women as well as men—were every bit as intimidating as Red Shirts. One report said a group of women with "hatchets and large sticks" warned "those who voted Hampton should be slaughtered." They had the sanctions of the bedroom too. Smalls appealed directly to the wives of turncoats: "Don't service them." Come election day, coastal freedmen turned out at the polls in force, and afterward planters gave in to the strikers' demands. South Carolina's attorney general noted, "Laborers are at work again . . . upon terms that are very onerous to the planters."[88]

Elsewhere in the state, however, what white violence could not achieve, fraud did. Democrats voted early and often. More people voted the Democratic ticket in Edgefield than actually lived there—and Edgefield was a black-majority county. During the ensuing chaos, both Hampton and

Chamberlain claimed victory. It was a similar split picture in Louisiana. Meanwhile, the presidential election could not have been closer. Republican candidate Rutherford B. Hayes needed to carry both Louisiana and South Carolina to claim victory. A Republican-majority commission called the election for him, but as a gesture of compromise, Hayes let Democrats "redeem" Louisiana and South Carolina. He judged that Democratic control would spare freedmen future violence. But freedmen in South Carolina begged to differ. "To think that Hayes could go back on us," complained one, "when we had to wade through blood to help place him where he is now."[89]

The Democratic victory did not end the troubles in the South; it just changed the balance of power within which battles over the meaning of freedom were fought. Hampton removed all Republicans from state offices and dismissed all black members of the state militia. He set up a chain gang and started an investigation into Republican corruption. Smalls was charged with taking bribes, while journalists—seeing an opportunity to pile on—charged that he had not piloted *The Planter* but had hid in the ship's boiler room. For his part, Smalls claimed Hampton's men offered him $10,000 to step down. In 1877 a judge sentenced Smalls to three years' hard labor. The former war hero had escaped slavery, wielded political power, and enjoyed economic reward, only to face the prospect of forced labor once again. His life served as an apt story of the black experience in the South after emancipation. He appealed the sentence, and in 1878 he lost his congressional race in an election that was so corrupt he was sure Congress would intervene. It did not. In 1879 he was pardoned as part of a deal that saw the final pardon of Democrat rebels.

As for the coastal lowlands, Hampton left much of the region's governance to local black officials. But the balance of power had shifted here too. The state passed laws that favored landowners, and the white state militia sided with the planters. In 1878 the Columbia *Daily Register* crowed, "Employers . . . have never had so little trouble with their hands since the war as during the last year."[90] That year, Hampton went to the Senate. His replacement as governor started to remove black officials along the coast. Black schooling survived the backlash, however. Democrats did not want to provoke Congress, and with victory assured, they no longer saw black schooling as a political threat anyway. Inadvertently, the 1875 civil rights act's failure to require integrated schooling took the heat off public education.

Meanwhile, in Georgia, Henry Turner had long since headed out of Macon, and away from electoral politics, to pastor a prestigious church in coastal Savannah. But he was already looking even further east, across the Atlantic, back to his first love, Africa. In 1878, and through to the end of the century, he would champion calls for mass emigration. True to form, Turner's new approach reflected growing support for emigration out of the South—especially among African Americans in the low country. In the meantime, Turner worked with black artisans to build up Savannah's black economy; Grant appointed him inspector of the customs house. He encouraged black men to defend their homes with guns, although he became the first black Methodist to appoint a female deacon. He called on white Americans to pay reparations to former slaves. And he preached that the "All-Seeing Eye" belonged to a black God. Across the South, African Americans would continue to build their communities, and resist those who interfered, as best they could.[91]

In Washington, Frederick Douglass came out in support of Hayes—a decision sweetened by his appointment to the lucrative position of marshal of Washington. In a foretaste of future factional divides among black Americans, many condemned Douglass's misplaced loyalty. One correspondent told him that when Hayes recognized Hampton, he recognized "the worst enemy a race battling for freedom can find . . . it appears to be growing dark again."[92] The bright news of a prestigious post was no compensation for this growing darkness. In a final irony, Hayes downsized Douglass's job in order to prevent him from mingling with white visitors. For the first time, the marshal of Washington was not invited to receptions at the White House.

In October 1871 nine black student singers from Fisk went on tour across the North. Like most new black colleges, Fisk was teetering on the brink of bankruptcy. One teacher explained her request for back pay was because she had worn through her only pair of shoes. The Jubilee Singers hoped to raise money to build a new hall. They also hoped, said one student, "to ameliorate . . . caste prejudice."[93] Concerts by black-faced minstrels were common, but a concert by accomplished black musicians was—to quote the tour organizer—a "new thing" entirely. Considering the deteriorating image of black Americans in U.S. culture, this new thing seemed opportune. The following year, the singers headed to Britain—the first black American performing group to travel the Atlantic. In 1874 they returned to tour in America, and then they headed to Europe for a three-year tour.

In America, the first reviews were mixed. The *New York World* thought the group "sung with mellowness and life"—not bad, for a group that "had the air of well trained monkeys." The musical press was decidedly cool to their classical numbers. But initial disapproval of black performers gave way to acceptance. Crowds warmed to the Jubilee Singers' slave spirituals. The influential abolitionist and preacher Henry Ward Beecher adored "the wild slave songs, some of which seem like the inarticulate wails of breaking hearts made dumb by slavery."[94] President Grant invited them to sing at the White House (though they were expelled from their District of Columbia hotel because of their race). Yet even the praise for authentic slave music confirmed stereotypes of black simplicity and emotionalism. The *New York Evangelist* thought the "wild and plaintive" melodies were "born of that sound of music which seems to dwell in these simple children of nature."[95]

By contrast, in Europe the Jubilee Singers became a sensation, welcomed by the great and the good. Britain was in the grip of revival, and preachers warmed to their religious message. Welsh audiences—who had a vibrant hymnal tradition of their own—related the slave experience to their own suffering at the hands of the English. Scottish audiences compared the spirituals to their highland laments. Musicians acclaimed the music's authenticity. The composer Antonin Dvorak would later praise black spirituals as "the folksongs of America . . . the product of the soil." The singers raised £10,000 during their 1873 tour. In 1876, Jubilee Hall opened at Fisk University.[96]

The story of the singers is a reminder that black Americans used many means to battle for their livelihood, to build community, and to challenge a racist world. Reconstruction was an extraordinary era of political drama, but it was not simply a story of high politics. It is a reminder, too, that battles were fought in the arena of public opinion as well as at the workplace or voting booth. In years to come, black performers would seek to overturn negative racial stereotypes in American culture, in the hope that this would advance the wider struggle for meaningful freedom. But the fate of Reconstruction also gave early warning of the limits of this strategy. The Jubilee Singers won praise at precisely the moment that northern Republicans turned their back on southern freedmen, at precisely the moment that former slaves faced economic catastrophe, and, curiously, at precisely the moment that the black image in the white mind was taking a downturn.

The northern tour of a southern group is also a reminder of the national scope of the struggle, not least because black Americans faced racial barriers across the country. Their success in Britain and Europe pointed to the international scope of the struggle, too. For years to come, black Americans would seek inspiration and support from abroad. Even so, despite offers to stay in Europe, the singers returned home. Their success in raising funds for Jubilee Hall showed there were victories even in the midst of political defeat. Community institutions, not least colleges, would sustain black Americans in the dark years to come. But the construction of Jubilee Hall also served notice that black victories, and black community building, were never far apart from politics. During the last days of Reconstruction, white vigilantes destroyed hundreds of black schools and churches. So Jubilee Hall was built with fifteen-inch-thick walls.

CHAPTER THREE

Resisting the Juggernaut of White Supremacy, 1878–1906

In 1889 Oliver Cromwell encouraged black farmers in black-majority LeFlore County, Mississippi, to trade directly with white farming cooperatives rather than their landlords. Cromwell was a traveling organizer for the Colored Farmers' Alliance—an organization claiming a million members. By sending Cromwell a letter inscribed with skull and crossbones, local "white citizens and planters" made their intentions clear. By replying with a letter signed by "Three Thousand Armed Men," so too did black Alliancemen. One hundred black farmers marched "in regular military style" to deliver the letter. What started as a struggle over trading rights soon became a full-scale battle. Mississippi's governor, three companies of the state's National Guard, and a local white posse joined together and killed some twenty-five black farmers. Planters warned white farmers to stop trading with the Colored Alliance, because the organization's defiance had "produced a feeling of uneasiness . . . as to the welfare of our wives and little ones."[1]

At the turn of the century, black Americans were more likely to be lynched in Oregon than in Mississippi, or in Iowa than in South Carolina.[2]

In 1894 the outspoken Ida B. Wells toured Britain to win support for her anti-lynching campaign. The celebrated abolitionist William Lloyd Garrison wrote approvingly to the London *Times* that Wells "found deaf ears to her complaint in the United States. Spoken from the vantage point of London, her faintest whisper goes like an arrow to its mark."[3]

In 1896, the Supreme Court in *Plessy v. Ferguson* ruled that "separate but equal" provisions for black and white travelers on public transport did not contradict American law. The majority opinion explained that "legislation is powerless to eradicate racial instincts." Considering that Harvard University's evolutionary display cabinet placed the Negro between the chimpanzee and the white man, and that the majority of the justices had been to Harvard Law School, it was hardly a surprising judgment.[4]

On September 22, 1906, a white mob wreaked havoc on
Atlanta's downtown business district. Three days later, in
Tennessee, when thirty-five black prisoners in the Knox County
jail heard the news, they refused to go to their cells. The jailers
turned a hose on them to force them back, but the prisoners
captured the hose, turned it on the officers, then threw bottles
and broom handles with knives attached. Three officers were
hemmed in. Two hours later—after the police arrived—order was
restored.[5]

At first light, on April 21, 1878, thousands of African Americans
thronged the banks of Charleston Harbor. Many would have been in the
crowds that had cheered the return of the *Planter* thirteen years before.
Now, they came to watch the *Azor,* a speedy clipper, sail away from
Charleston, and away from the South, to Liberia. Anticipation had been
building for weeks. Parents brought their children to look at the *Azor*
and imagine the journey. On departure day, scores of people tried to stow
away. The crew called in an armed guard. At 8 a.m., the *Azor* set sail.
Two steamers, packed with black excursionists, accompanied the *Azor*
out of the harbor, while those on shore waved hats and handkerchiefs.
The 206 passengers hoped to build a new life in Africa. As one emigrant
put it, in an appeal that would be heard in generations to come: "We
want a country of our own."[6]

The coming and going of boats in Charleston Harbor spoke to the rise,
and now fall, in the tide of fortune for African Americans. The wartime
escape of *The Planter* had been a symbol of the slaves' contribution to
their own freedom. The celebrated return of *The Planter* had signaled the
hope of Reconstruction. Now, the departure of the *Azor* reflected the
despair of Redemption—nowhere more than in South Carolina, scene
of much brutality during the recent restoration of Democratic control.
Ironically, a tug named *Wade Hampton* pulled the *Azor* out to sea—just
as the election of Hampton as governor had prompted the *Azor's* passengers to head east. (In a further irony, the *Azor* had originally been built to
carry slaves from Africa—hence, its suitability for the reverse journey.)

Many of the greatest champions of Reconstruction now supported emigration. Henry Turner, recently a legislator in Georgia, consecrated the
Azor in front of five thousand people. Martin Delany, previously a passenger on *The Planter,* joined the crowd to wave the *Azor* away. He told
reporters of the "apprehension on the part of the blacks that they could
not live in a subordinate position where for ten years they held the reins
of government."[7] Both Turner and Delany had set their sights on Africa

before the Civil War. Now, to their minds, the future for black Americans in America looked every bit as bleak as it had in slave days.

The trip was organized by the black-owned Liberian Exodus Company—a venture that grew out of local enthusiasm for emigration. Liberia seemed the obvious place to go. It rivaled Haiti as an overseas icon of black freedom—the company formed after four thousand people celebrated thirty years of Liberian independence in July 1877. Africa as a whole was increasingly alluring at this moment, as rescue parties searching for the explorer David Livingstone sent reports of untold potential in the interior. Liberia in particular had the reputation of being a promised land of abundance. Rumor had it that a single potato could feed a whole family for a day. Word spread, too, that the Liberian government was keen to welcome American settlers.

As they had during Reconstruction, freedmen's groups petitioned Congress, the president, and northern allies for support—in this case for emigration. They even petitioned the British government. As they had during Reconstruction, freedmen and women also organized for themselves. Traveling lecturers spread the news. So too did kinship networks. Most church leaders were initially hesitant. But their congregations were not. So ministers started exhorting for an exodus that was going to happen anyway. Some saw God's hand in the turn of affairs. In Bible times, hadn't God's chosen people suffered for a little while after freedom, before entering into the Promised Land? Local people hastened the day. After settling up with landlords at the end of 1877, hundreds headed to Charleston to catch a boat. The problem was, there wasn't one. So the Liberian Exodus Company hurriedly raised money by selling stock, bought the *Azor,* and hoped to send many thousands to Africa.

In the event, the enterprise was short-lived and seemingly ill-fated. The *Azor* ran out of good water. There was barely enough food, and what there was, said one report, was "only fit for hogs to eat." Twenty-three people died en route (and two babies were born). A white Charleston journalist who boarded the *Azor* wrote in disgust (yet with barely concealed delight), "The negroes were . . . so filthy and lazy, that it is only wonderful so few of them died."[8] Unexpected costs put the company into debt, forcing it to sell off the *Azor* on the ship's return. The company planned to buy the ship back later, but a combination of a financial swindle and a legal tangle conspired against it. As for the emigrants, most may have settled well.[9] One became Liberia's chief justice; another built the first Liberian steamship. But the earliest stories to reach America were complaints from a dozen angry returnees about a "Liberian fraud."

One year, and one harvest, later, a new exodus began, when black Mississippians headed to Kansas. It was a similar story. The so-called Exodusters were running from the reversal of fortune after Reconstruction and the prospect of worse to come. One migrant gave an affidavit about receiving the following threat: "We white folks are going to have it our own way or kill you all __ ___ Republican niggers."[10] Emigrants were also running toward the promise of prosperity. Word spread of available land, and of transport and supplies provided by the government. "Free Kansas" held a special place in the black imagination, too. Before the war, the famous John Brown had battled, and beaten, those who wanted to make Kansas a slave state. Those who stayed in Kansas may well have prospered—later census reports suggest that far higher numbers of Mississippi emigrants to Kansas owned their home compared with those who remained (though the records do not show whether emigrants were relatively better off in the first place).[11] But the story published at the time was of those who returned, penniless and bitter.

More people made it to Kansas than to Liberia—perhaps 25,000 moved in 1879. Still, this was hardly an earth-shattering total. After all, some six million African Americans stayed in the South. The so-called Great Migration of black southerners to northern cities would not begin for a couple of generations. Thus, it would be easy to dismiss the exodus movements as mere curiosities of no consequence. But it would also be a mistake.

Although only thousands moved, hundreds of thousands discussed the exodus, celebrated it, and seemingly, desired it.[12] One black South Carolina politician thought emigration aroused religious "enthusiasm very much like fanaticism." Many spoke of "Kansas fever." Exodus clubs sprang up across the South—especially in states where the reversal of Reconstruction had been swift and brutal. From the North, Sojourner Truth acclaimed "the greatest movement of all time" in verse: "The prison doors have opened, and out the prisoners went. To join the sable army of African descent, for God is marching on."[13] Ultimately, what slowed the exodus was not the lack of intent, but the lack of a promised land or the means to get there. Moving was risky and costly. In this context, what was significant was how many did try to leave. "Not a few seemed willing," wrote one northern missionary, "to suffer any hardship, even to death itself." This was no exaggeration. One man left Edgefield County, South Carolina, after Christmas, in the pouring rain, with two young children, to walk 750 miles west. By the time he reached Georgia, one child was barely alive.[14]

Migration out of the South continued after the Exoduster movement of 1879 had died down. A new fever seemed to break out every couple of years or so—after a poor harvest, or an outbreak of violence, or a new round of restrictions on black labor. Within the South, perhaps a third of rural workers moved at the end of each year in search of better conditions. Georgia sharecropper Ed Brown likened himself to a rabbit, moving in a "zigzag, dodging one hunter then the next."[15] Sometimes large groups moved en masse. Early in 1887 a local white newspaper reported in horror the "perfect swarms"—five hundred people a day—heading from the Mississippi hills to the delta.[16] More black migrants left bloody Edgefield County—perhaps one fifth of the black population—than virtually anywhere else. One astonished white reporter, unwittingly echoing the migrants' millennialism, reckoned there had been "nothing like it since the days of Pharaoh."[17]

Such mass movement showed that the post-Reconstruction South was anything but settled. Redemption crushed Republican rule in state government, but it did not crush black southerners' Reconstruction struggles to make freedom work in their localities. Emigration groups often grew out of freedmen's political societies. Moving to make a decent living was akin to Reconstruction struggles for land and against planters. A group of South Carolina families headed to Arkansas in 1886 because landlords had taken first lien and political power. They wanted to "leave planters without help."[18] Mass movement also showed that white elites had not regained full control, despite the Democratic "redemption" of state politics. In Washington County, Texas, from where a thousand black farmers moved in 1879, planters slashed rental prices from five to three dollars per acre. In Louisiana that same year, freed people moved en masse ahead of a constitutional convention that had been called to disfranchise all black voters.[19] Fearing a further loss of labor, the convention pulled back.

Thus, after Redemption—even because of Redemption—black southerners continued to challenge the economic and political order. And while many moved, others stayed and fought—especially in those parts of the South where Redemption had been less brutal (often white-majority states where Redemption came early) or where black southerners had been able to stand their ground against vigilantes (often counties with a large black majority). In diverse ways and diverse places, they continued to seek a better life and resist those who interfered.

Consider just a few examples: in Galveston in July 1877, black washerwomen went on strike; the following year, black and white Alabama coalminers joined together for higher pay and against convict leasing; in the 1878 elections, black voters in the black-majority "Senegambian" district of east-central Texas supported the insurgent Greenback Party; after the 1878 elections, a Young Men's Protective Association in New Orleans complained about violence and fraud; the following year in Virginia, black voters swung behind the insurgent Readjuster Party; that same year, a National Conference of Colored Men met in Nashville and delegates called for the same rights "accorded the other nationalities of our country"; in 1880 black sugar workers in Louisiana went on strike; in 1881 black washerwomen in Atlanta launched the most determined labor protests in the city's history. "We will have full control of the city's washing at our own prices," the Atlanta ladies insisted, "as the city has control of our husbands' work at their prices."[20]

It is telling just how worried planters and politicians were by the limits of Redemption. The Reconstruction experiment may have been over, but the Reconstruction electorate, a free labor workforce, and resilient black institutions remained. One informant in Orangeburg, South Carolina, told his Democrat boss in 1880 that "I've pried into their camps . . . *We are in danger.*"[21] Planters in Hinds County, Mississippi, appointed a "Committee of 15" to deal "in a becoming style" with anyone who helped workers move.[22] In the Alabama mining district, black labor organizer and brilliant orator Willis Thomas worked to such effect that "true Democrats," wrote one local paper, feared *"Reconstruction days had come again."*[23]

Southern Democrats had rational reasons to worry. After Reconstruction was over and the hated Yankee troops had departed, they were anything but a solid coalition. In fact, in Virginia in 1879, it seemed that Reconstruction days had come for the first time. Virginia had been the only southern state not to have an elected Republican government during Reconstruction. But now, splits among Virginia's white voters over the question of the state's wartime debt gave rise to the Readjuster Party, which did not want to pay the debt in full. With majority black support, the Readjusters won both houses of the state legislature in 1879, then the governorship in 1881.

Virginia seemed to be a harbinger of things to come in southern politics, at least in the upper South. In Tennessee, Democratic divisions over the state debt allowed Republicans to win the governorship in 1881 after ten years of Democratic control. "It means," commented the *New York Times,* "the first step towards the dissolution of the solid South on real, pressing, practical questions."[24] Most of these practical questions concerned money matters. The post-Reconstruction southern economy had more years of bust than boom, and poorer white farmers regularly locked horns with the "better classes" in politics and at work. Over one fifth of white southerners voted against the Democratic Party at some stage in the 1880s.[25] Many poor white families—far more than black families—left the South.

Splits in the white vote reopened the possibility of biracial anti-Democrat coalitions across the South (often insurgent parties rather than Republicans). Such coalitions were especially strong in black-majority regions of black-minority states. In the Senegambian district of Texas, for example, biracial alliances kept local politics out of the Democrats' control for a generation after Reconstruction. Indeed, more black candidates won state office in Texas, Arkansas, Tennessee, Virginia, and Florida in the first elections *after* Reconstruction than during it. And even in the states of the lower South, where the blood shed during Redemption violence lay fresh on the ground, black voters in many black-majority counties held firm. More often than not, local Democrats came to "fusion" agreements with black voters to share out offices.

Where black voters retained political influence, or where black workers were hard to replace, then black protest remained effective. In Virginia, black legislators demanded—and won—a $100,000 appropriation for a new black college and the foundation of an asylum for the African American mentally ill, who had previously been kept in jail. The editor of the Petersburg *Lancet,* the aptly named George Bragg, attributed gains "to the manly stand taken by the colored people."[26] In Louisiana, sugar workers were able to strike because of the centralized production system (which helped with organization and self-defense), the technical requirements of sugar rolling (which made it hard for planters to bring in strikebreakers), and the presence of a black sheriff (which was a consequence of their numbers and economic strength). A Senate investigation into the bloody Louisiana elections of 1878 noted that wealthy sugar planters had actually opposed violent "bull-dozing" of black voters because "demoralization of agricultural labor . . . would bring ruin."[27]

Elsewhere, black southerners exploited opportunities as and when they arose. There were victories aplenty—or at least successful rearguard defenses. In 1878 in Memphis, an outbreak of yellow fever played into the hands of black political leaders. The city government had refused to appoint black policemen. Now, as white residents fled the city, the (also aptly named) Mayor John Flippin changed his mind.[28] In 1881 in Atlanta, when black washerwomen struck ahead of the World Cotton Exposition, the city government tried to regulate the "Washing Amazons" but found it hard to land a punch—their organization was decentralized, their lowly work made them impossible to replace with white women, and trusty scare tactics about promiscuous black men were irrelevant.[29] City officials backed down. All the while (as in Reconstruction) black southerners used the spoils of their political and labor activism to build up community institutions, which in turn provided the foundations for the defense of freedom.

As had been the case during Reconstruction, black actions in the South captured national attention. Each bout of migration fever hit the front pages of the major newspapers—and thus so too did the freedmen's tales of woe. As in Reconstruction, the movement of former slaves along southern roads forced Congress to take note—in 1880 the Senate set up a committee to investigate the exodus. As before, northern allies used the freedmen's testimony to demand action. Some joined mass meetings called by northern African Americans. A leading New York minister, Theodore Cuyler, charged, "This Negro exodus ought to be a voice of thunder in the ears of influential white leaders in the South."[30] Others provided charity. Former abolitionists in Great Britain—so recently entranced by the Jubilee Singers—sent clothing to help destitute emigrants (or as the London *Times* called them, in an otherwise heart-wrenching account, the "foolish wanderers").[31]

Quite what effect this national, even international, lobbying had on southern leaders is impossible to measure. In fact, the greatest pressure on southern planters came from international cotton traders, who wanted a stable supply line as quickly as possible. There were plenty of existing reasons why Democratic leaders might want to watch their step anyway—not least because they were chary of provoking federal interference under the provisions of the Reconstruction amendments. Still, it is striking how many Democratic spokesmen were at pains to placate northern opinion. In a roundtable discussion of black voting in the influential *North American Review* in 1879, Mississippi Senator L. Q. C. Lamar knew of no "southern man of influence" who believed black disfranchisement to be a "political possibility." (Lamar's moderate line served him well—he would later become the first southerner appointed to the postwar Supreme Court).[32]

And yet, for all its vibrancy, the first post-Reconstruction protest also revealed the new constraints faced by black southerners. The fact that so many hoped to leave the lower South told its own story. The passengers of the *Azor* guessed right—the Redemption era turned out to be a time of desperately defending rights rather than advancing them, of occasional victories interspersed by regular setbacks, and of enclaves of strength in an otherwise unforgiving world.

In national politics, the Democratic capture of both houses in 1878 confirmed the passing of Reconstruction. The Senate Committee on Migration deemed the exodus to be a Republican conspiracy to move gullible black voters north—notwithstanding the fact that Kansas was already comfortably Republican. Hearings were full of laughter at the migrants' expense. The only positive action Congress took on their behalf was to suspend import duty on charitable donations from Britain. The Republicans regained both houses in 1881, but the parties split the houses for the next three Congresses, and traded the presidency too. What this meant was that Republicans were in no position to help black southerners even if they wanted to. But after Reconstruction, it was clear that most did not want to. Party platforms dropped the suffrage question during the 1880s.[33] Lack of Republican interest translated into a lack of regulatory interest. Although the Department of Justice mounted nearly five thousand criminal indictments in the South between 1870 and 1894, only a quarter came after Reconstruction.[34] As for Republican President James Garfield (1881), he admitted he "never could get in love with [the] creatures."[35]

While Congress retreated from Reconstruction, the Republican-majority Supreme Court began to reverse it. In the civil rights cases of 1883, the Court ruled the federal government could not intervene against private (as opposed to state-sanctioned) acts of discrimination, and that freed slaves could no longer be "a special favorite of the laws."[36] Noteworthy here was public reaction—or rather, the lack of it. The *Nation* noted "the calm with which the country receives the word that the leading section of the celebrated Civil Rights Act of 1875 has been pronounced unconstitutional."[37] African Americans were far from calm. Black Texans rioted. In a widely reported speech, Henry Turner said the decision should be "sawed, cut and carved with the most bitter epithets and blistering denunciations that words can express."[38] But neither rioting nor rhetoric could restore Reconstruction Republican radicalism to national politics.

Nor could black ballots or biracial politics restore Reconstruction days back in the South. In 1883 Democrats overthrew the Readjusters in Virginia, regained the governorship of Tennessee, and then knocked back the insurgent challenge in every other state for the rest of the decade. They did so by playing on Reconstruction-era fears that black gains caused white pain. In South Carolina, Democrats warned that the insurgent Greenback Party wanted to "Africanize the state." It was an irrational claim. The Greenbackers were led by white men opposed to the power of corporations. But so soon after the bloody racial battles of Redemption, when anti-Democratic voting or white control had seemed a zero-sum game, the claim resonated. Ahead of the 1883 election in Danville, Virginia, Democrats produced a list of outrages that resulted from black political power—the influx of "idle and filthy negroes," and "*Negro women* have been known to *force ladies* from the pavement." Four black Americans were killed in the violence that followed. Democratic Party publicists called it white self-defense. News of the "riot" swung the election. Black men still voted in force, but white voters turned out in greater numbers.[39]

Across the South, little by little, Democratic leaders took steps to contain the power of the anti-Democrat vote. Because of the Reconstruction amendments, they could not target black voters explicitly. But they manipulated election machinery to their advantage. The South Carolina legislature redrew the electoral map to squeeze black voters into a single black-majority district, the so-called Black Seventh, that snaked its way bizarrely across the state. In Mississippi, stray mules happened to eat some ballot papers that happened to come from black-majority counties.[40] Though fusion continued in black-majority areas, it usually meant, to quote Senator W. B. Roberts from Bolivar County, Mississippi, "the Negroes . . . have some of the offices, and the whites of course [have] the best ones."[41]

After Reconstruction, Democratic legislatures quickly passed a welter of legislation to contain insurgent workers, too. Alabama's legislature banned the nighttime transport of seed cotton in Black Belt counties only. Violators could face up to twenty years in prison.[42] Prisoners returned to the land to pay off their fines, by way of the chain gang. To one British visitor, Sir George Campbell, the convict-lease system "does seem simply a return to another form of slavery." It was probably worse. Over a quarter of convict-lease workers in Tennessee died during 1884–85. And Tennessee had a reputation for being one of the better state systems.[43]

Hard times left black southerners with hard choices. Black voters split between Republican and insurgent parties. Black spokesmen split on protest tactics. Some (such as Delany and Turner) supported emigration. Others (such as Smalls or Turner's main AME rival, Bishop Daniel Payne) advised staying put. Some condemned Democratic scaremongering. Others chastised the black poor for letting the race down. Such divisions were rarely so clear cut in practice. But what was clear was that the days when prominent black spokesmen and organizations could claim to speak for the entire race were long gone, if they had ever been there at all.

Still, if the heady days of southern Reconstruction were now a memory, the decade after Redemption did not see a return to slavery either. Even in these constrained times, black men could vote, black workers could contract their labor, black families could move, and black communities could build institutions and garner resources. Thus, while the passing of Reconstruction changed the terrain of the struggle for freedom, it didn't end it. In many localities, the end of Reconstruction was not even a clear watershed in everyday black life.

Indeed, in black-majority areas, black voters continued to hold local political power. Ironically, gerrymandered districts in the South ensured black representation into the next century. Twelve of the fourteen terms served by black congressmen after 1879 were in gerrymandered districts.[44] As late as 1890, Kansas Senator John Ingalls reckoned that disfranchisement would be "impossible." A renowned intellectual and a scathing critic of Democratic fraud, Ingalls was no misty-eyed idealist. His study of the world taught him that "no race has ever been deprived of rights . . . once solemnly conferred."[45]

As a historian, Ingalls was right. But as a prophet, he would be completely wrong. By the end of the century, in the North and the South, the African American freedom struggle would become a desperate rearguard resistance.

The Triumph of White Supremacy in the Northern States

Writing in the New York *Age* in May 1887, T. Thomas Fortune called for a National Afro-American League to fight racial injustice in the South. Born to slavery in Florida, Fortune left the South soon after Reconstruction, settled in New York, and founded the *Age,* which by 1887 was the most widely read black newspaper of its day. A tall man with wayward hair (and a lifestyle to match), the irascible Fortune was one of the most outspoken critics of southern racism. He had no doubt that the Redeemers' victory—for all their honeyed words—meant that Reconstruction was "a revolution gone backward." He castigated electoral fraud, mob violence, inequities in school funding, chain gangs, and the "tyranny" of segregated railroads.[46] In his 1884 book *Black and White,* Fortune had urged black southerners to arm themselves, and had called on the poorer black and white "dangerous classes" to join together. Now, at the league's first meeting, Fortune called on the delegates, mostly from the northern and western states, to stand "as representatives of 8 million freedmen" and "face the enemy and fight inch by inch for every right he denies us."[47]

Yet just over a decade later, Fortune found himself fighting racial oppression inch by inch much closer to home. On the evening of August 15, 1900, white mobs ran riot in New York City's Tenderloin District. Tensions had been rising for some time. Between 1880 and 1900, New York's black population increased from 65,000 to almost 100,000 people. In the big picture, this was not much of an increase—from 1.3 to 1.4 percent of New York's total population. But in the Tenderloin, the city's squalid vice district, where recent immigrants from Europe and black newcomers (including Caribbean immigrants) scrapped for housing and jobs, it mattered.

The New York summer of 1900 was the hottest in memory. So too was racial tension. As people stayed late on the streets to escape the stifling heat of decrepit tenement apartments, street fights were common. A seri-

ous outbreak of violence was entirely predictable. So too was its trigger—
a fight over a woman. In the early hours of August 13, Arthur Harris—an
odd-job man from Virginia, with no prior convictions—was drinking in a
bar. His wife, May, came to find him, and then waited for him outside.
When Arthur came out, he saw a white man hassling May. He rushed to
defend her. When the white man clubbed him, Harris pulled out a knife
and "cut him twice." The white man turned out to be a policeman, Robert Thorpe, the son-in-law of the local police captain. Thorpe had mistaken May for a prostitute and was trying to arrest her. Harris fled the
city. Thorpe died the next day.

On the third day, reported the *New York Times,* a crowd of a thousand
people "started to clean the side streets of Negroes.[48] An excited *New
York Tribune* correspondent called it a "real, live, nigger hunt."[49] One
man tied a clothesline to a lamppost, looking for someone to lynch. The
mostly Irish police force encouraged the mob. A lawyer who collected the
testimony of eighty victims concluded "it was the night sticks of the police that sent a stream of bleeding colored men to the hospital."[50] No records were kept of how many people were hurt. But despite the fact that
most black victims stayed at home, "afraid to trust themselves to the
mercy of the crowds," the emergency staff of three New York hospitals
worked through the night to treat cracked skulls.

Black New Yorkers fought back. One reporter was shocked at the sight
of Vincent Streets, a black painter, emptying his pockets after being arrested. "He was a walking arsenal. First came from his pockets a huge
loaded revolver, then a razor, after that a dirk knife, and finally a dozen
cartridges."[51] Fights between black men and the police, and between
black and white gangs, continued through the summer. Meanwhile, black
leaders demanded justice. Fortune, along with local ministers, organized
a Citizen's Protective League which held a mass meeting of some 3,500
people at Carnegie Hall. But city officials depended on the votes of the
very white workers who were most fearful of black migrants. Not a single policeman was indicted. As for Harris, he was arrested and sentenced
to hard labor. He died in prison.

The violence in New York was repeated across the North and West.
Not all black northerners lived in the equivalent of the Tenderloin, and
not all cities experienced a riot. But many did. A week later, in Akron,
Ohio, a white mob went on the rampage after a newly arrived black migrant was arrested for assaulting a four-year-old white girl. In cruel irony,
stray bullets killed two more white children. And in a further irony, one
of the worst riots occurred in Springfield, Illinois, in 1908 while the city
was preparing to celebrate the centenary of native son Abraham Lin-

coln's birth. When there wasn't a major riot, anti-black violence was still common. White gangs "hunted the nigs."[52] With the exception of New England, African Americans were almost as likely to be lynched in the North as the South, and more likely to be lynched out West. (There were many more lynchings in the South than elsewhere, but that was because most black Americans lived there.) Even in New England, a black person was over a hundred times more likely to be lynched than a white person.[53] Ida B. Wells bemoaned the fact that "lynching mania has spread throughout the North and middle West." Such violence set a chilling pattern for twentieth-century race relations in the North.

The pandemic of anti-black violence reflected a wider story of aggressive white supremacy. The North had never been a particularly safe haven or just environment for black Americans. But toward the end of the nineteenth century, a bad situation got worse. In politics, city councils sought to minimize black voting power. At work, white unions sought to force black workers from those jobs where they had already established a foothold. In education, local school boards moved toward segregation. In 1890 the *New York Times*—which had previously advocated integrated schools—approved of the shift: "Whoever insists upon forcing himself where he is not wanted is a public nuisance."[54]

Why African Americans came to be perceived as a "nuisance" subject to such intense racism was due to a powerful combination of forces that were at once local, national, and global. This was an age of empire, of racialist thought. In London in 1892, the young Winston Churchill, watching the great black heavyweight Peter Jackson, sketched a picture of an apelike figure.[55] Ideas of white supremacy crossed and recrossed the Atlantic, seemingly picking up force with each journey. Social Darwinists judged that black people had lost out in the "survival of the fittest." Scholars in Berlin hypothesized that people of African origin were innately better at manual labor in hot climates. Railway magnates in Canada liked the thought of cheap black workers so much that they considered annexing a Caribbean island. White railwaymen in Canada disliked the thought of black rivals so much that they fought for, and won, exclusive white control of skilled and semi-skilled jobs.[56]

The United States' own imperial ambitions (such as its armed occupation of the Philippines in 1899) justified racial hierarchies at home.[57] So, too, did the aftermath of Reconstruction. National reconciliation—inluding the rehabilitation of Confederates in public life—was a lily-white affair.[58] Intellectual and popular culture reinforced racial stereotyping. Doctors reported blacks' higher susceptibility to sexual diseases, preachers explained the divine ordering of the races, and entertainers fanned a new coon song craze.[59] In 1906 Fred Fisher, a German-born crooner, sold over three million sheet music copies of his first hit, "If the Man in the Moon were a Coon." (The era was already in a moon craze— Fisher's success lay in spotting the rhyme.) The coon was not just the traditional ignorant and indolent figure of fun—he was devious, dangerous, and sexually on the prowl. "Dey all know dat I'm a hot potato," boasted De Swellest Ladies' Coon in Town, "Wid a razor . . . or shootin' dice."[60] Songs were more powerful than reasoned racial arguments: moving their bodies to the beat, dancers accepted the message. It was just common sense.

Racial hierarchies made sense to white northerners because of the conditions in American cities. The U.S. economy went into severe recession in 1893 and stayed there until the end of the century. Only the Great Depression saw worse unemployment figures in modern times. As in New York, poor European immigrant workers lashed out at rivals and interpreted job competition in racial terms—against the Chinese out West, against Mexicans in the Southwest, and against black migrants everywhere. White workers justified their behavior as a response to black criminality and sexual deviance. Setting a pattern for the future, the oppressed racial and ethnic groups battled against one another too. Meanwhile, worker unrest made business and political elites wonder whether popular democracy had become rather too popular. By 1891 some thirty northern and western states had adopted the secret ballot, which prevented illiterate voters (disproportionately immigrant or black) from voting.[61]

As in New York, some African Americans responded with fists and guns. A hundred Exodusters, unable to find steady work in Kansas, headed to Omaha, Nebraska, and—armed with rifles—forced their way into a smelting works.[62] Blacks also continued to organize politically. Almost half of Seattle's small black community were members of political clubs at the end of the nineteenth century. Black northerners looked to the law, too.[63] And as in New York, whole communities joined together. City officials segregated the schools of Alton, Illinois, in 1897 to prop up real estate prices in white neighborhoods. The town's Republican mayor promised "to keep the niggers out of [white] school . . . if I have to use every policeman I have got." He needed them. Black children sat-in at the white schools. According to the *Washington Post*, they overpowered the janitor at one school and struck the lady principal.[64] One black parent filed suit. Black children then boycotted their schools—290 of 300 school-age children stayed away. Eleven years later, less than half the town's black children had returned. Black newspapers across the country championed the boycott, and black communities sent money to pay for private schooling.

On occasion—as in the South—divisions among white voters gave black voters some leverage. In Ohio in the 1880s and Detroit in the 1890s, black voters exploited close elections to gain electoral victories and Republican patronage.[65] At the height of black influence in Cincinnati, there were 164 black municipal and county employees earning in total over $120,000 per year.[66] On occasion—usually during strikes by white laborers—black migrant workers won new jobs and forced concessions from bosses.

But for the most part, black protest did little to slow white supremacy in the North and West. The problem for black Americans was not any lack of will power but lack of real power. In part, this was a simple matter of numbers. On the streets, black men were able to defend themselves in one-on-one fights, but they couldn't repel a mob. In city politics— run by multimillion-dollar political machines—black voters in the North were too few to hold much leverage. In the workplace, strikebreaking was a hazardous business. White bosses usually employed white workers to preserve calm. In the courts, the law proved to be a weak ally. Between 1884 and 1905, some seventeen states and towns adopted civil rights laws of some sort—the legacy of Radical politics and black lobbying. In practice, though, as a group of New England black men complained in 1886, "the colored citizen is discriminated against in so many depressing and injurious manners notwithstanding the letter of the law." In Ohio, the Equal Rights League actually opposed the state's first civil rights law for failing to include restaurants, barbershops, or juries and for making plaintiffs liable for all costs.[67]

The course of the Alton protests is a case in point. The litigation should have been successful, because school segregation violated Illinois' antisegregation law. But the trial court rebuffed the complaint seven times in a row. Each time the state Supreme Court asked the trial court to reconsider, and in 1908, having finally ran out of patience, the state court ruled for the plaintiffs. The school board accepted the decision but applied it to only the two children first named in the case—who by this time were twenty-one and nineteen years of age. When nineteen-year-old Minnie Bibb tried to call the board's bluff, she was told she would have to enter the third grade. Bibb refused to join a class with eight-year-olds. The community readied to protest again, but the riot in nearby Springfield put an end to the saga.[68]

Assertiveness by black Americans fueled white supremacy at least as much as it restrained it. One Indianapolis resident felt the city's "increase in its colored population by the increase in racial discrimination."[69] National newspapers headlined their coverage of the Alton boycott as "race war"—reason enough to denounce the protesters. This is not to say that black activists were authors of their own oppression. Rather, it showed just how little room they had to maneuver. Desperate for a job, one black miner near Seattle said, "Let them call us scabs if they want to."[70] In the context of rising fears and racism, blacks were called many other things besides scabs. The New Lexington (Ohio) *Tribune* described migrants as a "horde of barbarian niggers" ready to take homes and daughters as well as jobs.[71] Little wonder that most lynchings were against new black male migrants—the mob could unleash all its anxieties, imagined and otherwise, onto the male body of a stranger.

Little wonder, too, that many of the more prosperous black Americans, the so-called "aristocrats of color," tried to sidestep the racist onslaught. None more than the "black 400" in Washington, D.C.—in practice about a hundred mostly light-skinned elite families, out of a black population of 75,000 in 1900. Drawing on the promise of Reconstruction, they hoped to assimilate into elite white society. After all, many had such light complexions as to be able to pass for white on the street (and seemingly some did so). Black elites also lodged integration suits, appealing to their higher-class status rather than universal human rights.[72] If the number of magazine articles and novels is any guide, white Americans were fascinated by the mixed-race "mulatto" figure—but both the law and custom now put mulattoes firmly on the dark side of the color line. By the end of century, most elite blacks recognized that integration with the "better sort" of whites was a vain dream, and they turned instead to uplift the race by promoting black learning, publicizing black achievements, and reforming the masses.

For African Americans in the West and North, rising racism had catastrophic consequences. At the top of the list was poverty. For example, though only 4 percent of Philadelphia's youth population in 1890, black children filled almost a quarter of the places in the city's House of Refuge.[73] Many of the "aristocrats of color" held their own, and the segregated turn of the century saw the rise of black businesses aimed at a black clientele. The growing economic strength of separate black communities would provide the foundation for northern protest in years to come. But the exclusion of black workers from unions and major sectors of the economy during a period of rapid industrialization also set far-reaching precedents. Out West, white unions forced black employees out of California's food industry during the 1890s, and black women in northern cities were as likely to be domestic servants as their southern counterparts. Stigmatized as strikebreakers, forced into "dirty" jobs and dirty areas to live, black workers became associated with lowly status. It was a vicious, self-perpetuating, downward spiral of racism. Meat-packing employers in Illinois quite openly presumed that only "Negroes did not object to performing low-paying . . . unpleasant tasks."[74]

In the larger cities, segregated housing became the pattern, especially once improved transport allowed people to travel further to work. School boards drew school catchment areas that were all-white or all-black. In the smaller towns, the pattern was exclusion. Some five hundred "sundown" towns in Illinois required black migrants to leave before dark. In politics, the few elected representatives from local black districts became fewer. Black voters in Boston had been unusually well represented politically before 1897, often holding at least one seat on the City Council. But the council redrew electoral districts to black voters' disadvantage. Decline in patronage followed. In 1894 the new Republican council in Seattle appointed only one black man, as a dogcatcher—and his salary was cut in half. It may have been only because black voters in the North were so few that there was no talk of outright disfranchisement—an omission that would have significant consequences after the Great Migration in years to come.

White supremacy in the West and North had important consequences for national politics. It was not that the national government had been a strong advocate of racial equality after Reconstruction. But the end of the century witnessed an altogether more decisive retreat. In its landmark *Plessy v. Ferguson* decision in 1896, the Supreme Court ruled that public transport—and by extension wider society—could be racially segregated without violating the Constitution. Congress pulled back from Reconstruction, too. In 1889 Republicans gained control of Congress and the White House for the first time since Reconstruction and proceeded to pass such wide-ranging measures as the Tariff Act. But they did not manage to pass the Lodge Bill, which would have increased federal power to secure African American voting rights. When the Democrats swept back into power in 1893, they quickly repealed Reconstruction election laws. Republicans gained control of the federal government again in 1896 and retained unified control for another fourteen years. But their secure majority (because of support from new western states) allowed them to drop the thorny issue of black voting in the South. Republican President Benjamin Harrison (1889–1893), who had supported the Lodge Bill, began to withdraw patronage from black southerners in an attempt to attract Democrat dissidents.

Because the federal government pulled back from Reconstruction,

southern white supremacists were emboldened to act. One black Charles-
tonian wrote to Henry Lodge in despair that "the failure to pass [your]
Election bill has knocked us completely out in this state."[75] Rising black
anger against Republicans was palpable. A black Floridian informed
President Harrison in writing that "the negro [will] have nothing to do in
the future with the White Louse [sic]."[76] Because black subordination
and separation came to be seen as normal across the country, the task of
southern white supremacists became that much easier. Because migration
was not an attractive option, most black southerners were stuck in the
South, and would take their stand there.

The Triumph of White Supremacy in the South

Just a few months after Thomas Fortune in New York first called for an
Afro-American League, black sugarcane workers in southern Louisiana
demanded a modest increase in wages and payment in cash rather than
scrip (pay that could only be used at plantation stores). Some planters offered a compromise, but none gave in. The workers threatened a strike
starting November 1, 1887. A group of "influential [white] people" met
together in the town of Thibodaux and threatened to evict any strikers
from their plantation homes within twenty-four hours. The showdown
was set. Perhaps ten thousand black workers stayed home. "No power
on earth could remove them unless they were removed as corpses," said
one worker. His words would prove as prophetic as they were defiant.

Exactly what happened next is not known. Surviving newspaper accounts are far too partisan to be reliable. One Methodist newspaper
judged, "As usual, the Negroes . . . were treated with . . . barbarity."[77] But
the *New York Times* reckoned Thibodaux was "full of idle negroes, who
each day become more and more audacious."[78] Planters brought in white
strikebreakers and private militias. Strikers fought back. Many were arrested. Some wives joined their husbands in jail voluntarily. As rumors
spread, Thibodaux's "influential people" formed a risibly named Committee of Peace and Order, backed up by armed patrols, and prepared for
battle. On November 21, the first frost of the season warned that the
sugar crop was in serious danger of being lost. With time running out,
evicted workers, private militias, and white men from Louisiana's major
cities gathered in Thibodaux. To quote the *Times* again, "The outlook
is very dark . . . the most trifling incident will bring about a terrible massacre."

The "terrible massacre" started before dawn on November 23. The
"trifling incident" was the sound of gunshots, when a group of strikers

fired at white deputies standing at their post. Return fire killed six strikers. "This opened," wrote Mary Pugh (wife of a wealthy planter) to her
son, "the *Ball*." Armed white men rounded up strike leaders, took them
to the railroad tracks, placed each victim ten paces in front of them, and
shouted "run for your life," before shooting them dead. By the time the
state militia arrived, the mobs had done their worst. The militia disap-
proved, anyway. At least thirty people were killed, and many others fled
to the forest swamps. Mary Pugh was "sick with the horror of it." But
she thought the massacre would "settle the question of who is to rule, the
nigger or the White man?" and was relieved that "the negroes are as
humble as pie today." Out in the woods, vigilante hunters tracked down
their prey. Rotten corpses would be discovered long after the massacre.[79]

In many ways, the Thibodaux "sugar war" was just the latest—or
rather the final—chapter in an old story. There had been worker protest
in the sugar plantations since the end of the Civil War. But the sugar war
also had some new twists. The workers didn't just want more pay, they
wanted a different method of pay—every fortnight rather than every
month, in cash rather than scrip. They didn't just protest sporadically,
they joined with white workers in a massive strike coordinated by the
Knights of Labor—a regional workers' movement. And they didn't just
protest at planting time, they waited until the rolling season—thereby
putting the entire crop in jeopardy. In other words, black workers flexed
their economic muscle as never before.

What was new, too, was that by 1887 planters had won political
power in the sugar parishes, and they had allies in state government.
Thus, they were free to deploy their own militias and call on the state militia if need be. Northern opinion seemed to have swung behind them. In
national politics, the incoming House of Representatives had a Democratic majority, and the sitting president was a Democrat. In other words,
planters were in the strongest position they had known since the Civil
War.

This changing balance of power helps explain why the protest started,
and why it was put down. Emboldened sugar planters first introduced
scrip and made less regular payments after Redemption. Thus, black
workers were simply trying to draw a line in the sand, to defend their
hard-won Reconstruction gains. A strike was not so much a gamble as
the only option other than folding. It was now or never. The arrival of the
Knights of Labor in southern Louisiana in 1886 (to organize railroad
workers) suggested it might be now. The Knights' "producerist" rhetoric
calling for unity of honest toilers, its reputation for successful strike action, and its organizational know-how allowed it to channel worker dis-

content into a mass worker movement. But ultimately, cane workers lacked the firepower or political support to win the day. Their defiant stand-off proved to be their last stand. There would no more strikes in the cane fields for half a century.

In many ways, the story of the turn-of-the-century South was the story of the cane fields writ large. Those with a vested interest in white supremacy gained the power to settle Mary Pugh's question of who was to rule once and for all. The answer would be the "white man," not "the nigger." To be sure, the Reconstruction amendments remained, promising an expansive view of citizenship regardless of color (and these amendments would come back to haunt segregationists in the mid-twentieth century). But in practical terms, black southerners became denizens rather than citizens. To quote Thomas Fortune, this was indeed "a revolution gone backward." And at least outwardly (and certainly compared with the belligerence of Reconstruction and its immediate aftermath), many black southerners seemed to become "humble as pie."

Exactly how white supremacy was imposed played out differently in different places. Sometimes—as in the cane fields—the struggle was settled in blood. Thibodaux was followed by a series of anti-black riots, notably in Wilmington (1898) and Atlanta (1906). In the period between the Thibodaux and Atlanta riots, some two thousand black southerners were lynched—more than one victim every four days. At other times, the struggle was settled by new legislation that restricted black labor (especially in the countryside), segregated public space (in the cities), or disfranchised black voters. Exactly when white supremacy was imposed varied too. Just sixty miles east of Thibodaux, in the New Orleans docks, black longshoremen demanded, and won, higher wages to the end of the century. In politics, Mississippi disfranchised black voters in 1890, while Georgia did not finish the job until 1908. But for all the twists and turns, the so-called Jim Crow South of racial disfranchisement, segregation, and subjugation was firmly in place by the dawn of the twentieth century (Jim Crow was the name of a stock minstrel figure).

As in the cane fields, the gradual, changing balance of power in southern politics and society after Reconstruction made the rapid reversal of Reconstruction possible at the end of the century. Rather like in a boxing match, there was a long softening up process before the final, dramatic, knock-out blow. In the case of disfranchisement, the removal of black voters in each state was as swift as it was devastating. In Arkansas, for example, 71 percent of the black electorate voted in 1890. Four years later, after the introduction of a poll tax, only 9 percent voted.[80] Such rapid disfranchisement was possible only because black voting power had already been reduced. First violence and fraud cut into black voting and returned Democrats to power. Then Democrats contained the opposition vote by redrawing electoral districts and through control of the election machinery. Shifting political power hastened the imposition of new segregation and labor laws and provided cover for white vigilantes. In turn, violence and labor laws undermined the ability of blacks to defend the vote, making the final solution of disfranchisement possible. Once they held a preponderance of power, white supremacists could seek absolute power.

As in the cane fields, black defiance sometimes triggered the final push to settle the struggle for mastery. There were the old-time fights over livestock and fights on the streets, aggressive gestures and assertive glances—no doubt what reporters meant what they wrote of the "audacious" behavior of cane workers in Thibodaux. What was new was that such protest merged with the mass workers' movements and insurgent politics that convulsed the late-nineteenth-century South. In the midst of a landscape that seemed as old as time—the sun up to sun down backbreaking routine in the fields, church on Sunday, a diet of grits, black-eyed peas, and peaches—the South was changing fast, and racial politics changed with it.

Some landowners and entrepreneurs looked longingly to the coming of a New South, a South of industry and trade. But many southerners feared the march of progress. The turbulent 1890s saw more years of recession than prosperity, where local people felt adrift in national and global markets as never before. Hence the rise of workers' movements. Because black workers were so numerous in the South, they joined this protest nearer the center than the margins occupied by their northern counterparts. The Knights of Labor oversaw major biracial strikes in the docks of New Orleans, the lumberyards of Florida, the coalmines of Alabama, the tobacco factories of Virginia, and the levees of Memphis (not to mention the cane fields of Louisiana). In the countryside, the Knights were matched by (and sometimes overlapped with) the Farmers' Alliance—a million producers pushing back against the power of merchants and large landowners. The alliance was lily-white, but a Colored Farmers' Alliance emerged alongside which claimed over a million fee-paying members by 1891, including 300,000 women.

Biracial unions and farmers' alliances were no bastions of racial camaraderie. Richard Davis, who helped organize black miners in Alabama during the 1890s, observed that "blacks and whites worked together underground" but "wouldn't ride together on work-train, or eat together—even in dirty clothes."[81] In the countryside, many white Alliancemen were landlords who refused to lease land to black farmers. But "the fact is," wrote the editor of one farm journal, "that the law of self-preservation compels the southern white farmer to take the southern black farmer by the hand."[82] In any case, black workers demanded justice from the workers' movements every bit as much as they used the movements to seek justice from bosses and planters. The Colored Farmers' Alliance strongly supported the Lodge Bill, even though the white Farmers' Alliance opposed it. Black miners in Wolf Den, Alabama, in 1890 refused to fund the white checkweighman's salary after their calls for a black checkweighman had been rebuffed.[83] Soon afterward, in an early case of affirmative action, the United Mine Workers in Alabama made a constitutional provision for a black district vice president.[84]

In politics, the People's Party, also known as the Populist Party, grew out of the revolt of the countryside. Populist leaders appealed to the "common farmer" who felt buffeted by price swings of the global market and bitter toward predatory merchants nearer home. As with the Farmers' Alliance, the People's Party started off as a white peoples' party. Or as a Georgia black Republican, William Pledger, put it, Populists were "the men who have lynched the colored people in the past."[85] But as with worker movements, political insurgents in black-majority areas needed black support. The result was a series of pragmatic alliances, with strength in such black-majority strongholds as southern Louisiana and Grimes County in the Senegambian district of Texas. In North Carolina, a Populist-Republican alliance controlled the state government from 1894 to 1898.

Biracial, confrontational movements triggered a backlash. Reporting a possible Farmers' Alliance protest in September 1891, an apocalyptic *Atlanta Constitution* headline screamed, "The biggest agricultural strike in the history of the world is imminent."[86] In November in central Arkansas, a white plantation manager called Tom Miller agreed to a wage increase to 60 cents per pound for his black workers. Emboldened, black workers nearby struck for 75 cents. One Democratic newspaper reported a virtual standstill across one stretch of thirty miles. The usual sheriff's posse arrived, killing at least fifteen strikers. They murdered Miller, too, for breaking ranks.[87] It was a similar story in politics. Insurgent victories led to campaigns of violence. In Grimes County, a White Man's Movement won the election for sheriff in 1900. The following day, a white posse killed the remaining insurgent officeholders and drove other insurgent leaders (white and black) out of the county for good.[88]

But it was not only dramatic, political protest that triggered supremacist violence. So too did everyday, gradual economic progress and institution-building. As Robert Smalls put it in a letter near the end of his life, "I believe that the prejudice against the Negro today in this country is because he is improving . . . For this reason he is feared."[89] In the country-side, many slipped toward debt slavery—or, as Henry Turner loudly condemned it, "peonage." But according to the 1900 census (the first to report farm ownership), almost a quarter of black farmers owned the land that they worked.[90] In the lower South, black farmers held on to the (mostly marginal) land they had gained during Reconstruction. In the upper South, they gradually increased their landholdings. Farmers' access to credit and equipment was underpinned by mutual aid societies based on old kinship networks.[91] Landless farmers made some progress, too. In 1880, two thirds of rural African Americans in the cotton states were laborers. But by 1900, over half were renters or sharecroppers or owned their land.

In the cities, black poverty was rife. Some sought relief through readily available cocaine and cheap liquor. But many made a steady living, and some prospered from the segregation—and dollars—of black communities. By 1891, 75 of Atlanta's 450 retail grocery stores were black-owned. One sign of rising prosperity was the increase in black property ownership. Fewer than two thousand heads of families owned their homes in cities of the lower South in 1870. By 1890 nearly sixty thousand did—more than one in eight family heads. The numbers doubled again during the next twenty years, and the situation was even better in the upper South. In his farewell speech to Congress in 1901, the last remaining black congressman, George Henry White of North Carolina, defiantly trumpeted black achievements. "My parting words are in behalf of an outraged, heart-broken" people, but they were also a "rising people, full of potential force." One symbol of rising prosperity was Atlanta businessman Alonzo Herndon. Born a slave, Herndon cut hair at a white hotel, set up his own barber shops, then invested his profits in real estate. By 1900 his net worth was $12,750 (a millionaire in 2010 money). Herndon's flagship barbershop had imposing front doors of solid mahogany and plate glass, a marble floor, and a chandelier.[92]

In the countryside, some poor white farmers blamed black famers for the debts they faced. Some joined Whitecap oath-bound paramilitary associations, promising—to quote one Mississippi Whitecapper—to "assist in every way directed by the organization to compel negroes to vacate any and all property owned by merchants, and to assist to put out of the way any and all obnoxious negroes."[93] In the cities, mob violence was directed at black businesses and schools as much as people. In 1906, white vigilantes hacked their way through Herndon's barbershop doors and smashed the chandelier.[94]

With hindsight, the vicious imposition of white supremacy might seem

the inexorable culmination of the Redemption era—because the slave society that had provided the foundation for antebellum political order no
longer existed. By the end of the century, white men at last had sufficient
power to demand absolute mastery, and African Americans' attempts to
build up and resist proved futile and provoked violence.

At the time, however, white supremacy seemed anything but assured. Its proponents fretted about black tenacity and federal interference right up until disfranchisement, segregation, and worker restrictions
were finally in place. Above all, they knew full well there was no united
support for, or even a united agenda called, white supremacy. To be sure,
racism was ubiquitous—a legacy of slavery and a product of late-nineteenth-century ideas. But support for a violent, absolute hierarchy of
domination was not ubiquitous. Indeed—as the biracial workers' revolts
showed—white men and women in the New South had priorities other
than race, and enemies other than black rivals. Restrictive labor laws and
disfranchisement devices such as the poll tax hurt poor white southerners
almost as much as black southerners.

For the most part, it was Black Belt elites who were at the forefront of
disfranchisement; it was planters who sought to control black labor, and
it was urban progressive reformers who promoted segregation. They had
to work hard to craft an ideology, and create a coalition, to win the day.
In other words, they had to work hard to ensure that Mary Pugh's question about who should rule would play out in racial terms as a choice between the "white man or the nigger" rather than, say, the laborer or the
landowner, the farmer or the merchant, the Black Belt conservative or the
city modernizer, the boss or the worker, even the white woman suffragist
or the male patriarch. Thus, the triumph of white supremacy was the
construction of a new order at least as much as the restoration of an old
one. It was a triumph every bit as far-reaching as Reconstruction or Redemption. In fact, it was not just a triumph of white supremacy, but of
white male elite supremacy. Yet by the turn of the century, virtually all
white southerners—wealthy and poor, rural and city folk, men and women,
even adults and children—believed they had a vested interest at various
times in different aspects of white supremacy. Therein lay its power.

In the rural Black Belt, no individual contributed more to this triumph
than Ben Tillman. The South Carolina governor spent his childhood as a
member of the wealthiest slaveholding family in Edgefield County, and he
spent his adult life trying to reconstruct white patriarchal power. He
fought in, and later rejoiced in, the bloody Red Shirt campaign that overthrew Reconstruction. But he was not satisfied by Redemption. He railed
against the urban "fogies" who controlled the Democratic Party—gran-

dees like Wade Hampton, who were prepared to deal with black voters. He claimed to speak for the farmers (he called them "real Democrats and white men") who were "in hopeless servitude" to "money power," who struggled against the federal government, white traitors, and African American power, and who needed to "Organize! Organize! Organize!" or "remain slaves." He called for the bleaching of the ballot. Opponents mocked his shameless self-description as a "clodhopper—a poor farmer boy." No matter. He won the election for governor in 1890, and his forces took control of the Democratic Party. In 1895 South Carolina disfranchised black voters.

Tillman's victory is instructive. It showed—as was often the case—how the wealthy spoke in the name of the masses. It showed the enduring power of racism. But it also showed how issues other than color were integral to his appeal. Indeed, Tillman's success was precisely because he folded concerns over men's status and economic survival into a package called white supremacy. In Tillman's world, farmers and real Democrats were, by implication, white farmers and white Democrats who would not stand for fusion or compromise. Thus, Tillman's definition was both capacious (poor and wealthy men) and restricted (white men only), drawing sharp color lines but blurring class division.[95]

Scare stories about black crime helped the cause. Ahead of the Wilmington election of 1898, Democratic publicists reported black women shoving white ladies, or in one case, hitting a white lady with an umbrella. "Such exasperating occurrences," wrote a Democrat journalist, Josephus Daniels, "would not happen but for the fact that the negro party is in power in NC."[96] The scariest stories told of rampant black sexuality. Tillman spoke of his opponents as "political miscegenationists." Frederick Douglass countered that if black men really were bent on having sex with white women, they would have done so during Reconstruction.[97] Still, incessant, sensational reports in cheap, mass-circulation newspapers warned doubters that for black men it was but a step from an interracial strike to interracial sex, or from the voting booth to the bedroom. In a new twist in Arkansas, Democratic propagandists warned that white insurgents believed "the time is not far distant when the [Negro] and the white man would . . . sleep side by side in the same bed."[98]

Once created by propagandists, the monster of white supremacy took on a life of its own. In Wilmington, as in Grimes County, white mobs set to their deadly task a few days *after* Democrats won back control of government. Across the South, Populists turned against black voters, ironically because racial scares and fraudulent manipulation or miscounting of black votes had enabled Democrats like Tillman to win the day. Thus, black men were the victims, but they were also to blame. It was a similar story with lynchings. Mobs killed in response to news of murder, accusations of rape, or other crime. Yet lynchings shaped racism as much as they were caused by it. Often they turned into public spectacles of the most horrific torture, including mutilation of the victim's genitals. Sometimes crowds arrived on special trains. On a few occasions schools were given the day off so children could watch. Entrepreneurs sold body parts, photographs, even recordings of a final scream. The watching crowd learned that black men must be capable of unspeakably bestial crimes to deserve such brutal punishment. And if that was so, disfranchisement, segregation, and labor laws were not just necessary—they were vital.

The Black Belt demagogues hankering after the Old South found unlikely allies in urban progressives desperate for a New South of industrial progress. So unlikely, in fact, that they didn't see themselves as allies at all. Henry Grady, the self-styled "spokesman of the New South," was Tillman's antithesis. The son of a Georgia merchant, Grady's skill with words allowed him to become a reporter and editor of the influential *Atlanta Constitution* in 1880. He saw industrial progress in close union with the North as the South's future, and he distanced himself from what he called the honest mistakes of slavery and Civil War in the past. To reassure potential northern investors, he praised the loyalty and labor of black workers, waxing lyrical about happy southern race relations. (One thousand black Bostonians turned up to disagree when he spoke in their city.) Grady promised decent wages, modern schools, and the defense of civil rights. It was just that Negroes were inferior and easily led, so, for the time being, there should be disfranchisement. He supported segregation, too, as a sensible way to impose order on bustling southern cities. Grady's honeyed words sounded different themes to Tillman's rabid diatribes. But on closer inspection, Grady's assertion that "supremacy of the white race of the South must be maintained" could have been Tillman's own.[99]

The unfolding of white supremacy reached a climax in Atlanta, the self-proclaimed capital of the New South. Here was a growing black community where migrants fought with white newcomers over space and jobs. Here were successful black colleges, black businessmen like Herndon, and—according to one Atlanta native in 1897—"more eminently cultured Negroes than any city in the union." Yet here too was a stigmatized community, where black districts had a reputation for dives and vagrants, and where preachers and reformers like Grady linked purification of the suffrage and public space to purification of the city's morals. And here was a closely contested election for governor where the Democratic candidates (with the support of former Populists) tried to "outnigger" each other for votes. A competitive daily press took full advantage. The day of the riot—Saturday, September 22, 1906—there were four separate rape stories. That night, white mobs smashed black businesses and—to shouts of "Save our women"—attacked black Atlantans traveling on streetcars. One black woman defended herself with a hatpin, another "fought like a savage wildcat with an umbrella." Ten black people were killed.[100]

After the riot, disfranchisement in Georgia and prohibition in black Atlanta soon followed, and segregation became more entrenched downtown. Democratic Party publicists hoped the example of Atlanta would settle the race question for the whole region.[101] A. J. McKelway, a southern Presbyterian reformer who supported child labor laws, prohibition, disfranchisement, and the Wilmington revolution—all to "save civilization"—concluded, "In anything like a race war the negro has everything to lose. It means, for him, not battle but extermination."[102]

Fighting Back

The fall of Atlanta to white supremacy sealed the triumph of Jim Crow across the entire South—a bleak new order would last generations. Yet the Atlanta riot also taught a different lesson—of continued resistance even in the eye of the mob. Black Atlantans battled and were not exterminated. On Sunday, they smuggled hundreds of guns into the city. That night, black families defended their homes, black professors patrolled their college campuses, and black prisoners rioted. From New York, Thomas Fortune applauded, while white northern journalists followed the fast-moving events with fascination. On its front page, the *New York Times* reported on black gangs wanting to "get even," readying to "drive out [white] families from their homes," and shooting two white policemen who interrupted a black meeting.[103]

Beyond Atlanta, there was plenty of retaliation against white violence. A third of lynchings were reportedly in response to murder, often of a brutal white boss. Lynchings were less frequent in black-majority areas—precisely because of the danger of black retaliation. For example, on August 21, 1899, in McIntosh County, Georgia, Henry Delegale, a locally prominent black man, was put in jail on the charge of rape. When the sheriff tried to sneak him out and release him to his white accusers, the bell of the local black Baptist church sounded the alarm. Hundreds of African Americans, many armed, surrounded the jail. Delegale himself was later tried and released.[104] Where such confrontation was too dangerous, there were anonymous ways to strike back. In 1891, the sheriff of Baldwin County, Georgia, shot an unarmed black man dead. A few days later, the sheriff's cotton mill burned down.[105] Such "coincidences" were particularly common a day or two after landlords evicted uppity tenants. The specter of black violence would continue to haunt the New Jim Crow South.

Still, what was also clear was that the balance of gunpower had shifted decisively, especially after disfranchisement. Atlanta's black community fought back, but Wilmington, the Reconstruction home of black militias, was cleaned out. In the countryside, burning a barn after dark was not the same as facing down a mob in the daylight.

What was true of black self-defense was true more generally. Black southerners resisted the imposition of Jim Crow. They boycotted segregated streetcars in at least twenty-five cities, sometimes for several years, sometimes with success.[106] Black southerners appealed to the law too, again with some success. In ten of eleven ex-Confederate states, African Americans took public, legal action against disfranchisement, and in Maryland black voters knocked back all three attempts. Some urban elite leaders played the class card. Arkansas State Representative John Gray Lucas asked sponsors of a segregated transport bill whether "a drunken white man is preferable, as a fellow passenger, to the most genteel negro."[107]

At best, though, black southerners could only slow the juggernaut of white supremacy. In transport, even the successful boycotts merely delayed, rather than derailed, segregation.[108] In voting, Maryland proved to be an exception due to high levels of black literacy, income, and arms in Baltimore, a curious state statute that banned the poll tax, and the presence of a sizeable number of immigrants unwilling to relinquish their vote for the sake of white supremacy. On the class issue, segregationists mocked black elite attempts "to draw the soap line." The Arkansas bill passed with only three white legislators opposed. In the courts, the law proved a fleeting ally, reflecting black southerners' deteriorating status. Tellingly, the *Plessy* decision provoked little attention among New Orleans Democrats. The leading local paper ran only a brief editorial and was not too sure what the case was about.[109]

In many ways, the final appeals for justice underlined just how weak black southerners had become. In South Carolina, the elderly Robert Smalls took his place as one of just six black delegates, out of 106, at the 1895 state constitutional convention called to introduce a literacy test. For comparison, there were seventy-one black delegates to the 1868 convention. With typical bravery, he spoke up. The Democratic *Charleston News and Courier* reported somewhat wistfully on the last hurrah of an

old foe: "No one can fail to be impressed with Gen Smalls' earnest pro-
testation, before God." Maybe so, but delegates failed to be moved. All
but the six black delegates voted for disfranchisement. Smalls refused to
sign the new constitution. When the convention proposed not to pay the
travel costs of anyone who refused, Smalls—in a final gesture of defiance—said "he would rather walk home than sign." As it turned out, in
the rush to disfranchisement the convention failed to vote down his
costs.[110]

In a sign of changing times, Democratic publicists—not black southerners, as during Reconstruction—now used southern white violence to
appeal to the nation as a whole. It worked. *Outlook* magazine—a liberal
religious journal founded by former abolitionists—published a
roundtable on the Atlanta riot. Writing as the "northern black" voice,
women's reformer Carrie Clifford pointed out that violence was "directed at the . . . progressive negro [and not] the vicious negro" and reminded white Christians of the command to love thy (Negro) neighbor.
But the response of a "southern white" laid the blame for the violence at
the feet of black men: "If there had been no assaults upon white women
there would have been no mobs." The editor concluded by calling for
black self-restraint, thus accepting the demonization of black men as de-
based criminals. In the light of the riot, Clifford reckoned the "lecture to
blacks on self-restraint becomes indeed a roaring farce."[111]

To win support, black critics of white supremacy looked abroad. The
foremost anti-lynching campaigner of the day, Ida B. Wells, traveled to
England. Born a slave and orphaned in her teens, Wells began her career
as a teacher while she supported her siblings. She then switched to journalism, and in 1889 she was elected as the first woman secretary of the
Afro-American Press Association. Fortune reckoned "she has plenty of
nerve; she is smart as a steel trap, and she has no sympathy with hum-
bug."[112] Though Wells had long challenged racism (she once bit a conductor who threw her off a segregated train, and then sued the company),
it was the lynching of three friends in Memphis on account of their business success that prompted her campaign. She thundered that the charge
of rape was a "threadbare lie"—most lynchings were not on account of
interracial sex; and where sexual encounters did occur, it was to satisfy
white women's longings rather than black men's lust.

Both the message and the messenger (a single black woman with a confrontational style) provoked far more criticism than support among
white Americans. Her enemies—who included some nervous black leaders—called her a "black harlot." Not so in England. During a four-
month tour in 1894, Wells gave over a hundred lectures, breakfasted
with MPs in the Houses of Parliament, was interviewed by leading news-

papers, and inspired the formation of an influential anti-lynching committee. By now a celebrity, Wells took the opportunity to denounce the leading American white women's temperance leader, Frances Willard, who happened to be in Britain at the same time. Willard was a social reformer who did not condone lynching, but to boost her cause she criticized black men for their love of "demon rum" and their resulting lust for pure white women.

Wells hoped Americans would "not ignore the voice of a nation that is her superior in civilization."[113] The *Washington Post* reckoned that "nobody in the United States cares three straws about the opinion of a lot of English gossips and busybodies."[114] Actually, the governor of Alabama did care—he wrote to the British press asking whether the queen would welcome his advice on Britain's handling of Ireland or India, adding that lynching was preferable to rape. As for Wells, said her critics, she was more bothered about "her income than the outcome." It would be half a century before world opinion would begin to influence domestic race politics. Willard got her own revenge, too. Back among temperance friends at the end of 1894, she suggested, patronizingly, that Wells' "zeal for her race . . . clouded her perception as to who were her friends," and repeated her call for an end to "the unspeakable outrages" against white women.[115]

Willard was one of many white reformers who affirmed stereotypes of black depravity even as they condemned white violence. Such reformers called on "respectable" black leaders to put their race in order. After the Atlanta riot, only one local white minister spoke up to call white men to repent. But two thousand white Atlantans, mostly businessmen, formed a Civic League to meet with black community leaders to address black delinquency and so ease race tensions. There was self-interest aplenty here. Atlanta's Chamber of Commerce worried about the city's credit rating. There was plenty of paternalism, too. One speaker explained, "The Negro race is a child race. We are a strong race, their guardians."[116] Some black leaders accepted (in public) the responsibility for reform in return for aid to do so. This appeal, or even manipulation, of paternalism could be heard elsewhere in the South. Rural workers appealed to landlords for protection against Whitecappers. But such deference was a far cry from the bold demands of Reconstruction days. And in Atlanta, the pay-off was shortlived. The City Council refused to increase funds for black education, despite talk of ignorant blacks becoming a criminal class.

As conditions deteriorated at home, support for African emigration revived. Henry McNeal Turner led the call. Ever in the center of the action, Turner had taken up a pastorate in Atlanta shortly before the riot. He was unimpressed by meetings with Atlanta's mayor after the riot, reckoned the comforts of hell were preferable to those on offer in the United States, and declared the U.S. flag a "dirty and contemptible little rag." Such talk prefigured the seemingly sudden surge in black nationalist and emigrationist movements to come after World War I.

Yet for now, most black southerners stayed put. They continued to build their lives, and communities, as best they could, but in more difficult circumstances than most had known. White supremacy seemed assured. But not quite: the Reconstruction amendments remained in place, and the memory of protest lived on. So too did Democratic dissidents and black rebels. White planters did not have complete control over their labor, let alone their livelihoods—black workers' wages in the Louisiana cane fields continued to rise and fall with demand from the global market. And all the while, separate black communities built up their strength from within.

Appropriately enough, in segregated Atlanta, the city that had supposedly risen like a phoenix from the ashes of the Civil War, black businessmen and women rebuilt their livelihoods by relying on black customers. Four years after the riot, Alonzo Herndon completed a new luxury home—a fifteen-room, two-floor Gothic Revival building complete with two-story Corinthian columns flanking the front door. Soon after, he became Atlanta's first black millionaire. In the years ahead, Georgia's white supremacists would worry more about Atlanta's thriving black community than any other threat. Rightly so. This community would nurture, among many others, a young college teacher named W. E. B. Du Bois (the most influential activist of the early twentieth century), a young Communist worker named Angelo Herndon (one of the most celebrated militants of the 1930s), and during the 1940s a minister's son named Martin Luther King Jr.

CHAPTER FOUR

Black Leaders Reckon with Jim Crow, 1893–1916

In 1901 the all-black Tuskegee Institute, in Alabama, celebrated the opening of its new library. The institute was the best resourced black college in the country. The handsome brick building, complete with an imposing Ionic portico, overlooked a quadrangle that called to mind the layout of the University of Virginia. Except in one respect. The portico faced away from the public road. Thus, a passer-by would only see a nondescript back wall, and have no idea of the learning and beauty that lay on the other side.

"Nothing more exasperates the better class of Negroes than this tendency to ignore utterly their existence. [They] are aroused to righteous indignation when they see that the word Negro carries most [white] minds to . . . the police courts." W. E. B. Du Bois, from a study of Philadelphia in 1899[1]

Black educator Nannie Burroughs cherished the story of former student Bettie Reed. A white family hired Reed as domestic help for a summer trip in Maine. The vacation home had only one bathtub. When the family refused to let Reed use it, Reed refused to stay. The family relented, reluctantly. After the vacation, the family wrote to Burroughs. "We are begging her to go back with us next season . . . she is a great deal cleaner than we are . . . Our objection was based on mere hearsay about colored people."[2]

In 1891 the black jockey Isaac Murphy became the first winner of three Kentucky Derbies. In 1899 Marshall Taylor became the first black world sprint cycling champion. Two years later William Lewis became Harvard's first black football coach. The *AME Zion Quarterly Review* asked, "How can it be reasonably argued that the race will never amount to anything? It would really seem the chief trouble is the race is amounting to too much."[3]

In 1913 some of Democratic President Woodrow Wilson's cabinet appointees segregated their departmental employees. Wilson's treasury secretary (and son-in-law), William McAdoo, defended the measures in a letter to the African American *World*: "*Separate toilets* . . . assigned to the blacks are just as good as those assigned to the whites . . . I do not know that this can properly be called segregation."[4]

At noon on Wednesday, September 18, 1895, seemingly every steam whistle in Atlanta sounded forth. At one o'clock, twenty-five military companies led a procession from the city center to the grounds of the Cotton States and International Exhibition. On arrival, the platform party assembled on the "profusely decorated stage," the soldiers headed straight for the barbecue stand, and a 60,000-strong crowd gathered in temperatures that visiting journalists complained were too hot for comfort. The exhibition grounds looked resplendent, complete with 347 flagstaffs, a 100-foot water slide, and a host of gleaming buildings that showcased the very latest technologies. At his home in Massachusetts, President Cleveland stood by to start the exhibition by pressing a specially installed golden button. First, though, it was time for a prayer of dedication, the reading of an exposition ode, and six speeches.

City leaders expected the exhibition to tie the regional economy firmly to the new industrial era. (The New South still kept the old race relations and religion, though—the exhibition was segregated and was the first industrial fair of the era to close on the Sabbath.) But they did not expect the exhibition to provide an extraordinary personal boost to an African American leader, Booker T. Washington, an educator from Alabama, who gave one of the speeches on behalf of "the masses of my race." Most in the crowd had not even expected a black speaker. When the master of ceremonies, former Reconstruction governor Rufus Bullock, introduced a "great southern educator," the crowd had cheered. When a black man stood to speak, the applause turned to suspicious silence (although black spectators cheered from their section).

That soon changed. With a bluntness that would have made Bullock wince, Washington dismissed Reconstruction as a "strange" mistake. He denounced black leaders who complained about white supremacy. He then called on black southerners to stay in the South and remember that "no race can prosper till it learns that there is as much dignity in tilling a field as writing a poem." (A national group of poets later pointed out, wistfully, there was certainly more money in tilling a field.) In turn, Washington called on white southerners to employ black workers, assuring his hearers of "devotion that no foreigner can match." Holding one hand high above his head, Washington promised, "In all things that are purely social we can be as separate as the fingers, yet one as the hand in all things essential to mutual progress." That way, he declared, sectional and racial strife would end and material prosperity would "bring into our beloved South a new heaven and a new earth."[5]

The crowd's response was as delirious as it was deafening. One observer said even "the fairest women of Georgia stood up and cheered. It

was as if the orator had bewitched them."[6] Bewitched indeed, considering that black men were supposedly such a grave danger to southern
belles. Acclaim surged out from Atlanta, via the press, right across the
country. "The speech," reported the Boston *Transcript,* "seems to have
dwarfed . . . the Exposition itself."[7] After reading the speech (which, with
characteristic self-promotion, Washington had sent him), President
Cleveland agreed. On the strength of the speech, Washington would become the dominant black figure of his generation, the black adviser to
presidents, and in due course, an international celebrity.

Not all black leaders shared the enthusiasm. Henry Turner reckoned
Booker "will have to live a long time to undo the harm he has done our
race."[8] Turner was also livid at the portrayal of Africans as cannibals in
one Atlanta exhibit. But most skeptics held their tongues, or at least their
pens, to see what would pass. In any case, critics were rendered mute by
the cacophony of praise from white commentators. Here was a diplomat
to replace the outspoken Frederick Douglass, who had died earlier that
year. Washington's manifesto—industrial progress rather than political
rights, industrial education rather than a classical education—promised a
painless resolution to the intractable "Negro problem." In their delirium,
some reporters let their imagination run wild. The *New York World* described the 5'6" classically African-featured Washington as "tall, bony,
straight as a Sioux chief, high forehead, straight nose [and] the sinews
stood out on his bronze neck."[9]

But the reason Washington rose so high, and for so long, was very
much his own doing. The Atlanta speech was the moment he had been
planning for—he had first used the hand and fingers analogy in a letter to
a Montgomery newspaper a decade before.[10] He was a brilliant orator,
lacing his arguments with humor and metaphors. He capitalized on his
fame by publishing an international best-selling autobiography, *Up from
Slavery,* by peppering the press with articles, and by making speeches
across the country, and Europe, with the energy of a modern-day presidential campaigner.

What made his message seem so credible, and so compelling, was
the evidence of his life story. *Up from Slavery* was a rags-to-renown narrative that even Horatio Alger—the popular contemporary author of that
genre—might have rejected as too fanciful. The rags were, literally, the
"torture" of flax shirts that were the lot of slave children. Washington
had little idea of his birth date, less idea who his (white) father was, and
he was born with no surname at all. The renown by 1901, when his autobiography was published, included an honorary degree from Harvard,
tea with the queen of England, and dinner at the White House. In Wash-

ington's telling, the "Negro" was lucky because out of the "unusual struggle through which he is compelled to pass, he gets a strength."[11] Washington's struggle including leaving his small-town Virginia home at age sixteen to seek an education at Hampton industrial school, some four hundred miles away. En route he slept rough, loaded up boats to earn money, and gained admittance to the school after proving he could clean a room—he swept it three times and polished it four. He impressed his teachers so much that in 1881 he was invited to run a new industrial school in Tuskegee, Alabama.

One London writer called the growth of the Tuskegee school a "veritable romance."[12] In Washington's hands, it was a didactic romance. The Alabama state legislature established the school soon after Reconstruction. (For all Washington's talk that the vote did not matter, the bill's sponsor had promised to create a school in order to win black votes.) At first, the school was just a few old shacks, with one teacher and a handful of part-time students surrounded by "an ignorant, degraded Negro population of twenty-five thousand." "But gradually [by] hard work, we brought order out of chaos, just as will be true of any problem if we stick to it."[13] By the end of the century, the school had a thousand students, a hundred teachers, a $2 million endowment, thousands of acres, a handsome campus (with red bricks fired by the students), and the blessing of local white leaders. President McKinley even made a visit. Washington told him in advance what to say. From Tuskegee, Washington organized farming conferences and a National Negro Business League, while finding time to solicit donations from millionaires or advise local people on killing vegetable bugs.

Washington's philosophy—a renunciation of rights, silence on abuses, and disparagement of higher education—could hardly have seemed more different from Harriet Tubman's derring-do or Henry Turner's thundering rhetoric. In fact, in secret he financed legal challenges to segregation. And in public, he occasionally spoke out against segregation laws, and even lampooned the emerging idea among whites that one drop of "African blood" made a person a Negro (the so-called one drop rule), by expressing amazement at the weakness of white blood. Still, the overwhelming balance of his message was to accommodate white supremacy. He earned praise from white Americans in direct proportion to the extent he eschewed problems facing black Americans. He delivered his Atlanta speech while South Carolina's politicians were disfranchising black voters. He didn't mention it. The day after the speech, a friend who was accompanying his twelve-year-old daughter on a train was beaten so badly by the conductor he was disfigured for life. The friend's crime? Refusing to move from his seat when requested. Washington didn't comment on that either.

But if Washington tiptoed around white supremacy, he was not the self-serving sell-out that critics would later accuse him of being. Washington saw himself as a race man in the tradition of Frederick Douglass, a race man committed to race progress, and—most important of all— a race man with the only practical plan to bring that progress about. His new approach marked a dramatic tactical change from previous leaders. But that was necessary, he argued, because the circumstances had changed. Black southerners had to face up to the triumph of white supremacy. It was a time for conciliatory platitudes rather than confrontational protest.

Washington's silences were strategic. He believed that if black southerners could not have the democracy part of the American system, they should at least seek the capitalist part. With some three fourths of black southerners barely eking out a living on the land, he judged the capitalist part more pressing anyway. Moreover, he believed that the only way to get the capitalist part was to renounce the democracy part. In education, he saw a choice between industrial schools and no schools at all. A Republican Congress had recently failed to pass the Blair Bill for black education; northern philanthropists had lost interest in black schools; and some southern politicians were clamoring to close them. With no state help on offer, self-help made sense.

If Washington was fighting for scraps, he thought they were scraps worth fighting for. His life had taught him the lacerating harm of poverty. He hated the new slavery of debt with a passion—debt threw black workers on a downward spiral of dependency, and dependency made freedom a sham. But Washington thought he was fighting for far more than scraps. His was a sure-fire formula to trump race prejudice. Working hard from the bottom up would lead to prosperity. He told the story of illiterate local farmer Willis Ligon, who refused to borrow money to buy a mule, put the plow harness across his shoulders, staggered across fields by the light of the moon—and was now the proud owner of several farms. Prosperity, in turn, would lead to power, and then to respect, rights, and race harmony.

In the context of rising white supremacy, this was a giddy vision. The age in which Washington lived presumed that the black race was heading down. Washington wanted to prove that the race was heading up.[14] Hence the title of his autobiography. Hence the significance of his Tuskegee "experiment." Or as the school song put it, written by the foremost black poet of the era, Paul Lawrence Dunbar, to the tune of "Fair Harvard":

Oh Mother Tuskegee, thou shinest to-day
As a gem in the fairest of lands;
Thou gavest the Heav'n-blessed power to see
The worth of our minds and our hands.

Washington had some grounds for hope. With white families resisting industrial education to enable their children to get ahead, he sensed an opportunity. His philosophy was in step with contemporary political thought. This was an era when intellectuals increasingly looked to pragmatism, not ideals, for guidance, when industrialists looked to the market, not the state, for solutions, and when moralists looked to hard work, not charity, for reform. The influential treatise *On Heroes* by the Scottish writer Thomas Carlyle, which addressed the need for great men to serve as examples, may well have informed Washington's self-promotion, too. The Tuskegee school day, starting with the morning bell at 5 a.m., was the triumphant Protestant work ethic in all its glory that the German sociologist Max Weber would write of soon after a three-day visit in 1904. Washington was clearly awe-struck by the self-made millionaires he met, too, even as he won their hearts and opened their purses.

Washington's vision was also in step with the aspirations of the nation's small but growing black business community. Black funeral directors, grocers, dressmakers, and the like profited from urban migration and, ironically, segregation. By 1900 the number of black-owned businesses in the South's ten largest black communities had doubled to two thousand since Reconstruction, serving half a million people. His emphasis on progress resonated with black publicists.[15] Two years after his Atlanta speech, some of black America's leading intellectuals set up an American Negro Academy in Washington, D.C., to chart black achievements through history and thus "destroy racism." His conciliation resonated, too, with many leaders of the black church. In 1895 the National Baptist Convention merged with two other black Baptist groups to make it by far the largest black institution in America. The convention's president, Elias C. Morris, urged his members not to suffer "inhuman treatment" without protest. But otherwise he told them to "be law-abiding, no matter how much they may suffer." Many local ministers went further. After a lynching in Arkansas in 1892—three years before Washington's speech—AME church leader James Conner warned black voters "to hold the ballot is death." "Time, education, wealth and religion are the only solutions of the race problem."[16]

Not all members of the self-styled better class of black southerners were wedded to all aspects of Washington's philosophy. Conner still hoped for "free expression of political sentiment." ANA intellectuals and many teachers deplored his focus on industrial education. A few businessmen, and some clergy, spoke out against Jim Crow. Some black clergy also condemned his materialism. For his part, Washington often worked outside the church through his business league, and he scorned incompetent clergy. Though deeply religious in his personal devotions, his rhetoric was strikingly humanist, setting the scene for a secular turn in race leadership that would last until Martin Luther King Jr. Even so, for many better-off black southerners, his tactics of hard work and acceptance of Jim Crow made sense for the moment.

What marked Washington out from his peers was that his ideas were not just tactics. They were—as critics later charged—a "veritable way of life." Whereas protest leaders since slavery had connected political rights to manhood, Washington argued that leaving politics to one side was the new business of black men. He cherished a magazine article that praised his 1901 Business League meeting for not condemning white violence. "Their conduct [showed] the supreme power of manliness that is recognized in self-restraint."[17] Thus, in some ways he anticipated the thinking behind the nonviolent protest of the 1960s Civil Rights Movement—though self-restraint then would mean remaining nonviolent, not eschewing protest altogether. With regard to womanhood, though, Washington stood firmly in the tradition of male leaders. He praised the noble character of his mother and the sacrificial work for Tuskegee of his three wives (two died)—thereby rejecting contemporary contempt for black women. But he saw himself as a patriarchal figure, master of his family and father of the race.

What marked Washington and his peers out from the vast majority of black southerners was their insistence that power lay in loyalty rather than disruption. In other words, Washington and his supporters placed themselves on a collision course with the black workers' protest tradition. Washington really ought to have crossed his fingers in Atlanta when he called on the New South's industrialists to employ those who "without strikes" had been the most "patient, faithful people that the world has seen." Precisely because he knew it wasn't true, he took every opportunity to lecture workers on becoming patient and faithful. *Up from Slavery* taught that "miners were worse off at the end of a strike"—they never won, and they were left in debt.[18]

Washington's philosophy, therefore, challenged the nature of black leadership and black protest even as he hoped to promote black welfare. Whether his new approach would take hold depended on whether his scheme succeeded. The first few years after his speech gave him grounds for confidence.

Washington could point to a steady increase in black land ownership. Between 1900 and 1910, black farmers increased their overall portion of farm wealth from 5 to 6 percent, and the number of black-owned businesses in the South's big cities tripled to six thousand.[19] The most thorough contemporary academic survey of black institutions judged Washington's Business League—with its 450 local affiliates—"the most virile institution of a purely secular nature among Negroes of the present generation."[20] Far more black Masonic groups emerged during the ten years after Washington's speech than in any other decade, and perhaps a third of black men and women joined.[21] The trajectory was indeed up.

Washington could claim some credit for the survival of black education in the South, too. The mantra of industrial education proved sufficiently nonthreatening (just) to reconcile enough southern white leaders to some sort of state-funded black schooling. At Washington's urging, the retail tycoon Julius Rosenwald funded construction of six schools in rural Alabama under Washington's supervision. Rosenwald would fund 5,352 more schools in his lifetime. In fact, local people more than matched Rosenwald's contribution, continuing a long tradition of grassroots giving. But Rosenwald provided seed money for their efforts. Black illiteracy fell to barely 30 percent by 1915.

Washington also took pride in the impact of Tuskegee on racial thought.[22] The question of whether "there lay in the colored race capacity for improvement," declared steel colossus and major donor Andrew Carnegie at Tuskegee's silver anniversary in 1906, "is no longer open."[23] Even European imperialists took note. They had long dreamed of growing cotton in the warm soils of Africa, but they did not think Africans were up to the task. The Tuskegee experiment made them think again. Imperialists assumed (as did Washington) that all black people shared the same essential characteristics. So cotton entrepreneurs took Tuskegee graduates to African plantations. Excited by the implications for black status back home, Washington warned his three graduates in Sudan against "going native" or you will do "your school, and the race a grave injustice."[24] He need not have worried. The leader of the Togo expedition wrote, "We are all doing all that there is in our power to reflect credit upon our race in America, and above all, credit upon Tuskegee our dear old Al."[25]

Washington's greatest grounds for confidence, though, lay in his own achievements. He became Theodore Roosevelt's right-hand race man. On September 14, 1901—the very day of his inauguration—Roosevelt wrote to Washington, "I must see you . . . to talk over . . . future appointments in the south." That meeting turned out to be dinner—a dinner that outraged white southern opinion. From then on, Washington peppered the president with advice. He even suggested ways to not seem to be "dictating" to the president. During Roosevelt's first term, the advice seemed to count. Roosevelt closed down a post office in Indianola, Mississippi, after white residents bullied the black postmistress into resigning. In 1905 Washington reckoned, probably rightly, that Roosevelt was the most popular president among black Americans since Lincoln. Some years later in south Georgia, Mallie Robinson named her young son (and future baseball star) Jackie Roosevelt Robinson in Teddy Roosevelt's honor.

Washington's prestige in white circles allowed him to assume the mantle of race leadership. To make the point, he wrote the first biography of Frederick Douglass. He came to dominate the Afro-American League (through friendship with Fortune) and took control of several newspapers, by investing strategically. After the dinner with Roosevelt, even Henry Turner congratulated "the great representative and hero of the Negro race, not withstanding you have been very conservative. I thank you, thank you, thank you."[26] From the Caribbean to South Africa, black leaders sought details of Washington's Tuskegee Institute in order to replicate it. A young soon-to-be-famous Jamaican called Marcus Garvey first headed to America to visit Tuskegee. Washington's control of federal patronage enabled him to control dissenters, too. The wealthy Arkansan John Bush had business concerns around the world, yet he relied on Washington for his appointment to the Federal Land Office in Little Rock. So, when Washington asked Bush to support Roosevelt's preferred white Republican candidates in 1906, Bush replied, "Speak and your order shall be obeyed."[27] Those who didn't obey soon found their jobs gone, and sometimes their secrets exposed in the press.

The problem for Washington, though, was that he was a client first and a boss second. After winning election to a second term (1905–1909), his patron Roosevelt tossed aside much of his counsel. In August 1906 the president heard reports of fighting between black soldiers and white residents of Brownsville, Texas. Ignoring Washington's pleas, he discharged virtually all the soldiers without honor or pensions. To add insult to injury, Roosevelt told Congress later that year that the "greatest existing cause of lynching is the perpetration, especially by black men, of the hideous crime of rape." Black leaders felt betrayed. Washington admitted in private that Roosevelt had made a "great blunder," but out of loyalty he decided, "I must keep my lips closed."[28] Unwilling to break his ties to the President, Washington would share the scorn.

To make matters worse, Washington's schemes did little to lessen white racism. For many, his maxim that "the only time my neighbors bothered me about my color was when I became broke" was the exact opposite of their experience. Even John Bush admitted it was "virtually impossible to please the white man." The voices of the few "best white men" who spoke up for civility were drowned out by the voices of the worst. In 1905 the novelist Thomas Dixon warned in a national newspaper that Washington's secret plan was to "destroy the last vestige of dependence on the white man."[29] It was a self-serving rant (though in fact with more than a grain of truth). Dixon had just published his novel, *The Clansman,* a romantic history of the Klan. But it was a powerful rant nonetheless. Dixon's previous paean to white supremacy, *The Leopard's Spots,* had outsold *Up from Slavery* (ironically, released in the same year by the same publisher) by four to one.[30]

Some of Washington's schemes turned out to be embarrassing flops. Of the nine graduates who ventured to Togo, five returned quickly and the other four died. The final victim was swept away by a fast river, and his body was never recovered. When German officials refused to issue a death certificate, his widow was left without compensation (she hired a Berlin lawyer to sue).[31] Progress in landownership—though impressive in the context—was still desperately slow. Even progress in black education, Washington's signature issue, was paltry at best. Black schools survived, but only white schools improved—and thus black students were doubly disadvantaged by their skin and lack of schooling.

Such discrimination wasn't Washington's fault. The vain attempts of so many—from sugar workers in Louisiana to Ida Wells' campaign against lynching—exposed just how weak black Americans were at the turn of the century. As Washington acknowledged to Fortune in 1902, "It is hard to give an individual or race influence that it does not intrinsically possess."[32] Even so, the hubris at the heart of Washington's rhetoric was that accommodating Jim Crow would usher in—as he put it in Atlanta—a "new heaven and new earth." It didn't. The New South was still the Old South when it came to white supremacy, with all its pain and tears.

For black workers, Washington's philosophy actually hindered their struggles. It was not that he changed many workers' hearts and minds. Ten years after his Atlanta speech, he complained that "too many of them yield to the temptation to go off on excursions, picnics etc., when their work demands their time."[33] But wider support among black leaders for his philosophy altered the balance of power between black workers and white bosses. Nowhere more than in Birmingham, Alabama, home to the largest concentration of black industrial workers in the country. It was also a city, wrote one black visitor, where the black middle class was "utterly Booker-T-Washingtonized."[34] Captains of industry relied on cheap black labor to keep down costs and undermine white unions. During a miners' strike in 1908, black ministers and the black press sided with the operators against the unions, causing the strike to collapse. What was true in Birmingham was true around the world. Imperial entrepreneurs deployed Washington's conservative views on labor, just as they embraced what they believed to be his advocacy of racial segregation.

In Birmingham, the mine operators and city fathers may have won out anyway. Jim Crow was as much about the subjugation of black labor as it was the segregation of black society. But black workers fumed. One miner condemned preachers as "nothing more than stool-pigeons for the coal companies" who "instead of preaching the Gospel of the Son of God [preached] the doctrine of union hatred."[35] Still, the workers' efforts in Birmingham and elsewhere pointed toward more protest to come. After World War I, Alabama miners would lead some of the most disruptive strikes in the country. And when this protest came, it would be directed against black accommodationists every bit as much as white operators.

In December 1906 Washington returned for another major speech in Atlanta, this time to a mostly black audience. A decade earlier, he had charmed a white crowd and city leaders when calling for racial tolerance. But barely a month before this latest speech, the crowd had become an anti-black mob, whipped up by city leaders. Nevertheless, Washington gave much the same message as always. But after the flames and the fury of the riot, it was a message whose time had passed, delivered by a messenger whose influence was on the wane. The Atlanta rioters tore down Washington's reputation as surely as they tore down the black side of town.

By this time, Washington had plenty of rivals ready to celebrate his demise. He became the focus of some of the most vicious personal attacks from other black leaders in American history, his speech derided as the "Atlanta Compromise." But the story of black leadership in the Washington era was far more than the rise and fall of Washington. Though it was a time for speeches rather than strikes, there were other prominent black voices, with other strategies to reckon with Jim Crow.

"Lifting as We Climb"

On the evening of May 18, 1893, the black writer Anna Julia Cooper addressed a crowd of some five hundred women at the International Congress of Women—a congress that met in Chicago during the city's World's Fair. Delegates from twenty-seven countries representing over a hundred organizations were present. The previous gathering of the congress, in 1876, had excluded black women. This time, one session was devoted to "the intellectual progress of the colored women of the United States." The session was part of a broader theme entitled "The Solidarity of Human Interests" which celebrated women's progress in "all civilized parts of the earth." But this solidarity did not extend to black equality. The civilized parts of the earth did not include Africa and Asia. The organizers simply wanted to show that women of all colors shared a "passion for independence."[36]

Invited to speak on the thorny topic of race progress before a mostly white audience at an International Exposition, Cooper might seem to be a female counterpart of Booker T. Washington. In many ways, she was. Born to slavery, Cooper was the child of an errant white master. Despite poverty (her mother became a domestic servant) and trials (her husband died barely a year into their marriage), she gained an education, and in 1902 she became head of the M Street School in the nation's capital— the foremost "colored" high school of its day. She later became only the fourth African American woman to earn a doctorate—from the Sorbonne in Paris. Like Washington, Cooper was in demand as an orator at home and abroad. Like Washington, she wrote a race book, *A Voice from the South* (1892), which praised the progress of black southerners, extolled the virtues of black workers, and even complimented Washington on his Tuskegee Institute.

The greatest similarity between the pair was that Cooper also claimed the mantle of race leadership. But there the mirror image ended. In Atlanta, Washington sought to represent the whole race. In Chicago, Cooper sought to "speak for the colored women of the South." Washington praised the possibilities of a New South. Cooper spoke of the South "because it is there that the millions of blacks in this country have watered the soil with blood and tears." Washington muted his criticism of white supremacy. Cooper thought "the despairing fight, as of an entrapped tigress," of black women to resist rape provided "material for epics." Washington affirmed his audience's view of what black men's priorities ought to be. Cooper challenged her female hearers to broaden their vision. "The sentiment of her constituency . . . demanded an entrance not through a gateway for ourselves, our race, our sex, or our sect, but a grand highway for humanity."[37]

Cooper's message did not provoke Atlanta-style acclaim. Even so, at least one member of the audience was exultant. The aged Frederick Douglass, invited in recognition of his support for women's rights, took the platform. The sight of "refined, educated colored ladies addressing— and addressing successfully—one of the most intelligent white audiences that I ever looked upon" thrilled him. "My heart is too full to speak," he concluded, before characteristically speaking some more of the coming "new earth . . . when prejudices . . . will all pass away."[38]

Cooper's speech and career reveal there were prominent leaders other than Washington acolytes or critics, even in Washington's heyday—and many of these leaders were women. While Washington built his school, prominent black women built clubs across the country. In 1892 Cooper founded one of the first, in Washington, D.C. Four years later, the National Association of Colored Women formed to bring local clubs together. By 1916 some 1,500 clubs had affiliated. These organizations ran any number of programs, from jail visits to kindergartens to black history lectures. Together, they reached into the neighborhoods of virtually every sizeable American town. In other words, clubwomen's networks rivaled those of Booker T. Washington. They forged links abroad, too. Cooper earned quite a reputation. The West African radical Edward Blyden wrote an American pastor, "I can never forget Anna J. Cooper, brilliant, thoughtful."[39]

Because Washington cast such a long shadow over the era, black clubwomen's work inevitably related to him in some ways. Many women shared his enthusiasm for industrial education. Nannie Helen Burroughs, founder in 1909 of the so-called 3B school of "Bible, Bath and Broom" in Washington, D.C., earned the nickname Mrs. Booker T. Her mantra, "Until we realize our ideal, we are going to idealize our real," would have earned Washington's approval. Her work ethic would have, too. In one year, when she was just twenty-two years old, Burroughs traveled 22,215 miles, gave 215 speeches, and wrote 9,235 letters.[40]

But other clubwomen came out against Washington. Cooper, for example, denounced the "colored leader of white American thought" who allowed (referring to his famous analogy) "the domineering *thumb* to over ride . . . every finger weak enough to give up the struggle." She condemned his contempt for higher education—"We are building men, not . . . farmers"—and his meddling, which hastened her dismissal from M School in 1906.[41]

Yet for all the support for, or opposition to, Washington, what is striking is how few clubwomen fit neatly into either camp. They had pressing agendas of their own. Clubwomen were for racial uplift, which had many guises (including industrial education). For most clubwomen it meant teaching their "lowly" sisters a better lifestyle—high morals, clean living, and thrift. Or, as the NACW's motto put it, "Lifting as We Climb." Once blacks were suitably civilized, there would be no more justification for Jim Crow. Thus, uplift was, in many ways, a plan with which Washington concurred—and not just the thrift part. Tuskegee Institute's devotional life taught, and its disciplinary code required, exemplary moral behavior. Washington emphasized hygiene as well as hard work, too. "The gospel of the toothbrush," he told a Birmingham audience in 1899, put Tuskegee students "on the highroad to civilization."[42]

For many clubwomen, racial uplift was a case of necessity in response to the triumph of Jim Crow. "We may wish to . . . hold ourselves entirely aloof from . . . the lowly, the illiterate and even the vicious," explained the first NACW president, Mary Church Terrell (a light-skinned member of the capital's so-called elite 400), but with the drawing of the color line "we cannot escape the consequences of their acts."[43] For many, the NACW's motto should have been, "Only by Lifting Can We Climb." Racial uplift was also a response to wider trends in American society. The early twentieth century was a so-called Progressive Era when white reformers spoke of social justice and preachers spoke of a social gospel as never before. Clubwomen's emphasis on hygiene mirrored the Victorian belief that cleanliness was next to godliness. Or in the case of the toothbrush, clean breath bespoke a clean heart. In 1896 the Colgate company seized the moment by launching toothpaste in a tube. There was a practical health issue here, too. Cooper and Washington were shaken by the deadly spread of disease in urban slums and rural shacks. Soap and toothpaste saved lives even as they civilized souls.

Above all, black clubwomen were right in step with the turn of the century's so-called Women's Era. "To be alive at such an epoch is a privilege," wrote Cooper in *Voice*, "to be a woman, sublime."[44] It was an era when white women were in the vanguard of social reform, and an era that measured the civilization of any given society by the civility of its women. As Cooper explained, "In order to reform a man, you must begin with his great-grandmother." It was but a step for black women to appropriate Women's Era rhetoric for their race work. "What a responsibility then to have the sole management of the primal lights and shadows!" wrote Cooper. "Such is the colored woman's office. She must stamp weal or woe on the coming history of this people."[45]

Defending their reputation was a case in point. Black women suffered the worst insults from (as Cooper called them) the "angry Saxons," so it was vital to the race as a whole for black women to rebut them. Indeed, the NACW formed in furious response to the claim by a prominent Missouri journalist, James Jacks, that all black women "were prostitutes and were natural thieves and liars." The NACW, declared Terrell, would "face that white man and call him a liar." More often, though, clubwomen busied themselves with the everyday tasks of social reform. In so doing, they faced white America and called all Jim Crow stereotypes a lie. By pursuing what the historian Evelyn Brooks Higginbotham has aptly called a "politics of respectability" through their efforts to reform the lowly, black clubwomen also sought to showcase their own noble characters. Respectability compensated for lack of material possessions. And by respectably, respectfully, joining the wider reform movement, clubwomen sought material rewards for the race, too. Even in the South. There, the exclusion of black men from formal politics opened up a space for black women to represent the race.[46]

In practice, though, clubwomen often found themselves caught between, rather than abreast of, movements for race equality and women's rights. "The black woman," wrote Cooper, is "an unacknowledged factor in both." For Cooper, there was no question what the main enemy was: white supremacy in all its manifestations. In one moving story, she wrote of a train journey to a small town where she suffered the agony of being thrown out of the first-class car, of watching black convict laborers from the train window, and of being turned away by the hotel proprietor. Yet she still found time to ponder the particular problem of the black woman's split identity. At the railway station, "I see two dingy little rooms with "FOR LADIES" swinging over one and "FOR COLORED PEOPLE" over the other; while wondering under which head I come."[47]

Little surprise then, that even as clubwomen sought to raise black womanhood to challenge white supremacy, they presented a challenge both to black men and to white women reformers. Cooper's *Voice* critiqued the sexism of the former and the racism of the latter. To take the case of sexism first: Cooper argued that "our present record of eminent men, when placed beside the actual status of the race in America to-day, proves that no man can represent the race." Because that "actual status" was to be found in the "homes of the rank and file . . . Only the BLACK WOMAN can say "when and where I enter, in the quiet, undisputed dignity of my womanhood . . . the whole *Negro race enters with me*."[48]

Seeing the black woman as the representative of the race did not in itself challenge gender norms. Cooper still promoted women's domestic duties, and her working life followed the conventions of her day—she was able to pursue a career only because she was a widow (in D.C., married women were not allowed to teach). But Cooper called for more opportunities in education—"not the boys less, but the girls more." Seeking "more" for the girls was not the same as seeking independent rights. But it did mean that what Cooper called the "thumping within" could at least begin to be "answered" by "beckoning from without." And it meant throwing down the gauntlet to black men who "drop back into sixteenth century logic" when they "strike the woman question." Cooper even contrasted some black men's weakness in selling their vote to Democrats to black women's strength: "You do not find the colored woman selling her birthright for a mess of pottage." Where you found them was knocking some backbone into their husbands to vote the right way. And while Booker Washington might think "it is good policy to cultivate one's neighbors . . . the black woman can never forget."[49]

Leaving aside particular arguments, the sternest challenge to male leadership was simply the rise of so many women activists in the public square. Between 1890 and 1910—the period that literary scholars now call the Black Woman's Era—black women writers published more works of fiction than black men had during the previous half century. They were as proficient as they were prominent. Cooper's *Voice* reached back to Tacitus and the Nordic age, contrasted Eastern and Western cultures, and quoted liberally from contemporary thinkers. "Her criticism in excellent English," wrote the Boston *Transcript* reviewer, "is a manifest of the ability and cultivation of those she represents." While white women reformers tended to write homely narratives to make a broader point, Cooper followed male writers in presenting a tighter, deductive argument. It was an old habit. She had given her graduation address "mannishly," not "pretending to read . . . as a lady properly should."[50] (Washington took the less threatening, and more "feminine," approach.)

While they challenged their menfolk, black clubwomen upbraided their white women counterparts. Given their analysis of women's role in shaping society—a society that now embraced violent white supremacy—it could hardly be otherwise. "Am I right in holding the American Woman responsible?" asked Cooper. "I think so." Cooper thought the "irresistible spell" of southern racism had captured the hearts of the American woman who was now "as fearful of losing caste as a Brahmin in India."[51] She could point to plenty of racial slights. Adella Hunt Logan was told she couldn't address the 1897 convention of the National American Women Suffrage Association because if she proved to be an "inferior speaker . . . it would militate so against the colored race." (This was hardly likely, given that Logan was a former lady principal of Tuskegee Institute.)[52] Black clubwomen confronted racism in the women's movement in different ways. Wells challenged it directly. Terrell tried diplomacy. Cooper used *Voice* to prick the conscience of the "pure gold" northern reformers, urging them to embrace a woman-led movement for human rights.

While black clubwomen questioned the right of black men or white women to speak for them, most didn't question their right to speak on behalf of poor women—even though in any given town at the turn of the century, some 80 percent of black women workers were in domestic service, but barely 2 percent were in professional work, such as teaching.[53] The voice that Cooper "demanded to be heard" was that of "women who are so sure of their own social footing" that they are ready to declare *"I am my Sister's keeper!"*[54] Racial uplift forced the classes together, but it didn't blur them. The motto "Lifting as We Climb" made it clear who was doing the lifting and climbing. Ironically, by trumpeting their mission to reform the mass of unrespectable black women, clubwomen reinforced negative stereotypes. Tracts like "Take a Bath First" hardly helped.

Some clubwomen worked sacrificially among the poor, especially those—like Cooper—who held deep religious convictions or had known poverty. Cooper wondered how many black leaders had "ever given a thought to the . . . down-trodden colored woman bending over washtubs . . . with children to feed and house rent to pay."[55] Because respectability was based on virtue rather than wealth, even the poorest could, in theory, become reformers. Laura Bagg, a domestic, was a founding member and later a vice president of Atlanta's main uplift club, the Neighborhood Union. But in practice, many clubwomen—and their husbands and fathers—desperately preserved social distance. One black editor in Arkansas reckoned, "No one will call . . . 'nigger' so quickly as a light colored dude."[56] Even Cooper's moving mention of the "down-trodden colored woman" was just that—a mention, the only mention in nearly three hundred pages.

Clubwomen's confidence in racial uplift matched Washington's optimism for industrial education. As the Baptist's Women's Convention, founded by Nannie Burroughs, put it, "Fight segregation through the courts . . . ? Yes. But fight it with soap and water, hoes, spades, shovels and paint, to remove any reasonable excuse for it. That is a fight that will win."[57] By speaking of women's reform rather than political rights, local clubs did make significant gains across the country—especially in the context of rising racism. Atlanta politicians, for example, put the Neighborhood Union in charge of settlement work in black districts. Clubwomen used the funds (which increased after the riot) to develop kindergartens that cared for some three thousand poor children.[58] Through their words and their work, clubwomen won respect from some white women reformers and race men too. White suffragists worked closely with Terrell, and Washington praised the work of the Tuskegee women's club—as so he should. His wife, Margaret, was one of the NACW's leading lights. The American Negro Academy invited Cooper to address them—the first woman to do so.

Ultimately, though, clubwomen's vision of race progress foundered on the rock of white supremacy—just as Washington's method had. Cooper later wrote that the "colorphobia" and the "accursed hunger for gold" of the Progressive Era made it the "most trying period in all [colored people's] trying history in this land of their trial."[59] Though they won precious resources for hard times, clubwomen's hard work at lifting the masses did not enable them, let alone the race as a whole, to climb. The clubwomen's vision foundered along the fault lines of race and gender, too. Some white reformers cooperated with their black sisters, but few embraced Cooper's broad vision of human rights. Sympathetic male leaders still assumed male leadership, and the American Negro Academy did not invite Cooper, or any other woman, to speak again. Some race men turned women's rhetoric against them—if the status of the race depended on its women, then black women must be responsible for its decline.

Meanwhile, clubwomen found uplift easier said than done. Many among the "unrespectable" did not want to be "lifted," and many who chose respectability (often churchwomen) did so without need of telling. Sometimes the lowly confronted their "betters." After clubwoman Mamie Garvin Fields straightened the hair of one girl in rural South Carolina, the girl's mother (Fields remembered with a wince) "la[id] me out."[60] More often, the "lowly" just ignored the lessons on offer. Baptist clubwoman Jane Edna Hunter warned that going to dance halls meant a "voluntary return to the jungle."[61] If so, the Progressive Era saw a charge back to Africa. Atlanta, home to the Neighborhood Union, was also home to more juke joints than any other southern city. Dances that went by the name of the Grind, or Funky Butt, were as far from the clubwomen's vision of respectability as it was possible to be.

Clubwomen were also held back by practical constraints. When Cooper took in five orphaned relations in 1915, she had to stop her traveling. At times, clubwomen did not help themselves. They were not immune from the philosophical conflicts swirling among their male counterparts. Margaret Washington came under attack for being too conservative (although, in the manner of her husband, she took control of the NACW anyway, in 1912). They were not immune from personality conflicts either. Cooper and Wells bitterly condemned Terrell's attempts to seek an unconstitutional third term as president of the NACW in 1899. Terrell admitted later she did not have a friend in Washington, D.C. Male critics chortled over the supposedly gentler sex's "unseemly scramble for office."[62]

Still, it would be wrong to pin their struggles on internecine squabbles. Personality conflicts were present in every generation of race protest (not to say American life). If anything, the clubwomen's movement was notable for its unity of purpose. And with hindsight this era would turn out to be a high point of higher-class black women's attempts to speak for the race as a whole. Before long their voices would be forced to the margins. A world war and its aftermath—when heroic black men would come to represent the race, and when white women would jettison their black sisters as they grabbed for suffrage—would see to that.

Fighting Booker T. Washington and Jim Crow

On the evening of July 30, 1903, Booker T. Washington gave a speech to some two thousand people packed in Boston's AME Zion Church. He was at the height of his power, and he expected to be among friends. This was a meeting of his Negro Business League. His supporters had advertised endorsements by prominent black Bostonians ahead of the speech (the first that most knew of their endorsements was when they read their names in the local paper). In short, all seemed set for a celebration of the man and his message. Instead, the speech would mark the beginning of open warfare among black leaders that would follow Washington, perhaps even hasten him, to his grave.

The Boston meeting could hardly have been more different from the Atlanta triumph. When Thomas Fortune introduced him, there was hissing from the crowd. When Washington stepped forward, there was a scuffle. Two dozen police restored order. When he began with an ill-judged joke about a mule, there was some jeering. Boston's leading black journalist, William Monroe Trotter, shouted out loaded questions, such as: "Are the rope and the torch all the race is to get under your leadership?" Pandemonium ensued. Someone threw cayenne pepper and stink bombs on the stage. Trotter was arrested and sentenced to thirty days in prison. His supporters in New York and Chicago held church services in solidarity.[63]

Trotter's militancy ran in the family. His father, James, was a leader of the 55th Massachusetts' strike for full pay during the Civil War. James's postwar earnings as register of deeds in Washington, D.C., then gave young Monroe unmatched opportunities. An outstanding student, he took them. The same summer that Washington spoke in Atlanta, Trotter became the first African American Phi Beta Kappa graduate of Harvard. Trotter then founded a newspaper, the Boston *Guardian*, which suited his purposes and personality. He was a talented critical writer, he was anything but a team player, and he was appalled at the rise of Jim Crow in Boston. In his hands, the *Guardian* became one of the most influential newspapers of the era, vowing "to protest forever against being proscribed or shut off in any caste from equal rights."[64]

A believer in the highest liberal arts education, an advocate of race rights, and a man with a hot temper, Trotter seemed destined to confront

Washington. Paraphrasing the infamous *Dred Scott* decision, Trotter complained that "the northern Negro has no rights which Booker Washington is bound to respect." Whereas Washington's other early critics focused on his philosophy, Trotter got personal. A *Guardian* report of one speech in 1902 commented on the look in Washington's "eyes that would leave you . . . restless during the night if you had failed to report [him] to the police." While on the subject of Washington's face, Trotter added, "Those eyes along with an enormous nose and mouth seemed huddled together."[65] So Trotter determined to face down the man he called the Great Traitor, Pope Washington, and a miserable toady (and these were just the names he used in public).

After the so-called Boston "riot," Washington rushed to limit the damage. Protesting rather too much, he told a local newspaper, "I have rarely received a more hearty and welcome reception on the part of the masses than I received tonight."[66] But the damage was done. Trotter's stunt brought black critics to the notice of white Americans. Even Teddy Roosevelt expressed concern. Washington replied casually, "I do not suffer myself to become very much vexed with these people."[67] Little did Roosevelt know that a much vexed Washington was plotting with allies, that very week, to disgrace the rioters.

As it turned out, Trotter did not remain Washington's main opponent for long. The bull-headed traits that prompted the riot prevented him from leading a broad anti-Washington coalition. That role fell instead to W. E. B. Du Bois, a scholar-activist based, in 1903, at Atlanta University. Within a decade, Du Bois would replace Washington as the dominant black leader of the era, and for a further half-century he would remain a pivotal figure in black protest. But back in 1903, Du Bois first rose to prominence as the champion of Washington's critics.

In his telling, Du Bois' early life could hardly have been more different from that of his Tuskegee rival. He was born to a respectable family line, "by a golden river and in the shadow of two great hills" in Massachusetts in 1868.[68] There were hardships. His father—a mulatto from Haiti—walked out soon after his birth. His mother—semi-paralyzed after a stroke—had to work as a maid. And his white classmates kept him at a distance. Still, he had opportunities Washington never had. He earned his first degree from Fisk University, his second (in philosophy) from Harvard University, then studied as a graduate in Berlin, before becoming the first black man to gain a doctorate (in history) from Harvard. By the time he moved to Atlanta, he had acquired the academic hauteur, trimmed beard, and pince-nez to go with the degrees, not to mention a taste for fine wines and expensive cigarettes. A man of the soil he was not.

What he shared with Washington was a conviction that the future of the race lay in his hands. "Is it egotism," he wrote on the eve of his twenty-fifth birthday, "or is it the silent call of the world spirit that makes me feel that I am royal and that beneath my sceptre a world of kings shall bow?"[69] But from the outset it was clear that Du Bois' calling would take him far from the road to Tuskegee. His first widely read article, "The Strivings of the Negro People," published in *Atlantic Monthly* in 1897, urged black Americans to ponder their grievances: "How does it feel to be a problem?" Whereas Washington celebrated the promise of America, Du Bois was torn: "One ever feels his two-ness—an American, a Negro; two souls . . . two warring ideals in one dark body." Washington shared Du Bois' wish "to be both a Negro and an American without being cursed." But whereas Washington believed real power would come from material progress, Du Bois believed in the power of ideas.

Not surprisingly—given his time in Berlin—many of Du Bois' first ideas drew from the idealist philosophy of Georg Hegel. Hegel had taught that human history was progressing from a time of bondage toward an ever clearer manifestation of the true (or divine) Spirit of Freedom. The realization of this spirit came through successive cycles of conflict, reaction, and resolution, and each cycle resolved itself through the development of nations at six different times in history—from the Chinese via the Greeks to the Germans. Du Bois adapted Hegel's schema for his own purposes. "The Negro is a sort of seventh son"—the next in line to realize full freedom and also (according to the Caribbean tradition of seventh son) the most blessed. His philosophy enabled him to find solace in the present and take hope for the future. The Negro's current "warring ideals" were a step toward a "higher synthesis of civilization and humanity."[70]

Du Bois' brilliant intellect marks him out as one of the most original contributors to American political thought in the modern era. Yet in his early years especially, he was also a man of his time. The coterie of intellectuals that formed the American Negro Academy shaped his first ideas on race and progress. His call for a "talented tenth" of "gifted minds" to lead the race echoed Cooper. Though he wrote the first critical review of *Up from Slavery,* he did not begin on a collision course with Washington. His first plans were "to make a name in science, to make a name in literature and thus to raise my race." Washington was sufficiently impressed by the young scholar to offer him a position at Tuskegee—no doubt the principle of holding potential enemies close was at play here, too. Du Bois declined, politely, and, as it turned out, with stunning irony: "You will always have . . . my sympathy & cooperation."[71] But he was initially generous in his praise of Washington—a man of such "evident sincerity" and "tact and power," he wrote in his review of *Up from Slavery,* that he "commands . . . the respect of those who do not" share his vision, Du Bois included.[72]

With the publication in 1903 of Du Bois' *The Souls of Black Folk,* the differences between the men became more forthright. Du Bois devoted a whole chapter to a critique of Washington's methods. "All men cannot go to college," he agreed, "but some men must." The Atlanta Compromise had strengthened rather than subverted white supremacy, ushering in disfranchisement, segregation, and fewer funds for black higher education. It was not Washington's fault alone, "but his propaganda" allowed "whites, North and South, to shift the burden of the Negro problem to the Negro's shoulders." *Souls* could hardly have been more different from Washington's autobiography in style as well as substance. The chapter "on the training of black men" finished thus: "I sit with Shakespeare and he winces not. Across the color line I move arm in arm with Balzac and Dumas . . . I summon Aristotle and Aurelius and what soul I will, and they come all graciously."[73] The thud of Washington's jaw dropping when he read it must have shaken Tuskegee's red brick walls.

Yet even at this stage, Du Bois and Washington were not at daggers drawn, at least not publicly. They still had much in common—a passion for education, the goal of equality, skepticism toward the black church, and a belief in progress. They shared a global vision, too. Both spoke (as did Cooper) at the Pan-African Conference in London in 1900. They met for supper soon after *Souls* was published. What turned the rivals into enemies was their jockeying for power within black institutions—and Du Bois' resentment at Washington's monopoly on it. And what brought this struggle to the fore was the night Washington was shouted down in Boston.

Before the Boston riot, Du Bois and Washington agreed to attend a conference, in early 1904, of leading colored men. It would be a chance, as Du Bois described it, for a "heart to heart" and, as Washington put it, to "correct mistakes."[74] Perhaps the 1904 reconciliation conference would never have worked. But the Boston riot ensured it could not. After Boston, Washington hounded Trotter even as he courted Du Bois. "The real issue," complained Trotter, is "his clandestine methods of attempting to crush out all who will not bow to him."[75] Du Bois agreed—he saw Trotter as a martyr. At the conference, delegates found common cause, and in any case, Washington did not oppose higher education for the elite. A three-man steering group—including Du Bois and Washington—was established to oversee the next steps. But when Washington molded the resulting Committee for the Advancement of the Race in his own image, Du Bois resigned in disgust.

From that moment on, to quote Kelly Miller, a Howard scholar and

friend of both men, it was "war to the knife, and knife to the hilt."[76] In
time to come, the war would be characterized as industrial education ver-
sus classical education. But at the start, the war was not so much about
strategy—though Du Bois accused Washington of diverting funds away
from higher education. It was not even that Washington's strategy didn't
seem to be working—though this was vital for bringing latent criticism
into the open. Rather, in Du Bois' telling, it was Washington's authori-
tarian nature that made younger activists cry out, "I have a right to
think!"[77] To be fair to Washington, his plan depended on a united front
of conciliation. But Du Bois was in no mood to be fair. In April 1905 he
wrote in fury to Oswald Garrison Villard—the New York editor and
grandson of abolitionist William Garrison, who was a keen supporter of
racial justice and both men: "Mr. Washington heads an organization . . .
whose purpose it is to ruin any man who openly criticizes his methods."[78]
After her firing from M Street, Cooper could have added "any woman,
too."

In June, Du Bois joined openly with Trotter at a meeting of some thirty,
mostly northern, black leaders. They met by Niagara Falls, on the Canadian side, symbolic of the "mighty current" of protest they hoped to unleash. (It was also a pleasant venue—to quote Du Bois—for "croquet,
tennis and fishing.")[79] The so-called Niagara movement was born, a
movement to fight both white supremacy and Washington's methods. In
fact, Niagara had more in common with Tuskegee than both sides realized. Though Niagara's Declaration of Principles praised "uplift in home
life" and called on unions to include black workers, the founding delegates were all professional men, who made no overtures to clubwomen
or workers—just as Du Bois had paid no attention to Washington's
sidelining of women's leadership or workers' struggles in *Souls*.

Washington fought back. He kept the black press mostly silent on Niagara. With help from the famous Pinkerton detective agency, he tried to
discredit Du Bois, and ironically the Atlanta riot played into his hands.
Washington denounced the "agitators of both races" who attracted "attention to themselves." To some extent, the fightback worked. The Niagara movement fell apart—it didn't develop a base in the South, and it
split into factions. Du Bois fell apart emotionally, too. The Atlanta riot
taught him the futility of political protest and the fragility of white support. Still struggling with grief and recrimination over the death of his
first son (his wife had blamed his work schedule), Du Bois sought psychi-
atric help and poured his energies into his studies.[80]

But if Washington held off Niagara, he couldn't hold back the sentiments, or the people, that had given rise to it. Du Bois compared "King

Booker's" "Tuskegee machine" of patronage and intimidation to the very worst of corrupt city politics. Trotter formed a Negro Equal Rights League—with protest, and Trotter, at the center of operations. Meanwhile, Villard and other heirs of the abolitionist movement called a Conference on the Negro in 1909. Niagara had revealed the depth of black opposition to Washington, while the Springfield riot of 1908 had exposed the crisis of northern racism. The conference gave rise to the National Association for the Advancement of Colored People (NAACP), which cast itself as "an aggressive movement" (to quote Villard) "on behalf of the Negro's rights," committed to fighting lynching in Congress, fighting Jim Crow in the courts, and fighting racism in general. Du Bois joined from the outset. Most members of the Niagara movement followed him in.

Villard was adamant the NAACP was not to be "a Washington movement, or a Du Bois movement."[81] He allowed no criticism of Washington initially, and so did not include Trotter or Wells among the dozen black delegates to the first steering committee (neither forgave Villard for the slight). But it soon became a Du Bois movement. His appointment as the editor of the NAACP's journal, *The Crisis*, told Washington all he needed to know. Washington fought back again. He complained that whites were trying to control the race through Du Bois. (Trotter agreed.) But it was a patently hypocritical case for Washington to make.

What was true, though, was that Washington was losing his grip on patronage. Roosevelt's successor, William Howard Taft (1908–1913), supported the lily-white campaigns of southern Republicans. The 1912 Republican platform did not even mention black voting rights. (Du Bois, Trotter, and 100,000 black voters switched their support to the Democrat Woodrow Wilson—much to their later regret.) Washington was losing his reputation, too. Early in 1911, as he peered at an apartment keyhole in New York, Washington was beaten up by a "big German" dog dealer called Henry Ulrich, who thought Washington was looking for a white woman. For the diplomatic race leader, the national front-page attention was as painful as the bruises. The fact that, while minding his own business, he was attacked in a northern city on suspicion of intent to rape simply because of the color of his skin was a cruel rebuttal of his life's philosophy. When a New York court cleared Ulrich, it just added insult to the injury. (Ulrich was immediately arrested for desertion of his family—Washington's digging into Ulrich's private life saw to that.)

Ironically, Washington's fall occurred at just the moment he began to condemn the fire of white supremacy. In 1912 he wrote an article for a national journal with the title "Is the Negro Having a Fair Chance?" (His answer: no.) He stepped up his legal challenges to segregated transport. But it didn't wash with his opponents. Du Bois scoffed in *The Crisis,* "We note with some complacency that Mr. Booker T. Washington has joined the ranks."

In November 1915 Washington died of an illness resulting from high blood pressure. In a final twist, his doctor blamed his demise on "racial characteristics." He may have just meant that black men could not cope with stress—unbecoming enough for a man who had worked so hard for so long. But he may have been trying to imply that sexual disease was at play—even more unbecoming for a man who had built his life on propriety.

Washington's death left the way open for Du Bois to assume the mantle of race leader and the NAACP to shape black protest. In due course the NAACP legal team would direct the cases that undermined Jim Crow; southern NAACP branches would sustain protest through to the Civil Rights Movement; and the NAACP leadership would represent the voice of black America to the federal government. But the story of the rise of the NAACP would be anything but inevitable. Washington's strategy of accommodation lived on and lived strong among southern black elites— not surprising given that he was as much a reflection as the cause of a more conciliatory response to Jim Crow. Meanwhile northern black elites (though mostly Southern-born) and white liberals founded the National Urban League in 1911—a counterpart to the NAACP that would focus on philanthropy and black economic development.

As for the NAACP, its early record showed no more success than Washington's. It established few branches in the South. NAACP lawyers won cases against peonage (*Bailey v. Alabama,* 1911), and the grandfather voting clause (*Guinn v. Oklahoma,* 1915), but these victories were more symbolic than substantive. In any case, many national leaders— from Trotter to Cooper to Wells—were independent of (or at least not dependent on) the NAACP. Above all, none of the leaders jockeying for power had anywhere near as much influence as they wanted over local people. The emergence of a black hero cut from an entirely different cloth from Washington, Cooper, or Du Bois would make that abundantly clear.

Outraging Jim Crow

"How do you feel, Jim?" "How do you like it?" So spoke the most famous black man in America, on Independence Day, 1910, in front of a crowd from twenty thousand in Reno, Nevada. This was a rather different speech from those of Washington or Cooper. The words were not addressed to the crowd but to Jim Jeffries, the greatest white heavyweight boxer of the day. They were not the words of conciliation or challenge—they were taunts. The most famous black man in America was no longer Washington, nor the upcoming Du Bois, but boxer Jack Johnson. It was Round 14 of a projected 45-round fight for the heavyweight championship of the world.

In Johnson's telling, this was the moment fate had decreed for him. Born in Texas in 1878, he first learned his trade in the alleys near his home. His father, Jack wrote later, was a "pious" school janitor, somewhat crippled by the time the Galveston storm of 1900 destroyed the family home. Jack would be anything but pious. As did many pugnacious black activists, Johnson attributed his toughness to his mother, Tiny. She warned Jack that if a white boy ever whipped him, she would give him a bigger whipping. She never had to. Tall for his day and with muscles to spare, Jack could beat up anybody.

Johnson's fists brought him money, attention, and women—rewards that he prized in equal measure. To begin with, the money was a few pennies thrown by jeering white crowds at the fighters in so-called "Battle Royals"—street fights where black men or boys, sometimes deformed, often blindfolded, were forced to hit until only one was left standing. In Galveston, the one still standing was usually Jack Johnson. Yearning for dollars rather than cents, Johnson traveled the country, ending up in Chicago but staying nowhere for long. First, he beat the main black heavyweights. Then he went in search of white prey, where the big money was to be found.

Heavyweight prizefighting was supposed to be segregated. But Progressive reformers had fought boxing with such ferocity that purses for punching were shrinking fast—too fast for world champion Jim Jeffries, who retired in 1905. So some second-rank white heavyweights were willing to fight a black man for a price. Johnson beat them all, and humiliated most, including Jack Jeffries, a mediocre fighter trading on his brother's reputation. Refusing to play the submissive role assigned to black boxers, Johnson feinted and counterpunched, waiting for his opponents to tire. (Legend had it that he kissed some opponents during clinches, to drive them to frenzy and exhaustion.) Then he hit and hurt until they bled and fell. All the while he taunted.

Johnson's rise shocked the white American public because black fighters were supposed to have weak wills and soft stomachs—top scientists and boxing experts both said so. But Johnson's personality shocked white Americans more. He was brash to the point of outrageous. Commenting on Johnson's pajama-style shorts after one fight, a *Los Angeles Times* reporter fretted that they were not just pink but "one of those screaming, cater-wauling, belligerent pinks."[82] Outside the ring, he flaunted his wealth—drinking fine wine (through a straw), flashing his gold teeth, buying fast cars, and changing his suit three times a day. He flaunted his women, too, never traveling without one "Mrs. Johnson" and a few mistresses besides. His women were former prostitutes—and worst of all, they were white. The story was widely told of Johnson booking a room in a white hotel. When the clerk explained that "We don't serve your kind," Johnson replied, "I want it for my wife—she's your kind." Johnson's women had to wait day and night for a short visit, never knowing whether their lover would bring them gifts or fists, or both.

In 1907 Johnson deposed Tommy Burns, the world champion. True to form, Johnson humiliated him. "You a woman, Tommy?" he called. Johnson kept the fight going longer than needed, probably to inflict maximum damage on Burns's face. He became the most divisive figure in American life. After the fight, Johnson walked off a vaudeville tour when a theater manager would not allow him into the white-only—and the only warm—changing room. He was arrested for beating a black man in a drinking argument, for owning a dog that ripped open a man's arm, and for any number of speeding offenses. He claimed ever more white women—including at least nine members of the most exclusive white escort agency in America. (The girls were fired for sleeping across the color line.) Johnson's antics confirmed the stereotype (to quote Virginia lecturer Dr. Thomas Murrell) that black men's "sexual powers are those of a specialist in a chosen field."[83] To advertise his specialist powers, Johnson stuffed bandages down the front of his tight shorts.

A frantic search began for a white boxer to stop Johnson. But the stronger the challenger, the harder he fell, and in the case of Stanley Ketchel in 1909, the more teeth came out. Johnson pulled them out of his glove while standing triumphant. Hence the call for Jim Jeffries, the last and best White Hope, to come out of retirement. The Chicago *Tribune* carried a picture of a blond girl pleading, "Please, Mr. Jeffries, are you going to fight Mr. Johnson?"[84] The old-time message of white men needing to protect their daughters could hardly have been clearer. When a purse of $100,000 was promised—by far the largest to date—Jeffries agreed to "fight for the sole purpose of proving that a white man is better than a Negro."

As the fight approached, Americans agreed about what was at stake. "The biggest battle of modern times," former champion John Sullivan explained in his expert newspaper column, "is really between representatives of two races."[85] The arrival of Halley's Comet in April, and a solar eclipse in May, added to the sense of foreboding. Black pastors set aside time for prayer. Black punters set aside large sums at the inviting odds of ten to six against Johnson. In Africa, a prince reportedly bet five hundred elephant tusks. Across the country, crowds gathered around telegraph services. Henry Turner installed a press wire service in his church. So too did Booker T. Washington at his institute.

They need not have bothered. The news from Reno was entirely predictable. Johnson dressed up for the occasion—he wore a Stars and Stripes belt. White supremacy was on proud display—a brass band played "All Coons Look Alike to Me." And the fight was an anticlimax. Jeffries had been out of the ring for five years, and it showed. In the second round, Johnson closed Jeffries' right eye, and by the thirteenth Johnson was punching him at will. In the fifteenth, Jeffries hit the canvas for the first and last time in his career. Jeffries conceded afterward that even in his prime he would not have won. Johnson was unusually warm in his praise of Jeffries' courage, too.[86]

The crowd, becalmed by the mismatch (and by the provision of lemonade rather than beer), shuffled quietly back into town.[87] But the Reno stadium was the calm eye in what became a national storm of racial violence. "That Mr. Johnson should so lightly and carelessly punch the head of Mr. Jeffries," reported the New York World, "must have come as a shock to every devoted believer in the supremacy of the Anglo-Saxon race." There were enough shocked believers to make revenge inevitable. The celebrations of black Americans (with black women and men, complained one newspaper, "losing respect for the police") made that revenge deadly. More than twenty-five black Americans were killed, more than five hundred were injured, and more than five thousand people—mostly African Americans—were arrested. It would remain the most widespread moment of anti-black violence until Martin Luther King Jr.'s death nearly sixty years later. Five thousand miles away in London, a white gang attacked a black music hall performer as he walked across Leicester Square.[88]

Worried authorities in most cities banned the film of the fight. The South African government followed suit. But the violent backlash, and the censorship, could neither erase the result nor dim the memory. Breakfast customers in black restaurants would ask for coffee as strong as Johnson and eggs as scrambled as Jeffries' face. In black folklore, the second line of a favorite hymn, "Amazing Grace, How Sweet the Sound," got a new lyric: "Jack Johnson knocked Jim Jeffries down." In many towns, over half the black population turned out to cheer a visit from the man some called "the King of the black race."

It wasn't all praise. Black commentators were unhappy about the white women. But even the disapproving were proud of his achievements. And for years to come, any challenge to authority was called a "Jack John-

son." He seemed beholden to nobody. A favorite story told of Johnson
giving a confused southern sheriff a $100 bill for a $50 speeding fine.
"Keep the change," he explained, "I'll be coming back this way." He was
not even beholden to his nation. "What has America ever done for me or
my race?" he said to one overseas reporter.[89] Some fifty years later, Muhammad Ali would explicitly claim Johnson's mantle as "the greatest,"
and echo his anger. (By contrast, Joe Louis, world heavyweight champion
in 1937, would distance himself from the elderly Johnson to protect his
patriotic reputation.)

Addicted to the limelight, Johnson went in search of ever more thrilling
highs. On a lucrative "Wine, Women and Song" tour, he hooked up with
chorus girls and infuriated theater owners. He toured Europe. The newly
inaugurated "King George should be glad to meet Jack Johnson," chuckled the *Chicago Defender,* a black newspaper, "to break honors even."[90]
In New York he raced, and lost to, the world driving champion (who was
stripped of his racing permit for racing a black man). In Chicago he
opened a café near the vice district and talked of buying a home in an exclusive white suburb. He lectured in churches on his favorite Bible pas-
sages. He married a long-standing mistress, Etta Duryea, who on September 14, 1912, suffering from depression, blew her brains out. Two weeks
later, Johnson appeared in public with a new belle—an eighteen-year-old
from Minnesota, Lucille Cameron. Federal agents arrested him for
breaking the newly passed Mann Act which was intended to stop the
trafficking in women for prostitution. Over half of the twenty states that
allowed racial intermarriage introduced bills to ban it.[91]

In some respects, Johnson saw himself as a race leader. At his Chicago
homecoming, he compared himself to Napoleon, and at Christmastime
he played the role of a black Santa Claus. When campaigning for the
black Republican Edward Wright in his bid for Chicago alderman in
1910, Johnson sounded Washington's themes of race progress—albeit
more brashly. "In every walk of life there is a black man coming out the
winner . . . black school teachers and black bicycle riders." True to form,
he had a special message for the ladies: "Go home to your sweethearts . . .
as a personal favor to me, and see they [elect] Mr. Wright." Like many
uplift reformers, he believed an upright example would change racial stereotypes. Because he had refused bribes to lose to Jeffries, he told his Chicago homecoming crowd: "I have shown the world that there is one
black man who loves honor more than money."[92] Like Du Bois, he turned
against the Republicans, and then against Washington. As he put it in his
autobiography, Washington has "not been altogether frank in the statement of the problem or courageous in the formulation in his solutions to
them."[93]

Johnson's rise even helped forge national protest networks. Founded in 1905 by the pugnacious journalist Robert Abbott, the *Chicago Defender* used its hometown hero to establish itself as the leading protest paper of its day. It offered readers an eighteen-inch statue at discount price. The *Defender* became the first black newspaper to reach a quarter of a million sales (and maybe twice as many readers). Perhaps two thirds of the papers found their way to the South. In turn, the rise of the *Defender* helped turn Johnson's life into legend. The story was told, wrongly, that Johnson had tried to board the *Titanic,* only to have the captain tell him "I ain't hauling no coal." "Black man oughta shout for joy," sang blues man Blind Lemon Jefferson. "Cryin', fare thee, *Titanic,* fare thee well."[94]

For the most part, though, the "King of the black race" expended little energy on the race question. One of the most striking things about his autobiography (the one comment about Washington aside), or his life more generally (the odd election speech aside), was his silence on white supremacy. His eyes were ever on a financial prize and the fame and female conquests that came with it. In fact, white supremacy shaped even those aspects of his life—he embraced white women as more beautiful and loyal, and he had to fight the color line to become boxing champion. But once he was champion, he drew the color line by fighting only white men (there was more money and less decent opposition).

Johnson's lifestyle presented a major challenge to conventional race leaders. With his unfettered hedonism, contempt for race taboos, and lack of patriotism, Johnson was Booker T. Washington's worst nightmare come to life—in pink pajama shorts. After Johnson's arrest for sex trafficking, Washington put out a plaintive press release: the "sober element of the Negro people of the United States is . . . severe in condemnation of the kind of immorality with which Jack Johnson is at present charged." He even used Johnson's example "to prove my contention" that "no one can do so much injury to the Negro race as the Negro himself."[95] The problem for Washington, though, was that Johnson was almost as shrewd a self-publicist as he was, and more popular among black Americans than he ever had been. The *Akron Journal* reckoned interest in Johnson's footwork "entirely eclipsed the interest in the headwork of Washington."[96] Many condemned Washington for criticizing Johnson. He never did it in public again. Johnson counterpunched anyway. "I never got beat up because I looked in the wrong keyhole," he said, referring to Washington's own scandal.

NAACP leaders joined the chorus of disapproval against Washington. Du Bois judged it was only Johnson's "unforgiveable blackness" which led to the Progressive hue and cry against boxing—a pastime no worse than football and better than war.[97] But Johnson gave the NAACP plenty of problems, too. Through *The Crisis,* Du Bois tried to rally opposition to the proposed legislation against intermarriage. Such laws would leave the "helpless . . . colored girl" at the mercy of the "lust of white men." The case against white men's lust was a staple of black rhetoric. With Johnson in the headlines, however, it was an impossible case to make.

Above all, Johnson threatened the work of clubwomen. He won acclaim through punching, not politeness. He celebrated machismo. He even justified his preference for white women by slandering black women as unfaithful. What made matters worse was the attention Johnson drew to the underworld he moved in. In his disdain for the lifestyle of the black bourgeoisie, Johnson was as much everyman as maverick. He was popular in places—bars and backstreets—that reformers couldn't reach, and where *The Crisis* wasn't read. Johnson's exploits, and the boisterous reaction to them, lifted the veil on aspects of black urban life as something other than the industrious, respectable, talented version that Washington, clubwomen, and Du Bois so desperately wanted to promote. Within a generation, a great migration would make this world much larger—and much more visible.

In the end, reformers needn't have worried about Johnson. His fall was as swift and as headline-grabbing as his rise, with a heavy dose of federal pursuit and white supremacist glee thrown in. Lucille Cameron's mother worked the media to good effect. "Jack Johnson has hypnotic powers," she told reporters, through tears. He boasted, "I could get you, too, if I wanted."[98] In fact, Lucille was already a prostitute, she had traveled to Chicago before meeting Johnson, and she married Johnson soon after his arrest. No matter. Federal agents turned up a spurned former lover who was eager to testify against him, and Johnson was sentenced to a year in jail for abetting prostitution. He jumped bail, fled abroad, became bored, lost his title in Cuba, returned to the United States, did his stint in prison, and went on tours for ever decreasing fees. Later in life, white children paid a dollar for the privilege of hitting him. He compared his woes to Job in the Bible (though with characteristic self-absorption, he reckoned he had it worse). In 1946 he died in a car crash, ending his life as he had always lived it—at high speed.

White Supremacy in a Progressive Era

On February 8, 1915, a silent movie premiered in Los Angeles. *Birth of a Nation* told a harrowing story of the Civil War and its aftermath through the lives of two white families, one from the South, one from the North. It was brilliantly innovative—the first movie with panoramic scenes, an orchestral score to fit the screenplay, and a running time of more than an hour (it ran for three). It was also the single most effective piece of white supremacist propaganda of the Jim Crow or any other era—certainly far more powerful than any speech by a black leader could ever be.

Based on Thomas Dixon's novel *The Clansman, Birth of a Nation* exploited race stereotypes at every turn. The southern hero of the movie, Ben Cameron, is brave in war and noble in defeat. Black men (or rather, white actors in black face) are depraved and dangerous. Dim-witted Reconstruction legislators put their feet up, drink whisky, and pass legislation approving intermarriage. Black men with guns stop white men from voting. A cunning mulatto lieutenant governor tries to marry Cameron's sweetheart, Elsie. (The politician's mixture of white and black blood combined to give him both intelligence and perversion.) A simple black soldier, Gus, tries to rape Cameron's younger sister. After an absurdly lengthy chase, she jumps to her death off a cliff to preserve her honor. There was a lesson for southern white women, too. The girl had refused to obey her brother's order to stay inside, and suffers the consequences.

A despairing Cameron seeks inspiration. He finds it when he sees a group of white children hide under a sheet to scare off black bullies. The Ku Klux Klan is born. In a rush of derring-do, the Klan rescues Elsie, lynches Gus, defends the Camerons, and restores white control. In case the audience hadn't yet grasped the point, the figure of Christ then appears in the sky. As for Elsie and Ben, they are last seen sitting happily by the seaside. Dixon was thrilled with the movie, telling a friend, "Every man who comes out of one of our theatres is a Southern partisan for life." At the New York opening, horsemen dressed in Klan regalia trotted through Times Square.

Black leaders responded to the new technological racism in characteristic fashion. Washington hoped that ignoring the movie would deny it publicity. Du Bois and the NAACP publicized the threat of anti-black riots—Boston's mayor asked sarcastically if Macbeth should be banned in case it incited prejudice against whites.[99] Trotter led a march at the Boston premiere, and was punched by a policeman. One of Trotter's allies managed to sneak in and threw an egg at the screen during the rape chase; he was ejected. From Chicago, black preacher James Webb went on a speaking tour trumpeting "The Black Man's Part in the Bible" (or more precisely, his new book by that title) as the "greatest defense against *Birth of a Nation.*"[100] In Philadelphia, a thousand black Americans tried to smash their way into the premiere. The police beat them back.

The black press celebrated any good news they could lay their hands on. The *Chicago Defender* trumpeted the "greatest slap" for the movie when Brazil banned it, following protests in Rio de Janeiro.[101] Even so, a slap abroad and an egg at home hardly hurt the box office. White critics praised it, and white crowds flocked to see it. The NAACP campaign to ban the film soon became a damage-control exercise to cut some of the worst scenes (and even then only a few review boards agreed). Director D. W. Griffith professed shock at all the fuss. Calling him racist "is like saying I am against children, as they were our children, whom we loved and cared for."[102] For black Americans, such patronizing paternalism was part of the problem.

Grudgingly conceding victory to the "mighty genius," Du Bois called on black Americans to forget Griffith's "cruel slander" and popularize their own black aesthetic (a call that would be echoed by activists in future generations). Both Du Bois and Washington explored the possibility of a counterweight movie. The NAACP version—*Lincoln's Dream*—never got off the ground. The underfunded Tuskegee version, *The Birth of a Race,* would have been better if it hadn't. One *Variety* reviewer called it "the most grotesque cinema chimera in the history of the picture business."[103] Its premiere and final showing were one and the same event. The NAACP learned its lesson and kept a close eye on Hollywood for decades to come. Away from the silver screen, Du Bois promoted his own three-hour spectacular pageant, *Star of Ethiopia*—a theatrical celebration of black history. Some thirty thousand people watched a production at the New York State Fair. An impressive number, until it is put alongside the one million viewers of *Birth of a Nation* in New York theaters in the first year alone. Dixon's epic became the most successful silent movie of all time.

What was true for the movies was true for the White House. Woodrow Wilson had run for office speaking of a "New Freedom" "that releases men and women from all that pulls them back." He then presided over the racial segregation of government departments, virtually cut off patronage for black Americans, and sent troops into Haiti and the Dominican Republic. Trotter complained in a meeting with Wilson that the presidential seal of approval for segregation meant "a 'new freedom' for white Americans and a new slavery for your African-American fellow citizens."[104] Trotter provoked Wilson to anger. But he had no power to press him to change course. Wilson had no need of black voters, and the Democratic Party controlled both houses of Congress.

Birth of a Nation brought together white supremacy in popular culture and presidential politics. Wilson screened the movie at the White House. Reports said he thought the movie "is like writing history with lightning. And my only regret is that it is all so terribly true." He was hardly going to think otherwise—Griffiths had cannily taken many of the movie's quotations from Wilson's 1902 *History of the American People*. The uproar from black Americans may have prompted Wilson to leak a letter three months later calling the movie an "unfortunate production."[105] But it was far too little far too late.

Birth of a Nation and Wilson's actions showed just how comfortably white supremacy sat with the new urban, technological, Progressive Era. In the name of efficiency, direct democracy, reforming the poor, removing vice, cleaning up politics, calming urban tensions, and seeking international freedom, Progressive reformers formalized the color line in many aspects of American life. Or as the Atlanta *Independent*, a black newspaper, put it in 1907, "Reform legislation . . . means special favors for white people and the downright outlawry of the black man's rights."[106] Atlanta reformers used fears of tuberculosis—supposedly a "Negro disease"—to regulate the movement of black women domestics. In other words, cries for social reform, underpinned by medical opinion, empowered—at long last—those seeking to control the labor and behavior of black working women. Atlanta's main white newspaper spoke cheerfully of domestics wearing badges that "resemble those kept on hand for the city's canines."[107]

The reaction to Wilson's actions and *Birth of a Nation* also showed that black Americans continued to protest. Even at the height of Jim Crow, some fought, some tried to disrupt, some appealed for justice, some challenged stereotypes, some prayed, some moved, and many kept their heads down and tried to carve out a life and a community as best they could. The philosophies embodied by Washington, Cooper, Trotter, Du Bois, and Johnson would remain influential for years to come. Still, the success of the movie and the actions of the president showed just how little power black Americans possessed in their fight for a more meaningful freedom. Whereas the bravery of black soldiers had challenged negative race stereotypes during the Civil War, the notoriety of Jack Johnson and the popularity of *Birth of a Nation* now reinforced white prejudice. And whereas freed slaves had been able to force the hand of the federal government during Reconstruction, the most prominent race leaders could only provoke Wilson to anger, not action. What black Americans needed was leverage—not just over the federal government but over local politicians, white bosses and workers, popular culture, and hearts and minds. America's entry into the First World War would give them that power sooner than anyone could have imagined.

CHAPTER FIVE

Great War and Great Migration, 1917–1924

"Mr. President, Why Not Make AMERICA safe for democracy?"
Banner carried during parade in New York, 1917

In 1917 the Illinois 8th Regiment traveled through Arkansas and Texas to Houston. At one stop, a soldier called Jeffries tried to buy a Coca-Cola in a small store. The storekeeper said he would sell him a Coke but he couldn't drink it in the store. Jeffries replied that he knew his place and would drink it outside. When the storekeeper placed the bottle on the counter. Jeffries took it and smashed it over the storekeeper's head, and then, with his buddies, proceeded to wreck the place.[1]

In Durban, South Africa, in October 1920, one thousand people turned out for a meeting of the African National Congress. The highlight was an appearance by a black American sailor called Moses, recently arrived from New York. Moses told the audience "that their leader Marcus Garvey was the man they relied upon, and who would free Africa: that the first vessel of [Garvey's] fleet was named 'Frederick Douglass,' and this vessel had been sailing to different places."[2]

In May 1923 blues singer Bessie Smith released her first record—
"Down Hearted Blues" and (on the flip side) "Gulf Coast Blues."
By the end of the year, it had sold nearly a million copies.

During the war and its aftermath (1917–1923), more than a thousand black Americans were killed by white mobs in the United States, compared with 773 black Americans killed by German soldiers in Europe.[3]

Saturday, July 28, 1917, New York City. First came the sound of muffled drums—four black men beating a rhythm, their drums draped with black material. Then came the sight of ten thousand people—most were African Americans, some were Caribbean immigrants—marching in silence through Manhattan, down Fifth Avenue from Central Park. Hundreds of children, dressed in white, walked behind the drummers, a dozen to a line, holding hands, with an adult at either end of each line. Behind them followed row upon row of women, also dressed in white. Thousands of men marched at the rear, dressed in dark suits, as if in mourning. A crowd of perhaps twenty thousand people lined the route, watching in silence. This Silent Protest Parade was by far the largest public protest march by black Americans since the end of Reconstruction.

The parade was organized in response to a race massacre in East St. Louis, Illinois, at the beginning of July. Trouble had been brewing there for months, in response to black migration. In 1916 Democrats claimed that Republicans were bringing in black voters ahead of the presidential election. The following year labor leaders claimed that factory owners were bringing in black workers to crush the unions. In late June rumors spread that black migrants had caused an outbreak of smallpox, planned an armed insurrection, and—the trigger for the riot—murdered two policemen. Once the riot began, the baying of the crowd took the violence to shocking levels. At least two hundred houses were burned down. Women, fleeing their homes (said one reporter), "were shot down like rabbits."[4] One young boy was thrown into a fire to die. White women attacked black women. The police disarmed black men but stood by as white mobs did their work.[5] First news reports estimated at least a hundred deaths.

Black Americans were outraged. Prisoners in a Chicago jail rioted. Many black leaders and journalists called on black men to arm themselves.[6] The NAACP in New York—in liaison with local churches and civic groups—called for the parade. "We march," the NAACP explained, "because we deem it a crime to be silent in the face of such barbaric acts." A delegation went to the White House and urged Woodrow Wilson to denounce the violence and support a federal anti-lynching bill.

By marching silently in Manhattan the marchers fairly shouted their anger. They carried hundreds of banners. There were appeals to God ("Mother, do lynchers go to Heaven?") and to humanity ("We want our children to live in a better land"). There were reminders of black patriotism ("We have fought for the liberty of white Americans in 6 wars") and black achievements ("Our music is the only American music"). There were references to international freedom movements ("India is abolishing caste, America is adopting it") and solidarity with black nations (some marchers carried the flags of Haiti and Liberia). And there were complaints aplenty ("Repelled by the unions we are condemned as scabs"). All the while the steady beat of the drums sounded an insistent call for justice.

Yet the scale of the parade was not just a reflection of outrage but a response to the opportunities of the moment. After all, there had been many, far too many, barbaric acts since Reconstruction. Black Americans had long sought justice, and the banners repeated old arguments. By the summer of 1917, however, there was a belief that change was possible. By the summer of 1917, America was at war.

In April, Wilson had called on Americans to fight Germany "to make the world safe for democracy." The marchers seized upon the rhetoric and gave it their own meaning. One carried a banner showing a black woman kneeling at the feet of the president, pleading with him to enforce democracy in America before exporting it abroad. It was the only banner that the police deemed objectionable, and it was soon taken down. No matter. The *New York Age* had already printed a similar cartoon.

The Silent Parade turned out to be the first of many marches and parades during the war era. If the previous generation had been marked by speeches, the new way was spectacle—which bespoke new opportunities for black Americans to protest publicly. America's wartime rhetoric and wartime needs gave them the power to challenge white supremacy. With pens in hand, black journalists deployed the language of democracy in their calls for meaningful citizenship. With guns in hand, black soldiers fought discrimination in the army and—on their return—at home. When wartime production opened up new jobs, over a million African Americans left the rural South in search of a better life. When white workers and white women used the war to push their own democratic agendas, black workers and black women demanded inclusion. When Wilson sought a democratic postwar peace for the world, black leaders pursued their own global, anti-imperial vision.

African Americans who lived through these tumultuous years saw them as pivotal for American race relations. The verdict of the Silent Parade organizer, James Weldon Johnson, is a case in point. Born in 1871, Johnson taught in the rural South, wrote an influential novel, worked for the Republican Party, served as consul in Cuba, and toured Europe in support of his brother's vaudeville show. Before the war, he was best known as a songwriter. "Under the Bamboo Tree" became an international hit, "You're All Right Teddy" became Roosevelt's campaign song, and "Lift Every Voice and Sing" became known as the "Negro national anthem." In 1916 he became field secretary for the NAACP, and four years later, the first black executive secretary. Johnson met with U.S. presidents and visited local NAACP branches. Few people were in a better position to assess the significance of the Great War era. "At no time since the days following the Civil War," Johnson concluded in his autobiography in 1934, "had the Negro been in a position to make greater gain or sustain greater loss in status."[7]

For Johnson, an NAACP-sponsored conference of black leaders in

1916 meant that "the Negro" seemed particularly well placed to make "great gain in status." A year after the deaths of Booker T. Washington and Henry Turner, the conference at Amenia, New York, was an attempt to overcome the bitter factionalism of previous decades. Unlike most nineteenth-century black leaders, Johnson did not believe in an active God. But the timing seemed providential, so the conference "took its place in the list of important events in the history of the Negro in the United States."[8] In fact, Wells and Trotter were absent, the conference was male-dominated, and it was hardly representative of the masses of black Americans. Everyday local battles for justice continued irrespective of a meeting in Amenia. Still, the NAACP's Du Bois enthused that after Amenia, the "Negro race was more united and more ready to meet the problems of the world."[9]

Yet Johnson was right: the turmoil that offered "great gain" also threatened "greater loss." East St. Louis turned out to be the opening battle in a bloody domestic race war that outlasted the Great War. America's wartime needs and wartime rhetoric also gave new power to defenders of race hierarchy. Southern politicians and northern industrialists used wartime legislation and the language of democracy for their own ends. Many white workers and white women actually embraced white supremacy in pursuit of their own democratic agendas. At every stage the federal government tried to stifle black dissent for the sake of national unity. After the Silent Parade, Wilson claimed he could find no constitutional basis for federal action against lynching, a crime that, in his view, fell under the jurisdiction of the states. Kelly Miller, a leading black educator, complained acidly, "The black man asks for justice and is given a theory of government."[10]

Ultimately the losses in status more than canceled out the gains. In the long view, the Great War was but a hiccup in the life of Jim Crow. But that should not distract from the drama, and the significance, of the moment. The crucible of war ushered in changes in the nature of protest—especially the adulation of fighting men and the celebration of blackness. The audacity of public protest exposed the depth of black resentment—a resentment hidden from view in less tumultuous years. Thus, the legacies of wartime protest—for both opponents and advocates of white supremacy—would last long after the coming of peace.

Fighting White Supremacy in the Army

August 23, 1917, Houston, Texas. "To hell with France," said one soldier. "Let's get to work right here." Late in the evening, about a hundred black soldiers from the 3rd Battalion of the all-black 24th U.S. Infantry Regiment marched downtown. They wanted revenge.

Earlier that day, a white policeman had slapped a black mother who had complained when he barged into her house, searching for a criminal. The policeman had called the woman a "God damn nigger bitch" and complained that "these God damn sons of bitches of nigger soldiers . . . are trying to take the town." To put the woman back in her place, the policeman arrested her—and pushed her child, who was reaching for her, onto the sidewalk. When one of those "nigger soldiers" happened to come by and told the policeman to hand the woman over, the policeman smashed him with his pistol. Back at base, the soldiers fumed. This was just the latest fight with local police, and it came less than two months after East St. Louis. That evening, when rumors spread that a white mob was coming toward them, the soldiers grabbed their guns, formed ranks, and headed to the police station. Shooting anyone who got in their way, they killed seventeen people.[11]

The soldiers knew their revolt could not last long. They were soon outnumbered and outgunned by white police and the National Guard. Three hours later, the mutiny was over. Two black soldiers died in the shootout (most likely the ringleader shot himself to avoid capture). The army then sentenced thirteen soldiers to death, sent forty-one to prison for life, and moved the rest of the battalion away from Houston. But the end of the fight was far from being the end of the story.

The Houston mutiny cast its shadow over wartime America and beyond—inspiring some, haunting others. At stake was the place of young black men in American life—and by extension, the place of African Americans more generally. So much of the justification for Jim Crow had been built on the need to keep dangerous black men under control. Much of the response of black leaders had been to sidestep the issue of black manhood. Washington called on black men to work hard and remember their place, Du Bois called on the better sort of black men to take a lead, Cooper reckoned women were best suited to uplift the race, and in many southern communities (with black men excluded from politics) black women represented the race to white officials.

With the coming of war, however, black men—and ordinary rough, tough, armed black men at that—stepped forward and demanded full rights of citizenship, just as they had during the Civil War. Across the country, African Americans applauded. In Texas, Clara Threadgill-Dennis—a college graduate and school principal's wife—wrote an open letter to the Houston rebels in her local paper: "Every woman in all this land of ours, who dares feel proud of the Negro blood that courses through her veins, reveres you . . . because you dared protect a Negro woman from the insult of a southern brute."[12] Threadgill-Dennis and the newspaper's editor were arrested for their trouble. To avoid a stint in prison, most black newspaper editors condemned the mutiny—yet as they did so they took the opportunity to articulate, at length, the soldiers' grievances.

Thus, wartime mobilization shook both white supremacy and black responses to it. Even before the start of war, southern politicians had raised the alarm about black soldiers. Mississippi Senator James Vardaman— never one to miss a chance of demagogic scaremongering—could think of "no greater menace to the South," not even a German victory, than black conscription, and presumed that a black soldier would come "to the conclusion that his political rights must be respected."[13] He was right. As Perry Howard, chairman of the black Liberty Bond Committee in Jackson, Mississippi, argued: "If the Negro . . . furnishes his quota of fighters, man for man, he expects the ballot."[14] Vardaman proposed a bill to ban black men from the draft, but it failed to pass. Wilson's Selective Service Act of April 1917—which introduced the draft—made no mention of race. Even so, the federal government, out of deference to southern interests, did not induct black men into the army until the following spring. (The Houston troops were one of three regiments of standing black troops.)

In fact, black men were in no hurry to sign up. More than 100,000 failed to register for the draft, or failed to report for duty when called up. They did not see the squabble between European powers as one worth dying for. Nor, for that matter, did many poor southern white men. Indeed, it was white resistance to the draft that led southern politicians to change their minds about black conscription. During 1918 local draft boards began to call up black men in disproportionately high numbers. After all, there were advantages to drafting black men, too. Some sheriffs acted like bounty hunters by rounding up black (but never white) deserters to claim a $50 reward each time. Black leaders complained that black workers on white land were often given exemptions, yet black independent farmers were invariably called up. A one-armed black Texan was told that the reason he gave for refusing the draft—his disability—was "not satisfactory."[15] By the end of the war, some 357,000 black men had served in the army.

Nonetheless, southern segregationists were right to worry about armed black men—to quote one official—"strutting in their uniforms." Strut they did. Haywood Hall—son of former slaves, and a future Communist leader—signed up for the 8th Illinois Regiment. "Patriotism was the least of my motives," he said. He wanted to see France and get a better life.

Late in 1917, Hall's regiment headed to Houston. At stops along the way, the soldiers stole from shops and blew kisses to white women, intimidating local people as much as angering them. Hall remembered his fears as they approached Houston. But "to our surprise . . . the whites, especially the police, had learned that they couldn't treat all black people as they had been used to . . . Houston blacks were no longer the cowed, intimidated people they had been before the mutiny." From Hall's perspective, "The girls were especially proud of us."[16] Membership in the local NAACP surged.[17]

The problem for black conscripts was that many more got to carry a shovel than a gun. Many didn't even wear a uniform. One soldier reckoned the army wanted their "manpower . . . but not their manhood."[18] Almost half of all black conscripts were put to service work in America (though, considering how deadly the war turned out to be, this was a blessing in disguise). Officers in Camp Gordon, Georgia, hired former chain gang bosses to handle black recruits—who subsequently rioted. For many of the 200,000 black servicemen who went to France, army life seemed more like a convict labor camp than a chance for glory. Secretary of War Newton Baker warned black leaders that the army was not "trying by this war to settle the Negro problems."[19] But by claiming neutrality on the race issue, the army ended up expanding the reach of white supremacy. Officials ordered soldiers not to protest segregation in the South, they imposed segregation on the ships crossing the Atlantic, and they warned French officers to segregate black soldiers from white servicemen.

Despite—or rather because of—these hardships, army life profoundly affected black recruits. Two black YMCA support staffers in France, Addie Hunton and Kathryn Johnson, thought the troops developed "a racial consciousness and racial strength that could not have been gained in a half century of normal living in America."[20] Hunton and Johnson reckoned that as black men from different backgrounds shared mud, fear, exhaustion, insults, and anger, they united along the color line. The women could just as well have been talking about themselves. Both were "better-class" reformers—Hunton a former teacher, Johnson an NAACP worker. Both had expected to boost the race, and their own careers, by lifting up the lower types. A few weeks in France changed their minds. Appalled at the treatment of black soldiers, and envious of the resources available to the thousands of white YMCA workers (there were only a dozen black staff members), the women applauded the soldiers' militancy. They even waved back when the soldiers shouted oh-la-las. When the war was over, they dropped their previous appeals to white paternalism and condemned discrimination in the social services.[21]

Ill-treated and away from the front line, black soldiers seemed to fight American soldiers more than Germans. Hunton and Johnson felt "we were living close to the edge of a smoldering crater." Predictably, the volcano erupted in clashes over French women. Black soldiers also fought against discrimination in a way that would have been unthinkable in the Jim Crow South. For example, at the end of the war, black laborers—and only black laborers—had to exhume American corpses to rebury them in military cemeteries, while, back at camp, white troops relaxed. When one white group put a "No Negroes" sign on a large recreational tent, black troops burned the tent to the ground. White officers had to mount a machine gun to stop further trouble.[22]

Some forty thousand black troops did end up fighting the Germans, but most did so under the French flag. General John Pershing placed four black infantry regiments under French command, and the French—well used to deploying colonial troops—sent them into battle. One U.S. official worried that black soldiers "enjoy unrestricted social equality among the French." Black American soldiers enjoyed the sight of uniformed French colonial troops in action, too. Few knew that these troops were fighting their own battle to win meaningful citizenship. In the minds of black soldiers, France became a country without a color line—a country that exposed both the immorality and the abnormality of American practice.

If southern Democrats feared black soldiers, the thought of black officers made them apoplectic. By the same token, African Americans prized black officers as irrefutable proof of their responsible manhood. Initially the War Department ducked the issue by retiring Lieutenant Colonel Charles Young—the highest ranking black soldier—on the grounds of illness. Young claimed foul, rode on horseback from Ohio to Washington, and joined the NAACP board. Intense lobbying from the NAACP eventually led to the training of black officers. But the training camp at Fort Des Moines was segregated, and officers were then sent to the all-black 92nd Division under white superiors. Some were replaced by white officers once they arrived in France. Black spokesmen split down the middle over whether to support Fort Des Moines. As it turned out, the war's end in 1918 meant that the camp closed after graduating just one class. It would take another world war to raise the issue again, and more years still to resolve it.

On November 11, 1918, America and its allies signed an armistice with Germany. Baker hoped the end of the war would be the end of the race problem. In the foreword to an official history of the black contribution to the war, he recommended, "If there have been some things which you think were not as they should have been, you must try to forget them."[23] To help induce amnesia, he sent Robert Moton—Washington's successor at Tuskegee, who was angling to succeed Washington as confidant to white leaders—to tour France. Moton dutifully called on soldiers to "find a wife . . . and settle down." The problem for Baker was that black soldiers would not even settle down for Moton's speech. One private, Ely Green, shouted out, "Why in the hell did President Wilson send you over here to tell us how he honors the Negro?"[24]

Ely was clearly no exception. At the end of the war, when Du Bois traveled to France and met with black soldiers, "Before the war there was but one radical in a thousand negroes," observed Du Bois. "Now there are at least 25 in every hundred . . . filled to the boiling point with hatred for the white Americans never before dreamed of."[25] In fact, white southerners did dream. Many had nightmares. Georgia Senator Thomas Hardwick worried, "What will be the result when tens of thousands of Negroes come home from this war with a distinguished record of honorable military service? I can conceive that a new agitation will arise as strong and bitter as the agitation for Negro suffrage which swept the North after the Civil War."[26]

Fighting for Democracy at Home

Hardwick was right. The war did lead to strong and bitter agitation. But he got his timing wrong. African Americans did not wait for soldiers to come home. James Weldon Johnson noticed the difference as he traveled the country to drum up support for the NAACP. His 1916 tour had not been particularly successful; there were only six NAACP branches in the South. But by the end of the war the NAACP had some 165 branches and more than forty thousand members, almost half based in the South. NAACP leaders boasted of their southern empire. "Did you ever know a race to awake as our race has awakened?" asked one member in Augusta, Georgia. "The old spirit of humble satisfaction, of let-well-enough-alone is dying out."[27] This was no magic of new organization or charismatic leadership—there were only three people working in the head office during 1917. One Fisk University professor observed, "The negro leaders are really now being led by the masses in this spirit of bitterness and unrest."[28]

The spirit of bitterness stemmed from the belief—to quote one Texas preacher—that America was yet to honor "the rights of the race which had been bought by blood [of black soldiers]."[29] Bitterness led to unrest because the social upheaval of the era gave black Americans new power to press their longstanding demands. Some hoped that support for the war effort would earn a reward. The New Orleans NAACP newsletter read, "If we keep the Huns on the run, we will get everything that we have been desiring."[30] Johnson was less sanguine. "If loyalty to the nation and fighting its battles could give the American Negro his full rights," Johnson told one audience, "he would have had them long ago." But Johnson did think "circumstances were combining to put a higher premium on Negro muscle, Negro hands, and Negro brains than ever before; all these forces had a quickening effect that was running through the entire mass of the race."[31]

The quickening effect was shown most dramatically in the movement of black Americans from the countryside to the city. During a massive relocation that would become known as the Great Migration, some 1.5 million African Americans left the rural South, so that by 1920 one third of African Americans lived in cities. Most moved to southern cities, but nearly half a million left the South altogether. There were many reasons why people moved. Some left the rural South to flee violence. Others left because the price of cotton collapsed from 1913 to 1915, and the boll weevil wreaked devastation soon after. Many headed north dreaming of freedom. Most joined family members who had already moved. The *Chicago Defender* claimed some of the credit, having launched a "great northern drive" in May 1917. With the help of black railroad porters, the *Defender* reached parts of the South that other newspapers couldn't reach. Headlines like "Flight Out of Egypt" invested black migration with divine approval.

Yet black southerners had been vulnerable and poor before the Great Migration, and this was not the first time they had been urged to head north. Many elite black southerners, and a few thousand poorer African Americans, had already done so. What was new was that jobs had suddenly become available in previously all-white northern industries. European immigration plummeted because of the war, at just the moment that wartime production stretched American industry to its limit. The introduction of the military draft in 1917 shrank the labor pool still further. The primary cause of the Great Migration, then (given that there were few incentives to stay in the rural South), was the promise of a half-decent wage in the city. This was true for poor southerners regardless of color—indeed, more whites than blacks left the South.

The Great Migration marked the beginning of some fifty years of black migration away from the rural South that would ultimately affect race relations in the United States as much as the Civil War or the Civil Rights Movement. For each individual, the move was a form of protest in itself, a rejection of the oppressive terms of the plantation system. But the movement of so many, so quickly, also had a cumulative effect, just as it had during the Civil War. Johnson thought the Great Migration "tantamount to a general strike"—the "most effective protest against Southern lynching, lawlessness, and general devilry."[32]

Those who moved tended to be younger and slightly more skilled than those who remained—exactly the sort of people one might expect to strike out for a better life. But many who stayed behind exploited the resulting labor shortage to make their own demands for change. Black miners in Alabama exploited the government's wartime support for labor to forge a union. Black washerwomen across the South exploited the army's laundry needs to strike for higher wages. Wives of black soldiers took advantage of the 1917 War Risk Insurance Act, which was designed to soften the blow of the draft by enabling housewives to stay at home. The biggest federal investment in local affairs since the Freedmen's Bureau (the sums involved were over half the entire prewar budget), it inadvertently enabled black women workers to become housewives for the first time (or take better-paid, but riskier, short-contract work by providing a financial safety net).

Overall, the wartime gains for southern black workers were impressive. Wages doubled in the Alabama coalfields and tripled on some southern plantations. In the Arkansas delta, black sharecroppers forced a switch from annual to weekly pay. Many rural workers were able to pay off debts. One visiting reporter marveled that African Americans in the delta, as "never before," bought "organs, talking machines . . . guns and other luxuries of life so profusely."[33]

An unwritten rule of southern history was that any major challenge to the racial status quo prompted panic. So it was in this era. Word spread of a secret society called WWTK—White Women to the Kitchen. Many suspected that Germans must be behind the trouble—one rumor had a German–African American coalition poised to take over Texas. Some southern officials hurriedly tried to stem the outgoing tide of migrants through conciliation. For example, Florida's governor, Sidney Catts, first elected on a platform opposing black schools, now pleaded with African Americans to stay.[34]

But if southern white leaders pulled their punches, they didn't change their attitudes. Their feeling of victimization, their assumption of black treason, and their anger at the federal government's intrusion combined to harden their resolve. And just like black workers, southern officials used the wartime emergency to their own advantage. In May 1918 the federal government issued "work or fight" orders, empowering local defense councils to arrest anyone who was not doing essential wartime work six days a week. It was virtually an invitation to control black labor. The marshal in Pelham, Georgia, arrested the agency director for Standard Life Insurance Company, Rufus McCrary, who had a staff of twenty-five, for doing a nonessential job.[35] Violence continued, too. There were over seventy recorded lynchings in 1918—almost double the previous year's total, after twenty years of gradual decline. In May, a Georgia mob lynched eleven black men after the murder of a white farmer. The wife of one of the victims, Mary Turner, who was eight months pregnant, pledged to swear out warrants. The following day, several hundred men and women hung Turner upside down, doused her with gasoline and set her on fire. One man slashed open her abdomen in a deadly caesarean. A reporter who witnessed the killing wrote, "Out tumbled the prematurely born child. Two feeble cries it gave—and received for the answer the heel of a stalwart man, as life was ground out of the tiny form." In the crowd, fathers lifted their children for a better view.[36]

A generation before, legal repression and extra-legal violence had served the cause of white supremacy well. Yet the circumstances of war had changed—however slightly—the balance of power. The new wave of public protest continued. The NAACP's campaign against lynching even gained momentum in response to the increased violence. Georgia's Federation of Negro Women's Clubs sent many telegrams of complaints against lynching, including one to Wilson (though to no avail).[37]

Wartime attacks on black workers changed relationships within the black community. Previously, many "better class" black southerners had urged poorer African Americans to improve themselves and prove their worth to white bosses. That situation did not change overnight. But the heavy-handed treatment of black workers helped forge a stronger sense of racial consciousness across class barriers. The NAACP's protests against the application of work or fight orders to domestics underpinned its rise across the South. Some were successful—Atlanta's city government relented, recognizing that the argument that black domestics were essential war workers could not stand scrutiny (though the argument that black women were not entitled to a minimum wage would be heard again).

Those who migrated to the northern Promised Land did not find deliverance from white supremacy. The teenager Langston Hughes, who would later become one of America's greatest poets, tried to explore the areas around his house during his first weekend in Chicago. But he was beaten by some white boys, "who said they didn't allow niggers in that neighborhood."[38] At work, migrants soon found that the North was no Land of Milk and Honey. To be sure, some of the industrial wages on offer were unheard of in the rural South. But high wages were swallowed up by high living costs. Discrimination was rife, too. In 1918 the journal *Industrial Management* reminded bosses that "the mistake most foremen make is that they use the same method with the negro that they use with white labor."[39] Many black women fled sexual exploitation by planters only to be molested by the masters of urban houses. Trouble in the cities, not to mention the East St. Louis massacre, gave warning of violence to come when the war was over.

Wartime Appeals to the Government

In July 1918 Newton Baker wrote to the president: "My anxiety is growing at the situation in this country among the negroes."[40] As Secretary of War, Baker knew of the militancy of black soldiers, the apathy of black draftees, the demands of black war workers, and the complaints of white southerners. He suggested that Wilson write an open letter denouncing lynching. A few days later, Wilson did so. Thus—as was the case in the Civil War and Reconstruction—African American demands at the grassroots filtered through to the highest levels of government. And as in the Civil War era, it was the need to win a war, and anxiety about black violence and disloyalty, which led policymakers to take note.

Because black opinion mattered, the black press mattered. The early twentieth century saw a spectacular increase in the circulation of black newspapers. By the end of the war, both the *Chicago Defender* and the NAACP's *Crisis* magazine had over 100,000 subscribers and a much larger readership. Black newspapers had a field day with wartime rhetoric. They dressed up their demands in the language of democracy, just as previous black leaders had adopted the language of freedom. They demonized southern white supremacists by comparing them to the hated Huns, a tactic that would be repeated with the Nazis in the next World War. (In fact, the hated Huns bombarded black soldiers with leaflets, asking, "Do you enjoy the same rights as the white people do in America, the land of Freedom and Democracy?") War Department officials singled out the *Defender* as "the most dangerous of all Negro journals" and blamed the *Crisis* for "exciting the colored races to acts of violence."[41] Such assumptions revealed the ignorance of policymakers. The mainstream black press reported, rather than incited, black violence.

But the war also gave the government new justification to clamp down on dissent. This was part of a wider effort to enforce national unity that culminated in the Espionage Act of June 1917. War Department officials wooed the black press by inviting forty editors and prominent leaders to

Washington, D.C., in June 1918, to discuss black support for the war. But they warned the press by suspending the socialist Harlem *Messenger* for calling on America to make "Georgia safe for the Negro" before fighting in France. The *Messenger*'s young editors, A. Philip Randolph and Chandler Owen, spent the rest of the war in jail.

Government interference had an impact. Contrary to black public opinion, the vast majority of black newspapers backed the war. Du Bois, editor of the *Crisis,* admitted to one correspondent in August 1918, "THE CRISIS will never say anything that it does not believe: but there are a great many things which it does believe which it cannot say just now."[42] In fact, Du Bois most likely already had said what he did not believe. Under pressure from leading white NAACP financers, and with the offer of an army captaincy dangled in front of him, Du Bois had urged his readers in July: "While this war lasts [to] forget our special grievances and close our ranks shoulder to shoulder with our white fellow citizens." War did not excuse social injustice, but "we will not bargain with our loyalty."[43]

The "close ranks" editorial was the stuff of government propagandists' dreams. The furor Du Bois' words provoked would follow him to his grave.[44] But many black spokesmen were not prepared to "forget our special grievances." Some of them denounced Du Bois. As they had done during the Civil War and would do again during World War II, many were quite ready to "bargain with our loyalty." They didn't threaten mutiny—after Houston, they didn't need to—but they did demand rewards. Even the editors at the government-sponsored conference, after declaring support for the war, called for a "clear word on lynching from the President" and an end to discrimination in war-related industry.[45]

Such tactics may have had some effect. Perhaps as an attempt to justify his own stance, Du Bois pointed to "one thousand negro officers . . . higher wages and better employment . . . a strong word from the President against lynching. Blessed saints! Is this nothing?"[46] Government bureaucracies began to address African American concerns. Baker appointed Emmett Scott, Booker T. Washington's former secretary, as an adviser. The Department of Agriculture Extension Service tried, for the first time, to help poor black farmers. The Department of Labor created a division of Negro economics "to see as far as possible that Negro workingmen are given a square deal."[47] Ultimately, though, there were few spoils of war. Black workers didn't come close to getting a square deal. Baker chose Scott because he was a loyalist in the image of his late master. Wilson's condemnation of lynching did not specify violence against African Americans. He said, and did, nothing about war-related industry.

Still, while there was war there was hope. John Mitchell, editor of the influential *Richmond Planet,* had long campaigned against disfranchisement and segregation. He recognized that the government's reluctance to act was matched by its eagerness to silence dissenters. "Go into your closet and shut the door," he warned despairing readers, "else someone other than God may hear you and arrest you when you come out." But he believed the war was bringing progress. "The longer the war and the bloodier," Mitchell wrote in October 1917, "the better it will be for the colored folk."[48] Unfortunately for Mitchell, by the end of 1918 the troops were ready to come home.

A New Negro Returns Marching, Dancing, and Fighting

February 17, 1919, New York City. One thousand soldiers from the all-black 369th Infantry Regiment marched along Fifth Avenue. This was no grim silent protest parade. This was joy, loud and unrestrained. After 197 days of fighting, the soldiers were ready to party. In the postwar euphoria, perhaps half a million people—black and white—turned out to welcome the first New York regiment to come home. They cheered for Sergeant Henry Johnson, a former chauffeur who fought twenty Germans single-handedly. And they stomped to the new jazz music of the regimental band, conducted by Lieutenant James Europe—the first black officer to lead men under fire in the war. Tall, dark, and broad-shouldered, the Alabama-born pianist had been a well-known musician in America before the war. He returned as an international superstar. His syncopated march music delighted French audiences. By the end of the war, James Europe was quite possibly the most popular American in France.

It was not just the noise level that was different from the Silent Parade. Then, women and children had marched at the front. Now, the march was a celebration of manhood. Wives and girlfriends jumped on their men, said one reporter, like tacklers in a football game. Scores of little boys, bursting with pride, wore mini-uniforms complete with the regimental emblem—a rattlesnake—sewn on the shoulder. In the Silent Parade, marchers had headed down Fifth Avenue to midtown Manhattan. Now, they headed up Fifth Avenue to Harlem. When they got there, Europe's band played "Here Comes My Daddy Now." The crowd's response, said the *Age,* "bordered on a riot." The Silent Parade had protested racist violence. This homecoming parade, said nineteen-year-old private Melville Miller, was the "most wonderful day of my life . . . That's one day that there wasn't the slightest bit of prejudice in New York City."[49]

7. During Reconstruction (and beyond), African Americans sought economic progress as much as civil rights. Baltimore caulker Isaac Myers formed a 300-strong cooperative and called for white unions to include black workers. (Courtesy of Dr. Suzanne Chapelle)

8. At the turn of the century, black clubwomen sought to challenge white supremacy by uplifting the moral and material standards of the black poor. Prominent clubwoman, author, and educator Anna Julia Cooper was outspoken in her call for both civil rights and women's rights. (Moorland-Spingarn Research Library)

9. Booker T. Washington's success in building up the Tuskegee Institute and his message of race progress through hard work rather than protest earned him the confidence of senior politicians. Governor Joseph Johnston and President William McKinley joined him on the platform to watch a procession in honor of McKinley's visit to Tuskegee on December 16, 1898. (Library of Congress)

10. World heavyweight boxing champion Jack Johnson flaunted his white wives and mistresses. After his very public liaison with eighteen-year-old Lucille Cameron in 1912 (just two weeks after his wife, Etta, committed suicide), federal agents arrested him on charges of trafficking women or prostitution. (Library of Congress, U.S. News and World Report Magazine Collection)

11. Some ten thousand people marched in silence through New York City on July 28, 1917, to protest a recent race massacre in East St. Louis, Illinois. The Silent Parade was the first march organized by the NAACP, and the largest black protest march since Reconstruction. (WGBH Educational Foundation)

12. After taking France by storm during World War I, celebrated band leader James Reese Europe (on the left) sought to "jazz away" racial prejudice with his army musicians during a tour of America in 1919. (National Archives and Records Administration)

This joyous, boisterous parade reflected the optimism of the postwar moment. Europe returned "more firmly convinced than ever that negroes should write negro music" and that this music could transform the place of black Americans in society. He didn't have to teach improvisation, he explained to one reporter. His rehearsals were all about reining it in.[50] Europe took his band on tour. After one concert in Chicago in May, the *Defender* reckoned he was "Jazzing Away Prejudice." Even "the most prejudiced enemy is compelled . . . to see us in a new light . . . Europe and his band are worth more to our race than a thousand speeches from so-called Race orators and uplifters."[51]

The problem was, however, that this "most wonderful day" without prejudice in New York was just "one day." It must have seemed most wonderful in hindsight precisely because the moment proved to be so rare and fleeting. For all the optimism, James Weldon Johnson remembered, "Clouds were gathering that, within twelve months, would blot the light from the skies for the Negro."[52] The dark storm of violence was horrifying. On account of the blood that flowed, Johnson called the summer of 1919 the "Red Summer." There were eighty-three lynchings, the highest number since the founding of the NAACP. Mob violence moved to the cities with the Great Migration. Between May and October 1919 at least twenty-five anti-black race riots broke out across the country. Hundreds were killed.

If there was such a thing as a typical riot, it started on a summer's evening, in response to a story of sexual assault, following rising tensions among working-class white men who saw black assertiveness as a challenge to their honor, their neighborhoods, and their livelihoods. Veterans were prominent on both sides. In Washington, D.C., in July, mobs went on a rampage after newspapers published the sensational sex crimes committed by a "negro fiend." In September, violence broke out in Omaha after black workers broke the strikes in the big meatpacking factories. For many, the riot in Chicago was particularly galling. Just two months after Europe jazzed away prejudice there, a week of violence left thirty-eight people dead. Chicago, the "land of hope," had become a land of horror. As for James Europe, at the end of May his drummer—in a fit of jealousy—stabbed him to death.

Red Summer was the deadly expression of wider repression to stop African Americans—especially black veterans—from stepping out of their place in southern society or from invading white residential space in big cities up North. In the South, white mobs stripped returning black veterans of their uniforms, and murdered at least ten of them. In everyday life, returning black veterans found the struggle for a decent home and job tougher than ever. Because of migration to cities and the return of white veterans, the competition for housing became especially bitter—a rational battle for a limited resource, compounded by a hysterical fear of race mixing. Between 1917 and 1921 some fifty-eight homemade bombs were thrown at the homes of black migrants who spilled into white areas of Chicago.[53] It was an ominous portent of the way that the battle for urban resources would be played out in racial terms for generations to come.

Yet in the midst of the terror, as Johnson declared proudly, African Americans resolved "not to run, but to fight." During the Chicago riot, Haywood Hall and army friends set up a machine gun by an upstairs window.[54] In Washington, D.C., some three hundred African Americans were wounded on the first night of violence. The following night, more whites than blacks were wounded.[55] These pitched battles were markedly different from the black anti-property riots that would sweep big-city America in the late 1960s.

The Jamaican-born Harlem poet Claude McKay famously wrote in celebration, "If we must die, let it not be like hogs . . . Like men we'll face the murderous, cowardly pack, Pressed to the wall, dying, but fighting back!"[56] According to the Kansas City Call, the fightback showed that the "The NEW NEGRO . . . does not fear the face of clay."[57] Talk of a New Negro caught on seemingly overnight. The Harlem intellectual Alain Locke, who popularized the term, believed the New Negro had "a spirit to seize, even in the face of an extortionate and heavy toll, a chance for the improvement of conditions."[58] By this definition, there were, in fact, many very old New Negroes. (The Cleveland Gazette first wrote of a New Negro back in 1895, after protest there led to a local civil rights law.) Even so, the sudden prominence of the term is telling.

What was new (and a contrast to the 1960s riots, too) was just how many black leaders celebrated this new assertiveness. Previously, advocates of armed self-defense such as Ida B. Wells and Henry McNeal Turner had struggled to get their voices heard above talk of "separate as the fingers" and "closing ranks." Now, even the Episcopalian minister Francis Grimké—a leading light in the capital's elite—told his congregation, "Oh, I thank God! . . . The pent-up humiliation, grief and horror of a lifetime . . . was being stripped from me."[59] What was new, too, was just how many local protest groups sprang up across the country. The number of NAACP branches more than tripled between 1918 and 1919 and swelled with workers as well as professional recruits. They called for better jobs as well as civil rights, and they joined up in remote parts of the rural South as well as in big northern cities. When the NAACP head office received a request for a charter from fifty-eight African Americans in

Silsbee, the staff had to get a map to find out where Silsbee was. It turned out to be a tiny town in Texas, with a black population of 158 people.[60]

In part, the postwar surge in protest came because the constraints of wartime were over. Regretting "close ranks" (he never did gain a captaincy), Du Bois let rip in the *Crisis* in May 1919. "We are cowards and jackasses if . . . we do not . . . fight a sterner, longer, more unbending battle against the forces of hell in our own land. *We return. We return from fighting. We return fighting.*"[61] In part, the postwar surge came because hundreds of thousands of black veterans did indeed return fighting. In 1919 perhaps a thousand black veterans in Phillips County, Arkansas, formed a union that demanded the right to sell crops directly to market. At stake were the profits from the most valuable cotton crop in southern history. At stake, too, was the freedom of black labor. On September 30 a white mob broke up a planning meeting in a local church. The farmers fought back, killing a white man. According to the *Memphis Press*, "The negroes are well drilled and armed."[62]

Above all, the surge in protest showed that African Americans believed the postwar months offered a genuine "chance for the improvement of conditions." They had good reason: postwar America witnessed an unprecedented pursuit of democracy. In 1919 unions led the most determined campaign for workers' rights in American history to date. Suffragists seemed set to win their campaign for the vote, and President Wilson traveled to France to negotiate a peace to promote democracy worldwide. In turn, African American workers, women, and national leaders all sought to assert their own vision of what democracy should mean.

Even the horror of Red Summer suggested progress might be at hand. The militant Chicago *Whip* reckoned that white rioters "fear that the Negro is breaking his shell and beginning to bask in the sunlight of real manhood."[63] In 1919 nothing was certain, yet many things seemed possible.

Strikes, Suffragists, and the Paris Peace Settlement

September 1, 1919, Bogalusa, Louisiana. Two thousand five hundred lumber workers marched through the town for a Labor Day parade. Set in a rural backwater, Bogalusa was home to the world's largest lumber mill. Great Southern, formed by New York investors, founded the town in 1908 and controlled it thereafter. Most of the town's wage earners— three thousand or so at the end of the war, a small majority of which were African American—worked for the company. Great Southern owned their workers' homes. They tried to own their hearts, too, by providing schools, parks, and even prizes for the best-kept gardens. But behind the smiling face of modern management was an old-fashioned controlling fist. What Great Southern gave it could take away if workers stepped out of line. Just to make sure they didn't, the company employed a large private militia. The plan was simple: keep morale up and dissent down. It had worked perfectly, until now.

In June, when the company raised rents to offset wartime pay increases, the American Federation of Labor began to sign up white workers. When Great Southern shipped in nonunion black men to replace white union men, the AFL reached out to black workers. Great Southern distributed pictures of an interracial meeting with the caption, "The South will get it if it don't watch out. Get what? Social equality, niggers and whites, men and women, all mixed up together like potatoes in one bin."[64] The company next turned to intimidation. On the day before Labor Day, a white mob lynched a black veteran (for the alleged rape of a white woman), attached the corpse to the back of a car, and drove through the black side of town. That same day, the Town Council warned white unionists that the inclusion of black men in the Labor Day parade would be intolerable. So when the workers marched, black and white together, they marched in rebellion—against the company and against racial custom.

Many postwar unions did not follow the Bogalusa biracial model. At the height of the Bogalusa campaign, white shipyard workers in Pensacola demanded the expulsion of black workers from skilled "white work."[65] James Weldon Johnson often heard white workers say, "Never let a nigger pick up a tool!"[66] Biracial unions seemed more likely to develop when the work environment was all male and when black workers were restricted to unskilled jobs, were well-established, and were so numerous as to be indispensable to the Union cause.[67] Even where biracial unions did develop, they were hardly places of interracial utopia. Bogalusa's union had white leadership and racially separate locals, and they opposed social integration. In Alabama, the Christmas lists of toys for striking miners' children were separated by race.[68] Even so, a mixed picture was an improvement upon a decidedly unmixed picture previously. After Samuel Gompers, the head of the AFL, excused the East St. Louis mob, Du Bois had complained that organized labor found "killing Negroes a safe, lucrative employment."[69]

Why this change mattered is that unions seemed poised to make advances in postwar America as never before. During the war, the increase in industrial production, support from Wilson's administration, and talk of industrial democracy strengthened labor's hand. After the war, the return of veterans, a rise in inflation, and employers' refusal to meet workers' demands fed into unprecedented worker protest. During 1919, one in five workers went on strike.

Labor's first steps toward biracialism mattered too, because the New Negro was very much a proletarian. Of course, black migrant workers had to be convinced that joining a union was in their own interest. One newcomer to the Chicago stockyards reckoned unions were "no good for a colored man. I've seen too much of what they don't do for him."[70] After the Chicago riots, most black workers there agreed. Even so, in some industries the prospect of the union making gains offered black families the hope of better wages and a safer world. In New Orleans, black and white dockworkers struck often and with success. In Alabama, twenty thousand black and white miners stopped work for six months in 1920. As workers talked with one another and as their families made sacrifices together, the color line lost some of its power. For some black families the union became the most progressive force in their lives.[71]

Ultimately, the biggest problem facing black workers was the weakness of the labor movement as a whole. The postwar moment of labor insurgency gave way to a decade of employer control. The Red Scare of 1919 (following the Bolshevik Revolution in Russia and an anarchist bomb plot at home) enabled employers to position themselves as defenders of democracy and smear restive workers as revolutionaries. The New Negro fightback allowed employers to play the race card. The withdrawal of government support once the war was won, and just as a recession was starting in 1920, weakened the hand of labor further.

Back in Bogalusa, Great Southern spread word that the union was financed by Russians set on giving one prominent black unionist "any woman he desires."[72] It evicted militant workers and sent gunmen after union leaders. Following a gun battle in November—when four white unionists died in defense of a black colleague—the game was up. One black union leader filed suit against the company, seeking compensation for mob violence. Almost a decade later, the Supreme Court ruled the militia a justifiable private police force.

By this time, biracial unionism was but a memory. Yet even then, it was a positive memory only for some. One black strikebreaker told white steelmakers in Pennsylvania, "You would not work with me before the strike. Now I have your job and I am going to keep it."[73] By this time, black workers—men and women—had reverted to old protest strategies of moving for better wages and conditions if possible, and sabotage and subterfuge if not. Even so, the brief moment of biracial unionism served notice of what might be possible. A generation later—during the New Deal and a greater war—that possibility would return.

While workers struck, suffragists celebrated. In June 1919 Congress proposed a Nineteenth Amendment to enfranchise women. The amendment was ratified the following year. For black women reformers, the timing seemed opportune. Before the war, especially in the South, they had begun to forge relationships with their white counterparts. They were mostly client-patron relationships, but they were relationships nonetheless—ones that allowed black women to divert some Progressive Era spending toward reform projects of their own. During the war, black and white women reformers institutionalized these relationships through patriotic work. In North Carolina, one white home demonstration agent invited black teachers to her office to teach them hatmaking. Historian Glenda Gilmore noted, "Twirling ribbons, making velvet flowers, and gluing feathers, these women ostensibly made hats, but they also trimmed the racial divide."[74] Trimming the racial divide led to tangible benefits—the state appointed six black agents.

Such cooperation across the color line emboldened black clubwomen to seek their share of the suffrage. Back in North Carolina, Charlotte Hawkins Brown, president of the state association of Colored Women's Clubs, addressed her white counterparts at their annual convention in May 1920. Before the war, the consummate networker had won funds for her rural vocational school through deferential appeals to white beneficence (in fact, the school's curriculum was mostly academic). Now, she demanded "the right of the negro woman to share equally the franchise."[75] Some clubwomen hoped that the suffrage would bolster their claims to represent the race, too. Even so, black spokesmen mostly supported women's suffrage. Du Bois—no doubt influenced by white suffragist backers of the NAACP—thought the issue straightforward: "Votes for women, means votes for Black women."[76]

The course of the suffrage campaign, however, gave warning that the issue would be anything but straightforward. Whereas biracial social work had gone under the radar somewhat, anti-suffragists made sure the prospect of black women voting became headline news. Predictably, Senator Vardaman stoked the fears. "The negro woman," he explained, trying to rekindle the frenzy of disfranchisement days, "will be more offensive, more difficult to handle at the polls than the negro man."[77] As it turned out, "votes for women" did not mean very many "votes for black women," at least not for a decade or two. Thousands of black women tried to register—the first major attempt by African Americans to register since disfranchisement. Hundreds of black women actually voted in Nashville, Tennessee, where white women voters welcomed black women's votes in support of a local reform ticket, which duly won. But Nashville was not just the exception in Tennessee, it was the exception in the South. Southern registrars began to disfranchise black women before the ink had dried on the Nineteenth Amendment.

The suffrage question exposed the limits of women's biracial alliances. When black women looked to white women reformers for support, their erstwhile allies looked away. Calling to mind post–Civil War friction between white feminists and black leaders, white suffragists even fanned fears of black women voters to raise the turnout of white women. Alice Paul, head of the National Women's Party—the most strident suffragist organization—did not invite a single black woman to address the party's first post-amendment convention. According to Addie Hunton, now an NAACP field secretary, who led a group of sixty black women to the convention, her group "harassed [the delegates] very thoroughly" until they agreed to consider a resolution calling on Congress to investigate disfranchisement. Hunton was proud of her efforts. But the convention rejected her resolution. It should not have come as a surprise: the party journal, *The Suffragist,* contained only two positive references but plenty of negative references to African American women during 1914–1919.[78]

The furor over women's suffrage did not destroy the embryonic tradition of interracial cooperation. Even at the height of Red Summer—or, rather, because of the violence—black and white social reformers worked together. In Atlanta in August 1919, a Commission of Interracial Cooperation formed with the express aim of easing urban tensions. Georgia's commission persuaded Governor Hugh Dorsey to publish a booklet documenting racial atrocities. But for the most part, the white voice of reform was but a whisper compared with the deafening defense of white supremacy. In any case, the aim of reform was to do just enough to make the black masses easier to manage (though wartime dissidents had given early warning of how difficult this would prove to be). Most white reformers defined interracial cooperation in the same narrow terms as they had before the war. The CIC did not speak out against segregation in society or discrimination at work, and the occasional training program or clean-up week did not begin to tackle black poverty. In 1922, the City Council in Norfolk, Virginia, voted to provide a park for African Americans. Five years later the black community was still waiting—though by this time there were twenty "white" parks.[79]

While workers and women sought democratic rights at home, Woodrow Wilson promoted democracy abroad. In January 1919 he headed to the Paris Peace Conference with a Fourteen Point Plan, which included the formation of a League of Nations. Many black American leaders determined to go to Paris, too—so many, in fact, that the *New York Age* worried they were "making themselves ridiculous."[80] Trotter's National

Equal Rights League sent delegates (including Ida B. Wells and A. Philip Randolph) to add a fifteenth point: "Elimination of civil, political, and judicial distinctions based on race or color in all nations for the new era of freedom."[81]

Few black Americans actually made it to France. Randolph was livid that the State Department gave passports only to "good niggers," which included Moton and Du Bois. The "bad nigger" Trotter stole across the Atlantic as a potato peeler on a cargo ship. By the time he got to Paris, ragged and penniless, the action was all but over. Trotter caused a stir in Paris, nevertheless. He bombarded delegates with calls for justice and ended one open letter to Wilson with "Yours for world democracy." He received a hero's welcome on his return to Harlem, too. But Trotter was very much shouting from the sidelines.

It would take half a century before black Americans would be able to decisively sway U.S. foreign policy (with a campaign against South African apartheid). Nevertheless, the Paris settlement marked the moment when the major civil rights organizations took an active interest in global politics. From this moment on they hoped the government's concern with democracy, or rather America's image, abroad would help their struggle for democracy at home. They hoped the League of Nations might pressure the American government to act in its own backyard. They hoped, too, that if they could gain equality in the United States, this might have a knock-on effect for oppressed people of color around the world. In fact, in years to come the knock-on effect would be the other way round, from postcolonial nations to the United States.[82]

Ironically, at just the moment black spokesmen tried to lobby the federal government overseas, the federal government used news from abroad to justify clamping down on black protest at home. During the Red Scare, the country's political intelligence system came of age. Attorney General A. Mitchell Palmer used black undercover agents to report on supposedly subversive race organizations. In 1919 Palmer warned the Senate that "the Negro is 'seeing red.'" History would show that Palmer was the one who was seeing things. The notorious Palmer Raids of November 1919, when ten thousand suspected Reds were arrested, turned up almost no Communists. His belief that black Americans were on a mission for Moscow was especially misguided. As one agent on the trail of black Bolshevism in Pittsburgh reported, the "chief slogan to be heard here is 'where can I get a job?'"[83] Still, perception was as damning as reality. By the end of 1919 the New Negro carried the stigma of two colors—black and red.

Thus, wartime talk of democracy proved to be illusory. While black

Americans used the rhetoric of democracy to push for full citizenship, the federal government used it as a way to ignore the color line, and employers and suffragists used it to defend the color line. Continued racist violence did its deadly work too. Back in Phillips County, Arkansas, a mob of over a thousand armed white men used machine guns to seek vengeance on defiant black farmers. An NAACP investigation reported at least two hundred deaths in what may well have been the single worst race massacre in twentieth-century American history.

With few allies and many powerful opponents, postwar New Negroes would have to carry the fight for justice on their own.

Marcus Garvey and the United Negro Improvement Association

Sunday, August 2, 1920, Harlem. At 2 p.m., under a clear blue sky, another procession rolled through the streets of New York. The parade celebrated the opening of the United Negro Improvement Association's First International Convention of Negroes. Like the return of the 369th Infantry, this was no silent parade. For three hours, bands played, choirs sang, and groups of children "whooped it for themselves." But this show was for black New Yorkers only—the march started and finished in Harlem.

Four black mounted policemen rode at the head of the parade. Behind them marched the UNIA's African Legion, each man smartly dressed in a dark blue uniform with a red trouser stripe. The officers carried dress swords. Next in line marched two hundred Black Cross Nurses, dressed in white. Behind them marched delegates representing twenty-five countries and all the American states. A motorcade of some five hundred cars brought up the rear. The star of the show was Marcus Garvey, the president-general of the UNIA, who sat in an open-topped car. Onlookers saw a fairly short, stocky man, dressed extravagantly in purple, black, and green military regalia with a white feather in his helmet. Enterprising shopkeepers sold Garvey cigars, complete with his picture on the band.[84]

The parade ended at the UNIA's Liberty Hall, where a capacity crowd of twelve thousand heard Garvey formally open the convention. That evening, some twenty-five thousand people attended a "monster public meeting" at Madison Square Garden, while thousands more stood outside.[85] According to a UNIA report, when Garvey arrived "men and women cheered, waved handkerchiefs, threw their hats into the air and did everything else they possibly could to give vocal expression to their feelings of delight."[86] The convention lasted for a month. For the first week, delegates reported on the poor conditions of black people in their home states and countries. The following week, delegates agreed a 54-

point Declaration of Rights, the "Magna Carta of the Negroes of the World." Speakers stressed the themes of economic progress, global black unity, and armed self-defense. The keynote demand was the redemption of Africa. The convention elected Garvey provisional president of Africa.[87]

In fact, Garvey had never been to Africa. Born in 1887, he grew up in Jamaica, one of only two of eleven children who survived to adulthood. As a young man he took a minor job in journalism, then traveled to London in 1912, where he fell in with a group of activists drawn from all parts of the black Atlantic. Two years later he returned home and founded the UNIA, hoping to unite "the four hundred million black people of the world." The UNIA hardly caught on. Inspired by *Up from Slavery,* Garvey traveled to the United States. He planned to stay briefly, meet Booker T. Washington, and raise money. But he arrived after Washington's death and, impressed by black prosperity in the northeast, decided to build the UNIA in America.

Garvey took America by storm. At the end of 1921, the *Nation* concluded that he had "founded so large a power in the English-speaking world as to add to the current vocabulary of that language a new word, 'Garveyism.'" Garvey's power base was Harlem, where he was one of over thirty thousand West Indian immigrants. But his support spread across the country and around the globe. By the mid-1920s, there were some eight hundred UNIA divisions in America.[88] Such numbers dwarfed support for the NAACP even at its postwar peak—and by this time the NAACP branches were in rapid decline. Over half of the UNIA divisions were in the South, with an influence beyond their numbers—many members were property owners and heads of kin. When Garvey visited Los Angeles in 1922, some ten thousand people turned out to greet him— almost half the black population of southern California.[89] In a back-handed compliment, the federal government's Bureau of Investigation (the forerunner of the FBI) judged him "the cause of the greater portion of the negro agitation in this country."[90] Across the globe, those who associated with Garvey formed perhaps a thousand chapters in forty-three countries and territories.[91]

What attracted so many people to him? In America, he tapped into long-standing currents in black protest. In the South he borrowed the mantle of Booker T. Washington (through his emphasis on individual hard work and black economic ventures) and Henry McNeal Turner (through his emphasis on black unity and African redemption). He tapped into the New Negro zeitgeist, too, telling the UNIA convention, "We meet . . . not as cringing sycophants, but as men and women standing erect and demanding our rights."[92] He also drew on a new race consciousness: at the end of the war, Americans thought of race in terms of white vs. black as never before. Immigrant groups like the Irish, who had previously occupied a somewhat fraught position between Negroes and Anglo-Saxons, were now considered "white," thanks to government restrictions on immigration after 1924, the publication of best-selling pseudo-scientific books proclaiming a single Nordic race, and the arrival of belligerent black migrants in northern cities. In the South, the black-white binary dated back to slavery, but even there, ideas of race hardened after the First World War ended. Virginia adopted a racial purity law in 1924 that defined a negro as anybody with any nonwhite ancestor after 1684. Some tried to push the date back to 1620, until they realized that the race of three former governors and two former presidents would change to negro.

For their part, black leaders embraced the black-white binary, but for different ends. In the late nineteenth century, Du Bois had taken the view that there were at least fifty races. Now, he thought there were five, and after the brutality of the Great War, and race riots at home, he condemned the white world as essentially barbaric. Ironically, the end of the war was also the moment that black intellectuals first turned to science to argue that the environment, not race, shaped character. But this argument would not gain wider traction for a decade or so.

This new race consciousness was also born of anti-imperialism. In Du Bois' case, he had long thought Jim Crow was "but a local phase of a world problem." The war confirmed his thesis. "Ownership of materials and men in the darker world," he wrote, is the "real prize that is setting the nations of Europe at each other's throats."[93] All the while, black mariners, returning veterans, and other travelers spread news of white atrocities and black resistance around the world, from Memphis to Marseilles to Mombasa. News of Australian troops attacking veterans of the British West Indies Regiment in Wales hardened the resolve of veterans in Trinidad as they joined strikes for better wages. Local authorities complained the strikers "were imbued with the idea of a black world controlled . . . [by] black people."[94]

It was an idea that resonated strongly in Harlem, home to numerous African American and Caribbean immigrant radical groups. And from Harlem, the idea reverberated across black America. Moreover, news from Haiti suggested that the United States was behaving as a colonial power at just the moment it opposed European imperialism. In 1915 U.S. troops had moved onto the island to restore peace. After a fact-finding mission in 1920, James Weldon Johnson accused U.S. officials of corruption and U.S. troops of murdering at least three thousand local people. "To England's India," declared the NAACP, "the United States has added a perfect miniature in Haiti."[95]

So Garvey's race conscious, anti-colonial, global vision perfectly captured the moment. He spoke, as had Turner, of a black God; he celebrated dark skin color; and he was quick to praise other anti-imperial groups, such as Gandhi's movement in India and even the Irish. (He named Liberty Hall after the Dublin original and persuaded black New York dockers to support their hated Irish counterparts' patriotic strike of 1920.) As he often put it, if two million Irish could repulse the British, there was no telling what 400 million black men and women could do. Garvey called on some skilled black workers to go "back to Africa."

How Garvey moved from surfing the zeitgeist to shaping its course is harder to explain. As a recent immigrant, he was not an obvious leader of black America. Initially, he relied on support from existing organizations, from the NAACP to radical Harlem groups. He was not particularly handsome, and surviving tapes of his speeches suggest that he spoke in a somber, though somewhat passionate, monotone. Yet within a couple of years, the UNIA began to squeeze out other race organizations. To some, Garvey became a "Negro Moses"—as Belle Beatty, a rural Georgian put it—"a God-sent man to lead his race back to their native homeland."[96]

Part of the answer was that Garvey was a master of flamboyant performances that dramatized black American hopes. He thought big, and acted bigger. His Black Star Line Steamship Corporation—a fleet of ocean liners, each named after a black hero—sought to link the Caribbean, Africa, and the United States. In an age when large ships were symbols of national power, this was black business laden with meaning—as striking for its time as a space rocket named after Malcolm X would have been in the 1970s. By 1920 there were between thirty thousand and forty thousand stockholders in the Black Star Line. Those unable to speculate were still enthused by the ambition. One Clevelander, recalling the "hungry days" of 1921, remembered that "when Garvey rode by in his plumed hat, I got an emotional lift, which swept me above the poverty and prejudice by which my life was limited."[97]

Yet Garvey crashed almost faster than he rose. He delighted in making enemies. Once established, he seemingly took on every black leader who was not a paid-up Garveyite, and even some who were. He denounced black clergy as hypocrites, and Du Bois as a hater of black people. As for the NAACP, one banner at his 1920 convention read "Nothing Accomplished After Considerable Pretence."[98] For good measure, during a brief return home in 1921, he described Jamaica as the most backward country in the Western Hemisphere. There was a sinister edge to his verbal jousting, too—he warned rivals in 1922, "If you desire to keep your limbs as they are, please find some other occupation."[99] That same year, he fired James Eason, the leader of the UNIA in America. Eason was murdered shortly afterward. No evidence linked the murder to Garvey. He gloated nevertheless.

Garvey's enemies sought to bring him down. The resulting bitterness made the Washington–Du Bois feud seem like a lover's tiff in comparison. The *Defender* charged him with corruption in 1919. The *Age* described the UNIA convention as a "huge joke" because the international delegates were all Jamaican immigrants.[100] In June 1922 the black press gleefully reported Garvey's acrimonious divorce from his first wife. Later that month, Garvey met with the deputy leader of the Klan (both agreed on the need to preserve racial purity). The *Messenger* launched a "Garvey Must Go" campaign. Even so, Garvey may have trounced his critics had his economic schemes succeeded. But they crashed—as did most of his ships. The postwar recession probably doomed the company anyway, but Garvey had bought ailing ships, at high prices, and managed them poorly. The Black Star Line was suspended in April 1922—a fiasco symptomatic of Garvey's inability to manage the UNIA.

In the end, the Justice Department—which considered him a Bolshevist—intervened by arresting Garvey for the capitalist crime of mail fraud. He was convicted in 1923. For some supporters, Garvey's suffering reinforced his Messianic role. But many deserted him. Garvey recognized that his moment had passed: "1919 up to 1922 presented the one glorious time and opportunity for the Negro," he wrote in 1924. Now, "the world has practically returned to the normal attitude."[101] That same year the Liberian government reneged on a deal to allow him to buy land there. In 1927 Coolidge commuted Garvey's sentence and then deported him. He tried to drum up support in Europe, Canada, and Jamaica, but these were years of decline. Garvey died in 1940, following two bouts of pneumonia. He never did see Africa.

In the end, Garvey was the proverbial comet who lit up the sky before crashing to earth. But the crash was not the end of race consciousness or black America's global vision. After Garvey, the *Crisis* and *Defender* printed many more stories celebrating blackness—even running regular black baby competitions and beauty pageants. The middle of the decade would see a celebration of black artists in Harlem. The NAACP and other organizations continued to promote news from Africa and the Caribbean. Du Bois sponsored three pan-African congresses during the 1920s. In the late 1960s the call for "a black world controlled by black people" would return, strongly, in the Black Power era.

Garvey's crash was not even the end of Garveyism. By 1926 there were still 423 southern divisions of UNIA. His influence lasted even longer. Rural Garveyites joined the agrarian unrest of the Great Depression, and Garvey supporters from Africa, the Caribbean, and Europe attended the pan-African congresses. In 1936 a black woman informed Charleston's police chief that black men "call their meeting place the UNIA . . . they have their firearms hid in their meeting places." In 1965, at Garvey's shrine in Jamaica, Martin Luther King Jr. (who knew a thing or two about dramatizing black sentiment himself) reflected that Garvey "was the first man on a mass scale and level to give millions of Negroes a sense of dignity and destiny, and make the Negro feel he is somebody."[102]

Bessie Smith, the Blues, and Black Culture

In May 1923 Columbia Records released the debut disc by blues singer Bessie Smith. This was not the first blues song. Mythology has it that twenty years earlier, blues man W. C. Handy spotted a poor black man slumped on a delta station platform, pressing a knife on the strings of a guitar and singing the classic AAB blues rhyme. Nor was it the first hit blues record—that distinction belonged to Mamie Smith in 1920. Even in her heyday, Bessie Smith was only one among many popular blues women. But what a heyday it was. She soon became the undisputed Empress of the Blues, releasing twenty tracks a year. Her fame coincided with a boom in consumption, which included purchasing "race records" by the major labels and readily available wind-up gramophones. Black sharecroppers' homes were more likely to have a gramophone than electricity. In other words, far more people were listening to Bessie Smith than were reading *The Crisis* or going to UNIA meetings.

On the face of it, Smith could hardly have been more different from Garvey, Du Bois, and their ilk. Her music did not address the debt America owed black veterans, the possibilities of pan-Africanism, or the hypocrisy of American democracy. In fact, early blues music barely addressed any social issues at all. Blues men did not want deliverance from racial segregation so much as deliverance from sexual frustration. Blind Lemon Jefferson's popular (and none too subtle) "That Black Snake Moan" wailed, "Uum, better find my mama soon / I woke up this morning, black snake makin' such a ruckus in my room." Blues women sought sexual fulfillment too, and deliverance from unfaithful partners. In "Downhearted Blues," Smith warned, "I got the world in a jug, the stopper's in my hand / I'm gonna hold it until you meet some of my demands."

Yet for all their differences, Smith and the race-conscious political leaders had much in common. She sang a pride in blackness. Indeed, blues women did at least as much as race leaders to forge a national black culture—not just in churches and schools but in dance halls and bars after dark on the "wrong side of town." Touring blues women followed the Great Migration and brought the sound of the rural South to the black side of segregated cities across the nation. Depending on where he or she lived, the New Negro might or might not join a union or support the UNIA, but the New Negro almost certainly danced and drank the blues. Having a separate black experience was about seeking pleasure as well as building protest organizations.

Even so, by dressing up and stepping out on a Saturday night, black men and women asserted their rights to a lifestyle of their own choosing. Finding sanctuary in urban nightlife went hand in hand with the struggle for a better life in the daytime. Black domestics in northern households sought—and mostly found—jobs that enabled them to live out rather than live in. Living out was no easy life—the travel was time-consuming, as was the responsibility of looking after two households. But it was a freer life, and in some cases it meant freedom from sexual abuse. Aggressive blues women embodied this assertion of freedom within the constraints of race and sex discrimination. To be sure, record companies exploited the performers on their race records lines and paid artists only a small fixed fee. But rather like minstrel figures before them, and hip hop singers in years to come, blues women exploited racial stereotypes for their own ends, too.

Bessie Smith's life was a case in point. Born to poverty in Tennessee, probably in 1894, she was only eight when her mother died. A year later, she started touring with a vaudeville show. She never stopped touring. By 1919 Smith was the star of her own "hip-shaking" show in Atlanta. An extraordinarily gifted singer, her powerful voice combined clarity of diction with spine-tingling emotion. Her appeal was erotic, too. Smith was tall, large, and—in the eyes of many—highly desirable. She also had a violent, jealous husband. Gossip suggested there was much to be jealous about. Alcoholic, moody, and ruthless, Smith made enemies as quickly as friends. Most of her songs were "stolen" from rival blues women. Yet she made herself into a star.

For white authorities, the image of debauched blues women reinforced their concern with black urban life. Some blamed idle, immoral, migrant women for poverty and the spread of sexual disease. And indeed, during the postwar recession, some migrant women faced a cruel choice between poverty and prostitution. The postwar era marked the beginning of the collocation of inner-city life with blackness, depravity, and danger. It was an image that would harden with the later flight of white residents to the suburbs. To be sure, there was fascination mixed with fear. White customers made their way to black juke joints, whose forbidden pleasures were all the more seductive during Prohibition. Smith even held performances for white customers only. But whereas James Europe was supposedly "jazzing away prejudices," the heavy-drinking, loose-living Bessie Smith seemed to be confirming them. Just as black workers were stuck with the dirtiest jobs, black artists sang the dirtiest music, and so the vicious circle of racial prejudice was perpetuated.

Black reformers shared the moral panic, fearful for the reputation of the race. Some clubwomen tried to help newcomers adjust to city life. In Chicago, Ida B. Wells founded a Negro Fellowship League whose members met migrant women at the train station, took them to safe lodging, and tried to find them jobs. Concern for migrants' welfare was matched by condemnation of migrants' morals. The Cleveland *Gazette* urged long-standing black residents to explain to newcomers "how to conduct themselves in public places so as to help and not hurt our people of this community."[103] But migrant women did not seek lessons in proper conduct. Some already cherished the respectable model of church attendance, faithful marriage, and godly living. Others turned to exuberant storefront religion, or scratched out a living as best they could in the underworld of gambling and sex work.

In this period, black clubwomen found themselves increasingly marginalized. Because the New Negro was male, the new woman voter was white, and the new migrant woman was assertive, there was little space left for them to lift as they climbed—or even just to climb. New organizations such as the NAACP and the NUL took over many of their campaigns, contributing to the National Association of Colored Women's virtual collapse. In Chicago, Ida Wells believed the Urban League had been formed to knock out her Fellowship League, and the NAACP did not even invite the great anti-lynching champion to its National Conference on Lynching in 1919. Women reformers were relegated to the second tier of NAACP leadership as fund-raising "crusaders." More radical organizations made little provision for female leadership either. Garvey paid lip-service to the dark-skinned "Black Queen of beauty," but the queen he had in mind was a lover, not a leader.

There were still some prominent women leaders. None more so than Madame C. J. Walker, the extravagant, outspoken, self-made beautician and America's first female millionaire of any color. Walker was the largest donor to the NAACP, a member of the Silent Parade delegation to the president, the host for Trotter's meeting ahead of his trip to Paris, and a key supporter of Garvey in the early days. Black women continued to work within the new black organizations, too—even within Garveyism. Garvey's second wife, Amy Jacques—Jamaica-born into a family where women lived as equals—effectively ran the organization during his stretches in prison.[104] As associate editor of the *Negro World,* she introduced a new section called "Our Women and What They Think." Far from writing the standard column on fashion and fancy, she penned profiles of inspiring women around the world. For Amy Jacques Garvey, feminism and pan-Africanism went hand in hand.

Even so, the tumult of war and its aftermath had clearly shaken up relationships among black Americans as well as between black Americans and the wider American society. As the rise of Bessie Smith and Marcus Garvey showed, there were many competing voices in black America, and many ways of seeking a better life.

On May 30, 1922, Washington society gathered for the dedication of the new Lincoln Memorial. The white marble shrine, wrote one reporter, was "compelling in its purity of line and . . . glistening as a flawless gem" as it "perpetuates . . . the spirit of Abraham Lincoln."[105] Dignitaries from home and abroad took their seats in front of the platform; African American guests found that they were assigned seats in a separate section at the rear (many left in disgust before the speeches began). Wilson's successor, the Republican Warren Harding, gave the main address. He barely mentioned emancipation. Robert Moton gave the "negro's tribute," and spoke of slavery and the urgency of bringing an end to mob lynching. But true to his conservative form, he called on black Americans, more than any other group, to repay the debt they owed American democracy.[106]

Five years after the Silent Parade, black Americans seemed as subjugated and constrained as ever. It was almost as if the wartime turmoil hadn't happened. NAACP membership, especially in the South, fell back to prewar levels. Even the contribution of black soldiers in France was airbrushed from national memory. Black Americans remembered with pride the French government's award of the prestigious Croix de Guerre to three black regiments. But white Americans heard another story—of the black 368th retreating under fire. After interviewing the disgraced troops, Du Bois explained to *Crisis* readers that the soldiers had been sent over the top without maps, wire cutters, or grenade launchers. He exposed a campaign to defame black soldiers, publishing a letter from one southern colonel to a senator which claimed that "colored officers . . . have been engaged very largely in the pursuit of French women." A Harlem black veterans group wanted the "scoundrel and liar court-martialed." Newton Baker dismissed the call, but he did advise clemency for four black officers who had retreated. The fact that Baker responded shows that grassroots pressure still had some impact. But the fact that he left the colonel in his post shows just how limited that impact now was.[107]

In economic terms, black Americans generally were little better off than they had been before the war. In the South they were worse off. Before the war, black and white workers got the same wages for the same job (although black workers mostly had inferior jobs). After the war, black workers began to get lower wages for the same job for the first time—a further strengthening of a segregated society.[108] In the North, black migrant men got a permanent place in the industrial workforce— this would prove to be one of the most important legacies of the war era—but James Weldon Johnson complained that ethnic workers saw black workers as rivals at best, and scabs at worst. Thus black industrial workers were trapped, to quote one Milwaukee steelworker, in the "jobs that even Poles didn't want."[109] For example, the number of black iron and steelworkers jumped from 18,220 in 1910 to 52,956 in 1930, from 4.5 to 8.5 percent of the total. Yet the percentage stuck as unskilled laborers only dropped from 73.6 to 73.5 percent. The lowest paid jobs were the most vulnerable to technological innovation. They were also the most dangerous. "Our lives are short," complained one black steelworker. "You get hot on the job, your heart beats way too fast, you suffer from cramps."[110] Meanwhile, some black women even lost their jobs as domestics to white women, as white veterans returned and white women workers had to leave the factories.

In 1924 the *Crisis* reminded "the new immigrants to the north as well as Negroes living there that the greatest significance of this migration is the increased political power of black men in America."[111] First elected in 1915, Chicago Mayor William Hale "Big Bill" Thompson served three terms by keeping black support. His enemies likened City Hall to Uncle Tom's Cabin because so many black people seemed to get a job there. Some black officials were elected too—a congressman in Illinois, a few aldermen in Chicago, some councilors in West Virginia coal towns, the first black assemblymen in California and New York.[112] Black voting in northern cities was a promising portent of things to come. But in the early 1920s, the overall picture showed limited progress. Black voters were still very much a minority in the North and remained disfranchised in the South. Even Thompson's leadership is better known for the free rein he gave to Al Capone than for progressive racial policies—and the riot happened on his watch. At a national level, the Republican sweep of elections at the end of 1920 made little difference to the everyday lived experience of black Americans. With the help of Republican allies, in 1922 the NAACP pushed an anti-lynching bill through the House. But the bill failed to pass the Senate. James Weldon Johnson despaired. "The Southern Democrats roared like a lion and the Republicans lay down like a scared 'possum."[113]

As for the new president, Harding knew "absolutely nothing about the race question," according to Johnson. He had never even heard of Booker T. Washington. Nevertheless, Johnson was pleased to see the back of Wilson, to whom "[I] came nearer to constituting keen hatred for an individual than anything I have ever felt."[114] Harding at least denounced lynching. But he told Johnson that "colored people in the South should willingly accept white leadership until such a time as prejudice was worn down."[115] Given the bloodlust of the era, that time was hardly imminent, and Harding did not seem overly concerned to speed the day. During one visit to Houston, the president reached over the heads of black children to greet white children. Christa Adair, a black teacher, had arrived early to secure the front row for her class. She later became a Democrat.[116]

Yet if wartime protest ultimately had its limits, it left important legacies. The nature of African American protest changed in many ways—the era hastened the rise of a starker race consciousness, stronger national links, an enhanced global vision, a more proletarian, urban, and secular orientation, and new claims on American democratic values. The force of wartime protest warned that white supremacy—in all its various, powerful guises—still needed to be updated and enforced at every turn. And the memory of wartime protest lingered—an unsettling thought for defenders of discrimination, but a precious resource for African Americans during the dark days of depression and repression ahead.

CHAPTER SIX

Renaissance in Harlem, Dark Ages Elsewhere, 1924–1941

In 1928 black investors provided money for the first black beach club near Los Angeles. The club was launched to much fanfare, including the largest black beauty competition in state history. Soon after, arsonists burned the club down. The local black press, very briefly, pointed the finger at the Klan. It later transpired that few people had joined the club, and many of the investors had faced bankruptcy. But because of the fire, they got all their money back from insurance.

Late on July 17, 1931, in a church in rural Alabama, a few dozen black sharecroppers met together to protest the death sentence handed down to a group of black boys. On August 3, on the South Side of Chicago, a few hundred unemployed men and women tried to prevent the eviction of a 72-year-old grandmother. In both places, the police broke up the protests and armed black men fought back. In Alabama, the sheriff's men killed Ralph Gray—a local leader of the movement and a member of the Communist Party. In Chicago, police killed John O'Neil, Abe Gray, and Thomas Paige—all three born in the South, all three Communists. In Alabama, armed white men forced many black sharecroppers to flee. In Chicago, some twenty thousand people turned out for the funeral, and white officials met with black leaders and agreed to funnel more emergency relief to the black community.[1]

"We got it hammered into us to watch our step, to stay in our place, or to get off the street when a white woman passed." Mississippi civil rights leader Charles Evers, reflecting on his inter-war childhood[2]

On October 3, 1935, Italy invaded Ethiopia, causing fights between black and Italian youths to break out across America. Ten percent of New York's police force headed to Harlem. In the weeks that followed, Harlem residents raised money for two tons of medical supplies to send to Ethiopia.

"Is this living here holding our empty hands . . . And every so often crawling to plead for a handout of crumbs." "Rise and Live," by Richard Wright, published in 1934[3]

On March 21, 1924, some one hundred black writers and white publishers met for dinner in Manhattan's Civic Club. A five-course meal of bonhomie and literary chat, it was a far cry from recent race riots. The master of ceremonies, Alain Locke, could hardly have been further from the stereotype of a dirty black migrant. Born in 1886 in Philadelphia, the only child of well-educated parents, Locke was suave, elitist, gay, and somewhat eccentric in the manner befitting a professor of philosophy. (After his mother died, he invited colleagues to tea in his rooms while her corpse sat comfortably in an armchair.) Locke was also one of the most learned black men in America. After taking an undergraduate degree at Harvard, he was the first—and for nearly sixty years the only—black Rhodes Scholar to Oxford, England. He then studied philosophy in Berlin and earned a doctorate at Harvard before taking a chair at Washington's all-black Howard University. Locke styled himself as the "philosophical midwife" for a new generation of writers. He pored over his children's texts and fussed over their needs.[4]

The dinner was arranged by Charles Spurgeon Johnson. Born in 1893 in Virginia, the son of a forthright Baptist minister, Johnson trained as a sociologist in Chicago. After the riot there, he helped write a postmortem report, attributing the violence to misunderstanding between the races. Johnson moved to New York in 1921 to direct research for the National Urban League and to edit the league's journal, *Opportunity*. He was convinced that interracial dialogue would lead to better understanding, and that changing the black image in the white mind would lead to a better world. White philanthropic support for *Opportunity* augured well.

Officially Johnson called the dinner to celebrate the publication of Jesse Fauset's first novel, *There Is Confusion*. Young and ambitious, Fauset was literary editor of the NAACP's *Crisis* magazine. Her novel was a rather melodramatic tale of a well-to-do black woman whose ambition for her man spurs him to succeed. Ahead of the dinner, Locke hailed *There Is Confusion* as the novel the "Negro intelligentsia has been clamoring for."[5] But Locke used the dinner to promote other writers. No one mentioned Fauset until near the end. She never forgave him for the slight.

Still, for Johnson and Locke, the dinner was a resounding success. The editor of *Survey Graphic*—an illustrated magazine concerned with social problems—offered to devote a special issue to black writers. Locke gathered the essays and introduced the March 1925 issue. *Survey Graphic*'s circulation doubled. The following month, at Johnson's instigation, *Opportunity* hosted a literary awards dinner which more than three hundred people attended. It was a "magnificent assemblage," said Johnson, again a mixture—as some put it—of "Negrotarians and Niggerati." The brilliant young poet Langston Hughes won first prize for *The Weary Blues*. The publisher Alfred Knopf snapped him up. Years later Johnson reflected on the awards dinner: "It was intended as the beginning of something and so it was."[6] The Harlem—or as some called it, the New Negro—Renaissance was born.

In fact, the Renaissance was rather less geographically restricted and less original than its names might suggest. Writers came and went, and there were outposts in Washington, Philadelphia, Atlanta, and even Europe. Cooper, Washington, Du Bois, and many others had previously written to critical acclaim. What was new, though, was that the Harlem sponsors of the Renaissance saw black literature as an integral part of the struggle for black equality. As James Weldon Johnson explained in the preface to his 1922 *Anthology of Negro Poetry,* "No people that has produced great literature . . . has ever been looked upon by the world as distinctly inferior." What he called the "art approach to the Negro problem" combined various protest ideologies with an added literary twist.[7] Black Americans would gain rights once they had proved their worth. The talented would take the lead. But now, they would fight with the pen.

With hindsight, such optimism appears naive, even bizarre. But for Harlem's literary lords, it seemed perfectly reasonable. Irish nationalism had been marked by a literary renaissance. C. S. Johnson believed literature was "the soft spot . . . in the armor of the nation."[8] After the anything-but-Great War, and taking heed of Freud's warning that a suppressed id led to neurosis, modernist writers worried that white culture tottered on the edge of a nervous breakdown. F. Scott Fitzgerald's *The Great Gatsby* (1925) exposed the vacuous underbelly of the Jazz Age, as did the writings of H. L. Mencken and Sinclair Lewis. Black artists, by contrast, believed that their culture was on the way up. Following Du Bois' lead, Renaissance writers extolled their African heritage and their contribution to virtually all the original aspects of American culture, from spirituals to cakewalks. Thus, full acceptance of black artists could redeem wider American culture and society, too. It was up to white America to respond. "How would you have us?" asked Weldon Johnson. "Rising or falling? Men or things? / . . . Strong, willing sinews in your wings, / Or tightening chains about your feet?"[9]

Encouragingly for black leaders, evidence suggested that cultured white Americans were leaning toward the "sinews in your wings" option—quite a contrast to the behavior of white workers, women, and government officials after the war. Hughes believed the "Negro was in vogue."[10] In 1921, *Shuffle Along*—the first musical written and performed by black artists—opened at an unfashionable uptown theater. No matter: it became a smash. A year later, Claude McKay's *Harlem Shadows* was the first book of black poetry published by a white publishing house for a generation. In 1923 Harlem's famous Cotton Club opened to rapturous acclaim. In 1924 the Georgia-born tenor Roland Hayes sang to sellout crowds in 54 cities.

If 1924 seemed to be the right time to launch a literary movement, Harlem was the right place. An urban neighborhood where most people came from elsewhere, Harlem was something new, a place of possibility—not "typical," wrote Locke, but "prophetic," black America's Dublin.[11] Just 4,000 African Americans and Caribbean immigrants at the turn of the century had become almost 200,000 by 1930. When King Solomon Gillis, the protagonist of Rudolph Fisher's *City of Refuge* (1925), fled the South, he was exhilarated to find "Negroes . . . overwhelmingly everywhere . . . In Harlem, black was white."[12] Black mingled with white, too. Fitzgerald became friendly with McKay after meeting him at a party (though he had first mistaken McKay for a servant). Hordes of white New Yorkers journeyed to Harlem on weekend nights in search of a fantasy land that was exotic, erotic, and easy to reach by subway. Fisher concluded, "Negro stock is going up, and everybody's buying."

Promoters of the Renaissance hurried to capitalize on this cultural capital. But they disagreed about the best way to do so. A special *Crisis* forum in 1926 on "The Negro in Art" elicited a wide range of answers. Du Bois called for art as propaganda; Locke, ever the cultural elitist, called for art for its own sake—poets should focus on the meter rather than the message. That same year, younger Harlem writers launched their own journal, *Fire!* With its earthy realism, secularism, and exploration of homosexuality, *Fire!* threw down the gauntlet to the old guard. "If white people [or] colored people are pleased we are glad," Hughes explained. "If they are not, their displeasure doesn't matter."[13] (It was a good thing it didn't. The *Baltimore Afro-American* reviewer threw the first edition of *Fire!* into the fire.)[14] But even the younger writers had vastly different approaches. Hughes' poem "The Negro Speaks of Rivers" asserted a timeless dignity to a noble people. The light-skinned Jean Toomer's experimental novel *Cane* explored the mulatto's ambiguous identity. (Toomer chose to be white and left Harlem soon afterward.)

Thus, the Renaissance was far from being a carefully coordinated assault on white supremacy. Even the propagandist work that tackled the "Negro problem" head on diverged drastically. *Fire in the Flint* (1924), by the young NAACP official Walter White, was basically *Birth of a Nation* upside down. White's hero, medical doctor Kenneth Harper, is almost a parody of respectability who finds himself in a southern white world of unrestrained vice. White thugs rape his sister. Still, Ken helps a sick white woman, only to be murdered by the Klan for consorting with her. (Ken fights to the death, manfully.) Journalist George Schuyler, on the other hand, preferred propaganda by pantomime. In *Black No More* (1931), Dr. Junius Crookman discovers a way to remove black pigmentation. The main black-to-white character, Max Disher, teams up with the head of a Nordic League to make millions from ignorant whites worried about Negroes in their midst. Pompous black leaders lament the end of oppression, while white Senator Rufus Kretin complains, "You can't preach that white supremacy stuff . . . when they ain't no niggahs." In a final twist, Crookman's procedure turns people a little too white—prompting a stampede for skin darkeners.

Yet for all its energy and expectation, the Renaissance was soon over. Hughes dated the end to 1931, as the Great Depression settled in on America. "We were no longer in vogue . . . Sophisticated New Yorkers turned to Noel Coward."[15] By that time Hughes had left for Cuba, *Opportunity* and *Crisis* had stopped giving prizes, C. S. Johnson had left the NUL, and James Weldon Johnson had retired from the NAACP.

Judged by the early hubris of its champions, the Renaissance achieved little. Poignantly writing in the *Survey Graphic* one decade after the New Negro issue, Locke found "it hard to believe that the rosy enthusiasm and hopes of 1925 were more than . . . a cruelly deceptive mirage."[16] Fauset complained that "publishers best preferred Negro literature that bordered on the pornographic."[17] By far the biggest selling book about Harlem itself, *Nigger Heaven* (1926), by white author Carl Van Vechten, follows the demise of a black writer as he becomes entangled in the sordid black underworld. Du Bois advised his readers to "drop it gently into the grate."[18] Someone took the advice further and burned Van Vechten in effigy. Renaissance writers did not even establish a new tradition in black literature—later writers would mock their romantic racialism. The great cultural legacies of these years were blues and jazz, which promoters of the Renaissance often criticized and which found their freest expression far away from Harlem.

Yet to write off the Renaissance as a flash-in-the-pan is both too harsh and too simplistic. If the new black stereotype was primitive and exotic, it was an improvement on the fool or rapist of tradition. Renaissance writers did not all capitulate to the white aesthetic or prejudice. They influenced, just as they were influenced by, America's emerging literary modernism. Even *Nigger Heaven* was not the calculated insult it seemed. The title referred to the segregated balcony in theaters where blacks looked down on their supposed superiors. Van Vechten's previous novels with white characters had been just as lewd (he was only respectful of cats). To be sure, his initial fascination with Harlem grew out of a craving for novelty rather than a condemnation of racism (he was the first New Yorker to wear a wristwatch). But it was no passing fancy. [19] He was intimately involved with Harlem's elite and its gay underworld, and he wrote about both. James Weldon Johnson rather liked the book.

Above all, a small, literary movement in Harlem was hardly going to overturn race stereotypes that were deeply entrenched throughout the Western world. For all the excitement of the first gala dinners, most Renaissance artists never claimed it would. Black artists in Paris also struggled to transform the black image—though France held far more promise than America did. The French public had thrilled to black jazz during the war, officials had quickly banned *Birth of a Nation,* and black artists were very much in vogue—no one more so than Josephine Baker. Born in 1906, she grew up in East St. Louis (she was there during the riot), left school for the stage at thirteen, and headed to New York (where she starred in *Shuffle Along*) before settling in Paris in 1925. She was an overnight sensation, top of the bill at the famous Revue Nègre. But even Baker's image was decidedly ambiguous. Topless, wearing a skirt made of large bananas, and moving frenziedly to her *danse sauvage,* her performance fairly screamed primitive sexuality. It dovetailed with Parisian artists' portrayals of the primitive female body—such as Matisse's *The Blue Nude*—and the image of Africa in the minds of French men and women.

The problem for the Renaissance, then, lay as much in the timing as the tactic. Long after Harlem's vogue had passed, protest leaders would continue to champion black artists and challenge cultural stereotypes. In due course, a vastly improved black image in popular culture would go hand in hand with gains in civil rights. But in the 1920s, Nordic superiority held sway; 1924 was the year when the Ku Klux Klan, mixing white supremacy with anti-Catholicism and anti-Semitism, was also in vogue. In Indiana, one white man out of three was a member of the KKK. The main intellectual challenge to white supremacy would come from the hard sciences and anthropology. Even the champions of the Renaissance realized that a black literary canon could only be one weapon in a wider arsenal. At the height of Harlem's vogue, Charles Johnson and the NUL still fought for better jobs, Weldon Johnson and the NAACP still campaigned for political rights, and Alain Locke still believed that pan-Africanism offered the best hope of all.

In this context of overbearing cultural racism, it is striking that black artists did, just occasionally, challenge race stereotypes. In 1924, the influential *World* columnist Heywood Broun, after watching the petite, exuberant Florence Mills in *Dixie to Broadway,* admitted that he found "certain reservations in the theory of white supremacy."[20] In London, the Prince of Wales watched Mills sixteen times. As only British royalty could, he pronounced her "ripping."[21] Even so, the rhetoric of the Renaissance stood in stark contrast to the reality of everyday black life in 1920s America. Langston Hughes concluded, "The ordinary Negroes hadn't heard of the Negro Renaissance. And if they had, it hadn't raised their wages any."[22] Hughes wasn't quite fair to entirely divorce the ordinary Negro from the artist. McKay's poems were read out in mass meetings, and over 100,000 people turned out to mourn Mills' premature death in 1927.[23] But his point about wages was spot on.

In 1926 the National Industrial Conference Board estimated that a Manhattan family of four needed a minimum income of $33 a week.[24] But a 1927 Urban League survey found that over half the black men in Harlem earned less than $23 a week. It was not that they were paid less for the same work, it was just that two thirds of employed black men in New York did unskilled work. Thus, the majority of married black women worked (unlike married white women). But some 80 percent labored in domestic service, for long hours and a pittance. Low earnings led to low quality of life—and shorter lives, too. Black children born in Harlem were twice as likely to die in infancy as white children born elsewhere in the city. Housing was so poor that the city housing commission chairman reckoned "the State would not allow cows to live in some of these apartments."[25] Harlem's problems of cocaine addiction, prostitution, and homicide belied its reputation for carefree abandon. Black writers took note. Fisher's optimistic migrant King Solomon Gillis was soon fighting a West Indian, was fooled into selling drugs, and wound up in the hands of brutal policemen.

If the Renaissance didn't improve wages, it didn't improve race relations either. White travelers to Harlem mostly came to gawp, like tourists on safari. Many clubs, even the Cotton Club, were white-owned for a white clientele. Little wonder, wrote Hughes, that black Harlemites were bitter behind their smiles. As if to mock the hopes of Renaissance propagandists, the real-life drama that captivated the New York public in 1925 was the marriage of "Kip" Rhinelander, scion of a wealthy Manhattan dynasty, to Alice Jones, the daughter of a cab driver—who turned out to be black. Sensational press stories of Kip's imbecility and Alice's deception soon followed. So too did divorce. One exasperated black reporter reckoned Alice deserved a "medal for her bravery" in marrying "this millionaire boob."[26] Still, the moral of the scandal for white readers was clear.

What was true for Harlem was true across the country. America's supposed boom decade was bleak and bitter for most black Americans—the postwar backlash gradually became a way of life. Heartrending tales from communities north and south—more gripping than any penned by Renaissance writers—warned of the destructive power of racism run wild, and the weakness of black Americans to tame it.

On September 9, 1925, in Detroit, a young black doctor and his wife—Ossian and Gladys Sweet—moved into their new home, in a white neighborhood. Ossian was making good money, and Detroit seemed a good place to make it. The mayor had won election on an anti-Klan platform. Still, the Sweets expected trouble. Ossian asked friends to join him, with guns. On the second night, they used them. A mob circled the Sweets' home, determined to restore the purity of the neighborhood and the value of their houses. When rocks shattered a window, one of Sweet's men shot back and killed a white man. The police charged Sweet and his friends with murder.

The NAACP backed the defense, turning the case—to quote James Weldon Johnson—into "a fight in behalf of justice for the Negro as had not been fought since the Civil War."[27] Early in 1926, the Sweets won. Their victory pointed to future NAACP legal challenges to racial discrimination. With matching support from the left-wing Garland fund, the NAACP used the Sweet case to raise $65,000 to finance a permanent legal defense fund. But for now, the episode exposed what the NAACP called "segregation by terrorism." As for the Sweets, Gladys picked up TB during her months in prison, passed it to her child, and they both died. Years later, Ossian shot himself.

Barely a year after the Sweet case ended, the Mississippi River burst its banks, and terrifying torrents of water swept over the levees. As man desperately battled nature, some black writers hoped white southerners would at last recognize their common humanity with their former slaves. After all, planters near Greenville, Mississippi—the worst affected area—prided themselves on their benevolent paternalism. They had even repelled the Klan. But when nature won, man battled man along the color line. Rescue boats evacuated white women and children, then white men, then livestock, before returning for black families. Thousands died. Fearing mass migration, the leading Greenville planter, William Percy, ordered that African American refugees—almost 100,000 people—be held at gunpoint and obey his work orders to earn relief. Some fought back, while others ran away. Black northerners raised money, and the NAACP investigated the mistreatment of black victims and lobbied for government aid. Secretary of Commerce Herbert Hoover, in charge of relief efforts, appointed black advisers and promised fair resettlement. But as the waters receded, so too did his promises. In a well-worn excuse, Hoover insisted he was not to blame "for the economic system which exists in the South." Nor, seemingly, for the justice system, which saw National Guardsmen shoot down resisters.[28]

Mobs in Detroit and concentration camps in Greenville were a world away from gala dinners in Harlem. Literary prowess proved no substitute for economic or political power. Faced by discrimination in the North and Jim Crow in the South, most black Americans had to rely on long-standing, everyday tactics to fight for equality, or even just to survive.

Surviving Jim Crow

In 1928 Charles S. Johnson left New York for Nashville. He had lost confidence in the art approach, and—more practically—he had lost funding for *Opportunity*. But he still believed in the power of black writing and interracial dialogue. Johnson accepted the position of chairman of the Sociology Department at Fisk University and turned to research the rural South. The change in focus made sense. Johnson—complete with narrow-rimmed round spectacles and conservative suits—was an academic at heart. The South was home to over three quarters of black Americans, two thirds of whom lived in the countryside. Through a detailed survey of six hundred families in Macon County, Alabama, Johnson hoped to publicize examples of bad and good racial practice. In other words, what Johnson had previously tried to do with poems, he now proposed to do with statistics. (Unbeknown to Johnson, Macon County was home to the very worst practice: as part of a medical experiment, government health officials were withholding treatment for four hundred black men suffering from syphilis.)

Johnson would not be alone. Anthropologists and sociologists, black and white, headed South between the wars to study the "Negro problem." They shared received scientific wisdom that racial difference was the product of the environment, not innate. They shared, too, the hope that their work might improve that environment. It didn't. It didn't even overturn racial barriers in American scholarship. At the American Sociological Meeting of 1935, Johnson was asked to enter by a back door. But he had never expected, nor advocated, anything other than incremental change. He believed that presenting the facts to the better sort of policymakers—his "method of indirection"—would ultimately undermine southern racism. Thus, he was content to be a "sidelines activist"— fittingly enough for a man whose mentor at Chicago, the sociologist Robert Park, was once Booker T. Washington's ghostwriter. Fittingly, too, Du Bois denounced Johnson for being too conservative.

As they expected, the social scientists found a world of appalling discrimination and abject poverty, a world where black adults were denied the titles Mr., Mrs., or Miss, where half of black adults were barely literate and where more black people than not lived under a roof with a leak. One woman told Johnson, "It just rains in here and leaks outdoors."[29] The scholars disagreed in their interpretation of the problem—some called it caste, Johnson called it "class . . . complicated by race." But all agreed the problem was not so much segregation—there was little to segregate in the rural South—but exploitation. They blamed the plantation system but also powerful white southerners, telling tales of vanity and hypocrisy. White planters, in hock to the banks, took advantage of illiterate black farmers, while white men, in fear of black men's sexuality, still took black women as their mistresses.

What the social scientists hadn't expected to find was just how many black southerners had adapted to Jim Crow without accepting it. "What constitutes the race problem," wrote Johnson, "is not the fixed character of the relations, but their dynamic character. There would be no race problem if the Negro group uniformly accepted the status assumed for it."[30] Stories of resistance were legion: of a group of boys directing white strangers looking for black prostitutes to the smartest white section of town; of parents calling their baby daughter "Misjulia" so that whites would have to address her with dignity; of a black driver, arrested for skipping a stop light, pretending he thought red was the sign for Negroes to go; of a woman thrusting a hot iron on the back of a white salesman intent on rape; of a woman repelling her amorous white boss by saying she disagreed with racial equality; of children stealing a drink from a white water fountain; of a black miner who broke a white water hydrant so that all the town had to drink from the "colored" one.[31]

Such stories were a far cry from an overt, coordinated protest movement, the sort of movement that shook the South during World War I and would soon shake the South again. Rather, they were reminiscent of slave-era stories of sabotage. But such stories mattered. They unnerved white southerners. The sociologist John Dollard found that whites in Mississippi had an "unshakeable conviction . . . that danger lurks in the Negro quarter."[32] And they sustained black southerners, perpetuating a resistance tradition that connected generations. Seemingly every figure in the rural southern Civil Rights Movement of the 1960s treasured memories of their parents' or grandparents' defiance.

Such was the force of white supremacy, Johnson thought it inevitable that acceptance, not confrontation, was "the most common type of response to the personal implications of the race system."[33] But even here there were stories of feigning compliance, of foot-dragging and stealing.

If anything, though, this secret world sustained black southerners even more than public gestures. One laborer boasted to Johnson, "I can make them think they own the world. It is nothing but a lot of jive that I hand them." White southerners were certainly thrown off balance. "The sober fact is we understand one another not at all," admitted William Percy of Greenville, not long after the flood. "Just about the time our proximity appears most harmonious something happens—a crime of violence, perhaps . . . and to our astonishment we sense a barrier in between."[34]

Behind the barrier, black southerners built their own lives, their own way. Through the blues, they transformed their experiences of oppression into music. Through humor, they mocked Jim Crow bitterly. One well-known folk tale spoke of the harvest settlement: "Ought's a ought, figger's a figger; all for de white man, none for de nigger." They mocked each other, too. Anthropologists recorded the game "the dozens," where young men took turns insulting each other (or rather each other's mother's sexual organs). Through kinship networks they shared news and built institutions—from fraternal lodges to beauty parlors to rustic speakeasies.

The black church remained central to community life. Some three quarters of black women, and half of black men, went to church at least once a month.[35] Church buildings provided a meeting place for other organizations, while church services provided a message of hope. Where white preachers thundered hell, black preachers promised justice in heaven. The anthropologist Hortense Powdermaker was impressed by one sermon where a black cook ended up living in her white mistress's house—and vice versa. If Christianity offered hope for the future, education offered hope for the here and now. Many people, observed Powdermaker, were "convinced that if illiteracy were removed, the rest would vanish with it."[36] Being unable to read left black farmers at the mercy of their landlords' "figgers." Local people (as had Johnson's parents) scrimped and saved to keep their children in school and to keep their schools in repair.

Even so, the twin tormentors of southern poverty and racism meant that black institutions were as much about survival as progress. Average state spending on southern black schooling, for example, actually declined during the 1920s—by 1930 it was less than half, per child, than that for southern white schools, and less than a quarter of the national average. Quality declined with it. Johnson noted that the average test score for rural black Alabama teachers in 1930 was below the national average for ninth-grade children. Just getting to school was hard. A fourteen-year-old Alabama girl, Beulah King, told Johnson it "don't seem fair to me for them to let the white children ride and make us walk." That walk was often five miles or more. Miss King admitted, "I want to cry when it is rainy and cold."[37] During harvest season, most rural black children had to stay in the fields anyway (as did many white children).

Little wonder that tens of thousands of black southerners continued to move in search of a better life. One 1926 survey found that black tenants and sharecroppers moved every 4.3 years on average (poor white farmers moved even more frequently). Most moved within the South, pressuring planters to promise better terms and punishing those who did not keep them. With the passage of immigration restriction in 1924 and northern industry's need for cheap labor, migration to the North also resumed, at even higher speed—as many people moved in the 1920s as in the previous and subsequent decades combined. Once there, they competed with white workers for decent housing and jobs and sought employers who offered the least bad deal. They voted in blocs—in 1929, Chicago's Oscar De Priest became the first black congressman of the century to win election. The following year, NAACP leaders celebrated when pressure from black voters helped derail the appointment of racist Judge John Parker to the Supreme Court. Black voting foretold significant political influence in the future. But for now, even in Chicago, black voters were very much the junior partner in a corrupt Republican coalition, while Parker's defeat owed more to labor's opposition. In economic terms, the situation for migrants actually deteriorated. The percentage of the total black workforce in the manufacturing and mechanical industries fell during the decade, from 58.5 percent to 48.6 percent. Three quarters of those who did find industrial work earned their dollars for pouring hot iron, breathing black dust, and carrying heavy loads. Rural black southerners passed along the news that "A nigger is a nigger even in Chicago."[38]

Of those who stayed in the South, what concerned Johnson was that amid the defiance and subterfuge some came to "believe in the inferior role of the Negro."[39] Churches preached liberation for the future, not for now. School boards demanded black children be taught manual labor. Langston Hughes complained that even colleges like Fisk were "doing their best to produce spineless Uncle Toms."[40] How many black southerners surrendered to Jim Crow is impossible to know. The visiting social scientists—for all their confidence in their latest research techniques—had little chance of penetrating deeply into the secret world that they found. (Dollard and Powdermaker, who studied the same small town in Mississippi, presented strikingly different surveys.)

What was clear was that even those black southerners who were angry or impatient were also vulnerable. The NAACP was run right out of the Deep South. One angry and impatient southern labor organizer complained that if "a Mississippi sharecropper stuck his head up . . . he got it shot off."[41] As they kept their heads down, many suffered deep wounds to their self-esteem. In the end, black southerners carefully balanced their resentment with resignation, and tempered their hopes for the future with the need to survive in the present. "If I was a little better off," one laborer told Johnson, "all of the white folks could kiss where the sun don't shine . . . a man has to be less than a man to get along most of the time."[42]

With the onset of the Great Depression, black laborers were soon a lot worse off. The stock market crashed in 1929; national income halved in three years; cotton prices fell from 18 cents per pound to 6 cents; unemployment rose to 25 percent. Drought in the Mississippi Valley in 1930—so cruel after a flood—made matters worse. Some joked that the long-running black depression only became "Great" when it "hit the white man."[43] There was truth in this, but it was gallows humor all the same. Nonwhite workers were fired first; unskilled workers and domestics lost their jobs to unemployed white men and women. "At no time in the history of the Negro since slavery," wrote T. Arnold Hill of the Urban League in 1931, "has his economic and social outlook seemed so discouraging."[44] Black unemployment reached 60 percent in some cities. Life expectancy dropped to less than thirty years in some ghettoes. What the statistics cannot convey is the sheer desperation of mothers hunting for scraps of food in trash cans, of children scavenging for coal at train depots, of the elderly shivering in boarded-up buildings.

Depression bred racial tensions. In the cities, black and white migrants poured into overcrowded and underemployed neighborhoods. In Atlanta, fascist-style blackshirts marched with placards, "Niggers, back to the cotton fields, city jobs are for white folks."[45] White demagogues ran "nigger" campaigns, promising to defend white jobs, white poverty relief, and, as ever, the purity of white women if elected.

And yet an irony of the Depression was that it would provide—in due course—opportunities for poor black Americans too. Because the Depression hurt the black middle class, it forced them to give attention to the economic agenda of the black poor. Because the politics of hunger bred left-leaning radicalism, it raised the prospect of interracial workers' alliances. And because poverty stalked black and white alike, it forced government officials to turn their attention to the economic suffering long faced by black Americans. On his inauguration in 1933, President Franklin Roosevelt promised a New Deal for the American people—the most momentous growth of government-sponsored relief and recovery programs in American history. These would, in due course, bring some benefits to black Americans and bolster their struggle for equality. But only after a fight.

Challenging the New Deal

On March 31, 1933, President Roosevelt signed into law an act creating the Civilian Conservation Corps. Designed to give useful work to unemployed youth, the act decreed (following an amendment introduced by De Priest) that "no discrimination shall be made on account of race, color and creed." Within a fortnight, some 180 black men from Harlem traveled to Fort Dix, New Jersey, for training.

At Fort Dix they found simmering racial tensions. Early in May, a hundred black recruits from Newark went on strike, complaining that food was scarce and disgusting. The *New York Times* scoffed that perhaps the "filet of sole was under-done."[46] Army officers defended their fare, telling reporters that one company of 200 men ate 2,200 hotcakes for breakfast.[47] They defamed the strikers, pointing out the presence of nine abandoned cars outside the camp, stolen after an unauthorized trip to Newark. The Newark recruits begged to differ. All was fine, they insisted, until they were thrown out of their barracks to make way for white recruits and had to give up their hot meals for raw potatoes. The Harlem recruits, though, stayed out of trouble. They formed into company 235-C (for "Colored"), under the command of a local white major, Roland Shrugg, and were posted to upstate New York to plant trees.

On a nondiscriminatory federal program, earning $30 a week, far away from the South, under the command of a New England officer— this seemed about as good as it could get for unemployed young black men during a depression. For a few weeks, it was. Then Shrugg brought in twenty white recruits and replaced the company's two black clerks. The Harlem recruits refused to work. State police arrested six "ring leaders," including the two dismissed clerks, because they "had threatened violence." The six pointed to their "outstanding" record at Fort Dix, even in the midst of the food protests. It made no difference—they were sent home. Thirty-five men still refused to work. Shrugg's defense against charges of racism hardly helped morale: "This camp is operated on merit and the negro clerks are not capable of handling their jobs." Shrugg's superior, General Charles Roberts, promised all would be forgiven for those who returned to work. Just one man did. Thirty-four men were sent home on the next train, with little prospect of finding work.

To pacify the remaining recruits, a senior CCC officer transferred the white recruits out of the company. But this was not the end of the story. CCC reports warned of a "somewhat nervous" local white population fearful of the "possibility of rape," and so Company 235-C was sent to Long Island, far from white towns. This was no isolated incident: white communities in Gettysburg, Maine, and Washington all demanded the removal of black companies. The head of the CCC was only too happy to oblige. Robert Fechner told one senator he was "a Southerner . . . who clearly understood the Negro problem." To preempt tensions with local people, Fechner promised that "Negroes would not be widely employed . . . in any position of authority." Roosevelt backed him—though he asked that his name "not be drawn into the discussion." Black commentators were livid. The *Richmond Planet* complained that "War Department policy is segregation from top to bottom in everything it handles."[48]

In many ways, the racial impact of the early New Deal was the story of Company 235-C writ large. Writ very large, in fact. Congress passed an unprecedented amount of legislation leading to the creation of a dizzying array of agencies—to rescue the banking system, to reform agriculture, to revive industry, to provide relief for the poor, insurance for workers, and jobs for the unemployed. On paper, Roosevelt's plans were color-blind. In practice, they were anything but. The New Deal's social security provisions (including unemployment insurance and old age pensions) did not apply to domestic work or agricultural labor—and so did not apply to roughly two thirds of black men and women. "From the Negro's point of view," wrote NAACP lawyer Charles Houston, the social insurance program "looks like a sieve with the holes just big enough for the majority of Negroes to fall through."[49] It could have been a comment on the entire first phase of the New Deal.

The Agricultural Adjustment Act compensated farmers for planting less cotton, and thus increased prices. Southern landlords duly pushed 100,000 black tenants off the land, without passing on the checks. The National Recovery Act, which mandated a minimum wage, did not apply to domestic or agricultural work. Where black workers did qualify, most found themselves working fewer hours (at less pay) to accomplish the same tasks, and some half a million black workers lost their jobs altogether to unemployed white men and women. Some called the NRA the Negro Removal Act, or Negroes Roasted Again. Emergency relief was distributed via local agencies, and much was lost in transmission, especially in the South. None of the early New Deal agencies contained antidiscriminatory enforcement provisions. Indeed, the only measure that explicitly called for action on race actually reinforced discrimination. Federal Housing loans were required to preserve the racial composition of neighborhoods—in effect, they built walls around black slums. To add insult to injury, Roosevelt ignored black calls for anti-lynching legislation, for termination of the poll tax, and for an end to segregation in the army.

When pressed, Roosevelt explained that he was constrained by the power of southern Democrats. "I did not choose the tools with which I must work," he told Walter White, famously.[50] In some ways, he was right. Only when southern Democrats lost their hold on Congress some thirty years later would a president be able to pass strong civil rights legislation. Much New Deal discrimination was not solely attributable to racism. The treasury secretary demanded the exclusion of agricultural and domestic workers from social security provisions simply because he thought the legislation unworkable otherwise (other countries also excluded such workers at first). Most racist discrimination was the work of local officials. Some Roosevelt appointees held enlightened views: for example, Harold Ickes, secretary of the interior and a former head of the Chicago NAACP, desegregated his department cafeteria and appointed a Negro adviser. At Roosevelt's instruction, the government spent more on black schools in his first term than it had in all the years since the Civil War. First Lady Eleanor Roosevelt held the most enlightened views of all.

Nevertheless, in reality, Roosevelt's excuses did not quite stand up to scrutiny. He was a man of his time, telling nigger jokes in private and happy to use his wife as cover in public. (Even Eleanor's circle showed the limits of liberalism. After touring the South, her friend Lorena Hickok sympathized with white anger about raising black wages—though she was "raised in the sentimental traditions that all men are created equal." "SUCH Negroes!" she wrote Eleanor. "Many of them look and talk and act like creatures barely removed from the Ape."[51]) For every Ickes, Roosevelt appointed several segregationist or indifferent officials. Even Ickes was unwilling, or unable, to make major changes in employment practice initially. His Negro adviser, Clark Foreman, was white. His massive Boulder Dam public works project employed four thousand workers, but only eleven of them were black men.

The most telling lesson of Company 235-C, though, was not New Deal discrimination but the black response. Roosevelt's recovery programs spurred the most concerted protest in a generation. Black farm workers decried their displacement; black industrial workers challenged their exclusion; the black unemployed demanded relief; and black spokesmen opposed discriminatory legislation. In many ways, these were old-time protests updated for the latest outrage. But there was much that would be new. In the depths of the Depression, black protest took a proletarian turn. As in World War I, even civil-rights-minded black leaders switched their focus to black workers. For their part, black laborers would join with left-leaning groups—even Communists—as never before. When they did so, they began to reshape the New Deal.

Challenging the New Deal in the Countryside

In the summer of 1931, *Opportunity* magazine pondered the startling rise of a Communist-led Sharecroppers Union in Alabama. Elmer Carter, Johnson's successor as editor, reckoned the farmers knew nothing of Marxism. But "they know of grinding toil at miserably inadequate wages."[52] By the summer of 1931, they knew quite a lot about Marxists, too. And they clearly liked what they learned—allies prepared to fight with them, even die for them. It was mutual admiration. Communist organizers found black farmers seasoned in resistance, and adapted their programs accordingly. As a result, the radical left began its move toward the center of southern protest politics, organizing some, influencing many.

The rise of red politics in the black South was as unexpected as it was dramatic. Communism had put down roots in Harlem during the radical ferment of World War I, but there had been no growth thereafter. Communists held little appeal for black Americans; white and mostly foreign, they were pariahs who spoke little English. Or spoke so much Marxist jargon that it must have sounded like a foreign language in any case. A 1926 outreach meeting in Chicago complete with ballerinas and a performance of Pushkin—in Russian—hardly helped. By the end of the decade, the party could claim only fifty black members. But a policy change at the Sixth Comintern (Communist International) meeting in Moscow in 1928 saw a new focus on the American South. At the suggestion of the black Communist Haywood Hall—in Moscow just years after fighting white mobs during the Chicago riot—the Comintern declared black southerners had the right to self-determination. The timing was opportune. With the onset of the Depression, plenty of southerners were desperate for support.[53]

By the summer of 1931, few people seemed more supportive than the Communists. That spring, nine vagrant black youths were charged with raping two young white women on a train near Scottsboro, Alabama. Communist lawyers moved in where the NAACP feared to tread. It seemed an ideal case, exposing the interwoven problems of racism and poverty. So it proved. Scottsboro became the main story in the American press for the next two years. As details emerged, the frame-up became ever clearer. The girls were unhurt, were also vagrants, had criminal records, and were sexually active. The last time they had sex was before the train ride, and one admitted to making up the charges anyway. Through party publicity, the racism of Alabama's courts was soon on full display. Rallies were held across America and around the world. In Germany, demonstrators hurled bottles at a U.S. consulate, one marcher was killed, and Albert Einstein headed a support committee. Walter White tried to muscle the NAACP back into the case, accusing Communists of opportunism, but he was too late, not to mention hypocritical. In any event, no one could dispute that Communist action had saved the boys' lives, and ultimately won them their freedom. (The last of the nine was released in 1950.)[54]

Communist organizers led by example, too. That same spring, one hundred miles or so south of Scottsboro, a black sharecropper, Ralph Gray, beat his corrupt landlord, joined the party, formed a 1,000-strong union of black farmers, shot the sheriff, and was killed by a posse. His corpse was dumped outside the county courthouse. But Gray's nascent Sharecroppers Union didn't heed the warning. Haywood Hall visited one meeting and was astonished to find "a small arsenal . . . of shotguns, rifles and pistols." They would need them. The next shoot-out followed in 1932, in nearby Reeltown, after the union sought to protect the land of a debt-ridden farmer. At least three croppers died. The movement went underground. But the martyrs' memory lived on. In South Carolina, croppers sang "Do lak Alabamy boys an' win or be foun' dead." Five union leaders were arrested. Despite roadblocks, black Alabamians packed the court.[55]

What Scottsboro and Reeltown meant was that when landlords began to turf their tenants off the land using the New Deal, black sharecroppers were ready to listen to left-leaning radicals. They wanted their share of compensation. By the fall of 1934, the Sharecroppers Union had eight thousand members in Alabama—men and women, who marched on relief offices, struck against vindictive landlords, and won a smattering of wage increases and compensation payments. In turn, Communists embraced black southerners—their kinship networks, their culture, even their churches. So too did other left-leaning groups. The socialist-led Southern Tenant Farmers Union gained a foothold in Arkansas. This merging of old traditions, new organizations, and dire circumstances saw the rekindling of late-nineteenth-century farmers' producerist politics which had been squashed by Jim Crow and squeezed by Garveyites and the NAACP. Rural families demanded their rights as citizens because of their toil on the land. In southern cities, it was a similar story. Groups like the NAACP and NUL and their methods of resistance were thin on the ground. Birmingham had upwards of three thousand Communist members early in the New Deal. It had only six NAACP members.[56]

Radical protest groups did little to improve the lot of southern farmers in the short term. They failed to stop the eviction of tenants or to sustain their members through the bitter winter of 1934–35. Black croppers may have been desperate, but they were also weak. Landlords controlled local relief committees, sheriffs owned the better arms, and politicians blocked the more egalitarian aspects of New Deal policy. Perhaps because of this power imbalance, radical protest groups gained only a few thousand members each at the start. They were rarely interracial in practice, save for white leaders. Because of Communist dogma, radical groups even refused to work together.

But rural protest had an effect that outstripped the size of its membership or the success of its first campaigns. It meshed with the millennial revival that swept many thousands in the rural South. Communists won admiration from black reformers. NAACP Field Secretary William Pickens admitted, "As long as I have a fighting corpuscle in my blood, I will feel a kinship with the courage of people like that."[57] By bringing southern discomfort to national attention, rural protest also had a gradual impact on federal policy. "There can be no doubt," wrote the *New York Post,* in one report, "of the reversion to slave law, mob violence and fascist methods in Arkansas."[58] Liberal reformers in the agricultural department admired the croppers and pushed to protect their rights. By Roosevelt's second term, the federal government paid half the money due to tenants directly to tenants (though this prompted a further round of evictions). In 1935 Roosevelt created a Resettlement Administration to help those who had lost their land, and black farmers received some 23 percent of all loans—their proportion of the rural population (albeit not their proportion of the rural poor).

Challenging the New Deal in the Cities

Early in June 1930, Mrs. Fannie Peck called a founding meeting of black housewives in the gymnasium of Detroit's influential Bethel AME church. Born in Missouri in 1879, Peck was fairly new to Detroit—her husband had recently been appointed pastor there. A few days before the meeting, she had heard a lecture about black housewives in Harlem who had pooled their spending power to support black-owned stores. Peck took it upon herself to organize something similar in Detroit. Her husband had founded the city's Booker T. Washington Trade Association, and she hoped this might become the women's counterpart. It soon became much more than that. Fifty women turned up at that first June meeting. By 1935 there were some ten thousand members of the Detroit Housewives League, and local leagues in some thirty major cities across the nation.

Peck was a canny strategist. Adopting the nonthreatening posture of a group of housewives, she insisted the league was not seeking "to right the many injustices . . . within the field of civil and property rights." Peck was at pains to join forces with other black groups, promising to be a rival to none. She was an adroit organizer, too. Her committee formed sixteen units across Detroit, devolving power to poorer working women in their neighborhoods—here as so often, racial segregation bolstered racial association. The league awarded prizes to those who recruited the most new members. Yet Peck rightly attributed the organization's growth to a new mood born of the Depression—a "realization on the part of the Negro woman that she has been . . . making sacrifices to educate her children with no thought as to their employment."[59]

In many ways the Housewives Leagues was clubwomen's work, church work, Washington's business league, and Garvey's race pride all rolled into one. Certainly many of the members had roots in one or all of these traditions. But in other ways the Great Depression, the Great Migration, and the New Deal prompted something new. With jobs the issue, gone was the focus on respectability. With huge black urban communities to build from, gone, too, was any need for polite requests. Housewives Leagues across the country launched "Don't Buy Where You Can't Work" campaigns. The plan was simple: boycott stores in black districts until they agreed to hire black workers. With city officials disbursing New Deal relief and setting wage limits, housewives demanded a fair deal from local government. After Cleveland officials cut the wages of black garbage collectors in 1934, league members dumped garbage in the streets.[60]

The rise of the Housewives Leagues reflected a wider revival in black nationalism. In 1934 Du Bois told *Crisis* readers: "It would be idiotic simply to sit on the side lines and yell: 'No segregation' in an increasingly segregated world."[61] "It is the race-conscious black man cooperating together in his own institutions and movements who will eventually emancipate the colored race."[62] He should have said woman too, but he got the point about putting black dollars to work. It was not that all black reformers switched to the new style. Walter White threw Du Bois out of the NAACP, telling *Crisis* readers that separation "means spiritual atrophy for the group segregated."[63] In some cities, elites condemned the confrontational turn, and the lower-class membership, of Housewives Leagues. Still, the point is that many did switch their strategy—even reformers in the NAACP. In branch after branch, a "New Crowd" of younger, more strident activists challenged "Old Guard" leaders for control.

If reformer types turned their attention to the economic crisis, the economic crisis turned people's attention to long-standing militants. And none were more militant than the Communists. Modeled on the Russian example, Communist unemployment councils led hunger marches, blocked rent evictions, and demanded relief funds for black and white equally. As in the South, Communists embraced the existing workers' culture of opposition, and once again their impact exceeded their numbers. The black press followed the Communists' every move, often in admiration. Communist-led protests turned the spotlight on black suffering. After a mass eviction protest, fighting, and the deaths of four Communists in Chicago in 1931, city leaders called in their traditional black allies to restore calm. But the black clergy, educators, and journalists refused to do their bidding. "I can't tell a hungry man to be patient," explained one minister.[64] The delegation explained that the "only cure" for radicalism was unemployment relief. The conservative black newspaper, the *Chicago Bee,* thought the situation so dire it was a wonder the whole race hadn't turned red.

In fact, the whole race was turning in many different directions. The itinerant black mystic Father Divine told people to turn to him. "I take your poverty," he told a rally of some ten thousand in Harlem in 1932, "and give you peace and prosperity."[65] No one was quite sure where he came from, and Divine wasn't telling—the history of God, he explained, could never be understood by mere men. (He seems to have started life as George Baker in the South, working first as a gardener.) With a message of communitarianism, celibacy, and positive thinking, his movement spread. The *New York Times* reckoned his followers numbered two million, though it was probably a lot less.[66] But Divine's following was just the most prominent of a multitude of religious sects—including a small, but destined to be famous, Nation of Islam. (Divine's movement later collapsed in a storm of financial and sex scandals, and he retreated from public life. During the Civil Rights Movement, one aide explained, "Father has said everything there is to say about everything.")[67]

The mix of strategies, from Communists to housewives to the NAACP, was sometimes combustible. Garveyites broke up Communist meetings. Some Communists condemned Don't Buy boycotts as "an attempt to utilize the misery of the masses for the strengthening of the Negro petty bourgeoisie."[68] Yet for all the differences and divisions, protesters found they had much in common. The pain of the Depression and the promise of the New Deal saw to that. Communists formed an alliance with Divine and often joined Don't Buy boycotts. Divine promoted black cooperatives. New Crowd NAACP types used their power as representatives of ever increasing blocs of black—segregated—voters even as they sought integration in New Deal projects. Reformers even defended workers' violence. After black Harlemites rioted in March 1935, city officials blamed the Communists. Not so Harlem leaders. The *Amsterdam News* blamed "the oppression of 204,000 American citizens in the most liberal city in America."[69] As so often happened, the spark for violence was news of police violence—in this case, the murder of a boy arrested for shoplifting, at a store that had been the focus of a Don't Buy campaign.

Together, urban protests pressured local governments to channel federal funds to black causes. After the Harlem riot, Mayor LaGuardia, a keen New Deal supporter, created a multiracial commission to investigate. He valued black votes, and he feared black violence. He even appointed a black sociologist, E. Franklin Frazier, to serve as its chairman and Alain Locke to implement the findings. The commission applauded the work of the Communists for preventing trouble and blamed employment discrimination, racial segregation, and police brutality. LaGuardia rejected the findings. But during the next two years, relief money channeled to black workers, schools, and youth clubs almost doubled. It was a similar story elsewhere. Little wonder that black voters switched to New Deal candidates. The Reverend Samuel Proctor, a pastor in Harlem, explained that there was still plenty of discrimination, but "black folk have never been so crazy to wait for things to be perfect."[70] Nor were they so crazy to allow policymakers to ignore them—black lobbyists headed to Congress.

Challenging the New Deal in Government

While untold numbers—so often the poor, so often women—challenged the New Deal in the countryside and cities, the story in Congress was entirely different. Only two young black men, both Harvard educated, challenged New Deal policy at its source. Robert Weaver had a doctorate in economics. John Davis was a lawyer, a former contributor to *Fire!*, and a champion debater. Calling themselves the Negro Industrial League, they trudged from congressional hearing to congressional hearing during Roosevelt's first one hundred days, pressing politicians to consider the racial impact of the NRA.

Two men representing twelve million people would have been almost comical, except that so many of the twelve million were making their own voices heard. As in Reconstruction days, the power of these lobbyists lay in the complaints they conveyed. They collated shocking data about NRA discrimination in southern mills. They made the case against lower wages for black workers in NRA codes—not an easy case to make, since equal wages would lead to more black unemployment. But it was vital to prevent race discrimination from becoming embedded in federal policy. Policymakers were persuaded, and the NRA mandated equal wages for black and white workers, though the resulting layoffs, regional wage differentials, and the exclusion of domestics and agricultural workers still had a devastating effect.

In the summer of 1933, Clark Foreman co-opted Weaver as his assistant in Interior, and the NIL disbanded. But its influence lived on. In the first place, Weaver's appointment marked the first of some forty-five appointments of black government officials during Roosevelt's first term. (It marked the start of his own long career in government too—some thirty years later, he would become the first black cabinet member, as Lyndon Johnson's secretary of the Department of Housing and Urban Development.) Such appointments made a stunning contrast with the bleaching of the bureaucracy under the previous Democratic president, Woodrow Wilson. The advisers were anything but the yes men of yesteryear, too. Within a month of representing black waitresses during Washington's Don't Buy boycotts, black lawyer William Hastie was appointed assistant solicitor in the Department of Interior.

Black advisers also gave outside agitators the inside track on the workings of government. J. Max Bond, a former teacher, was virtually a double agent in the heart of the New Deal's Tennessee Valley Authority—a massive hydropower project that would displace many rural people. On paper Bond was "supervisor of Negro training." In public he supported the program, so much so that some black journalists rebuked him. In private, he prodded officials to include local blacks in its rehousing programs, without much success. In secret, he tipped off the NAACP about racial exclusion, and in true espionage style his NAACP contacts sent letters in plain envelopes to his home address. When the NAACP threatened the TVA with legal action, TVA officials called on Bond to write and pacify the NAACP. He did—but he covertly sent word that "this situation should be exposed."[71] Using Bond's information, the *Crisis* ran an exposé on black displacement, entitled the "Alley in the Valley."[72] A congressional committee called for better treatment for black people, and—though discrimination continued—the TVA began to watch its step.

Meanwhile, the NAACP ramped up its legal campaign for civil rights. In 1934 its board appointed Charles Hamilton Houston as its first fulltime counsel. Houston was a veteran of Jim Crow army camps in World War I France, "damned glad I had not lost my life fighting for this country."[73] He was also a brilliant legal scholar, the first black member of the *Harvard Law Review*. (There wouldn't be a black president of the *Review* until 1990, when a 28-year-old former community organizer called Barack Obama got the job.) Houston set the NAACP strategy to challenge education segregation as the means to dismantle Jim Crow and to champion local cases in order to "arouse and strengthen the will of local communities to demand and fight for their rights."[74] In due course, the strategy would do both, with spectacular success. As dean of Howard University Law School, he also nurtured a new generation of civil rights lawyers—including Thurgood Marshall, who graduated top of the class in 1933 and would go on to lead the seminal *Brown* case in 1954 and become the first black Supreme Court Justice in 1967.

By 1934, Weaver—to Davis's annoyance—had moved into government. Davis maintained his watch on Capitol Hill. With the backing of the NAACP and some twenty other organizations, he formed a Joint Committee on Negro Recovery. His alliance with the NAACP was crucial. In the pages of the *Crisis,* Davis presented his research to a wide audience. Much wider than he could have imagined, in fact. Eleanor Roosevelt read his 1934 article "NRA Codifies Wage Slavery" and passed it to NRA officials.[75] Davis and the NAACP did not sit easily together: Davis was outspoken and impressed by the Communists, and at the end of 1934 the NAACP pulled its support from the JCNR, which duly collapsed. But what rose in its place in 1936 was a National Negro Congress—a massive militant alliance focused on jobs and economic justice that showed both the desperation and possibilities of the moment.

Uniting around Workers' Rights

The Negro Congress was Davis's brainchild. In May 1935 he co-hosted a conference with Weaver and the black economist Ralph Bunche on the "Position of the Negro in Our National Economic Crisis." Some 250 delegates, black and white, from Communist to liberal, discussed the New Deal's record to date. The verdict was unanimous. "For the Negro," said Bunche, "the New Deal means the same thing, but more of it."[76]

Davis was particularly despondent. Since 1933 the number of African Americans claiming relief had almost doubled to 3.5 million—yes, the New Deal was serving the black poor, but it was not creating jobs for them. Davis thought New Deal slogans masked the same old "raw deal." As things stood, there seemed little prospect of change. "Hardly anywhere in America does there exist for Negroes an effective weapon to compel respect and justice." A few advisers notwithstanding, blacks had "no voice in the government" either. Hence the call for a meeting of all protest organizations to "work for the solutions of basic problems facing the Negro."[77]

The Depression and New Deal made an unprecedented gathering of diverse groups a real possibility. But it would take seismic events overseas to make it certain. During the summer of 1935, as Italian troops readied to invade Ethiopia, black America held its breath. Ethiopia, the historic home of black Christianity, was the last remaining independent black African nation.

Tens of thousands of black Americans rallied in support. On August 18 America's main black churches held a day of prayer. At the start of October, the black press reported "joyous enthusiasm" among Ethiopians at the prospect of war. Within days, the Ethiopians got their wish. Italian troops poured over the border. More than half a million Ethiopian troops advanced "bravely," wrote one black reporter, "into the barrels of the Italian's death-dealing machine guns."[78] "I'd like to go to Ethiopia and fight," wrote one Mrs. Wimley Thompson from New Mexico to the *Pittsburgh Courier*.[79] Harlem youths didn't have to travel that far: they fought Italians on the streets of New York. Black leaders petitioned Roosevelt and the League of Nations to sanction Italy. But Roosevelt stood aloof. In the spring, superior Italian firepower—including chemical weapons—won the day.

Ethiopia's fight marked a turning point in the longer history of black internationalism. Before the Ethiopian war, black Americans had celebrated Africa's past, not its present. They had pondered how to uplift the dark continent, not how Africa could light their own path to freedom. After Ethiopia, anti-colonialism became integral to the black American freedom struggle. The rise of the black press, now with a readership of over two million, made this international vision possible—in turn, editors sent reporters to Ethiopia when they saw the impact on circulation figures.

In the short term, Ethiopia caused "the fever of race consciousness," to quote the *Courier,* to "spread like an epidemic."[80] Race fever brought disparate black organizations closer together. So too did events in Europe. Fearful of Adolf Hitler, in August 1935 the Seventh Comintern called for a Popular Front against Fascism. What this meant in America was that Communists were free to ally with other left-leaning groups and black reformers—even the black church and New Dealers—in their battle for jobs and justice. It also meant these other groups felt free to work with Communists. In practice, such alliances had begun on the ground anyway. Now, they could develop formally. The stage was set for the Negro Congress.

In February 1936, some five thousand men and women from more than five hundred organizations representing three million people converged on Chicago for the founding convention. Walter White stayed away, but almost everyone else was there. Some pawned their valuables to pay their way. Delegates shared a "flaming resentment" at black suffering, but also a genuine hope they could influence the New Deal. It was the broadest such gathering in living memory, broader than the founding of the NAACP. It was also strikingly different. Whereas the NAACP saw political and legal rights as the means to make economic gains, the Negro Congress saw economic power as the means to win full citizenship.

Davis was the national secretary, but the chairman was A. Philip Randolph. It was a natural choice. Randolph's track record of pushing economic rights was second to none. Born in Florida in 1889, Randolph had served the socialist cause in Harlem in World War I. A decade later, in Chicago, he organized the first Negro Labor Conference. Since 1925 he had led the Brotherhood of Sleeping Car Porters on behalf of the twelve thousand black porters who worked long hours on Pullman trains. The brotherhood, Randolph believed, was on a "quest for the holy grail of economic freedom."[81] Along the way Randolph had fought white unions for recognition, Pullman bosses for better conditions, and virtually all black leaders and the black press in Chicago—who applauded Pullman for employing blacks at all, at slightly better than rock-bottom wages. Only Chicago clubwomen supported Randolph at first. But now, with the New Deal turning its attention to workers' rights and black leaders turning their attention to economic justice, the holy grail seemed within reach.

Randolph was a suitably charismatic leader—tall, handsome, and a gifted orator. So gifted, in fact, that the BSCP treasurer advised local leaders to take collections before Randolph spoke, else the audience might whip into a frenzy, rush into the street, and forget to donate. Randolph had first moved to Harlem as an aspiring actor, fitting in performances as Othello between his socialist duties. He was not a particularly good organizer, however, and made some tactical mistakes in the early days of the BSCP. But he was tough, as befits a man who remembered his mother with a shotgun on her lap when his father set out, with a pistol, to prevent a lynching. And he couldn't be bought—perhaps a legacy of his parent's devout Christian faith and his own secular commitment to the workers' cause.

Randolph's opening address set the contours of the movement. He began by invoking the tradition of slave rebellion (though any mention of God was absent). He spoke at length of Ethiopia and the spread of Fascism. He surveyed the double burden of black workers—as workers they were "robbed, exploited," as Negroes they were "hated . . . and murdered." He dismissed the New Deal as "no remedy . . . it does not place human rights above property rights." Then he set forth remedies of his own, remedies shared by those in the hall. He endorsed workers' and farmers' movements, civil rights organizations and housewives' leagues. He sought integration of the unions, a focus on nitty-gritty issues of jobs and housing, and a campaign for a real New Deal. Above all he called for a united front dedicated to "mass protests . . . and legal action." After Scottsboro, it was clear that protest and legal action were no longer strategies at odds with each other. The *Defender,* so recently a staunch opponent, positively purred at his "pulse-tingling, spirit inoculating exhortation." (In fact, Randolph didn't make it to Chicago—a colleague read his speech aloud.)[82]

The Negro Congress would be short-lived. Randolph was busy with the brotherhood. Davis found it impossible to get the various groups to work together effectively. It was not just that the NAACP was keen for the congress to fail—many congress activists had some enthusiasm for the New Deal. Thus, the congress soon contracted from a mass united front, to focus on workers' organizations, thereby moving from a race organization to one much more dependent on white allies, especially Communists. But Randolph had long despised the Communists. After the surprise of the Nazi-Soviet pact of 1939 he felt no obligation to even tolerate them. Speaking at the April 1940 congress, Randolph denounced both Fascism and Communism and condemned the national congress as no longer Negro. It was time the "darker races . . . look to themselves . . . Freedom is never granted, it is won."[83] By the time he finished speaking, two thirds of the audience had walked out. Randolph couldn't care less. He resigned and the congress collapsed. So too did Communist influence in mainstream black protest across the country.

The congress's importance, though, lay in its wider impact. This extraordinary show of commitment to black workers and to confrontation altered the complexion of mainstream protest politics. Even Walter White changed his tack. Fearing isolation, he addressed the second congress in 1937. He was, in fact, catching up with the militancy of local NAACP branches. To be sure, he still hoped to lobby the government— he became a confidant of Eleanor Roosevelt and gained the ear of the president by the end of the decade. But in April 1941, White was to be found on the back of a union truck outside a Ford factory in Michigan, supporting some nine thousand striking black workers, warning white bosses, black clergy, and black business leaders alike that "Negro Ford workers . . . cannot afford to rely on the personal kindness of any individual when what the workers want is justice."[84] Soon after America joined the war, Randolph and White would threaten Roosevelt with a massive workers' protest, and win.

Why the proletarian, confrontational turn in protest mattered was because it coincided—and partly caused—a slight turn in the New Deal toward racial justice. Black voters left their traditional Republican home to support Roosevelt in 1936. It was the most dramatic shift of an electoral bloc in American history, and coincided with the declining influence of southern Democrats: in 1936 southerners made up less than half the Democratic Party's congressmen for the first time in forty years. Though Roosevelt remained chary of alienating the larger pool of white workers, he worked hard to get black votes and intended to keep them. Late in his 1936 campaign he addressed his first all-black audience, at Howard University, promising "no forgotten men and no forgotten races." There was a major difference between not being forgotten and being central, and many of Roosevelt's actions were more gesture than substance. But it was a start.

The second phase of the New Deal addressed some black concerns. The Department of the Interior imposed racial quotas on WPA contractors; the CCC virtually doubled black recruitment; new departments such as the Resettlement Administration and the National Youth Administration worked to avoid discrimination; department heads appointed more than a hundred black administrators; some agencies sidestepped southern politicians; and the Justice Department created a civil rights section. There were significant symbolic gestures too. Late in 1938, the Daughters of the American Revolution barred the brilliant black contralto Marian Anderson from singing in Washington's Constitution Hall. Walter White lobbied with Eleanor Roosevelt and Harold Ickes to stunning effect: Roosevelt resigned from the DAR, and Ickes arranged for Anderson to sing from the steps of the Lincoln Memorial. Some 75,000 people, black and white, came to hear her—quite a change from Warren Harding's segregated dedication of the memorial.

Using the New Deal

In practice, the egalitarian turn in the New Deal was only slight. Local abuses continued, especially in the South. African Americans continued to fight New Deal discrimination. But the turn was just enough to give black activists new weapons in their battle for economic justice and civil rights.

Within the government, black advisers were precisely that—advisers, not policymakers. But at least they had some influence on the inside, and they continued to ally with the NAACP on the outside. None more than Mary McLeod Bethune, who hosted Friday evening meetings of a self-styled black cabinet at her home. Bethune was a self-made woman, the fifteenth child of former slaves, a seasoned southern educator, and a devout Christian, who built up a college for girls in Florida and became president of the NACW as well as a friend of the first lady. In 1935 she formed a National Council of Negro Women to voice black women's concerns to New Deal policymakers. Bethune played her cards well. The head of the Urban League reckoned she had the "most marvelous gift of affecting feminine helplessness in order to attain her ends with masculine ruthlessness."[85] Roosevelt appointed her head of minority affairs for the National Youth Association. Her department became one of the most racially evenhanded in its distribution of funding, though it didn't challenge segregation.

As the government offered more relief to minorities, local campaigners took advantage. The percentage of black workers in the WPA jumped from 8 to 15 percent in two years (though no more than 5 percent of black WPA workers had supervisory roles).[86] By the end of the decade, black income from NRA work and relief almost equaled black income from agriculture and domestic service, and black families lived in one third of low-income PWA housing units. Black southerners tended to fare worse when programs were administered locally. But even in the South the relative rates of black and white infant mortality remained in alignment (though the black rate was higher), suggesting that basic needs were met, even if greater needs were not addressed.[87] And the New Deal clearly changed expectations. In 1939 black Louisiana sharecropper Willie Dixon wrote directly to the attorney general, after his landlord had stolen his crops, "I am told that President Roosevelt is a true friend to the negro people. I want you and him to aid me, please."[88]

New Deal programs empowered some black Americans to aid themselves. The Federal Theater, Music, and Writers' projects (1935–1939) provided unheard-of financial support for black artists. One generation after Woodrow Wilson applauded *Birth of a Nation* in the White House, federal money now supported plays with such provocative titles as *Black Empire* and *Run Little Chillun* (not that Roosevelt himself would have known: before the Marian Anderson performance, the closest he got to a black cultural production was a concert by the Fisk Jubilee Singers).

In the countryside, left-leaning farmers' groups swelled in numbers with the creation of the Resettlement Agency. By 1936 the Southern Tenant Farmers' Union (STFU) claimed more than twenty-five thousand members. After a flood in Missouri in 1937, state STFU leader Owen Whitfield, a black gospel preacher, spoke for some six thousand members—in practice, loosely affiliated kinship groups linked together by radical politics and religious revival. When the Bankhead-Jones Act authorized loans for tenants in the summer of 1937, poorer white farmers joined them for the first time. Whitfield was delighted. The rural poor needed to gain the "balance of power" in alliance, he exhorted, "before we can obtain . . . land, mules and hogs." After Whitfield contacted Roosevelt directly, FSA officials opened a government cooperative farm for a hundred families. The movement splintered due to socialist-communist infighting at the end of the decade. But when local planters resumed evictions, more than a thousand black and white farmers set up a homeless camp on the edge of a highway. And when, to Roosevelt's horror, police and terror groups drove them off, the FSA offered food and loans for resettlement.[89]

The key constituents of the later New Deal, though, were industrial workers. Randolph's Pullman porters took advantage of amendments to the 1934 Railway Labor Act, which forced companies to recognize representative unions. Pullman had faced down the Brotherhood of Sleeping Car Porters in 1929. In 1935 bosses had to face up to 4,165 members of the brotherhood, backed by the federal government. Two years later, the company signed a contract with the union that increased wages by over a million dollars, and—just as importantly—halved working hours. The victory carried enormous symbolism. Previously Pullman porters had to smile as they served and, as Randolph put it acidly, they had to beg white men for tips. It was slavery updated for an industrial age. Now porters could work as free men. The victory also confirmed Randolph's confidence in mass protest. He told the Second National Negro Congress triumphantly, "True liberation can be acquired and maintained only when the Negro people possess power; and power is product and flower of organization."[90]

Away from the Pullman cars, the story of black workers was more complicated. The New Deal empowered unions through a series of startling measures, including the Wagner Act of 1935—legislation of such significance that union leaders called it labor's Magna Carta. The problem was, most unions excluded black workers as a matter of policy. Thus, the New Deal labor measures that empowered unions also empowered white workers' hold over industrial jobs. This was no accident. The question of race came up explicitly in discussions of the Wagner Act. The issue at stake was Section 9, which would enable unions to have exclusive rights of bargaining, as long as they were elected by a majority of workers in any given company. NAACP and NUL lobbyists argued that this closed shop would be a closed white shop, and called for an explicit nondiscrimination clause. But the American Federation of Labor—the national union body—"fought bitterly" against it, admitted one union official. White labor had far more clout than black lobbyists. The AFL won. Randolph despaired.

But black migration that forced the hand of relief agencies also began to force the hand of labor. As luck would have it, the AFL lost its dominance, which provided a further opening for black workers. After a series of arguments (including a fistfight at the national convention), a new body—the Congress of Industrial Organizations—broke away from the AFL. Rather than the AFL's craft unions, the CIO promoted industrial unions, whereby an entire plant, rather than particular groups of workers within a plant, would be covered. The intention was to give labor more bargaining power. So it proved. In a sequence of stunning victories, CIO unions won recognition in industrial plants across the country.

Because some bosses had welcomed cheap black labor in the past, black workers had become part of the industrial workforce. In the South and Midwest, one in five packinghouse workers was an African American, as were one in ten coal, iron, and steel workers. In other words, in some industries, CIO organizers needed to include black workers whether they wanted to or not. Black strikebreaking in the past, and the threat of the AFL, made the matter all the more pressing. Because of the Communist Party's popular front, some of the most influential agitators within the CIO wanted to include black workers anyway.

Even where they did reach out, there were limits. More often than not, black workers confronted racism, segregation, and marginalization. The president of Chicago Steel Union's women's auxiliary admitted, "I know that Negroes *are* workers . . . but there's just something about them— that black skin." Many refused to join, and many black leaders—especially clergy and businessmen—urged them not to. Still, the simple facts were that the Depression revealed the sharp limits of bosses' beneficence, the New Deal boosted the power of labor, and the CIO promised inclusion. John Davis told Chicago steelworkers in 1936 their choice was stark: "between joining the union with their white fellow workers and taking the side of their slave driving employers."[91]

At its best, biracial organizing changed race relations. After visiting the steelworkers' Chicago office in 1937, black reporter Dan Burley was "struck with the lack of friction present among . . . Mexicans, blacks, Polish, Italians, Germans and Irish." Breaking news that bosses' pay had risen to $125 an hour certainly helped.[92] Biracial organizing could be effective, too. In the mines of Alabama, tobacco houses of Virginia, and steel works of Illinois, black and white workers won wage increases together. In the titanic struggle between the CIO's United Automobile Workers and Henry Ford in Detroit's car factories in 1941, interracial unity held firm—despite black churches' support of Ford, despite the UAW's acceptance of separate black and white seniority lists, and despite Ford's bringing in black strikebreakers. The UAW won recognition, and the contract raised wages, established a grievance procedure, and banned discrimination. It didn't address the lack of black promotions, though. With the battle lost against the union, Ford soon stopped employing black workers anyway. Even at its best, biracial organizing left plenty more battles for black workers to win.

The labor movement didn't address the particular economic problems facing poorer black women, either. In fact, the New Deal as a whole did little for women of any color. Most universal programs applied to work done by men; most women-specific programs (such as Aid to Dependent Children) were administered locally. But the combination of the Depression and a New Deal that focused mostly on white workers had disastrous consequences for black women, and thus for black families. During the 1930s, black women's participation in the labor force actually fell as more white women needed jobs. A desperate dawn sight on city street corners was black women huddled together, hoping a local housewife might hire them for an hour or two. Even if they got work, pay was meager. Black women made 23 cents for every dollar made by white men (white women made 61 cents).[93]

To make matters worse, black women's movements struggled during the New Deal. The NACW's rhetoric of women's respectability and resourcefulness had little to offer during a depression. Bethune's NCNW didn't fill the breach, and was not helped by Bethune's own abrasive manner. Meanwhile, poorer women workers, black and white, had no language of welfare rights to match their predicament.[94] Movements for black women's equality, and for poor black women's welfare rights, would not re-emerge in force until after the Civil Rights Movement. Still, as wives of strikers, as leaders of store boycotts, as domestics who refused to live in, black women shaped the New Deal at the grassroots.

The "better class" of black women reformers played active roles in the New Deal apparatus of southern cities by disbursing relief. Ironically, they gained inclusion by invoking the old rhetoric of black uplift—and thus poor-black delinquency—for a white audience. Atlanta's Neighborhood Union told New Deal officials that only they could "help the Negro masses to adjust themselves to the type of world in which they must live."[95] The old rhetoric served subtly new purposes. A generation before, women reformers thought they were "lifting as we climb." Now, by joining New Deal bureaucracies that separated off poorer black neighborhoods, they hoped to climb without lifting. It certainly suited New Deal officials to appoint black reformers rather than address the underlying causes of black poverty themselves. Thus, the New Deal marked the widening of class divisions in southern black communities—divisions that would undermine workers' protest during the civil rights years.

Native Sons

Just seven years after Langston Hughes declared Negro writers out of vogue, a Negro writer in Harlem came into vogue as no black writer ever had before. Early in 1938, Richard Wright's short story "Fire and Cloud" won first prize in a national magazine competition. Later that year, it was published with three other short stories as *Uncle Tom's Children.* Two years later, Wright's novel *Native Son* was published—the first book by a black author ever to be chosen by the Book of the Month Club. It sold 200,000 copies in just three weeks.

Wright's success went beyond the Renaissance promoters' wildest dreams. But for those like C. S. Johnson who hoped to narrow the racial divide, Wright's subject matter was the stuff of nightmares. "There is nothing" in *Uncle Tom's Children,* wrote one reviewer, "about the happy cullud folks singing in the cotton fields."[96] Nothing indeed. In the four stories, a teenager flees after his friend is lynched; a flood victim shoots a white boat owner so that he can take his wife to a hospital, but she dies and he is killed; a man murders the white salesman who seduced his wife, then dies fighting a white mob; and a black minister chooses to represent his angry people rather than deal with the sweet-talking local mayor, and is badly beaten for his trouble. Even so, Wright was frustrated because it was a "book which even bankers' daughters could . . . feel good about." So he determined that "no one would weep over" his next book—"that it would be so hard and deep that they would have to face it without the consolation of tears."[97]

Native Son was harder and deeper than any race book ever published. The *Washington Post* called it "a super-shocker."[98] The opening scene set the tone. In a squalid Chicago apartment, amidst a family he hates without understanding why, a young migrant called Bigger Thomas kills a rat by crushing it. During the two weeks that follow, Bigger gets a job (via a New Deal agency) as chauffeur for a white liberal family, hacks their film-star daughter to pieces, burns her body parts, tries to extort money by pretending she has been kidnapped, murders his black girlfriend by smashing her skull, is chased by the police, kills one policeman, and is caught and sentenced to death. Along the way Wright spares no one. Bigger's employer (who donated ping-pong tables to the local NAACP) made his fortune from renting out substandard apartments to black families, including Bigger's. The daughter, drunk, is about to have sex with Bigger when they are disturbed; he murders her in panic. A white woman sacks her domestic servant on hearing of the murder. A black preacher offers Bigger nothing but platitudes. A sincere white Communist lawyer helps Bigger but cannot fathom him. The biggest shock is that Bigger first finds meaning to his life—and power over others—through the pain he inflicts.

Wright's super-shocker was a deliberate rejection of what he called the "humble novels, poems and plays" of the Harlem Renaissance's "prim and decorous ambassadors," who had been "received as though they were French poodles who do clever tricks."[99] (He exempted Langston Hughes from this criticism.) His shocking prose had far more impact than the Renaissance on subsequent black literature. His stories were also a more realistic commentary on black life. Whereas Renaissance writers focused more on the exceptional and noble, Wright focused on the masses—their suffering and anger, defiance and despair. His exploration of self-defense, race consciousness, and left-leaning politics all rang true.

Wright could speak about the masses because he had lived their lives. Born in 1908 to near poverty in rural Mississippi, his mother's ill health and his father's desertion prompted an early sense of responsibility coupled with hopelessness. As a youth, he almost suffered a nervous breakdown. He was brought up by his grandmother, whose overbearing Seventh Day Adventism prompted his early hatred of religion. As a child he "learned to lie, to steal, to dissemble . . . to play the dual role which every Negro must play if he wants to eat and live."[100] He reported that his move to Chicago as a young man "depressed and dismayed me, mocked all my fantasies."[101] He failed the medical examination for a post office job because of being malnourished. When he got the job after fattening up, he railed against the relentless drudgery. He survived the Depression working on federal projects, including the Writers' Project, and joined the Communist Party without ever feeling tied to its dogmatism. His writing on alienation, sex without intimacy, and female betrayal all drew on his life experience too.

If Wright was everyman, Bigger most certainly was not. But Wright explained later that even Bigger was born from the many Biggers he had met in his life, "more than I could count and more than you suspect." Through Bigger, Wright sought "to tell the truth as I saw it and felt it" and so "to register the moral—or what *I* felt was the moral—horror of Negro life."[102] The truth and the horror won acclaim from white commentators, who compared Wright to Chekhov and Dostoevsky, Dickens and Faulkner (more acclaim, in fact, than from black commentators, whose pride was matched by their fears of fueling prejudice—though the NAACP showed its new militancy by awarding him its prestigious Spingarn Medal for outstanding achievement in 1940).

In part, Wright won acclaim because realism in fiction—works such as John Steinbeck's *Grapes of Wrath*—had become an established literary genre of the Depression. But white readers were ready for black realism because black protest and poverty were already in the news. Wright's urgent, graceful, bleak prose, drawing upon Hemingway's simple, naturalistic style, made him a masterful messenger of dark tidings. Eleanor Roosevelt found Wright's work "so vivid that I had a most unhappy time reading it."[103]

Critics pointed out that Wright's success showed that racial hatred was not the only story of New Deal America. It was funding from the Federal Writers' Project, after all, that had given Wright a start in his literary career. Such inclusion, and his sales, pointed ahead toward black claims on the American state and public in the years to come. Nevertheless, Wright's shock value pointed out another path to progress, one where angry protest forced change. In some ways his work proved to be singularly prophetic. In prison, Bigger told his lawyer he had wanted to join the army, but "Hell, it's a Jim Crow army. All they want a black man for is to dig ditches."[104] Within a year, thousands of black men would be fighting for the right to fight.

A Communist writer, voicing such anger, would have been out of the mainstream during the Renaissance. But by the end of the Depression decade, Wright was not alone. In a talk to black educators in 1938, even Mary McLeod Bethune admitted despair. "We are losing our homes and our farms and our jobs . . . We are scorned of men; they spit in our faces and laugh. We cry out in this awesome darkness."[105] As Davis had done at the start of the New Deal, Bethune organized a conference on the status of black Americans, in 1939. White, Davis, Weaver, and Randolph all joined her. As befitted a government insider, Bethune's report to the president praised his best efforts. But she charged that he had not addressed the "fundamental problems of the Negro." Weaver thought even the quota system in WPA contracts (which often didn't work in practice) was just a "device to regain lost ground; [not] to open new types of employment." The NAACP had won some symbolic victories in court, but for now they had done no more, said the Howard sociologist Kelly Miller, than "keep open the door of hope."[106]

Another recession, starting in 1936, hit black workers hard. In most cities, upwards of a third of black men were unemployed at the end of the decade. The percentage of black workers in manufacturing actually fell from 7.3 percent in 1930 to 5.1 percent in 1940, and as bad luck would have it, the percentages were lowest in the war industries that were soon to boom.[107] By this time, Congress was rolling back relief funding, and as bad timing would have it, this was just the moment some agencies sought to be evenhanded. The Resettlement Administration gave black farmers a fair shake of tenant loans. But this meant only 3,400 black farmers, out of nearly 200,000 who lost their land.[108] The fact that Missouri farmers had gained Roosevelt's attention when homeless, camped out on the edge of a highway, told its own story.

On the ground, black Americans expressed their anger. "The officials of the W.P.A.," one group of Chicago workers wrote to Roosevelt, "are not treating us as God's children, but as God's step-children."[109] The report card on the South was worse. A Mississippi black Republican, S. D. Redmond, told Ralph Bunche, "The New Deal agencies haven't meant a goddamned thing to the Negroes."[110] Little wonder that two million people signed a petition in 1939 calling for federal aid for anyone willing to move to Africa. One Illinois petitioner explained, I would "rather be any place than here working on W.P.A. and starving to death."[111] Bethune concluded, to the president, there was still "much—very much—to be done."[112] Another world war would soon give black Americans the power to begin to do it.

CHAPTER SEVEN

World War II and Its Aftermath, 1941–1948

On the morning of May 5, 1941 (before America joined the war), thousands of black women in Cleveland picked up their telephones, dialed 0, and jammed the switchboard of Ohio Bell Telephone. They were angry at the company's refusal to hire black women. At the same time, pickets outside Ohio Bell's offices likened the company's policy to Hitler's. Within a week, the company agreed to hire black women as elevator operators (though not as clerical workers).[1]

A black man in Detroit whose loyalty to America was "beyond question" admitted to researchers, "I was really ashamed of myself the day Pearl Harbor was hit. When I heard the news I jumped up and laughed. 'Well, sir,' I said, 'I don't guess the white folks will say colored people can't fly airplanes from now on.'"[2]

Detroit, June 20, 1943. A night of violence left at least twenty-five African Americans and nine whites dead. African Americans dubbed it "Black Pearl Harbor." One federal official reported Detroit "closely resembles bombed-out London." The Dayton *News* reported, "We have done for Hitler what Hitler could not do for himself." Detroit's mayor admitted, "I was taken by surprise only by the day it happened."[3]

Black soldier Charles Jones from Mississippi, stationed in England, was invited to dinner by a local family. He was surprised when he, and only he, was seated on a large cushion. His hostess explained that white GIs "told us you had tails."[4] Another British resident said, "I don't mind the Yanks, but I don't care much for the white fellows they've brought with them."[5]

During October 1944 a white streetcar conductorette struck black passenger Mrs. Alice Burke with a door handle. Burke tossed her through the window and was later found guilty of aggravated battery.[6]

New World A-Coming. So ran the title of black journalist Roi Ottley's 1943 prize-winning popular history of Harlem. For a few weeks the $3 book reached the bestseller lists (behind Robert Carlson's exposé of U.S. fascism, *Under Cover,* but ahead of Colonel Robert Scott's *God Is My Co-Pilot* and Dr. David Fink's much-needed wartime blockbuster *Release from Nervous Tension*).[7] Born to West Indian parents in Harlem in 1906, Ottley's concern for social justice and his punchy prose helped him rise swiftly to become the editor of New York's *Amsterdam News.* After the war, he would become a prolific author on race matters. This first book was a characteristically witty and colorful history of the long struggle for "democracy—cleansed and refreshed." But Ottley believed that this moment, this war, was fundamentally different from all that had gone before. World War II was a "'People's War'—for in spite of selfish interests a new world is a-coming with the sweep and fury of the Resurrection."[8]

At the height of World War II, who could disagree? The old European empires teetered on the brink of collapse. America's president called for a new world based on "four essential human freedoms": freedom of speech and religion, and freedom from fear and want. At home, the American economy swapped bust for boom virtually overnight. In 1940 America's standing army was smaller than Portugal's, but by the end of the war some sixteen million Americans had served in the armed forces. More than five million people moved to towns, and three million left the rural South for good. Women entered the factories. European immigrants, previously treated with suspicion, became accepted citizens of America at war.

With hindsight, it is easy to presume that America's "last good war" was good for racial equality too—at the very least, a key stepping-stone to a belligerent Civil Rights Movement. Hitler gave white supremacy a bad name. The black press launched a Double V campaign, for democracy's victory at home as well as abroad. NAACP membership swelled from 50,000 to over 400,000, while Roosevelt issued the first Presidential Proclamation for civil rights since Reconstruction. As black workers moved in droves to get new industrial jobs, the average income of African Americans rose faster in the 1940–1950 period than in *any* other decade during the twentieth century. After the war, black veterans returned home fighting for freedom, and Roosevelt's successor, Harry Truman, quickly set up a President's Committee on Civil Rights. In the wider world, India's bid for independence in 1947 heralded the collapse of imperialism.

But drawing a straight line from the war to the Civil Rights Movement is an oversimplification, and in many ways wrong. War did not initiate militant protest, and organizational growth was not the same as new mobilization. Black young men didn't just return from the army fighting; they went into the army fighting. Black workers did not need a war for democracy to discover the failures of American democracy. While black Americans adopted the new language of war, they articulated very old goals. Leotha Hackshaw, a binocular inspector, framed long-standing black hope for security and prosperity in the rhetoric of Roosevelt's Four Freedoms; "The Negro has attained one of these [religion] and part of another [free speech]. Freedom from fear and freedom from want he is fighting for now."[9] There were some important developments in black protest: hitherto-moderate race leaders applauded the aggressive protest of soldiers and workers and they connected their cause with nationalist movements around the globe. As in the First World War, black workers, black migrants, and soldiers set the agenda. But when the war was over, race leaders would move toward a more narrowly focused agenda.

Although there were significant wartime gains, they were often partial and temporary. There were plenty of setbacks too. Black men had to wait their turn to pick up new jobs. Black women struggled to get new jobs at all. Migration did not end white supremacy in the South, though it did provoke white mob violence in the North and West. Federal support for civil rights was grudging at best. Although the Supreme Court swung in favor of equal treatment, army chiefs were resistant, and an increasingly powerful conservative bloc in Congress stood guard over white supremacy throughout the war and beyond. In American popular culture, the perpetuation of many racial stereotypes in new media, such as radio and television, helped segregationists more than it hurt them. In the global arena, Roosevelt's alliance with Britain meant he kept quiet on the question of colonialism.

Above all, to focus on the eventual impact of the war is to miss the uncertainty of the time. To be sure, some were optimistic. At the end of 1943, the great jazz musician Duke Ellington put Ottley's book to music for a performance at New York's Carnegie Hall. Ellington's "New World A-Comin'" added an upbeat finale heralding a postwar "land of beautiful happiness."[10] But many feared the new world coming could turn out to be worse than the old one. By 1943, surveys suggested that only one third of black southerners thought they would be better off after the war.[11] The longer black soldiers served in the army, the more pessimistic they became.[12] Ottley feared that "the Negro stands at the door of a fretful future."[13]

African Americans had good reason to fear the impact of war. The aftermath of World War I held bloody memories. This time around, antiblack violence came sooner. During 1943 black researchers recorded 242 major racial clashes, most in the North and West. Detroit was the bloodiest. There, wrote the black journalist Louis Martin in 1944, "the Negro has lost ground during the war period despite the surface gains in employment." The "solution which seems most acceptable to the white majority is the Jim-Crow pattern of the South."[14] Many feared a segregated army would march Jim Crow into new regions, even into Europe. "The noose of prejudice," wrote Ottley, "is slowly tightening around the necks of American Negro soldiers."

What *was* different about wartime, however, was that black activists gained new power to fight for equality. From black passengers in the bus and black workers on the shop floor to black soldiers with guns in hand to black officials in the War Department, they used their new power to gain better jobs and housing, to end discrimination in the army, to seek global freedom, and to challenge racial stereotypes. America's wartime need to mobilize all its people, including the black tenth of the population, meant that black disruption mattered, so black demands could not be brushed aside. The wartime growth of black organizations and a further doubling of the circulation of black newspapers meant these demands were heard. It also enabled black activists to connect their struggles to each other and around the world. According to government polls, a startling 72 percent of black Americans read a black newspaper regularly.[15]

The new power of black protest meant that black Americans were not the only ones to fear the racial impact of war. One 1942 poll showed that less than a quarter of white Americans thought black Americans were dissatisfied. But just two years later, almost three quarters of whites thought blacks were dissatisfied.[16] Little wonder Ottley's book sold so well. It "tells a story," wrote the *New York Herald Tribune,* that "America cannot afford to ignore."[17] *New World* was followed by other wartime "blackbusters": Gunnar Myrdal's 1944 *American Dilemma,* a mammoth empirical study of race relations, Lillian Smith's rather more racy *Strange Fruit,* a novel about interracial sex, and Richard Wright's autobiography, *Black Boy.* In an urgent search for answers, a southern publisher commissioned a collection of essays by a wide range of black leaders entitled *What the Negro Wants.* As it turned out, what they all wanted was full rights of citizenship, now. In a panic, the editor distanced himself from the essayists.

Southern segregationists feared the end of an era. To be sure, a visitor passing through Bessemer, Alabama, on Independence Day 1944 would have presumed white supremacy was secure. A festive crowd cheered three black prisoners as they each tried to grab a watermelon while being pummeled by fire hoses. (Successful, they were given thirty-day reductions in their sentences, and the melons.)[18] But segregationists feared that the days of incarcerated watermelon-chasing were numbered—they feared federal interference, the loss of workers and domestics, even an armed rebellion. In a widely reported speech to Bessemer's leading men, lawyer Horace Wilkerson warned that the end was nigh. Noting that black men were brazenly blowing kisses at white college girls, Wilkerson called for "a League to Maintain White Supremacy."[19]

White residents of northern and western cities feared the influx of black migrants. Myrdal's optimism that the American dilemma—commitment to a creed of equality *and* to white superiority—was rooted in white American minds rather than the result of competition seemed well wide of the mark. One liberal editor in Hartford, Connecticut, admitted to the British journalist Alistair Cooke that "we want to keep our reputation as abolitionists and humanitarians with a conscience about the Southern Negro, but the new Negroes in town constitute a nuisance." White working men feared for their jobs, their neighborhoods, their schools, and their daughters.[20]

Few Americans were more paranoid about black unrest than J. Edgar Hoover, director of the Federal Bureau of Investigation. True to form, Hoover quickly commissioned a survey to check up on black patriotism. The results: "Negroes . . . represent a large apathetic and seditious minded group."[21] Less than a third of African Americans thought they would be worse off if Japan won the war.[22] "Black children were inclined to pretend they are Japanese soldiers."[23] A majority of black GIs in Britain believed "that this war is not worth fighting" (less than a third of white troops felt the same way). Race fights on military bases undermined their efficiency, while fights between industrial workers threatened war production. Federal officials calculated that the Detroit race riots alone lost more than a million man-hours of work. One official clipped out the *Chicago Sun* headline, "Hitler won a battle in Detroit today."[24]

This climate of fear about the "new world a-coming" explains the prominence of the "Negro question" during the war. C. S. Johnson, who spent much of the war researching black and white opinion, summed it up well. "War did not so much change the fundamental dilemmas of American race relations, or the respective viewpoints of the persons involved, so much as it brought them out into the open."[25] All sides tried to turn the exigencies of war and the language of democracy to their own advantage. Black Americans fought for full freedom and resisted those who interfered. In the South, white supremacists defended the color line. In the North, they defended the privilege of better neighborhoods and jobs. White moderates were caught in the crossfire, as the Roosevelt administration strove to keep a lid on trouble. Thus, the war was the latest battle in a long saga. It was just that this battle seemed as though it might be the decisive one. As Ottley's *Amsterdam News* warned black readers one week after Pearl Harbor, "That which you fail to get now you won't get after the war."[26]

A Place to Work, a Place to Live

A year after Pearl Harbor, government pollsters asked black Americans: "What do you feel worst about right now?" Two thirds said low wages and employment discrimination.[27] The initial wartime boom was a Jim Crow boom, ending the Depression for white workers only. One survey found that less than a third of wartime industrial firms in the Midwest employed any black men. Virtually none employed black women. By mid-1942, the black unemployment rate across the country was triple that of whites. In New York, the proportion of African Americans relying on New Deal projects for their livelihood was actually higher than during the Great Depression. To make matters worse, a growing conservative coalition of southern Democrats and northern Republicans in Congress flexed its muscle, using the excuse of a booming economy to destroy New Deal relief programs. "When the defense program got under way," wrote a despondent Robert Weaver, black Americans "seemed to be losing ground daily . . . The forces of racial reaction felt that their position was secure."[28]

The most-publicized economic protest came in a march on Washington that never happened. In May 1941, A. Philip Randolph threatened Roosevelt with a march of over 100,000 black workers unless the president outlawed discrimination in defense employment and the army. In due course the march would be remembered as the prototype for Martin Luther King's celebrated March on Washington in 1963. Randolph's insistence on an all-black movement—partly to keep Communists out of the picture—also prefigured the Black Power era. But in fact, the march was as much the end of something old as the start of something new. It followed a decade of Don't Buy Where You Can't Work campaigns and Randolph's own fight for the rights of Pullman porters. The idea of mass civil disobedience was borrowed from Gandhi, although the actual plan was suggested by an unnamed black woman at a union meeting. But unlike the New Deal protests, the threat of a public demonstration in the nation's capital forced a reluctant Roosevelt to act decisively. He issued Executive Order 8802, which required nondiscrimination in defense employment and established a Fair Employment Practice Committee (FEPC) to check for violations (though it ducked the army question). "St. Philip," the man who faced down the president, became a hero.

As it turned out, Randolph's star soon began to fade. The *Chicago De-*

fender criticized his all-black "Ku Klux Klanism in reverse." His call in 1942 for marches on city halls across the nation got little response, and the movement, out of funds, was soon eclipsed by the NAACP. By 1945 its headquarters in Harlem had become a bookshop. But this did not mark the end of the campaign for economic justice. Quite the opposite. It provided a glimpse of a much wider struggle for jobs at the factory, on the farm, and in union halls. And with the creation of the FEPC, the march on Washington reshaped—to black workers' benefit—the economic landscape on which this battle for jobs raged.

The FEPC was perhaps the most controversial federal agency in U.S. history. Segregationists resented government interference. Black activists resented Roosevelt's grudging manner and the FEPC's limitations. *Fortune* magazine agreed that it was "a compromise" put forward by "necessity rather than by political or industrial statesmanship."[29] Initially, the FEPC conducted a series of hearings in major cities. But it soon became clear the FEPC could bark but not bite—it could act only after receiving complaints, and even then it could not penalize a firm. Before a year had passed, the FEPC lost its bark as well. Roosevelt shunted it under the control of the unsympathetic War Manpower Commission. Facing renewed pressure, and with elections looming, Roosevelt re-established the FEPC in 1943 on a larger scale. But again, the FEPC had no power other than persuasion, publicity, and, *in extremis*, reporting industries to the president.

Consequently, its impact was decidedly mixed. Two unusual and contrasting cases make the point. In August 1944, white transport workers in Philadelphia, the City of Brotherly Love, went on strike when eight black men were employed as trolley operators. The FEPC referred the case to the president, who in turn passed it to the secretary of war with instructions to get the city moving. In a remarkable display of federal support for black workers' rights, army chiefs took over the transit system, threatened strikers with conscription, and then posted armed guards on trolleys. By contrast, when the FEPC referred the problem of southern railroads to the president, nothing happened. Management and unions ignored FEPC directives to promote black workers.[30]

Black Americans bombarded the FEPC with complaints about discrimination, and they were damning in their assessment of the commission's response. The FEPC's self-assessment was more upbeat, claiming that 1,723 of 3,703 valid complaints received "satisfactory adjustments"— reasonably spread across the country. It is impossible to gauge just how much credit, if any, the FEPC should get for these adjustments. It seems likely that in some cases, when management was weighing whether to hire African American workers, the threat of FEPC-generated bad publicity (and the offer of FEPC advice) may have tipped the balance in favor of hiring black workers.

The key point, though, was that at best the FEPC only tipped the balance—it was hardly decisive. More generally, Executive Order 8802 had little impact at the start of the war. Weaver worried that one survey, two months *after* the order, showed that half the openings expected to occur in war plants were barred to black workers as a matter of policy.[31] In Michigan and Indiana, nearly 90 percent of jobs were white-only. One federal investigator, John Beecher, called many training programs a "pathetic farce: the few black men who got on training programs did so for the lowest jobs, and black women rarely got on at all."[32] Discriminatory training compounded the problem that the biggest wartime demand for jobs was in precisely the sorts of skilled and semi-skilled industrial jobs from which black workers were traditionally excluded.

Ultimately, it was the escalation of the war that came to the rescue of black workers. Once the reserve of white labor—male and female—was used up, employers were forced to turn to black men. Some black Detroiters thanked Hitler for providing "more jobs than the Urban League, YMCA, and NAACP put together."[33] In the summer of 1942, African Americans were only 3 percent of the workforce in defense industries. Two years later 1.5 million black workers formed 8 percent of the defense workforce. San Francisco's mayor called for an end to the "Negro invasion," but the black population of San Francisco quadrupled nevertheless. Southern planters persuaded Roosevelt to require agricultural workers to get a "Statement of Availability" from their landlord before leaving. Many dodged it. "Defense migration" to industrial centers surpassed even the Great Migration in size and scope. By 1950 nearly two thirds of African Americans lived in cities, and one third were in cities outside the South.

Moving to the big cities and getting jobs was not the end of the struggle. To borrow Winston Churchill's wartime phrase, it was not even the beginning of the end. Initially, the only jobs available were the dirty, dangerous, poorly paid ones that white men left behind and white women couldn't fill. And white workers, South and North, were determined to keep it so. On May 24, 1943, Alabama Dry Dock in Mobile upgraded twelve black men, in a segregated gang, to become welders (alongside seven thousand white welders). The next morning, to cries of "Get every one of them Niggers off this island," white men attacked any black worker they could find. A month later on the West Coast, three hundred white workers at Vancouver shipyards stormed into the black mess hall to warn off new arrivals.[34] More commonly, skilled white workers simply refused to work alongside black men. During 1943 there was an epidemic of what the black press dubbed "hate strikes." They were effective. A black worker in Detroit acknowledged that promotion was unlikely: "Mr. Chrysler isn't going to close the plant down for one Negro."[35] Down in Mobile, a spokesman for Gulf Shipping admitted that the risk of hate strikes meant it "was much simpler not to hire them [blacks] in the first place."[36]

The situation was even worse for black women. Job openings, such as they were, mostly came in heavy industry and were reserved for black men. White men accepted unskilled black workers in their midst, just not black promotion. But, claiming the risk of venereal disease and contamination, white women (and white men on their behalf) would not tolerate black women workers at all. At Detroit's U.S. Rubber plant, two thousand white women walked off the job in March 1943 because of shared bathroom facilities.[37]

Finding a decent place to live was as hard as finding a decent job. Workers of all colors suffered the shame of America's wartime slums. But black migrants suffered most of all. One white San Franciscan asserted in 1943, "I wouldn't even want Marian Anderson as a neighbor."[38] White homeowners policed their privilege. In Los Angeles, restrictive covenants barred 95 percent of housing to black migrants—the only minority housing available there belonged to interned Japanese-Americans. Following the pattern of the tensions between African Americans and other racial minorities, black migrants refused to give up their housing after the war was over. In Chicago during 1944–1946, there were forty-six reported fire-bombings of black homes in white neighborhoods. In New York, housing officials enthusiastically supported—with tax exemptions and land grants—the Metropolitan Life Insurance Company's plan to build homes for 24,000 white people. It was not a question of white supremacy, the company president explained; it was just that "whites and blacks don't mix. Perhaps in a hundred years they will."[39]

Hemmed in to inadequate spaces, black migrants paid exorbitant rents for—to quote the deputy mayor of Los Angeles—a "life as no human is expected to endure."[40] In Mobile, one investigator found twenty-seven people sharing one toilet and one hydrant. Sleeping in "hot beds" (where lodgers took consecutive eight-hour shifts), under canvas, or in an open field was all too common. The effects on health and education were as predictable as they were depressing. Ottley reckoned "a tenement was a hundred delta cabins, plus tuberculosis."[41]

Tension over housing and jobs was as old as migration, but the sheer speed of defense migration made the problem unmanageable. To few people's surprise, there was an outpouring of racial violence in 1943. And to no one's surprise, Detroit got the worst of it. *Fortune* magazine blamed the racism of poor white men who enjoy the "satisfaction of kicking someone who is socially even lower than oneself."[42] The NAACP condemned the police, the "Gestapo of Detroit." A federal investigation found "most explanations of the hatred for Negroes finally end up in the argument that the Negro males want to . . . enjoy the pleasures of marriage with white women."[43] Whatever the cause, it was clear that the promise of wartime jobs had been overtaken by the pain of violent discrimination.

In response, African Americans resorted to a range of strategies they had followed for generations. Some fought back. On August 1, 1943, Harlem erupted in violence, following a rumor that a white policeman shot a black soldier in the back, in front of the soldier's mother, for trying to protect a black woman. But the fighting was not quite spontaneous. Armed black men had been warning, "We'll give them Detroit in reverse."[44] One middle-aged, well-paid black longshoreman, smashing a window, said, "I don't have to do this . . . I'm doing this for revenge." North and South, there were countless fights and arguments in the overcrowded wartime buses. Workers, many carrying knives, fought back on the shop floor, too. One alarmed federal official witnessed a white girl, having banged her head against a wing tip carried by black workers, pick up a sixteen-inch bolt and hit the nearest black man. "Instantly . . . whites and Negroes in the plant left their machines and formed lines." Only the military guard prevented a full-scale fight.[45]

Self-defense had a long history (and a long future) in American race relations. What was new in wartime was that employers needed black laborers and could not ignore their complaints. Black workers matched hate strikes with counter strikes. Sometimes this tit-for-tat degenerated into farce. In July 1943 in Maryland, Bethlehem Steel Company admitted three black men to a new riveter's school, one of the better-paid steel jobs. The existing riveters, all white, demanded that the school close. Management yielded. Black laborers stopped working. Management yielded again. Soon all seven thousand workers, black and white, massed in opposite corners of the yard. Management called in the police. The union worked out a compromise deal making seniority the basis for promotion, regardless of race.[46]

Worker unrest and urban violence forced city authorities to take notice, too. In the wake of the riots, virtually every city created a race relations committee. As happened often in America's urban history, white moderates sought to better manage white supremacy rather than end it. The black novelist Ralph Ellison caustically belittled the committees as "frantic efforts . . . to discover a foolproof technique of riot control."[47] He had a point. In Los Angeles, the Beverly Hills Civic Association, which sponsored the Mayor's Community Council on Anti-Racial Discrimination, simultaneously spearheaded a campaign to keep Beverly Hills "Caucasian." Frantic and self-interested as these organizations were, though, local black leaders used them to push for better jobs and housing.

Race leaders continued to put pressure on the federal government. Weaver and others lobbied from the inside. Meanwhile, complaints poured in from around the country, often couched in the language of the war effort. One black businesswoman in Indianapolis wrote bitterly about a government loan to build homes for "members of the white race." "This is an outrage . . . You boldly classify the Negro with the Japs whom he is expected to hate and fight."[48] The combination of riots, hate strikes, black votes, and the need for war mobilization pressured the government to respond. Early in the war the government decided to build the Sojourner Truth Housing Project for black workers in Detroit. After angry demonstrations by local whites the government backed off. When frustrated black Detroiters lobbied the government, held daily mass meetings, and picketed City Hall, the government reversed itself again.

Building on their later New Deal experience, black industrial workers also fought through the labor movement. Unions provided both the best and worst of times for black workers. At best, left-leaning biracial locals (mostly CIO)—from meatpackers in Chicago to tobacco stemmers in Winston-Salem—championed black rights in the workplace and in the wider community. At worst—and more commonly—locals were the institution through which white workers kept their hold on skilled jobs. Out West, Local 72 of the Boilermakers Union (which controlled two thirds of ship building) accepted black members only as auxiliary members, with no vote. When three hundred black workers refused to pay dues, they were sacked. Union leader Tom Ray rallied white workers with the familiar "Would you let a Negro marry your sister?" argument.[49]

But as black workers swelled the ranks of industrial labor, even hardened CIO and AFL officials realized that naked white supremacy was no longer in their self-interest. Though most locals retained segregated meetings, white union leaders often tempered hate strikes, which in turn allowed some black workers to take the first steps up the occupational ladder. Mainstream black leaders—many previously suspicious of labor—approved. The NAACP's Walter White proclaimed the CIO "our natural ally" in 1943. As for black workers, they were not naive. "A man doesn't kick you in the ass," said one black worker in Detroit, "and then you turn around and kiss him." Nevertheless, black union membership increased. In 1935 there were 150,000 black members of the CIO and AFL. By the end of the war, there were well over a million. In some cities, such as Detroit, the labor–civil rights alliance became the foundation of black activism during the war and beyond.

The vast majority of black workers—especially women and rural workers—were not covered by the labor movement. But they, too, turned the war to their advantage. Black laundrywomen in Atlanta won a 25 percent pay increase at the end of 1944 after a year-long dispute. (This was not as generous as it sounds. By 1945, domestics still received only about one eighth of the average pay of white working women.)[50] In the countryside, planters retained their supremacy and pocketed most of the profits from the wartime tripling in the price of cotton. Yet even in Mississippi, as one in ten black laborers left the delta, the balance of power shifted slightly. A rejuvenated Southern Tenant Farmers' Union presented planter abuses to the government and even organized a picking strike. Ultimately, planters held much greater sway over the government than rural workers. They also undermined the STFU by forcing thousands of croppers to join their own, decidedly conservative, union. Still, the government's raising of the wartime pay ceiling in September 1944 doubled the wages of cottonpickers. Many workers refused to pick even at this new rate—and planters complained that up to a third of the cotton harvest was left to rot in the fields.[51]

At the end of the war, Weaver was pleased with black progress: wartime changes "represented more industrial and occupational diversification for Negroes than had occurred in the seventy-five preceding years." Black unemployment fell from nearly a million in 1940 to 151,000 in 1944.[52] Black Americans began to move into semi-skilled and skilled occupations, and even unskilled work paid well during wartime. The average income of urban blacks more than doubled. Yet Weaver also drew attention to important limits. The actual proportion of skilled and semi-skilled workers among the growing black industrial workforce changed little. The number of black female domestics decreased, but the proportion of domestics who were black increased. And a rise in salaries was more than offset by the problem of poor housing.

The War's Greatest Scandal

In his contribution to *What the Negro Wants* in 1944, A. Philip Randolph wrote: "Pivotal and central to the whole struggle in the Negro liberation movement at this time is the abolition of Jim Crow in the armed forces."[53] Coming from the pen of a man committed to the labor struggle, Randolph's words were all the more significant. The black press devoted far more column inches to black soldiers than to the war itself. "What made Harlem mad?" asked one federal investigator after the riot there. Answer: the "treatment of Negro soldiers."[54]

Civil rights leaders believed that winning the right to fight would advance the struggle for equality more generally. As ever, Du Bois put it best: "This is no fight merely to wear a uniform. This is a struggle for status, a struggle to take democracy off of parchment and give it life."[55] Before the fighting started, black leaders sensed Jim Crow's vulnerability in the army, just as in defense employment. With the 1940 elections looming, Roosevelt made his customary symbolic concessions on the race issue. He ordered the recruitment of black troops in proportion to the population, he appointed the forthright lawyer William Hastie to a new position as "Negro civilian aide to the secretary of war," and he promoted the army's most senior black soldier, Benjamin Davis, to the rank of full general.

By the same token, race leaders feared that a defeat in the army would set back the wider war on white supremacy. They soon realized that Jim Crow was well dug in. Just one day after Pearl Harbor, army chiefs warned a group of black leaders that the "army is not a sociological laboratory." Military wisdom held that black soldiers were inferior fighters; that military efficiency demanded stability; and that military commanders should thus defer to racism in the ranks. One 1944 internal review concluded: "Segregation makes difficulties, but mixing units would create even more."[56] In turn, Roosevelt deferred to his generals. Although the army recruited nearly a million black Americans, they were put in segregated units, and virtually all were assigned to service details rather than combat duty. Initially, the marines and air force took no black recruits at all. It seemed to be the Civil War and World War I all over again.

Randolph called Jim Crow in uniform "the war's greatest scandal." In a military hospital in Tampa, Florida, German POWs refused to work in the kitchen because they would have to serve black as well as white patients. To appease the Germans, the black patients were duly separated into a new mess hall.[57] Worse still, Jim Crow in uniform marched across the United States, into segregated camps from Staten Island to Alaska. To the horror of civil rights leaders, Jim Crow even invaded North Africa and Europe. From Morocco in March 1943, one captain wrote of three fellow officers at a restaurant loudly forcing the proprietor to "kick the black bastards out." "This, I repeat, was only one of many incidents."[58] In Britain, when rural police arrested copulating couples for damaging the crops, they seemed to think that interracial couples were the only ones who did the damage. Worst of all, black men in uniform were attacked, off and on base. The Purple Heart–winning Mississippi soldier Henry Murphy said he feared America's 1st Infantry Division more than the Germans. "They were castrating [us]—hit your seeds with a razor."[59] There were reports of white children throwing stones at black soldiers.

With guns in hand and the training to use them, black soldiers returned fire. As new recruits told the black journalist H. C. Brearley, "When we get to the front the first thing we'll do is to shoot our white officers; then we'll start shooting Japs and Nazis."[60] Fights off base were legion. From Louisiana to Leicester, England, a pattern was established: local police or white soldiers would beat a black soldier for being with a white woman or protecting a black woman, and then battle would be joined. In Mississippi in May 1943, skirmishing escalated into virtual civil war. The previous fall, the notoriously belligerent black 364th Infantry Regiment had wreaked havoc in Phoenix. For reasons best known to themselves, army chiefs transferred the 364th to Camp Von Dorn in Mississippi, the very heart of white supremacy. Right after the regiment arrived in late May, the local sheriff murdered one private. On their first Saturday night at the base, a hundred black soldiers marched in formation to "clean up" the nearby town of Centreville. From this point on details are confused. Military records show that four black soldiers were killed in a shootout with police. Rumors spread that hundreds were killed. Black newspapers reported further killings that summer—allegedly because a 364th solider said "yes" instead of "yes sir" to a white man.[61]

Black soldiers volunteered their support to local community protesters. Time and again they joined the battle over housing, the ballot box, and segregation. Simply by walking down a street (worried whites called it strutting) they made an impression. Decades after the war, black residents of Savannah, Georgia, remembered with pride the night that troops drove into town, set up their machine guns, and forced city policemen to run for cover. Black soldiers made an impact in communities beyond the United States, too. In Britain, the question of race had traditionally been raised in the far reaches of the empire rather than at home. In 1940 there were fewer than eight thousand black Britons. But the arrival of 130,000 black GIs forced Britons to take a position on race. In general, the upper classes supported Jim Crow, while working-class Britons sided with black GIs against white soldiers, whom they regarded as insufferably arrogant.[62] The births of a thousand brown-skinned wartime babies tell their own story.

While black soldiers fought, black leaders lobbied the president and the War Department. Walter White traveled overseas to collect, and then publicize, soldiers' complaints. But the key pressure came from within the War Department. At the start of the war this hardly seemed possible. Roosevelt created the post of Negro aide to divert complaints from his own in-box. The first aide, William Hastie, resigned in disgust when he discovered that the Committee on Army Race Relations had been set up without his knowledge, and without him on it. But his successor, Truman Gibson, served on the committee and stayed the course, making himself such an irritant that he helped prod the army forward.

Gibson was a jack-of-all-trades. After growing up in the South, he moved to Chicago where—among other things—he took on civil rights cases as a lawyer and ran the Negro World Fair of 1940 (a Miss Nude Negro America section ensured extensive publicity) before Hastie recruited him as his deputy. After the war he would manage boxer Joe Louis, help launch television's Friday night fights, be convicted for extortion, and then return to the law. With a precise mind, a flair for presentation, and a very thick skin, Gibson was an ideal person to deal with the military machine.

Judging that "no revolution was possible in the army," he aimed for a "slow chipping away at [army] attitudes." He soon realized the army's public egalitarian stance was not matched in private—he saw a memo where Roosevelt scribbled "ok" on the War Department's policy "not to intermingle colored and white enlisted personnel."[63] In response, Gibson played the army at its own game. In public he was unfailingly loyal, so much so that the black press criticized him at times. But in private, he "chipped away" at the wall of discrimination with the persistence of a prisoner seeking freedom. Through internal memos, Gibson highlighted countless cases of discrimination and trumpeted black achievements. At one press conference, he quoted a training officer's endorsement of integration. "It don't matter who's firing next to you when you're both killing Krauts."[64] The "getting along" bit stretched the truth. Censorship reports on GI mail in Europe found that where white or black GIs referred to each other, 90 percent of comments were unfavorable. But the argument held a certain logic in wartime.

Gibson's strongest card, though, was not logic but the anger of black soldiers. As early as 1942, he warned Secretary of War Stimson that many black soldiers "would much rather fight their domestic enemies than their foreign foe."[65] Initially, army leaders thought they could contain the trouble, but by the time Gibson was promoted this was clearly wishful thinking. Some officers confiscated ammunition from black soldiers guarding Japanese POWs for fear they would join together. Thus, army leaders were open to advice, especially from a loyal official. At Gibson's prompting, the army committee on race relations called for equal access to camp facilities and to buses from camps to local towns.

Ultimately, as with defense employment, it took the demands of war to open the door for major black advances. The generals needed more troops to fight, and they needed their troops to stop fighting one another. Thus, sending black troops to Europe and North Africa solved two problems in one go. The first officer to use black soldiers in combat was General John C. Lee, grandson of Confederate General Robert E. Lee. No advocate of race equality, Lee was prepared nevertheless to use black troops to fill spaces in his regiments. General Dwight Eisenhower, commander of European forces, overruled him, but two black units still fought on the frontline. In inimitable style, General Patton gave his seal of approval to a black tank unit. "I don't give a damn what color you are as long as you . . . kill those sons-of-bitches."

Many others did give a damn. By the end of the war progress was both limited and confusing. The navy and air force accepted black recruits, but on a segregated basis (the Tuskegee-trained pilots would shoot down over 100 German aircraft by the end of the war). Back home, on military bases outside the South, black soldiers often gained access to all facilities. Yet injured black veterans still could not get a haircut at the government's Walter Reed Hospital in the nation's capital, because barbers were for whites only. The battle for the army would continue past the war.

A Triple V

Walter White claimed that each black American during the war sought "simple justice . . . not alone for himself, but for all other disadvantaged peoples of the earth."[66] Given how difficult it was proving to be to get simple justice in Detroit and Alabama, it might seem fanciful for White to have raised his eyes to Delhi and Algeria too. But this was no idle rhetoric. White, a pragmatist, had been following the mood of black Americans, who—building on recent interest in Ethiopia—were connecting their battles at home with anti-colonial struggles as never before. The *Chicago Defender* ran as many editorials on the mistreatment of colored nations as the mistreatment of African Americans. For the first time, most major black newspapers filed reports from overseas correspondents, who joined a dense nexus of colored journalists from London to Lagos. In surveys during late 1942, nearly 90 percent of black Americans supported Gandhi's call for the British to "Quit India" immediately (less than half of white Americans did).

The Council on African Affairs (CAA)—the leading institution devoted to anti-colonialism—was founded to little acclaim in 1937. But the war gave it prominence and credibility, as did its chairman, Paul Robeson. A supremely gifted athlete, singer, actor, lawyer, and orator (to mention a few of his talents), the dashing Robeson was America's most famous black celebrity, seemingly admired and desired in equal measure. By the outbreak of war, Robeson was probably the most famous black American in the world. (The fact that he spoke fifteen languages endeared him to local people on his travels.) Other celebrities, including the singer Marian Anderson, were more than happy to help raise money for the cause. Meanwhile, a galaxy of black political stars joined the CAA leadership. California publisher Charlotta Bass, black women's organizer Mary Bethune, and the venerated W. E. B. Du Bois all worked for the council—Du Bois as Robeson's deputy.

Thus, the wartime Double V was really a Triple V—victory for democracy abroad, victory for democracy at home, and victory against colonialism everywhere. The sociologist Horace Cayton wrote in 1943, "The Negro had placed his problems in a new and larger frame of reference . . . through an identification with the exploited peoples of the world."[67] This larger frame of reference still had vestiges of Garvey's and Turner's presumption of American leadership. Richard Wright judged "the Negro in America" as the most important "phase of this general problem . . . telescoping the longings in the lives of a billion colored subject colonial people into a symbol."[68] But more than before, black Americans drew strength from abroad. America's black press applauded bus boycotts in South Africa, strikes in Uganda, and colored trade unionists at the World Trade Union Congress. They juxtaposed stories of black candidates in Massachusetts and Vermont winning elections to their legislatures for the first time with news of Africans winning their first elections in Kenya, and islanders winning their first majority in Barbados.

Joining the worldwide struggle radicalized mainstream American civil rights organizations. White threw his support behind the CAA and brought Du Bois back into the NAACP, which awarded Robeson its prestigious Spingarn Medal. White was an avowed supporter of integration and suspicious of left-leaning politics. The CAA, by contrast, reorganized in 1942 to become an exclusively black-led organization that supported armed resistance struggles. Its leaders understood racial oppression in class terms and saw the global labor struggle as the way to oppose it. Robeson himself had met with the Abraham Lincoln brigade of African American volunteer fighters during the Spanish Civil War and had forged a close alliance with striking miners in Wales. Many of the CAA's leaders, not least Robeson, were moving toward a Marxist analysis of white supremacy. The CAA did not hide its links to Communist activists. In short, the war pushed left-leaning politics further into the mainstream of black activism—though the Cold War would soon send it back to the margins.

The black press also took advantage of America's global ambitions to challenge white public opinion. Editors used the loathing of fascism to discredit their opponents just as often as they used the language of democracy to justify their goals. The essence of the Double V was not merely that black activists were on the side of American ideals but that white supremacists were little different from the Nazis. Langston Hughes wrote, "You tell me that Hitler is a mighty bad man / He must have taken lessons from the Ku Klux Klan."[69] Newspapers juxtaposed stories of Nazi atrocities in Europe with news of supremacist outrages in the South. Thus, in different ways, the languages of anti-fascism, democracy, and anti-colonialism empowered workers, soldiers, and other activists. After all, no one read black newspapers more avidly than officials in the War Department. And black leaders knew that government officials worried about America's image abroad. One federal report into the race riots concluded, "Axis radios have exactly the information they need to discredit the United Nations Four Freedoms Policy."[70]

Selling the Race

In his contribution to *What the Negro Wants,* the black historian Rayford Logan called for economic justice, army integration, and political equality. Then he told a story: "A young woman informed me in all seriousness that her whole attitude changed when she saw a colored girl in a class at Columbia University wearing better clothes than she did."[71] Logan's logic was simple. Much of the problem of race started in the white mind, and if white people would just recognize the humanity and talent of black Americans, then the color line would surely fade.

Logan was out of step with most black Americans at the grassroots, who saw racism in terms of competition for resources. But he was in step with white liberal intellectuals such as Gunnar Myrdal and with black intellectuals of the past—not least during the Harlem Renaissance. And it was certainly true that "What Every White Man Thinks He Knows about Negroes," to quote the sociologist Guy Johnson, affirmed race discrimination in practice: "The Negro is lazy . . . cannot manage complicated machinery . . . is dirty, smelly . . . fond of loud colors . . . a naturalized clown . . . inordinate sexual passion . . . His mind works like a child's."[72]

The coming of war offered hope of change. Black soldiers and defense workers provided compelling propaganda. New media—especially movies, the radio, and glossy magazines—provided vast outlets for this material. Intellectual culture had already changed. Surveying recent findings on "race inferiority" in the journal *Scientific Monthly* in 1943, W. Krogman concluded, "In words of one syllable *there is no such thing*."[73] It was time to sell the race.

Civil rights leaders and artists peddled their propaganda. The National Urban League established connections with major radio networks. Walter White courted Hollywood, telling NAACP colleagues that the "treatment of the Negro in the motion pictures . . . takes rank over some other phases of our work," and telling the Screen Writers Guild that the "media by which ideas are formed and propagated is more crucial than the making of guns and planes."[74] The consistent aim was to portray black men (and it was mostly about men) as worthy soldiers, high achievers, and everyday guys.

The movie *The Negro Soldier* did all three. When Gibson suggested making a movie to improve the morale of black soldiers, officials at the Office of War Information were enthusiastic. It hardly seemed a risk—they insisted it avoid contentious subjects (like segregation) and planned to show it to new black recruits only. But the movie came back like a boomerang to strike a blow against army segregation. Officials handed the film to Frank Capra, the greatest moviemaker of his day, who in turn delegated it to Carlton Moss, a black producer known for his patriotic Harlem revue *A Salute to the Negro Soldier*. But Moss crafted a script that would "ignore what's wrong with the Army and tell what's right with my people." *The Negro Soldier* both ignored army segregation and made a mockery of it. Against a background of stirring music, patriotic black soldiers were shown in thoughtful worship and on the shooting range. They read poetry and chased only black girls (and even then ever so politely). Moss also inserted a review of historic black patriots, contemporary scientists, and lawyers. The black man didn't just step out of his usual place, he leapt out.

Civil rights leaders knew that the 43-minute film, to quote White, "does not tell the truth" about racial discrimination. But they believed it the best they could get, and demanded the movie be shown widely. The army was caught in a trap of its own making. The War Department made the movie compulsory viewing for all new recruits, black and white, and put it on general release. Not surprisingly, the department did nothing to promote the movie. But it had Capra's name on it, and White called in his Hollywood contacts to endorse the film. Harry Cohn, president of Columbia Pictures, described *The Negro Soldier* as "the greatest war department picture ever made."[75] NAACP branches called on theaters to show the film. Some four thousand "white theaters" showed a shortened version.[76] In Manhattan, *The Negro Soldier* played alongside *Snow White*.[77] This was far from being a blockbuster. But compared with previous attempts to praise black men on the silver screen, this was quite a triumph.

Nothing in mainstream popular culture matched *The Negro Soldier*, though there were some positive signs. In the movie *Sahara* (1943), an African soldier called Tamboul (Rex Ingram) helped a lost tank crew (led by Humphrey Bogart's character) find water. In Harlem, children watching the movie cheered. On radio, NBC broadcast the landmark radio series *Freedom's People* documenting the contribution of African Americans to American life.[78] The popular *Ladies Home Journal* even ran a positive story about a middle-class army wife and her daughters, "Meet the Hinksons of Philadelphia."[79] But a few pioneer programs and articles did not herald a rush of egalitarian productions.

The government did far more to camouflage black soldiers than praise them. Black faces were deleted from newsreels heading to white theaters. On propaganda posters, the only colored faces to appear regularly were those of Japanese soldiers. And in the wider popular culture, the black soldier was conspicuous by his absence. During the final year and a half of war, when black soldiers were in combat, the influential *Life* magazine published a mere ten pictures of black men in uniform, out of some fourteen thousand photographs in total. Most of these ten pictures were very small. One black soldier carried an accordion; none carried weapons.[80] In the national press, there was a revival of stories about "savage," cowardly, or incompetent African American soldiers. Polls found that less than half of white Americans thought that African Americans were doing enough to support the war.[81]

Shapers of the popular culture did little to promote the image of black civilians either. Movie moguls were more concerned about profits and southern censors than taking a lead on race. For every *Sahara*, there were many more films like Universal's *Captive Wild Woman* (1943), where a mad scientist transforms a gorilla into an attractive mulatto woman— a stereotype compounded by her regression to an ape as soon as the thought of sex crosses her mind. For children, Warner Bros. put out a popular cartoon, *Coal Black and de Sebben Dwarves* (1943). The aim was patriotic—and Coal Black's pigtails turned into U.S. flags at the end—but African Americans were incensed at the caricatures. A Columbia University study in 1945 found that of one hundred black appearances in wartime films, seventy-five perpetuated old stereotypes, thirteen were neutral, and only twelve were positive.[82]

The negative image on the silver screen was reflected across American popular culture. By far the most famous black character on radio, Rochester of the hit comedy *The Jack Benny Show,* sent decidedly mixed messages. Played by an African American actor, Rochester was integrated into the cast and intelligent. Nevertheless, he was a domestic servant whose sexual prowess was the foil for Benny's problems in that department. "The gags about gin-drinking and crap-shooting are usually good," the actor and director Orson Welles warned Benny, but they "perpetuate a dangerous myth."[83] National magazines were little better. *Life* published fewer pictures of black Americans as skilled workers or at leisure in the final eighteen months of the war than across a similar period at the end of the 1930s. As for readers of *Ladies Home Journal,* after meeting the Hinksons in 1942 they did not meet a single black character during the rest of the war.

Because of the massive growth of popular media, more white Americans actually saw more negative stereotypes of African Americans during the war years than ever before. Far from enabling black Americans to break out of their assigned place in American society, the rise of popular culture locked them in. Only the great black entertainers, such as boxer Joe Louis and musician Duke Ellington, regularly crossed over into white popular culture. By becoming wartime patriots, they became national heroes. Before joining the army, Louis pummeled Hitler's hero Max Schmeling in a world heavyweight bout that was billed as America vs. the Nazis. Ellington became a fixture on army radio. Both hoped to use their popularity to shame white supremacy. "You can say anything you want on the trombone," explained Ellington, "but you gotta be careful with words."[84]

Yet even the rise of black entertainers did not, of itself, undermine wider stereotypes. One *New York Times* sports reporter considered the question of Louis's "Color? Only in the tint of his skin. He doesn't drink or smoke. He doesn't turn racing cars upside-down. He doesn't sing . . . He never has been sued for breach of promise."[85] Indeed, praise of black entertainers, and only entertainers, confirmed racial difference more than it challenged it; Ellington complained that "the Negro is not merely a singing and dancing wizard."[86] It suggested race hierarchy too. In 1941 sports writer Dean Cromwell mused that the black man's "ability to sprint and jump was a life-and-death matter to him in the jungle."[87] It was no coincidence that jazz and boxing had associations with low culture.

In any case, white propagandists also used the war to shore up the color line. Thomas Dixon's 1939 *The Flaming Sword* (his twenty-eighth and last novel) saw a combination of black Americans, Communists, and assorted bad guys try to overthrow the American government. War against Japan reinforced the idea of nonwhite deviousness and danger— Langston Hughes wondered, "How come we did not try [atom bombs] out on Germany?"[88] Southern politicians played the patriotism card to defend the color line—bus signs in Charleston, South Carolina, urged passengers to observe Jim Crow laws, since "co-operation . . . will make the war shorter."[89] They played the victim card too, against government interference and black aggression.

For segregationists, civil rights inevitably meant sexual wrongs. Asked by C. S. Johnson to comment on the Negro and the war, the secretary of Birmingham's Chamber of Commerce replied, "There's no white man down here going to let his daughter sleep with a nigger . . . The war can go to hell."[90] What the wartime black writer Sterling Brown called the "black herring of intermarriage" had long been a powerful supremacist cry. But in the turmoil of war, southern supremacists found it easy to portray any step toward black rights—be it the FEPC or black voting—as a leap toward the bedroom. In response, race leaders did not deny—as they often had in the past—that they sought social equality. Instead, they pointed out, to quote Brown again, that "crowded buses" are not "marriage bureaus." To those forewarning the fall of southern white civilization, Brown scoffed, "Vicksburg will decline to the level of . . . New York."[91] Mockery was a well-established survival strategy. But it didn't erase the color line.

The enduring strength of segregationist ideology had practical consequences. In 1944 a team of black sociologists found that "nigger-baiting" had been revived in southern elections. In fact, many—maybe most— white southerners disavowed Klan extremism. Leading white moderates formed the Southern Regional Council, to call for fairer treatment of African Americans. Yet the supremacists' argument that supporters of interracial organizations were really seekers of interracial orgies, as ridiculous as it may seem in hindsight, was hard to rebuff at the time. White reckoned "the highest casualty rate of the war seems to be that of Southern white liberals." Even Eleanor Roosevelt advised, in an essay entitled "If I Were a Negro," that "things such as social relationships might well wait."[92] But caught up in the turmoil of war, many moderate black leaders were no longer willing to wait, or to be told what to wait for. The old way of managing white supremacy, through a judicious mix of paternalism and control, was out of date. As the middle ground between civil rights activists and segregationists gave way, confrontation in the South, rather than gradual change, seemed ever more likely.

In the nation as a whole, there is little evidence that the wartime image of black Americans improved dramatically.[93] One postwar poll found that 53 percent of whites thought black Americans were "potentially" as intelligent as whites, a step up from 42 percent in the only wartime poll to ask the question, in 1942. But "potential" was not the same as the end of racism. British journalist Alistair Cooke was struck by "the persistence of lazy clichés among the whites," especially in northern cities.[94] Federal investigators reported a Detroit policeman telling a group of black children, "Get out of here, you little black bastards before I kick you in the ass."[95] Nor did "potential" mean a willingness to change practice. In the North and West, anti-black sentiment grew in response to black migration and the scramble for resources. By the end of the war, more than three in four white Americans supported residential segregation—more in the North than the South.[96] A majority thought job openings should go to white workers first. Even when black and white workers labored alongside one another, it didn't automatically result in camaraderie. As the black writer Constance Nichols put it in a poem about the Civil Service in 1945:

> You send your memos on a metal tray,
> And coldly kill each overture I've tried.
> Why hope to rid charred continents of gloom
> 'Till *we* have learned to smile across a room?[97]

Leading the Race, Following the Masses

Under Jim Crow, many prominent race leaders had emphasized respectability. Some of this persisted during the war. The *Chicago Defender* warned Negro "zoot-suiters" to mind their "P's and Q's." The Double V was partly an attempt, to quote the black journalist George Schuyler, "to bag concessions out of the white folks while holding the disgruntled Negro masses in check."[98] But the "Negro masses" were soon very much out of check. The new symbols of race protest were young, militant, and decidedly macho. Those organizations and race leaders that wanted to prosper had to get in line.

Consider, for example, Adam Clayton Powell Jr., the first black man elected to New York City Council (in 1941) and the first black congressman from the Northeast (elected 1944). According to Ottley, who knew him well, the light-skinned, blue-eyed Powell was "born with a silver spoon in his mouth which he is using as a lever to lift himself up in the world." As pastor of Harlem's Abyssinian Baptist Church, the Protestant church with the largest membership in the United States, Powell had a ready-made power base. Powell also had Garvey's flair for showmanship, with the added bonus that he, unlikely Garvey, was well over six feet tall and extremely handsome. Women sometimes called him "Mr. Jesus." He started the war married to former Cotton Club dancer Isabel Washington and ended it married to jazz singer Hazel Scott, famous for her hit "Tico Tico."[99]

Powell's showbiz status alone, though, did not guarantee his popularity. As Horace Cayton observed "The Negro lower class is as cynical in its appraisal of Negro 'big shots' as it is of white folks."[100] The secret of Powell's success was that he embraced the militancy of wartime Harlem. He compared racist New York police to Nazi stormtroopers. He shared a platform with Liu Liang-Mo and Krishnalal Shridharani, well-known Chinese and Indian freedom fighters.[101] He worked with black Communist activists. It was a wise choice—along with Los Angeles, Harlem was the main urban hotbed of black left radicalism. When Powell left the New York City Council, the Georgia-born, Harvard-educated black Communist Ben Davis won his vacant seat. Davis's wartime pamphlet, *Lynching Northern Style: Police Brutality,* spoke to the concerns of many. Powell claimed later that "we used the Communists more than they used us."[102]

The war's biggest winner, though, was the NAACP. Having struggled during the 1920s and much of the 1930s, it ended the war as the undisputed champion of black rights organizations. This was no accident. Walter White, whose skin was even lighter, eyes even bluer, and ego as big as Powell's, astutely repositioned the NAACP. Previously hesitant about confrontational protest, White eagerly partnered with Randolph for the March on Washington. He praised militant unions and the anti-colonial struggle, fought for black soldiers, and backed the New Crowd militants in many local branches. In a sense, White became a race leader by following the masses. And as the masses gained in power, the NAACP reaped the benefits. With higher wages brought about by war mobilization, more people could afford NAACP membership fees and finance litigation.

This is not to downplay the role of national spokesmen and organizations entirely. White was an enthusiastic lobbyist. The NAACP's legal arm enjoyed a string of successes, winning a remarkable 90 percent of cases before federal courts during the war era. *Gaines v. Canada* (1938) ruled that states must provide education for black graduates; *Smith v. Allwright* (1944) outlawed the all-white Democratic primary in the South (a ruse to keep black voters from the elections that mattered). In *James v. Marinship Corp.* (1944), the California Supreme Court ruled that the Boilermakers Union—as the only union on offer to workers in the industry—must accept black members. With no fear of re-election, and with no blocking southern vote, justices played fast and loose with precedent. In practice, many of their decisions had little immediate impact. A decade after *Gaines,* for example, not a single southern state had admitted a black student to a doctoral program. But these cases gave optimism for the future and allowed NAACP lawyers to link with local communities in the present.

As the NAACP rose, other organizations fell, and once-prominent black women's organizations fell furthest of all. On the ground, black soldiers and male workers were the new symbols of protest, and high politics remained a man's game. Yet no one was more responsible for the growth of the NAACP than a woman organizer, Ella Baker, director of branches from 1943. Baker longed to place the NAACP "on the lips of all people, the uncouth MASSES included."[103] Born in the South, Baker moved to Depression-era Harlem as an adult and became involved in cooperatives, education, and unemployed councils. By the time she joined the NAACP, Baker was convinced that effective leadership came from local people. As she traveled the country, she went where other NAACP leaders wouldn't go. One man in a Baltimore nightclub told her, "You certainly have some nerve coming up here, but I'm going to join that doggone organization." Her leadership training programs inspired, among others, a young Montgomery seamstress called Rosa Parks. Her job done, Baker left the organization soon after the war, having become disillusioned with the NAACP's limitations and above all with White. "He was very much in love with himself."[104] She would help launch another grassroots wave of protest, by students, a generation later.

Thus, the absence of women's organizations did not simply mean the absence of black women activists. Across the country, women persuaded men to take a militant stand at the workplace, they used the household budget to promote community goals, and some confronted segregation. Irene Morgan was not a member of any protest organization; the 27-year-old mother was just trying to make ends meet as a cleaner. On a stifling hot summer day in 1944, she boarded a Greyhound bus in Virginia, heading home after a check-up following her recent miscarriage. Half an hour later, when a white couple boarded the bus, the driver told Morgan to move further back. Feeling unwell, she refused. At the next town, a police officer appeared with a warrant for Morgan's arrest. She ripped it up and threw it out the window. When the officer tried to pull her off the bus, she kicked him between the legs. He staggered away. Another policeman scuffled with her and took her to jail. With the backing of the NAACP, Morgan sued, and two years later won her case, *Morgan v. Virginia,* in the Supreme Court. Her actions prepared the way for the famous Freedom Rides of 1961.

Nonetheless, the marginalization of black women's organizations, and of black women within organizations run by men, meant that the call for black women's rights also became marginalized. The legacy would be a postwar generation of protest dedicated to race rights rather than women's rights, and a postwar feminism that catered to white women only. There was also a dark side to the celebration of macho: during this period, black women writers movingly discussed, often in sympathetic terms, domestic violence by men who were unable to vent their anger against white tormentors at work.

The changing fortunes of the major organizations showed that ultimately the key struggles for racial equality occurred at the local level. In turn, the black press, black organizations, and black family networks connected local activists with the nation and the wider world. Each state, each town, each neighborhood had its own story to tell. In Washington and St. Louis, a newly formed pacifist organization, the Committee (later the Congress) on Racial Equality (CORE), experimented with sit-ins at segregated restaurants. In Hillburn, New York, black children boycotted their inadequate school and demanded admittance to the better-equipped local white school. After an NAACP appeal to the state board of education, and rallies in Harlem, they won, although—in a portent of things to come—white parents promptly moved their children to nearby private schools.[105] In Texas, black voters tested *Smith v. Allwright.* Across the breadth of a nation at war, black Americans had more resources to organize and more power to disrupt. Whether they would retain that power in peacetime was a different question.

Fighting to Win the Peace

In 1945, using $500 that he borrowed against his mother's furniture, the black publishing entrepreneur John H. Johnson launched the first black glossy magazine, *Ebony.* Its aim was not to "get all hot and bothered about the race question . . . EBONY will try to mirror the happier side of Negro life—the positive, everyday achievements from Harlem to Hollywood."[106] Actually, *Ebony* featured achievements that were anything but everyday. First features included an armless businessman in Chicago and a deaf book salesman in Oklahoma. But its format—glitzy interviews with black entertainment stars and a catalog of rags-to-riches stories— was a hit. *Ebony* became the best-selling black magazine in America.

Even so, the glitzy optimism of *Ebony* could not hide the "unhappier side of Negro life." Each issue carried a single page of serious editorial comment tucked between photographs of smiling celebrities and dream homes. Like a jolt from a daydream, the first editorials were unfailingly despondent. "What are the bulletins from America? Not good. The tap-tap-tap of the news ticker spells out a hymn of hate." The Klan was on the rise. "In New York and Cleveland, students fresh from history classes on the Bill of Rights have clashed in pitched battles because of different skin color."[107] Black housing in Chicago was worse than Calcutta. Massive black unemployment loomed. Unless America created "sixty million jobs," it would be "a lonesome tramp down a lonesome track once again."[108]

As for the rest of the black press, it remained very hot and bothered indeed about the race question. Typical end-of-war headlines ran "Race Discrimination Ends—In Germany, Not America." There was little comment on America's triumph (although newspapers expressed pride in the fact that 179,000 black workers had helped make the atom bomb). But there was outrage that black soldiers who fought on the beaches in Europe were not able to bathe on the beaches in New Jersey. Attention turned to the immediate postwar peace. Across the country, activists sought to preserve wartime gains at work, at home, in the army, in the government, and in the global anti-imperialist struggle.[109]

As with the war, peace offered black Americans both promise and problems. The promise included a new language of rights, a record of service, growing electoral influence upon northern Democrats, and America's need to project positive race relations during the Cold War. The first moves of Harry Truman—who succeeded FDR after his death in 1945, just six months into his fourth term—offered hope. Truman had no track record on civil rights. Black Americans were, to quote *PM* magazine, "just mild about Harry." But prodded by unprecedented demonstrations outside the White House, the importance of black votes, wartime talk of race justice, and Soviet criticism of America's race problem, he quickly (unlike Roosevelt) became a forthright advocate of civil rights (though his wife, unlike Roosevelt's, tried to hold him back). In December 1946 Truman created a President's Committee on Civil Rights. The following year he urged Congress to implement the committee's report *To Secure These Rights*—calling for equal opportunities in housing and employment and stronger federal agencies to protect civil rights.

The problem was, most wartime advances, such as they were, had resulted from wartime necessity. As the Double V campaign became a single V, necessity evaporated, and with it went the power of blacks to disrupt the war effort. At the local level, if World War I was any guide, the imminent return of veterans and the inevitable fight for peacetime jobs heralded trouble. A *Newsweek* poll showed that two thirds of white Americans expected postwar race relations to take a turn for the worse. In Congress, the conservative coalition of southern Democrats and northern Republicans finished the war with a larger majority than it had when the war began. As for the president, his new doctrine to challenge Communism posed as many constraints as opportunities. He became the first of many presidents to subordinate civil rights to anti-Communism. The hounding of Communists at home meant the government turned against some of the most forthright advocates of race equality—advocates who had also pressed mainstream organizations to focus on workers' rights as well as civil rights. Truman's attorney general collated a list of "subversive" organizations which included the National Negro Congress. Any government employee who had ever been a member of an organization on the list could be investigated.

The promise and problems facing black activists explain the rollercoaster course of protest in the very first years after the war. Initially, campaigners seemed poised to make great gains. But they were soon rebuffed. And as a result, the nature of protest would begin to change, setting a trend for the decade to come. Black workers, soldiers, and anticolonial campaigners would no longer set the agenda. To consolidate the NAACP's mainstream position, its leaders would retreat from their wartime emphasis on the workplace, self-defense, and global solidarity—and loosen the connection between the American freedom struggle and anticolonialism.

This pattern of promise, rebuff, and retreat held true for both the issues of human rights in the new world order and workers' rights in America. In the case of the global anti-racist struggle, the idealistic turn of international politics augured well at first. In 1945, the United Nations Educational, Scientific and Cultural Organization (UNESCO) declared that racial theory was not only unsupportable, it was to blame for World War II. The United Nations, formed in San Francisco by fifty nations in May and June 1945, was intended to build a more secure and better world. The U.S. delegation invited the NAACP to send three delegates— White took Du Bois and Bethune—to act as consultants.

High expectations for San Francisco made the outcome all the more disappointing. When the UN tempered its support for decolonization and human rights, the NAACP delegation was livid. White called South African premier Smuts—who led the obstructionists—a "jackass." To mock Smuts's racism, Du Bois told the story of being mistaken for Smuts at the conference. White complained that the State Department used the NAACP consultants as "window dressing," just one of forty-two organizations invited to act as consultants to the U.S. delegation, which included the chair of the Senate Foreign Relations Committee, Tom Connally, an ardent Texan segregationist. The U.S. delegation even opposed immediate independence for subject territories. The army wanted a free hand over nonwhite territories in the Pacific, and the State Department sided with European colonial powers in the standoff with Russia. Three years later, the United States was instrumental in eliminating social and economic rights from the UN Declaration and Covenant on Human Rights.

Despite the San Francisco debacle, black organizations continued to appeal to the UN. In 1947 the NAACP wrote a lengthy petition entitled *An Appeal to the World,* which called on the UN to intervene in American race relations. The appeal marked the beginning of the NAACP's Cold War campaign to press the United States to practice at home what it preached abroad. But it also marked an end to its wartime embrace of global anti-racist movements. The new focus was on civil rights rather than human rights, on African Americans' identity as citizens of America rather than as a people connected with Africa through common descent. That same year, Du Bois was dismissed from the NAACP again, never to return. The 80-year-old champion of pan-Africanism went to work fulltime for the CAA. In the context of the Cold War, however, the CAA was on the wrong side of the now-hot Communist question. Du Bois passed his last days in Ghana, still shouting with erudition, but from the margins. As for Robeson, the State Department revoked his passport in 1950, explaining that his "criticism of the treatment of blacks in the United States should not be aired in foreign countries."[110] His films and recordings were also pulled from circulation. The NAACP fell into line, revoking Robeson's Spingarn Medal and keeping its distance.

At the workplace, peacetime biracial unionism seemed more promising than ever immediately after the war. In 1946 more than 200,000 black workers joined the greatest strike wave in U.S. history. The CIO launched Operation Dixie, a million-dollar attempt to unionize the South, promising—in the words of CIO President Philip Murray—a "civil rights crusade." In black-majority left-leaning unions, there were some startling advances at the workplace and beyond. That summer in Winston-Salem, North Carolina, tobacco stemmers of United Tobacco Workers Local 22 struck, and black women pickets fought with police. The stemmers won a partial wage increase and three paid holidays each year. Black voters elected Winston-Salem's first black alderman since Reconstruction.[111]

Yet the postwar years soon marked the end of militant interracial unionism. In the South, Operation Dixie, by focusing on the white textile industry, avoided the race question. In any case, it soon petered out. Even the more inclusive unions ducked the issue of seniority, which meant that the longest-serving workers (in other words, white workers) retained jobs and won promotions. Congress used the postwar strikes and the bogeyman of Communism to roll back New Deal labor laws. The Taft-Hartley Act (1947), which passed despite Truman's veto, forced union leaders to affirm that they were not members of the Communist Party. As a result, CIO and AFL leaders purged those labor organizers most committed to the rights of black workers. They centralized union structures, too, thereby undermining the local militancy that was often associated with black activism. Local 22 in Winston-Salem, and most other left-led unions across country, didn't stand a chance.

Meanwhile, black activists called on the government to make the wartime FEPC permanent. The *Pittsburgh Courier* called it "the Battle of the Century." Robert Weaver warned of the high "probability of extreme job displacement of colored workers during reconversion"—most gains had come in defense industries preparing to cut their workforce.[112] Last hired, mostly unskilled black workers were liable to be the first fired. An FEPC report in January 1946 found that black workers accounted for a fifth of those who had lost a job since VJ day.[113] A seasonal tobacco worker from Winston-Salem, Christine Gardner, the mother of three children, made a heart-wrenching plea before one Senate committee. "My husband and I have been married 10 years . . . His greatest ambition is to buy for me a Christmas present and for himself a complete set of clothes."[114] As it turned out, there was no recession. But there was no permanent FEPC either. In peace, unlike war, workers' pleas could not be backed up with the threat of disrupting vital military production. Conservatives in the Senate quashed the idea by means of a filibuster—whereby senators could talk *ad infinitum* to prevent a vote, in this case talk that included a discussion of the position of commas and semicolons in the Senate chaplain's prayer. Activists would have to wait a generation for the federal government to act.

By the end of the decade, only a third of black workers who entered war industries held onto their jobs (compared with just over half of white workers).[115] Yet there was no mass unemployment, either. The average income of black families reached half that of white families by 1950—the highest it had ever been. And just as black workers in World War I got their foot in the door of unskilled industrial jobs, black workers in World War II began to fill some skilled and semi-skilled positions. More than ever before, there were black winners and losers. Unskilled black women lost most. The proportion of domestics who were black women rose from 45 to 60 percent, as virtually all clerical and sales positions went to white women only. By contrast, the black middle class prospered—hence the rise of *Ebony*. Whereas only 5,000 African Americans attended college in 1910, more than 88,000 did so by 1948. As better educated, more affluent black citizens emerged, the rights of laborers slipped down the agenda of the prominent civil rights organizations. The next nationwide wave of civil rights protest in the 1960s would start with a push for integration of public space rather than with a demand for justice at the workplace.

The first postwar hopes for human rights and biracial unions were not matched by hopes for the army. Considering the grudging and stuttering moves toward military desegregation at the height of combat, there seemed little prospect of forcing change during peacetime. In the first postwar review, army divisions were integrated, but the regiments that made up the divisions were segregated. The loyalist Truman Gibson resigned, frustrated that "the army demonstrated the agility of a gymnast in presenting an enlightened acknowledgement of the clear evidence at one moment and then falling back the next moment on any excuse to continue the status quo."[116] It would take further moves from the president, two more army reviews, and the Korean War before Jim Crow finally demobilized.

In the meantime, the end of the war triggered a battle over the place of black soldiers in public memory and of returning veterans in everyday life. The black press and welcoming crowds on the black side of towns celebrated black heroism. But in the South, white mobs often forced returning veterans to take off their uniforms. In the White House, there were "no Negroes among the heroes," complained black journalist Harry McAlpin, after watching twenty-eight white soldiers receive the Congressional Medal of Honor.[117] (Seven black soldiers did eventually receive Medals of Honor for World War II bravery—in 1997.)

The GI Bill, signed by Roosevelt in June 1944, provided federal aid for veterans' education, regardless of color, and over half of all veterans took up the offer—black veterans more so than whites. But if the GI bill prepared black veterans for better-paying jobs, racial discrimination prevented them from taking them. Because there were few colleges open to black veterans in the South, and because there were fewer higher status jobs open to black workers anywhere, the GI Bill actually widened the gap between black and white incomes. Black veteran Henry Hervey used the GI Bill to go to Northwestern University in Chicago, and—armed with a degree—went to the city's banks looking for a job. "I got the same job offer I would have gotten if I had not gone to college or had not gone in the Army: it was either a janitor or a mailroom clerk."[118]

Still, the vast majority of black veterans who did use the bill later described it as a life-changing event. Even those southern black veterans who could attend only segregated vocational training programs benefited from higher real wages (even if white veterans benefited more). In an unintended consequence, over a third of veterans who used the GI Bill for further training went on to participate in civil rights protest (compared with fewer than one in ten black soldiers who did not make use of the bill). In Mississippi, Medgar Evers, a black veteran, tried to cast his ballot even though local whites threatened to shoot him. He used the GI Bill to go to college and became a forthright NAACP civil organizer in the state. To quote Hervey again, "By that time you learn that you can fight city hall . . . there are ways you can bring pressure."[119]

With the coming of peace, fighting city hall and bringing pressure at the local level remained the key battlefields. In cities and neighborhoods, North and South, activists did not retreat in their demands (in many rural parts of the South, the war had not made much difference anyway). They continued to use the diverse strategies of the New Deal and war years, from lobbying and litigation to boycotts and building community to fighting back. In the Upper South in 1947, CORE volunteers embarked on a Journey of Reconciliation or Freedom Ride to test the *Morgan* decision on interstate travel. Eight black men sat at the front of a bus, eight white men sat at the back. As they rode, they sang in tribute to Irene Morgan (a song that would remain a protest classic), "Get on the bus, sit anyplace, / 'Cause Irene Morgan won her case. / You don't have to ride Jim Crow." The riders were arrested six times, and some were sent to the chain gang for a month.

As in previous years, local activists often deployed different—sometimes conflicting—tactics. Atlanta's Reverend Martin Luther King Sr. admired veterans for being "eager and unafraid."[120] But he condemned their mass demonstrations for the hiring of black policemen (they were successful, and later King conceded they were right). Just as tactics varied, so too did results. There were as many setbacks as gains, and often gains and setbacks at the same time. The Klan rose for a third time in the South, making full use of anti-Communist rhetoric. Overlooking patriotism and racism, Georgia's Grand Dragon declared at a ceremony in 1946: "The Klan opposes all isms except Americanism." By 1948 as many people belonged to the Klan as to the NAACP. Yet in the wake of *Smith v. Allwright,* black voting tripled to 750,000 between 1940 and 1948. In cities such as Atlanta and Savannah, black voting (often allied to demonstrations) led to the appointment of black policemen, the creation of biracial councils, and increased spending on black schools. Though gains were small, they had lasting significance. A generation later, civil rights protests would flourish in precisely those cities where black activists had already forced change.

The most decisive postwar breakthrough came in popular culture. In 1947 the Brooklyn Dodgers became the first major league team to sign a black player. This was not simply a consolation prize—black newspapers devoted more column inches to the question of integrating American's national pastime than any other single topic during 1945. Lobbied by black journalists, white owners of northern teams realized it was in their own interests to tap into the Negro Leagues. Despite the furor Robinson's debut provoked (he would be spat upon and ostracized), a black baseball player was not a practical threat to the northern residential color line—hence the lack of opposition to sports integration compared with the integration of northern factories and neighborhoods. During the war, GI Jackie Robinson had been involved in fights and was court-martialed for refusing to sit at the back of a bus. But he carried himself with such dignity, and played with such skill (he was voted Rookie of the Year), that he won over critics.

Roi Ottley reworked *New World A-Coming* for publication in 1947. He changed the title to *Black Odyssey* and added a downbeat conclusion. Much of American society had changed because of the war. But in the race arena, much had stayed the same. For all the lofty wartime rhetoric, America had not resolved her dilemma of promising democracy yet practicing discrimination. Du Bois, scarred by World War I, predicted that black Americans would gain equality by 2045 at the earliest. But many African Americans, fighting simply to make a living and raise a family, had never expected anything other than a long haul. During the war, a young black woman called Hortense Johnson moved to Washington to take a job inspecting boxes. It was tedious; she worked long hours; she had a long commute. "I'm not fooling myself about this war. Victory won't mean victory for Democracy—yet . . . by doing my share today, I'm keeping a place for some brown woman tomorrow, and for the brown son of that woman the day after tomorrow."[121]

13. In the 1920s, the flamboyant performances and loose-living reputation of Bessie Smith—"Empress of the Blues"—challenged the values of middle-class black reformers. (Library of Congress, Carl Van Vechten Collection)

14. Membership of the NAACP expanded dramatically in parts of the South during World II. The Savannah NAACP Youth Council was the largest in the country in 1942. Members are pictured here with Ella Baker (leaning against the car), national director of branches and youthwork. (Courtesy of W. W. Law)

15. White communities in northern and western cities often defended the "racial purity" of their neighborhoods against black migrants. On February 28, 1942, white residents attacked the first black tenants at the federally funded Sojourner Truth Housing Project in a formerly white area of Detroit. (Corbis)

16. Robert C. Weaver, at his desk in April 1942 as chief of the Negro Employment and Training Branch of the labor division in the federal Office of Production Management. In 1966, during the Johnson administration, he became the first African American cabinet member. (Bettmann/Corbis)

17. Union leader A. Philip Randolph—the foremost civil rights spokesman on the eve of World War II—proposed a March on Washington of 100,000 black workers in 1941. To avoid it, President Roosevelt issued Executive Order 8802, which required nondiscrimination in defense employment—the first presidential directive on behalf of civil rights since Reconstruction. (Moorland-Spingarn Research Library)

CHAPTER EIGHT

Three Steps Forward, Two Steps Back, 1949–1959

One morning in March 1949, hundreds of black longshoremen marched onto the New York waterfront to "force hiring of some of our men." The all-black local was the only longshoremen's local without a pier. Barely one in ten of the men had regular work. The longshoremen picketed the waterfront for three months. Some sat-in at the office of King Joe Ryan, the self-declared "president for life" of the International Longshoremen's Association. Ryan hired thugs to throw them out. He accused the protesters of being Communists. Five years later, a city Waterfront System Commission took over hiring. An Urban League study reckoned that the new "seniority" hiring system merely "formalizes a pattern of discrimination." The commission investigated the black local for communism.[1]

One evening in July 1949 in Winston-Salem, North Carolina, five hundred African Americans threatened to hang a white man for shooting a young black woman. The police rescued the white man.[2]

Ruling in the *Brown v. Board of Education of Topeka* school segregation case in 1954, Chief Justice Earl Warren declared: "In the field of public education, the doctrine of 'separate but equal' has no place." In response, the Harlem Tenants Council wrote to the state legislature, "Segregation in education . . . cannot really be eliminated until segregation in housing, too, is outlawed."[3]

"Thar he." The words of a 64-year-old Mississippi sharecropper and minister, Moses Wright, in August 1955, as he pointed at the two white men accused of murdering his nephew, Emmett Till. Wright said he could feel the "blood boil" in the white spectators in court. He fled the state soon afterward.

"We're beginning to feel that this attitude among white liberals is never going to get us anywhere and what we need is not opportunity but power." Democratic Minority Conference, black political organization in Los Angeles, 1957.[4]

Soon after dark on January 3, 1949, the biggest tornado in Arkansas history wreaked havoc on homes in the small lumber town of Warren. Or rather, on white homes. As it zigzagged through the town, the death-dealing wind side-stepped black districts, sometimes by just a few yards. "It was the work of God," said King Evans, owner of the O.K. Hotel, "and we have much to be thankful for." It called to mind the Old Testament, when God's judgment passed over his chosen people before setting them free. In one miracle, the "big wind" picked up two young African American boys, stripped off their clothes, and put them down unhurt a hundred yards along the road. The *Chicago Defender's* editors put the story on its front page, knowing that readers would chuckle over the headline, "Freak Storm Skips Negro Section, Kills 52 Whites."[5] But it also fit with the *Defender*'s optimism for the year ahead—because the "civil rights gains made by Negroes in 1948 were greater than at any time during the 86 years since the issuance of the Emancipation Proclamation."[6]

This was a turnabout. The war and especially its aftermath had been disappointing. But the *Defender* judged 1948 a banner year. Star running back Levi Jackson became the first black captain of Yale's football team. The UN appointed Ralph Bunche as its mediator in Palestine, and two years later, he would be the first nonwhite person to win the Nobel Peace Prize. The South's last remaining white state primary, in South Carolina, fell. The NAACP won a key housing case, *Shelley v. Kraemer* (1948), that barred injunctions to enforce racially restrictive covenants.

Above all, in 1948 President Truman moved on civil rights. In July, with one eye on America's image abroad, he issued executive orders requiring nondiscrimination on government contracts and in the military. After police in South Carolina struck and permanently blinded Isaac Woodard, a returning black soldier who had won a military good-conduct award, Truman told his aides, "This shit has to stop." But his gaze was also fixed on the black vote—if just 300,000 black voters had switched to the Republican candidate in 1944, Roosevelt would have lost the election. Facing the extra challenge of a Progressive Party to his left and a breakaway southern Dixiecrat party to his right, Truman reached out to black voters. He even campaigned in Harlem—the first sitting president to do so. Truman's gamble worked. He lost four Deep South states to the Dixiecrats, but two out of three black voters supported Truman, and he won the election. Northern Democrats reached out to black voters too. Because of black migration, black voters held the balance of power in twenty-five districts. Over howls from southern Democrats, liberal Democrats inserted a civil rights plank in the 1948 party platform.

Their gains in the North gave Democrats control of both chambers of Congress. "Encouraged by the progress we have toward full citizenship," the *Defender* concluded, "we may look forward to the New Year with our hearts full of hope."[7] And as the Arkansas storm seemed to show, God was not just on their side, He was ready to wreak vengeance on their enemies.

For the black press, the NAACP, and black labor leaders, the top postwar priority was to make the Fair Employment Practice Commission permanent. Congressional procedures provided the major obstacles. Congress's committee structure, where leadership was based on seniority, bolstered the power of rural, and thus mostly conservative, members to shape the legislative agenda. The filibuster allowed the southern Democratic minority in the Senate to block civil rights bills that did get through committee. Responding to the challenge of the 1948 election, southern senators sought to tighten up the procedural rules to make it nigh impossible to override a filibuster.

Thus, the test of 1949's promise was the question of the congressional filibuster. NAACP leaders called the filibuster proposal the issue of the year—as important as lynching or segregation. They lobbied Congress. They joined with representatives of twenty religious, workers', and other progressive organizations to make the case. They had support from newly elected liberal northern Democrats who challenged institutional blocks so forcefully that conservative opponents called them "bomb throwers." And yet they lost. The most acute black political commentator of the era, Henry Moon, lamented in the *Crisis* that congressional procedures allow a "mad minority . . . to dictate the legislative program of the entire nation."[8]

Without a war, black activists struggled to force the government to act. In 1950 the NAACP tried to repeat the March on Washington. In January some four thousand delegates, representing dozens of civil rights and workers groups, gathered as part of a National Emergency Civil Rights Mobilization. It wasn't nearly enough. The FEPC was not even introduced as a bill.[9] To make matters worse, overzealous union leaders looking for Communist sympathizers denied entry to hundreds of delegates. Walter White offered his resignation to the NAACP board—after his affair with, and then marriage to, a white woman, his reputation was in tatters anyway. In 1955 the St. Louis–born black journalist (and former *Crisis* editor) Roy Wilkins succeeded him.

With the election won, and an intransigent Congress and a Cold War to deal with, Truman did not vigorously pursue the agenda of *To Secure These Rights,* which had called for equal opportunities in employment and housing and federal protection of civil rights. When his successor as the Democratic nominee in 1952, Adlai Stevenson, opposed a compulsory FEPC law, Adam Clayton Powell threatened to leave the party in disgust.[10] But he had nowhere else to go. The Republican nominee, the war hero Dwight Eisenhower, also opposed a compulsory FEPC. During the eight years of his presidency (1953–1961), "Ike" did not believe it was the government's business to legislate on race matters either. Wilkins complained that "if he had fought World War II the way he fought for civil rights, we would all be speaking German today."[11]

Of the branches of the federal government, only the Supreme Court would act in line with Gunnar Myrdal's call for black rights to match American rhetoric. Not accountable to an electorate—for whom the issue of race was more often a practical struggle over resources than a theoretical discussion of rights—Supreme Court justices felt unconstrained by legal precedent. The NAACP would win every single case it brought during the 1950s.[12] But the Court didn't enforce rights. Taken as a whole, the federal government did not live up to the expectations of 1948, and not even to the example of the later New Deal and war years.

Thus, local struggles for equality (out of which Supreme Court rulings grew) remained as important as ever. Because of the changes of the New Deal and war years, protest played out differently in different places. In northern cities, activists sought local fair employment and housing legislation. In some southern cities, activists confronted segregated schools and buses. In the Deep South, activists struggled to hang on.

Yet for all the differences, local people remained connected by family, news media, popular culture, institutions such as the church, and protest organizations. North and South, local people faced discrimination, too. Writing in the *American Mercury* in June 1949 for the "millions of complacent white folk in the big Northern cities," the now-conservative black journalist George Schuyler listed a litany of racial injustices: jail sentences for intermarriage were longer in some northern states than in the South; more than half of northern cities had no black clerks or store salesmen whatsoever; 95 percent of New York's parks were for whites only. In a Washington, D.C., dog cemetery, "even a white dog is barred if its owner is black!"[13] Such racism, wrote the novelist James Baldwin in 1953, gave black Americans across the nation "a kind of blind fever, a pounding in the skull and fire in the bowels . . . There is not a Negro alive who does not have rage in his blood."[14]

Thus, in practice, activists across the country shared many of the same broader goals. In the North they fought against segregation in schools and public facilities as well as for jobs and housing. The NAACP's leading lawyer, Thurgood Marshall, told colleagues that "it is just as important to fight the segregated school system in the North and West as it is to fight for equal schools in the South."[15] In southern cities, they fought for jobs and housing as well as against segregation in schools and public facilities. The issue of segregation was not a question of social mixing, and not just a question of rights. Rather, the battle against segregation was a battle for equal resources. "Throughout these times," reflected Mississippi activist Aaron Henry, "I don't think we had a great desire to integrate just for the sake of being with white people. We wanted integration to better our position . . . the whites had proved to us that there could never be a 'separate but equal' society."[16]

North and South, local activists shared the new context of a Cold War, too. Anti-Communism may have allowed mainstream black leaders to cast segregationists as un-American, but it also allowed defenders of race privilege to conflate black agitation with red agitation. Ultimately the Cold War context would help black leaders more than segregationists. A decade later, President Johnson would call supremacist vigilantes un-American. But for a time it was a close-run thing: Eisenhower called black agitators un-American. Meanwhile, fear of the taint of subversion saw mainstream 1950s protest, North and South, depart from the labor-left-nationalist militancy of the New Deal and war years. When the NAACP passed an anti-Communist resolution at its 1950 convention, only a small minority, including Rosa Parks, voted against it. The Harlem branch purged Ben Davis, a city councilor, much to the later regret of branch president Ella Baker. The NAACP switched focus from economic rights to civil rights, and they severed their links with the left-leaning anti-colonial struggle, too. In 1955 Du Bois wrote: "One of the curious results of the current fear and hysteria is the breaking of ties between Africa and American Negroes."[17]

In the end, the 1950s would prove to be the classic case of three steps forward and two steps back—winning rights but still facing discrimination in everyday life. Stepping forward, black celebrities broke through into popular culture, most northern cities passed fair employment laws, the 1954 *Brown* decision ruled against school segregation, black residents of Montgomery won bus desegregation in 1956, and President Eisenhower intervened to secure integration of schools in Little Rock, Arkansas, in 1957. But stepping back, negative race stereotypes persisted, local fair employment laws were barely enforced, the 1955 *Brown II* decision refrained from demanding swift school integration, white southern segregationists mobilized in defense of the status quo, and white residents of northern cities fought to preserve the *de facto* color line.

Breaking into Popular Culture

In January 1949 the Brooklyn Dodgers announced that their spring training would include a game against the Atlanta Crackers. Apoplectic at the thought of Jackie Robinson strutting his stuff on a southern diamond, Klan Grand Dragon Samuel Green warned, "The Atlanta baseball club is breaking the traditions of the South and will have to pay for it." Green was shouting against the wind. A local white reporter mocked him: "It sure would be a terrible thing for me, sitting there in the bleachers, to be contaminated by that darky out there playing second base."[18] The Crackers did the opposite of pay for it. Some 25,000 people came to watch—more than double the stadium's capacity—and over half the crowd were black supporters. "The real story," according to the *Atlanta Constitution,* "is any time certain forms of Jim Crow are proven unprofitable, the South finds a way to do away with them."[19] As for Robinson, he stole home in the first inning.

That same year, Fox Studios released *Pinky*—a box office hit about a young mulatto southern woman. Pinky's grandmother, a selfless washerwoman, saves her pennies to send Pinky up North for a decent education. There, Pinky becomes a nurse, people presume she's white, and a white doctor falls in love with her. On a return South, Pinky ends up caring for an elderly plantation mistress, inherits the woman's estate in her will, then faces the woman's relatives in court, who claim the "colored girl" manipulated the old woman. Pinky loses the case but discovers pride in her blackness and learns to stand up for her rights. If this plot seemed custom-made for the civil rights cause, that was because it was. The studio chief, Darryl Zanuck, consulted Walter White about the movie during production, and White's daughter Jane helped to sharpen up the black characters in the script. White was exultant, writing to Zanuck, "It begins to look as though what [we] have been working for all these years is beginning to show results."[20]

With the success of Robinson and *Pinky,* race leaders redoubled their efforts to improve the black image in popular culture. Walter White, in particular, still believed that the problem of racism started in the white mind, and thus black achievers could win victories for the race as a whole. In 1948 he presented broadcasters with a list of "words which are objectionable to Negroes," not to mention the stereotype that they were "addicted perpetually to the use of dialect and the eating exclusively of water melon." The following year, the inaugural conference of the Committee for the Negro in the Arts met to discuss how best to use black consumer power to effect change.[21] The black press made the integration of sports a top issue, while black magazines like *Ebony* called for black stars on screen. In 1950 when black New Yorkers picketed a movie theater over the re-release of *Birth of a Nation* (complete with new sound features), the run was cut short. In 1956 when the minor league New Orleans Pelicans refused to field the black baseball players assigned to them by their major league team, the Pittsburgh Pirates, black attendance in New Orleans, normally over 40,000, dropped to only 3,400. The boycott spread to other cities in the Southern Association. In 1961 the league disbanded.[22]

Following Robinson and *Pinky*, black performers smashed the color barrier in popular culture—partly because of protest, and partly because white businessmen recognized the power of black consumers and the competitive advantages of black performers. Hollywood changed only slowly—and pulled back from message movies (and Pinky was played by a white actress to placate southern censors). But in baseball, by 1960 every major league team had a black player. Willie Mays became the greatest baseball star—black or white—of his generation. Even the game itself changed, as the major leagues added speed and base running (adopted from the Negro Leagues) to their own power-hitting style. By the end of the decade, black athletes were found in many professional sports—all but one major league football team had a black player, black golfer Charlie Sifford had won a major PGA event, and black tennis player Althea Gibson had won the U.S. Open. After she took the Wimbledon doubles with Angela Buxton, a British Jew, one newspaper ran the headline "Minorities Win."

But no medium changed more during this period than radio. In 1946 not a single radio station catered to black audiences; yet by 1955 many stations devoted at least thirty hours a week to black programming, and twenty-eight stations, including twenty-two in the South, devoted most of their airtime to a black audience. Most of these stations were white-owned, but the owners recognized that an audience with a collective income of $15 billion by 1953 should not be ignored.[23] Black music crossed over to white audiences as never before. By the end of the decade more than 90 percent of the top-selling records on the (black) national Rhythm and Blues charts also appeared on pop charts, and almost one in three Top Ten hits was by a black artist.[24] White teenagers listened to Little Richard's "Tutti Frutti" and tuned in to black DJs like Shelley "The Playboy" Stewart of WEDR in Birmingham. The greatest pop star of them all, Elvis Presley, was the answer to record producer Sam Phillips' search for a "white boy who could sing like a nigger."

Stewart reckoned that "music really started breaking down the barriers long before politics in America began to deal with it."[25] The baseball broadcaster Ernie Halwell trumpeted in 1957, "Here the only race is the race to the bag . . . Color is something to distinguish one teams' uniform from another."[26] Whether black sports stars and performers changed the racial views of white fans is impossible to gauge. What is clear is that the black image in the white mind changed dramatically in the post-war generation. Whereas fewer than half of those polled in 1942 thought blacks "can learn things just as well as white people if they are given the chance," by 1956 some 80 percent did. Such changes undermined the power of segregationists.

Still, some caution must be attached to this picture of progress. Popular adulation of black performers and entertainers did not end racist stereotypes. America's main sports newspaper celebrated Mays' break-through with a cartoon, "Ah gives base runners the heave ho!"[27] The most popular "black" television program of the early 1950s, the *Amos 'n' Andy* show, portrayed two of the three male characters as buffoons. NAACP-led protests forced CBS to pull the show from the air in 1953, though it stayed on re-runs until 1966. NAACP leaders worried that black DJs' colloquial style ("Great googly-moogly, that was the Swallows with 'It Ain't the Meat, It's the Motion'") hardly led to the acceptance of African Americans in respectable circles.[28] The popularity of some black musicians bolstered the image of black men's sexual prowess. Little Richard hailed from a cross-dressing, female-impersonating musical scene in parts of the black South, and while most of his fans did not know of this affinity, his sequined tops and barely restrained performance gave plenty of clues. As for Elvis, he didn't just "sing like a nigger," he gyrated like one, too.

Meanwhile, some aspects of popular culture remained no-go areas for African Americans. Jim Crow kept them out of the finer arts—black painters rarely showed in major galleries in the 1950s, there was only one black musician among the twenty-five city orchestras, and not a single professional black ballerina. In due course, television news would be a precious resource for publicizing the causes of black demonstrators, but in the 1950s normal Americans were portrayed on TV as white. In any case, most black performers saw integration as only a means to an economic end. Poorer musicians shunned it, actively seeking a separate union from their white counterparts to help preserve their "Chitlin" performance circuit.

Some resented integration. A character in a short story published in the *Harlem Quarterly* complained that "the thing we likes most, we can't have to ourselves" since "it belongs to everybody."[29] He was referring to

music, and to the growing number of white artists who were covering
black songs and stealing the spoils. But the same was true in sports—the
integration of the major leagues led to the demise of the long-standing
Negro leagues. On the other hand, black crossover artists had to embrace
white styles to secure their success. The recorded lyrics of Little Richard's
"Tutti Frutti"—desexualized from the first version he sang in gay bars
across the South, to great acclaim—ended up making no sense whatsoever.

Nor did acceptance of black performers in popular culture mean acceptance of black Americans in everyday life—not even acceptance of
black performers in everyday life. Willie Mays couldn't buy a house in an
affluent white neighborhood until San Francisco's mayor intervened, and
a brick smashed his front window soon after he moved in. By 1960
Boston's Fenway Park employed just one black man on its staff—a
cleaner. Disneyland, which opened soon after the *Brown* decision, did
not employ even one. Meanwhile, the American Federation of Musicians
estimated that 18,000 out of 22,000 musicians who had been in the or-
chestra pits of movie theaters—a common black profession—lost work
once recording technology became commonplace.[30] As for segregationists, the popularity of black musicians added fuel to their racist fire. By
the end of the 1950s, segregationist groups warned that "Jungle Music
promotes integration." During a Nat King Cole concert for whites only
in Birmingham, Alabama, in 1956, someone shouted "Let's go get that
coon," and a group of white men forced Cole off the stage. The fact that
he was midway though singing "Little Girl" was unlikely to be a coincidence.[31]

Tellingly, even the most successful black performers were as likely to
embrace protest as they were to become satisfied with their success. Louis
Armstrong refused to travel to Russia on a good will tour after the Little
Rock school crisis in 1957, saying, "The way they are treating my people
in the South, the government can go to hell."[32] Those who were most
critical of American race relations fell foul of the red scare. Ironically, the
very man who at first held his tongue for the sake of integration later became the most outspoken critic of American race relations of all. "As
long as I appeared to ignore insult and injury, I was a martyred hero,"
wrote Jackie Robinson. "But the minute I began to sound off—I became
a swell-head, wise guy, an 'uppity' nigger."[33]

A Place to Live and Work

At the start of 1953, Donald and Betty Howard lived with Betty's grandmother in Chicago. As proud parents of two young children, they were

keen to find an apartment of their own. Donald was a postal worker, so financing a move should not have been too difficult. Except that the Howards were "Negroes." Donald found that suitable apartments were unavailable in the white sections of town, and too expensive in the over-crowded black sections. So when Betty happened to see a sign advertising apartments outside the Chicago Housing Authority's new Trumbull Park, she stopped by to put her name down. What Betty didn't realize was that it was an all-white housing project. And what the receptionist didn't realize was that light-skinned Betty was black.

When the Howards realized the mistake, they expected some trouble. They went ahead anyway. They moved on July 30 and had a pleasant surprise. Local children (some with darker skin than Betty and her children) helped them unload their van. But when word got out, the project manager told them to leave. They refused. On Wednesday, August 5, a paving stone crashed through their window.

A two-week carnival of violence followed. Some evenings the mob swelled into thousands. It was as if a besieging army had set up camp, demanding surrender. Bricks and foul-smelling sulphur bombs rained down on the house. The Howards barricaded their windows and at the worst moments shut their children in a closet for safety. White gangs attacked passing black motorists at random—one report noted "a gray-haired woman of about 65 fell prostrate in front of the car . . . When the halted car began to inch ahead the woman clung to its front bumper." By August 11, one third of the city's police were on duty, implementing the department's Plan 5, reserved for the most serious emergencies. The "cops," complained Donald, "seemed more intent upon protecting white families from contact with us than in protecting my family from the white mobsters."[34]

At the start of September, after meetings with local race leaders, the CHA announced that its four remaining all-white projects would open to African Americans—but only "when law and order could be maintained."[35] Local NAACP president Willoughby Abner was livid. He judged, correctly, that it was an invitation to white vigilantes to break the law and be disorderly. On cue, white mobs lit fires in all four projects. In December the CHA sought to evict Donald for "failing to submit proper information in his income status."[36] The following spring, Chicago police arrested him for firing shots at a gang. Donald denied both charges. Meanwhile, some seventeen thousand white Chicagoans signed a petition calling for less protection for the Howards, so that police could focus on crime elsewhere.

The Howards' case outraged Chicago's black community. The *De-*

fender condemned immigrants fighting to defend the purity of white neighborhoods, when their own "mastery of the English language is confined to the one word 'Nigger.'"[37] Black gangs came to Trumbull Park to fight back. Abner shared the anger. A union man and a friend of A. Philip Randolph, the fiery NAACP president had been elected on a platform to confront segregation directly. For the first time in its history, the Chicago NAACP fought in the streets as well as in the courts.

At the end of March, some 1,500 people, representing approximately two hundred black and progressive organizations, marched on City Hall. Mayor Martin Kennelly, whose political base was white Irish voters, affirmed his support for the principle of integration. Black leaders damned it as spin with no substance.[38] Next, the NAACP turned to the federal government, which had financed the housing project; the attorney general promised to keep an eye on the situation. The NAACP also turned to the courts and filed a $100,000 suit to desegregate other all-white CHA projects. The *Defender* seized on the comment by one CHA leader that anyone found guilty of mob action might be evicted, and helpfully named every person who had been arrested, complete with their full address (a tactic that segregationists used to good effect against black activists in the South). Black Americans also turned to God. Ministers designated August 22 a National Day of Prayer for Trumbull Park, since the "efforts of men" had done nothing.[39]

In May 1954, just as the *Brown* decision was being handed down, the Howards moved out. "We just couldn't take it anymore," Betty Howard explained to a sympathetic journalist. "I am very bitter toward the majority of white people. I used to be very broadminded . . . But now, well, I just didn't think this was possible." As they left, a rally of white homeowners cheered. But by this time a handful of other black families had moved in, and the affair rumbled on. As of the end of 1954, the cost of policing Trumbull Park had exceeded the cost of building it.[40] There were plenty more fights as black youths—encouraged by Abner—gathered in the project to play baseball. In 1955, some five thousand people marched on City Hall. The new Democratic mayor, Richard Daley, was caught between the anger of his two key voting blocs—blue-collar white voters and black voters. So he left via a backstreet exit and shunted the problem to a committee.

Unofficially, a deal was struck with white homeowners that violence would end as long as not more than a handful of black families moved into each section of the park. It was hardly an adequate resolution for aspiring black homeowners, since CHA housing was less than 2 percent of the city's housing stock. By this time, the local NAACP was virtually bankrupt, and Abner was soon ousted by the black Democratic leaders who favored working with the Daley machine. Racial violence—to quote one resident—had "became normal." As for Daley, he would later see off Martin Luther King's campaign for fair housing in Chicago.

The Howards' story encapsulated many of the issues of protest beyond the South between World War II and the Civil Rights Movement. It told of the battle for resources—a decent house or job—that lay at the heart of struggles along the color line. It told of the persistent efforts of African Americans to gain their fair share. It told of the wider resonance of individual struggles, and of divisions among black activists. And it told of the opposition to change—from prevaricating politicians to white supremacist violence on a par with anything to be found in the South.

Each northern city had its own story to tell. Some, like the larger Rust Belt cities, suffered massive industrial decline, while others, like the newer cities of the West Coast, did not. In some cities, such as Detroit, Chicago, and New York, alliances between civil rights advocates and labor unions anchored protest. In others, such as Philadelphia and Pittsburgh, labor unions stood at the front in defending the color line.

Overall, though, similar patterns of protest revealed the new voting power of black northerners to demand rights in the postwar city, but also their inability to translate those rights into practice. Seeking to redeem the postwar promise of liberalism, activists lobbied Democratic officials for city and state fair employment and fair housing laws. Local politics in the North and West (unlike Congress) was free from the conservative clutches of southern segregationists. Postwar black voting carried real power as part of a Democratic coalition based on workers—black migration saw Chicago's population more than triple in size in the postwar generation, while San Francisco's quadrupled. When campaigners met opposition, they invoked the Cold War imperative of living up to American ideals. One NAACP press release asked Illinois' stonewalling Republican governor, William Stratton, "to explain to the Russians why his state failed to pass a law guaranteeing the right of nearly a million citizens to obtain work."[41] In terms of winning formal civil rights, protest in the postwar city was a remarkable success story. By the time Illinois' fair employment law passed in 1961, nineteen states—and many more cities—had passed fair employment legislation, and every state beyond the South had banned school segregation.[42]

With rights guaranteed in practice, the important question was implementation. In place of the mass demonstrations of the New Deal and war eras, there were hundreds of smaller campaigns and thousands of individual protests (like the Howards'). This was protest pied-piper style—where pioneer families and workers fought to breach the color line in the hope that thousands of families and workers could then follow. Because respectable middle-class mothers were supposed to stay home, it meant many of these pioneer activists were women—as were many of their fiercest opponents. The results would be mixed. But in the longer term these small campaigns would lead to an escalation of tactics and goals—to grassroots protest that would eventually force both the state and federal government to act.

Segregation of public facilities fell quickly, under pressure from court challenges, direct protest, and local ordinances. More often than not, local chapters of CORE headed protest campaigns—picketing, leafleting, or staging sit-ins at white-only department store lunch counters. A pacifist organization, CORE provided a model for the southern sit-in movement of the 1960s (its leader, Bayard Rustin, would influence Martin Luther King Jr.). Even so, there were fights aplenty. In the Rosedale neighborhood of Washington, D.C., in 1952, a "pilgrimage" of parents and children sought unsuccessfully to open up an all-white playground. A few days later, a black youth climbed the park fence, fell in the swimming pool, and died. From then on, black children climbed the fence daily. When white youths hit the fence-climbers with baseball bats, a black man pulled out a gun to stop the attack. CORE workers were critical of such violence, but local people were not. The park opened up for black children. By 1963, integrated eating places were so normal that the incoming president of the Chicago Commission on Human Relations was astonished to learn that in 1946 the commission had given an award to a restaurant that welcomed black customers.[43]

In terms of living and working, however, activists made little progress. Partly this was because local legislation was too weak, thereby exposing the limits of liberalism—the belief that racial discrimination was a matter of principle rather than practice. In New York, the State Commission against Discrimination pointed with pride, not embarrassment, to the fact that it had not forced compliance in a single instance. The presence of an FEPC law in any given town made no significant difference whatsoever to patterns of African American employment during the 1950s. In part, it was because neighborhood and workplace opposition was so strong, undergirded by white workers' fears for their status and livelihoods and, as ever, for their daughters. Local white newspapers deliberately ignored white violence (although two weeks of rioting in Cicero, Illinois, in 1951, was reported as far afield as Singapore). But taken together, street by street, factory by factory, the appalling degree of urban violence during the 1950s rivaled anything in the South. In Chicago, the city's Commission on Human Relations recorded a serious incident on average every ten days between the war and 1960.

Activists were also hamstrung by division. The battles for the mantle of black leadership sometimes seemed as bitter as battles against the color line. Some tensions were the usual personality politics, others were the old story of class politics—as labor leaders jostled with the "better classes" for leadership. Abner's ascent to power within the Chicago NAACP was as fraught as his fall. One ally—NAACP executive secretary Benjamin Bell—physically attacked branch president and liberal lawyer George Leighton in 1952. Bell intended to join Abner's labor forces in the 1953 branch elections, but he shot himself in the groin while cleaning his revolver shortly beforehand.[44] Above all, anti-Communist pressures ripped wartime alliances asunder.

Even so, limited legislation, strong opposition, and internal divisions were nothing new. The main reason why activists failed to bridge the color gap was because of economic and demographic forces beyond their control. In the Rust Belt especially, this was a devastating decade of recession, automation, and the movement of industrial jobs out of town. Detroit suffered four recessions during 1949–1960. The number of manufacturing jobs almost halved—a downturn affecting workers of all colors, but black workers hardest of all because they lacked seniority. And the loss of entry-level jobs in heavy industry meant unemployment for new black migrants. In Detroit in 1960, 15.9 percent of black adults were out of work, compared with 5.8 percent of whites.

That the problems facing black Americans were about more than just racism is shown in the uneven pattern of black unemployment. Construction unions—with the short-term nature of hiring, high wages for skilled workers, and a tradition of father-to-son apprenticeships—were most resistant to black workers. But some important industries, notably the major car plants on the West Coast and in the Midwest, did alter their hiring practices. In cities where black votes mattered, public sector employment saw significant changes. By 1961, black workers made up more than a third of Philadelphia's municipal workforce.[45] Even these positive stories, though, tended to feature lower-paid jobs, and not nearly enough of them to keep up with the numbers of new migrants from the South.

Civil rights organizations, such as the NUL, NAACP, and unions, lobbied, litigated, and provided vocational training. Some workers complained directly to FEP commissions, and perhaps a third of cases taken up locally led to employers eventually agreeing to hire a black worker. In the context of recession and discrimination, however, a few token appointments here and there proved about as helpful as planting the odd flower on a landslide. In 1958, the black economist Dr. Irwin Sobel observed, "The Negro is . . . economically all dressed up with nowhere to go."[46] Worse still, a few token appointments cleared companies and unions of charges of racial exclusion.

Housing segregation compounded the problem of unemployment. As jobs moved out of the city, black workers could not. In the mid-1950s, over three quarters of black adults in one North Philadelphia ghetto were not in regular employment.[47] Calls for housing desegregation, then, were about access to resources, not a desire for social mixing. One 1956 survey of black families in Los Angeles found that 84 percent would move to a "nonminority" area if they could.[48] White homeowners' resistance and urban zoning policies meant they could not. Federal agencies refused to intervene—yet after the 1956 Federal Highway Act, massive federal grants subsidized urban renewal programs that often led to the bulldozing of downtown black residential areas. The burden of housing segregation, wrote James Baldwin, revealed "unbearably, the real attitude of the white world, no matter how many liberal speeches are made."[49]

Housing segregation compounded the problem of economic inequality, too. In postwar America, a home was a family's primary financial asset. The 1949 Housing Act provided generous mortgage subsidies to improve housing, yet most of those subsidies went to white homeowners. One survey found that 50 percent of all 1950s construction was supported by government mortgages—and black Americans received barely 2 percent of that money (and that was mostly for segregated housing in the South). Jim Crow housing also had a knock-on effect on schooling, because school boards drew school catchments to reflect housing segregation, and local people funded their schools through property tax. To complete the dismal picture, overcrowding meant that black tenants faced high rents for squalid accommodation.

The rise of black ghettoes was partly caused by racist attitudes, but it also created racist attitudes. White city dwellers passed jobless black men hanging around on street corners at so-called "slave markets" in the hope of picking up day work. They saw black neighborhoods fall into disrepair. And they read about black teenagers dropping out of substandard schools and joining gangs. At the very moment when black celebrities achieved unprecedented popularity, black inner-city residents provoked unprecedented fears. This dichotomy explains polls that showed rising numbers of white northerners who believed black people could be as intelligent as white people, but also a rising number who supported housing restrictions. It explains, too, differing white attitudes depending on economic background (and thus where people lived). In one 1951 survey in Detroit, 85 percent of working-class whites expressed negative views toward blacks, compared with 43 percent of upper-income whites (most of whom lived in exclusive enclaves segregated by wealth if not strictly by race).[50]

Ironically, the postwar city actually had wealthier black residents than ever before. Educated African Americans made gains in municipal employment; many of the breakthrough appointments in industry were for skilled black workers; and black businessmen prospered in the context of segregation. Whereas fewer than one in six black men worked in middle-class occupations in 1950, one in four did in 1960 (and one in three by 1970). Some found homes in isolated black suburban islands. But for the most part members of the rising black middle class distanced themselves from the ghetto by pushing into white neighborhoods. In a typical week in Chicago during the 1950s, three-and-a-half blocks shifted from white-majority ownership to black-majority ownership. Real estate agents encouraged this "blockbusting" since it guaranteed property turnover and sales commissions. Allegedly some agents even paid black women to push their babies in prams through nearby white neighborhoods, in order to create a panic and induce white flight.

Little wonder, to quote Robert Weaver soon after *Brown,* that black reformers identified housing as the nation's "number one civil rights problem."[51] In 1950 the NAACP helped found the National Committee against Discrimination in Housing. If access to the fast-expanding suburbs was the key battle, then the major battlegrounds were Levittowns. By the 1950s, their founder, William Levitt, was the self-styled "leading builder of the country." *Time* estimated that the "Henry Ford of Housing" had built one in eight suburban houses—or, as Levitt boasted, a new house every sixteen minutes. Levitt's approach was to combine good design and good value, "the most house for the money." He offered his clients government-backed mortgages and a variety of homes to choose from. The most popular was the ranch-style bungalow—an open plan laid out around a fireplace, with floor-to-ceiling picture windows.[52]

Levitt didn't just plan perfect houses. He advertised his Levittowns— such as the one in Bucks County, Pennsylvania, built to service the new out-of-town U.S. Steel Plant—as "the most perfectly planned communit[ies] in America." His perfect communities had schools, parks, shops, and churches in all the right places. But his suburban idyll was what some called segreburbia—Levittowns were for "members of the Caucasian race" only. Levitt insisted that, as a Jew, he understood discrimination and that he had "no room in my . . . heart for racial prejudice." It was just that his customers did. "We can solve a housing problem, or we can try to solve a racial problem, but we cannot combine the two." His company even refused to renew the leases of residents who had black guests to dinner in his Long Island Levittown in the early 1950s.[53] As one journalist later put it, Levittowns offered "nothing less than Jim Crow with a two-car garage."[54]

As with employment, housing activists tried to win legislation. The NCDH lobbied public officials. The NAACP complained to President Eisenhower about "Jim Crow Levittowns." Docudramas and stories placed in popular journals showed respectable black families merrily moving in to white neighborhoods. As the upbeat narrator in one 1958 movie, *All the Way Home,* concluded (in a way that would have amazed Betty Howard): "Together a way of life emerges that is good for everybody."[55] The NCDH persuaded sympathetic whites to sell homes to blacks and even ran courses to enlighten unsympathetic white homeowners. As in employment, activists won a spate of local fair housing laws—twenty-one cities and eight states by 1954.

Yet in terms of dampening white opposition, or opening up new neighborhoods, such campaigns achieved little. Levitt, and others like him, simply removed explicit references to race. As with the Howards, it was individual families who finally forced the issue. In Levittown, Pennsylvania, in 1957, it was William and Daisy Myers' turn. With the help of Quaker activists, this middle-class college-educated American couple bought a pink and white ranch-style house from a white owner who was in a hurry to sell. Three nights later, a mob of three thousand people surrounded the house. Stones smashed the Myers' prized picture window. One stone-thrower admitted to a reporter, "He's probably a nice guy, but every time I look at him I see $2000 drop off the value of my house."[56] "We expected some trouble," Daisy explained later, "but nothing like this."[57]

The Myers' persistence forced state officials to act in order to uphold the promise of liberalism. When the state attorney general banned large gatherings, the rioting stopped, and a state court affirmed the Myers' right to live free from harassment. The NAACP followed up with a suit against the new Levittown in New Jersey. Daisy Myers went to visit activists there, warning that the Levitt policy "gives a go-ahead to the biggest race haters."[58] By this time, she could claim victory at home—she told reporters that the trouble was over, some people were being friendly, and her children were settled in the local Bible class. In 1961, the family moved away. In 1999 the town council finally apologized to Myers for discrimination and harassment.

Actions by people like the Myerses prompted the national government to act, too. As so often in American history, grassroots pressure, and local violence, opened up space for protest organizations to press their case. In the presidential election of 1960, both candidates sought the northern black vote—and both focused on the housing issue. Two years later—after considerable black lobbying—President Kennedy signed Executive Order 11063 guaranteeing equal opportunity in federally funded housing. It was still weaker than activists hoped (it did not cover single-family and two-family dwellings, and only covered future transactions, for example). But a dozen years after the founding of NCDH, and following the battles of hundreds of families, it was quite a triumph—one that provided a platform for future protest to erase the urban color line.

The troubles in "Levittown . . . and other localities," argued Tennessee's Governor Frank Clement, "have proved . . . that the problem of mixed races living in a single place is not a Southern problem."[59] The struggle beyond the South also pointed to just how far the nationwide struggle for equality had to run. Legal segregation in the North (as it would be in the South) proved a far easier foe than resource discrimination. "I just didn't think this was possible," said Betty Howard. "I expected trouble," said Daisy Myers, "but nothing like this." Such opposition, and the ineffectiveness of legislation, woke activists up to the limits of liberalism. It pointed to more widespread, confrontational protests to come in the 1960s. The battle to breach the northern color line would soon become a militant battle for results. But it would take events in the South to provide the spark for the next chapter in the northern story.

Brown, Montgomery, and Little Rock

In some respects, the postwar South could hardly have been more different from the North. Northern activists hoped local politicians would iron out the defects in democracy. Southern activists faced state politicians who championed white supremacy and failed to punish vigilante violence. On Christmas Day 1951, a bomb killed Florida NAACP president Harry T. Moore as he lay in bed. His wife, Harriet, died a few days later. No one was ever convicted. Looking back on Mississippi during the 1950s, Aaron Henry recalled, "It was plain that we could expect no help from local, state or federal authorities, and those of us who were in the fight were in it all the way. We had to hang on."[60]

Some—to Henry's great sadness—did not hang on. An NAACP official reckoned the movement in Augusta, Georgia, collapsed because "Negro spies and informants have a demoralizing effect upon the mildly interested people." But some fought back. In Columbus, Georgia, in 1951, black veterans—fresh from Korea—blew up the sheriff's car with a hand grenade.[61] As in the past, most African Americans despised the Jim Crow system but played along with it. Henry suspected "that every Negro maid in Mississippi has been asked at some point how she felt, and most of them obligingly told the white lady boss that they were happy as could be."[62] Henry didn't condemn them for it. As Sammie Hatcher, reflecting on his time working at Union Camp paper factory, explained, "You couldn't raise too much sand, a man say you gone, you just gone. I didn't like it but . . . I needed to work . . . I had six children at the time."[63]

Henry's description of 1950s protest fit his home state of Mississippi perfectly. But in many parts of the South, especially in cities in the upper South, African Americans were able to do more than just hang on. As in the North, they pressed on against segregation, and for more resources, too. "It is not so much the sheet waving . . . of the Klan which is dangerous," wrote William Foulkes, a black reporter in Atlanta, but the "systemized job and economic sanctions which mean strangulation and death for any Negro who dares compete with the supremacy system."[64]

As in the North, postwar changes strengthened the hand of many southern activists. At the outset of the 1950s, white attitudes seemed to be changing. Polls suggested that over half of white southerners thought that African Americans could, potentially, be as intelligent as whites (up from 20 percent during the war, though less than nearly 90 percent in the North).[65] Some moderate politicians spoke less about the "Negro problem" and more of good government. When Adam Clayton Powell came down to address a mass meeting in Montgomery in 1954, Alabama's Governor Jim Folsom invited him to the governor's mansion for a drink. Few southern liberals, and no southern moderates, advocated integration. Segregation seemed as natural a part of southern life as biscuits and gravy. But changing attitudes did offer black southerners the promise of progress and the opportunity to organize.

So too did changes in the southern economy, brought about by mechanization. Every time a farmer bought a tractor, ten people had to pack up and head for the city. By 1960, almost three in five black southerners lived in an urban neighborhood, a few of which prospered. In 1956 *Fortune* magazine lauded Atlanta's Auburn Avenue as the "richest black street in the world," home to multimillion-dollar businesses and churches, including Ebenezer Baptist, pastored by Martin Luther King Sr. Some segregated communities began to influence municipal elections and even elect black officials, such as in Greensboro, North Carolina. By 1956, some 20 percent of black southerners voted. While this meant that

80 percent did not, still (as one observer concluded), black citizens in Atlanta, Memphis, and New Orleans "may qualify with as much ease as in any northern city."[66]

Black voters were in no position to demand the end to segregation, let alone fair employment laws. But they did make some gains within the context of Jim Crow. When African American leaders first approached Atlanta's Mayor William Hartsfield during World War II, he told them to come back with ten thousand votes. When they returned a few years later, they had over twenty thousand. Hartsfield duly purged the Klan from the police force and appointed black officers. Atlanta's black leaders boasted that they held "the most powerful bloc south of Chicago." The Atlanta story played out across the South. Few towns had black policemen before the war, but by 1954, 143 southern towns did. Usually, black officers were segregated and were not allowed to arrest white people, but they made a difference nevertheless. In Greensboro, as the Reverend J. J. Green observed in 1955, "East Market Street was so dangerous that you didn't dare walk down it with your wife. Now . . . You don't even hear bad language."[67]

Thus, some cities became islands of progress in a region more associated with hate and violence (though the year 1952 was the first one without a lynching since recordkeeping of lynchings began). To quote William Foulkes again, "Most Negroes in the cities do laugh at and ridicule the occasional Ku Klux Klan parades . . . They can see through the inferiority complexes of the wearers of sheets." Black Atlantans called their city an "oasis" in Georgia. In reality, southern cities were hardly the stuff of peace and abundance. Atlanta was home to some of the worst slums in America. Two hours to the west of Atlanta by car, black residents of Birmingham renamed their city Bombingham in grim tribute to the experience of so many homeowners as they tried to cross the residential color line. Still, growing black urban communities and moderate municipal politics made diehard segregationists very nervous. Roy Harris, a prime mover in segregationist resistance, warned his supporters that "Atlanta could be the Achilles heel in the fight to keep segregation in Georgia."[68]

Harris was right. Protest was most likely to flourish precisely where black Americans had already managed to gain leverage, rather than where they were most oppressed. Aaron Henry reflected later, "Where there was the most progress, there was less intimidation and harassment, and the opposite for other communities, so the better got better and the worse became worse."[69] But in the midst of this mixed picture of local protest—from hanging on in the rural South to pressing on in some southern cities—a series of thunderbolts flashed across the sky of the region's racial history. The *Brown* decision of 1954, the Montgomery bus boycott of 1955–56, and the Little Rock school crisis of 1957 jolted the race question in the South almost out of recognition. These headline-grabbing events grew out of local struggles, and in turn reshaped the terrain of local struggles. And all the while, they taught activists important lessons about the limits of gradualism, the power of resistance, and the potential of the federal government to bring about change if it could be forced to act.

The *Brown* Decision and the Power of White Supremacy

On Monday, May 17, 1954, Chief Justice Earl Warren delivered the Supreme Court's opinion in the case *Brown v. Board of Education, Topeka, Kansas.* The case was a conflation of five cases, brought by the NAACP to challenge school segregation. Warren concluded, "Separate educational facilities are inherently unequal." *Brown* reversed the court's support for segregation that had stood since *Plessy v. Ferguson* in 1896. Ralph Ellison mused: "What a wonderful world of possibilities are unfolded for the children."[70]

Brown was a pivotal moment in southern history, a moment after which nothing seemed quite the same again. The battle for integrated education was the culmination of the NAACP's long-term master plan to invalidate Jim Crow. From 1938, the legal arm of the NAACP had been led by Thurgood Marshall, who hailed from a middle-class background and had studied at Howard University, the nation's elite black institution. Marshall was tall, handsome, and popular, equally at ease in the rural South and among Washington elites. A motivator with an earthy sense of humor, he called himself the Head Nigger in the office. Others called him "Mr. Civil Rights." As a lawyer Marshall was cautious, careful to take cases only when he was confident of winning. For many years, Marshall and his team had focused on the equal part of the separate but equal doctrine. Both their victories and their frustrations along the way finally persuaded Marshall to challenge the separate part of the formula as well. After consulting branch presidents and the NAACP board, in 1950 Marshall decided it was time to act. The Cold War helped. The Justice Department's brief for *Brown* urged the Court to view the case "in the context of the present world struggle between freedom and tyranny."

Brown was also the result of long-term grassroots protests. Local struggles over education had traditionally been for better black schools, not integrated schools. But because of discriminatory spending, these local struggles evolved into struggles for integrated schooling. In rural

Prince Edward County, Virginia, in 1951, black children—outraged by the provision of a modern school for white children nearby—refused to turn up at their old shack of a school. Black parents wrote to a firm of black lawyers in Richmond to ask them to file an integration suit, and as a courtesy gesture Oliver Hill, a partner in the firm, agreed to visit. "When we got there," he remembered later, "they had such high morale, and were so well organized, and could state their case so nicely, we didn't have the heart to turn them down."[71] The suit became part of *Brown*.

Mr. Civil Rights appreciated that NAACP legal victories were dependent on such grassroots initiative—and on great sacrifice. The Delaine family in Clarendon, South Carolina—who initiated a suit that also became part of *Brown*—had their house burned down and were forced to flee the state. Plaintiff Harry Briggs was fired from his job as a gas station attendant. His wife, Liza, lost her job as a chambermaid. Still, when the case reached federal court in 1951, some five hundred people made the journey to witness the arguments. "Imagine oneself in their position," Marshall explained, and "ask the question: 'Would I have that much courage?' If you are honest with yourself the answer would most probably be 'No!'"[72]

For all the bravery of the Delaines and Briggses, and for all Marshall's skill, the victory was also dependent on the changing outlook of the Court. After all, in *Plessy*, the Court had endorsed segregation as "natural." As chief justice, Warren took much of the credit and criticism for the decision, though in fact his main contribution was to turn a majority decision into a unanimous one. Virtually all the Supreme Court clerks supported school integration, and the justices all subscribed to the liberal view that the problem of racism could be overcome eventually by bringing children together. They even accepted the NAACP's assertion that because a dozen or so black children in South Carolina chose white dolls over brown dolls in tests, segregated schools produced an inferiority complex. (No one thought to test black children in integrated schools to see if other factors, such as advertising or everyday discrimination, might be causal.)

At a celebratory party after the decision, Marshall warned his staff, "You fools go ahead and have your fun . . . we ain't begun to work yet." But even Marshall thought school segregation would be gone across the country in "up to five years." Segregationists, on the other hand, railed against "Black Monday." Mississippi's Senator Eastland sent out 300,000 copies of a speech that exposed *Brown* as "based on the writings and teachings of pro-communist agitators."[73] But yelps from white supremacist politicians were to be expected. As one reporter put it, "Eastland . . . jumps to the call of segregation like Pavlov's dog to the sound of a bell."[74] Less predictable was that some white groups came out in support of *Brown*. The Southern Baptist Convention voted by a massive majority (only fifty out of nine thousand dissented) to affirm *Brown*. The most common position, though, was neither rejoicing nor rebellion but resignation. As Jim Folsom reckoned, "When the Supreme Court speaks, that's the law."[75] School districts in parts of the South made plans to desegregate.

Yet ten years later, only one southern black child in every hundred attended school with white children. Many black southerners remained unconvinced about integration (almost half, according to one 1955 poll), and some, quite rightly, feared the repercussions. More important than black ambivalence, though, was white intransigence. A year after *Brown,* the Court issued a follow-up decision that refused to put a date on implementation, calling only for "all deliberate speed." Perhaps some of the justices were naive, or sympathetic to white southerners. Most likely, they were simply in step with liberal sentiment that supported equal rights but not government-led enforcement. Whatever the reason, it was but a small step from all deliberate speed to all deliberate delay. "The Supreme Court had given us a beautifully wrapped gift," reflected Aaron Henry, "but when we removed the shiny wrappings, the box was empty."[76]

In the Deep South, segregationists declared war on *Brown*. In July 1954 segregationists in Indianola, Mississippi, formed the White Citizens' Council. By 1956 it had 250,000 members, three times as many as the southern NAACP. Strongest in the Deep South, the council lobbied state governments to pass new segregation measures. Month by month, so-called "massive resistance" seemed to grow in intensity and scope. On March 12, 1956, all but three southern senators signed a "southern manifesto" promising to use "all lawful means to bring about a reversal of this decision." Later that year, Virginia's legislature passed measures to prevent desegregation. When NAACP lawsuits forced three school districts to admit black students in 1958, Virginia's governor shut down public education.

Those who had hoped for gradual change were puzzled by just how massive segregationist resistance was. One reporter, John Martin, traveled around the Deep South to find answers. In *The Deep South Says Never,* Martin explained that the WCC "is every bit as righteous, determined and sure of success" as civil rights activists. The WCC was respectable—less hooded sheets on a hilltop than suit and tie in a social club. The movement was well-funded and politically savvy, basing its position on powerful appeals to science, history, and religion, with a dash of anti-communism, anti–rock and roll, and foreboding about declining school standards thrown in for good measure. Predictably, the WCC also warned that "interracial mating" would follow integrated schools as surely as night follows day. One woman told Martin that whenever WCC meetings got boring, they just started talking about black men having sex with white girls, and passed around glossy pictures of black men and white girls dancing.[77]

Most of these were old arguments. *Brown* did not create white supremacist angst, and the Dixiecrat movement of 1948 had already shown that segregationists were politically well-organized. What *Brown II* gave segregationists was confidence in victory. There was nothing subtle about this. John Patterson won election as governor of Alabama in 1958 on a "Kill the NAACP!" platform. Thus, instead of fighting for integration, the NAACP was soon fighting for its life. Between 1955 and 1957, membership in the South fell by almost half, the organization was outlawed in Alabama, and it was tied up in litigation in most other southern states. Politicians called for the publication of NAACP membership lists, in the name of preventing secretive Communist activity. Aaron Henry remembered that "the whites had won a big round, and, for several years after early 1956 . . . we moved under a cloud, and we moved cautiously."[78]

The cloud darkened further after the murder of Emmett Till in August 1955. A fourteen-year-old boy from Chicago, sent to visit his Uncle Moses Wright in the small delta town of Money, Mississippi, Till had embarrassed a white woman in a local store soon after arrival. Till's friends said later he whistled at her on a dare. She claimed that he grabbed her and said "unprintable" words. A few days later, the woman's husband returned. With his half-brother, they abducted Till, beat him to a pulp, and threw his body in a nearby river. When the corpse surfaced, the face was so disfigured that Till could be identified only by the ring on his finger. His mother, Mamie, insisted that the corpse be displayed in an open casket ahead of the Chicago funeral. The black press published the picture, which was seen around the world.

So too was a picture of Moses Wright, pointing out the murderers in what was a mockery of a fair trial. Despite overwhelming evidence to convict, the all-white jury took sixty-seven minutes to agree on a not-guilty verdict. "If we hadn't stopped to drink pop," said one juror, "it wouldn't have taken that long."[79] Mamie traveled to the delta to testify too, though her dignified appeal for justice outside the courtroom was even more significant. Many student activists in the Civil Rights Movement said the Till case was the moment they resolved to protest one day.

Soon after the trial the murderers confessed all to *Look* magazine for $4,000, but under America's double-jeopardy provision in the Fifth Amendment they could not be tried a second time.

Yet in many cities—precisely where black activists had already secured gains—massive resistance to school desegregation and the ensuing white violence did not have the destructive impact that the headlines might suggest. For activists in cities like Atlanta, Nashville, and Greensboro, the importance of *Brown* and its aftermath lay in the lessons it taught. The silence of white moderates was as deafening as WCC rhetoric. In Mississippi, journalist Hodding Carter could not find a single white minister or union leader who had spoken up against massive resistance.[80] "I don't like 'em," one woman told John Martin, "But you wouldn't dare say so. It's too late."[81] Southern moderates' fatalism trumped their gradualism, because few were prepared to countenance anything other than (benign) segregation.

The moderates' dilemma had political consequences. In Alabama, Folsom initially mocked the WCC as "haters and baiters." Maybe so, but they were powerful. After a mob prevented Autherine Lucy from becoming the first black student at the University of Alabama in February 1956, Folsom's days were numbered. It didn't help that he had been away in the country during the riot, doing a little fishing and rather more drinking. After the riot, Folsom vowed to defend segregation, but he still lost the 1958 election to WCC cheerleader John Patterson. Another loser in that election, George C. Wallace, learned his lesson. "They out-niggered me that time, but they will never do it again," he said. In his inaugural address as Alabama's governor in 1962, Wallace would declare, "Segregation now! Segregation tomorrow! Segregation forever!"

Black leaders were shocked by the moderates' surrender. In 1963 the influential black journalist Louis Lomax wrote that we "had faith in a class of white people known to Negroes as *good white people . . .* It was incredible to a Negro woman who had been a servant in a white home for twenty years that her employers would cringe and hide while white trash threw bricks at her grandson on his way to school."[82] They also lost faith in the president for (to quote Henry) his "weak and ineffective domestic leadership."[83] At no point did Eisenhower endorse *Brown.* He later told friends that appointing Earl Warren as chief justice of the Supreme Court was the "biggest damn fool mistake" he had ever made. After all, he had told Warren that the main thing white southerners "are concerned about is to see that their sweet little girls are not required to sit in school alongside some big overgrown Negro."[84]

Massive resistance, the moderates' silence, Eisenhower's prevarication, the NAACP's weakness—not to mention the example of the North and West—meant that many black activists in the South began to lose faith in the liberal promise of government-led gradual change. To quote Lomax again, *Brown* "was the day we won . . . we were proud. But we were also naive."[85] Maybe, but not for long.

The Montgomery Bus Boycott

In 1954 the elders of Dexter Avenue Church in Montgomery, Alabama, sought a new pastor. They had fallen out with the previous incumbent, the Reverend Vernon Johns, for any number of reasons: his fiery sermons, his loud criticism of distinguished church members, his habit of selling vegetables in the church basement and frequent references to discount prices in sermons, his part-time work as a fishmonger, and his provocation of the Klan. One sermon title on the church billboard read, "It's Safe to Murder Negroes in Montgomery." Church elders were proud of Dexter's reputation as the home to the high-standing. So they went looking for a new pastor who would cause less trouble. They found a 25-year-old man by the name of Martin Luther King Jr.[86]

King fit their requirements splendidly. He was from respectable stock —the son of one of Atlanta's leading ministers. He was well-educated, first at Atlanta's elite Morehouse College and later at Boston University, where he received his doctorate. His wife, Coretta, was an Alabama native who had been studying music in Boston's New England Conservatory when they met. He preached well at his trial sermon. But unbeknown to the Dexter elders, King's journey to faith had taken a few side turns. His initial decision to be a minister was partly a way to appease his father after a policeman caught him drinking beer. As a seminary student he was drawn to a liberal theology out of step with the certainties of the black Baptist tradition. He had doubts about the emotionalism of the black church, and many doubts about himself too. Behind his public gravitas, he was bedeviled by inner conflict. As a youth he twice flirted with suicide. A struggle with depression would mark his adulthood. (As for Coretta, she urged Martin to take a job in a northern city instead.)

Still, from what the elders could see, King seemed ideal. They were in for a shock. In a foretaste of his presumption of leadership, King quickly faced them down and took full control of the finances and committees. But the bigger shock was still to come. In late 1955 King led a city-wide boycott of Montgomery's buses. During the next year, his house would be bombed, he would go to jail, and he would emerge a hero hailed around the world. The mass circulation black magazine *Jet* would put King on the front cover, calling him "Alabama's Modern Moses." Huge crowds would gather around the country to hear him speak. The wealthy would open their wallets to support him. Some women would swoon.

King did not create the desire to challenge bus segregation in Montgomery. African Americans had boycotted the city's public transportation for over a year when segregation was first introduced in 1900. Since then, there had been plenty of fights. Black passengers were required to pay at the front and then get off the bus in order to board at the rear. Sometimes the driver took the fare and drove off before the passenger could get back on. If the seats in the black section of the bus were full, black passengers had to stand, even if the white section of the bus was empty. A local Women's Political Council, led by an irrepressible teacher, Jo Ann Robinson, sought more black drivers, more courtesy from white drivers, and the option of expanding the black section if need be. In short, they sought to make segregation less harsh, rather than remove it. This seemed reasonable—the bus system in Mobile, Alabama, which was run by the same company, had a moveable line to keep blacks segregated from whites.

Recent developments in local politics meant that adjusting bus segregation suddenly seemed possible, too. Black voter registration had increased tenfold between 1950 and 1955. In 1953, black voters provided the margin of victory for a moderate city commissioner, Dave Birmingham. By 1955 the city commission had appointed black policemen, made some provision for the black poor and sick, and had upgraded black schools. The baseball team added two black players to the roster. These changes hardly added up to revolution. But at the time they seemed startling. One local black editor thought: "Montgomery is fast taking the lead as Alabama's most enlightened city." In turn, such developments emboldened activists, such as the Women's Political Council, to demand more improvements.[87]

The planning for a boycott also predated King's arrival in Montgomery. In the 1955 city elections, a segregationist candidate, Clyde Sellers, beat Dave Birmingham for a seat on the City Commission. Riding the back of massive resistance, Sellers calculated (rightly) that he could afford to ignore the black vote as long as he secured enough white voters. Suddenly, black leaders faced the prospect of no more gains through negotiation with the City Commission. By this time, the local NAACP was led by a forthright union man, E. D. Nixon—a stocky, tough railroad porter. Nixon started looking out for a potential plaintiff to challenge bus segregation. And when Adam Clayton Powell came to visit later that year, his stories of boycotts in New York added fuel to Nixon's plan.

On the evening of December 1, 1955, Rosa Parks boarded a bus downtown. It would become the most famous bus ride in American history. At the time, Parks was a 42-year-old returning home, weary from her day's work as a seamstress and in some pain from an inflamed shoulder. She took her seat just behind the sign marking the colored rear section of the bus. As more white passengers boarded the bus, the bus driver moved the sign back a row and told Parks to give up her seat. As there were no black seats left either, Parks would have been forced to stand. She refused to move. Technically, she was within her rights, but the driver called the police, who arrested Parks and took her to the city jail.

When the driver decided to challenge Parks, he picked the wrong person. Her biography was a lesson in the long history of protest. One of very few blacks in the city to complete high school, she was also one of the most active opponents of white supremacy in the state. Her grandfather had been a supporter of Marcus Garvey. Her husband, Raymond, helped found the local NAACP. She had attended meetings to protest the trials of the Scottsboro Boys in the 1930s. After the war she became one of the first black women in Montgomery to register to vote. She had also helped run what the *Defender* called "the strongest campaign for equal justice to Negroes seen in a decade"—to convict the men who gang-raped a married black Montgomery woman (they weren't convicted). Unable to get a job as a stenographer on account of her color, she put her typing skills to work in service of the local NAACP. Parks was secretary of the branch, adviser to the branch's youth council, and a leader of the voter registration effort. She had also attended a two-week training course for civil rights campaigners at the Highlander Folk School in Tennessee. "I did not get on the bus to get arrested," Parks explained later. "I got on the bus to get home."[88] But she knew that the Women's Political Council hoped to launch a boycott, and that the NAACP hoped to file a test case. She also knew the teenage girl who had been planning to file suit, until she became pregnant. Parks was also still seething at the acquittal of Till's murderers just two months before.

The opportune arrest of this mild-mannered, well-known, committed Christian outraged the local black community. The Women's Political Council distributed leaflets calling for a boycott. Nixon called a meeting of local black leaders. But by the time they met, and to the consternation of some, community support for a boycott was unstoppable. A Montgomery Improvement Association was founded to organize it, and after a heated meeting between rival factions, King was appointed leader. On December 5, Parks appeared in court. She was fined $10 plus costs. She refused to pay. The boycott started the same day. It lasted for another 380 days.

That it went on so long had as much to do with local politics as local protesters. Just two years before, black residents of Baton Rouge, Louisiana, had launched a similar boycott, led by a charismatic preacher, seeking better treatment. But city leaders quickly made concessions (including, some said, buying off key black leaders). The resulting compromise to end the boycott angered some activists—an anger that would remain for at least a generation, especially in light of what happened in Montgomery.

By contrast, Montgomery's City Commission took a hard line. Sellers was constrained by his tough campaign rhetoric, and the other commissioners felt intimidated by members of the WCC (which had not been a factor in pre-*Brown* Baton Rouge). Rather than seeking to defuse protest, they sought to trample it. It almost worked. Shortly after the boycott began, the commissioners found three ministers willing to denounce the action and prepared a story for the local paper saying the boycott was over. But when King got wind of the ruse, he spent the evening traveling to local taverns and juke joints to let people know the boycott was still on. The commissioner's gamble backfired. Protesters who had sought the right not to have to stand for white passengers now sought the right to sit beside them throughout the bus. Police harassment, and a bomb thrown at King's house, served to unite the movement further. The MIA filed suit. Through mass meetings and car pools to get people to work, the boycott endured. On November 13, 1956, the Supreme Court upheld a district court ruling against segregation, which led to a new city ordinance. By December 20 the boycott was over.

The movement made King a national figure. If he hadn't chosen Montgomery (against his wife's wishes), and if he hadn't been chosen as MIA president (because he was too new in town to be aligned with any faction), he may have been barely a footnote to history. He was in the right place at the right time. But in many ways, he was also the right man. He had thought deeply about issues of social justice and Christianity. His theological search convinced him that evil lay in the human heart, but that it could be overcome by righteous resistance. Hence, his nonviolent confrontational approach, which sought to redeem the oppressor—and purify the oppressed—through resistance founded on Christian love. He combined genuine intellectual insight with unsurpassed rhetoric. His biography meant that he could speak in the southern black church and to white northerners as well. His genius was in the way he managed to combine the two. He showed great courage after the bombing of his house. For all his flaws, King would shape the tactics of civil rights protest across the South and around the world. In particular, he would become the spokesman for (or rather interpreter of) black southerners' grievances and aspirations to white America.

Still, the reason why the boycott developed was not so much due to King but to organization by the Women's Council, the institutional strength of the black community, and the sacrifice of thousands. The reason why it carried power was the clout of black consumers. Segregationists did not have a comparable capacity. The WCC pleaded with white housewives not to pick up their maids, but to no avail. As the black journalist Louis Martin observed, "When there is no power behind your very fine argument, the knuckleheads don't listen . . . There are two instruments of power in our hands which we are beginning to learn to use, the vote and the wage dollar."[89] It was a lesson King took to heart. As he told a mass meeting in 1956, "Until we as a race learn to develop our power, we will get nowhere. We've got to get political and economic power for our race."[90]

The Little Rock Nine

On September 4, 1957, teenager Elizabeth Eckford was understandably nervous about going to her new school. As one of the first nine black children to be accepted to Little Rock High School, she anticipated a hostile reception. Still, she knew that the governor had called out the National Guard to protect them, and she was excited at the prospect of making a difference. She had even badgered her parents to let her transfer. She had her new dress ready. Before dawn she had read Psalm 27, "The Lord is my light and my salvation—whom shall I fear?"

Her faith was about to be tested. What Elizabeth didn't know was that the other eight children had arranged to go together by car—but since the Eckfords didn't own a telephone, she didn't get the message. She also didn't know that the governor, Orval Faubus, had instructed the National Guard to block the black children from school.

When Elizabeth reached Little Rock High, two guardsmen forced her to turn around and walk back through a mob. She looked to a gray-haired older woman who seemed to be sympathetic. The woman spat in her face. When Elizabeth walked to a nearby store to call a taxi, the store shut her out. To cries of "Go back to the goddamn jungle!" she walked to the closest bus stop and sat down. A local civil rights leader sat down beside her, showed his gun, and offered to take her home. She declined. After some time, the bus came. Elizabeth headed to the laundry where her mother Birdie worked, and as her mother held her close, Elizabeth wept.[91]

Horrifying and heart-wrenching as her experience was, Elizabeth would not be the only child to shoulder the burden of integration. Three years later, six-year-old Ruby Bridges, wearing cute pigtails and a new starched white blouse, would brave a mob of housewives and teenagers in New Orleans. The novelist John Steinbeck would compare the scene, which he witnessed, to "vomitings of demoniac humans."[92] Yet Elizabeth's trial, and the Little Rock story, stood out. Over 250 reporters and photographers descended on the city like a flock of vultures, sensing a kill. Above all, though, Little Rock stood out because it led to federal action. On September 24 Eisenhower ordered one thousand paratroopers to enable the nine black children to go to school. It was the first time a president had sent troops to defend African Americans since Reconstruction.

The Little Rock crisis fit the pattern of southern public protest. As in Montgomery, it was the relatively moderate nature of local politics, rather than new oppression, that prompted protest to develop. In the 1954 election for governor, Faubus skirted the issue of *Brown*. He then appointed six African Americans to the state Democratic Committee, prompting the WCC to call him Awful Faubus. With the rise of massive resistance to integrated schools, Faubus created a state commission to defend segregation. Even then, his posture may simply have been a way to ensure support for the passage of an expensive package of socially progressive reforms—just a week before the integration of Little Rock High, he had still not made appointments to the segregation commission. As for admitting the Little Rock Nine, he warned the WCC that he couldn't intervene. "Everyone knows no state law supersedes a federal law."[93]

Local black activists had been organizing in the city long before the confrontation. A veterans group, for example, was working with poorer neighborhoods on the east side. But the NAACP was the key organization in town. Since 1952 the local branch (and state conference) had been led by Daisy Bates. Young, petite, and beautiful, Bates was also bold and charismatic, able to hold a crowd and sweep it into action. She had nursed anger against white people ever since she learned that white men had raped and murdered her mother. Daisy was married to newspaperman L. C. Bates—he was the man with a gun at the bus stop who offered to help Elizabeth Eckford. The Bateses were never quite accepted as part of Little Rock's black elite. But then again, they never sought to be—

Daisy was impatient at the gradualist approach of so-called race leaders. In any case, once the crisis developed, the black community swung behind the Bateses. Armed men set up an all-hours vigil round their house.

Starting in 1952, the Little Rock Council on Schools (an umbrella group that included the NAACP) had called for integration. They had met with Virgil Blossom, the superintendent of schools, who was clearly trying to stall and limit integration. He suggested attendance zones, which meant that only two hundred black children would be eligible to apply for transfer, and only to Central High rather than to a school in the suburbs serving wealthier white families. And on top of these restrictions, applicants would be screened for suitability. But the fact that Blossom met with the council at all was a start, and *Brown* and Montgomery gave activists added confidence. By 1956, some other Arkansas school districts had put in place plans to desegregate, with no problems, and that same year Little Rock had desegregated its buses peacefully.

As in Montgomery, activists moved from appeals to confrontation when progress suddenly stopped. With the rise of massive resistance, the school board swung in line with the WCC. When Daisy Bates and the NAACP filed suit for full integration, the judge ordered a version of Blossom's original plan, which meant that only nine students would be able to transfer. WCC leaders visited Little Rock and whipped up large crowds to oppose even this token desegregation. On August 27 a church-based Mothers' League filed suit to keep Central High white only, warning of sexual diseases. Angry that they were not allowed to transfer their children to the all-white suburban school, these women appealed to their menfolk to act. They also called on Faubus to be a witness in their suit.

Faubus calculated that he had the most votes to gain by throwing his lot in with the segregationists. He argued that violence would occur if integration went ahead—and then he helped ensure that it did. On the eve of the transfer, his televised warning of likely violence sent viewers a clear message. Early on September 4 a white reporter raced to Daisy Bates's house, pleading with her to keep the children back. "I've never seen anything like it . . . People I've known all my life—they've gone mad." Bates took the eight children anyway.

Faubus learned his lines quickly, promising Eisenhower to his face that he would control the situation. But back in Little Rock, he flaunted defiance, cocksure that Eisenhower would not get involved. For two weeks the students stayed out of school. After a federal judge ruled on September 20 that Faubus had used troops to prevent children from going to school, not to preserve law and order, Faubus duly removed the troops.

He then flew out of town for a governors' meeting. Three days later the nine children re-entered the school. But with a thousand-strong mob threatening to overpower the city police, the students withdrew at mid-morning. Some black reporters were beaten.

Eisenhower said it was "disgraceful." While he did not approve of school integration, he felt it his duty as president to uphold the law. And as a general used to obedience from subordinate, he was enraged by Faubus's deception. Eisenhower also felt that the eyes of the world were on Little Rock. *Ebony* magazine described "Little Rock" as "the two-word satellite that circled the globe."[94] It was an apt analogy. Just before the crisis, the Russians had celebrated the launch of *Sputnik 1,* which had given them the lead in the space race. To rub America's nose in it, Radio Moscow included Little Rock in the daily itinerary of major cities passed over by the Russian rocket.

The next day, the president ordered in the paratroopers. Facing a mob in Little Rock was child's play compared with facing an armed enemy in the Korean jungle, and the troops quickly ensured the students' entry into the school. Thus, Little Rock became a pincer movement against segregationists—an assault by black southern protesters on one side and by the federal government on the other.

As with many transfer students across the South, the first year was full of insults for the Little Rock Nine. Bates encouraged them not to retaliate but to complain to school staff. The feistiest student, Minnejean Brown, eventually snapped. At lunchtime one day she tipped a bowl of chili over two of her tormentors and soon afterward was expelled. (The girls' vice-principal wrote admiringly in her diary, "I can't help liking her natural reaction . . . This bowl of chili no doubt has been heard around the world!")[95] Some children started a chant, "One nigger down and eight to go." But the other eight made it. Ernest Green was the first to get his diploma. Martin Luther King Jr. joined Bates at the graduation.

The Limits of Protest

Because the southern Civil Rights Movement would follow in the early 1960s, it might be tempting to see the high-profile confrontations of the 1950s as stepping-stones toward triumph. But Montgomery and Trumbull Park, Little Rock and Levittown, showed that progress seemed anything but inevitable at the time. White violence in the North surprised the first pioneer families in white neighborhoods. Violence in the South did not surprise anyone, but it continued to shock nonetheless. Between the *Brown* decision and the closing of Little Rock's high schools, there were 225 recorded instances of attacks on civil rights activists, private homes, and institutions.[96]

There was certainly no sense of steady gains during the decade. Black urban areas—and thus black voting blocs—grew in size, and the black middle class grew in numbers and consumer power. But in terms of earnings, labor-force participation, and occupational attainment, black workers were further behind white workers in 1959 than they had been at the end of the war. In northern cities, housing and school segregation and black unemployment actually increased during the 1950s. And in the South, Jim Crow seemed secure. One speaker at Fisk University's Fifteenth Annual Conference on Race Relations in 1958 worried that "integration is moving backwards." One national poll at the end of the decade found that 61 percent of respondents thought "white people have a right to keep blacks out of [their] neighborhoods."[97]

Even the victories in the South were followed by setbacks. After the bus boycott, Montgomery's WCC vowed to make their city the historic place where "integration efforts were stopped cold." It's hard to imagine a boast that would be proved more spectacularly wrong. But at the time, it was plausible. Segregationist hardliners won the first council elections after the boycott. The NAACP was still barred from the state. Snipers shot at black passengers sitting on the front seats of buses. Six bombs detonated near buses in January 1957, and service was temporarily suspended. Later that month, when the Klan heard that a black truck driver was dating a white woman, they captured Willie Edwards Jr. and forced him to jump to his death off a bridge across the Alabama River. But they got the wrong black truck driver. The Montgomery *Advertiser* reported, "The issue now has passed beyond segregation. The issue *is whether it is safe to live in Montgomery, Ala.*"[98]

In Little Rock, voters approved Faubus's closure of all four public high schools for the 1958–59 school year. Forty-four teachers who had supported the Little Rock Nine lost their jobs. Congressman Brooks Hayes, who had tried to broker a deal between Eisenhower and Faubus, lost his seat to a write-in candidate from the school board (one of only three write-in victories in the second half of the twentieth century). The Reverend Dunbar Ogden, who supported integration, was dismissed from his church, and his son committed suicide. So too did Little Rock's police chief, Gene Smith, who had held back the mob; segregationists accused him of being a Judas. Smith shot his wife dead before turning the gun on himself. As for Faubus, he played the role of tough, aggrieved victim well—and thus fit the trope of the white hero in the westerns that dominated TV schedules in the 1950s. Wary of alienating white southern viewers, news reporters mostly treated Faubus with respect. One poll at the end of 1958 ranked him in the top ten admired figures in America. Faubus would serve as governor for twelve years in total, helped by a switch to a moderate stance in the early 1960s. (His last run for office was in 1986, when he was beaten by a young opponent by the name of Bill Clinton.)

Yet for all the brouhaha, the protest in northern cities and even the set-piece southern confrontations also exposed the limits of old-style white supremacy. By the end of the decade, legal segregation was a thing of the past in the North, and segregationist violence was proving counterproductive in much of the South. The NAACP's Roy Wilkins reckoned that when "some outrage occurs, white people send the NAACP checks." He praised Faubus for "clarifying the issue of segregation" and so "educated to our point of view millions of people in America."[99] In some cities, business elites urged a move away from violent, unyielding segregation for the sake of civic progress.

The problem for all-or-nothing segregationists was the lack of alternatives to closing the schools (or, for that matter, closing the local pool or park). In Little Rock, the Supreme Court rejected segregationists' plans to convert the public school system into a taxpayer-funded private school system. At that point Faubus proposed a constitutional amendment that would end the state's obligation to provide free education. In other words, white parents faced a choice between integration or no schools at all. In Little Rock's most exclusive suburbs, a Women's Emergency Committee formed "neither for integration nor for segregation, but for education."[100] Token integration held no terrors for them—it would not affect their school. Their husbands approved, and the president of Little Rock's Chamber of Commerce called for the schools to stay open—the crisis had already cost the city five new industrial plants. Three diehard segregationists on the school board were replaced by three pragmatists, and in 1959 the city duly implemented a token "controlled integration" plan without trouble.

The resolution in Little Rock pointed to the new battles ahead for southern activists. The alternative to massive resistance was not massive integration but minimal compliance. Little Rock also opened its zoo to black visitors—on Thursdays. In other words, African Americans in southern cities faced much the same issues as their northern counterparts. In 1959 a group of younger black businessmen in Atlanta published a pamphlet calling for A Second Look at Atlanta, the self-styled "city too busy to hate." One of the authors, Whitney Young (soon to be president

of the National Urban League), complained that "Atlanta was comparing itself to Mississippi and saying how enlightened it was [but] nothing
was really integrated."[101] Black Atlantans were more than one third of
the city's residents but occupied less than a sixth of the land, had access
to less than a sixth of the hospital beds, and had virtually no representation on city boards or the Chamber of Commerce. The black vote, in alliance with middle-class white voters, had kept Atlanta free from demagogues, but this alliance was effectively "whitemail," with black voters
the junior partners.

The lessons of the postwar decade, then, were that gradualism was not
the same as progress; that allies in the North supported rights rather than
enforcement; that moderates in the South sought token changes to avoid
confrontation rather than embrace integration; that opponents would
fight for control of resources; that state politicians in most of the South
championed massive resistance; that Jim Crow was entrenched in the
Deep South; and that the president did not see civil rights as a moral
cause (he even lumped the NAACP and White Citizens' Council into the
same category of overzealous militants). It was a far cry from the expectations of civil rights leaders in 1948, or even after *Brown*.

What it meant was that many activists' patience in the promises of
gradual change began to wear thin. It meant, too, that many activists—
like Bates in Little Rock, like Abner in Chicago—began to denounce the
traditional black leadership in their town. *A Second Look* was as much a
criticism of Atlanta's black elite as it was a criticism of the city's political
leaders.

With the hindsight of the Civil Rights Movement, an upsurge in protest might seem inevitable at the end of the 1950s. Certainly more confrontational protest was likely. As the 1950s had shown, activists—especially workers, voters, and consumers in the cities—had new power to
demand change. Local legislation in the North, and federal legislation for
the South, meant that activists had the law on their side. Of course defenders of the color line also held power, especially those who accepted
minimal compliance to retain maximum discrimination. They, too, could
vote, organize, and appeal to American values. But diehard white supremacists would struggle to make their case in the context of the Cold
War, and in the face of developments in popular and intellectual culture.

Yet at the end of the 1950s, a nationwide, massive outbreak of confrontational protest was anything but inevitable. The *New York Times*
reported a higher number of civil rights demonstrations in 1946–1948
than in 1957–1959.[102] In Little Rock, the Bateses hung on, but their business went bankrupt, and segregationists crushed demonstrations in 1960.

In Montgomery, the black movement fell apart after the boycott. Parks' husband had an emotional breakdown, and the couple left for Detroit. Nixon resigned from the MIA, angered at its lack of recognition from King and for "being treated as a child" by some of the ministers.[103] With the militant labor organizer gone, more conservative leaders assumed control. Some suggested filing for school integration, but no one had the stomach for the fight.

As for Martin Luther King Jr., he formed the Southern Christian Leadership Conference in January 1957. The SCLC reflected the struggle's national links. King took advice from northern activist Bayard Rustin, who persuaded King to appoint Ella Baker temporary executive secretary. (King would have preferred a man to fill the post, but Rustin himself would have been a liability—openly gay and recently arrested for sodomy.) The SCLC reflected King's Christian background, too. He hoped the organization would be the political arm of the black church—virtually all the officers were churchmen. The SCLC accepted King's theology of nonviolent confrontation to win over opponents and purify self. And it reflected King's sense of personal destiny: more than any other protest organization, the SCLC revolved around one person.

In time, the SCLC would play a pivotal role in southern protest. But in its first years it planned little and achieved less. Copycat bus boycotts were few and far between (the victory in Montgomery meant activists elsewhere only needed to litigate). The National Baptist Convention, the largest black organization in America, kept the SCLC at a distance, despite King's lobbying. The SCLC's planned mass march on Washington in 1957 (in liaison with the NAACP and A. Philip Randolph) was undermined by tensions between the main leaders. Only twenty thousand or so turned up. The SCLC's 1958 plan to launch a Crusade for Citizenship in twenty-one cities was undermined by the lack of an office, staff, or phone. Ella Baker had to take change to a public telephone booth to make her calls. Later that year King was stabbed by a deranged black woman in Harlem. During his recuperation, the SCLC lacked direction.

As it turned out, much of the SCLC's activity at the end of the 1950s was the old, unglamorous story of local organizing, networking, and encouraging—the sort of work at which veteran activists like Ella Baker excelled. King cared little for such an incremental approach, and with his presumption of male leadership, he didn't care much for Ella Baker either. The feeling was entirely mutual. Believing that "strong people don't need strong leaders," Baker resented King. She resented, too, some male leaders' assumptions that women activists were best suited as secretaries or lovers, or both. Baker may have had a blind spot about King. But she was right that local people did not need a national organization or national leader in order to act. As she traveled the South and followed the news, Baker learned of the persistence of local activism.

Variety of Protest on the Eve of the Civil Rights Movement

Because the southern Civil Rights Movement of the early 1960s was nonviolent, led by the "better classes," and opposed to segregation, it would be easy to presume that the protest on the eve of the movement was cut from the same cloth. It was anything but. The SCLC and NAACP were indeed peaceful and respectable movements seeking civil rights. But during 1959, the year before civil rights protests surged across the South, there were plenty of other strategies on offer.

Late on Saturday evening, May 2, 1959, two African American couples shared a ride home to the Florida A&M University campus. They were returning from a ball—the men were still in their tuxedoes, the women in their dresses. On a lonely road, four white men stopped the car at gunpoint. The men had made a pact to "go out and get a nigger girl." They "got" nineteen-year-old Betty Jean Owens and raped her seven times. Outraged, Ella Baker wrote that "Negroes all over the South would watch developments closely." At first, they saw a trial that was as predictable as it was sickening. The jury was all-white. The defense counsel shouted at the still bruised Owens: Was she a virgin? "Didn't you derive any pleasure from that?"

In other ways, though, "Negroes all over the South" saw something as uplifting as it was surprising. Over a thousand students met in protest on campus, refusing to "sit idly by and see our sisters, wives, and mothers desecrated."[104] Four hundred students sat outside the court in silent vigil. The world's press carried the story. The jury found the men guilty—though they recommended mercy (perhaps because two of the men were mentally retarded). The judge sentenced them to life imprisonment, and recommended that they face up to their Maker, and fast.

On May 14, 1959, in Biloxi, Mississippi, nine African Americans waded into the ocean from a white-only beach. They were forcibly removed. The Biloxi confrontation was independent of any organization—it could hardly be any other way, since the NAACP was barely hanging on in the state, and the SCLC had no affiliate there. The prime mover in the struggle was Dr. Gilbert Mason, a Howard University–trained Biloxi native. The traditional black leadership warned him not to protest. White leaders on the County Board of Supervisors warned that if he did, "There's going to be bloodshed." Mason remained defiant. When the board asked how much beach he wanted, he replied, "All twenty-six miles, every damn inch of it." Some months later, more than a hundred black men, women, and children waded in from the beach. The official police plan was to "go out and beat the hell out of any Negro found on the beach." Two black teenagers were killed.[105] Mason defended himself with a pool cue. An armed group of "Black Angry Men" formed to defend him from future violence.

In June 1959 Baker met with the Reverend Fred and Mrs. Ruby Shuttlesworth in Birmingham. Since the Montgomery boycott, the Shuttlesworths had held weekly mass protest meetings. Like King, Fred Shuttlesworth was a devout Christian—he too believed he had a calling to lead a movement. (When another minister said God had told him to cancel the first mass meeting, Shuttlesworth replied, "Now just when did the Lord start sending my messages through you?") But unlike the Kings, the Shuttlesworths were from humble stock. They bypassed the city's "respectable" black leadership and based their movement in the working class, calling for better jobs at least as much as for integration. By the end of 1959, they had survived a bombing that ripped apart their home, Fred had spent ninety days in prison, they had desegregated the buses, and Fred had fallen out with black lawyers who charged full fees for civil rights cases. He had also lost faith in the promises of white moderates. After meeting with the city commission to request black policemen, he learned "that a white man smiles like he means 'yes' but he means 'hell no.'"[106]

On the eve of the civil rights movement, there were well-known militant rivals to King and Roy Wilkins too. No one more than Robert Williams, branch president of the NAACP in Monroe, North Carolina. Just four days after the Tallahassee rape, a white man was found not guilty of attempted rape in Monroe. It was time to "meet violence with violence," Williams told reporters. "We must be willing to kill if necessary." Williams had hardly been a shrinking violet before the case. During the war, he had battled white workers in a Virginia navy yard, fought in the Detroit riot, and spent three months in an army stockade for insubordination. After the war, he had enrolled in college, condemned "most students" in a left-leaning journal for "thinking [of] becoming a third class aristocracy in a Jim Crowed world," and founded his NAACP chapter by recruiting from local bars and pool halls. Shortly before the rape trial, he marshaled an armed guard to protect his vice president from the mob, and defended two boys (age eight and eleven) who were arrested for kissing a white girl. But it was the anger of local black women toward Williams for not seeking revenge on the Monroe rapist that "made me realize that this was the last straw, that we didn't have as much protection as a dog down there."[107]

Wilkins suspended Williams that same day and arranged for King and Daisy Bates to denounce him at the NAACP annual convention as dangerous and unrepresentative. (Bates was dependent on Wilkins and the NAACP for financial support after her family business collapsed.) Dangerous maybe—though he advocated self-defense, not aggression—but Williams was hardly unrepresentative. Biloxi's Dr. Mason had an armed guard, as did Bates. Ella Baker's good friend, the feminist lawyer Pauli Murray, represented Williams when he appealed to the NAACP national board. Baker herself spoke out in sympathy, albeit not full support. Williams became one of the most admired figures of his generation—so significant that King debated him in print.[108] Many NAACP delegates supported him at the 1959 convention. When Williams later fled to Cuba, to avoid arrest for kidnapping a white couple—he insisted he had been protecting them—and started broadcasting music and messages to the South, his mythic status and influence only increased.

Williams wasn't the only popular militant drawing Wilkins' anxious fire that summer. In July 1959 CBS aired a *60 Minutes* documentary on the Nation of Islam, entitled "The Hate That Hate Produced." The Nation's spiritual leader, Elijah Muhammad, warned, "We are going to treat the white man as he deserves," and predicted "there will be bloodshed." The light-skinned, slight-framed Georgia-born Muhammad was a former Garveyite who had known poverty, alcoholism, and white violence by the time he took over the Nation in Detroit in 1934. At that time, the Nation was one among many small black religious sects. Muhammad developed a theology around the notion that black people were the original tribe of Shabazz who had lived righteous lives for trillions of years; then an evil scientist-god named Yakub created the devilish white race to torment black people for six thousand years. The Shabazz tribe now had to stand firm against white devils before regaining paradise.

Wilkins dismissed Nation members as wacky racists. But the organization was both popular and powerful. Muhammad recruited among the poor and prisoners who were drawn to his condemnation of American institutions, his mockery of Christian hypocrisy, his promise of a triumphant black nation, his praise of black women, his calls for strict personal discipline, and his promotion of the Fruit of Islam—uniformed armed groups designated to protect members of the Nation, especially women. (As so often happened, praise for and protection of black women also meant male authority over them.) By 1959, *Time* magazine reckoned that the Nation of Islam had at least seventy thousand members and many more sympathizers (the CBS documentary led to a surge in both). Muhammad claimed a quarter of a million followers.

By this time, through canny investments in real estate, the Nation of Islam had become one of the richest black organizations in America, too. Muhammad forged connections with black leaders abroad, wrote his own column in mainstream black newspapers, and received praise from the black press when the Fruit of Islam faced down the police in Harlem. "I have a sinking feeling that Elijah Muhammad is very significant," admitted Chicago Urban League director Edwin C. Berry. He "makes a lot more sense than I do to the man in the street who's getting his teeth kicked out."[109] It would be his protégé, Malcolm X, who would soon make even more sense to the downtrodden.

Meanwhile in 1959, "Queen Mother" Audley Moore of Harlem presented a petition to the United Nations to force the American government to give land and pay reparations for slavery—precisely the opposite strategy to Wilkins' efforts to work in alliance with sympathetic politicians, and far from King's focus on southern civil rights. Moore was the embodiment of the long radical tradition. Born in Louisiana in 1898, granddaughter of a lynch victim and great-granddaughter of a slave who was raped by her master, Moore moved to Harlem. Among many causes, she was present at the opening rally of Garvey's convention, joined the Communist Party after Scottsboro (until it dropped its call for self-determination), lobbied the WPA to give sewing jobs to black women who would otherwise be domestics, led rent strikes in Harlem, served on the executive board of the National Council for Negro Women, accompanied some seven thousand war brides from Europe to reunite with black soldiers in America, campaigned against police brutality, and founded the Universal Association of Ethiopian Women which called for welfare rights and prisoner rights. She worked with Robert F. Williams and Malcolm X, too. In 1955, she founded a Reparations Committee of Descendants of U.S. Slaves—and her work for reparations would influence activists for generations to come.[110]

There were plenty of other local protests, too, during Baker's short tenure in the SCLC. From rent strikes in Harlem to sit-ins in segregated restaurants in a handful of southwestern towns to a 100-city boycott of Anheuser-Busch beer, in support of jobs at the company's all-white brewery in California. Indeed, there were anti-racist protests around the world, and the black press covered them in some depth. In the *New York Age*, columnist Chuck Stone wrote, "We must continue to realize that the black man who digs in the diamond mines in Johannesburg, who toils over the Ghana cocoa trees . . . and who drives a bus in London is our brother."[111]

The good news was the brothers in Ghana won independence in 1957.

The next year, Guinea followed suit. Audley Moore and Malcolm X applauded the Mau Mau resistance in Kenya, too. The bad news was that black Londoners suffered a race riot in 1958, and the lynching of black immigrant Kelso Cochrane in 1959 was Britain's first. Because Britain—with a minority black population in a liberal society—and not Africa was the analogous case to America, this racial violence was particularly worrying. But even so there were examples to inspire. The black press reported on black Londoners who fought back against white mobs, and of the dignified anger of over a thousand mourners at Cochrane's funeral.

Thus anyone watching the turn of events in 1959 might have concluded that more confrontational protests were imminent, and that some of those protests would be directed toward ending segregation in the South and demanding equality in practice, not just rights, everywhere. But even Ella Baker was taken aback by what happened next.

18. During this 1959 rally against school integration at the State Capitol in Little Rock, Arkansas, marchers held placards equating "race mixing" with communism and the coming of the antichrist. (Library of Congress, U.S. News and World Report Magazine Collection)

19. In 1963, to an unprecedented blaze of publicity, a quarter of a million people marched on Washington for better jobs and housing as well as for civil rights. (Library of Congress, U.S. News and World Report Magazine Collection)

20. This photograph of a police dog jumping at a teenager on May 3, 1963, in Birmingham, Alabama, provoked outrage around the world and put pressure on the federal government to act on behalf of black equality. (Bill Hudson/AP/ Press Association Images)

21. In 1964, in an address covered by major television channels, sharecropper Fannie Lou Hamer appealed, in vain, to the Democratic National Convention to seat delegates from the Mississippi Freedom Democratic Party rather than the regular lily-white state delegation. (Library of Congress, U.S. News and World Report Magazine Collection)

22. Malcolm X, who understood the domestic struggle for black equality in global terms, visited Oxford University in 1964, where he called for people to use "extreme methods" to change "this miserable condition that exists on this earth." (Hulton Archives/Getty images)

23. In Harlem in 1964, at the height of the nonviolent Civil Rights Movement, angry crowds surged onto the streets in response to the shooting of a black teenager by a policemen. (Library of Congress, U.S. News and World Report Magazine Collection)

24. Martin Luther King increasingly focused on the issue of poverty. In 1966 he toured the Vine City slum in Atlanta and met with residents who were protesting against exploitation by landlords. (Kenan Research Center at the Atlanta History Center, Bill Wilson Photography Collection)

25. Many of those involved in urban riots used violence as a means of protest, especially against police brutality, as in this case during the disturbances in Atlanta in 1966. (Kenan Research Center at the Atlanta History Center)

26. On March 12, 1966, after the heyday of the southern Civil Rights Movement, state NAACP field secretary Charles Evers (front left) led marchers at the all-black Alcorn College in Claiborne County, Mississippi—part of a local campaign for integration, better jobs, and black policemen. (Courtesy of Mississippi Cultural Crossroads)

CHAPTER NINE

The Civil Rights Movement, 1960–1965

"Africa in Big Surge Toward Freedom." Front-page headline, *Chicago Defender,* February 13, 1960

During a student sit-in in Nashville in 1960, a gang of white youths started to menace the peaceful demonstrators. A watching white minister, Will Campbell, was drawn to two figures. One was a "little old gray haired lady" who kept asking gang members, "How would you feel if that was your sister?" The other was a white student who turned up when the gang started fighting like "a wild animal mob." He punched the ringleader in the eye and said, "If you don't get out of here, I will stomp the piss out of you." (The ringleader suddenly noticed the police were outside, and told his gang it was time to go.) "There is no doubt" that both "prevented serious injury," Campbell mused, but "which one of these two made the proper ethical decisions, or did they both?"[1]

Atlanta, the self-proclaimed "city too busy to hate," desegregated its public schools peacefully in 1961. The following winter, the mayor erected a wooden street barricade in a southwest neighborhood to assuage white fears of black people trying to move in. By the next day, grateful white residents had wrapped the barricade in Christmas paper. Black Atlantans demonstrated. Critics called it Atlanta's Berlin Wall. A few nights later, "persons unknown" smashed the barricade. The next morning, white residents chopped down trees and rebuilt it, and Klansmen patrolled the road. One person carried a sign, "Whites Have Rights, Too." Soon after, the court ordered the barricade removed, and within a month, most homes were up for sale. Between 1955 and 1970, nearly one third of Atlanta's white residents moved to the suburbs. Some called Atlanta "the city too busy moving to hate."[2]

"Why has the Negro revolt come *now*? The late fifties and early sixties have been good years, relatively speaking, for Negroes, and even white liberals are hard-pressed to understand why better conditions for Negroes have served only to usher in a new Negro militancy." Louis Lomax, African American journalist and author, 1963[3]

groes in Birmingham [in 1963] began to stab the
in the back and bust them up the side their head—yes,
That's when Kennedy sent in the troops, down in
Birmingham. After that, Kennedy got on the television and said
'This is a moral issue.' That's when he said he was going to put
out a civil rights bill." Malcolm X, Message to the Grassroots,
Detroit, 1963

On February 3, 1964, an estimated 464,361 students stayed out
of New York Schools to protest segregation. It was most likely
the largest civil rights demonstration in American history.[4]

On Monday morning, February 1, 1960, four black men from historically black North Carolina Agricultural and Technical College walked into Woolworth's department store in downtown Greensboro. They bought toothpaste and school supplies, kept their receipts, and moved to the lunch counter. When they were refused service, one of the four, Ezell Blair, said to the cashier, "I beg your pardon, but you just served us at [that] counter. Why can't we be served at the [food] counter?" The manager asked them to leave. Instead, they just sat—and sat—and sat. The next day, twenty-five students joined them. On Wednesday, black students occupied virtually all the lunch counter seats. On Saturday, after dozens of young white men tried to block the protests, the A&T football team formed a "flying wedge" to enable students to sit-in.[5] Woolworth's closed after a bomb scare. At a mass meeting that evening sixteen hundred students voted to halt the sit-in to allow negotiations.

The "lunch counter demonstrations," wrote the *Chicago Defender*, two months later, "ripped through Dixie with the speed of a rocket and the contagion of the old plague."[6] The tactics spread too. Soon there were wade-ins on the beaches, pray-ins in churches, read-ins in libraries, and piss-ins in restrooms. Whereas African Americans in Montgomery had protested segregation by staying away, this was protest by confrontation. By August 1961, over seventy thousand people had participated in some kind of direct-action protest. Hundreds of thousands more joined economic boycotts supporting the sit-ins. Within a year, over a hundred communities had desegregated their lunch counters, some—starting with San Antonio, Texas, in March—to preempt sit-ins from even starting.[7] On July 25, 1960, after renewed demonstrations, the lunch counter in Greensboro's Woolworth's served its first black customer. (The lunch counter itself is now in the National Museum of American History on the Mall in Washington, D.C.)

The sit-ins brought a dynamic new protest organization into play. On Ella Baker's initiative, some two hundred student leaders, men and women, gathered in Raleigh over Easter weekend 1960. King addressed the meeting, but at Baker's prompting the students formed an independent organization, the Student Nonviolent Coordinating Committee (SNCC, pronounced "Snick"). The first staff members worked on a shoe-string budget. Three quarters of them were under twenty-one years old. They were idealistic, committed to nonviolent confrontation and going to jail rather than taking bail. John Lewis, who was elected SNCC's chairman in 1963, embodied all these attributes. Raised in rural Alabama, Lewis was a devout Christian and vegetarian (a painful childhood memory was accidentally drowning a chicken as he was trying to "baptize" it). At Fisk University, he led sit-ins alongside the heroine of the Nashville movement, the determined beauty queen Diane Nash. He believed in the possibility of an interracial "beloved community." And he seemed to get beaten up more than anyone. He once gave a talk at a mass meeting shortly after having his skull cracked, before staggering to a nearby hospital.

The sit-ins galvanized other civil rights organizations. The NAACP leadership was initially hesitant—worried that the new strategy might be counterproductive, dismissive of naive youthful exuberance (Wilkins patronized it as "blowing off steam"), and envious of all the fuss, and finance, that SNCC received. But NAACP youth councils led many local direct-action protests, and the head office soon embraced the sit-ins—and claimed to have come up with the idea in 1959. CORE joined the action. Its leader, James Farmer, decided to test a December 1960 Supreme Court decision, *Boynton v. Virginia,* which ruled that interstate commerce must not be segregated. On May 4, 1961, fourteen volunteers, including John Lewis, gathered in Washington, D.C. After spending some time in silence rather than prayer, since many were atheists, they boarded a Freedom Bus (the black riders in the front, the white ones in the back) and set off for New Orleans.

The group had a fairly trouble-free ride through the Upper South, although predictably Lewis was beaten up at an early stop. Farmer reckoned that "those thugs did not know what *Boynton* was. They probably did not know what the Supreme Court was."[8] But in Alabama they met appalling violence. Outside Anniston, a pack of fifty cars hunted down the bus. Someone threw a Molotov cocktail through a window and the bus caught fire. It was all too reminiscent of the public burnings of yesteryear. In Birmingham, Police Chief Eugene "Bull" Connor kept his men away for fifteen minutes, while he telephoned local hate groups to let them know which bus station to go to. The resulting beatings were so brutal that the Freedom Riders aborted the trip. Some never recovered. Nashville students—led by Diane Nash—flew in to resume the ride. In Montgomery, there were more beatings, and Lewis was knocked unconscious for twenty minutes. A mass meeting welcoming the riders turned into a terrifying all-night siege. In Mississippi, Governor Ross Barnett promised President John Kennedy and his brother Robert, the attorney general, that there would be no violence. In turn, the Kennedys let him ship the Freedom Riders straight into Mississippi's notorious maximum-security Parchman farm jail.

Aside from race protest, the sit-ins marked the reawakening of college campuses after the quiet years of McCarthyism. During the 1960s, hundreds of thousands of students protested a range of civil liberties issues, from the death penalty to the Vietnam War to (only in California) having to wear clothes to lectures. In turn, American campus protests influenced the global youth demonstrations of 1968.

This sudden emergence of protest prompted the obvious question, why? At the end of March 1960, the *Defender* sent one of its top reporters, Lu Palmer, to visit the hot spots. His baffled conclusion: it was "as though someone was pushing freedom buttons on a giant freedom switchboard." As to who that someone was, Palmer groped for a familiar divine explanation: it was "a massive revolution with God as the only mastermind."[9] Quite a few of the students told him they found Christ's teaching inspiring, and their faith strengthened. Mass rallies in churches, with preaching and singing, resembled revival meetings. But personal faith and the institution of the church dated back decades, and hardly explained what was new about the 1960s (not least because the main black Baptist organization kept its distance from the new protest).

In any case, Palmer's students mostly offered human reasons for their action. Many praised Martin Luther King Jr. Ezell Blair remembered, "I could feel my heart palpitating" when he heard King speak in Greensboro in 1958.[10] One of the Greensboro Four had read a CORE leaflet, and all four had read books on black heroes. Some spoke of Gandhi. Many talked about the frustrating lack of progress after *Brown*—one student worked out that at the current rate of desegregation, American schools would need seven more millennia before they were integrated. Some pointed to inspiring parents, while others criticized the failings of middle-aged leaders. Echoing the words of previous generations, Franklin McCain (one of the Greensboro Four) reflected later, "I felt as though I had gained my manhood." Some got involved by chance. Diane Nash had only recently transferred to Fisk from a northern college—to recuperate after splitting up with her boyfriend. Above all, the students spoke to Palmer about the march to freedom of African nations. James Baldwin, the literary voice of the movement, concluded in a review of the sit-ins for the *New York Times,* "This searching disaffection has everything to do with the emergence of Africa . . . at the rate things are going here, all of Africa will be free before we can get a lousy cup of coffee."[11] The story was widely told of Vice President Richard Nixon, attending Ghana's independence celebration, asking a black man what it felt like to be free. "I wouldn't know," he replied. "I'm from Alabama."

In the midst of the heroic stories and beatings, few noted the most important reason of all. By 1960, African American students now had the opportunity to protest publicly as never before. Southern defenders of old-style "No not one" segregation were fast losing their dominance throughout the region—because they were losing the argument. Popular opinion on race undertook one of the most dramatic shifts of opinion on any issue in modern times. Less than half those polled in 1944 thought "Negroes are as intelligent as white people." By 1956, 80 percent did, including a majority of southerners. A majority of those polled in 1942 supported segregated transport and public accommodations. By 1956, barely a third did—and only a small majority of white southerners. These results need to be treated with caution. Most respondents, nationwide, did not think the government should intervene to enforce integration. And fewer than one in twenty white people nationwide approved of intermarriage.[12] But changing opinion provided an opportunity to challenge southern segregation nonetheless—not least because white northerners saw segregation (wrongly) as a southern problem.

Public opinion had swung so dramatically for many reasons. The intellectual debunking of race differences filtered through to high schools— young, educated whites were the least committed to segregation of all white southerners. Black entertainers were stars in mainstream culture. Country soul singer Solomon Burke may have been naive when he said that "if everybody was to sing" (or preferably buy) his latest hit "Everybody Needs Somebody to Love" "it would save the whole world."[13] But black music did crossover to such an extent that in 1963 *Billboard* combined its black and white charts. The major religious denominations came out in clear support of the *Brown* decision, and while few segregationists had Damascus Road conversions on race, some stopped defending it at all costs, on account of their faith. That's not to say that most white Americans approved of the sit-ins—they didn't. But white mobs beating dignified protesters now produced a guilt-inducing moral drama on the nightly TV news. As the conservative southern editor Jack Kilpatrick ruefully observed, "Here were the colored students in coats, white shirts, ties, and one of them was reading Goethe . . . and here on the sidewalk was a gang of white boys come to heckle, a ragtail rabble."[14]

Changing opinions, though, were only part of the story. After all, the deepest sections of the Deep South still held firm. There, politicians, publishers, and local preachers thundered against interracial sex, Communists, and rock 'n' roll. White supremacists added the example of jungle-style politics in newly independent Africa to the list of the inevitable consequences of black advancement. In 1962 the *Southern Conservative* reported with delight that the president of Gabon had been imprisoned for "eating his mother-in-law."[15] Segregationists still had some brilliant intellectuals and constitutional scholars on their side, while southern Democrats in Washington held the line, and disproportionate power, too. In 1957 and 1960 they watered down civil rights bills so far that black leaders wondered whether the bills were even worth supporting.

The key change, then, was that those still defending total segregation had less power to do so. Times definitely were a-changin'. The southern economy was modernizing out of recognition—as one quip put it, "Cotton is going West, Cattle are coming East, Negroes are going North, and Yankees are coming South."[16] The dethroning of King Cotton and the decline of sharecropping meant that the need for cheap, controlled black labor was in decline. The South's growing dependence on northern and federal investment meant that insistence on "the southern way" had potential costs.

Southern politics was changing too. The so-called Solid South, once dominated by white elites in the rural Black Belt who had disproportionate influence in state politics, was breaking up from within. A series of court rulings in the early 1960s reapportioned electoral districts to reflect urbanization. In the cities, chambers of commerce held power. White business elites were not eager to desegregate downtown. But faced with unremitting demonstrations, they judged that social stability—and economic prosperity—required a change in racial customs. For members of country clubs who drove their own cars, this change came at a low cost—they had little stake in segregated downtown public parks or segregated buses. They had no need for massive resistance because they had no fears of massive integration in the circles (and exclusive suburbs) where they lived. Thus, working-class white urbanites who did have a stake in public segregation found themselves fighting a two-front battle—against the protest of black rivals and the indifference of white elites. It was an unwinnable war—and most southerners knew it. In one 1958 poll, only a third of white southerners did not believe the "day will come" when "whites and Negroes . . . will generally share the same public accommodations."[17]

As die-hard segregationists weakened, black activists gained strength. The largest demonstrations occurred in southern cities such as Atlanta, Nashville, and Savannah, where growing black communities had already made gains. Once black voters became a part of the governing coalition with white business elites, city politicians could not afford to dismiss demands to desegregate public space out of hand. Average black income rose by a third during the 1950s (even though it remained stuck at barely half the income of whites). White businesses took note. The *Wall Street Journal* reported in 1961 that black purchasing power was "almost equal to that of all Canada."[18] Thus, black boycotts mattered, especially when the Klan's counter-picketing kept worried white customers away too. In June 1960, the manager of Greensboro's Woolworth's pleaded with the mayor to "do something, my business is going to pot."[19] Increased black resources helped finance protesters, from feeding picketers to finding bail money. The development of black institutions also provided experienced leadership—not just ministers but church women's group organizers, teachers, and social and neighborhood club leaders.

Protest leaders coined a slogan, "Freedom Now," that resonated. It asserted a new sense of self, of being and acting "free."[20] Black ministers fashioned a powerful theology of liberation. The growing number of black-oriented radio stations and newspapers took up the beat. Improved black schooling during the 1950s (due to a frenzy of spending in the South, initially designed to show that separate could be equal and thus preempt *Brown*) prepared a larger group of black students than ever before. "Pop had only the Bible," said James Farmer, "but we have the Bible and a college education."[21]

In other words, the student protests flourished because, for the first time, they could. Perhaps the more interesting question was why this new wave of protest was seemingly so moderate in its approach and limited in its goals. After all, 1959 had promised rather more militant alternatives—from Robert F. Williams's armed resistance, to mass protest against rape in Tallahassee, to labor unrest in Harlem. During the sit-ins, there were plenty of radical voices still around. Baldwin told *Times* readers of "the Nation of Islam movement" "at the other end of the pole" from the students. "The Muslims do not expect anything at all from the white people . . . the Muslim movement has all the evidence on its side."[22] Prior to the sit-ins, the issues had been schools, jobs, housing, the vot and self-defense. Now the issues seemed to be the right to eat at a lunch counter, ride on the front of an interstate bus, or pray in a white church.

Part of the answer was that protest emerged on campus, as opposed to the union hall or the veterans' club. "College students," noted Palmer, were "often referred to as the 'country club bunch,'" hence the surprise that they "erupted like fanatic Latin American collegians."[23] Still, these fanatics were mostly respectable, optimistic, and middle-class, unschooled in the economic, radical, or armed dimensions of black struggle.

The main point, though, to quote Baldwin again, was that "the movement does not have as its goal the consumption of overcooked hamburgers and tasteless coffee at various sleazy lunch counters."[24] "Freedom Now" meant more than civil rights; it meant the positive power to influence. When Atlanta University students explained their protest in a widely publicized document, they called it "An Appeal for Human Rights." According to Gloria Richardson, the leader of a movement in Cambridge, Maryland, that soon trumpeted armed self-defense, "Public accommodations was the easiest thing to attack . . . as merely a spearhead . . . [for] schools, the manner in which the welfare and employment offices were operating, and housing units."[25] Her own polling found that nearly half of African Americans saw jobs as the top priority, while only one in twenty prioritized access to public accommodations.[26]

The southern sit-in movement connected with northern city movements too. According to James Farmer, "To move from supportive demonstrations for the southern campaigns into northern employment and housing projects was a natural progression."[27] In Philadelphia, explained young minister Leon Sullivan, "some of us were picketing the five-and-ten stores to support the lunch counter sit-ins in the South, when we realized that the North and East had problems that were just as acute."[28] Sullivan formed a new organization of four hundred ministers and targeted firms that relied on black customers. First on the list was Tastykake, maker of a popular donut. Sullivan demanded that the company hire black sales clerks and van drivers and adopt a nondiscrimination policy; 150 black-owned grocery stores agreed not to take Tastykakes during summer vacation, and by August Tastykake had given in. "After the Tasty victory," Sullivan said, "black people were walking ten feet tall."[29]

The story of the Philadelphia boycott was replayed in different formats across the North and West. In the first months of 1960, perhaps a quarter of a million African Americans joined Don't Buy Where You Can't Work boycotts. In May 1961, some 2,500 African Americans from Chicago's Southside rode forty-six buses on a Freedom Ride to city hall, carrying

banners calling for better housing, jobs, and the vote.[30] Many of the protests were a far cry from the first Greensboro sit-in. In Detroit, the militant minister Albert Cleage formed a Freedom Now political group in
1961. In liaison with black Muslims, trade unionists, socialists, and civil
rights leaders, Cleage mobilized support to swing the mayoral election
to the liberal candidate, Jerome Cavanagh. The following year, Cleage
sponsored an independent black slate for congressional elections. By that
time, he ran the largest race organization in the city.

Clearly there were differences between southern student protest and
northern city movements. Northern activists sought to gain jobs in formerly white industries and to force school boards to act. As one poster
during the Philadelphia campaign put it, "Tokenism Is Not Enough."[31]
Postwar northern reform organizations had won local fair employment
measures. But as Whitney Young, the new leader of the National Urban
League (NUL), argued in 1962, black northerners had "a mouthful of
rights and an empty stomach."[32] An NAACP survey found that the status
of black labor actually declined in states with fair employment laws.[33] In
contrast, southern civil rights activists still hoped that ending legal discrimination might open up new opportunities. The West was somewhere
in the middle. California protest leaders were still pushing for equal employment rights in 1960. They won them in 1961, and confrontational
protests demanding results soon followed.

Even so, the differences among the regions should not be overdrawn.
Southern sit-in protests soon demanded black employment behind the
lunch counter, and they meshed with local struggles for school and housing desegregation. Activists learned from one another, too. Martin Luther
King invited Philadelphia's Leon Sullivan to address the SCLC in 1962,
and later adopted Sullivan's program in forming Operation Breadbasket.
Figures such as Ella Baker, and organizations such as CORE, transcended
region. The main city campaigns North and South still embraced the
American dream and the promise of postwar liberalism, even as they
fought against those who would deny it. Activists shared a protest culture
(they sang the same freedom songs) and a popular culture (they listened
to the same hits and read the same magazines). That's not to say that
all black Americans felt part of a national movement, though. In 1963,
the student magazine at Washington's prestigious Howard University reminded "Howard men and women . . . to avoid any contact with movements, causes, and ideals. Things may be rough in Mississippi but that
does not concern US."[34]

Local activists, North, South, and West, also felt part of the same international movement. In Cuba, Fidel Castro came to power in 1959,

outlawed segregation, condemned American white supremacy, and promoted Cuba as a land "free of racism" that represented the promise of Third World liberation. Some went to visit—from baseball star Jackie Robinson to freedom fighter Robert Williams, who later went into exile there. The black press followed global developments closely. Following the Sharpeville massacre in South Africa in March 1960, the *Defender's* six-inch headline ran simply, "Africans Vow to Fight On." The other front-page story was the sit-in movement.[35]

These were not just background news events "over there," accessible only to the globally minded. They played out on American soil, not least because of the presence of the United Nations in New York City. On September 19, 1960, Castro (who cannily brought his dark-skinned general with him) moved to Harlem's historic Theresa Hotel while visiting the UN; Malcolm X led a welcome party of thousands. By inviting the leaders of Russia, Egypt, and India to his hotel, Castro made Harlem the temporary center of anti-imperial global politics. International issues even took root in southern soil. In Macon, Georgia, black students protested the exclusion of visiting Ghanaian student Sam Oni from the city's main Baptist Church—Oni had been converted in Ghana by missionaries from that very church.[36] Broadcasting from Cuba, Robert Williams filled *Radio Free Dixie* with news of the international struggle.

Activists North and South also shared the same frustration with the federal government. Kennedy's electoral platform—the most pro–civil rights in U.S. history—included a promise to end federally funded housing segregation at the "stroke of a pen." But it took him two years (and the receipt of thousands of pens from protesters) to make the stroke. Kennedy's focus was on Cold War politics. His assistant attorney general remembered that Kennedy's team saw the Freedom Riders "as a pain in the ass," given Kennedy's upcoming meeting with his Russian counterpart, Nikita Khrushchev. Kennedy felt constrained by southern Democrat opposition, too. Civil rights leaders had little sympathy for these delays and excuses. Farmer judged his meeting with Kennedy in 1962 "the most insulting session I've ever had with a government official"—Kennedy worked on papers while Farmer spoke to him.[37] By the start of 1963, Kennedy had not come out in favor of the Civil Rights Movement, let alone proposed legislation. Meanwhile, Attorney General Robert Kennedy had authorized FBI Director J. Edgar Hoover to spy on Martin Luther King.

Activists North and South also shared disappointments locally. The sit-in protests fizzled out, and students won small concessions at great cost. In New Orleans, Little Rock, and Atlanta, they didn't win any concessions at all. In Philadelphia, Sullivan's campaigns forced three hundred companies to hire black staff, but these turned out to be token appointments, not a breakthrough. In the rural South, student activists soon found that sit-ins were not just impossible but irrelevant to the main problems local people were facing.

Toward the end of 1962, an unexpected drama at the University of Mississippi seemed to sum up what little progress had been made. In 1961 James Meredith, a 29-year-old air force veteran, sought transfer from all-black Jackson State College to Mississippi's revered university, Ole Miss. The strong-headed Meredith had not consulted with NAACP lawyers (who joined the case), or even with Mississippi civil rights leaders. After a year of wrangling, the Supreme Court ruled that Meredith must be admitted on September 30, 1962. Governor Barnett framed the transfer of one student—a veteran and family man—in apocalyptic terms: "We will not drink from the cup of genocide." As the day approached, the local media whipped passions into a frenzy. "Meredith literally rocked and rolled this town out of its senses," wrote black reporter James Hicks. "They acted as if this young lone Negro was a man from Mars."[38]

On the eve of Meredith's admission, the Ole Miss Rebels hosted the Kentucky Wildcats in a football game. The Rebels went into the game unbeaten, but the Wildcats promised to be their toughest opponent yet. The combination of football and race sent testosterone levels soaring. At halftime, Barnett took the microphone and declared: "I love Mississippi! I love her people! I love our customs!" The roar of the crowd drowned out anything else he might have wanted to say. But he'd made the point. Love for Mississippi meant defense of white privilege and defiance of the Supreme Court. It was an invitation for Mississippi men to take their stand. The Wildcats didn't have a chance against the Rebels; the final score was 14–0. And that evening a race riot broke out. Barnett's deputy ordered the state patrol to withdraw, and federal marshals were hopelessly outnumbered by the mob. Bobby Kennedy ordered in troops, but by the time thirteen thousand soldiers arrived early the next morning, the damage had been done. Over a hundred federal marshals were injured, and two people were killed. Veteran journalists wept at the sight.

Different people drew different lessons from the riot. Black Americans praised Meredith but condemned President Kennedy's lack of leadership. Segregationists took heart that resistance could still work. Deep South politicians learned that defiance was still a prerequisite of popularity. The few outspoken white dissenters concluded there was no room for them in the combustible atmosphere. Ira Harkey, a maverick small-town Mississippi editor, asked if Jesus Christ "were to visit us . . . by whose side would He stand, beside the . . . slavering members of the mob and their 'nice-folk' eggers-on, or beside the trembling victim of hate?" Harkey won a Pulitzer Prize for his editorial—and a one-way ticket out of Mississippi. Previously, his readers had just barely tolerated his provocative views—even his publication of a letter by the fictional bigot Colonel Myopia Heartburn. But that was before the Ole Miss riot.

On September 30, Meredith took his first class—in American history. He probably realized he would soon be on the curriculum, even at Ole Miss. (Forty years later, his own son would graduate from the same university, at the top of his class.) Barnett's continued shenanigans forced Bobby Kennedy to keep three hundred soldiers on campus far longer than he wanted to. As for the Rebels, they went on to win the Sugar Bowl in their best season ever.

The Cries of Birmingham and Elsewhere

One name conspicuous by its absence from the story of protest during 1960–1962 was Martin Luther King Jr. He remained a popular figure. His advice column in *Ebony* tackled subjects ranging from nuclear war to "What should I do if my husband is having an affair?" (Answer: make yourself more attractive.) At the Montgomery Freedom Rider rally, his speech encouraged the fearful and calmed the angry. Yet he was a somewhat peripheral figure to the surge of protest. SNCC asked him to be an official adviser, but Ella Baker was a bigger influence. Thanks to Baker, the SCLC had developed a promising scheme of citizenship schools (to help adults pass literacy and citizenship tests), but they lacked the fame of the student movement. When King moved to Atlanta in 1960, it was on the understanding (with his father, among others) that he would not get involved in local demonstrations. He met the Freedom Riders for a meal there (though Farmer was surprised when King left the tab to him to pick up). But to their disgust he refused to board the bus. Like a messiah, he said his time had not come.

By the end of 1962, the SCLC was struggling. King joined a campaign in Albany, the largest town in Georgia's Black Belt, but the campaign ran into trouble. King's team annoyed SNCC workers already there, and he met a canny foe in Laurie Pritchett, the chief of police. Pritchett's men were restrained in front of the media, which allowed him to point out black youths throwing "nonviolent" rocks. But he shipped demonstrators to rural jails; and one woman miscarried after a beating. To King's annoyance, Pritchett turfed King out of jail by arranging for an "anonymous black man" to pay bail. Hundreds did go jail, and the memory of those days lived long in the city. But the campaign won no concessions (although city fathers in other Georgia towns met with local leaders to avoid becoming an Albany). Slater King, vice president of the Albany movement, estimated that 20 percent of maids who had joined marches lost their jobs permanently.[39]

The SCLC left Albany virtually broke and unsure where to go. Where they ended up was Birmingham, Alabama. The magic city was barely a two-hour drive north of Montgomery. But "Bombingham" was far more hostile territory for a protest movement. It was also a city in rapid industrial decline, where seven out of ten black miners had lost their jobs during the 1950s.[40] Even so, by early 1963 local hopes were raised by the prospect of a change in the city government—once again, new opportunities rather than new repression prompted protest. Birmingham had been run by three city commissioners, one of whom in 1963 was "Bull" Connor. Local businessmen pushed through a referendum to replace the system with an elected mayor who they hoped would be business-oriented. Black activists spotted an opportunity, and Fred Shuttlesworth invited King—a personal friend—to spearhead the campaign.

The movement's manifesto, released April 2, spoke of a desire to enjoy the "American dream." King hoped to force the city to desegregate all public facilities and schools and introduce fair hiring. As in Albany, the campaign stuttered. Attendance at mass meetings dwindled. Soon only a few dozen marched. An economic boycott had little effect. More moderate black leaders in the city—including most pastors—remained aloof. Although the movement had the largest "working-poor" membership of any organization in the city, it did not involve the so-called riffraff—the tens of thousands of unemployed.[41] King went to jail over Easter, but even this did not mobilize support. In his famous "Letter from Birmingham Jail," he wrote that the "Negro's great stumbling block in his stride toward freedom is not the . . . Ku Klux Klanner, but the white moderate, who is more devoted to 'order' than to justice."[42] The movement turned its attention to voter registration.

Then King got a couple of lucky breaks. First, Connor remained in office, pending an appeal against the change of government. Second, with few adults prepared to march, for fear of being arrested or losing their jobs, King's team asked schoolchildren to demonstrate instead of going to school. The children were only too happy to oblige. On Thursday, May 2, thousands of well-dressed children marched into the city's segregated Kelly Ingram Park and into jail. Faced by a second "Children's Crusade" on Friday, and with no space left in the jails, Connor felt trapped. One officer remembered "You could see Bull moving, looking concerned, fidgety. He was just desperate. 'What the hell do I do?'"[43] What he did was turn high-pressure water hoses on black boys and girls.

The old strategy no longer worked in a TV age. Cameramen took pictures of young marchers being knocked into the air. One policeman told his captain, "Ten or fifteen years from now, we will look back [and] say, 'How stupid can you be?'"[44] Actually, it would be more like ten or fifteen minutes. A large crowd on the sidelines—the "riffraff"—rushed in to support the children. As punches were thrown, Connor sent in police dogs, and his officers drew their clubs. A photograph of a police dog leaping at a black teenager was seen around the world.

Moderate black leaders swung behind the movement. White vigilantes mobilized, too. Over the following weeks, as the number of demonstrations, and fights, grew, the city fathers came, in secret, to the negotiating table. King joined the traditional black leadership in seeking a compromise, causing tensions to mount within the movement. One afternoon, SNCC's executive secretary, Jim Forman, happened upon King in his bathrobe, eating a steak, while children were marching downtown. He walked away in disgust. Shuttlesworth refused to negotiate. "Now Martin," he said. "You're mister big, but you're going to be mister S-H-I-T."[45] Nevertheless, on May 10 Shuttlesworth read out a settlement—which fell short of the movement's original demands—at a press conference. Soon after, he collapsed and was rushed to the hospital.

The deal did not end the confrontation. The city government denounced Shuttleworth's statement. So did two thousand members of the Klan, who assembled in nearby Bessemer on May 11 to "turn Alabama upside down for God."[46] Later that evening two bombs exploded in the black community—one at King's motel. Thousands of angry African Americans faced down the police, and some attacked white passersby. Violence continued throughout the summer. When two black children moved to a white school in September, more bombings and fights broke out. Then on Sunday, September 15, a bomb at a black Baptist church killed four young girls. Even as more fights followed, the city refused to integrate downtown.

But the movement had a profound national effect. Speaking on two local television stations in Mississippi (a significant sign of changing times in itself) on May 20, 1963, the long-serving black activist Medgar Evers argued that "history has reached a turning point, here and over the world."[47] Just a few months after the riot at Ole Miss, Birmingham showed that the days when unyielding segregationists could get away with brutality were numbered. On the ground, both sides threw punches, but the television audience saw only King vs. Connor, children vs. police dogs, nonviolence vs. bombings of little girls, order vs. chaos, good vs. evil. National journalists—often a target for white vigilante violence themselves—backed the movement. After the church bombing, Eugene Patterson, the editor of the *Atlanta Constitution* wrote, "A Negro mother wept in the street . . . In her hand she held a shoe, one shoe, from the foot of her dead child. We hold that shoe with her." He later read the editorial live on national television.

Birmingham also signaled the resumption of protest across the country. One monitoring group counted more than 930 demonstrations in at least 115 southern cities in 1963—more than any other year. No one counted demonstrations in the North and West, but there were likely at least as many. CORE Field Secretary Chet Duncan wrote to the head office in July, "The entire western region has come to LIFE!"[48] On the front pages of the *Chicago Defender*, the Birmingham campaign jostled for space with stories from around the nation—the arrest of a two-year-old girl on a picket line in Albany, Georgia; a selective buying campaign in Chicago; picketing of a white-only lakeside resort in Michigan; a blockade of a construction site in New York; fights between white mobs and evicted sharecroppers living in a tent city in Tennessee; and an attempted march across Mississippi by William Moore, a white Baltimore postman. Moore intended to deliver a letter to Ross Barnett urging the end of segregation. On the third day of his walk he was shot dead. A group of SNCC volunteers continued the march.[49]

Some African Americans remembered the Birmingham campaign as the moment when their anger first stirred—just as Emmett Till's murder had been a turning point for many in the 1950s. For singer Nina Simone, news of the church bombing set her in a "rush of fury, hatred and determination" as she "suddenly realized what it was to be black in America." She wrote her first civil rights song, "Mississippi Goddam" (so titled because Mississippi summed up for her the worst of white racism). Her patience had run out. "You keep on saying, 'go slow,'" she sang, but "I don't trust you anymore."[50] More often, though, anger about Birmingham meshed with longstanding local concerns. Indeed, some of the more highly publicized protests, such as in Philadelphia and Cambridge, Maryland, resumed before Birmingham hit the headlines.

Birmingham also affected figures on the national stage. Because of Birmingham, President Kennedy decided to act. One 1963 poll showed that 42 percent of people thought race was America's most pressing problem—compared with only 4 percent the year before. In the Cold War context, Kennedy felt the gaze of the world upon American race relations. Secretary of State Dean Rusk judged white supremacy "the biggest single burden that we carry on our backs in foreign relations."[51] After Birmingham, the burden became too heavy to bear. Ahead of a conference of African leaders in Addis Ababa, Prime Minister Milton Obote of Uganda released an open letter to Kennedy condemning the attacks on "our own kith and kin."[52] America's closest allies were concerned too. Residents of Llanstephan, a small Welsh village, sent money to furnish a new stained-glass window in the bombed church—a towering black crucified messiah, who looks down on the auditorium to this day.

Kennedy told his brother to get the "people off the streets and the situation under control." With typically shrewd timing, he addressed the nation on June 11—the very day that Governor George C. Wallace (whom Kennedy loathed) blocked two black students at the door of the University of Alabama, to fulfill his pledge of "Segregation forever." Kennedy appealed to morality "as old as the scriptures and clear as the American Constitution," while warning of the more practical problems of "fires of frustration and discord [that are] burning in every city, North and South."[53] The following week, he sent a civil rights bill to Congress. It was rather weak, but it did the job. African leaders praised the president. Thereafter American diplomats were able to deflect international criticism by telling a story of progress in the midst of conflict.

But for African Americans, Kennedy's rhetoric seemed a far cry from the reality of their lived experience. On the very night of Kennedy's speech, Medgar Evers was shot dead in his driveway in Mississippi by a white vigilante. The next night, African Americans in Cambridge, Maryland, battled police. Mississippi Senator Eastland said of Evers' murder, "Apparently it was a dastardly act . . . Too many such incidents are happening . . . including the race riot last night in Cambridge."[54]

Protests continued across the country. SNCC would pour in resources to challenge white supremacy in the Deep South. In southern cities, demonstrators would call for an immediate end to all discrimination. In the North and West, activists would demand results, not just rights. And bolstered by this local agitation, black leaders would try to force Kennedy and his successor, Lyndon Johnson, to champion meaningful civil rights legislation.

Fear, Frustration, and Freedom Summer in the Rural South

In 1962 SNCC launched projects in rural Mississippi and southwest Georgia, while in 1964 CORE headed to rural Louisiana. Each SNCC team initially had a dozen or so volunteers who promised to live, work, and suffer in some of the most notorious sections of the Black Belt—like

"Bad" Baker County in Georgia. One Southern Regional Council reporter noted that "even Albany Negroes characterize Baker County as being 'one step down from hell.'"[55] *Time* magazine crowned McComb—the site of SNCC's first Mississippi project—"the toughest anti-civil rights community in the toughest anti-civil rights area in the toughest anti-civil rights state."[56] Rather like in Reconstruction days, the idea was that the sheer numbers of votes—African Americans were a majority in many counties—could become a powerful weapon for the weak. The students hoped to transform the most oppressive region in America, and so transform American society as a whole. They also hoped to transform the nature of the Civil Rights Movement. As it turned out, their experience of rural protest ended up transforming them.

The students' nitty-gritty community organizing approach, one long favored by Ella Baker, sought to develop local leaders, men and women, according to local priorities. It was the antithesis of SCLC's community mobilizing approach, let alone the NAACP's focus on lobbying sympathetic elites. The project leaders epitomized this "trusting the people" mindset. Bob Moses, head of the Mississippi team, grew up in a Harlem housing project. First, his aptitude for mathematics took him to Harvard, and then his support for the sit-ins led him to Atlanta, where he met Baker, who pointed him to SNCC, which sent him to Mississippi. After meeting people like Medgar Evers and Aaron Henry, who had sustained the NAACP in Mississippi through the darkest days of Jim Crow, Moses was reluctant to impose his own plans. Moses' counterpart in Georgia, Charles Sherrod, grew up in a slum in St. Petersburg, Florida, then studied religion at Virginia Union, and promised to stay however long it took. He would still be there at the end of the century.

These rural projects were very much part of a national movement. They were funded by the Voter Education Project—a fund set up after the Kennedys encouraged students to focus on voter registration in the absurdly mistaken hope that this would calm tensions in the South. The heroism of some rural volunteers became part of movement folklore. Time and again the eyes of the nation would turn toward the drama of the rural South. Yet protest in the rural South had a story all its own. The work was slow and laborious—walking from house to house along hot, dusty lanes. Whereas city-based movements confronted segregation, the rural projects were more concerned about the self-belief of black southerners long schooled in subservience (at least in public) to Jim Crow. Sherrod insisted, "Our criterion for success is not how many people we register . . . we are in a psychological battle for the minds of the enslaved."[57]

There were plenty of victories. In Ruleville, Mississippi, the fervent

Christian Fannie Lou Hamer came from an activist tradition. Her mother—who had nineteen other children—"believed deeply that black was beautiful," carried a gun in her covered bucket to the cotton field, and taught the infant Fannie, "If you respect yourself enough, other people will have to respect you." As a young woman, Hamer found work measuring the pickings of local sharecroppers. She secretly added a weight to offset the owner's crooked scales. At age forty-four, she met Moses. "I didn't know that a Negro could register and vote." After that, "I could just see myself voting people outa office that I know was wrong and didn't do nothin' to help the poor."[58] Hamer would become a nationally famous rebel.

Considering Jim Crow's suffocating oppression of rural protest down the years, such victories were momentous. Yet for every victory there were plenty of setbacks. The hubris of the volunteers' first reports was soon replaced by a sober realism. For volunteers in "Terrible" Terrell County, Georgia, the highlight of December 1962 was the promise of a seventy-year-old blind man, Les Holly, to try to register. "This blind man can see a lot more than most of the people with two eyes," the students reported melodramatically. Two months later, Holly changed his mind.[59]

Project workers soon found that the potential power of black voters was more than counterbalanced by other weaknesses. At the heart of the problem was poverty. In Georgia, student Penny Patch observed, "When you work in the cotton fields all day and come home to nothing but pork and beans . . . it's hard even to think about registering."[60] Three quarters of black delta residents lived below the poverty line.[61] Most had less than six years of education, so students had to teach literacy before they could move on to voter education classes. The rural setting also presented problems. Distance mattered. With only a couple of cars for each project, Sherrod reckoned that lack of transport was "our most deadly handicap."[62] News spread slowly, especially because white businessmen owned the airwaves. Few rural black southerners felt connected to black activists in other southern towns, let alone activists around the world. Some teenagers had not even heard of Martin Luther King.

The all-or-nothing white supremacy that was becoming vulnerable in the city remained as strong as ever in the countryside. Seemingly any white resident who strayed from the party line was run out of town. In Greenwood—an early movement center in Mississippi—"Red" and Malva Heffner tried to get white leaders to speak to the students. And in Americus—the main focus of the Georgia project by 1963—Warren Fortson arranged a secret meeting between business leaders and movement leaders. Red Heffner was a successful insurance agent, whose daughter was Miss Mississippi in 1963, while Fortson was a lawyer and brother of Georgia's secretary of state. But when news of their actions became public, the men and their wives were shunned socially. "It was as if we didn't exist," said Betty Fortson.[63] Red and Warren found they had no clients, and after receiving death threats, both families left town to rebuild their lives elsewhere (with some difficulty).

Rural police had few qualms about using violence. Two days before Kennedy's televised speech, police arrested Fannie Lou Hamer. Promising "to make you wish you was dead," according to Hamer, they forced two black prisoners to beat her up, permanently damaging her kidneys. Then, Hamer said, one of the officers "tried to feel under my clothes." When SNCC worker Lawrence Guyot went to the station to seek her release, the police—as if to underscore the link between racial violence and sexual fears—beat him and tried to burn his genitals.[64] The presence of interracial teams fanned sexual fears further. In McComb, rumors spread of the planned rape of white women.

Hamer later turned the tables on her assailants by telling her story around the country. But fear of attack remained a deterrent for many, and the threat of unemployment was a deterrent for most. Applicants for voter registration had to state the name of their employer, which meant, said Hamer, "you would be fired by the time you got back home."[65] The students sympathized. In Georgia, Jack Chatfield's heart went out to one woman who had been warned that her husband would be fired if she voted: "One day of the year she will be at the polls [but] the other 364 are not accounted for."[66] Hamer's boss of eighteen years (she had helped care for his children) told her to choose between voting and her job. Hamer chose voting. Her husband, Pap, lost his job at the end of the harvest. Then the Hamers received a water bill for $9,000 for one month—even though they didn't have running water. Unable to pay, Pap went to jail.[67]

Despite the intimidation, hundreds did try to register to vote during 1963. The problem was, registrars used old-style citizenship tests to stop them. In Ruleville, the registrar asked Hamer to define a *de facto* law. "I knowed as much about a *facto* law," she recalled later, "as a horse knows about Christmas Day."[68] Authorities also used legal powers. In July 1963 four SNCC volunteers in Americus were charged with insurrection—which under Georgia's long-forgotten anti-treason act carried the death penalty. By time of their release four months later, local momentum had collapsed.

Little surprise, then, that the projects first made progress in larger towns. There was nothing moderate about race relations there—one student described Americus as a "shitty, terrible little town out in the middle of the country." But staff workers were able to build on the strengths common to urban black communities elsewhere—high school students willing to demonstrate, along with a few willing, economically independent adults. "These are the most amazing people we deal with," Sherrod wrote of Americus youth. "Nothing can defeat them." But even here progress was slow. City leaders were happy enough to fill the jails—in one case, twenty pre-teenage girls were held for six sweltering summer weeks in a cell the size of a classroom. Food was cold hamburgers. The toilets were stopped up.[69]

By the end of 1963, both SNCC projects could point to real achievements. They had survived. They had built up a core of activists—especially younger people and women. In Mississippi, SNCC had joined with the local NAACP and other groups to form an umbrella organization, the Council of Federated Organizations. COFO held its own election in November 1963, where 83,000 people voted for Aaron Henry for governor. Yet in many ways the projects had reached a stalemate. The potential voting power of black Americans remained just that—potential. Real power remained in the hands of others.

Little wonder that the projects began to reassess their efforts. COFO's prospectus for 1964 offered two choices: "Continue . . . with small progress in selected communities with no real progress [or assemble a] task force of such a size as to force . . . the federal government to intervene."[70] SNCC opted for the latter. That summer, some six hundred northern students—mostly white students from leading universities—headed South for what became known as Mississippi Freedom Summer. The ensuing drama would grip the nation and change the national movement.

In preparation, the Mississippi legislature passed laws to counter protest. A rejuvenated state KKK boasted a membership of nearly five thousand people. On June 20 the first batch of students headed to Mississippi. The next day, three volunteers disappeared in Neshoba County. Andrew Chaney was a 21-year-old local African American from a movement family. Andrew Goodman and Michael Schwerner were New York Jews. Forty-four days later, the bodies were found. One witness said Chaney's body was so mutilated it looked as though he had been in an airplane crash. By the end of the summer, there were at least three more murders and thirty-five shooting incidents. Chaney's mother, Fannie Lee, suffered more than most. She was no stranger to tragedy: her grandfather had been murdered by a white landowner. Soon after her son's murder, Chaney filed suit against five restaurants for discrimination. She lost her job as a baker, Klan members planted burning crosses on her lawn, and someone threw a firebomb at her house (it missed and destroyed her neighbor's house). She took her four children to New York and got a job as a cleaner.

Yet despite the violence, the movement endured. Volunteers pushed on with voter registration, set up freedom health clinics, started a traveling theater, and established freedom schools to teach black history. The murder of well-heeled white students won national and international attention. Building on the freedom vote of 1963, COFO formed a Freedom Democratic Party—an integrated alternative to the state Democratic Party. Two days after Chaney's body was found, the FDP held its first convention in Jackson and selected a delegation for the upcoming national Democratic Convention in Atlantic City.

"For many people," SNCC worker Joyce Ladner recalled later, "Atlantic City was the end of innocence." Yet at the start of the convention, delegates were optimistic. They had a strong moral case to be seated as the Mississippi delegation. With Hamer to the fore—she gave a nationally televised speech—they pushed their case with media savvy. But President Lyndon Johnson had other ideas. One year into the job after John Kennedy's assassination, and with an election coming up, Johnson was desperate not to lose southern white support. Texas Governor John Connally warned him, "If you seat those black buggers, the whole South will walk out." Johnson called a press conference during Hamer's testimony to divert attention. (New channels showed clips of her speech during primetime news instead.) Later that night, Johnson's team presented the FDP with a deal—the regular (white) delegates would be seated, but the FDP could have two at-large delegates. Some black leaders, including King and Henry, reckoned it was the best they would get. But most delegates rejected it. Hamer warned, "We didn't come all this way for no two seats."[71]

The next morning, the delegates discovered that Henry had agreed to the deal anyway. Johnson left Atlantic City with the election in the bag. SNCC left Atlantic City, one student explained, no longer struggling "for civil rights, but for liberation."[72] What liberation meant was a radical departure from early SNCC ideals.

In the months ahead, students would denounce the Democratic Party, the federal government, and the promise of postwar liberalism. On its own, Atlantic City was not the only decisive moment, but it confirmed what many were already thinking. During 1963 Moses had sought in vain to meet the president. SNCCers despised FBI agents, who stood by taking notes while white mobs beat them. It was time, said Moses, to "set up our own government and declare the other one no good." After the summer, he left Mississippi, and then America—moving to Canada and then Tanzania. Later that year, ten students and Hamer traveled to West Africa. As Forman expressed it, "We were strangers in a foreign land . . . We belonged here in Mother Africa."[73]

Many black students questioned the interracial ideals of SNCC's "beloved community." They were appalled when rural African Americans treated white volunteers with undue deference. Many black women were disgusted when black men sought sex with white volunteers, and when white women were willing to oblige. (Sherrod wrote to the head office in 1962, "Yeah, sexual relations. This is a hell of a problem.") In 1963 in Georgia, John Churchville was contemptuous of whites going native: "It makes you cringe to see them trying to catch the rhythm."[74] He would soon be home in Philadelphia, denouncing the Civil Rights Movement as a "trick" and helping to found a black nationalist movement.[75] Students rejected nonviolence, too. In fact, few if any local people had ever adopted it. Before long few if any students tried to persuade them otherwise. No weapons were allowed in COFO's freedom houses, but from the earliest days movement supporters guarded the houses with guns. Margaret Rose, a white freedom school teacher and a committed pacifist, admitted, "I cannot help feeling more secure knowing they are armed."[76]

Simmering tensions within the movement began to boil over. COFO had never been a stable alliance. But after "respectable" leaders agreed to the Atlantic City deal, Moses reckoned the "class thing . . . first came to a head." At a leadership meeting in September 1964, Forman was appalled by what he considered the NAACP's Gloster Current's "blatant 'Fuck-the-people' attitude."[77] In March 1965 the NAACP withdrew from COFO, and COFO disbanded soon afterward. Hamer stopped her membership. "There ain't nothing that I respect less than the NAACP."[78]

Rejection of American liberalism, acceptance of self-defense, an emphasis on blackness, and contempt for moderate leaders showed just how much the furnace of white supremacy had molded young black activists, and how much they had learned from those around them. Thus even during the heyday of Martin Luther King's nonviolent movement, there was a very different story unfolding in the South, one that would lead student activists easily into the Black Power era of the late 1960s.

The rural projects continued after Mississippi's Freedom Summer. What happened next simply accelerated the radicalization of the activists. Students came to understand racial oppression in material terms. In a widely circulated research pamphlet on southwest Georgia, long-term volunteer Jon Perdew concluded, "If you want to change things, you have to look at who owns what, for businessmen are the ones who really swing the billyclubs." Students also saw the rise of community-wide violence—and its effectiveness. In Natchez, Mississippi, local NAACP President George Metcalfe was almost killed by a car bomb. Yelling "We're going to kill for Freedom," hundreds of young African Americans took to the streets. Such fighting, in so many places, was unheard of since Reconstruction. It represented the triumph of SNCC's original aim of freeing enslaved minds—just not in the way SNCC had first imagined.[79]

The Deacons for Defense certainly weren't afraid. Founded in Louisiana in late 1964, the Deacons were the first organized, highly publicized regional armed group in the country. Mostly working-class veterans, in old mill towns like Bogalusa, the Deacons admired CORE activists. But they were not prepared to join nonviolent protest. So the Deacons patrolled CORE demonstrations instead. The activists appreciated the protection. Within months, the Deacons claimed sixty chapters and several thousand members. "Most whites do not admit it," reported the *New York Times,* "but the Deacons send a chill down their spines."[80]

The Deacons called on the wider movement to take up arms. Ernest Thomas, a Korean War veteran who had lived in Chicago, became a key spokesman. In a feature in *Life* magazine, Thomas insisted, "If we'd had the Deacons [in Mississippi], three more men would be alive . . . Or else a lot more would be dead." As had other spokesmen down the ages, he called on black men to assert their manhood through violence. In August 1965, even the *Times* reported that black men used to try and be "big enough not to hit back." Now "the Negro . . . can also dish it out." The Nation of Islam courted Thomas, but he declined the offer of a merger. He didn't like the sound of giving up drinking or learning Arabic. "I can hardly speak English," he reflected later. He declined a merger with left-leaning revolutionary groups too. "I'm just a capitalist that don't have a damn thing."[81] Still, the Deacons provided one bridge from the rural South to the armed politics in northern cities to come.

Demonstrations alone had prompted urban business elites to act. Sustained fighting finally forced rural elites into making concessions. In late 1965, after street fights in McComb, 650 "concerned citizens" signed a public statement requiring an end to intimidation and the fair treatment of African Americans. In Jonesboro, Louisiana, Governor John McKeithen rushed to negotiate improvements in the local school. Even the federal government intervened. During the McComb fighting, Johnson sent word he would dispatch troops unless the trouble stopped. In Bogalusa in 1965, the Justice Department filed five suits designed to cripple the Klan. It is striking just how quickly segregationists backed down in the face of determined federal action, suggesting a path not taken after *Brown.* Almost overnight, local authorities moved to comply with the law. In Jonesboro, a three-hundred-strong nonviolent "women's civilian patrol" replaced the Klan.[82] No doubt the Deacons chuckled at the emasculation of their opponents. With the Klan on a leash, the Deacons disbanded.

Ironically, at this very moment of opportunity, the student movement pulled back. Many local groups—farmers, laborers, and domestics—called for a second Freedom Summer. But the students were not so much tired of white supremacy as plain tired. Hamer was hospitalized for exhaustion. After the Mississippi Summer, SNCC had grown too big to function as a free-floating organization, yet it was too faction-ridden to unite into a disciplined organization. One SNCCer remembered a standoff involving "baseball bats, knives and a couple of pistols"—after an argument about meal tickets at a conference.[83] Forman blamed excessive pot smoking, a "luxury" for "anyone who is engaged in an intense struggle against the United States Government."[84] By the end of 1965, the rural projects had run their course (though some of the Georgia staff remained, separate from SNCC). Nevertheless, those involved learned lessons that would shape future protest in America. Hundreds of volunteers would go on to fight for social justice in politics, universities, or the feminist movement. Some women students, black and white, grew frustrated with the presumption of male leadership even as they learned the language and techniques of protest.

Those who remained in the black freedom struggle stopped talking about rights and started talking about power. At the end of 1965 in majority-black Lowndes County, Alabama, one activist wrote on a blackboard: "Get Power for black people." Forman remembered, as "I looked at the written words, something clicked in me." The project leader was Stokely Carmichael—a Trinidad-born, Howard-educated charismatic student nicknamed the Delta Devil for his seemingly miraculous ability to organize a movement. (As elsewhere, such miracles depended on long-serving local people.) Carmichael decided to run independent black candidates under the symbol of a Black Panther. It would be but a small step to the Black Power era, and Carmichael himself would first coin the term Black Power. But the small step was the culmination of a long journey for those first volunteers who had come to the rural South just a year or two before, to learn from those around them.

Impatience, Confidence, and Confrontation in the Cities

On June 23, 1963, at least a hundred thousand people in Detroit joined a March for Freedom to show solidarity with the Birmingham struggle.

There were so many people that the march had to start an hour early. Martin Luther King flew in as a celebrity speaker. All the main protest organizations in the city were involved—from the NAACP to the Housewives League to black nationalist Albert Cleage's Freedom Now Party. That evening, 12,500 people jammed into Detroit's Cobo Hall arena for a mass meeting. Another ten thousand filled an overflow hall. Police reckoned at least thirty thousand more stood in the parking lot. By all accounts, King mesmerized the crowd with an early version of his "I Have a Dream" speech.

The Detroit march was a far cry from the Birmingham campaign. King left behind a snarling police chief who had turned fire hoses on children, to be welcomed by a smiling police chief who escorted him to the march. Detroit's liberal mayor, James Cavanagh, joined King and urged white Detroiters to march—some ten thousand did. Even so, "We have served notice on . . . the City of Detroit that we are part of the freedom struggle," Cleage said to cheers. "We must FIGHT and FIGHT and FIGHT."[85]

The march marked the twentieth anniversary of Detroit's wartime riot. Many said little had improved. Violent white neighborhood groups that blocked black homebuyers, urban renewal programs that bulldozed black districts, federal mortgages that subsidized white flight to the suburbs, tax breaks that encouraged new industries to set up there, recessions that reversed black wartime gains, automation that reduced the entry level industrial jobs available for black migrants, union efforts to preserve jobs for their (white) members, and the school board's siting of schools to reflect residential segregation that created a two-tier system had all combined to leave black Detroiters in—or rather to lock them into—inner-city poverty. The Urban League reckoned Detroit "seems to be an explosive situation." March organizers pointed out that black Detroiters represented less than a third of the population, but two thirds of those prosecuted, three quarters of those unemployed, and four fifths of those claiming relief. King had clearly been well-briefed. He declared: "I have a dream this afternoon that one day right here in Detroit, Negroes will be able to buy a house or rent a house anywhere that their money will carry them and they will be able to get a job."[86]

In 1960 the new Chrysler Freeway replaced Hastings Street, the "central artery of black nightlife in Detroit." Black music collector Joe Von Battle lost his record shop. "A way of life had been totally destroyed," his daughter remembered bitterly. "The white man decided to get rid of Hastings because the community was becoming too strong."[87] But the Motor City's bulldozers didn't crush black music. In 1963 Berry Gordy Jr.—a sharecropper's son turned entrepreneur who founded the Motown record label in 1958—bought the previously lily-white Graystone Ball-room downtown. Three days before the Freedom March, the thirteen-year-old black pop sensation Little Stevie Wonder—fresh from his num-ber one hit "Fingertips"—played to a sellout crowd. Detroit's vibrant black music scene was a reminder that African Americans fought for free-dom in culture as well as politics. The Graystone provided pleasure, a place for free expression, and a chance to celebrate community.

But hot nights at the Graystone gave way to cruel days in the city. Thir-teen days after the march, police shot and killed a black woman, Cynthia Scott, claiming that the imposing six-foot-tall sex-worker had pulled a knife on them. A witness said Scott was running away. It was just the latest in a series of police fights. City records listed over 1,500 clashes between police and residents during 1961–1964. But the fact that a young woman had been killed, hot on the heels of the Freedom March, sparked action. The NAACP demanded an investigation. Cleage called for a picket of police headquarters. Three thousand people turned up, shouting: "Get killer cops." That summer, mass rallies and boycotts con-vulsed the city. One angry white resident called on the mayor to put an end to the trouble or "our civilization will go back to jungle law and can-nibalism."[88]

To quote Cleage, Detroit was part of an "epidemic of militant action" beyond the South after Birmingham.[89] In one year, there were as many school protests in northern cities as there had been in the past century. Rent strikes in New York were the largest for a generation. By the sum-mer of 1963, said one movement leader in Seattle, "the Civil Rights Movement had finally leaped the Cascade Mountains."[90]

Seattle was not Detroit. But for all the differences between protests in the North and West, some general patterns emerged during the summer of 1963. Outrage at Birmingham meshed with outrage at local problems. "The Negro in Detroit," the *Defender* aptly summarized on the eve of the Freedom March, "feels chief concern in three areas: housing, education and jobs."[91] The Scott murder was a reminder that police brutality was a chief concern, too. These problems were as old as migration, but the situ-ation had deteriorated. In the battle over housing and jobs, it was not the case that all white workers won (although those who moved to the sub-urbs prospered). But it was definitely the case that most black migrants lost. Mass migration had led to more housing segregation—in 1960 the most segregated city in the country was Los Angeles. The passage of state fair employment and fair housing laws, and the triumphs of a few pioneer black employees, homeowners, and schoolchildren, had not re-shaped the postwar city. Thus, during the new wave of protests in 1963, northern activists demanded immediate, substantial results in schooling, in housing, and at work. As they did so—as in the rural South—demonstrations turned to scuffles, and the established civil rights organizations turned their attention to the poor.

In short, the new protests reflected new disillusionment with the limits of the supposedly race-neutral New Deal state and postwar liberalism. (An even harsher critique of liberalism was still to come.) Yet they also reflected new confidence that black communities had the power to force change. The Don't Buy campaigns of the early 1960s had shown the potential of the black dollar. The combination of black migration into the cities and white flight out of them meant that the urban black vote mattered more year after year. In Detroit, black voters had tipped the balance for the liberal mayor Cavanagh. Now they were claiming their reward. Northern activists also believed that the global zeitgeist—from Alabama to Accra—was on their side. "Civil rights is so red-hot just now," reported CORE fieldworker Genevieve Hughes in the Bay Area, "that the white folks are scared out of their minds. We can do anything we want."[92]

In education, doing anything we want meant challenging whole school systems rather than particular schools. After school protests across the country, some thirty activists (including representatives from SCLC and SNCC) met in New York in January 1964 to discuss a coordinated national boycott.[93] The Cleveland delegation feared their city's conservative "power structure" would withstand a boycott. New York's Reverend Milton Galamison was more confident. After a decade leading a parents' movement, he had become exasperated by the school board's litany of committees, consultations, and deliberations. In January 1963 he rejected the board's suggestion of yet another survey. On February 3, 1964, virtually all the black children in the New York system skipped school.

All the major race organizations in the city backed the boycott. Bayard Rustin, back from Montgomery, took charge of the planning. Following the southern example, he established networks with over five hundred churches to provide freedom schools. Rustin was exultant. "The civil rights revolution has reached out of the South," Rustin told reporters, "and is now knocking on our own door."[94] With nearly half a million children staying away from school, it was kicking down the door of segregation. The board quickly put forward a school-pairing integration plan.

In most cities, jobs became the biggest issue of all. The NAACP's labor secretary Herbert Hill predicted that "timid" fair employment laws would soon be "obsolete" as a "Negro mass movement will proceed to the attack in its own way." Some said Hill was outspoken to compensate for being a white man in a black movement. Maybe so, but he was on the mark. The movement's "own way" included boycotts, dumping garbage, blocking traffic, and in some stores filling up shopping carts, taking them to the checkout lane, and then abandoning them. It included calls for industry-wide solutions. In San Francisco in 1964, hundreds of demonstrators occupied the prestigious Sheraton Palace Hotel to demand black staff in the hotel industry. And it included demands for a wide redistribution of jobs. The National Urban League's Whitney Young called for a Domestic Marshall Plan, and "a decade of discrimination in favor of Negro youth" to close the gap left by "300 years of deprivation."[95]

Protesters also occupied construction sites for the first time. In the longer term, these protests would shape federal policy on affirmative action—the most important economic consequence of the civil rights era. In 1963, construction seemed to be the most important, the most resistant, and seemingly the most vulnerable industry of them all. Skilled construction workers took home good wages during an era of industrial decline. Many building projects were funded by the state, so the city could not shirk responsibility. Yet construction remained a virtually lily-white industry, especially at the skilled and semi-skilled level, even though some building projects were in black areas.

In Philadelphia, Cecil B. Moore led the fight. A charismatic former marine, the self-proclaimed "goddamn boss" of North Philadelphia (the poorest part of town) was a man for all people—a snappy dresser and a street-talker, a "self-avowed heavy drinker" willing to negotiate in respectable circles, a black nationalist who supported integration, and a NAACP leader who focused on the ghetto. In response to Birmingham, Moore called a huge rally and warned, "The only difference between Birmingham and Philadelphia is geography." Migrants called Philadelphia "Up South." (Mayor Tate also made the link, telling reporters that protests "made us fear another Birmingham.") Moore then threatened the Board of Education with mass protests unless it started hiring black workers at all of its construction sites. The board demurred. On Monday, May 24, 1963, he targeted the building of a ghetto school. The merging of the two hot issues of jobs and education galvanized support. Local clergy, the NAACP, and ghetto residents—from grandmothers to schoolchildren—all joined in. Moore called for nonviolence—if possible. Early on Friday morning, pickets fought police. The school board agreed to hire five black workers immediately, with the promise of more. Moore told a jubilant crowd, this is "just a first step in the march to freedom."[96]

It is hard to exaggerate the scale of the protests and sense of the moment in cities across the North and West in the year after Birmingham. It was a similar story in southern cities. Still saddled with Jim Crow, demonstrators called for an end to *de jure* segregation in public space and schools, and for breakthrough black appointments in the workplace. In many southern cities they also demanded access to more homes, jobs, and meaningful school integration—in Atlanta, civil rights leaders presented the mayor with a document titled *The City Must Provide*. Meanwhile, SNCCers joined existing neighborhood groups in Atlanta's Vine City, just a few miles from Martin Luther King's home. After a visit, King admitted, "I had no idea people were living . . . in such conditions." The problems, wrote one SNCCer, "were the same as any other city where forgotten Negroes live." And so the goals were much the same. To quote one pamphlet:

> We protest
> Because our houses are condemned
> Because we have no heating system
> Because we have rats and roaches
> Because we have holes in the floor.[97]

As in the North, many southern protests teetered on the edge, and often over the edge, of violence. Some nonviolent protesters marched, but—as in Birmingham—more lined the streets who were willing to fight. Cambridge's Gloria Richardson thought it was "simply fantastic" that "men slept in the day" and defended black homes at night.[98] And like their northern counterparts, southern city protests were caught up in the global moment. In 1964, for example, a UN delegation came to assess race relations in Atlanta. Students and the KKK marched, and then fought, outside the delegation's hotel. (On leaving, the UN delegates pronounced themselves impressed with the city's progress.)[99] In turn, American protests continued to have global resonance. There were copycat protests in the Caribbean, Canada, and Europe.

Yet what this latest nationwide surge of urban protests had in common, above all, was just how little they achieved—apart from the end of *de jure* segregation in cities away from the Deep South. Once the boycotts were over, the New York Board of Education pulled back from its school-pairing plan.[100] In Philadelphia, Moore's "first step" turned out to be the last step—by the end of the summer, there were only six skilled black workers on sites across the whole city. Retail employers began to take on more black workers—St. Louis protests won particularly impressive results. But construction unions remained virtually lily-white. In Atlanta, only nine of the first 123 black applicants to white schools won a place. By 1965, only 2.3 percent of black children in the South attended desegregated schools—actually fewer than in 1954. In January 1966, a man froze to death in a Vine City apartment because the landlord failed to provide heat.

Protests North and South were hampered by their own weaknesses. Civil rights organizations found it hard to organize poorer areas. "When the immediate grievance is removed," lamented one CORE worker, neighborhood "councils collapse."[101] Meanwhile, rivalry was rife. In Atlanta, the old guard met secretly with the mayor to agree on the terms of a token deal ahead of biracial negotiations with the more militant crowd. In New York, Galamison was livid when NAACP leaders withdrew their support for a follow-up boycott. (They may well have been paying him back for leaving the organization a few years before.) His committee switched their protests from the school administrator's offices to the NAACP headquarters. "My immediate reaction was that it was foul and below the belt and despicable," Galamison reflected later. "The years have given me time to think, however. And my long-term reaction . . . is that it was foul and below the belt and despicable."[102]

Internal divisions were nothing new, though. The main obstacles came from without, not within. Although polls showed that a sizeable majority of white Americans opposed racial segregation, the same polls showed that the key questions now came down to where and what and when. A majority supported the principle of black rights in the Deep South or the inner city, in theory and in the future. But most white Americans opposed black rights in their own neighborhoods and workplaces, in practice and right now. One poll at the height of the New York schools crisis found that 80 percent of white parents opposed the board's school-pairing plan. Large majorities opposed the intrusion of federal or municipal government into housing arrangements (even though the federal government had helped fund residential segregation, and municipal governments had helped enforce it in the first place).[103]

Little surprise, then, that white city residents who were most likely to be affected by black demands mobilized in force. One month after the school boycott in New York, 15,000–20,000 white parents marched on City Hall and followed up with their own boycott—a quarter of the city's schoolchildren stayed home. After the appointment of skilled black craftsmen at a Philadelphia school, white craftsmen walked off the site. White residents' associations proliferated. Some local courts came down hard on protesters, and the leader of one peaceful protest against a San Francisco car dealership was sentenced to nine months in prison. James

Farmer was furious: "San Francisco is the worst city in the country."[104] (Quite a criticism, coming from a Freedom Rider.)

Some of the language of opposition dated back generations. Parents spoke of vulnerable white girls at mixed schools; homeowners and workers warned of the dangers of black crime and laziness. But unlike diehard racists in the Deep South, urban segregationists also developed a powerful new rights language that resonated with American ideals and complied with federal law. City residents spoke of homeowner rights and freedom of association to secure neighborhood house prices. Unions spoke of color-blind hiring by seniority and the passing of apprenticeships from father to son, which perpetuated a formerly color-sighted system. And parents spoke of freedom of choice to go to neighborhood schools, allowing school boards to draw districts that overlapped precisely with segregated neighborhoods.

While segregationists fought to block black goals, moderates sought to contain them. In city after city, North and South, politicians met with race leaders, sympathized with their demands, and agreed to gradual integration of houses, schools, and workplaces. But the emphasis was on the gradual part. In other words, many promised minimum concessions to preserve the maximum privilege. Georgia Governor Carl Sanders (whose conservative opponents tarred him as a "nigger lover") said in 1962, "I am a segregationist but not a damned fool." One exasperated activist complained in 1965 that Atlanta's school transfer screening process was so tough that successful black candidates needed to be a "blend of Joan of Arc and Albert Einstein."[105] Thus, the moral crusade against segregation missed the point—because the alternative did not have to be full integration. As a 1964 poll revealed, roughly a quarter of white Americans supported segregation, the same proportion supported desegregation, but half wanted something in between.[106]

As northern black activists refused to settle for tokenism, Democratic politicians found themselves caught between the proverbial rock (white pressure) and a hard place (black demonstrations). In other words, the New Deal coalition of black and white ethnic workers was fast unraveling. Considering that defenders of the status quo formed larger voting blocs, paid more taxes, and provided the bulk of the skilled workforce, it was little surprise that politicians chose the rock. In some cities, voters chose for them. In 1964 referenda, voters in California and Detroit overturned fair housing legislation. Thus in the generation when black Americans began to break out of their inferior place in the white mind, they found themselves confined to an inferior space in the city (which in turn promoted racism in the mind).

Because of their numbers, and because they were part of electoral coalitions with wealthy whites, southern black urbanites had more success
in the wave of protests after Birmingham (in cities where they could vote
freely). Black Atlantans represented some 40 percent of city residents and
were able to push into white neighborhoods and schools. But many white
working-class Atlantans—angry that elites shunted the burden of desegregation onto them—fled the city they felt had let them down. The
process happened far quicker than in the North, because the issue was
desegregation (a sudden change during the late 1950s) rather than employment (a longer term, factory by factory battle in northern cities). But
the end result was much the same. White workers moved to suburbs
where they could draw a new line in the proverbial sand (or rather, in Atlanta, on the asphalt of the I-285 perimeter road). Our aim, one spokesman explained, is to "build up a city separate from Atlanta and your Negroes and forbid any Negroes to buy, or own or live within our limits.
You have forced this on us and we will fight to the finish."[107] The warning would prove prophetic.

Frustrated by the obstacles they faced, the new northern activists
(as had their rural counterparts) took stock. Half a year after Detroit's
March for Freedom, Albert Cleage organized a Northern Grassroots
Leadership Conference. At least seven hundred people from eleven cities
attended. The conference could hardly have been more different from the
Freedom March. First of all, only black delegates attended. The president
of the meeting began by saying "Welcome to the revolution!" This was
followed by an opening prayer that included a Muslim invocation. Top of
the bill was a speech by Malcolm X. His "Message to the Grassroots"
talked about what the black revolution should look like—not "going to
the toilet with white people" but "completely changing the Negro's position." The conference ended by passing militant resolutions: support for
existing radical protests, black workers, and the exiled Robert Williams;
a Christmas boycott of white stores; solidarity with all colored people of
the world; and advocacy of armed self-defense. (This final resolution
earned a four-minute standing ovation. The Reverend Cleage explained
that nonviolence was not Christ's way.)[108]

Just as the March for Freedom had revealed black frustration at the
limits of liberal politics, the Grassroots Conference told of a willingness
to reject liberal politics altogether. It was not that any of the ideas at the
conference were new. Quite the opposite. Calls for self-defense, racial
pride, global solidarity, and workers rights were echoes of the wartime
March on Washington, the National Negro Congress, Garveyism, the
New Negro, the Colored Farmer's Alliance, Henry McNeal Turner, black

Reconstruction, Civil War fighting, even slave rebellions. Cleage himself had previously been accused of being a racist for calling on black voters to vote for black candidates.

What *was* new was that increasing numbers joined with, or at least sympathized with, protest that stressed black unity, linked with anti-racism struggles abroad, and pressed black city-dwellers to confront the power structure and take control of the state. The full flowering of what would come to be called Black Power would occur later in the decade. But these local trends anticipated the later national shift in ideology. In Philadelphia, Sullivan sought to build the black economy as a rival source of power. In New York, black writer Amiri Baraka left the interracial literary scene of Greenwich Village to found the Black Arts Repertory Theater/School (BARTS) in Harlem early in 1965. BARTS did not last long, but it would inspire some eight hundred black regional theaters. Fights during protests became commonplace. After traveling fifteen thousand miles across the country late in 1963, the black reporter John Williams was struck by a rising gun culture and reckoned that "grim anarchy" was but one crisis away.[109] As in Mississippi, violence often had a political purpose. During three days of rioting in Philadelphia, over a hundred businesses were destroyed—but not a single black one. Crowds shouted "We want Freedom."

In Detroit, Cleage's black critics dismissed him as unrepresentative. Arthur Johnson, executive director of the local NAACP, insisted that "ours is the voice of the Negro population." With 22,000 fee-paying members, he had a point. The Detroit branch would stay loyal to the Democratic Party and the promise of postwar liberalism. So too would the national NAACP, the NUL, and virtually all existing black politicians. In popular culture, the mainstream emphasis in 1963–1965 was still on integration. Although Gordy at Motown cut a disk of King's Detroit speech, he initially avoided association with the movement, and the 1964 hits of his star act, The Supremes—tunes like "Where Did Our Love Go?" and "Baby Love"—were hardly the stuff of Simone's "Mississippi Goddam." Still, even the Detroit NAACP ratcheted up criticism of the city government. One NAACP official complained after yet another inconclusive meeting, "Even reasonable, honest, long-suffering negroes like me are beginning to lose patience and hope." Across the country, many other "reasonable negroes" were losing patience too. For the elderly poet Langston Hughes, the murder of a teenager riddled by bullets from the gun of an off-duty police officer in Harlem (which led to the 1964 fighting there) crystallized his thinking. "How many bullets does it take," he asked, "to kill me?"[110]

Cleage's Grassroots Conference also showed that local advocates of a new politics were increasingly connected. Malcolm X's star turn at the conference was fitting, for it was he more than any other figure who bound them together. In his own telling, Malcolm's life was an epic journey through American racism to self-discovery. Born Malcolm Little in Nebraska, the child of a murdered Garveyite, Malcolm was brought up by a white family in Michigan. He excelled at school, then rebelled, and ended up in Boston's Roxbury neighborhood. When he was called up for a draft interview, he said he would be delighted to join the army so that he could shoot white GIs (he was turned down). The silver-tongued, jazzy-dressing, drug-dependent young Malcolm was soon on the run from an anti-drug squad, Italian gamblers, a hustler he had punched out, and a West Indian called Archie. When he returned to Boston, he was arrested for burglary, and because his partner in crime was a married white woman, he received a ten-year sentence. He was not yet twenty-one.

In prison, Nation of Islam leader Elijah Muhammad helped Malcolm channel his rage toward study. On his release, Malcolm became the Nation's leading spokesman, and built its newsletter to a circulation of half a million. But as Malcolm's rising star eclipsed Muhammad's fading sun, his position became perilous—especially when he discovered that Muhammad was not practicing the Nation's moral code. Muhammad censured Malcolm for speaking out about John Kennedy's assassination—members of the Nation were supposed to shun American politics. But Malcolm held the spotlight, befriending champion boxer Cassius Clay (later called Muhammad Ali) and traveling to Africa. Malcolm left the Nation in 1964, after his view of white people had moderated somewhat. He remembered telling a white female student—who wanted to help his cause—that she was a white devil and so could do nothing. If he were to meet her again, he mused, he would tell her she couldn't help black people but she could change her white community. Malcolm X was assassinated on February 21, 1965, most likely by Nation loyalists, though some suggested fearful drug barons.

His autobiography—published soon after his death—would become required reading for would-be black revolutionaries during the later 1960s. During his lifetime, however, mainstream civil rights leaders belittled his influence. James Farmer, who respected Malcolm X (and whose wife reckoned that Malcolm bested Farmer in debates), said, "Malcolm has done nothing but verbalize."[111] It was certainly true that after leaving the Nation, Malcolm struggled to develop his hoped-for program to "eliminate the political oppression, the economic exploitation, and the social degradation suffered daily by twenty-two million Afro-

Americans."[112] His two main attempts—the formation of Muslim Mosque Inc. and the Organization of Afro-American Unity—attracted but a few hundred members. It was nothing for the half-a-million-strong NAACP to worry about.

But such criticism missed the point. Major Black Power organizations would only emerge later in the 1960s, when a critical mass at the grass-roots rejected the promises of liberalism. Before then, Malcolm was a roving ambassador for radical protest. He turned up wherever militant protest occurred—at Cleage's conference, on a Harlem picket line, as a preacher at Galamison's church. He welcomed Hamer to a New York rally as "the country's number one freedom-fighting woman." He went to Selma, Alabama, in 1965, during a campaign by King there. The *New York Herald Tribune* reported that the "young crowd cheered him repeatedly, and for hours afterward other speakers tried to simmer off the steam that Malcolm had generated." His visit to the English town of Smethwick in 1965, scene of a recent "Do you want a nigger as neighbour" election campaign, inspired the influential activist Michael X and radical organizations there. Malcolm even happened to meet with SNCC visitors in West Africa. In John Lewis's view, "Malcolm's impact on Africa was just fantastic."[113]

Moreover, to suggest that "verbalizing" was "nothing" misses the power of Malcolm's words. One SNCC admirer explained, "Malcolm X said aloud those things which Negroes had been saying among themselves."[114] He critiqued the civil rights crusade. "Whoever heard of a revolution," he asked Cleage's conference, "singing 'We Shall Overcome'? You don't do that in a revolution. You don't do any singing, you're too busy swinging."[115] He mocked King "as a chump, not a champ. Anybody who puts women and children on the front line is a chump." To white audiences, however, Malcolm held up attacks on the nonviolent King as proof of the pervasiveness of white racism. He was a regular speaker on television and white student campuses across the nation, as well as Europe.

By the time of his death, Malcolm X championed a rejection of the American liberal state and the futility of interracial alliances. Yet, as he explained in an interview shortly before he died, "I still would be hard pressed to give a specific definition of the over-all philosophy which I think is necessary for the liberation of the black people in this country."[116] This lack of dogmatism anticipated the experimentation that would become the hallmark of the Black Power era.

Even so, he embodied some of the key aspects of protest that would dominate the later 1960s. He called on black men to defend their homes.

He encouraged spirituality. He condemned the American political system. He praised blackness, telling crowds "You're better than the white man." He saw in black culture and radical politics a means to link their domestic struggles with imperialism and exploitation abroad.[117] He recognized that newly emancipated African countries tended to embrace socialism. "The civil-rights struggle must be expanded beyond the level of civil rights to human rights," he explained to a black workers' group in mid-1964, to enable "our brothers and sisters in Africa and Asia, who have their independence, to come to our rescue."[118]

Forcing the Hand of the Federal Government

The cumulative impact of demonstrations in 1963 thrust the issue of race to the forefront of conversations. As one southern mayor recalled later, "It was like 95% of everything anybody thought about."[119] Most activists sought local change (even as they saw themselves as part of a wider movement). But some sought to present their case directly to a national audience and national politicians.

None more than Martin Luther King Jr., who quickly realized that local problems also needed a federal solution. And never more than at the March on Washington. On August 28, 1963, in sweltering afternoon heat, over 200,000 people (perhaps a quarter of them white) marched to the Lincoln Memorial. The marble Lincoln had gazed down on quite a few demonstrations since Marian Anderson first claimed the site for black freedom. But this was by far the largest civil rights march Lincoln had seen. For the first time, viewers across the country shared his vantage point. CBS provided live coverage, including innovative overhead shots using a mounted camera. Thanks to the recent launch of a communications satellite, six other countries followed the march live. Millions watched Marian Anderson sing once again, saw black and white celebrities make an appearance, heard messages of support from religious and labor leaders, and heard speeches from the leaders of the main civil rights organizations. (James Farmer, who was in prison, was represented by his deputy Floyd McKissick.) But the grand finale was left to Martin Luther King. He delivered his "I Have a Dream" speech with all the eloquence of a preacher, the vision of a prophet, and the strategy of a politician. The electrifying speech dominated the evening news and crowned King as the spokesman for black America.

Carefully choreographed, respectable protest on the sunny streets of Washington was a far cry from tense confrontations across the nation. One reporter called it a cross between a fish fry and a church picnic.

Malcolm X called it a "farce on Washington." The all-male roster of speakers did not reflect the prominence of female activists on the ground —some of them complained to A. Philip Randolph, who planned the march (as he had the World War II version). He claimed that if he had asked one or two women to speak, others would have been put out. There was a tribute to black women, instead.

Nevertheless, in some ways the march did show local concerns writ large. It reflected the recent surge in action at the grassroots—in 1957 when King and others had called a pilgrimage to Washington, only a few thousand people turned up. It reflected local calls for economic change. Billed as a March on Jobs and Freedom, the platform of ten demands included better housing, more training, and a higher minimum wage. It revealed frustration at the limits of liberalism—SNCC's John Lewis asked, "Which side is the federal government on?" It showed the global impact of American protest—there were copycat marches by black activists outside U.S. embassies from London to Accra (which were far less restrained). Even though King's dream powerfully aligned protest with the promise of the American dream, he also warned of the "whirlwinds of revolt" and stressed the "fierce urgency of now."[120]

The march also exposed the depth of opposition to black demands. A majority of white Americans opposed the march. So too had Kennedy. Once it was clear the march was going ahead, Kennedy leaned on civil rights leaders to moderate their demands—and for good measure called up extra police and closed the liquor stores. The march exposed divisions within the civil rights coalition, too. Lewis had wanted to be even blunter, but some other speakers threatened to pull out unless he toned his message down. King advised him to do so, too.

What the television audience actually saw and heard, however, was rather different from the conclusions they drew. Rather than hearing the call for economic and social equality across the nation, they heard a call for moral change and an end to segregation in the South. Rather than heeding the demand for swift action, politicians congratulated the marchers on their respectable behavior. And rather than seeing the diversity of black activists in the crowd, media coverage focused on a single telegenic preacher on the platform.

Indeed, from this point on, the American public saw King as *the* leader of the movement. This perception was entirely mistaken. King's erstwhile colleague Ella Baker complained, "The movement made King, he didn't make the movement." The SCLC was closely involved in only a handful of demonstrations. Local leaders did not need King—and activists in some towns tried to keep him out. Some SNCCers mocked him as "De

Lawd," while the NAACP's Roy Wilkins' early dislike of King turned to outright animus when King hogged the headlines. King's nonviolent approach was increasingly out of step with everyday protest (even his colleagues disagreed with his opposition to smacking children). He didn't even craft all his own rhetoric. The heart-wrenching repetition of "Let freedom ring" in his Washington speech was first delivered by the black pastor Archibald Carey to the Republican National Convention in 1952.[121]

But King did bring many gifts to the movement. He was adept at handling sensitive male egos, and remained on courteous—often close—terms with potential rivals. He showed great stamina in the face of opposition, assaults, and bouts of depression. With his preaching background, intellectual training, and experience of life in Boston, he was a brilliant communicator to white America. Little wonder that one poll found that 95 percent of African Americans thought King was the movement's most effective spokesman. In fact, Baker was quick to praise King's contribution. She was just frustrated that by praising King she was causing people to misunderstand protest. It was certainly true that King and only King received the plaudits—*Time* made King its Man of the Year for 1963 (following Pope John XXII and John F. Kennedy). The Nobel Committee awarded King the Peace Prize in 1964.

Thus, what King said, and what he believed, mattered. Because of King, media coverage of the movement accentuated nonviolence, the positive role of religion, set-piece confrontations, male and middle-class leadership, calls for integration, and an optimistic faith in the potential role of government. One frustrated activist reckoned that white people thought demonstrators just wanted the right to "hug a white person." In fact, King also spoke out for economic justice and human rights. He called for economic power in Montgomery, and a Bill of Rights for the disadvantaged in Birmingham, and complained in his Washington speech that the "negro's basic mobility is from a smaller ghetto to a larger one." By 1964 King would be calling for a "massive assault" on poverty. But most white supporters saw a dreamer rather than a champion of the poor. "The Martin Luther King that people talk about," King told a friend, seems "somebody foreign to me."[122]

Thus, the national conversation about the nature of the Civil Rights Movement represented just one aspect of what was happening locally. Militant activists such as Malcolm X were widely known, but they were portrayed as being outside the mainstream of black thought. Skewed as it may have been, this perception of what African Americans wanted was vitally important. It provided the context for the struggle to pass national civil rights legislation—leading to the Civil Rights Act of 1964 and the Voting Rights Act of 1965.

Many African American leaders had an eye on forcing the federal government to act. The NAACP's Roy Wilkins had the greatest access to the White House. SNCC and CORE kept in touch, often testily, with the Justice Department. The novelist James Baldwin and other artists met with Robert Kennedy during the summer of 1963—the meeting turned into a shouting match over the president's reluctance to act. NAACP lawyers continued to bring cases, with success, before the Supreme Court. The Leadership Conference on Civil Rights—a coalition of civil rights groups—lobbied Congress. So too did the so-called "101st Senator," Clarence Mitchell, the NAACP's chief lobbyist. Within Congress, black politicians such as Adam Clayton Powell pushed legislation. But by the summer of 1963, Martin Luther King had the greatest influence over Washington lawmakers.

King and his team played the media with the consummate skill of seasoned politicians—much to the annoyance of seasoned politicians. He presented local dramas to a national audience. Never more so than in Selma, Alabama. At the start of 1965, King joined a local voter registration campaign there with the intention of provoking a crisis that would force the issue of black voting to the top of the legislative agenda.

King's colleague, Andrew Young, remembered that "we could not have found a more exemplary case of social polarity, or a more abused and oppressed black community."[123] The local White Citizens' Council was the largest chapter in the state. In Dallas County, where Selma was located, black residents formed the majority of the voting age population, but barely 1 percent of registered voters.[124] Selma also exposed the limits of federal power. In April 1961, Attorney General Robert Kennedy filed a voting-rights suit against Dallas County registrars. Yet between May 1962 and August 1964, seven out of every eight black applicants were rejected by the local board. King pointed out that at this rate it would take over a hundred years before black voting reached white levels.

A good drama needs an arch villain. By 1965, foolish foul-mouthed white sheriffs were very thin on the ground. Fortunately for King, Dallas County had one—Jim Clark. Wearing a "Never" button on his lapel and dressed in the style of a wartime general, Clark seemed to be a cracker sheriff drawn directly from central casting. A combination of racism, a red-hot temper, and a desire to impress rural white voters meant Clark was never far from losing control. Time and again the SCLC goaded Clark, and time and again Clark reacted. He ordered police to attack a crowd that included journalists, used electric cattle prods to round up a group of teenagers, clubbed a woman in front of a newspaper photographer as she was waiting to register, and appeared to punch one of King's colleagues in the face in front of a television camera (in fact, Clark's deputy landed the blow, but Clark took the credit).[125] When Clark wound up in the hospital for exhaustion, the SCLC sent him flowers and two thousand children to pray for him.

SCLC also chose Selma because they were impressed by the commitment of local campaigners. Mass meetings of the Dallas County Voters League numbered up to a thousand people. At the end of 1964, the veteran Selma activist Amelia Boynton invited King to join them. Although progress might have seemed excruciatingly slow to outsiders, Boynton believed there were grounds for optimism. In 1964 Selma's few black voters had been significant in the narrow victory of Mayor James Smitherman. Smitherman supported segregation, but he was more restrained than his predecessor. It was the by-now familiar split between moderates and hardliners—one that was most apparent in the rivalry between Wilson Baker, Selma's director of public safety, and Clark, the country sheriff.[126] Baker was no liberal. "If we can only get the bastards out of town without getting them arrested, we'll have 'em whipped."[127] But Baker ordered Clark's police to stay away from protests in Selma. The problem for Baker, though, was that once applicants for the vote reached the county courthouse, they came under Clark's jurisdiction. King's deputy Ralph Abernathy reckoned they "clearly hated one another more than they hated us."[128]

Thus, the Selma campaign was rooted in the politics of the county courthouse, the local churches, and the town square. But from the outset, the SCLC's focus was on national opinion, Congress, and the White House. The campaign proper started on January 18, when King and SNCC's John Lewis led four hundred applicants to the courthouse to register. By early February, more than 2,400 people had been arrested—including King—and Selma had become a front-page story. The *New York Times* published a letter from King where he pointed out that there were more black people in Selma's jail than there were registered to vote. Upon his release on February 5, King announced that he would be going to meet the president. Johnson chafed at King's presumption and refused the meeting. Recordings of his telephone conversations suggest he detested King as a rabble-rouser. Still, on February 9, they did meet, although Johnson insisted that King's visit should be billed as a meeting with the vice president. Afterward King praised Johnson—and so put Johnson's private assurances on record. "The president made it very clear to me that he was determined during his administration to see all remaining obstacles removed to the right of Negroes to vote."[129]

Back in Selma, King and his staffers discussed the question, "How far can Selma take us on the right to vote?"[130] The SCLC decided to broaden the campaign to the surrounding rural counties. On February 18, after an evening meeting in Perry County, protesters marched to the courthouse. Almost immediately the street lights dimmed and police attacked the crowd. Jimmie Lee Jackson, trying to protect his family, was shot and died. At Jackson's funeral, King announced to some two thousand mourners that there would be a march from Selma to Montgomery on Sunday, March 7, to demand the vote. It was the defining set-piece confrontation the SCLC had been praying for. As the six hundred marchers crossed Selma's Edmund Pettus Bridge on the road to Montgomery, Clark's police stopped them with tear gas. Wearing gas masks, the police attacked. Fifty-six marchers were taken to the hospital. John Lewis—true to form—suffered a fractured skull.

"Bloody Sunday" shook the nation. Some fifty million viewers watched the violence and heard Clark say, "Get those goddamned niggers." One of those viewers, Lyndon Johnson, recalled later, "I felt a deep outrage."[131] ABC broke into a movie called *Judgment at Nuremberg* to follow the story—and plenty of commentators made the connection. Even the conservative *Birmingham News* declared support for King. At least 450 white clergy from across America responded to King's call to come to Selma. After arresting a group of white northerners, Wilson Baker admitted to reporters that "this has ceased to be a Negro movement." Listening to their attempts to sing "We Shall Overcome," Baker reflected on a movement that was now beyond his control. "At least we had good music when the Negroes were demonstrating."[132]

Bloody Sunday, said Minnesota Senator Walter Mondale, "makes passage of legislation to guarantee Southern Negroes the right to vote an absolute imperative for Congress this year." Some 122 senators and representatives spoke out in support of voting rights. Few criticized the campaign, and most of those were from Alabama.[133] King sought to make the pressure irresistible. He rescheduled the march for Tuesday, March 9. Fearing an even bloodier Tuesday, Johnson sent an emissary to try to negotiate. King accepted a compromise: he led the marchers across the bridge, knelt to pray, and then turned the march around. Some SNCC activists were livid.[134] Later that evening, three white clergymen who had traveled to support the movement were attacked, and one of them, the Reverend James Reeb, died two days later.

The march was scheduled a third time for March 21. In the interim, President Johnson addressed a joint session of Congress to urge the passage of a voting rights bill. In front of a televised audience of seventy million, Johnson told Congress, "No delay, no hesitation, no compromise."

Johnson had invited King to be present, but King declined because it clashed with Reeb's funeral. As they watched Johnson's speech on television together, King's colleagues saw him weep for the first time. Johnson presented his proposals to Congress two days later. When the march finally began, it was a celebration. On arrival at Selma, King declared, "We Have Overcome today." Soon afterward, news filtered through that Viola Liuzzo, a white mother of five helping to transport the marchers, had been shot dead.

It would be easy to ascribe the passage of civil rights legislation to King's compelling presentation of the black cause and demonization of white supremacists. His letter from jail in Birmingham had prompted Kennedy to action. Johnson's first public commitment to introducing voting legislation followed King's release from jail yet again and his demand for a meeting. Johnson's announcement of a specific date for the legislation followed Bloody Sunday, which was precipitated by King's march. In the climax to his speech in Congress Johnson borrowed the movement's rallying cry, "We Shall Overcome." It was the most passionate speech of his presidency.[135]

A closer look at the passage of the Civil Rights Act and Voting Rights Act, however, shows that King had not stumbled across a magic formula to force change. Rather, he capitalized on the changing balance of power in Washington between those seeking reform and those defending the status quo. Southern segregationists had never been weaker in Congress. In turn, African Americans had never been stronger at any time since Reconstruction. The migration of African Americans to northern cities (where they could vote for liberal Democrats); the Cold War context; the precedents set by the Supreme Court; the rise of a sympathetic mass media; and declining popular support for strict segregation (seen as a southern problem) shifted the political winds toward civil rights. So too did the age-old fear of black uprisings. President Kennedy first acted in response to black fighting in Birmingham, and King played the fear card to good effect. "If sizable tangible gains are not made soon all across the country," King warned, "some Negroes might be tempted to accept some oblique paths such as Malcolm X proposes."[136]

This changing balance of power did not exactly give King an open door. But for the first time for a century, it was a door that would open under pressure. In the case of the Voting Rights Act, the Justice Department had actually prepared options for the president to consider before the Selma campaign had been announced. The final draft of the bill was prepared two days before Bloody Sunday. Unlike his predecessors, Johnson arrived in the White House with a genuine commitment to equal opportunities. A former teacher of poor Mexican children in Texas, Johnson used his first speech after Kennedy's assassination to urge the passage of the Civil Rights Act. Unlike Kennedy, Johnson was prepared to confront southern segregationists. After Bloody Sunday, Johnson summoned George C. Wallace to the White House, sat him in a squishy sofa, and gave him a long lecture littered with expletives. Three hours later, Wallace told reporters, "Hell, if I'd stayed in there much longer, he'd have had me coming out for civil rights."[137]

This is not to say that Johnson was a civil rights pioneer. He had opposed much of the 1957 Civil Rights Act and refused to seat the Mississippi Freedom Party delegation at Atlantic City. Nevertheless, Johnson genuinely believed the black vote was key to unraveling southern white supremacy. As he told his vice president before the Selma campaign began, when blacks get the vote "they'll have every politician . . . kissing their ass." Johnson also recognized that more black voters would benefit his re-election prospects—they had provided his margin of victory in four southern states. Of course, Johnson knew full well that pushing for civil rights legislation risked alienating southern white voters further. But he calculated that it would be a popular move outside the South.[138] Polls consistently found that the campaign to vote had more legitimacy than any other civil rights campaign.

The swift passage of the legislation was also dependent on the willingness of Congress to support the president. The 1964 election left the Democrats in firm control of the House and the Senate. Their 295–140 majority in the House was the largest since 1936. All in all, it added up to a rare opportunity for Johnson. The *Congressional Quarterly* calculated that 68.4 percent of proposals submitted by Johnson in 1965 were approved by Congress, the highest since the *Quarterly* started keeping a record in 1954.[139] The weakness of southern Democrats helped his cause. Northern liberal Democrats (many dependent on black voters) held a majority. Southern Democrats had lost some of their key positions of power. Prior to 1965, Senator James Eastland of Mississippi had used his position as chair of the Judiciary Committee to kill off over a hundred civil rights bills. But after the 1964 election, the committee had a liberal majority. The *de facto* senator for southern resistance, Georgia's Richard Russell, was ill. He was defeatist too. "If there is anything I could do," he told one colleague, "I would do it, but I assume the die is cast."[140] Johnson's overwhelming victory against Barry Goldwater, who had vehemently opposed the civil rights bill, gave him a personal mandate for further reform. He also invoked the need to win hearts and minds across the world in the battle against Communism.

What this all added up to by 1965 was two wide-ranging pieces of legislation. The Civil Rights Act of 1964 sought to end segregation. Title II outlawed Jim Crow in public accommodations. Title IV authorized the attorney general to file suits to enforce school desegregation. The act also targeted workplace discrimination. Title VII prohibited companies with fifteen or more employees from discriminating on account of race, sex, or religion. The Voting Rights Act of 1965 outlawed any voting test or qualification that would "deny or abridge the right of any citizen of the United States to vote on account of race or color." Section 4 suspended literacy tests in the six southern states where voter turnout in 1964 was less than 50 percent of the voting age population. The act allowed the attorney general to send in "examiners" and "poll watchers" to enforce voting rights in these states.

Passage of this legislation was a stunning victory for the Civil Rights Movement. The Voting Rights Act is "every bit as momentous," declared John Lewis, "as the Emancipation Proclamation."[141] At the start of 1963, let alone 1960, few people, if anyone, could have imagined such a victory so soon. At that stage, Kennedy was only considering modest proposals. But it was not the end of the story. The legislation had limits. Both acts focused mostly on the South. Title IV excluded any effort to "achieve a racial balance in any school by requiring the transport of pupils . . . from one school to another," thus allowing southern segregationists to move from massive resistance to minimum compliance. Title VII had no real enforcement power. Some sections of the Voting Rights Act were in place for only five years. In the meantime, Johnson's Justice Department chose not to send in voting "examiners" to many parts of the South. By this time, many activists no longer trusted liberal reform to provide a remedy for racial injustice anyway.

Johnson signed the Voting Rights Act on August 6. Five days later, near the Watts suburb of Los Angeles, police stopped a young black man called Marquette Frye on suspicion of drunk driving. Frye's mother arrived. She scolded her son, and, as tensions mounted, she hit one of the officers. The police grappled with the Fryes and arrested them. A crowd gathered. Rumors of police brutality spread. A week of violence followed, during which fourteen thousand National Guards were called out and thirty-four people died. The local police chief, William Parker, condemned the rioters as "monkeys in a zoo." Two thirds of African Americans in Los Angeles thought the violence was deserved. The beating—just the latest in a series of police brutality cases—occurred in the context of increasing segregation and rising black unemployment, despite local civil rights legislation. In 1964 three out of four white California voters had approved a proposition that overturned a fair housing law passed only the previous year.

The shock of Watts was not just in its timing but its location. Watts was not in the South. It wasn't particularly poor. Johnson called up King: "We've got so much to do . . . that I don't know how we'll ever do it, but we've got to get ahead with it."[142] As he would soon find out, many no longer trusted him—or any other liberal reformer—to "get ahead" and "do it." When King rushed to broker a settlement, he was in for a shock, too. Two years previously, he had been the celebrated speaker at a mass rally in L.A. Now, he was heckled. Five years after the first sit-ins, Watts showed that the struggle for equality was far from over, and that neither Johnson nor King held the initiative.

CHAPTER TEN

Black Power and Grassroots Protest, 1966–1978

"I started off on the concept that you attempt to do it the respectable way. Then, you move up to another level or less, maybe, accepted way, which was a sit-in. Then you find that that doesn't work but so much, so you move up to something else, which may be a civil disobedience-type of action. Then you find that doesn't work and then what do you do? You may have to come to that last resort, which is the revolutionary thrust."
Ella Baker[1]

In 1967, militant black leader Lemuel Chester was accused of starting a fire that destroyed two blocks in downtown Cambridge, Maryland. The following year, city officials appointed Chester director of an expensive new community centre.[2]

Interview with Ewart Brown, president of Howard University student union, 1968:
Brown: "The color of the skin is one what we call the natural instincts."
Interviewer: "Instinct is sort of passé in science, isn't it?"
Brown: "They say it's passé but when you turn on the Temptations you begin to question that."[3]

In Las Vegas in 1971, welfare mothers stormed Caesars Palace to protest the cutback of state welfare payments. The Nevada state government reversed its decision.[4]

In 1977 Congressional Black Caucus Chairman Parren Mitchell added an amendment to the Public Works Employment Act which set aside 10 percent of federal contracts for Minority Business Enterprises. Little noticed at the time, it was one of the most significant pieces of legislation for black employment of the civil rights era.

On a balmy Sunday afternoon, June 5, 1966, James Meredith set off from Memphis with the intention of walking to Jackson, Mississippi. Since graduating from Ole Miss in 1963, Meredith had traveled far and wide—giving talks across Europe, studying in Nigeria, visiting the Nile—before settling in New York to study law. Shortly before the march, his name was back in the news. In April, he announced his candidacy as an insurgent Democrat for a place on New York's upcoming constitutional convention—a direct challenge to Adam Clayton Powell. His memoir, *Three Years in Mississippi,* which revealed his "divine responsibility to advance human civilization," was just out.[5] The Memphis NAACP gave his walk extra publicity by criticizing him for not having the courtesy to let them know in advance. Meredith added his own theatrical touches by wearing a pith helmet and carrying mementoes from Egypt—an ebony cane and an African chief's tail (a stick with flowing hair at the top).

Meredith told reporters that he marched to challenge the "overriding fear that dominates the day-to-day life of the Negro in the United States . . . particularly Mississippi."[6] No doubt he remembered the tragic end to postman William Moore's 1963 March across Mississippi. To preempt trouble, Meredith had written to every sheriff along the planned route. Only one replied. The officer at his first stop, De Soto County, explained, "We are going to treat James Meredith just like any other nigger chopping cotton in the fields."[7] Meredith sought to highlight the problem of voting. He calculated that the 220-mile walk would take 450,000 steps—one for each unregistered black voter in Mississippi. Meredith also had a challenge for black men. "I am sick and tired of Negro men [hiding] behind their women and children," he explained, as he called on men, and only men, to join him.[8]

Meredith's march was far from the only race story of the week—it wasn't even the main one. Elsewhere in Mississippi, Freedom Democratic Party candidates canvassed voters ahead of the upcoming elections. In Watts, Barbara Deadwyler prepared to file suit for "wrongful death" against the patrolman who shot her husband as he raced her—then eight months pregnant—to the hospital. (Her lawyer, Johnnie Cochran, taking his first case, would later become the most famous black trial lawyer in America.) In Selma, black voters celebrated a federal court ruling to count contested votes in the election for sheriff—thereby ensuring Jim Clark's defeat. In Chicago, Martin Luther King's team readied to turn the city into the next Selma, this time to spotlight housing and economic problems. In Guinea, President Sekou Touré pulled back from plans to restore Ghana's recently deposed President Kwame Nkrumah to power. Meanwhile, commentators debated whether Lyndon Johnson's recent, much-heralded White House conference on civil rights had amounted to anything more than a talk-shop. Consensus was it hadn't. The panel on the family was so fractious it ended up discussing the less controversial topic of the Boy Scouts.[9]

On Monday, June 6, Meredith started his second day of walking. Hecklers spat at him. One called out, "You'll never make it past Batesville"—a town sixty miles further on. He was right. Twenty-eight miles into Mississippi, a car drove slowly past the entourage, then parked on a side road. A heavy-set white man climbed out, carrying a shotgun. Law officers accompanying Meredith were not concerned—a man with a gun was hardly an unusual sight in Mississippi, and he seemed just to be curious. Their concern was potential snipers in the woods a few yards back from the road. The man approached the marchers, called out, "James," and fired. The first two shots sprayed sixty or so pellets into Meredith's neck and back. Meredith lay writhing in the dust. The march to allay fears ended up increasing them.[10]

The march became the top race story. Still, it may have blown over in a day or two, since the attacker shot from too far away to do lasting damage. Meredith recuperated in style at the home of Juanita Hardy, better known as the ex-wife of movie star Sidney Poitier. He told reporters that white suburbanites rather than southern segregationists were the greatest threat to a just America.[11] But Meredith's fall led to a much bigger story—the public fracturing of the civil rights coalition and the public end of the nonviolent movement for integration. Against Meredith's wishes, civil rights leaders vowed to complete the march. The problem was, they were too divided to do so together. SNCC's new leader, Stokely Carmichael, demanded the exclusion of white people and protection by Deacons for Defense guards. He calculated it would force the NAACP's Roy Wilkins and the National Urban League's Whitney Young to pull out. They duly did so. King came to a compromise with Carmichael: he accepted the Deacons but refused to bar white marchers. Reporters picked up on the dispute.

On June 16 the march reached Greenwood. The police station there had a plaque in praise of a German shepherd called Tiger for the dog's role in stopping previous demonstrations. Police arrested Carmichael for putting up his tent on school grounds. After his release later that evening, Carmichael headed to a 3,000-strong mass rally. King was away recording a television show, so Carmichael had top billing. He told the crowd, "We been saying freedom for six years and we ain't got nothin'. What we gonna start saying now is Black Power!" Supporters roared back, "Black Power!" Carmichael said he knew instantly that "they could not bring [the civil rights slogan] 'Freedom Now' back. It was over. From now on, it was 'Black Power.'" He was right. For the next few years, Black Power would dominate the national discourse on race. The phrase symbolized the rejection of nonviolence, contempt for liberal reform, and the end of King's dream of a color-blind society. As the *Chicago Defender*—hardly the most radical black newspaper, and highly critical of SNCC's militant turn—wrote in an editorial three weeks later, "this is a new day . . . the doctrine of passive resistance as preached by Dr. King is ebbing." Instead, there is a "determination to meet fire with fire."[12]

In fact there was nothing new about the phrase "black power." Less than a week before the Greenwood march, Adam Clayton Powell had told four thousand Howard University students to avoid the "sterile chase of integration," and that "to demand these God-given [human] rights is to seek black power—what I call audacious power." Some Watts residents had told reporters that riots were "displays of black power."[13] Richard Wright had used the phrase as the title of a 1954 study of emerging African nations. Carmichael's colleague Willie Ricks had already used the phrase in speeches on the march. There was certainly nothing new about the idea of black power either. Black leaders from Martin Delany to Malcolm X had argued the case with force. Carmichael himself had developed black-only politics to "take over Lowndes County," Alabama. Harlem CORE leader Roy Innis told reporters, "Carmichael just gave a name to what a lot of people were already thinking."[14]

Nor did Carmichael's Greenwood speech lead to an immediate change in protest politics. When King spoke in Detroit a few days later, fifteen thousand people turned out to hear him. When Carmichael spoke there soon afterward, only a few hundred turned up. Moreover, the Black Power movement shared many of the same ideas as Freedom Now. Both called for more than rights or justice. They called for the power, or freedom, to make one's own decisions. Thus, both asserted a new sense of self-respect and new behavior—one could actually feel free or powerful (rather than just have legal rights). When demonstrators chanted "Black Power" outside Philadelphia's main post office in 1966, they were actually calling for the same things (more jobs) with the same tactics (picketing and disruption) as they had the previous year. Carmichael's speech did not even mark such a dramatic change during the Mississippi march. King rejoined the march, and warned that "black supremacy would be as evil as white supremacy." By the time they reached Jackson, Whitney Young had joined them. Soon afterward, the major leaders—including Roy Wilkins—found as much common ground as possible during a televised debate.

Still, this was to be the last coordinated march between the big organizations. From this point on, high-profile Black Power activists would denounce liberal reform tactics and moderate black leaders with equal vehemence. SNCC and then CORE would soon formally reject nonviolence and eject white members (though in the case of SNCC, by the narrowest of votes). And King would be left standing on increasingly precarious center ground.

Some race leaders and white liberals blamed the media for losing all sense of balance. "If Stokely Carmichael throws his shoe up in the air," one black educator complained, "the TV networks have 500 words on it before it hits the ground."[15] He had a point. When activists in the small town of Talbotton, Georgia, called NBC news to report the shooting of a black marcher, they were told, "A white man shooting a black man has lost its sexiness." What was sexy—and got on the news—was black aggression. Meredith reckoned that skewed media coverage left people thinking he had been shot by a rival black leader. Ironically, liberal and moderate overreaction gave the slogan air time. At the NAACP's 1966 annual convention, Wilkins condemned Black Power as "a reverse Hitler, a reverse Ku Klux Klan." After SNCC expelled white members, one of its founders (and future NAACP board chairman), Julian Bond, reckoned, "The crazies are taking over."[16]

Whatever the causes of the media frenzy, the die was cast. In any case, the media had plenty of material to paint a picture of a lethal Black Power epidemic. During the five years after Watts, there were over five hundred major violent uprisings by African Americans. The most deadly were in Newark and Detroit in 1967, where nearly eighty people died in total. But there were also riots in many small towns in the South, even in black suburbs. "Dig it, baby!" mocked one SNCC activist, about a riot in Des Moines, Iowa. "Didn't know there was even niggers out there, man."[17] Many—including Edward Brooke, the first black senator in the North—blamed the riots on Black Power.

There were plenty of individuals who spoke a new aggressive language, too. On May 12, 1967, the fiery, Louisiana-born H. Rap Brown succeeded Carmichael as chairman of SNCC. Carmichael warned that "people will be glad to have me back when they hear him." Brown didn't disappoint. At his first press conference he called Lyndon Johnson a "mad dog" and said "Violence is as American as cherry pie." One month later, Brown climbed atop a car in Cambridge, Maryland, and told a crowd, "Don't be trying to love the honkey to death. Shoot him to death." Later that night, two blocks of downtown Cambridge burned to the ground. The media blamed Brown for causing a riot. (In fact, the fire had nothing to do with Brown's speech, and there was no riot.) Critics renamed SNCC the Nonstudent Violent Uncoordinated Committee.

By this point, the Black Panther Party in California had replaced SNCC as the main Black Power bogeymen. The Panthers were founded in late 1966 by Bobby Seale and Huey Newton. Both grew up in poor southern families who moved to Oakland. Seale dropped out of high school because of racial prejudice and was then discharged from the air force for insubordination. The movie-star handsome Newton went to law school hoping to become a better criminal. Both were avid readers of black literature. Both dreamed of a global uprising of radical poor black youth.

Six months later, barely twenty people had signed up to their vision. But Seale and Newton soon proved as adept at street theater as King in his heyday. In May 1967 the Panthers—wearing leather jackets and berets and carrying guns—walked into the State Capitol in Sacramento. They were protesting against proposed legislation that would end the legal right to display guns. By accident, they found themselves in the main assembly rooms. Television channels interrupted regular programming to carry the protest live. Five months later, Newton was stopped by police late one night. A fight ensued, and a patrolman was killed. Newton spent the rest of the decade in jail. The Free Huey Campaign became a rallying cry for militant activists across America. In 1969 Black Panthers fought with supporters of a rival black radical group for control of UCLA's new Afro-American Studies Center. (Unknown at the time, the FBI carefully stoked the tensions.) Two Panthers were killed.

For a watching white audience, the Panthers raised the age-old specter of unrestrained black machismo. The title of black author and SNCC member Julius Lester's 1968 book, *Look Out Whitey! Black Power's Gonna Get Your Mama*, hardly helped. "Out of the depths of the swamp," wrote Lester, "the mire oozing from his skin, came the black monster and fathers told their daughters to be in by nine instead of nine-thirty."[18] The media fanned the fears of primitive danger. After the Sacramento showdown, a *Washington Post* editorial asked readers, "You thought something like that could only happen in Congo or Outer Slobovia?"[19]

Much of the mainstream representation of Black Power was of an incoherent, faction-ridden, anti-white, sloganeering, futile movement of hopeless youth. In other words, Black Power was the bastard son of the Civil Rights Movement. King was sympathetic—he called it the "cry of the despairing." But most white Americans were hostile. Lester reckoned, "Whites wanted to know only one thing: Does it mean y'all gon' kill white folks?"[20] In a 1967 poll in Detroit, a majority of white respondents thought Black Power meant a violent "black takeover." The *New York*

Times dubbed Newton's group the *"antiwhite* Black Panther Party."[21] FBI Director J. Edgar Hoover went one step further, dubbing the Panthers "the greatest threat to the internal security of the country."

This representation was important, for it framed grassroots white reaction, police overreaction, and political discussions in the late 1960s. But it was also entirely wrong, a fact that most African Americans knew well. In the same Detroit poll that showed white fear, only 9 percent of black respondents thought Black Power meant a violent black takeover. For the most part, grassroots Black Power groups were purposeful, practical, positive, and popular with black Americans. And far from being just the cry of the despairing, Black Power was also the call of the confident.

The Purposes of Black Power

The media's focus on factions and the incoherence of Black Power missed the point. To be sure, there were plenty of disagreements (some violent) over what Black Power meant. Some student leaders later regretted being vague in their explanations. But the supposed contrast with a clear and coherent Civil Rights Movement was a myth. As reporter Louis Lomax had commented in 1963, "I would wager that more than half of the Negro population . . . [is] incapable of articulating just what it is they seek under the catch-all label of integration."[22] Besides, if Black Power really could mean anything to any(angry)body, it is hard to explain why it resonated quite so powerfully with particular groups at that particular time.

In any case, Black Power had several clear themes. Carmichael tried to outline them in his book by that name in 1967. He was not anti-white, but he did critique the promises of liberal America. "The Democratic Party did not give black people the right to vote; it simply stopped denying black people the right to vote." He rejected nonviolence. "Nothing more quickly repels someone bent on destroying you than the unequivocal message: 'O.K., fool, make your move, and run the same risk I run—of dying.'" He rejected the interracialism of early protest, too. "Before a group can enter the open society, it must first close ranks." Instead, he stressed solidarity with international anti-colonial movements, called for majority-black communities to take political control, and focused on economic gains. Within this general framework, he expected to see "broad experimentation" by local groups.[23]

Experimentation was exactly what took place (some predating Carmichael's speech). Some militant groups were nationalists, who hoped for some form of black separatism, whether it be in the mind, in local communities, or in a separate territory. Others were pluralists, who called on

African Americans to "close ranks" and win their fair share in the struggle between different interest groups. In practice, most groups combined racial pride and political goals. Many focused on the poor, condemned middle-class black leaders, called for reparations to be paid for slavery, and identified with nonwhite protest abroad. Over time, many local groups—including the Black Panthers—moved toward revolutionary socialism. In Detroit, the Republic of New Africa (with "Queen Mother" Moore to the fore) called for land to create an African American nation in the Deep South, while the League of Revolutionary Black Workers developed out of radical autoworker movements and into a black Marxist movement. In Los Angeles, the flamboyant Ron Karenga founded US (meaning "us" as opposed to "them"). Karenga, who had been inspired by meeting Malcolm X, was a doctoral student at UCLA during the riot. He dropped out to launch a black cultural revolution based on "Nguzo Saba" (Swahili for "seven principles") and promoted an annual Kwanzaa holiday to celebrate African culture in America. Karenga quickly became the most influential advocate of cultural nationalism across the country.

These Black Power groups had plenty of slogans, but they went far beyond posturing. Black Power was often entirely practical when applied to a particular place at a particular moment. Revolutionary trade union movements demanded more black jobs and black representation in decisionmaking. Black Power student groups demanded more black faculty members, better treatment of black staff, and courses on black history. For all the hate-whitey rhetoric, explained Seale, "If you got enough energy to sit down and hate a white person *just* because of the color of his skin, you're wasting a lot of energy."[24]

The Panthers were a case in point. They had a ten-point platform, including full employment, end of police harassment, promotion of black history, decent housing, reparations for slavery, and a UN plebiscite for African Americans to determine their future. They ran breakfast programs for thousands of poor black schoolchildren—relying on (sometimes forced) donations from black businesses. To counter police harassment, Panthers patrolled police cars while carrying their own guns and tape recorders. When one Oakland policeman asked Huey Newton, "Who in the hell do you think you are?" Newton dropped a round into his gun and replied, "Who in the hell do you think *you* are."[25] The Panthers' language and gestures—revolutionary-style outfits, giving "the fist" rather than "high fives"—were designed to develop confidence and reassert black manhood. To strengthen their hand, the Panthers joined with SNCC and linked with the armed wing of the Chicano movement, the American Indian movement, and the Young Puerto Rican Brothers.

Even the urban uprisings were as aspirational as they were anarchic. There was plenty of indiscriminate looting, especially of liquor stores. But the federal committee that studied the 1967 riots—the Kerner Commission—reported in 1968 that those involved were often "politically sophisticated and ready to act on that basis."[26] One rioter in Washington, D.C., reckoned "the broadest motivation for anybody out there [was] that they'd blew up four young girls in Alabama." "We were only paying them back for the slavery and sufferings of our people." Even looters claimed moral justification. One middle-aged woman in Newark explained, "They rob us every day . . . What in hell do they expect?"[27] Another rioter, who condemned mindless looting, explained that she acted on need, not greed: "I went into the store and came out with a big sponge because I knew I needed something to wash the dishes with."[28]

Black Power protest was also popular. Local organizations did not have mass membership to rival the near half million member NAACP. Membership of the Panthers peaked at five thousand in forty-five cities. But the Panther newsletter had a circulation of quarter of a million by 1969, and polls suggested that a majority of African Americans sympathized with black nationalists, with revolutionary groups like the Panthers, and even with rioters. Meanwhile, the NAACP's approval rating among African Americans dropped from 80 percent in 1963 to just 20 percent in 1969.[29]

The Causes of Black Power

The rise and popularity of Black Power prompts the question (as with the rise of the sit-ins), why? Certainly, the theatricality of the Panthers attracted admiration. One eighth grade girl from North Carolina wrote the imprisoned Huey Newton that she was "very proud that I'm *black* (and I love you too)."[30] Black Power reflected the radicalism of the times. The year 1968 was the height of social unrest across America, with the rise of white militant organizations such as Students for a Democratic Society and a peace movement to end the Vietnam War. Many African Americans shared Black Power's outlook long before Meredith's march. John Oliver, an elderly Harlem resident, told one black interviewer, "I get tired of that one-nation-under-God boogie-joogie . . . If anybody can be the president, why all them dudes look like they do?" Sixty-one-year-old Harlemite Hannah Nelson agreed. A domestic worker and a churchgoer who taught music and black history in her spare time, Nelson explained, "We don't really agree with white people about anything important." As for the question "What do black people want?" Nelson reckoned, "Anything worth having."[31]

But these reasons alone do not explain why Black Power rose to such prominence so quickly. After all, radicals such as Queen Mother Moore, Robert F. Williams, and Albert Cleage, to name but three, had organized and performed before 1966. Indeed, the most charismatic proponent of Black Power was the late Malcolm X. Black Power groups mostly had a strained relationship with SDS, and few joined the peace movement.[32] And residual black support was a foundation for, not the cause of, Black Power's new prominence. Rather, Black Power (like the sit-ins) rose in response to the problems and opportunities of the moment—in the cities, the nation, and around the globe, and from politics and economics to culture.

In city after city, activists had demanded, and won, full legal rights in employment, housing, and schooling. But when they tried to make these rights real, success proved elusive. Thus, during the later 1960s, demonstrators ratcheted up their goals and tactics. Rather than calling for the employment of some skilled black workers, activists demanded quotas of black workers to fit the proportion of African Americans in the community. Rather than scuffles, there was a real threat of major violence. And rather than picketing individual sites, protests escalated to massive levels. In Chicago in 1969, local organizations shut down twenty-three construction protests simultaneously—leaving over a thousand workers idle.[33] At the end of the summer, black construction workers staged a national walkout.

Yet as protests mounted, conditions deteriorated. Black income crept up relative to white income during the 1960s, and economists would report that over two thirds of employed black workers were in the middle class by 1970. But black unemployment remained more than double white unemployment. In many ghettoes, a majority of young black men were unemployed. Urban renewal programs, zoning ordinances, the movement of industry to the suburbs, and white neighborhood groups continued to lock the black working-poor into jobless ghettoes. As the inner city gained a reputation for crime, unemployment, and family breakdown, and as racism assumed a spatial definition, the pattern of prejudice became self-perpetuating.

Thus, many black activists came to see liberal politics as part of the problem rather than the solution. "The white liberal," said Julius Lester, "has generally turned out to be more white than liberal whenever blacks assert themselves."[34] In national politics, Lyndon Johnson had pulled the rug from under the Mississippi challenge in Atlantic City, he had been slow to send registrars to enforce the Voting Rights Act, and the Civil Rights Act did little to enforce economic equality. Johnson's War on Poverty—the most ambitious federal social spending program in American history—did not address discrimination or deindustrialization. "We don't need a war on poverty," complained one activist, "we need a war on the rich."[35] The tokenism of moderate local governments seemed little better than the vitriol of segregationist governments of yesteryear.

In response to black militancy, vitriolic politics seemed to be on the way back, anyway. So, too, did heavy-handed policing. In Macon, Georgia, Mayor "Machine Gun" Ronnie Thompson blocked a 1968 demonstration with a tank—an obsession with tanks was one of the hallmarks of Black Power crowd control. In Philadelphia, Commissioner Frank Rizzo promised that "Philadelphia police will not permit rule by mob." On November 17, 1967, some three thousand black students marched peacefully to the Board of Education, and the school superintendent met with the leaders of the march. Rizzo's response was to tell his officers to "get their black asses." The ensuing brutality rivaled anything seen in the Jim Crow South. Rizzo claimed militants planned to start a riot and then poison rations for police on duty. In 1971, Rizzo was elected mayor.[36]

Rizzo's election was part of nationwide rise in conservative politics. "Law and order" became a shibboleth of political campaigns. In fact, the rise of conservatism was not simply a backlash against Black Power. Race had long been the faultline of the liberal Democrat coalition, as working-class white ethnic groups defended their status against black demands. "We knew all about the backlash, frontlash, sidelash, and all them other lashes," wrote Lester. "Hell, white folks hated niggers. So what else was new?"[37] Moreover, the rise of conservatism was as much a result of the new suburban politics of "middle-class entitlement" as of crude racism.[38] Even so, the specter of Black Power added spice to conservative rhetoric. The Republican governor of Maryland, Spiro Agnew, had won the support of black voters in his 1966 election because of his progressive record on civil rights. But after riots in Baltimore, he condemned the "circuit riding, Hanoi visiting, caterwauling . . . burn America down type of leaders."[39] "Why don't impoverished whites riot?" he asked (overlooking the fact that they often had). Two months later, Agnew would be elected vice president of the United States.

As Black Power activists turned against liberal politics, many turned against those black reformers who still subscribed to the old vision. Thus, Black Power was to be found on the campuses of black universities as much as on white ones. In March 1968 the Howard University student group Ujamaa (Swahili for "togetherness") demanded a relevant black curriculum. To shouts of "Think, Act, Be, Black" and "This is the Revolution," a thousand students took over the main "A" building for five days to make their point. The faculty gave in. Black Power groups challenged black reformers for control of the state, too. To ensure "maximum feasible participation" in the provision of services to the poor, Johnson's War on Poverty funded over a thousand local agencies. It also ensured that divisions between black activists would turn into bitter confrontations in a battle for funding. In Oakland, militant grassroots leaders won control of the local poverty board from city officials and liberal black leaders.

Entrenched poverty, the limits of liberalism, and the rise of state-sanctioned violence meant the Black Power critique of American life, and calls for reparations, resonated widely. Some talked of America as Babylon—a country where the jobless ghetto was surrounded by the "white noose" of prosperous suburbs, where the state favored those that had over those that had not.[40] (Even the Kerner Commission agreed that "white society is deeply implicated in the ghetto.")[41] Thus, many civil rights protest groups of the early 1960s moved seamlessly to a Black Power position. In Davenport, Iowa, the NAACP youth branch called itself the Black Power Youth Council—once again, local NAACP militancy ran ahead of national NAACP leaders.[42] In Greensboro, a new Association for Poor People was run by students from the same A&T campus that produced the first sit-in students. Even groups that did not explicitly adopt Black Power rhetoric came to share many of the same goals. In 1973 the head of Atlanta's NAACP, Lonnie King (the former leader of Atlanta's 1960 sit-in movement), agreed to a deal to slow school integration in return for black control over black schooling. "It's time to get out of the courts," he explained to an angry NAACP head office, "and move on to the more important issue of educating kids."[43]

What was true at the local level was true of national figures. In a well-reported 1967 speech at New York's Riverside Church, King criticized capitalism and called the American government, at the height of the Vietnam War, "the greatest purveyor of violence in the world today."[44] A hero when he bought into the American dream, he was branded a "traitor to the cause" by *Time* when he bought out of it. Lyndon Johnson called him "the crown prince of the Vietniks." In fact, King had long called for human rights rather than just civil rights. By the time of his Chicago campaign in 1966 he was calling for a higher minimum wage, guaranteed income for the unemployed, and open housing. The Chicago campaign had floundered in the face of hostility from Democratic politicians (black and white) and grassroots white violence—King's colleague Andrew Young called one Chicago demonstration "the march I would most like to forget . . . We felt like we were walking through a war zone . . . But this was America. In the 'enlightened' North."[45] In 1968 King laid plans for a mass gathering of poor people in Washington, D.C. With King at the helm, the campaign could have severely embarrassed the government and begun to forge an anti-poverty coalition across the color line.

But on April 4, King was assassinated in Memphis, where he was supporting a garbage workers strike. The outpouring of grief across the country at his death was matched by anger at his murder. Riots broke out in some 125 cities, the most widespread night of racial violence in American history. The irony of unprecedented levels of black violence marking the death of a man some called the "prince of peace" was not lost on commentators at the time. A more fitting tribute was Congress's passage of fair housing legislation on April 10, but it was in fact the rioting, not the assassination, which concentrated legislators' minds—National Guard troops were still patrolling the capital during the vote. That a bullet of hate felled a man dedicated to loving his enemies legitimized Black Power's embrace of self-defense. "Dr. Martin Luther King was the last prince of nonviolence," said Floyd McKissick, Farmer's successor as head of CORE, at a news conference. "Nonviolence is a dead philosophy, and it was not the black people that killed it." CORE prepared a publication to help black people "survive"—advising them to get hold of a weapon and prepare a first aid kit.[46]

Unlike King in his later years, the NAACP leadership did not budge. Wilkins thought the Civil Rights Movement had been a triumph. He despised the "young squirts" and "smart alecks" who denounced him and took attention away from his organization. The sharp-suited NAACP leadership who lobbied congressmen over wine and canapés could hardly seem more different from leather-jacketed Panthers who stormed state assembly rooms. But even here, there was much common ground. John Morsell, the NAACP's assistant executive director, admitted in private, "All of the goals which Mr. Carmichael . . . asserts . . . in the phrase 'Black Power' turn out, on inspection, to be merely restatements of goals pursued by the NAACP since its founding."[47] NUL leader Whitney Young was more frank. "If you think I am not as angry as Rap Brown," he told reporters, "then you misread me. I'm just no fool."[48]

Black Power also resonated because it fit the global moment. Black Americans opposed the Vietnam War more than any other group. Many were horrified by the disproportionate number of black draftees going to Vietnam—and thus the high number of black corpses returning in body bags. It is hard to overstate the importance of resisting the draft as a catalyst for Black Power groups, including the Panthers. For Carmichael, the draft was "white people sending black people to make war on yellow people to defend land they stole from red people." By contrast, the mid-1960s were heady days of postcolonial Africa and India, and revolutionary China and Cuba. On a world tour, Carmichael found it "both humbling and inspiring" as he realized that "our struggle in Mississippi and Harlem was part and parcel of this great international and historic motion."[49] Jim Forman, former executive secretary of SNCC and minister of foreign affairs at the Panthers, argued that black Americans were facing precisely the same problems as their global counterparts. During the summer of 1967 Forman traveled to a UN-sponsored conference in Tanzania to make the case for "The Indivisible Struggle against Racism, Colonialism and Apartheid."[50]

Militants found the case for an indivisible struggle compelling. Black nationalists believed the black American nation shared the sufferings of other nonwhite nations. Revolutionary nationalists believed the ghettoes to be urban colonies in need of liberation. Thus, black power advocates borrowed directly from revolutionary texts. The Panthers appropriated Mao's maxim, "Political power comes from the barrel of a gun." Most influential of all was the writing of the Algerian freedom fighter Frantz Fanon, whose call for a violent rejection of colonialism, *Wretched of the Earth*, was translated into English in 1965. Five years later, it had sold some 750,000 copies in America. Seale said he read it six times. One militant black journalist reckoned that "every brother on a rooftop can quote Fanon." Quotes included "Violence is a cleansing force . . . it restores self-respect."[51]

As black activists cast their eyes abroad to learn, they found plenty of people willing to teach. Prominent Black Power organizers met (in the United States or abroad) with foreign anti-imperial and anti-racist leaders. It was a collaboration that began before the Meredith march—even before the sit-ins. In 1960 (barely a year after Castro came to power), a group of black left intellectuals and activists traveled to Cuba. The prolific writer and music critic LeRoi Jones (later Amiri Baraka, a Black Power organizer) recollected that the trip "blew my mind; I was never the same again."[52] During the 1960s, Cuba would welcome (among others) leaders of the Deacons for Defense, the League of Revolutionary Black Workers, and Stokely Carmichael. From Ghana, black American expatriates (who had the most influence upon American activists of any African group) had been advocating a Black Power agenda since independence. Many had left the United States on account of harassment for their radicalism and so were firmly in a left-leaning nationalist tradition on arrival.

Still, their time in free Ghana underscored their commitment to an armed struggle and convinced them of an indivisible global struggle against racist exploitation.

If black Americans shared the same global outlook and faced similar domestic problems, they shared the same cultural trends, too—trends which in turn grew out of the domestic and global political moment. The mid-1960s saw the development of a distinctive black culture, a so-called soul culture, which became the imagined community of African Americans.[53] In religious life, a 1967 National Committee of Negro Churchmen called for a relevant black theology (they could have turned to Henry Turner's teaching at the start of the century).[54] Two years later, Detroit's Albert Cleage duly outlined his "theology of Black Power" in a series of sermons entitled *The Black Messiah* (including the notion that Jesus died "to lead a Black Nation to freedom"). Later that year, he was runner up in the election for the president of the fifty-million-member National Council of Churches.[55] Meanwhile, the Nation of Islam continued to grow despite losing Malcolm X. In literary culture, the late 1960s saw the flowering of the Black Arts Movement. The first Black Arts Convention was held in Detroit following the First World Festival of Negro Arts in Senegal and, as it happened, just a week or so after Carmichael's Greenwood speech. By this time, black artists had distanced themselves both from mainstream white literary culture and from white counterculture—or as one put it, from "suburbanite acne pickers."[56] Unlike the Harlem Renaissance, the artists were not trying to change white perceptions. This was a celebration of blackness, especially authentic, raw, black street culture. "We want a black poem," declared LeRoi Jones, "and a Black World."[57]

Black Americans also shared—and created—a popular culture that celebrated blackness and challenged white dominance in equal measure. The 1966 Howard University beauty queen, Robin Gregory, caused a sensation by wearing "a natural" ("Afro" hair style) at the annual pageant. One previous suitor asked her, "What have you done to yourself?" She answered that she had stopped doing things to herself. (Many more men rushed up to tell her how beautiful it looked.)[58] Across the country, men and women wore dashikis (African-style clothing). In sport, black football players refused to play in the 1967 American Football League All-Star Game in New Orleans because they were denied entry into social clubs. The commissioner moved the game. The following year at the Mexico Olympics, medalists Tommie Smith and John Carlos took the podium without shoes, wearing black knee-length socks and a black glove on one hand. As the American anthem was played, they did not look up at the flags but raised their fists. They explained that they were shoeless to show black poverty; they raised fists to show black unity; and they bowed heads out of respect for the late Martin Luther King Jr. and Malcolm X.

In music, artists turned away from the crossover pop of the early 1960s. "I was listening to a tune of mine playing on the radio . . . when the announcer interrupted with news about the Watts riot," recalled pop star Marvin Gaye. "I wanted to burn all the bullshit songs I'd been singing and get out there and kick ass with the rest of the brothers." Six years later, his politically sharp "What's Going On?" reached no. 2 in the album charts. In 1968, Motown's Berry Gordy, whose politics always followed profits, began to release message songs. Gordy's favorite band, Diana Ross and the Supremes, had a no. 1 hit, "Love Child," which addressed the problems faced by unwed ghetto mothers. Motown even developed a Black Forum label in 1970 to record the "ideas and voices of the worldwide struggle of Black people." First off the press was King's speech, "Why I Oppose the War in Vietnam."

It was not so much the explicit message songs that defined black music, however, but a new sound—a blacker soul music, and the rise of funk. *Billboard* reintroduced a separate R&B chart in 1965. When black consumers bought this sound—and they did in droves—they were also buying into racial pride. "Tell the world, sisters and my brothers," boasted Dyke and the Blazers in their 1969 hit "We Got More Soul." What made soul distinctive was hard to define. (Dyke and the Blazers didn't feel the need to try—they just knew that "when we walk" or talk or sing or dance—"we got more soul.") What was clear was that James Brown—the high-energy, raunchy, throaty-voiced performer who had grown up in poverty in the South—was the Godfather of Soul. Hits like "Sex Machine" (1970) transformed American music. His 1969 hit, "Say It Loud, I'm Black and I'm Proud," became virtually the anthem of the Black Power movement. *Look* magazine asked on its front cover, without irony, "Is He the Most Important Black Man in America?"[59] If Brown was soul's godfather, then Detroit's Aretha Franklin was its godmother. Her reworking of the Otis Redding hit "Respect" topped the July 1967 charts. Some said it was the summer of "'Retha, Rap [Brown] and Revolt."

For many African Americans, culture was not just the background to Black Power politics, it was a battleground of Black Power politics. Rioters in Detroit responded to heavy-handed police attacks on cultural institutions. Violence broke out late on July 23, 1967, after a police raid on a blind pig—a place of late-night illegal drinking and dancing. Four days later—at 4 a.m.—police destroyed Edward Vaughn's Forum 66 book-store, the only black bookstore in the city.[60] King returned to Detroit on February 16, 1968, to celebrate Aretha Franklin Day. Across the country, black leaders also called for the end of subservient black images. This was an old cry. But the new Black Power emphasis was not on changing white views; it was on asserting black pride. Carmichael thought it time African natives "beat the hell out of [Tarzan] and send him back to Europe."[61]

What was also new was that African American artists engaged in politics with an intensity unknown since the Harlem Renaissance. In Ben Caldwell's comical one-act play *Prayer Meeting*, a nonviolent minister falls to his knees in prayer in his bedroom. His eyes shut, the minister mistakes the sounds of a burglar for the voice of God. Realizing the mistake, the burglar tells the minister to preach violence. "Minister: But my people can't win with violence. Burglar: If you call what they doin' now, winnin', you the dumbest m.f. ever tried to interpret my word . . . The shit you preachin' gon' get MY PEOPLE hurt!"[62] Larry Neal, a leading BAM writer, wrote in 1968, "The artist and the political activist are one. They are both shapers of the future reality . . . Both are warriors, priests, lovers and destroyers."[63] Baraka agreed. He called for "poems that wrestle cops into alleys."[64] By this time, Baraka had founded the United Brothers—a coalition of radical black leaders committed to winning local political power.

The growth of soul culture, the promise of anti-colonial movements, and the practical programs of many militants meant that Black Power was far from the marginal, anarchic nihilism of stereotype. It was a response to the increased power of black workers, consumers, students, and voters in American cities and American culture. Thus, in some respects, Black Power was a statement of fact as well as a goal.

The high concentration of unskilled black workers in some of the older industries meant workers had power to disrupt production. Job training schemes after the riots meant that many auto plants had a majority-black workforce. On campus, black student numbers doubled between 1964 and 1970, when two thirds of black students attended integrated schools. In 1962 one man had struggled against the odds just to enroll at Ole Miss; eight years later, black student demonstrators there burned the Confederate flag, played "Mississippi Goddam," and marched on the chancellor's house.[65] In football, black athletes were a third of all players by 1967 and thus were able to force the switch of the All-Star Game.

Cities also presented possibilities. To be sure, there was plenty of anger and despair. Baraka wrote that "in the cities, which were once the black man's twentieth century 'Jordan,' *promise* is a dying bitch with rotting eyes."[66] Yet the combination of black migration and white flight meant that African Americans looked poised to take control of many cities. In 1970 black residents formed over a third of the population of Philadelphia and Cleveland, over 40 percent of Detroit and New Orleans, and over half the population of Atlanta and Washington, D.C. By this time Richard Hatcher and Carl Stokes had became the first black mayors of Gary and Cleveland, respectively. Both had links with local Black Power groups. In other words, even as they lost faith in liberal platitudes, activists gained faith in their own prospects for political power. And whereas previously civil rights advocates had sought to solve the problem of the ghetto by getting rid of it (hence the call for open housing), now they saw the inner-city as a promising political base.

Even—perhaps especially—riots showed the power of African Americans in the city. For all the mainstream's denunciation of violence as self-defeating, uprisings often had a positive effect, not least on the rioters themselves. An anonymous rioter in Washington told an interviewer, "It's a peculiar type of pride or dignity that one gets from destroying property that belongs to the enemy." They had a practical impact on local politics, too. The Washington participant added, "You'd be surprised at the number of doors that were opened up when people become violent."[67] Time and again, city politicians sought to prevent future violence by addressing complaints—be it the creation of a job training program or a community improvement agency. In 1968 Congress passed an Open Housing Bill. Congressman John B. Anderson admitted it was needed to "diminish the influence of black racists and preachers of violence."[68]

The steady growth of black consumer power also held promise. By the end of the 1960s, big business took note of the "soul market." The June 1969 issue of *Sales Management* ran an article for white business to explain the "vocabulary Soul Brothers cherish," including "Fox—A beautiful woman" and "Jive—A persuasive talker, but one prone to lies."[69] Scot toilet tissue offered posters of black history (in exchange for three wrappers and a dollar).[70] Television producers seemed to take note. The 1969 season had twenty-one primetime series with at least one black cast member, including Nichelle Nichols as Uhura (Swahili for freedom) on *Star Trek*'s starship Enterprise. (Uhura even kissed Captain Kirk, the first interracial television kiss on U.S. television—set centuries into the future in outer space.)

Forging a National Black Power Agenda

In response to widespread Black Power militancy, Adam Clayton Powell called a meeting to forge some sort of Black Power agenda. The first na-

tional Black Power Conference, held in Newark, followed—by chance—
hot on the heels of the 1967 riot there. It built on long-standing networks of black radicals and included representatives of traditional civil
rights organizations. Baraka spoke, his face still bandaged from a beating. Karenga was the fiercest speaker of all. The conference resolutions
showed that militant voices won the day: delegates affirmed the right to
revolt if necessary, they demanded the release of Newark rioters, and they
called on the UN to investigate the riot.

Perhaps even more importantly, the meeting set in motion a series of
conferences. Some four thousand delegates attended a follow-up convention in Philadelphia. Across the country, there were dozens of local and
regional meetings. King visited Baraka early in 1968. In public, he sought
common ground with Baraka's cultural nationalism. At a local school,
King declared, "I'm Black and beautiful."[71] In private, he stressed the
need for reformers and revolutionaries to find common cause. Baraka
agreed. He had been the prime mover in bringing Newark leaders together, and had managed the first Black Power conference. He would become the key coalition builder of the era.

Two years later, some three thousand delegates—black nationalists and
civil rights leaders—representing more than two hundred local organizations from at least forty cities met in Atlanta at the founding convention
of the Congress of African People (CAP). King's successor at the SCLC,
Ralph Abernathy, and Whitney Young joined young Nation of Islam
firebrand Louis Farrakhan and Malcolm X's widow Betty Shabazz. Banners displayed Baraka's catchphrase: "It's Nation Time." The conference
called for black leaders to build local black communities together. Some
militants complained that CAP marked the moderation of Black Power
radicalism. Yet equally, the meeting marked the radicalization of moderate race leaders. Both black self-determination and pan-Africanism were
central themes.

The CAP meeting spawned new assemblies and organizations. Baraka
linked with Gary's Mayor Richard Hatcher to host a National Black Political Assembly. In March 1972, some ten thousand people attended a
conference in Gary. Once again, the great and the good of black leadership were present, from moderate supporters of integration to militant
nationalists. As in Atlanta, militancy won the day. Even moderates joined
the chant "It's Nation Time!" The assembly called for the election of
black candidates and the formation of an independent black party. Two
months later, CAP organized the first African Liberation Day to support
black national parties in white-ruled southern Africa. Up to sixty thousand African Americans joined demonstrations around the country—the

largest black-led demonstration about an African issue since Mussolini invaded Ethiopia. The main rally in Washington ended with the chant "We are an African people."[72]

The Fall of Black Power

Atlanta, Gary, and the African Liberation Day represented the peak of national Black Power organizing. They also marked the beginning of its end. The Liberation Day idea rather fizzled out. Black politicians pulled back from forming an independent black party. Many of the more prominent Black Power groups were on the wane too. Some militant leaders moved into electoral politics and found a home in the Democratic Party. Other militant groups wilted under repression. Huey Newton and Ron Karenga broke down under the incessant pressure of confrontation and the influence of drugs. Faction fighting and local turf wars distracted some groups. In particular, cultural and revolutionary nationalists never reconciled their positions. Karenga reckoned the Panthers wore "some dead 1930s white ideology as a freedom suit." The Panthers called US "niggers with the bongos in their ears."[73] (It was members of US who had shot dead the two Panthers on the UCLA campus.)

Continued interest in soul culture failed to translate into a positive presence in mainstream culture. One 1973 survey found that there were more British people than African Americans on television in the United States. As for Hollywood, "Why can't Sidney Poitier, since he is such a superb actor, make love in the movies?" asked writer Calvin Hernton. To see him kiss a white woman, Hernton suggested, "would have caused a riot on Broadway and a slaughter in Alabama."[74] Away from mainstream movies, the early 1970s saw the production of some two hundred popular low-budget so-called blaxploitation films. Mostly set in the ghetto, they were the first movies to have black heroes who bested the white man. Melvin Van Peebles, director of the first blaxploitation hit *Sweet Sweetback's Baadasssss Song*, explained, "It's about rising out of the mud and kicking ass." But popular was not the same as positive. Often blaxploitation films merely replaced the fawning Uncle Tom stereotype with a foul-mouthed violent sex maniac—or, in the case of the most popular female star, Pam Grier (billed as "the baddest one-chick hit squad"), with a hard-punching buxom female fantasy figure. A coalition ranging from the Panthers to the NAACP coined the term "blaxploitation" and condemned it.

Nor did soul culture lead to black control of cultural production. At the start of the 1970s, African Americans owned only twenty of the fourteen thousand or so movie theaters in the country, and at most sixteen radio stations in 1970.[75] In the battle for "media control of Black minds," the Black Efforts for Soul in Television (BEST) watchdog—founded in 1969—lobbied the Federal Communications Commission, but with little success.[76] Worse still, the lure of soul culture attracted white businesses to previously black-dominated markets. George Johnson, the beauty product entrepreneur, complained that Whites "ignored this industry as long as they thought it was a nickel and dime business . . . Today, they are making strong efforts to take over every level of the kinky hair business."[77] At times corporate campaigns for the black dollar were as ludicrous as they were shameless. In 1979 one wig manufacturer told black consumers, "No price is too high to pay for your FREEDOM. This particular FREEDOM is $6.72."[78] As for soul music, cultural nationalists had been suspicious of white manipulation from the outset. (They preferred free jazz, which sounded the global vision, global connections, and radical politics of many of its greatest artists. But free jazz lacked soul's appeal to American consumers.) Over time, their suspicions increased. Black Panther Minister of Culture Emory Douglas complained, "You hear James Brown talking about Black and Proud, then you hear him on the radio saying 'Why don't you buy this beer?'"[79]

If corporate leaders tried to co-opt black power protest, white neighborhood groups in the cities continued to oppose it. Ironically, they borrowed tactics from, and legitimized by, the Civil Rights Movement. Antibusing leaders in Boston decided to "take a leaf out of Martin Luther King's book," holding sit-ins and even singing "We Shall Overcome." In Philadelphia, a crowd of over a thousand Italian-Americans chanted "White Power!" to demand the closure of their local school, after a spate of fights between black and white children.[80]

The shelf life of the Black Power movement—roughly six years—was similar to that of the Civil Rights Movement of the early 1960s. The legacy of Black Power would live on just as long as that of the Civil Rights movement, too. Many local groups continued. The celebration of African American culture—such as the Kwanzaa holiday—continued into the twenty-first century. Bobby Rush, co-founder of the Chicago Panthers, would become a long-serving member of Congress. In 2000 he would swat away the challenge of a young, aspiring politician called Barack Obama. Thus, the fall of Black Power was not the end of black power, just a fall from its dominating position in national discourse. But then again, the rise of Black Power did not mean the end of civil rights demonstrations in the South.

Surge of Protest in the Small-Town Deep South

On Friday evening, April 1, 1966, hundreds of demonstrators marched in the small town of Port Gibson, Mississippi. Tucked away in the southwest corner of the state, Claiborne County looked like it had missed out on the Civil Rights Movement altogether. One of the demonstrators, a student named James Miller, remembered that, in his childhood, stories of Montgomery and Little Rock seemed as remote as news from Africa. "It's just that far away. So never ever would that upset what was going on here." What was going on, Miller explained, was that his town was stuck in a "White is right . . . time warp." "If you have never been exposed to anything else . . . you assume that's the way it is."[81] With the onset of the Mississippi Freedom Summer in 1964 the news got closer. But the movement in Claiborne County that year was limited to a small underground NAACP chapter. Yet now hundreds marched, demanding the integration of public facilities, improved black employment, courteous treatment of black consumers, and the appointment of a black deputy police chief with full arrest powers (the existing token black policeman spent most of his time directing traffic near black schools).

The following Tuesday, over a thousand people marched across the campus of nearby Alcorn College—an all-black school whose conservative president had tried to prevent his students from joining the local movement. State troopers ringed the campus. Some demonstrators—mostly women and girls—confronted them. We said "derogatory things," one admitted later, about "their mamas and their daddies and their wives."[82] Campus police tried to disperse the demonstration. Unfortunately for them, they took their tactics straight from the Keystone Kops manual of crowd control. They shot tear gas downwind from the crowd, so the smoke just blew away. They then tried to set up water hoses, but by the time they switched them on, the crowd had moved. Some demonstrators started laughing. The on-looking state troopers joined in.[83]

At the head of the movement was Charles Evers, brother of the murdered civil rights hero Medgar Evers and his successor as state NAACP field secretary. Whereas Medgar was gentle and self-effacing, Charles was brash and self-publicizing. One local black critic called him "a hustler . . . he always has an eye out for things that will help Charles as much as the movement."[84] But no one could deny that he was charismatic. One seasoned black reporter called Evers "ruggedly handsome and dark, neatly cropped and mustached," a more powerful speaker than King who "tingled the spines of his listeners, thrilled their minds and souls and set their hearts beating faster."[85] At mass meetings, "young people scream with delight and elderly ladies . . . shower him with hugs and kisses."[86] Evers was too hot for the national NAACP leadership; but they wanted to regain control of protest in Mississippi, and so Evers was a risk worth taking.

Evers was also a shrewd enforcer, a testament to his days in the Chicago underworld. After the marches, the local movement launched a boycott of white-owned stores. Evers' well-publicized "goon squad" of sixty or so young men harassed any African American caught breaking the boycott. The owner of a local Piggly Wiggly supermarket admitted later, "The boycott nearly paralyzed our business." By January city fathers came to the table. They agreed to desegregate facilities, use courtesy titles, hire fifteen black clerks and appoint a black policeman to an active role. The deal was a compromise that didn't satisfy either the black or the white community. Still, both Evers and the merchants claimed victory.

In many ways, the Claiborne movement is instantly recognizable— comedy police notwithstanding—as a local protest from the southern Civil Rights Movement. Except the Claiborne movement happened after Selma, and after the passage of Civil Rights and Voting Rights Acts. It occurred after the famous Mississippi Freedom Summer disintegrated through battle fatigue, after Fannie Lee Hamer had been taken to the hospital with exhaustion, and just as the southern civil rights coalition crumbled. By the time marchers in Port Gibson started walking, the main direct-action protest organizations were looking North—King was in Chicago, and SNCC was setting up a base in Philadelphia. By the time Claiborne's merchants came to a compromise, Black Power was dominating the airwaves. Indeed, Carmichael first chanted Black Power just a hundred miles or so north of Port Gibson, while the Claiborne protest was at its peak.

Yet far from being exceptional, Claiborne was emblematic of a surge of demonstrations in the small-town South that emerged in the wake of the Civil Rights Movement and civil rights legislation. Because Charles Evers was particularly media savvy, Claiborne got some media attention. But for the most part, this southern surge went unnoticed by the national press. In most cases, media coverage amounted to a disparaging comment or two in the local newspaper. Even so, for hundreds of thousands of black southerners, this surge of small-town protests marked the moment when demonstrations began.

Local protests were mostly home-grown. They were a far cry from King's set-piece demonstrations or the mass influx of students during the Mississippi Summer. Indeed, Evers criticized Meredith's march for generating publicity for the leaders rather than winning rights for local people—he predicted it would turn "into another Selma, where everyone goes home with the cameraman and leaves us holding the bag." (There was some irony here. By the end of the summer, Evers was a prominent black face on local television, and his quip about Selma became a *New York Times* quote of the day.) Nor was the southern surge dependent on the example of Black Power. Evers denounced SNCC militants as "crazy." (This was partly turf war. As an NAACP man, and an empire builder in his own right, he didn't want any rivals in town.)

In practice, local movements borrowed from the examples of both civil rights and Black Power protests as appropriate. But they were not beholden to either. In Claiborne, the list of demands included integration, jobs, and courtesy—a throwback to the Civil Rights Movement. But Evers insisted he did not seek "civil rights" but "human rights." His opening-night march was against a conservative black institution—characteristic of the Black Power era. As for the question of violence, Evers told the white community, "We will remain nonviolent as long as you let us remain nonviolent," but "if you slap one of us, we will knock [the] hell out of you."[87] The movement had its own small, armed self-defense group, the Black Hats. The group leader falsified their minutes book to make them appear stronger than they were—and then ensured that the local sheriff stole it. This was hardly Black Power swaggering. Nor was it King's nonviolence. It was more akin to the Deacons for Defense model, and thus very much in the southern tradition.

After the passage of the Voting Rights Act, the SCLC's James Bevel commented, "There is no more civil rights movement. President Johnson signed it out of existence." Bevel was right that the days of using southern confrontations to force Johnson to act were over. But at the grassroots, the Civil Rights and Voting Rights Acts actually triggered much of the southern surge. Federally protected black voting gave local people the power to demonstrate against all aspects of white supremacy. Before the Voting Rights Act, African Americans in Claiborne had to appeal to white paternalism. After the act, Evers warned downtown merchants that African Americans were now a majority of eligible voters and "will have a powerful voice in the future affairs of the City and County."[88]

Small-town movements sprang up across the South after 1965 to enforce the promise of federal legislation. No issue was more contentious than schooling. A year after the Civil Rights Act, the school board in Crawfordville, Georgia (famous as the birthplace of Confederate Vice President Alexander Stephens, who declared slavery the natural condition of black people), made plans to comply. But the board then provided buses for white students to travel to white schools out of the county. Black students tried to board the buses. In response, the school board fired five black teachers, two bus drivers, and two cooks. Twenty parents lost their jobs and four families were evicted from their homes. In response, African Americans marched. They called for downtown integration, better jobs, and the introduction of a food stamp plan. Local leaders pointed out that "these issues were at stake long before the school question." Right on cue, a couple of hundred Klan members turned up. "Crawfordville, Georgia," wrote the influential Atlanta journalist Ralph McGill, "are two words now being printed around the world . . . the latest in a long procession of names—Little Rock . . . Selma . . . Watts." News coverage increased after a segregationist bit off part of a reporter's nose. The governor brokered a truce, and a federal court ruled against the school board. The issues of jobs and welfare remained unaddressed.[89]

Small-town movements also sprang up because the new legislation created as many problems as it solved. The integration of schools often outraged rather than appeased black communities. There was tension over selection for sports teams and cheerleading squads. Fist fights were common. Most galling of all, black principals of segregated high schools were always demoted to vice principal of newly integrated schools. In rural Pike County, Georgia, in 1969, black students walked out of school on the news that principal D. F. Glover would be demoted. The case was all the more poignant because Glover had the second highest academic credentials of any principal in the state. Within days, hundreds of students marched to the nearby white school in the county seat of Zebulon. After two black girls were attacked, thousands joined the march. The eventual compromise gave Glover a broader role, albeit still as deputy head.[90]

Meanwhile, as in urban Black Power protests, demonstrations focused on issues that had taken a backseat during the Civil Rights Movement. Top of the list was poverty. In April 1967, civil rights lawyer Marian Wright testified before the Senate Subcommittee on Employment, Manpower, and Poverty. "Starvation is a major, major problem now," she told them, and challenged them to come to the Mississippi Delta.[91] They agreed, and were appalled by what they saw. Mississippi's Governor Paul Johnson bristled at the publicity. "Nobody is starving," he told reporters, before adding that the only "nigra women I see" are "big, fat, black and greasy." In response, nearly a thousand African Americans from the delta marched on the statehouse to call for an end to hunger. The Poor People's March was the headline story in the black press nationwide. Evers explained that the march was to make the governor "sit up in that big fat office and see these people."[92]

The surge in southern protest was not limited to set-piece confrontations. After the Civil Rights Act, the American Friends Service Committee—a Quaker-based social justice organization—coordinated a Ten Communities Project to encourage students to apply to white schools and to prepare them for the trauma of transfer. After the Voting Rights Act, the Voter Education Project funded a second, larger round of registration projects. The first project had funded SNCC's rural venture—now fieldworkers faced many of the same problems. Potential voters feared losing their jobs or welfare benefits. The VEP reported that in many places, election officials remained "adversarial." Black voters in one county were told that if they wanted to oust the notorious segregationist candidate, they should "mark an X by his name." Rural African Americans continued to face intimidation, too. In Sylvester, Georgia, in December 1968, one of the first black girls to transfer to a white school was expelled for saying "goddamn." Times had changed—when the black community marched, white vigilantes did not attack. But they hadn't changed that much. The vigilantes placed beehives along the route, and lit them as people passed.[93]

The surge in southern protest was not united. After the fall of state-sanctioned Jim Crow, which had united black activists in opposition, long-running divisions came to the fore. As in the cities, factions battled for War on Poverty funding. Nowhere more than in Mississippi, where bitterness from COFO days still festered. Former allies fought for control of Head Start (preschool) programs. Eventually, the NAACP old guard won out over more militant groups.

Even when united, activists rarely achieved their goals. The traditional power structure remained intact, despite the new laws. Right across the South, politicians gerrymandered electoral districts to dilute the power of the black vote; educators established private school academies to sidestep the problem of school integration; and local councils reduced property taxes (which paid for public education) to allow parents to pay for private school tuition. Such tactics called to mind post-Reconstruction days. Little wonder that rural activists often encountered the same pessimism they had found earlier in the decade. From Cuthbert County in southwest Georgia, project worker Robert McClary reported gloomily at the end of 1967, "What is so striking is the great number of Negroes who simply do not believe they can do anything other than what the white man wants them to do."[94]

Even so, in the wake of the Civil Rights Movement, marches, boycotts, and picketing became a part of southern life in a way that was unimaginable just a decade before. In a sense, the movement made confrontation

seem legitimate—something to be expected on both sides after any fla-
grant incidents of injustice. Demonstrations would continue for years to
come. In 1974, Will Campbell—a clergyman who had worked with King—
visited the small town of Talbotton, Georgia, where local residents
marched for justice and for better jobs, schooling, and increased black
voter registration after the police had shot a black man in the back.
Campbell felt as though he had gone back in time. "The movement had in
fact arrived and in the same form as it had gone to Montgomery . . . Birmingham and scores of other towns." It just arrived a decade or so later.[95]

Each small-town campaign was not simply a final mopping-up exercise
after the main action elsewhere. Rather, it was the latest chapter in a
long-running local struggle for meaningful freedom. Back in Port Gibson,
the compromise of 1967 did not mark the end of the story. Claiborne
County won a reputation for being a more moderate sort of county, at
least by Mississippi standards. But this reputation hid continuing tensions. After the schools integrated, most white students moved to private
academies. When African Americans tried to visit a local Presbyterian
Church, an armed man blocked them, saying, "There are two Gods, a
black one and a white one." In 1969, after an unarmed black man was
shot dead, African Americans resumed a boycott. This time, merchants
filed suit to block it. The suit was thrown out only in 1982. As for
Charles Evers, he became mayor of nearby Fayette in 1969, failed to win
election for governor, and later threw his support behind Ronald Reagan.

Proliferation of Protest, Not Fragmentation, into the 1970s

In 1969 Richard Nixon became the first Republican president for eight
years. His campaign had appealed to the so-called silent [white] majority
that opposed government interference. When children are bused "into
a strange community," he told southern delegates to the Republican
convention, "I think you destroy that child."[96] His runningmate, Spiro
Agnew, was an outspoken critic of militant black leaders. At a press conference in February 1969, Nixon acknowledged that he was not seen as
"a friend by many of our black citizens." He added, "By my actions as
President I hope to rectify that."

Actually, many of his first actions did precisely the opposite. One year
on, the *Chicago Defender* complained, "On civil rights, President Nixon
is as silent as an Egyptian Sphinx."[97] In his first year, Nixon nominated a
southern segregationist, Clement Haynsworth, to the Supreme Court. He
did not appoint a single African American to his cabinet. He opposed the
renewal of the Voting Rights Act. And, for the first time, the Justice

Department opposed the NAACP in a civil rights suit. In 1969, 72-year-old Bishop Stephen Spottswood, national chair of the NAACP, accused Nixon of being "anti-Negro." In the early 1960s, student activists had criticized Spottswood for being too conservative. Now Spottswood told the NAACP annual conference, "The NAACP considers itself in a state of war against President Nixon."

If so, Nixon seemed to have a declining foe. The NAACP hemorrhaged members after doubling its annual dues in 1970.[98] Many of the other prominent protest organizations and personalities of the 1960s faded from view altogether. King and Malcolm X had been assassinated. The glamour of SNCC, CORE, and the SCLC was soon just a memory. In 1971 Ron Karenga, Huey Newton, Rap Brown, and Bobby Seale were in prison and Stokely Carmichael was living in Guinea. As for the Godfather of Soul, James Brown, he sang at Nixon's second inauguration.

As it turned out, the NAACP's war against Nixon would not last long. By the fall of 1974, Agnew and Nixon had resigned—Agnew for taking bribes, Nixon for the Watergate scandal. Some took pride in the fact that black security guard Frank Wills first spotted the burglary at the Watergate complex. The election of Democratic President Jimmy Carter in 1976 offered promise. As governor of Georgia Carter had declared, "The time for racial discrimination is over." Some black Georgians were less excited. State Senator—and former SNCC activist—Julian Bond told reporters, "Carter wouldn't be my first choice, he wouldn't even be my tenth." Still, Carter had the backing of the King family, and in a highly symbolic appointment he named Andrew Young (King's former colleague) as the first black American ambassador to the UN.

Whatever he may have wanted to do, though, Carter was soon preoccupied with stagflation, an oil crisis, and a hostage crisis. The economic downturn hit working-poor African Americans in the inner city and the rural South especially hard. Commenting on the oil crisis from the black perspective, energy expert Lenneal J. Henderson Jr. reckoned, "The word *crisis*, as strong as it is, is too tame, too abstract, too *white* to capture the economic terror of a state of siege." There were "poor men and women making cruel choices between fuel and food."[99] The 1970s saw a rise in inner-city poverty, gang warfare, one parent black families, and the numbers of young black men and women in prison. As for Andrew Young, he resigned in 1979 after an unauthorized meeting with a representative of the Palestinian Liberation Organization. As for Frank Wills, after being refused a pay rise, he left his job and was soon penniless.

Compared with the heady days of 1960s protest and progress, therefore, the 1970s might seem to have had little to offer. And yet . . . Nixon may have been as quiet as a sphinx, but local people continued to make loud calls for equality. Prominent leadership may have fragmented, but protest proliferated, from the streets of small towns to the corridors of power in Washington, D.C. "What's happened in the last ten years," observed Carl Holman, president of the National Urban Coalition, in 1978, "is that black leadership has diversified. There's no single figure who bestrides the landscape as Martin King did. We've got people working different vineyards."[100] For the many activists who had opposed the celebrity of a few charismatic men during the 1960s, this was no bad thing.

In fact, people had been working different vineyards for generations. What was new is that—for all the very real problems they faced—local activists were able to build on the very real achievements of the 1960s. Sweeping federal civil rights legislation gave them new power to stake their claims. The drama of the Civil Rights Movement and Black Power eras legitimized many of the tactics they used. The experience of the 1960s strengthened regional, national, and even global activist networks. And the fresh memory of urban riots continued to open up space for moderate reformers to make their demands. Nixon's adviser Daniel Patrick Moynihan recognized that ghetto uprisings "have given the black middle-class an incomparable weapon with which to *threaten* white America."[101] Surveys from the mid-1970s showed that the black middle class had never been more optimistic about their prospects.

Moreover, despite Nixon's posturing, the federal government continued to support civil rights. In Congress, liberal Democrats lost their dominance in the 1966 election—indeed, they lost more seats than they had won in 1964. But many of the new Republicans were racial liberals. Congress renewed the Voting Rights Act and rejected two of Nixon's judicial nominees (the first rejection of a Court nominee since John Parker in 1930). The Court continued to advance its post-*Brown* civil rights agenda. Responding to black demands, the justices called for equality of results rather than just fairness of procedures. In *Alexander v. Holmes County* (1969) the Court accelerated the timetable for school integration from at "all deliberate speed" to "at once." Two years later, in *Swann v. Charlotte-Mecklenburg Board of Education,* the Court unanimously approved a busing plan between Charlotte's city and suburbs as a means to ensure "the greatest possible degree of actual desegregation."[102] Whereas two thirds of black students attended schools with 90 percent or more nonwhite students in 1968, only one third did in 1980, and less than a quarter did in the South.

Somewhat surprisingly, Nixon actively enforced civil rights legislation, too. Left to his own devices, he would have taken Moynihan's advice that the race issue would benefit from a period of "benign neglect." Or as Nixon put it to aides who supported busing, "Knock off this crap . . . Do what the law requires and not one bit more."[103] But black protest ensured he wasn't left to his own devices. In 1969 NAACP lawyers won the *Alexander* case even though the federal government filed suit in opposition. Nixon fumed, calling the justices "clowns." That same year, massive protests over construction jobs around the country turned violent. Nixon realized he needed to act—and decisively. He reasoned that opposing the courts would only prolong the problem. It is "in our interest politically," he told an aide, to have the "confrontations this year rather than [the election year of] '72." And he calculated that his reputation would protect him from a white backlash. Unwittingly, black leaders helped his cause. In 1969 Roy Wilkins said Nixon's attitude is "almost enough to make you vomit."[104]

How the administration got the job done proved to be far-reaching. In education, Nixon publicly urged compliance, set up a Cabinet committee to supervise efforts to persuade southern leaders to comply, and approved an IRS ruling denying tax exempt status to segregated schools. He even persuaded his friend, the popular evangelist Billy Graham, to urge compliance on TV spots. In employment, Nixon believed that black economic progress would resolve much of the race problem. He approved a plan requiring contractors to include specific "goals" of nonwhite workers and specific "timetables" to achieve those goals. The plan was known as the Philadelphia Plan since it built on Lyndon Johnson's suggested (but quickly shelved) jobs plan for the City of Brotherly Love itself a response to black workers' demands during mass protests and violence there. The assistant labor secretary, African American entrepreneur Arthur Fletcher, had doggedly promoted the plan. The revived plan avoided talk of quotas (this would have been directly contrary to the Civil Rights Act) but spoke of acceptable percentage "ranges" of nonwhite workers (which was, in fact, still against the spirit of the Civil Rights Act).

The most significant government-sponsored advances, though, happened by stealth. The various administrative agencies that had been set up during the 1960s to promote racial justice developed a life of their own. They grew in size and stridency. Staff at the Equal Employment Opportunity Commission quadrupled during Nixon's first term.[105] Bureaucrats realized that if they didn't satisfy minority groups, the groups would just appeal to the courts. In any case, by the early 1970s—forty years after black officials first got a toehold within the federal administration—civil rights groups had taken control of the agencies. Black groups had been conspicuous by their absence from the drafting of the Civil Rights

Act or planning for the War on Poverty (not to mention the New Deal). But by the 1970s, representatives of the NAACP and other rights groups set the agenda for agencies with ever increasing budgets and ever expanding powers.

For example, the director of the Office of Federal Contract Compliance signed the Labor Department's Order Number Four which—among other things—applied the Philadelphia Plan to all federal contractors with contracts over $50,000 (the administration's plan had been for contracts over $500,000). This was hardly the stuff of facing down police dogs in Alabama. Only the most committed policy wonk would have noticed, let alone understood, the various technical changes. But such changes provided activists with federal backing to push for affirmative action in jobs protests across the country. Indeed, government agencies extended affirmative action policies—such as setting up bilingual schools —to other minority groups that hadn't even asked for them.[106] The fact that such radical changes were hidden in the minutiae of memoranda allowed the implementation of policies that were anathema to a majority of the population. The fact that it happened on the watch of a president who had campaigned against government interference (and may not even have been aware of the bureaucratic changes) just added to the irony.

Yet for all the progress, it was clear the civil rights legislative revolution of 1964–1972 still had limits. The Philadelphia Plan, for example, applied only to federal construction contracts—less than 5 percent of building industry work. Much of the language of employment legislation remained ambiguous. Title VII of the Civil Rights Act prohibited employment discrimination and approved affirmative action. But it did not define what employment discrimination or affirmative action actually was. Legislation often lacked proper enforcement procedures. There were only two officials designated to check up on the Philadelphia Plan for the half-a-billion-dollars' worth of federal contracts in the western region.[107] The ambiguity of federal legislation left it to activists to define the meaning of the law in practice. The lack of enforcement provisions left it to activists to enforce the legislation themselves.

What soon became clear, too, was that the Supreme Court (since 1969 led by the strict-constructionist Warren Burger, a strong critic of Earl Warren) had taken the legislative revolution as far as it wanted to go. In *San Antonio Independent School District v. Rodriguez* (1973), a 5–4 majority decided that affluent suburbs did not have responsibility to share property-tax school funding with poorer city districts. The following year, in *Milliken v. Bradley,* a 5–4 majority dismissed a Detroit desegregation plan that involved transferring students between the black inner city and white suburbs. One of the dissenters, Justice Thurgood Marshall (who had brought the *Brown* case), judged *Milliken* "a reflection of a perceived public mood that we have gone far enough in enforcing the Constitution's guarantee of equal justice." Marshall was downhearted. "It may seem to be the easier course to allow our great metropolitan areas to be divided up each into two cities—one white, the other black—but it is a course, I predict, our people will ultimately regret."[108]

Marshall was correct about the public mood. Ultimately, what constrained protest was not so much the new Republican president but the attitudes of the silent majority that he represented. In a 1972 national poll, 97 percent of respondents believed black people deserved an equal chance in getting a job (compared with only 49 percent in 1946). Well over 70 percent of respondents—North and South—agreed that black people should be free to live or go to school wherever they wanted (though barely a quarter of respondents agreed with the principle of intermarriage). But when it came to the question of implementation rather than principle, public opinion was opposed to equality (polls showed only a third, at most, in favor—and the trend was slightly down). "When the government tells the people what to do and think," said one opponent of fair housing legislation in California, "we have a dictatorship."[109] The silent majority was anything but silent. In South Boston in 1974, white mothers screamed abuse at black children being bused into their neighborhood.

Why such attitudes mattered was that the people who held them held power. Marshall's despondency about split cities proved to be on the mark. By the 1970s, new urban spatial arrangements, not old-style segregationist racism, provided the greatest obstacle to black activists. White city-dwellers followed jobs out to the suburbs, where they enjoyed better homes, schools, and parks and lower taxes. By 1970 the suburban population of Atlanta was three times as large as the city population. Fiercely protective of their suburban dreams, suburbanites fought to keep the nightmares (real and imagined) of inner-city life locked in place. Most Atlanta suburban counties were over 95 percent white. Neighborhood groups blocked black homeownership, suburban voters challenged suburb-city integration plans, and they rejected mid-1960s proposals to annex suburbs to the city. They even opposed the extension of the Metropolitan Atlanta Rapid Transit Authority (MARTA) rail system into the suburbs. Some white reactionaries dubbed its acronym "Moving Africans Rapidly Through Atlanta." One legislator explained in 1971, "The suburbanite says to himself, 'The reason I worked for so many years was to get away from pollution, bad schools and crime, and I'll be damned if I'll see it all follow me.'"[110]

Once the Supreme Court had backed the principle of suburban secession, there was little that black city activists could do to stop it. Because suburbanites spoke a language of individual rights (and even victimhood) rather than racism, the old moral arguments of the civil rights days lacked purchase. Talk of homeowner rights, freedom of association, and freedom of choice resonated with American values. James McDavid Jr., a white father from an affluent Charlotte suburb, explained in 1970: "I have never asked what anyone in government or this country could do for me, but rather have kept my mouth shut, paid my taxes, and basically asked to be left alone."[111]

The significance of suburban secession is shown by the success of school integration in a city where suburbs could not secede—in Charlotte, where North Carolina annexation law allowed automatic absorption of the suburbs. Initially, the course of integration protest was entirely predictable. In 1970 black parents forced two-way busing through the courts. Fights followed along the color line. White parents mobilized in a "struggle for freedom." But when new plans were drawn to protect the affluent suburbs from busing, white inner-city parents' groups turned their fire on the "limousine liberals." At one public meeting, black mother Kathleen Crosby spoke of the high burden on black students who were bused and the poor facilities for those remaining. White parents applauded. "I said to myself," she told reporters afterward, "Honey, this can't be happening."[112] The new coalition forced a busing plan that shared the burden across the city and suburbs. Charlotte showed that race politics, as ever, were anything but simple black vs. white. But it was also the exception to the suburban rule.

Overall, then, the post–Civil Rights and post–Black Power generation provided mixed opportunities for black activists. One journalist commented in 1970, "These are the days of good news, bad news and Agnews."[113] The turn against government intervention, and new spatial arrangements, constrained activists. But it didn't stop them. While news cameras focused on the white mothers who screamed against busing in Boston, forty thousand African Americans marched in support of school integration.[114] Activists pressed ahead on seemingly every issue—against South African apartheid, for better schools, against police brutality, for more jobs, against urban renewal, for more control over the radio industry.

The lack of a single, triumphant narrative should not distract from the diversity and creativity of the protest that did occur. Taken together, such activism shows that the 1970s was not just a decade of defending rights but a decade of seeking to expand rights further, and in some cases managing to do so.

Where they managed to do so would be especially in traditional industries and in central-city politics. In some workplaces and smaller communities, the legislative gains of the 1960s actually provided the springboard for first experiments in confrontational protest. Moreover, many previously sidelined groups within the African American community gained prominence during the 1970s. The celebrated figures of the 1960s were often civil rights clergymen, middle-class students, and—during the Black Power era—young male militants. But in the 1970s, African American groups such as welfare activists, feminists, and even the imprisoned were able to make demands for their distinctive causes with unprecedented force. Such groups would benefit from the triumphs and example of the rights revolution even as they reacted against the narrow vision of 1960s protest.

Grassroots Activism: Employment

Protest by African American workers had helped bring about the Civil Rights Act and the Philadelphia Plan. In turn, the Civil Rights Act and Philadelphia Plan gave workers new power in their long pursuit of workplace equality. As in the 1960s, African American workers focused on the textile industry in the South and the construction industry in the North. During the 1970s, seemingly each mill and each building site had its own story of confrontation and litigation. At a J. P. Stevens plant in North Carolina, A. C. Sherill's persistent requests for promotion had only earned him threats from management, assault from co-workers, and then redundancy. Before Title VII, Sherill would have been powerless to act. But the new law enabled Sherill to take on the company, and in 1973 to win. Sherill was just one of thousands of plaintiffs, many of whom joined together through local civil rights organizations to form class action suits.[115] As in previous generations, some of the most militant activists were veterans, in this case from the Vietnam War.

As in the 1960s, those on the front line received support from civil rights lawyers. In the South, the team of NAACP lawyers dedicated to the fight for textile integration was far bigger than the legal team working for the relevant government agencies. Lead NAACP lawyer Jack Greenberg reflected later that the campaign for textile integration was "almost on a par with the campaign that won *Brown*."[116] By the 1970s, workers received significant support from the state, too. As the number of cases and evidence of resistance mounted, both the federal courts and the federal bureaucracy came out in favor of industry-wide solutions, looking at results, not merely intent.[117] Whereas Title VII had called for "prospective and not retrospective change," the Court took the position that it was an "affirmative duty . . . to undo past discrimination." In 1971 a federal judge ruled the seniority system illegal because it perpetuated prior discrimination.[118] That same year, in a case brought by thirteen black janitors, the Supreme Court ruled against race-neutral tests that led to underrepresentation of racial minorities.[119]

Following a series of successful class action suits, companies took the initiative. In 1974 the major steel companies faced 408 cases pending with the EEOC. With the prospect of paying out massive compensation hanging like Damocles' sword over the industry, the companies and the union signed a consent decree with the federal government. The decree established goals and timetables for the admission of minorities and women to skilled jobs, and made over $30 million available as compensatory back pay. The attorney general, William Saxbe, claimed, "We are marking a new day with this decree."[120] The NAACP rightly suspected that negotiators had sought to do the minimum necessary to offset litigation. Still, it was progress. One black worker judged the decree "the most significant and just thing to happen to the American working people in 40 years."[121]

The struggle for workplace equality had mostly positive results. Black managers and professionals made stunning gains in firms covered by the EEOC. Minority hiring in steel rose quickly after the consent decree—far faster than it would have done without it. The integration of textiles was nothing short of historic. From being lily-white in 1960, some twenty percent of workers were African Americans in 1980 (and half of black workers were women). The construction industry proved to be more resistant. The proportion of black carpenters almost doubled between 1965 and 1980, but the proportion of African Americans in other crafts increased from 6.5 percent to just 7.8 percent. Many construction jobs required lengthy training, and the absence of large companies and the quick turnover of jobs undermined the litigation process.[122]

Overall, black workers moved into skilled and semi-skilled industrial work at a faster rate than at any time in American history. Unfortunately, they made their greatest gains in industries that were beginning to decline. Worse still, residential segregation meant they were unable to claim jobs in new suburban industries. Deindustrialization and recession packed a devastating one-two punch. The black economist Vivian Henderson observed in 1976, "It's as if racism having put blacks in their economic place stepped aside to see changes in technology and changes in the economy destroy that place."[123] Nevertheless, the protest of black workers in the industries that they could influence ameliorated some of the worst effects of the recession.

Grassroots Activism: Politics

African American protest had led to the Voting Rights Act, which in turn empowered African Americans to use politics to unprecedented effect—at least since Reconstruction—in the long struggle for meaningful citizenship. At the national level, the Congressional Black Caucus (CBC) formed in 1971 with a dozen members, and almost doubled in size during the decade. This still left black voters severely underrepresented in Congress. But the CBC was able to lobby the Democratic Congress in ways that many previous generations of civil rights leaders could have barely dreamed of.

The first chairman, Charles Diggs, earned the nickname Mr. Africa for his championing of the anti-apartheid movement on the Foreign Relations Committee. In May 1977, CBC chairman Parren Mitchell (who was 5' 5" tall) earned the nickname "The Little General" for adding an enormously significant amendment to the Public Works Employment Act that set aside 10 percent of federal contracts for Minority Business Enterprises. The amendment strategy was deliberately low key to avoid adverse publicity in white America. But Mitchell became a celebrity in black America—*Ebony* featured him in a glossy photo essay.[124]

Black candidates made spectacular progress at the local level. By 1977, over two hundred cities had black mayors. It was not that the issue of race had lost its salience—rare indeed was the African American candidate who won more than 15 percent of the white vote. But the difference was that black in-migration to the city and white out-migration from the city gave black voting blocs new power. Black politicians built on the networks and the know-how developed during the 1960s. Borrowing from both civil rights and Black Power strategies, campaigns relied on mass meetings, voter education classes, and self-consciously separate black voting blocs from which to demand inclusion in local politics.

As with black workers and affirmative action, black political activists got the right result at the wrong time. Suburbanization and deindustrialization had slashed the municipal tax base. The beginnings of a taxpayers' revolt reduced the tax base even further. A reduction in federal grants compounded the problem. In city after city, downtown became a ghost town. Hatcher's campaign slogan had been "Gary: A City on the Move." Cynics replied, "Yes, on the move out." One reporter asked, "Will the last one out please turn off the lights?"[125]

Still, African American mayors usually worked for a more equitable or even compensatory distribution of the resources that remained. Black residents benefited.[126] The proportion of African Americans in the municipal workforce during the 1970s rose fastest and furthest in those cities with a black mayor. Atlanta, Chicago, Cleveland, Detroit, Gary, Newark, and Washington had African American police chiefs within five years of their first black mayor. Some mayors took a lead in minority set-aside programs. When Maynard Jackson was first elected mayor of Atlanta in 1973, less than 1 percent of city business went to African American companies. By the end of his second term, one third did. Such local set-aside programs provided the model for Mitchell's PWEA amendment.

More generally, the number of black elected officials rose spectacularly from 1,469 officials in 1970 to 4,890 in 1980. The majority were in the rural South, where black candidates rarely won control of councils. By 1980, a black southerner was still sixteen times less likely to get elected than a white southerner (and most black elected officials held local minor offices rather than state-wide or federal positions). As in the big cities, rural black politicians also inherited costly social problems. Georgia's state NAACP President Robert Flanagan heard the common complaint, "You told me to vote and, hell, I'm still hungry and I look up there and see the sky through my house." "If a crow flew over some rural parts of the state," Flanagan continued, "it would have to pack a lunch."[127] Black elected officials were unable to overturn the recession of the 1970s. But they did seek to ensure that the recession was not disproportionately harsh on African Americans. Quite a contrast to the Great Depression and previous recessions, when local supremacist politicians had compounded black economic problems.

Welfare Campaigners

In 1968 Martin Luther King invited a group of welfare mothers to hear his plans for a poor people's campaign. He expected a grateful reception. But the mothers were angry that the campaign did not address their concerns. The spokeswoman for the group was Johnnie Tillmon. With a grandchild on her lap, she asked King some specific questions about welfare. King was nonplussed. "You know, Dr. King, if you don't know about these questions, you should say you don't know, and then we could go on with the meeting." King's colleague Andrew Young thought that the welfare mothers "jumped on Martin like no one ever had before." King confessed, "We are here to learn."[128]

Tillmon was in a good position to teach. As she later told *Ms.* magazine, "I'm a black woman. I'm a poor woman. I'm a fat woman. I'm a middle-aged woman. And I'm on welfare. In this country if you are any one of those things . . . you count less as a human being. If you're all those things, you don't count at all." Having grown up picking cotton, Tillmon moved to Los Angeles, where she worked in a series of poorly paid jobs. With the onset of various chronic illnesses, and with six children to support in the absence of a husband, she fell back on welfare. In Watts, Tillmon organized welfare mothers to work together. By 1971, some eight hundred welfare groups across the country had joined together as part of the National Welfare Rights Organization (NWRO). The NWRO claimed a total membership of 200,000. Tillmon became president in 1973.

As Tillmon's encounter with King showed, the welfare activists represented a group that had been sidelined during the 1960s. This had not been mere oversight. Black Power leaders addressed the problem of poverty, but their commitment to male supremacy meant they ignored welfare mothers. Civil rights leaders had feared the stigma attached to single welfare mothers. "I guess in the back of our minds we thought asking for welfare was tactically unsound," admitted Andrew Young. "If you asked for welfare, you might not get anything."[129]

Thus, welfare mothers took up their own cause. The NWRO's goals were "dignity, justice, full citizenship and an adequate income."[130] Ultimately, they didn't achieve these goals. Ronald Reagan would later deploy the image of a Cadillac-driving black welfare queen to good effect. But the rollback of welfare rights did not occur until the Reagan era, and even then it would be contested. Before that, welfare activists influenced welfare provision. "They say welfare is no longer a popular issue, but . . . I'd say it never has been popular," insisted Tillmon in 1973. "We have won some major battles and we plan to keep on fighting."[131]

When she spoke of major battles, Tillmon had in mind Nixon's Family Assistance Plan (FAP) of 1970. Some civil rights groups initially supported the plan. Although it was far from ideal, it was better than they expected. The NWRO, by contrast, denounced the plan. The proposed welfare allowance worked out to be less than the sum total of the various allowances already available. NWRO activists were angry, too, at workfare requirements without any guarantee of adequate childcare. A cartoon in the NWRO magazine called the FAP "Fuck America's Poor."[132] They determined to "ZAP FAP."

The testimony of welfare mothers in Congress made little positive impact on conservative senators such as Louisiana Democrat Russell Long. "If they can find time to testify and march," he scoffed (among other insults), "they can find time to do some useful work, like picking up litter." But the NWRO did persuade many mainstream civil rights groups to oppose FAP, even though some resented the NWRO tactic of making "everyone who supported [FAP] feel immoral."[133] These groups in turn influenced liberal senators wary of alienating black voters. Liberal opposition to Nixon's plan, coupled with conservative opposition for new welfare allowances, left FAP well and truly zapped by 1972.

The NWRO's ability to oppose FAP was not matched by an ability to push through something better in its place. There would be no welfare equivalent of the Civil Rights or Voting Rights Acts. At the local level, though, it was a different story. In the summer of 1970, some fifty mothers forced their way through the locked doors of Washington, D.C.'s welfare department and demanded grants for basic furniture. At the end of August, NWRO members sat-in at the office of HEW Secretary Robert Finch.[134] By the mid-1970s, such protests had translated into significant gains. In most states, welfare claimants won the right to have a male companion without forfeiting payments; officials were not allowed to raid welfare mothers' houses unannounced; and more women than ever before were deemed eligible. The NWRO's publicity prompted tens of thousands of eligible mothers to apply for welfare. Local chapters helped many with the application process. The black press quoted analysts who credited the NWRO with increasing the amount of welfare claims fourfold—which helps explain why welfare became such a hot issue in the 1980s.[135]

By the mid-1970s, the NWRO had fallen apart. But the welfare struggle continued locally, with some success, throughout the decade. The NWRO also spawned other anti-poverty movements. The Arkansas Community Organizations for Reform Now (ACORN) would develop into a leading advocate of low-wage workers and workfare employees into the twenty-first century (later renamed the Association of Community Organizations for Reform Now).[136] "I hear people saying that the welfare rights movement is dead," Tillmon complained in 1980. "The movement is different but still alive."[137]

Feminists

As with welfare activists, African American feminists came to the fore in the 1970s—indeed, there was some overlap between the two. Like the welfare activists, many African American women had sought to spotlight women's issues during the 1960s. SNCC women had raised the issue of gender equality. Veteran activist Pauli Murray had campaigned to add sex to Title VII of the Civil Rights Act. She then lobbied the EEOC commissioner for its strict enforcement; otherwise, "only half of the Negro population is protected."[138]

But as with welfare activists, feminists had been sidelined. The issue of race rights had so dominated 1960s discourse that there had been little space left for black women's rights. In any case, wrapped up in both the Freedom Now and Black Power slogans was a reassertion of black manhood and authority. Although he married a talented and independent woman, King presumed male leadership and preferred to work with male colleagues. In the early years, the Black Panthers were aggressively macho. Elaine Brown, a former lover of Huey Newton, reckoned that the first Panthers regarded a black woman leader as "an enemy of the black people." Some women complained that male leaders pressured them to have sex for the sake of the revolution. The Nation of Islam called on women to fulfill their natural role as homemakers. The National Council on Negro Women fell into line—in an inversion of clubwomen's philosophy at the start of the century, they accepted that women would only rise as high as the race. As for the EEOC, it virtually ignored sex discrimination in its first years.

During the 1970s the situation changed. The successes of the Civil Rights Movement opened up space for black women's groups (not to mention white women's groups, too). The limits of the Civil Rights Movement showed how necessary they were. The decline of national, male-led movements meant that community issues, and thus community groups, returned to the fore. And in every city, there were dozens of women-led local organizations. (Not everything had changed, though—black men were four times as likely as black women to get elected.) Some women's groups grew directly out of Black Power community projects. From 1974 until they disbanded in 1977, even the Panthers had a female leader—Elaine Brown. Other women-led community groups drew on much older traditions. But after the confrontations of the 1960s, they were able to adopt more aggressive tactics. In Harlem, Mothers Against Drugs (MAD) called on the police to account for their lack of action against (some said support for) drug dealers. One MAD leader told reporters, "The best news I've heard in a long time is that more white kids are getting hooked on heroin."[139] This way, she reasoned, the drugs issue would get attention from the powers that be. It was some change from the rhetoric of women reformers earlier in the century.

Some African American women articulated a distinct black feminist position. A few prominent black activists—like Pauli Murray and Fannie Lou Hamer—were founding members of the National Organization for Women. But most black feminists distanced themselves from the emerging white feminist movement. Murray left in 1967, frustrated that NOW's leadership included "no Catholic sisters, no women of ethnic minorities other than about five Negro women, and obviously no women who represent the poor."[140] One welfare mother wrote to NOW in 1973, "You speak of freedom and we are starving, begging, selling ourselves, scrounging for our very survival . . . How dare you call yourselves Sisters?"[141] Meanwhile Hamer distanced herself from the feminist platform. "I got a black husband, six feet three, 240 pounds . . . that I don't want to be liberated from." She also opposed abortion on the grounds that the unborn were the weakest of all in society. "If you give them a chance, they might grow up to be Fannie Lou Hamer."[142] Others took offense at the growing popular fascination with black macho. In 1970 Valerie Bradley warned readers of *Cosmopolitan* that the African American man was "big, black, virile, cool long before the white woman came to realize his assets . . . we intend to keep him."[143]

Thus, black feminists—many called themselves womanists—organized separate feminist groups. They defended themselves against the charge of holding back their men. And—as in the 1890s—they argued that the race could rise no higher than its women. In 1973 the National Black Feminist Organization held its first conference in New York City with some four hundred women. Local chapters hosted discussion groups and on occasion ran campaigns. The Atlanta chapter protested against the portrayal of Eloise "Mama" Curtis as a "castrating matriarch," on the popular television show *That's My Mama*.[144]

As with the NWRO, the NBFO fell as quickly as it rose. Critics condemned it for supporting white feminists (and thus undermining race protest), for supporting lesbianism (and thus "hating men"), or for its militancy (and thus promoting matriarchy). In any case, the organization had plenty of problems of its own: it was under-funded and undecided about its attitude toward poverty and homosexuality. But as with welfare activism, the collapse of a national organization did not mean the end of mobilization. Witness the outpouring of black women's literature by the end of the decade, such as some of the enduring classics in the field: Michelle Wallace, *Black Macho and the Myth of the Superwoman* (1978); bell hooks, *Ain't I a Woman* (1981); and Barbara Smith, *All the Women Are White, All the Men Are Black, But Some of Us Are Brave* (1981). A wide variety of local groups continued to organize. In Boston, the Combahee River Collective (so-named after Harriet Tubman's guerrilla raid) met at retreats during the 1970s—because "we realize that the only people who care enough about us to work consistently for our liberation are us." As they did so, they sharpened their critique of American society, the feminist movement, and the interconnected nature of race, gender, and class oppression around the world. Their published Combahee River Collective Statement would be a foundational document for black feminists into the twenty-first century.

Prisoners

From the end of the 1960s, the FBI's Counterintelligence Program (COINTELPRO) used lengthy prison terms as part of its assault on black militants. Take the case of the Charlotte Three. In 1972 federal agents sought the arrest of Jim Grant, T. J. Reddy, and Charles Parker. The three men had agitated, with success, for the establishment of a black studies program at UNC-Charlotte. In 1971 a local stable—known for its refusal to allow black riders—burned down. Fifteen horses died. Agents suspected the three activists. The only problem was they had no evidence. So they arranged for two black prisoners, one convicted of murder and the other of armed robbery, to meet in a cell to concoct a story for court. The convicted criminals were soon released and given an all-expense-paid trip to the beach. The Charlotte Three were imprisoned for a total of fifty-five years.[145]

Yet the 1970s saw another side to the place of prisons in African American protest. As the name "the Charlotte Three" suggests, questionable jurisprudence redounded to the benefit of activists. Civil rights protesters had first discovered the potential use of incarceration to aid their cause during the 1960s. Students saw a visit to the jailhouse as a badge of honor and used imprisonment as a way to galvanize support. But whereas 1960s demonstrators usually had brief stays in jail, 1970s militants often faced decades in prison. Thus, they came to see themselves, and be seen by some others, as political prisoners. The Wilmington Ten (sentenced to 282 years in prison for burning a grocery store in February 1971) were the subject of a *60 Minutes* documentary and their case was taken up by Amnesty International. The convictions were overturned in 1980.

Above all, Angela Davis's story won worldwide attention. Davis's picture—large Afro, raised fist, attractive face, defiant expression—was emblazoned on posters and t-shirts around the globe. The Rolling Stones released *Sweet Black Angel* and John Lennon and Yoko Ono released *Angela*. Davis was a brilliant scholar, a former student activist who took a left turn to Communism and began working with black prisoners including George Jackson, an outspoken militant accused of murdering a guard. When Jackson's younger brother, Jonathan, used Davis's gun in a courtroom shootout in 1970, she found herself number three on the FBI's Most Wanted list. She fled but was captured in New York. In response to public pressure, Davis was released late in 1972.

For many white Americans, such high-profile cases merely served to strengthen the association between black Americans and criminality. But some moderates were appalled. So too were African Americans. "The black community is in an ugly, dark, ominous mood," noted the *Chicago Defender*. "The belief in a widespread conspiracy to destroy the movement is indelible."[146] Some moderate civil rights leaders came to support militants that they may have otherwise ignored. Chicago's Coalition on Civil Rights opposed the imprisonment (for alleged murder) of local gang leaders Bobby Gore of the Conservative Vice Lords and Leonard Sengali of the Black P Stone Nation. The Reverend C. T. Vivian, a former colleague of King, was incensed to discover police had offered Sengali a reduced sentence if he would accuse Vivian of being a Communist.[147]

Meanwhile black prisoners sought to mobilize protest within prisons. As with welfare activism and black feminism, this too had a long tradition—Malcolm X had been recruited while in jail. But the 1970s saw an unprecedented level of collective action. Black Power rhetoric helped individual prisoners to see their incarceration as part of a systematic assault on black Americans. George Jackson was a case in point. Sent to Soledad Prison in 1969 for armed robbery, Jackson joined the Panthers and set about persuading his cellmates that prisons were a means of white repression. When Jackson and two inmates were accused of killing a prison guard, they became celebrity political prisoners known as the Soledad Brothers. They were acquitted, but Jackson was shot dead soon afterward (the guard feared Jackson had a gun hidden in his Afro—a plotline later copied by Pam Grier in the blaxploitation movie *Foxy Brown*).

Throughout the system, prisoners mobilized. In Attica, New York, prisoners fasted on August 27, 1973, to demand better conditions. When officials tightened restrictions, approximately 1,300 inmates took over the prison, holding thirty-nine guards and employees hostage. Prison protest did not lead to significant reform. After negotiations broke down, New York's Governor Nelson Rockefeller sent in the state police, who killed twenty-nine Attica prisoners, along with ten hostages. (The troopers used blood to smear epithets on the walls such as "Black blood will flow.")[148] Nevertheless, even the challenge to prison authority was a new departure. Considering the rapidly rising numbers of young black men in prison, such activism was important. Ben Chavis, one of the Wilmington Ten and future head of the NAACP, used the day-release program to earn a master's degree.[149] African American prison reform and prisoner support groups would grow in number, and prominence, during the rest of the century.

The small city of Tupelo stands in the middle of former sharecropping country in northern Mississippi, best known to some as the birthplace of Elvis Presley. During the 1970s, city fathers boasted of settled race relations. Schools had integrated without too much trouble. There had even been a black Miss Tupelo High. Then in 1978 demonstrations began, after city aldermen dismissed calls to fire two white policemen who had beaten up a black man. A charismatic leader, Alfred "Skip" Robinson, mobilized the "street people" who couldn't find a steady job. Robinson was a building contractor and head of the newly formed United League— a grassroots movement with seventy thousand members that championed the plight of poor African Americans in northern Mississippi. Unemployed Vietnam veterans led marches. The Klan countermarched. To "heal the sore" the city set up a biracial committee to consider voting, policing, and employment.[150]

That same summer, California voters approved Proposition 13, thereby amending the state constitution to prevent property tax exceeding 1 percent of the assessed value of any real estate. Opposed 4–1 by black voters, the proposition was a decisive rejection of postwar liberal growth politics. It was a reflection of the emphasis on individual rights that was the hallmark of suburban secession. And it marked the beginning of the so-called taxpayer's revolt, which in turn heralded the presidency of California conservative Ronald Reagan. The previous year, black lawyer Lionel Wilson had become the first black mayor of Oakland, California. His victory was dependent on support from two political traditions: the long-running Democratic coalition between middle-class blacks and blue-collar white union workers and the newer political mobilization of working-poor black voters (Elaine Brown was a key supporter). Wilson played down the "first black mayor" tag and ran as a moderate liberal. To try to slow the flight of business from the city, he opposed a payroll tax (which Elaine Brown had advocated to stop the suburban exodus of income). But it left him with the problem of a small tax base from which to tackle the increasing problem of inner-city joblessness and social service provision. The passage of Proposition 13 made the job that much harder.

The stories of Tupelo and Oakland reflected the persistence and power of black activism a decade after the heyday of civil rights and Black Power. As Robinson explained, "We are taking up where the movement of the 1960s left off." But Tupelo and Oakland also exposed some of the problems and constraints that activists would face toward the end of the century.

CHAPTER ELEVEN

Reagan, Rap, and Resistance, 1979–2000

"Fuck Tha Police." Title of N.W.A.'s (Niggaz With Attitude)
1988 hit rap song

On March 3, 1991, Los Angeles Police arrested Rodney King
after a high-speed car chase. By chance, a bystander videoed the
police beating King fifty-six times in eighty-one seconds. On
April 29, 1992, an all-white jury found the policemen not guilty.
The resulting violence was the worst urban uprising in U.S.
history. Angry youths attacked the police, passing motorists, and
Korean storeowners. At least fifty-eight people died, over five
thousand were arrested, and there was nearly $1 billion damage.
According to surveys, some two thirds of black Los Angelenos
thought "the targets of the rebellion got what they deserved." But
this was no simple black vs. white riot—in ethnically diverse
central Los Angeles, where the postindustrial economy hurt
residents regardless of color, it could hardly be otherwise. Of
those arrested, over half were Latino, and a third were African
American.

"I AM A BLACK GAY MAN. I AM A BLACK MAN. I AM A
MAN."
Banner at the Million Man March in Washington, 1995

During the summer of 1998, Emelda West—an elderly black
woman from rural Louisiana—met with executives of the
Japanese multinational company Shin-Etsuin in Tokyo. West
pleaded with officials not to build a huge PVC plant near her
home community. In September, the company withdrew plans to
build the plant.

One morning in November 1998, sixty of the seventy-three black
students at the University of New Hampshire marched into the
office of the university president. They refused to leave until their
demands were met—including the promise of a sixfold increase
in black student enrollment. University officers bought them
pizza for lunch, and by dinnertime they had agreed to a
compromise. Few, if any, other students noticed.[1]

In the summer of 1979, in a recording studio in New Jersey, Michael "Wonder Mike" Wright rapped these words over a bass line taken from "Good Times"—a recent disco hit:

> I said a hip hop the hippie the hippie
> to the hip hip hop, a you don't stop . . .

His new fifteen-minute version, "Rapper's Delight" by the Sugarhill Gang, entered *Billboard*'s R&B chart in November 1979. That same month, in a conference room in the New York Hilton, California Governor Ronald Reagan gave a more traditional speech. Launching his third bid for the Republican nomination for president, he promised to pursue the principle of "responsible liberty for every individual so that we will become that shining city on a hill."[2]

The rap from the Sugarhill Gang and Reagan's talk of the shining city on a hill seemed to mark the beginning of new eras in popular culture and national politics. "Rapper's Delight" was the first hip hop hit record, reaching number four in the U.S. charts. By the end of the century, hip hop dominated the music industry in terms of sales, awards, and advertising. As for Reagan, he won the election and (after a landslide victory in 1984) a second term. His time as president marked the triumph of conservatism in national politics. Reagan was succeeded by his vice president, George Bush Sr. In 1994, under the leadership of staunch conservative Newt Gingrich, Republicans won a congressional majority for the first time in forty years. Although Democrat Bill Clinton occupied the White House from 1993 to 2001, he distanced himself from Great Society liberalism.

On the face of it, hip hop and modern conservatism were two entirely unrelated movements. Reagan's optimistic campaign chimed with the aspirations of white-flight suburbanites. Hip hop emerged as the voice of African American inner-city poor. Grandmaster Flash's "The Message," one of the first major hip hop records, could hardly have been more different from Reagan's campaign theme of "Morning in America." Flash's "message" of warning for an innocent newborn child was that he would grow up in the ghetto, drop out of school, be unemployed, go to prison, and hang himself:

> Now your eyes sing the sad, sad song
> Of how you lived so fast and died so young.

Yet hip hop and modern conservatism had more in common than just the coincidental timing of their launch. Both benefited from a loss of faith in the old styles. In 1979, Democratic President Jimmy Carter faced an economic crisis at home and a hostage crisis abroad. That summer, teenagers held disco record demolition parties—a near riot broke out at one party during a ball game at Comiskey Park. Both hip hop and conservatism had already gained grassroots strength before the breakthrough. In the West and South, conservatives Barry Goldwater and George C. Wallace railed against the Great Society, high taxes, and forced racial integration. In the South Bronx, DJ's Kool Herc, Grandmaster Flash, and Afrika Bambaataa developed hip hop at house parties. Both movements integrated a wide variety of different components. The conservative coalition included the religious right and fiscal conservatives. Hip hop began as a mixture of graffiti artists, break dancing, MCing, and rapping. Above all, both modern conservatism and hip hop had important, interwoven implications for the struggle for racial equality at the end of the twentieth century.

After Reagan's victory, civil rights leaders saw the federal government as foe rather than (potential) friend. This was not the first time. In his last months, King had complained bitterly about the Johnson administration, and the NAACP felt at war with Nixon. But the unrelenting condemnation of a president by civil rights leaders called to mind the days of Woodrow Wilson. Reagan's campaign had set the tone. His New York speech did not mention civil rights. He then turned down a request to speak to the NAACP (he had already booked a holiday in Mexico). After winning the nomination, Reagan gave his first speech in Neshoba County, Mississippi—site of the unsolved murder of three student activists in 1964. Carter's team criticized Reagan for not mentioning the murders. What Reagan did instead was dust off old segregationist rhetoric, asserting, "I believe in states' rights."[3] The Imperial Wizard of the Klan endorsed the Republican ticket.[4] Reagan's team pointed out that he followed the trip to Mississippi with a speech to the National Urban League. He was hardly planning to stand at the White House door saying "Segregation forever." But most black Americans were anything but reassured.[5] In June 1980, Randall Robinson, a prominent opponent of South African apartheid, told a fundraising dinner, "I'm frightened at the prospect of Ronald Reagan."[6]

Reagan's time in office confirmed Robinson's fears. His administration pursued a policy of constructive engagement with the apartheid regime. He also appointed conservative judges to the federal bench; he promoted black conservatives who opposed affirmative action; and his Justice Department proved reluctant to protect minority rights. Black leaders were angry at the racial slights, too. Reagan famously failed to recognize Charles Pierce, the sole African American member of his cabinet, at a meeting of black mayors.[7] Above all, Reagan's mantra was, "Government is not the solution to our problems; government *is* the problem." By contrast, civil rights leaders had long seen federal intervention as key to solving racial inequality. They would be relieved when Clinton became president. John Jacob, the head of the NUL, gave President Clinton a "'B' . . . capable of doing a lot better."[8] Even so, in 1996, Clinton endorsed the new conservative consensus, declaring "the era of big government is now over."[9]

Mainstream civil rights leaders challenged the new conservative politics. The Reverend Jesse Jackson led the way. Born in South Carolina in 1941, by 1980 Jackson was based in Chicago working to improve the conditions of nonwhite poor people. Talented and telegenic, Jackson seemed the closest thing to Martin Luther King that the Reagan era had to offer. It was an image he cultivated carefully. Jackson had worked with King, often quoted King, and claimed to have cradled King as he lay dying (King's other colleagues that day begged to differ). At voter registration rallies, crowds shouted "Run, Jesse, Run." Jackson ran for the Democratic nomination twice, in 1984 and 1988, and was the frontrunner for a time in 1988, building a "rainbow coalition" of workers and radicals, and winning fifteen primaries and caucuses. A storm over anti-Semitic remarks and his links to controversial Nation of Islam leader Louis Farrakhan heralded the collapse of his campaign—though Jackson blamed the Democratic leadership. Just one generation after the Voting Rights Act, the emergence of a credible African American contender for the Democratic nomination was an impressive development. Yet for all his strengths, Jackson could not craft a winning coalition. Even the Democratic Party was reluctant to embrace his policies or campaign personnel.

Thus, it was ironic that at the very moment of the "Reagan revolution," African American artists reoriented national popular culture. Since the Harlem Renaissance, civil rights leaders had hoped that breaking through into popular culture would lead to advances in wider society. The 1980s and 1990s disproved the theory. Although white youths embraced hip hop culture and idolized black sports stars, few seemed interested in the problems of the ghetto. Black scholar-activist Kevin Powell complained in *Newsweek* that "this fascination with hip-hop is just a cultural safari for white people."[10] (The safari did not extend to film and television, though—only one of the 240 feature films released in 1981 had a black female in a leading role. An angry actor, Howard Rollins, asked why "E.T. couldn't have landed in a black family's yard."[11]) At election time, large majorities of white voters—including young people—

voted for the party that sought to roll back civil rights legislation. The African American public intellectual Cornel West commented, "The irony in our present moment is that just as young black men are murdered, maimed and imprisoned in record numbers, their styles have become disproportionately influential."[12]

Some black leaders blamed hip hop for turning young people away from tackling issues of racial injustice. "Oftentimes the music reinforces the very things that we are struggling against," complained Adrienne Shropshire, a 31-year-old community organizer in Los Angeles. "How do we work around issues of economic justice if the music is about 'getting mine'?"[13] By the end of the century, some pioneer artists agreed that hip hop had done more harm than good. "A lot of brothers and sisters," Afrika Bambaataa bemoaned, "they're losing respect of the 'us syndrome' and getting into the 'I syndrome.' You can't build a nation with an 'I' you got to build a nation with an 'us.'"[14]

For a time in the 1980s, it even seemed as though rappers might replace civil rights leaders as representatives of the race. With the release of "It Takes a Nation of Millions to Hold Us Back" in 1988, Public Enemy established itself as America's leading hip hop band. When Public Enemy paraded in open cars through Philadelphia that same year, the band's publicist, Bill Stephney, was astonished by the response. "You're seeing these graying forty-something Black men, tears in their eyes, throwing the Black Power salute like the revolution has come back." Lead rapper Chuck D complained the media "treat me like *I'm* Jesse Jackson."[15]

Yet it soon became clear that few early hip hop artists wanted to stand in the gap for political leaders. Stephney reckoned that "hip-hop was not just a 'Fuck you' to white society, it was a 'Fuck you' to the previous Black generation as well."[16] Rapper John Lewis Jr.—son of civil rights hero and congressman John Lewis Sr.—explained, "It's hard as hell growing up [with] pictures of your pops getting hit with billy clubs . . . that shit goes into your head."[17] Especially after the rise of gangsta rap in the late 1980s, rap seemed increasingly self-centered, self-harming, and self-defeating in equal measure. In N.W.A.'s 1988 hit "Gangsta, Gangsta," which mocked Nancy Reagan's Just Say No to Drugs campaign by saying "We're too busy saying 'Yeah!'" Ice Cube asked: "Do I look like a mutha fuckin' role model?"

A further irony of the era was that when at last black men came to dominate popular culture, they reinforced negative stereotypes that dated back to Jim Crow. Aggressive jewelry-laden men hardly made the case for government funding the deserving poor. The drive-by shootings of rivals Tupac Shakur (then the best-selling rapper of all time) and Notorious

B.I.G. in the mid-1990s gave rap's violent posturing real menace. Politicians pounced on rap's X-rated lyrics to promote themselves as defenders of family values. (2 Live Crew's 1989 album, *As Nasty As They Wanna Be,* famous for the track "Mc So Horny," was the first record to be banned on grounds of obscenity.) At Jesse Jackson's annual political convention in 1992, presidential hopeful Bill Clinton condemned Sister Souljah, a former member of Public Enemy. Clinton picked up on Souljah's widely reported comment, "If black people kill black people every day . . . why not have a week and kill white people?" Clinton lectured, "If you took the words 'white' and 'black' and you reversed them, you might think David Duke [a Klan leader] was giving that speech."[18]

For the traditional civil rights leadership, the rise of Reagan and rap spelled double trouble—an assault on the movement from without and within. The triumph of conservatism showed that a majority felt no obligation to compensate African Americans for slavery and segregation. The rise of hip hop exposed the weakness of traditional civil rights leadership, reinforced racist stereotypes, and suggested that the so-called hip hop generation had little to offer. NAACP executive director Benjamin Hooks complained, "The age of the volunteer is coming to an end."[19] By the end of the 1980s, NAACP membership had plummeted to barely a hundred thousand. The contrast with the 1960s was stark: majority support for nonviolent progressive students had been replaced by majority condemnation of violent idle young black men. The commemoration of the Civil Rights Movement during the 1980s—through museums, marches, and the introduction of an annual Martin Luther King holiday (signed into law by Reagan)—made the contrast all the starker.

Little wonder, then, that many traditional leaders and journalists hankered after the good ol' days of "the movement" and saw the Reagan era as one of atrophy and decline. The downturn in fortune experienced by many African Americans seemed to confirm the gloomy picture. The inequality gap in wages and employment that had been closing since World War II held steady from the mid-1970s through the mid-1990s. Inner-city poverty, family breakdown, and gang violence seemed entrenched. The arrival of crack cocaine in the mid-1980s compounded the problem. New get-tough crime measures led to an astonishing rise in numbers of young black men in prison. During the 1980s, sociologists popularized the term "underclass"—a group with no opportunity, or even desire, to break out of poverty and dependency. By the 1990s, large majorities of African Americans—including the black middle classes—told pollsters they did not expect the problem of racial inequality to improve in their lifetime.

Yet the despondency of the old guard tells only part of the story. In the first place, the Reagan revolution had its limits, especially in terms of its policy legacy. Reagan's election did not mark the overthrow of the Democratic leadership. In electoral terms, Democrats shared control of Congress and won sole control in 1986. In the judiciary, a number of federal appeals court circuits remained strongly liberal, and the Supreme Court swung to a conservative majority only after Reagan left office. Some critics from the American right castigated Reagan for not seeking a conservative enough revolution in the first place.[20]

Meanwhile, rap did not signal the decline of African American protest. Much of the criticism of rap lyrics missed the point. Hip hop was not produced to be debated in the cold light of day but to be danced to or listened to while driving the streets on sultry Bronx nights. The reason that Kool Herc first decided to play just the instrumental "breaks" of dance hits was because that was when dancers moved fastest (hence the name break dancing). At house parties, people wanted a sound, a beat, not political commentary. "It was impossible to put that type of shit in your rhymes," explained Chuck D. "You could throw in one line or two, like 'Reagan is bullshit.' Motherfuckers be like, 'Yeah, okay' [but] you better rock the fucking crowd."[21] In any case, many listeners understood that some of rap's boasting was a remake of "the dozens," a traditional, outlandish trade of insults. As rapper Ice T put it, "Rap is really funny, man. But if you don't see that it's funny, it will scare the shit out of you."[22]

Nor was hip hop to blame for inner-city tensions. The National Black Police Association defended Ice T's controversial 1991 hit "Cop Killer," stating, "There are no statistics to support the argument that a song can incite someone to violence."[23] Rather, hip hop was a reflection of existing tensions. On May 17, 1980—well before gangsta rap—hundreds of young African Americans in Miami fought the police and smashed shop fronts. Fifteen people died, and there was over $100 million of damage. The violence started after an all-white jury acquitted four white policemen of beating a black insurance salesman to death. After seeing two white victims on the street, 29-year-old Velderie Davis told reporters, "I'm glad it happened . . . we showed them we can hate too." As in previous years, this violence won wider sympathy. The *Washington Post* noted "ominous similarities" between the views of black "rioters and non-rioters."[24]

To be sure, rampant commercialism meant that tracks often presented a formula (or even self-parody) to satisfy consumers. By the 1990s, some music critics argued that rap had become an industry where middle-class black men made records with white producers for white suburban youth.[25] Even so, Chuck D's famous description of rap as "the Black

CNN" had merit, especially in the 1980s. "Rap gives you the news on all phases of life, good and bad, pretty and ugly: drugs, sex, education, love, money, war, peace—you name it." In fact, rap confronted the ugly stories that many civil-rights-leaders-turned-politicians—in a throwback to the days of respectability—were not prepared to confront. In contrast to earlier generations where they were ignored, the mainstream black leadership dictated the discourse on race in the Democratic Party about such sensitive issues as crime, family breakdown, and low educational achievement. Or rather, they dictated a lack of discourse on such issues. Rap had no such qualms.

Furthermore, the furor over rap meant it was all too easy for critics to dismiss the entire hip hop generation as defeatist. But Clinton's attack on Souljah took her quote out of context—she had been discussing the mindset of gang members, not her own opinion. Souljah was, in fact, one of the most politically engaged hip hop artists of her generation. She shot back that she was not the cause of police brutality or poverty, and that she—unlike Clinton—had never smoked drugs or had an affair. Souljah's bigger point was that Clinton's attack distracted from the issues at hand. "It is very shocking to me," said Souljah, that in a time of "inner city urban chaos . . . Clinton has chosen to attack not the issues, but a young African woman who is [a] very well educated, alcohol free . . . community servant."[26]

This was the key point. A representative "Black CNN" would have broadcast news of a continued, vibrant struggle for black equality. At the end of the century, there were numerous community servants attacking the issues. Even during the conservative era, even in the hip hop generation. The sheer scale of protest activity—from grassroots groups to national marches—was on a par with the 1960s. Indeed, in some ways, the conservative assault spurred rival groups to work together. Some activists continued to tackle old issues—the search for a decent wage and housing, a voice in local politics, a positive image, freedom from police brutality. Others addressed new issues, such as South African apartheid, environmental problems, AIDS, narcotics, and black imprisonment.

The importance of conservatism was that it framed this protest. Gone were the days of a national movement with the wind at its back, boldly seeking to advance the rights of all African Americans. The Civil Rights Movement was a distinct generation of protest, combining local activism with an effective national strategy to take advantage of the possibilities of the time. At the end of the century, at the national level, civil rights groups spent much of their time resisting the conservative assault on civil rights legislation. But such protest was no less important for being defensive. There were some successes too, such as the defense of affirmative action legislation. And at times, on specific single issues—notably the campaign against South African apartheid—activists were able to push a new agenda in national politics.

In general, though, the conservative resurgence in national politics meant that many of the most significant campaigns developed at the grassroots. Some of the themes raised in rap—unemployment, poor housing, prison, and the police—were very much the issues on the ground. Some of the tensions exposed in rap—sexism, homophobia, attacks on bourgeois African Americans—revealed the struggles within black communities. During the 1980s and 1990s, black women, homosexuals, and other marginalized groups fought to broaden the definition of racial equality to encompass a wide range of human rights. Thus, there was no single story of resistance. But local activists linked together through new human rights organizations; and in the era of globalization, local activists often developed an international vision, too.

Inevitably, this grassroots protest was hidden from public view. Yet in an age rightly associated with inner-city decline, local groups still made progress. In an age associated with conservative rhetoric, black intellectuals like Cornel West achieved unprecedented prominence in the public square. And in an age associated with young black men, many of the most effective local leaders were elderly black women.

Lifting Mandela's Spirits, Attacking Reagan

On November 6, 1984, Reagan won a landslide re-election victory. On Capitol Hill, members of the Congressional Black Caucus feared four more years on the sidelines. To make matters worse, despite Jackson's strong showing in the primary, the Democrats had played down civil rights issues. Congressman Ron Dellums of California felt "it was as if we had leprosy."[27] African American leaders met together, explained Congressman John Conyers of Michigan, to find "a strategy to begin our second term of office under this president." That strategy tackled Reagan on an issue that was eight thousand miles away—South African apartheid.

On Thanksgiving Eve, four black leaders met with the South African ambassador at the embassy. During the meeting, one of the four slipped out to alert the press that the other three would sit-in at the office to demand the end of apartheid. Television cameras were in perfect position to capture the unfolding drama. The police escorted the three dignified, handcuffed protesters to the police cars and then on to a night in the cells.

The Free South Africa Movement (FSAM) was born. Daily protests began outside the embassy and South African consulates around the country. During the next two years, some six thousand demonstrators would
be arrested.[28] The black journalist Juan Williams hoped that "after years
of looking for lightning to strike—the right issue at the right time to revive the moribund civil rights movement—black Americans have found
the issue in apartheid."[29]

In fact, black Americans found apartheid long before 1984. Back in
1912 the newly formed NAACP endorsed its South African counterpart, the African National Congress. Fifty years later Martin Luther King
and the ANC's chief, Albert J. Lutuli, jointly issued a call for sanctions against South Africa. During the 1970s the CBC and other groups
formed TransAfrica—the organization that launched FSAM. Jesse Jackson repeatedly raised the issue. But the reason that lightning struck late in
1984 was because the South African regime responded to a resurgence of
demonstrations with shocking brutality; five hundred black South Africans were killed. The South African newspaper *Sechaba* reported, "Afro-
Americans . . . regard an attack on the African continent as an attack on
them."[30]

As the CBC deliberations showed, though, the reason that this was the
right issue at the right time had everything to do with United States politics, too. *Newsweek* rightly observed that FSAM mobilized "against
South African racism—and against Ronald Reagan's approach to dealing
with it."[31] Reagan vetoed UN attempts to impose sanctions, preferring a
policy of "constructive engagement." After meeting Reagan, Archbishop
Desmond Tutu, the Nobel Prize–winning anti-apartheid campaigner, called
him a "racist pure and simple."[32] Randall Robinson, the director of
TransAfrica, even blamed Reagan for the recent "oppression" in South
Africa, since it "was almost pegged to the re-election" in America.[33]

The campaign against apartheid was also a chance to express anger
against conservatism. And therein lay its popularity. At a time when civil
rights leaders were on the defensive, this was one national policy where
they could go on the offense. Under liberal Democrat presidents, mainstream black leaders had played down their criticism of U.S. foreign policy so as not to jeopardize potential domestic gains. Under Reagan, they
felt they had nothing to lose. Reagan had refused to meet with the Congressional Black Caucus (even Nixon had extended that courtesy). Only
one of the state department's top hundred officials was an African American.

The Free South Africa Movement evoked memories of the 1960s Civil
Rights Movement. This was quite deliberate. Many leaders had first
tasted direct action during the 1960s, and they hoped to rekindle the

movement's spirit and inherit the movement's moral authority. The choice of four people to protest at the embassy was a reenactment of the first student sit-in at the Woolworth's lunch counter in Greensboro. Robinson told reporters outside the embassy, "If Martin Luther King were alive today, he would be here." Robinson arranged for the next best thing: Rosa Parks and Coretta Scott King joined the demonstrations. The crowds sang "We Shall Overcome."[34]

As with the famous civil rights campaigns, the focus was not on persuading the oppressors to relent but on forcing the U.S. government to do something about the problem—in this case, impose sanctions and make businesses divest from South Africa. As in the Civil Rights Movement, campaigners were media savvy. The first sit-in was scheduled for the lull in news between Reagan's election and the opening of Congress. On a typical day outside the embassy, the chanting would increase for a few minutes when the news cameras appeared, a celebrity would get arrested, the TV cameras would leave, and the protesters would head home to watch the clip on the evening news.

The reasons for the FSAM's success mirrored the Civil Rights Movement too. FSAM fronted a groundswell of grassroots action, in the churches, on campus, and among unions. The apartheid issue united anti-racists and anti-imperialists, leftists and liberals. Above all, apartheid—as with southern segregation in the 1960s—had few defenders left in the United States. As one black leader put it, "There is no question which side is the good side."[35] Even Reagan condemned apartheid. Thus, protesters did not have to change people's minds, just persuade them to act. Polls suggested that three quarters of white Americans who knew about the protests supported them.[36] Many Democratic politicians and even some Republicans were desperate to be photographed, or better still arrested, at the embassy. By 1986 more than half of the American firms and numerous states and colleges had divested from South Africa. California alone divested $13 billion.

Although the CBC felt marginalized, it led the congressional challenge to Reagan. Dellums introduced a sanctions bill during each session of Congress in the 1980s, gaining support year on year. Reagan tried to stall the movement by promoting a weak sanctions bill as an alternative. But in October 1986 bipartisan support forced through a tougher bill—inflicting on Reagan his most serious foreign policy defeat ever. The Senate voted 78–21 to override Reagan's veto. CBC member Mickey Leland of Texas was exultant: "This is probably the greatest victory we have ever experienced."[37] It was certainly the first time in American history that African Americans had decisively shaped U.S. foreign policy.

It is hard to measure the impact of the campaign on South Africa.

Apartheid would have crumbled without U.S. pressure. But American sanctions deprived the South African government of outside resources at just the moment when it faced its greatest challenges at home. Tutu was delighted. The American position is "not anti-South Africa," he declared, "it is . . . anti-apartheid." With the value of the South African rand plummeting, South African President F. W. de Klerk saw the writing on the wall. In 1990 he committed his government to move toward ending apartheid, and he released some political prisoners.

The most famous prisoner, and future president, was Nelson Mandela. As Mandela tasted freedom for the first time in twenty-seven years, he invoked King's famous phrase, "Free at last." When he later met Rosa Parks—by then a gray-haired grandmother—tears filled his eyes. In his first interview with African American journalists after his release, Mandela praised the FSAM. My "spirits were lifted," he said. "It was an impressive role for Black Americans to choose arrest."[38] His words were a reminder that struggles for racial justice were not bounded by national boundaries, not even by prison walls.

FSAM leaders hoped the victory would spawn a wider revival of the Civil Rights Movement. And to some extent, it did. Hundreds of students from UC-Berkeley picketed in support of longshoremen who refused to unload South African cargo. Activists tied the campaign to domestic issues. In 1985, twenty-two NAACP members completed the "longest civil rights march in history" (from coast to coast) to support sanctions and to encourage voter registration.[39] The anti-apartheid campaign also gave African American politicians the authority to speak out on other African issues. In 1985, Congressman Leland spearheaded a campaign that led to the passage of the Africa Famine Relief and Recovery Act, which provided $800 million for Ethiopian famine victims. As in the 1960s, other activist groups borrowed movement tactics for their own causes too. Shortly before Christmas 1984, three demonstrators were arrested at the British Embassy singing (to the tune of "We Shall Overcome"), "Ireland will be free one day."[40]

On June 20, 1990, Nelson and Winnie Mandela arrived in America to a heroes' welcome. Yankee Stadium in the Bronx was packed. Ever the showman, Nelson donned a Yankees cap. For many African Americans, it was an exhilarating moment of triumph. Over a hundred thousand people squeezed into Harlem's Africa Square to greet the Mandelas. After visiting twenty-seven cities in eleven days, they made one final stop at Oakland. It was an apposite farewell visit—home to Ron Dellums, the defiant longshoremen, and the campaign that won the most far-reaching state divestment legislation of all.

Yet the Mandela visit proved to be bittersweet, too. African American campaigners hoped the tour would help to transform the anti-apartheid campaign into a broader movement for human rights. Instead, the Mandela tour committee favored what some called a "Wall Street corporate approach." Bay Area organizer Myesha Jenkins was appalled when "Democratic Party advance men" arranged photo-ops of Mandela with local dignitaries at the expense of long-serving activists. Some blamed the ANC's desperate need for money to fight the forthcoming elections back in South Africa. Most blamed middle-class white liberals in the anti-apartheid movement. New York activists were incensed when members of the tour committee warned against fundraising in Harlem, because of the risk of money being stolen. Indeed, the tour committee was initially reluctant to have Mandela visit Harlem at all.

Mandela's tour sparked the unraveling of the anti-apartheid coalition. As in the 1960s, the unraveling was bitter. African American leaders resented white liberal anger at a problem across the ocean but indifference to race problems at home. White students resented African American demands to control student anti-apartheid campaigns. Yet for African American students, such control seemed only natural. Barbara Ransby, a leader of the Columbia divestment campaign, explained: "We argued that the anti-apartheid movement should be an extension of the Black freedom movement here, and that as a result Black students should be in the leadership."[41]

The Mandela tour also marked the end of FSAM's ability to pressure the American government to act. Mandela urged Congress to retain sanctions until South Africa promised open elections. But his arrival gave the impression that victory was already won. Bush lifted sanctions soon after he left. When the FSAM looked to Congress to raise a challenge, Congress looked away. The CBC's repeated attempts to pass tougher legislation (with backing from the black church for a national day of fasting) did not make it past the Senate. Meanwhile, the U.S. media's focus on "tribal" violence in South African townships—which fit well with the portrayal of hip hop gang violence in the United States—muddled the issue. (It turned out the South African government was responsible for fomenting the violence.) One African analyst put it, "The days of 'ANC good, apartheid bad' are over."[42] The days of FSAM, and the hopes for rekindling an old-style movement with a broad focus on human rights, were over too.

From Plantations to Chemical Plants

On the morning of September 15, 1982, ten yellow dump trucks set off toward a new landfill site at Afton, in rural Warren County, North

Carolina. Each truck carried six tons of soil that had been contaminated with polychlorinated biphenyls (PCBs)—a cancer-inducing toxin. Earlier that same morning, over a hundred people assembled in a black Baptist church two miles from the landfill. The group discussed plans, prayed, and then marched to stop the toxic dumping. They came face to face with sixty riot-equipped state patrol officers. When the trucks rumbled into view, many of the marchers pushed past the officers and lay down in the road. For a few minutes, the trucks stopped. The patrolmen arrested fifty-five demonstrators and cleared the road. The trucks rolled onto the site and dumped their toxic loads.

It was, said one reporter, like a "flashback to the 1960s."[43] Reporters often called any demonstration by African Americans a return to the 1960s. But in this case, the comparison would prove to be uncannily accurate. The Afton lie-down had a remarkably similar impact to the Greensboro sit-ins, just a hundred miles—and twenty-two years—distant. The lie-down escalated into a major confrontation, which in turn led to a nationwide movement, which in turn persuaded a president to act. And just as the 1960s sit-in movement developed into a wider assault on white supremacy, so too the environmental justice movement developed into a broader struggle for greater representation in decision-making.

The morning after the first lie-down, more demonstrators returned to halt the trucks. Within three weeks, over five hundred demonstrators had been arrested. At the request of local activists, civil rights leaders flew in from around the country. The protests hit the national news. They didn't stop the landfill—by the end of the year, trucks had dumped some forty thousand cubic yards of toxic soil. But the demonstrators did publicize the connection between race and toxic dumping. The state insisted that Warren County was picked for scientific reasons. Residents disagreed. Luther Brown, the local Baptist pastor, told reporters, "We know why they picked us . . . because it's a poor county [and] mostly black. Nobody thought people like us would 'make a fuss.'"[44] It turned out Brown was right. The Reverend Ben Chavis, a former Wilmington Ten prisoner and future executive director of the NAACP, directed the United Church of Christ's Commission for Racial Justice (which he chaired) to study the wider issue of "toxic wastes and race in the United States." The commission found that the most significant correlation in the location of waste facilities was not with poverty or with low population density but with the presence of a nonwhite majority population. By the end of the century, dozens of surveys had confirmed a racial divide in the way that authorities cleaned up toxic waste.[45]

Armed with that knowledge, nonwhite groups across the country began to make a fuss. African Americans had long sought to live in a decent environment. Under Jim Crow, neighborhood groups had called for proper sewerage. King's final campaign had been alongside sanitation workers in Memphis. But in terms of the focus on so-called environmental racism, and the sheer scale of inter-connected protests, this was very much a new national movement. In 1991, some 650 activists met together for the first national People of Color Environmental Leadership Summit. By the time of the second summit in 2002, over 1,400 delegates attended. Some three quarters of the delegates represented community-based organizations.[46]

As so often in the past, local people influenced national organizations. In this case, the protests changed the focus of two major social movements. Previously, African American organizations had focused on employment and civil rights, while white environmental groups focused on protecting wilderness. After Afton, both movements began to widen their vision. Congressman John Lewis, former head of SNCC, thought "the quest for environmental justice has helped to renew the Civil Rights Movement."[47] In turn, organizations like the NAACP and Greenpeace provided resources and expertise for local groups.

As with the Civil Rights Movement, the demonstrations put pressure on the federal government. Environmental justice advocates began to lobby the Environmental Protection Agency after the first Leadership Summit in 1991. The following year John Lewis and Senator Al Gore introduced an environmental bill in Congress. The bill failed, but when Gore became vice president the following year, environmental justice advocates gained favor in the White House. At Gore's urging, Clinton appointed Chavis and Robert Bullard (the leading academic advocate of environmental justice) to his transition team. In 1993 the head of the EPA made environmental justice one of her top four priorities, and she appointed twenty-five activists to a new EPA Justice Advisory Council. The following year, Clinton signed Executive Order 12898 directing federal agencies to identify and address any adverse environmental effects of their programs on people of color.

Thus, barely a decade after the first Afton lie-downs, the environmental justice movement had spawned national organizations and won influence (for the time being) in the highest level of the American state. As with the Civil Rights Movement, these national advances empowered grassroots activists. Campaigns fused the tactics and religious fervor of earlier protest with the global and technical realities of late twentieth-century industrial development.

More often than not, local leaders were elderly women who were angry at the degradation of their neighborhoods. Emelda West, a five-foot-tall grandmother, grew up in Convent, Louisiana—a mostly African American settlement of some two thousand people. For all the hardships of her childhood, she remembered happy times climbing trees for peaches or fishing for shrimp in the Mississippi River. But by the end of the century, the trees were mostly rotten, and no one dared eat the shrimp. Worse still, many children suffered from breathing problems and spontaneous nosebleeds. West lived in the heart of Cancer Alley—a group of twelve parishes with more than 150 major industrial plants. The four worst polluting facilities lay within three miles of West's home. In 1996 the multinational Shintech Corporation bought the last remaining greenfield sites outside Convent to build a huge PVC factory. Fearful of the links between PVC and dioxin, West took action.

Each time West walked past the proposed site, she muttered, "In the name of Jesus, I promise you, Shintech, you will *not* build here!"[48] West helped found the St. James Parish Citizens for Jobs and the Environment. The Citizens won support from celebrities, such as Stevie Wonder, from environmental groups such as Greenpeace, and from civil rights organizations such as the CBC. They also fought a canny propaganda battle. At public hearings they provided state officials with bottles of drinking water taken from a lake near a similar PVC plant. But moral pressure did not work. The head of Louisiana's (rather doublespeak titled) Department of Environmental Quality called the Citizens "little Hitlers." The governor criticized them for putting the environment ahead of jobs. The Citizens pointed out that the existing plants did not employ local residents anyway.

As the protests escalated, Greenpeace's southern field representative believed "the Shintech case emerged as the most important civil-rights case ever involving charges of environmental racism." With the free support of environmental justice lawyers, the group filed suit in 1998 under Title VI of the Civil Rights Act; then it appealed to the EPA, which in turn acted to slow down the approval process; and then it resorted to direct action, on an international scale. West flew to Tokyo to lobby Shintech's parent company. Each day, a Greenpeace representative called the company and said, "I have a 72-year-old African American grandmother who wants to meet with you."[49] After a few days, an assistant to the CEO agreed to a meeting. West presented petitions from over half the residents of Convent. Such was her pent-up emotion that West ended the meeting by slamming her fist on the table and pleading, "We don't want Shintech." In September, the company withdrew plans to build the plant.

Many campaigners believed the victory was every bit as significant as the *Brown* decision.

There were other victories too. Symbolically, in 2001 North Carolina began the process of detoxifying the Afton landfill. At the federal level, the Nuclear Regulatory Commission cited Executive Order 12898 as the basis for its denial of a permit for a facility in rural Louisiana—the first permit ever denied in the NRC's history.[50] More generally, local movements were most likely to stop a new facility from being built rather than remove an existing one. Even then, protesters sued, with some success, for compensation. In 2002 Shell agreed to relocate the citizens of Norco, Louisiana, who were sandwiched between a chemical plant and an oil refinery.

But overall, progress was mixed. The victories were more than matched by the rise in toxic dumping. One survey in 2000 revealed that nearly half the new public housing units for nonwhite poor were located within a mile of factories with toxic emissions.[51] Cancer Alley remained as lethal as ever. Shintech found an alternative site for a new, albeit smaller, facility. To be sure, companies began to sugarcoat their proposals with guarantees of jobs for local residents, which was better than nothing. In rural Burke County, Georgia, the majority-black county commission used money from a nuclear power facility to build a hospital.[52] Even so, being forced to choose between jobs and the environment was a cruel choice indeed—and not one that white suburbanites had to make.

One legacy of the environmental justice movement was a new generation of activists. It welcomed women as leaders at the national and international level and fostered multiracial coalitions. People of color found much to unite them and—unlike many other areas of racial politics at the end of the century—little to divide them. It also educated people in protest. In any given campaign, the first meeting would be held to oppose a hazardous facility. But before long, campaigners learned that the deeper issue lay with who made the decisions, and who held political and economic power.

Fighting Old Battles: Seeking Equality in the Workplace

In a confrontation that came to define the Civil Rights Movement, the city police of Birmingham, Alabama, used unnecessary force to tackle young demonstrators. One of the nation's finest civil rights museums, built in 1992, now commemorates the drama. In nearby Kelly Ingram Park—the site of the confrontation—metal statues of snarling dogs and defiant children evoke the pain and promise of the summer of 1963.

What isn't in the museum, though, is the story of the police force's symbolic role in the long-running struggle for economic equality.

During the 1970s African Americans sued to integrate the Birmingham police and fire service. As a result, the city signed a consent decree, promising to hire at least one minority applicant for every two white applicants; the city also agreed to a minimum quota of women. Then in 1984, ten white men who failed to get into the services filed suit against the consent decree, claiming "discrimination against whites and males." Reagan's Justice Department eagerly joined the suit. Birmingham's first African American mayor, Richard Arrington, who had helped negotiate the consent decree, was exasperated. The decree "could have healed a 100-year-old wound," said Arrington wistfully. "Now we will have to fight old battles."[53]

Fighting old battles was the order of the day at the end of the century. To be sure, the anti-apartheid and environmental justice campaigns showed that African Americans fought new battles when opportunities arose. But for the most part, the main battle in national politics was trying to defend the gains of the 1960s and 1970s. From the question of access to higher education to the drawing of election districts, civil rights leaders lobbied politicians, argued in court, and appealed to public opinion. But no battle was more contentious or important than the issue of affirmative action in employment.

There would be no repeat of snarling dogs. But the conservative rhetorical assault on hard-won compensatory legislation was ferocious. It enjoyed much broader support than had defenders of Jim Crow, too. Conservatives now spoke of the rights of hard-working white people (George Bush Sr. said, "I am concerned about the forgotten 90 percent"); they condemned affirmative action as reverse discrimination; and they spoke of quotas rather than targets. Prominent black conservatives (who received wide publicity despite being few in number) argued that affirmative action stigmatized African Americans. The Reagan administration's bite did not match the bark of conservative rhetoric (not least because support for affirmative action was embedded in some government bureaucracies). Even so, the administration sought to overturn Executive Order 11246, signed by Lyndon Johnson, which required federal contractors to implement affirmative action policies. As the Birmingham case showed, the Reagan administration also tried to win cases in court to stop private employers from pursuing affirmative action.

Civil rights activists pushed back. The battle over Executive Order 11246, said one civil rights veteran, aroused "the largest coalition ever on a civil rights issue."[54] The NAACP poured resources into defending affirmative action in court. Civil rights leaders fought in the battle of ideas, too. Julian Bond, chairman of the NAACP board, asked, "Which is better—to have a job and people look down on you, or have no job and people look down on you anyway?" In his stump speech, Bond argued that affirmative action was needed since past injustice still affected the present. "Imagine a football game in which one team owns the ground, the crowd, the equipment and the referees—and ties the legs of the opposing players together. The score is 100–0. And then in a pang of conscience, the winning team says we have been wrong, let's play fair from now on. It's still 100–0."[55] Civil rights organizations released compelling evidence of continued discrimination at the workplace, in housing, and in mortgage lending.

Although affirmative action advocates were on the defensive, they still had some power. As with anti-apartheid and the environment, civil rights groups joined with significant allies—particularly among Democrats and unions. Campaigners found some support from the courts, too. Although the courts ruled against general affirmative programs, in cases such as *Local 128 of the Sheet Metal Workers' International Association v. EEOC* (1986), the Court upheld affirmative action targets when there was specific evidence of intentional discrimination or severe underrepresentation. Opinion polls showed that although a majority opposed quotas, a majority still supported affirmative action. Or to put it another way, a majority opposed compensatory action but supported diversity. Thus, in 1996 California voters approved Proposition 209 which ruled against "preferential treatment" for the hiring of minorities in public sector employment. Yet the following year, Houston voters rejected a proposal to "end affirmative action programs."

In the final analysis, the battle over affirmative action added up to a stalemate in theory and something of a reversal in practice. Even a powerful conservative administration could not muster sufficient support to overturn Executive Order 11246. Republican Senate Majority Leader Bob Dole advised Reagan to "leave it as it is." A decade later Clinton pursued much the same line, promising to "mend it, not end it."[56] But Reagan's administration starved enforcement agencies of resources, leaving them limp and ineffective. Both Reagan and Bush appointed conservatives to the Equal Employment Opportunity Commission. The most controversial appointee of all, black lawyer Clarence Thomas as chairman, reckoned that to work with white conservatives "you must be against affirmative action." One economist commented in 1986, "If the tax laws of the United States were enforced as slackly as the antidiscrimination laws currently are . . . very few people would pay taxes."[57]

Civil rights leaders also complained that other disadvantaged groups—such as women and Latinos—adopted the tactics and lexicon of the movement, and then benefited from affirmative action at the expense of African Americans. Bond asked, "How did the civil rights road get so crowded?"[58]

One of the problems of having to fight old battles was that it held back consideration of more ambitious solutions. Even before the conservative assault, some questioned whether affirmative action could resolve entrenched racial inequality. In his seminal book *The Declining Significance of Race* (1978), the sociologist William Julius Wilson argued that affirmative action had a positive impact only on relatively well-educated black Americans. For the inner-city poor, the new deindustrialized, suburban, high-tech, highly skilled economy was a greater threat than racism had ever been. On Chicago's Southside, two thirds of adult black men had a job in 1960. By 1990, it was barely a third, and even fewer women. Wilson worried that joblessness produced "crime, family dissolution, welfare, and low levels of social organization." In an interview in 1997, Wilson admitted, "I am fighting pessimism right now. That's because we seem to be retreating from using public policy as a way to fight social inequality."

Some made bold suggestions. In 1990 John Jacob renewed the NUL's call for a domestic Marshall Plan—transferring $50 billion from the military budget to create full employment and provide training for nonwhite workers. The prominent journalist Ron Daniels backed the plan with a call to revive the "tactics of civil disobedience." "Are we prepared," he asked, "to surround the White House . . . and go to jail in MASSIVE numbers?"[59] The answer was no. But such talk missed the point. In an era of conservative ascendancy, national protests could expect little in return. African Americans had only once been able to face down the government over the issue of jobs alone—at the outset of World War II, when the government was at its most vulnerable and when the lily-white nature of defense employment made the issue clear-cut. In any case, issues such as Executive Order 11246 did not capture the imagination of African Americans at the grassroots. To make matters worse, complained Wilson, civil rights leaders became "so preoccupied with affirmative action that they didn't provide the kind of leadership that would help."[60]

What the calls for marches also missed was that mass mobilization around economic issues was already taking place, just not as a single, top-down movement. At times, grassroots campaigns influenced local and national economic decisionmaking—even when they were led by welfare recipients and the extremely low-waged. In the context of conservative ascendancy, they seemed to stand little chance of preserving their hard-fought gains of the 1960s and 1970s. In 1995 the crime-busting mayor of New York, Rudy Giuliani, pioneered a workfare scheme requiring welfare recipients—disproportionately black women—to work on public projects (mostly in parks) in order to receive benefits. The following year, President Clinton passed legislation that stopped Aid to Families with Dependent Children (AFDC), limited welfare receipt to five years, and promised to "end welfare as we know it."

The reforms attracted plenty of criticism. The Reverend Raphael Warnock, assistant pastor at Adam Clayton Powell's old church, complained that "workfare is a hoax . . . poor people are being put into competition with other poor people."[61] Senator Daniel Patrick Moynihan, the most prominent expert on poverty, condemned the "premise" that the "behavior of certain adults can be changed by making the lives of their children as wretched as possible." But talk of ending the culture of dependency and reducing the tax burden proved popular. By 1998 Giuliani celebrated slashing 400,000 people off the city's welfare rolls. His workfare scheme became a model for cities around the country.

Yet even in this context, the poor found ways to fight back. On February 2, 1997, New York's parks commissioner, Henry Stern, hosted the city's annual Groundhog Day Ceremony at Flushing Meadows Corona Park. Children watched with bated breath to see if the two prairie dogs, Flushing Meadows Phil and Corona Kate, would cast a shadow (if so, said the tradition, that would mean six more weeks of winter). As Phil and Kate emerged, workfare park attendants heckled Stern. The prospect of six more weeks of winter was precisely the problem. The workfare team wanted warm clothing. It was the latest protest in an ongoing campaign. One month before, workers had taken over ten of the park's district offices to demand hats and gloves. Then a group sat-in at Stern's office to demand a meeting. When they didn't get one, they chose to embarrass him during what should have been a cute ceremony.[62]

Groundhog Day heckling for hats and gloves hardly seems the stuff that social movements are made of. Yet as so often happens, an initial grievance led to wider action (think of Rosa Parks and the aggressive bus driver in 1955 in Montgomery). Two groups, Workers Together! and ACORN, tried to mobilize the workfare mothers. They started with hats and gloves. Then they turned to lunch breaks, sick leave, paid vacations, and childcare facilities. Then they organized marches calling for "A day's work for a day's pay."[63] Finally, the groups sought to win the right to shape policy. Workers blocked trucks from leaving sanitation garages to force welfare officials to meet with them.

This was the age-old struggle for better pay and decent working conditions. Whereas 1970s welfare protest drew on civil rights rhetoric, this latest effort drew on the labor tradition. With the backing of New York's largest union of municipal workers, ACORN sought to form a workfare union.[64] By June 1997 more than a third of workers had signed cards endorsing ACORN as their bargaining agent—the threshold required to call a union election. Giuliani and his administration insisted that those on workfare were not employees and were therefore ineligible to form a union. "Believe me," said one exhausted park cleaner, Elliott Roseboro, "we are workers." In an action reminiscent of the Mississippi Freedom Vote, ACORN held the election anyway. In October 1997, almost 17,000 workers voted for ACORN representation. Only 207 voted against.[65]

The protests took on a national focus. On Saturday, August 22, 1998, more than a thousand people, representing African American, Puerto Rican, labor, and feminist groups, marched on New York's City Hall. August 22 was the second anniversary of Clinton's signing of the welfare bill. Referring to the media and congressional focus on the president's recent sexual encounter with an intern, marchers held banners saying "Welfare is the real scandal." In Oakland, demonstrators marched in chains. By the end of the century, a wide range of organizations joined together as the National Campaign for Jobs and Income Support. The campaign lobbied to prevent the reauthorization of the welfare bill.[66]

Low-wage advocates did not win their main demands—the right to a union and the end of the welfare bill. But they did win some concessions. New York workers won hats and gloves—and a doubling of the budget for childcare. Ironically, such concessions undermined some support for the fight to form a union. Indeed, by 1998 Giuliani felt confident enough to target the end of welfare completely by expanding workfare into the private sector. But elsewhere, some fifty cities and states passed "livable" minimum wage bills by 2000. Meanwhile, in Washington Clinton duly signed legislation requiring a minimum wage for workfare workers. Most significantly of all, in 2000 he signed legislation that provided an extra $21 billion for earned income tax credits—a scheme designed to help working families rise above the poverty line.[67]

At the other end of the scale, high-achieving African Americans also continued to seek equal economic status. In their case, the problem was not a lack of decent jobs but the glass ceiling that restricted them from rising as high as they could. In 1993 a head-hunter for Texaco lured African American pension analyst Bari-Ellen Roberts away from Chase Manhattan. But from the start, Roberts felt she was working with a group of "neanderthals." When she suggested to the vice president of human re-sources that Texaco might want to develop its commitment to racial di-versity, he slammed his hand on his desk and accused her of wanting to see "Black Panthers in the halls of Texaco." When a less experienced white man was promoted to be her new boss—she was told she would have to train him—Roberts and five co-workers filed suit on behalf of Texaco's 1,500 African American employees.

On paper, Texaco was committed to diversity. Staff had to attend train-ing sessions where they discussed such issues as the complementary con-tributions of different colored jelly beans to a jelly bean bag. But Roberts and her lawyers pointed out that African Americans were promoted more slowly than white employees, were underrepresented in the higher wage scales, and tended to be paid less than white employees even in the same job category. So when Roberts filed suit in March 1994, she had reason to be confident of victory.[68] Two years later, she could be certain. The *New York Times* received a tape of three Texaco executives discuss-ing the "smart-mouthed little colored girl." The executives hatched plans to destroy documents relating to the case. One joked, "All the black jelly beans seem to be stuck to the bottom of the bag." Civil rights leaders threatened a national boycott. Texaco's stock fell by $1 billion in three days. A week later, Texaco agreed to pay out $176 million to minority workers and to improve human resources—the biggest discrimination payout in corporate history. Roberts went on to write an account of the case and became manager of her own company.[69] Some called her a modern-day Rosa Parks.

The various protests, from workfare park cleaners to Texaco's man-agement, demonstrated that black workers could win significant, some-times stunning victories on economic matters. They showed that vul-nerable workers could join together to influence the highest level of policymaking.[70] Yet the continued efforts also highlighted the seemingly intractable nature of economic inequality. In 2000, the median black household income was $30,400, compared with $44,200 for white households. Both white and black families had benefited from an eco-nomic boom in the late 1990s, but at the end of the decade African Amer-ican median household income was barely two thirds of white income (though this was the narrowest gap to date).[71] Although only a quarter of African American families were in poverty by 2000—the lowest rate on record—African Americans were nearly three times more likely than white families to be in poverty—the highest gap on record.

Behind the overall statistics there were winners and losers. The losers continued to be young black men, the less educated, and single-parent families.[72] The winners were the highly educated, government employees, and especially professional women. Indeed, by the end of the century the difference between winners and losers grew faster among black Americans than white Americans. The wealthiest quintile of black Americans secured almost 50 percent of the total black income—the highest to date—compared with 44 percent for the top quintile in the white population. Yet as the Roberts case showed, many of the winners still felt aggrieved. Black journalist Ellis Cose's 1994 best-selling book carried the title *The Rage of the Privileged Class: Why Do Prosperous Blacks Still Have the Blues?* Surely it couldn't be the case, he argued, that "black associates in law firms have such difficulty advancing because white partners fear that black lawyers will rape their wives."[73]

Worse still, the racial wealth gap remained a wealth chasm. By 2000, African American families were only two thirds as likely as white families to own their own homes, and their homes were on average only two thirds as valuable as those of whites.[74] Worst of all, the chasm was widening. The average net wealth of African Americans declined relative to that of whites, from one eighth in 1970 to one fourteenth by the end of the century. By then, African Americans inherited on average just eight cents for every dollar inherited by white Americans.[75] The less wealth, the higher the loans needed for college education and the higher the mortgage interest rate. In other words, the wealth gap was self-perpetuating.

Building by Building, Block by Block

The end of the century saw plenty of campaigns that rekindled memories of the 1960s. In 2000 the NAACP called a boycott of South Carolina's tourist industry to protest the flying of the Confederate flag over the statehouse. In 1987, in Forsyth County, Georgia, civil rights leaders led a nonviolent confrontation, like old rockers on a comeback tour. In 1912, white residents had expelled all black residents from the county. Seventy-five years later, the county was still virtually lily-white. Some twenty thousand people—led by King's former colleagues—joined a "march against racial intimidation." The Klan turned up, shouting obscenities.[76] The Pulitzer Prize–winning African American columnist William Raspberry was not especially impressed. "A 1960s-style march [was] a purposeless exercise in nostalgia."[77] A decade later, the county—the fastest growing in the nation—remained the whitest of America's six hundred largest counties, with only thirty-nine African American residents, out of a population of more than 75,000.[78] As for the flag controversy, it produced plenty of headlines—not least when South Carolina State Senator

Arthur Ravenel referred to the NAACP as the "the National Association of Retarded People," and then apologized to "retarded people" for the slur. On April 12, 2000, the state legislature offered to move the flag to a thirty-foot flagpole outside the state Capitol, next to a monument honoring Confederate soldiers. The boycott continued.

For the most part, however, grassroots campaigns were less concerned with set-piece confrontations and the politics of symbolism and more concerned with longer-term efforts to improve the everyday lives of African Americans. Such efforts were often based on traditional community institutions—the church, campuses, labor groups, women's groups, and tenants' organizations—and linked together through new social justice organizations. One campus activist explained, "Students are much more interested in volunteerism than in political action . . . What they've told us is, 'Our service work is not an alternative to politics—it is alternative politics.'"[79] What was true for students was true more generally. In an era ostensibly bedeviled by materialism and defeatism in equal measure, the struggle for racial equality was to be found in the age-old politics of building the community.

Nowhere more so than in the ghetto. Genevieve Brooks was the driving force behind the mid-Bronx Desperadoes Community Housing Corporation. At age seventeen, the diminutive, energetic Brooks left South Carolina for New York City. During the 1970s—in her forties and recently widowed—Brooks moved to a handsome integrated apartment in the mid-Bronx. But soon white tenants started moving out. Before long the landlord stopped cleaning the apartment block. When Brooks complained, the landlord suggested she move. The neighborhood was fast degenerating into a wasteland of boarded-up homes. Many apartment blocks were burned by landlords trying to pick up a final insurance check, or by tenants seeking priority on the city's placement list for units in new housing projects.

What Brooks faced was the classic problem of urban decay. By the 1980s the Bronx had become a byword for ghetto despair, just as Birmingham had once been the symbol of segregation. In 1977 as the New York Yankees hosted the Los Angeles Dodgers in the second game of the World Series, overhead helicopter cameras panned out from Yankee Stadium to a fire in a nearby school. Television commentator Howard Cosell famously told sixty million viewers, "Ladies and gentlemen, the Bronx is burning." In 1981 Hollywood released *Fort Apache: The Bronx,* a tale of violent crime and police corruption. Presidents Carter and Reagan both visited the Bronx: Carter called it the worst slum in America, and Reagan compared it to London after the blitz.

But instead of promising assistance, Reagan used the example of the Bronx to justify his attack on big government programs: "The government fought a war on poverty and poverty won." His administration cut spending on affordable housing by two thirds, and local governments followed suit. According to Brooks, city officials "thought that because this was a predominantly minority area it was just junkies and welfare folks." The emergence of hip hop from the Bronx served to confirm the stereotype.

Many of those who could afford to leave the Bronx did so. During the 1990s, African Americans moved to the suburbs at a faster rate than white Americans. But Brooks decided to stay. With the help of neighbors and members of her church, she formed a tenants' association. "We started sweeping our own streets, we went into the backyards and pulled the garbage out." By the start of the 1980s, hers was the only inhabited block in the neighborhood. Brooks linked with other tenants' groups in the mid-Bronx to create a safe neighborhood, "building by building, block by block." Because they were so desperate, someone suggested they call themselves the Desperadoes. The name stuck.

Brooks left her job to work full time for the Desperadoes. With her trademark gardenia in her hair, she spent time—in her words—"skinnin' and grinnin'" with local officials. Using tax shelters and state subsidies for low-income housing projects, the Desperadoes worked with developers and financiers to rehabilitate four abandoned apartment blocks. Brooks hired local gangs to protect the new buildings. The Desperadoes screened applicants and arranged childcare facilities for residents. As the Desperadoes proved their worth, the city government channeled millions of dollars into redevelopment. By the end of the century, the Desperadoes and similar groups in the Bronx had helped rebuild hundreds of homes for low-income families.[80] In 1997, President Clinton made the now customary presidential pilgrimage to the Bronx, but this time it was in celebration. "If you can do it, everybody can," said Clinton.[81] The only disappointed people were Japanese holidaymakers on *Fort Apache* bus tours.

Three presidential visits and one Hollywood movie were unique for a ghetto. Yet in many ways, Brooks' experience was emblematic of grassroots activism at the end of the century. Older women often took the lead. The work focused on pressing community issues. It was often painstakingly slow. But the Desperadoes showed that in the post–civil rights generation, there were still plenty of activists seeking a better life for people of color. Even in the ghetto. Even in the Bronx.

For the Desperadoes, the primary issue was housing. Around the country, local groups addressed a wide range of issues: from fighting drugs and improving schools and hospitals, to reforming prisons and college curricula, to winning childcare for low-income mothers or seeking compensation for displaced black farmers. The most high-profile issue was policing. Seemingly every city had its victim célèbre. On May 10, 1999, in Los Angeles, a thousand people marched to protest the exoneration of police who killed a nineteen-year-old woman, Tyisha Miller. The police fired twenty-one shots, some at the back of Miller's head. "If they get away with this," said veteran activist and comedian Dick Gregory, shortly before being arrested, "it'll be the babies next."[82]

Just as campaigns addressed a wide range of issues, they employed a wide range of tactics. Some of the newer social justice organizations, such as ACORN, saw the problem as essentially one of economic exploitation, irrespective of race; although its membership was predominantly African American, it sought links between low-income workers across racial lines. Other organizations, such as the Center for Third World Organizing, based on the West Coast, put race at the center of politics. Some groups identified with other nonwhite groups, and at other times African Americans competed with nonwhite communities. In 1991, Los Angeles' Brotherhood Crusade led a 110-day boycott against Chung's Liquor Store after the Korean American owner shot dead an African American alleged robber—one of a spate of murders between members of the Korean American and African American communities.

For all their diversity, one thread that linked the various campaigns together was their attempts to gain influence in decisionmaking. The passage of the Voting Rights Act allowed some access to power. During the 1980s, lawyers for the NAACP and other civil rights groups won hundreds of cases that led to the redrawing of voting districts and changes in voting systems. By the end of the century, there were nearly ten thousand black elected officials. Yet black electoral victories proved to be no panacea. Many black candidates won by playing down racial grievances, and in any case they rarely won state-wide elections. At the end of the century, Governor Douglas Wilder of Virginia (1990–1994) remained the lone elected African American governor in American history. Meanwhile, in 1994, the Supreme Court ruled in *Shaw v. Reno* that electoral districting should take no account of color, thereby ending the increase in African American officeholding. By 2000, less than 2 percent of all elected officials were African Americans.

Thus, local groups had to look beyond the ballot box to influence local decisionmaking. Social justice and human rights organizations helped. For example, ACORN's strategy was to "hear the grievances of the peo-

ple, address those grievances, and then educate to tackle the deep issues."
One African American woman in Boston, Maude Hurd, recalled the day
in 1982 when an ACORN fieldworker knocked on her door, asking Hurd
if she had any complaints about the neighborhood. Hurd did: city officials refused to clean up the debris-filled vacant lot next to her house.
The ACORN rep invited Hurd to a meeting—and asked her to chair it.
The 38-year-old was nervous. A widow with five children, she had never
been involved in community politics before. But within weeks she was
representing her neighbors in a meeting with the mayor. The trash got
cleaned up. Thirteen years later Hurd was dealing with politicians in
Congress—as president of ACORN.[83] By this time, ACORN had some
200,000 member families and had joined forces with low-income groups
around the world.

Through the networking of groups like ACORN, local campaigns regularly developed a wider influence. Major foundations took note. Between 1980 and 2000, the Ford Foundation gave $3 billion to groups like
the Desperadoes who were seeking to provide low-income housing. Social justice organizations even won concessions from the federal government. In 1986 Reagan signed legislation that enabled developers of low-
income rental housing to earn tax credits that could be sold to investors.[84] According to the National Association of Homebuilders, by the
end of the century tax credits were involved in well over 90 percent of all
affordable rental housing. In 1995 low-income groups successfully lobbied Congress to pass a strengthened Community Reinvestment Act—
ACORN arranged for activists to race in and take all the seats at the congressional hearings. The act rated banks according to the extent they met
the "convenience and needs" of low-income communities. In turn this
rating affected the government's decisionmaking on bank mergers and
new branches.[85]

In sum, the grassroots activism at the end of the century was as vibrant
as during the celebrated 1960s. Indeed, the protest bore striking similari-
ties to the Civil Rights Movement and Black Power protests. ACORN's
support for local protest continued SNCC's tradition of developing local
leadership, and the Ford Foundation's funding for local campaigns followed precedents set by philanthropic support for 1960s voter registration work previously. Some local campaigns led to important legislative
gains—just as civil rights protest won the Civil Rights Act and Voting
Rights Act. But as often as not, local movements developed in response to
the lack of action by the state—just as Black Power had done in the later
1960s. Many groups saw their own struggle for equality as part of a
global fight against racism and Western capitalism—just as Black Power
leaders had before them.

One March, Many Movements

On October 4, 1995, the former American football star, O. J. Simpson—an African American—was found not guilty of the murder of his wife, Nicole Brown Simpson—a blonde white woman. The trial revealed Simpson to be a wife-beater and the lead police investigator to be a racist. Pundits called it the trial of the century. Some 150 million Americans tuned in to hear the verdict. On campuses, white students groaned while black students celebrated. One poll found that three quarters of white respondents thought Simpson was guilty, while the same proportion of African Americans thought him innocent. Although Simpson was extremely rich and had distanced himself from civil rights issues, African American public intellectual Michael Eric Dyson reckoned that "O.J. was a term that represented every black person that ever got beat up by the criminal justice system."

Twelve days later, perhaps one in twenty adult black men joined a Million Man March in Washington, D.C. (estimates of the numbers range from 400,000 to over a million). Called by Louis Farrakhan—before the O.J. Simpson case—the march was billed as a day of atonement for black men, to take responsibility for their lives, their families, and their communities. On the platform, speakers included Christians and Muslims, celebrities and civil rights activists—even women, including Rosa Parks. On the streets, there were young and old, prosperous and poor, gay and straight. One young man from Oakland, David Muhammad, later recalled, when he "looked out into a sea of Black men . . . I knew this day would forever cause a change, if not in the world, certainly in me."[86] Over 100,000 men registered to vote on the day. Muhammad went on to start an organization helping young people after their release from jail.

For all the talk of color-blindness and movement fatigue, the response to the Simpson verdict and the sheer numbers involved in the march made it clear that race still mattered at the end of the century. Cornel West wrote in the *New York Times,* "The reason I will join the march" is to protest "the general invisibility of, and indifference to, black sadness, sorrow and social misery."[87] Surveys found that large majorities of African Americans thought American society remained unfair to black people and was unlikely to improve. In politics, over 90 percent of African Americans voted against the Republicans in congressional and presidential elections. This voting bloc was by far the most homogeneous of any ethnic or social group.[88]

Yet the media coverage of the march focused more on divisions than togetherness. Notwithstanding the presence of Parks and the promise of a follow-up Million Woman March, it was a march for men only. Marcia Gillespie, editor-in-chief of *Ms.* magazine, commented: "Black men are the leaders, and the women's place . . . is with the children, frying the chicken . . . I don't think so."[89] Many prominent African American figures criticized the march for seeking atonement rather than demanding change, or for being a high-profile moment rather than the start of a movement. The black economist Glenn Loury said caustically, "If I could get a million black men together, I wouldn't march them to Washington, I'd march them into the ghettos."[90] Some distanced themselves from Farrakhan for his occasional anti-Semitic, anti-gay, and anti-white rhetoric. The Reverend Joseph Lowery, head of the SCLC, endorsed the march but explained, "If my house is on fire, I don't care who brings the water."[91]

For those white Americans who viewed black Americans as one homogenous group, this public wrangling came as a surprise. But such disagreements were nothing new—just think of W. E. B. Du Bois, Anna Julia Cooper, and Booker T. Washington, or Martin Luther King Jr., Ella Baker, and Malcolm X. In the post–civil rights generation, African Americans continued to have a range of often-overlapping identities and goals. Making use of a detailed 1993–94 survey, the sociologist Michael Dawson calculated that among African Americans, 40 percent were disillusioned liberals, 37 percent were nationalists, 34 percent were Marxists, 19 percent were feminists, and 1 percent were conservatives (some had multiple identities). Such a diverse ideological outlook sat comfortably alongside race-consciousness. Dawson noted, "Even black conservatives put themselves in the middle of black-centered discourses."[92] The 2000 census recognized the ambiguity of the color line, asking respondents to select one *or more* racial and ethnic categories. Yet 34.7 million people identified (or in the case of minors, their parents identified) themselves as only "Black or African American," while just 1.8 million reported "Black or African American" and another category.

Even so, what was new was just how fragmented African American politics had become in the public square by the end of the century. In 1991, law professor Anita Hill accused Supreme Court Justice nominee Clarence Thomas of sexual harassment during his tenure as head of the EEOC. Some called it an unjustified slur on a successful black man. Over 1,600 women signed an advertisement in the *New York Times* defending Hill. Public wrangles over the treatment of black women were especially prominent in rap music. By the 1990s many rap videos showed the artist surrounded by gyrating, scantily dressed "nigga bitches." In the hit album *Amerikkka's Most Wanted,* when rapper Ice Cube finds out he has made the "neighborhood hussy" pregnant, he muses, "What I need to do is kick the bitch in the tummy." He doesn't, because—true to type—she turns out to be pregnant by someone else. Ice Cube maintained that such lyrics were a reaction to a crisis in masculinity. "She's bringin' home the bacon [so] the only way that you can show you're a man is through your penis."[93] Such pleas won little sympathy from black womanists; bell hooks denounced rap's "sexist, misogynist, patriarchal ways." Sheena Lester, culture editor of the LA *Sentinel,* was more down to earth: "If I'm a bitch, kiss my ass."[94]

Gender was only one prominent public division. Black conservatives called for color-blind legislation. Younger activists complained that traditional black leaders were still reliving the lunch-counter "hamburger wars" of the 1960s. Some black mayors—seeking the support of business—came into conflict with workers' groups. In many ways, the public divisions reflected the increased power of previously marginalized African American groups. Black womanists, for example, enjoyed a public voice that was unimaginable when they first started organizing in the 1970s. By the end of the century, Toni Morrison had won a Nobel Prize for literature, bell hooks was established as a public intellectual, Terry McMillan's novel *Waiting to Exhale* had sold three million copies and been turned into a movie, and Oprah Winfrey had become the highest-paid television performer. In music, Queen Latifah's 1989 platinum single "Ladies First" challenged male control of rap. In 2000, India Arie confronted rap's sexist lyrics, in her soulful, Grammy-nominated hit "Video." Flipping the music that had been sampled for rapper Akinyele's explicit "Put It In Your Mouth," Arie flipped the meaning too: "I'm not the average girl from your video / and I ain't built like a supermodel / but ... I am a queen."

Public divisions seemed set to continue into the twentieth century. Black women had joined the debate. But they were yet to end it. The scholar-activist Patricia Hill Collins warned that "coming to voice in the public sphere without coming to power in the social institutions that constitute it does little to challenge the injustices confronting African-American women as a collectivity."[95] The Clarence Thomas incident was a case in point. The furor over Hill's accusation actually worked in his favor. Given his strong opposition to affirmative action, it was by no means clear that the Democrat-controlled Senate would support him; but by claiming he was the victim of a "high-tech lynching," Thomas dared senators to risk a charge of racism. Mostly male, lily-white, and lily-livered, the senators ducked the challenge. Even in the academy, where black women made the most gains, they continued to be underrepresented at all levels. Black women historians pointed out they were vastly underrepresented in the award of prizes, too.

At the heart of public divisions was a debate over the meaning of race protest. Each group had its own agenda, but many groups sought to broaden the definition of racial equality to encompass a wide range of human rights. This was particularly true in the case of lesbian and gay African American activists. In raising the question of acceptable sexuality, they also challenged the established civil rights leadership's long-cherished commitment to traditional marriage, the nuclear family, and respectability.

During the Civil Rights Movement, influential figures such as Bayard Rustin and Aaron Henry were openly gay, but they subordinated the issue of gay rights to the quest for civil rights. Because white segregationists tried to tarnish the Civil Rights Movement with charges of homosexuality, James Farmer made sure none of the Freedom Riders were gay.[96] During the late 1980s, however, black gay activists brought the issue to prominence. In part it was because African American and gay rights movements had, respectively, put the issues of race and sexuality in the public domain. Yet neither of these movements acknowledged African American homosexual concerns. If anything, the end of the century saw a louder denunciation of the gay lifestyle from some influential African Americans. Farrakhan declared homosexuality unnatural, and rap artists declared it unmanly. To quote Ice Cube, "Real niggers ain't faggots."

It was, above all, the horror of AIDS that changed the issue from one of recognition and respect to one of life and death. The first media reports in the 1980s focused exclusively on white gay men. But the African American lesbian/gay community soon realized that AIDS was very much a black disease. By the end of the century, one in two HIV positive men was an African American, and two in every three HIV positive women were black. At the local level, AIDS support centers sprang up—often in church offices, almost always run by women volunteers. Black gay and victim support groups started lobbying for action, holding the first National Conference on AIDS in the Black Community in 1986.[97] When basketball star Earvin "Magic" Johnson announced he had HIV in November 1991, the movement gained national publicity.[98]

As with the environmental justice movement, this grassroots campaign began to influence two social movements. The white lesbian/gay movement began to share resources with African Americans, and civil rights leaders belatedly began to address the issue. In August 2000 Jesse Jackson shocked the crowd at the Black Expo in Indianapolis when he took an HIV saliva test—and urged all black men to do the same.

Yet at the close of the century, gay activists still felt they had a long way to go to win acceptance. In 2000 the campaigning journalist Earl Ofari Hutchinson wrote, "The national gay and lesbian publication, BLK, might as well gather dust in the Smithsonian Museum for all that most Blacks know or care to know of it."[99] Later that year, Coretta Scott King issued an "appeal to everyone who believes in Martin Luther King's dream to make room at the table of brotherhood and sisterhood for lesbian and gay people." But many civil rights leaders and most religious groups joined the fight against AIDS while refusing to accept the gay lifestyle. At the end of the century, polls showed a majority of African Americans opposed gay marriage. Gil Gerald, executive director of the National Coalition of Black Lesbians and Gays, even doubted the integrity of mainstream civil rights support for AIDS relief. At a meeting in 1987 at the Office of Minority Health, Gerald became "convinced they were all a homophobic bunch of people who had come to the table for money." He cried out, "Which one of you has ever held a person with AIDS in your hands, in your arms?" There was silence."[100]

"Black people face a deep crisis. Finding a way out of this mess requires new thinking, new vision, and a new spirit of resistance. We need a new movement of Black radicalism." So began a call for delegates—issued in late 1997—to an inaugural meeting of the Black Radical Congress. Earlier that year, a group of thirty-five veteran black activists had met in Chicago to plot a revival of black American left protest. They hoped to bring together a broad range of radical organizations and individuals. Hence they put out the call. "If you believe in the politics of Black liberation, join us in Chicago in June 1998 at the Black Radical Congress. If you hate what capitalism has done to our community . . . If you are fed up with the corruption of the two-party system . . . If you want to struggle against class exploitation, racism, sexism and homophobia, come to the Congress." On June 19, 1998, some two thousand people did so.

In many ways, the new movement stood in an old tradition. The date of the Chicago movement—June 19th or 'Juneteenth'—was the anniversary of the date when many slaves learned of their freedom. During the Chicago meeting, the historian-activist and co-founder of the congress, Manning Marable, invoked the long struggle for freedom. Marable compared the nascent congress "to the early development of the Congress of Racial Equality," "or the emergence . . . of the Student Non-Violent Coordinating Committee."[101] The congress's Black Freedom Agenda (the product of discussions lasting over a year) was inspired by the South African National Congress's Freedom Charter, the Black Panther Party's Ten-Point Program, and the Combahee River Collective Statement. Borrowing a slogan from student movements of yesteryear, workshop leaders at Chicago stressed the need "to struggle where you are." The purpose of the congress was to link existing struggles together—through workshops, conferences, networks, and publications. Activist-scholar and congress co-founder Barbara Ransby explained, "We will launch a campaign that will build upon work that is already going on across the country to challenge the criminalization of Black youth, police brutality and profiling and the government's virtual abandonment of public education."[102]

Yet for of all its connections with the past, the new movement was a product of the end of the twentieth century—a reaction against conservative politics and the ongoing problems faced by black Americans after the civil rights era. "Black America is in a fight for survival," asserted Marable. "We must challenge a system that places profits over the interest of the people." It was also an attempt to coordinate a movement in a generation that lacked what actor-activist Ossie Davis called a clear "moral assignment"—in the way that previous generations had squared up to slavery or Jim Crow.[103] Thus, the congress sought to take up where other recent attempts to build a radical coalition had failed—Jesse Jackson's rainbow coalition had been short-lived, while Farrakhan's coalition had excluded many people of color.

Above all, by building on "work that is already going on," the congress reflected the late-twentieth-century agendas of local activism—in all their diversity and vibrancy. The congress's Freedom Agenda called for human rights, not civil rights, for alliances among all people of color, for the end to the exploitation of all workers, for affirmative action, for gender equality, for an end to environmental racism, for an end to the two-party system, for the end of police brutality, for the right of self-determination for African Americans, for reparations for slavery and segregation, and for full acceptance for lesbian, gay, bisexual, and transgender people. The agenda placed black American rights firmly in a global perspective, too, and declared support for the liberation struggles of all oppressed people.

By crafting a broad agenda, the congress managed to bridge seemingly divergent constituencies. The initial group that conceived of the congress included democratic socialists, Marxist-Leninists, radical feminists, and left-wing trade unionists. As in previous generations, though, even the broadest organization could only include some black activists rather than all. The activist-scholar Ron Walters believed he had been excluded from leadership in the congress because he was a progressive rather than a radical—he had worked with Jesse Jackson, Democratic leaders, and the traditional civil rights organizations. So he decided not to attend the Chicago meeting. Still, he added, "I will be rooting for them."[104] His concern was not the congress's politics but its viability. "We need some serious opposition to the conservative policies and practices fostered by the politics of the Right Wing. But, the challenge of the Congress is whether they will do a better job of confronting it than other Black leadership formations are currently doing."

Of course, there was plenty of other "work that was already going on" outside the remit of the congress. Ahead of the Chicago meeting, Walters had hosted two hundred local organizers representing networks such as ACORN and National Welfare Rights. In August in Philadelphia, the National Urban League held its annual conference. Like the Black Radical Congress, the Urban League made economic injustice a top priority—the theme of the conference was "Economic Power: Leveling the Playing Field." Unlike the congress, the league believed the solution could be found within the capitalist system. As the CEO of the Chicago League, James Compton, put it, "African Americans must pursue economic power—the endgame in a capitalist democracy."[105] In October, the Congressional Black Caucus reported on a meeting with President Clinton in which they applauded his "Mend It Not End It" approach to affirmative action, called for the provision of free needles for drug users to combat the spread of AIDS, and urged Congress to use "the left-over surplus at the end of the fiscal year . . . to guarantee that there will be money" for after-school programs for inner-city youth and to resolve the social security crisis.[106]

Thus, far from declining, African American struggles for meaningful freedom continued in force at the end of the twentieth century. In the end, the so-called Reagan revolution turned out to be anything but on the question of race—the Reagan administration did not consistently seek to reverse the legislative gains of the 1960s and 1970s, and where it did it often found it lacked the power to do so. Community groups continued the fight to make rights real, and hitherto marginalized African American groups were able to assert their own agendas. The fact they still had to do so, with such urgency, showed the enormity of the problems and the barriers that many African Americans still faced. The fact that they did so, in such numbers and with some success, also showed just how much some African Americans had already achieved.

It would be little surprise, then, that such struggles would continue, and develop, into the twenty-first century. What would be a surprise, though, was the extent to which the question of racial equality would return to such prominence in mainstream American society. The devastation wrought by a fearsome hurricane and the election of America's first African American president would see to that.

27. Activist Johnnie Tillmon, president of the National Welfare Rights Organization from 1973, was an outspoken advocate of an adequate income for unemployed black mothers. (Moorland-Spingarn Research Library)

28. During his eight years in office, President Ronald Reagan met with the Congressional Black Caucus on only one occasion, February 3, 1981. (National Archives and Records Administration)

29. Emelda West (center), a resident of Louisiana's "cancer alley" and leader in the fight against toxic dumping, traveled to Tokyo in 1998 to press her case in person to the directors of a multinational company. (Courtesy of Elaine Osowski)

30. Bari Ellen Roberts was the lead plaintiff in a class-action suit charging Texaco with discrimination. Her victory in 1996 led to the biggest discrimination payout in corporate history and highlighted the problem of the "glass ceiling" faced by African Americans in private-sector employment. (Ted Thai/Time& Life Pictures/Getty Images)

31. Coretta Scott King—pictured here in 1983 with Gil Gerard (left), executive director of the National Coalition of Black Lesbians and Gays—was one of the first leaders of the 1960s Civil Rights Movement to embrace lesbian and gay rights. (Courtesy of Joan E. Biren)

32. Many of Kerry James Marshall's early paintings, such as this view of Altgeld Gardens (untitled, 1995), focused on the Civil Rights Movement and African American urban life. (Courtesy of the Artist and Jack Shainman Gallery, New York)

33. In Marshall's later work, such as the rococo-style *Study for Vignette* (2006),
he inserted black figures into genres that have historically been lily-white.
(Courtesy of the Artist and Jack Shainman Gallery, New York)

34. In the years following the devastation of New Orleans by Hurricane Katrina, black residents demanded the right to shape the rebuilding of the city. (Mario Tama/Getty Images News)

35. The swearing-in of Barack Obama as America's 44th President was watched by his wife, Michelle, daughters Malia and Sasha, and a record-setting crowd of nearly two million people. (Jason Reed/Reuters/Corbis)

Epilogue

"Is There Still a Reason to March in the 21st Century?" Question posed in the *Pittsburgh Courier,* the most widely read black newspaper for much of the twentieth century.[1]

Early in July 2006 hundreds of security officers, most of them African American, marched through downtown Los Angeles. They demanded better wages and the right to join a union. Nearly 70 percent of security officers in the county lived below the poverty line. The march was supported by the NAACP, SCLC, Nation of Islam, US, ACORN, religious groups, Gangsters for Christ, and many other local organizations. State Assembly member Jerome Horton, who joined the march, said, "Not since the civil rights movement has this community come together so strongly to fight racist policies."[2]

On May 16, 2006, Congresswoman Barbara Lee, chair of the Congressional Black Caucus, and six other Caucus members, were arrested outside the Sudanese embassy. They demanded more American action to stop genocide and support refugees in Darfur.[3]

In 2007 African American artist Kerry James Marshall received an unprecedented second invitation to Germany's prestigious twice-a-decade Documenta exhibition of leading artists, following a highly successful major solo show of his work that toured America. One prominent critic asked, "Can an artist get much more successful?"[4] Born in Birmingham, Alabama, in 1955, raised in Watts from 1963, and an avid student of earlier black artists, Marshall hoped his portrayal of unequivocally, emphatically black figures in his paintings would "reclaim the images of blackness as an emblem of power, instead of an image of derision."[5]

In the case *Pigford v. Glickman* (1999), groups of African American farmers won the largest civil rights settlement in U.S. history, after the United States Department of Agriculture admitted denying loans to black farmers in previous decades. Yet by 2008 more than 81,000 farmers had still not received compensation. To force the issue, campaigners marched outside USDA offices, even occupied USDA offices, lobbied politicians, and filed for damages.[6]

On August 29, 2005, Hurricane Katrina hit the continental United States with winds as strong as 140 mph and waves as high as 27 feet. One million Gulf Coast residents fled their homes; 1,836 people died. In New Orleans, the rising waters breached nearly every levee. As a city panicked, the waters came after everyone, regardless of color, and flooded 80 percent of homes. But not everyone had the same chance to escape. One in three black households had no access to a car, compared with one in six white households.[7] Three days after the storm, thousands fled on foot across one of the few secure bridges out of the city, to the suburban town of Gretna. Almost all in the crowd were African Americans. The mayor of New Orleans had promised that buses would be waiting for them across the bridge. But there were not nearly enough buses. County police, some firing shots in the air, turned the crowd back.

Most of those who died in the rising waters were elderly, trapped in care homes—as many white as black. But the watching world saw mostly black bodies floating in the streets, and mostly black families huddled on roof tops, under bridges, and later packed in the Louisiana Superdome under the supervision of the National Guard. Katrina's devastation, its disproportionate racial impact, and the temporary restriction of some twenty thousand displaced African Americans under armed guard called to mind the Mississippi flood of 1927. So too did some of the personal stories. The testimony of Pamela Mahogany, a middle-aged black nurse who lived in Saint Bernard Housing Development, was a twenty-first-century version of Richard Wright's "Down by the Riverside" from *Uncle Tom's Children*. As the waters rose, Mahogany and her son escaped—as had Wright's protagonist in Mississippi—in a stolen boat. Wright's family ended up in a relief camp among suspicious U.S. soldiers. In the Superdome, the "Army Corps, or whoever they was, only thing they did was stood at attention with rifles pointed at us," complained Mahogany. "I think I cried the whole three days I was in there," and was not allowed to leave. "It was just horrible . . . It was like we was dogs or something."[8]

Unlike black prisoners in the 1927 flood, though, Mahogany and her family were soon evacuated to Texas, where they received a warm welcome. Times had changed: New Orleans had a black mayor, and the federal relief effort did not rank victims on account of color. Barack Obama, the lone African American senator, quipped, "This administration was colorblind in its incompetence."[9] What Katrina did show, though, was the continued breadth of racial divisions in the United States at the start of the millennium. Polls found that three quarters of black Americans thought the government would have responded faster to white victims— and three quarters of white Americans disagreed. Above all, Katrina exposed the prevalence of inner-city black deprivation. Or as Obama put it, "The poverty and the hopelessness were there long before the hurricane. All the hurricane did was to pull the curtain back for all the world to see."[10]

What the world saw was the intersection of poverty, race, ethnicity, and gender in the twenty-first-century American city. It was mostly poor black women and their children who had to flee the housing projects— and it would be mostly Hispanic immigrant men who would be brought in to rebuild the city, often without contracts or protection. Seventeen days after the levees broke, President George W. Bush visited New Orleans and acknowledged in a prime-time speech that, as "all of us saw on television, there's . . . some deep, persistent poverty in this region," with "roots in a history of racial discrimination, which cut off generations from the opportunity of America."[11]

The world looked away soon afterward. Critics charged Bush with only mentioning domestic poverty six times during the following year.[12] But the problems persisted and in many ways got worse. "There is not a sign outside of New Orleans saying 'If you are poor, sick, elderly, disabled, a child or African-American, you cannot return,'" said William Quigley, professor of law at Loyola University in New Orleans and a Katrina evacuee. "But there might as well be."[13] A year after the flood, African Americans represented just one fifth of those who had returned to the New Orleans metro area—down from over a third of the population before Katrina struck.[14] In a widely reported remark, U.S. Congressman Richard Baker of Louisiana enthused, "We finally cleaned up public housing in New Orleans. We couldn't do it, but God did."[15] Citing the national emergency, the Department of Labor suspended Executive Order 11246 (signed by Lyndon Johnson and defended by activists during the Reagan presidency), which would have required all federally funded contractors to implement affirmative action policies in hiring workers to rebuild the city.

What the world didn't see, though, was the work of black activists before, during, and especially after the flood. Stephen Bradberry, a 45-year-old ACORN organizer for some nine thousand families in the city, reckoned that "this is the largest and most significant organizing opportunity this generation could ever hope to face."[16] It was an organizing opportunity reminiscent of the civil rights era—and some of the language used made the connection explicit. Common Ground Collective, founded in the wake of the storm by former Black Panther Malik Rahim, called its campaign to bring in student volunteers to help rebuild the city the "Second Freedom Rides."[17] In fact, it was more like a second Freedom Summer, as tens of thousands of volunteers came down to join a network of human rights organizations, including Bradberry's Katrina Survivors Association.[18]

The first battles were simply for survival. For example, Bradberry and fellow organizers sent hundreds of text messages via cell phone to thousands of families to direct them to emergency help and places to stay. Then came the battle to vote, to work, or to receive unemployment relief while evacuated. Jesse Jackson and Bill Cosby led a march across the bridge to Gretna in 2006, calling for satellite voting stations (away from New Orleans) for evacuees, and citing the recent precedent of such voting stations in Iraq, supervised by American soldiers.[19] They didn't get them. On the day of the 2008 presidential election, ACORN bused evacuees back to the city to vote. Last, and most important of all, was the battle to return and to have a say and a share in the rebuilding of the city. In many ways this was an age-old struggle—to live in environmentally safe areas, with decent schools, jobs, and housing. Activists used age-old tactics, too: lobbying local government, working with allies in Congress, scrutinizing the decisions of the relevant federal agencies, working through the courts, prodding public opinion, and pooling economic resources. Activists also used the tried and tested method of campaigning on the streets. In early January 2006, a coalition of local groups organized an emergency demonstration to block the demolition of the Lower Ninth Ward, home to Mahogany and other poor African Americans. Campaigners then won a settlement requiring city officials to notify those residents whose homes were targeted for demolition, so that homeowners would have a chance to fight the decision.[20]

The struggle to reshape the rebuilding of New Orleans was just one example of the continued work of black activists across a whole host of diverse issues as the new century began: from black janitors in Los Angeles trying to form a union to black politicians drawing attention to Darfur; from black artists promoting the black image on canvas to black farmers suing the U.S. Department of Agriculture. Some of their tools of protest were new. The Internet enabled activists to form global networks and spread information quickly, and to act independently of established organizations—though even the venerable NAACP took advantage of the Internet to add 100,000 online non-dues-paying members to its estimated roster of 300,000 members.[21] Some of the issues also seemed new. Following mass marches by Hispanics in 2006—now the majority minority group in America—black leaders had to take a stand on the question of illegal immigration.[22] But most protest stood in an organizing tradition that dated back generations, where activists sought to build a better world, and when necessary to challenge those who interfered. One of the most prominent campaigns—a call for reparations following the United Nations' 2001 condemnation of slavery as a crime against humanity— echoed the very first request of freedmen for forty acres and a mule after emancipation.[23] The question of how to relate to immigrant groups had a long, often fraught, history, too.

On November 16, 2005, at a ceremony on Capitol Hill, Stephen Bradberry became the first African American recipient of the Robert F. Kennedy Human Rights Award. "You deserve this day in the sun," Senator Barack Obama told him. Bradberry wasn't so sure. "I certainly don't consider the things I do to be anything extraordinary," he replied, echoing the sentiments of countless activists down the years. "It's just a matter of putting on my pants and going to work every day."[24]

Less than two months after Katrina struck, Rosa Parks died, aged 92. Her body lay in state in the Capitol Rotunda—the first woman, and the first person never to have been a government official, to be honored in this way. Her seven-hour funeral provided an opportunity to celebrate the victories of the Civil Rights Movement and the sacrifices of many that led to those victories. Barack Obama, one of many who spoke in eulogy, believed that "Parks embodied all those countless small acts of courage and determination and kindness that make a path through hardship and tragedy and make a way out of no way." Obama acknowledged "that I would not be here today [as a senator] were it not for this small woman, who lies before us."[25]

But away from the funeral, with bodies still being discovered in New Orleans, black leaders delivered plenty of critiques of twenty-first-century America alongside the nostalgia for times past. After all, Katrina had exposed structural inequalities to be a more deadly foe than prejudice or discrimination. The problem in New Orleans had not been where to sit on the bus; it had been a lack of buses and cars to help the urban black poor escape. While Parks' body lay in the Capitol, T. J. Crawford, the 29-year-old chairman of the National Hip-Hop Political Convention, told reporters, "Today you can eat at a lunch counter but you can't get an education that allows you to go to the next level."[26] There were even critiques of previous protest amid the praise for Parks. Van Jones, a 37-year-old environmental and civil rights activist who co-founded the influential campaigning website Color of Change in response to Katrina, complained that elder statesmen from the Civil Rights Movement had not made room for younger leaders with new ideas. "The older generation did not realize fast enough that it wasn't going to fix all the problems."[27]

Obama agreed. In his book *The Audacity of Hope,* which served to outline his political philosophy ahead of his presidential campaign, he cautioned against becoming "entombed in nostalgia" when "reminiscing about past victories."[28] Such divided assessments of the place of black Americans in the United States—the recognition both of past progress and present problems—echoed the views of African Americans in every generation since slavery. As a former slave put it in a prayer often quoted by subsequent black leaders, including Booker T. Washington and Martin Luther King: "We ain't what we ought to be, We ain't what we want to be, but thank God Almighty, we ain't what we used to be." Obama's verdict, nearly a century and a half later, was essentially the same. "I have witnessed a profound shift in race relations in my lifetime," Obama wrote in *The Audacity of Hope.* "I have felt it as surely as one feels a change in the temperature. But as much as I insist that things have gotten better, I am mindful of this truth as well: Better isn't good enough."[29]

On January 20, 2009, Barack Obama was sworn in as the forty-fourth president of the United States. The chosen theme for the Inauguration, "A new birth of freedom" (a phrase taken from Lincoln's Gettysburg address), seemed entirely fitting. Nearly 150 years before, Frederick Douglass, the first black marshal of Washington, D.C., was also the first marshal not to be invited to receptions in the White House, on account of his color. A century before, Booker T. Washington's dinner at the White House with President Roosevelt had provoked outrage. Nearly fifty years before, at the Lincoln Memorial, Martin Luther King had spoken of his dream of equality to a quarter of a million people. At the same event, student leader John Lewis had asked "which side is the federal government on?" Traditionally, the only black face in what some had called the Lily White House had belonged to the butler. Now, at the Lincoln Memorial, in front of a million people, with John Lewis among the assembled dignitaries, Barack Obama became the first African American president of the United States.

Obama's inauguration team chose to draw some explicit connections with the long freedom struggle. Many of the approximately three hundred surviving Tuskegee airmen marched in the Inauguration parade. Aretha Franklin, who had sung at rallies with Martin Luther King, sang "My Country 'Tis of Thee." The Reverend Joseph Lowery, a former president of the SCLC, gave the benediction, starting with the final verse of "Lift Every Voice and Sing," the historic Negro National Anthem. But it seemed as though fate had decided to make those connections even more poignant. The year 2009 was the bicentenary of Lincoln's birth, and Lincoln, like Obama, had come to the White House as a lawyer turned politician from Illinois. Inauguration eve fell on the annual Martin Luther King national holiday. The campaign trail, too, had taken Obama on a historic freedom tour. Early in the primaries, he joined a commemorative march in Selma; and as chance would have it, the first presidential debate was held at Ole Miss, scene of a deadly riot in 1962 when James Meredith, the first black student, was admitted on campus. (True to form, the idiosyncratic Meredith declined to attend the debate and made it clear he was not an Obama supporter.) Meanwhile, Obama's campaign message of hope for a "More Perfect Union" echoed not just the dream of the nation's founders but Martin Luther King's dream that "one day this nation will rise up and live out the true meaning of its creed."[30] And like King, Obama showed a rare talent for speaking his vision.

Yet during the campaign, Obama steadfastly rejected the mantle of civil rights leadership. He thought there was no movement left to lead. While a student at Columbia University, Obama heard an elderly Kwame Touré (formerly Stokely Carmichael) speak, and he concluded that Touré was out of date. "The movement had died years ago, shattered into a thousand fragments. Every path to change was well trodden, every strategy exhausted."[31] Obama rebuffed, too, presumptions that he was a new spokesman for black America. Indeed, Obama questioned whether there should, or could, be such a politician in the new century. "I reject a politics that is based solely on racial identity . . . or victimhood generally."[32] In turn, established black leaders such as John Lewis and Jesse Jackson did not initially endorse him (though virtually all black political leaders swung behind his candidacy once it gathered momentum). Many of Obama's greatest campaigning qualities—his steady demeanor, telegenic smile, appeal to the young, use of technology, adroit selection of (many white) advisers, and call for the kind of change that fit the mood of 2008—transcended race. When he did address race, Obama acknowledged white grievances as well as black grievances, and he balanced calls for society to take more responsibility for the disadvantaged with calls for deprived black American communities to take more responsibility for themselves. In a Father's Day sermon he chided too many black men for "acting like boys" in a generation where more than half of black children grew up in single-parent households.[33]

Instead, Obama spoke of a postracial America, one which he embodied himself, because he couldn't "even hold up my experience as being somehow representative of the black American experience."[34] He had a white mother from Kansas and a Kenyan father who had come from Africa to America on a student visa rather than a slave ship. Obama was born in Hawaii, raised for a time in Indonesia, and lived in relative material comfort. He attended college in California and New York, worked as a community organizer in Chicago, and studied law in Cambridge, becoming the first black president of the prestigious *Harvard Law Review*. His white grandparents, and then white tutors, were formative influences every bit as much as his African family or black faculty members. After Harvard he returned to Chicago, where he taught law at the University of Chicago Law School, worked as a civil rights lawyer, and served in the state legislature. In 2005 he was sworn in as U.S. senator from Illinois— only the third popularly elected African American senator in U.S. history.

Despite his unusual postracial story, though, Obama's autobiography, *Dreams from My Father,* related experiences that did, in fact, resonate with the testimonies of countless African Americans down the years. He wrote of his childhood frustration at the whiteness of popular culture, "that there was nobody like me in the Sears, Roebuck Christmas catalog . . . and that Santa was a white man." He could remember the moment when the force of the race problem first hit home, like an "ambush attack"—when he saw a story in *Life* magazine about the side-effects of skin bleacher. He knew the awkwardness of entering a mostly white school, when children sniggered over his name. He also shared a heritage of black pride. His white mother raised him on recordings of Martin Luther King's speeches and Mahalia Jackson's songs, on stories of Thurgood Marshall and Fannie Lou Hamer, and on the belief that "to be black was to be the beneficiary of a great inheritance, a special destiny, glorious burdens that only we were strong enough to bear."[35]

Though disavowing race leadership, Obama's story also overlapped with the experiences of celebrated black leaders. His childhood work routine while in Indonesia would have impressed Booker T. Washington. Because she couldn't afford to send him to school with other expats, his mother woke him each morning at 4 a.m. for three hours of English lessons, to make sure he would have the "life chances of an American." (When the young Barack complained, his mother would say, "This is no picnic for me either, buster.") His work among Chicago's poor called to mind Ida B. Wells, his legal training followed Thurgood Marshall, while his white lineage meant he shared Walter White's predicament of being able to "slip back and forth between my black and white worlds." Like Du Bois, Obama wrestled with his dual identity as a black man and an American, and like Du Bois, he often hovered above both worlds as he sought to resolve this dilemma. As a young man he found intellectual solace in Malcolm X's writings, shared Malcolm's loneliness at living in a white home, and identified with his anger at (to quote Obama) "always playing on the white man's court." At age twenty-one, living on the edge of Harlem, he would laugh when his roommate shouted "Scoop the poop, you bastards!" at the "white people from the better neighborhoods" who walked "their dogs down our block to let the animals shit on our curbs."[36] In the end, though, Obama judged black nationalism to be nothing more than "a cathartic curse on the white man." He believed "my identity might begin with the fact of my race, but it didn't, couldn't, end there."[37]

Above all, it was Obama's three-year stint as a community organizer on the South Side of Chicago during 1985–1988 that put him in step with black activists across the country. Obama and his colleagues worked with church leaders to improve schools, with ACORN to register voters, and with residents of a housing project to win funds for the removal of asbestos—the sort of unheralded campaigns that had been the hallmark of protest since the headline grabbing demonstrations of the civil rights decade. Indeed, Obama embraced his place in this organizing tradition. Back when he was preparing to graduate from Columbia, romantic images of the Civil Rights Movement—of students sitting at a lunch counter or canvassing on a Mississippi porch or singing freedom songs in prison—"became a form of prayer for me, bolstering my spirits, channeling my emotions in a way that words never could." He resolved to build up the Civil Rights Movement's "large" dream of a beloved community of "black, white and brown." In so doing, he hoped to earn his own place in that community. "It was a promise of redemption."[38]

Obama's work as a community organizer also led him to the same conclusions reached by so many activists before him about what made protest work. In his judgment, effective protest was dependent on activists having sufficient power to force change. "The problems facing inner-city communities," he wrote in an essay reflecting on his organizing experience in Chicago, "do not result from a lack of effective solutions, but from a lack of power to implement these solutions."[39]

How to achieve that power was a question that Obama pondered. While a community organizer, he recognized that, "as strained as race relations were, the success of the civil rights movement had at least created some overlap between communities, more room to maneuver for people like me."[40] But he saw limits in the judicial approach. "One of the tragedies of the civil rights movement," he argued in his 2001 campaign for state senator, was that it "became so court focused" and thus tended "to lose track of the political and community organizing and activities on the ground."[41] Nor did he believe (in what would have been a surprise to his most fevered supporters in 2008) that "charismatic leaders" "can knit together . . . diverse interests." Rather, Obama thought that the "only way for communities to build long-term power is by organizing people and money around a common vision," thus creating the "coalitions of powers through which you bring about redistributive change."[42] Less than a decade after his community work, though, Obama turned to what he called the "major arena of power," electoral politics.[43] According to one colleague, Obama "said you can only go so far in organizing. You help people get some solutions, but it's never as big as wiping away problems."[44]

When he ran for president, Obama's pledge to "wipe away the problems" characteristically balanced a recognition of the particular difficulties facing black Americans mired in urban poverty with a determination to remove the more general roadblocks confronting all disadvantaged Americans, irrespective of color. For example, he advocated affirmative action programs (structured to help qualified minorities without "diminishing opportunities for white students") as well as "strategies that help all Americans . . . schools that teach, jobs that pay, health care for everyone who needs it."[45] Obama's even-handed message—that a rising tide of opportunity would gradually lift all minority boats—fit his philosophy of social progress, his pragmatism, and his pressing political need to balance the demands of different constituencies. And it was a message that allowed Obama not just to tiptoe around the perils of racial politics but to prosper from the widespread hope that he just might resolve them.

Obama's victory seemed to mark the final defeat of the power of white supremacist sentiment. "This is the meaning of our liberty and our creed," he exulted in his Inaugural speech: "Why a man whose father less than sixty years ago might not have been served at a local restaurant can now stand before you to take a most sacred oath."[46] At every turn during the election, there were symbolic reversals from days past. Alabama Democrats who had backed George Wallace's segregationist candidacy in 1964 now backed Obama in the Democratic primary. There were no demonstrations at the Ole Miss debate, where Obama required no more security than his Republican opponent, the white Vietnam War hero John

McCain.[47] At that debate (indeed, in all the debates) there was not a single question asked about race. Obama's campaign was only briefly derailed when video footage surfaced showing his Chicago pastor, Jeremiah Wright, denouncing white Americans. Obama gave a well-received speech on race and later left Wright's church.

On election day, Obama's color cost him the support of some white voters, but it helped him gain others.[48] In fact, Obama gained more white voters—and most likely more blue-collar white voters—in the presidential election than had the previous Democratic candidate, John Kerry (though some political scientists speculated that, because of the Bush administration's unpopularity, Obama would have won an even greater majority if he had been white).[49] Obama also gained 95 percent of the black vote (up from 88 percent in 2004), and two million more black Americans voted than in the previous election. For the first time in U.S. history, younger black voters turned out in greater proportions than younger white voters, and black women were the most likely to vote of any racial, ethnic, and gender group.[50] Such influential black voting stood in stark contrast with the controversial election of 2000, in which George W. Bush's defeat of Vice President Al Gore was decided by a razor-thin majority in Florida. That election was described by Florida NAACP president Adora Obi Nweze as "illegal, immoral and undemocratic," on account of the disproportionate effect on black Americans of the state's decision to disqualify convicted felons from voting, not to mention the haphazard imposition of this disqualification, the high proportion of discounted ballots in some urban precincts, and a divisive Supreme Court decision to abort a recount.[51]

There were symbolic turnarounds on race matters beyond the presidential election, too. Four months after the Inauguration, and nearly fifty years after the murder of three civil rights workers there, the small white-majority town of Philadelphia, Mississippi, elected its first black mayor. The victor, Pentecostal minister and hospital worker James A. Young, hailed "an atomic bomb of change."[52] Retired school principal Dorothy Webb, a white woman, hoped the result would "erase the thought that we're just a Southern racist town."[53] The election followed the 2005 conviction of former Klansman Edgar Ray Killen for masterminding the murders—some four decades after an all-white jury had found him not guilty of civil rights violations. The new majority-white jury sentenced him to sixty years in prison. Even so, black residents complained that Killen was found guilty of manslaughter rather than murder. Fannie Lee Chaney, mother of one of the victims, was underwhelmed by the outcome. "Mighty long time," she told reporters. There were many other killers, but "most of them dead about now."[54]

Obama's victory prompted a surge in black optimism about race relations. Four months into the presidency, nearly two thirds of black respondents believed race relations were generally good—a startling jump from less than a third a year before. An even higher proportion of white respondents agreed, though that proportion had been high for many years.[55] The performance of the first black president clearly had the potential to change racial attitudes further. At a White House correspondents' dinner three months into his presidency, for example, the African American comedienne Wanda Sykes teased Obama about what was at stake. "I'm proud to be able to say the 'first black President'—that's unless you screw up and then it's going to be, 'What's up with the half white guy? . . . Who voted for that mulatto?'"[56] Michelle Obama, the first black first lady, commanded attention, and approval too. Writing in the *Nation*, Patricia Collins thought Michelle Obama provided an answer to Collins' longstanding question of lament: Where "is a picture of black femininity (in particular, that of darker-skinned, nontragic femininity) that might signify beauty, chic, elegance, vulnerability, sophistication?"[57]

Barack Obama himself, though, did not expect his victory to mark anything more than a small step forward in race relations. He was somewhat steeled to the euphoria, having previously attributed the "burst of publicity" surrounding his presidency of the *Harvard Law Review* to "America's hunger for any optimistic sign from the racial front—a morsel of proof that, after all, some progress has been made."[58] He warned reporters then, "It's important that stories like mine aren't used to say that everything is O.K. for blacks."[59] In 2008, during his landmark campaign speech on race, he insisted, "I have never been so naive as to believe that we can get beyond our racial divisions in a single election cycle, or with a single candidacy."[60] Two months after his inauguration, Obama reckoned that the "justifiable pride" Americans had taken in electing an African American president had only "lasted about a day. And right now, the American people are judging me exactly the way I should be judged, and that is, are we taking steps . . . to create jobs . . . and keep America safe?"[61]

Obama recognized, too, that racial divisions were not so much a consequence of attitudes—though clearly racial sentiment still remained an issue in politics; his ascent to the presidency left behind a Senate with not one African American member, and only one state, Massachusetts, had an elected African American governor. Rather, the problem of race in the

twenty-first century remained the embedded gap between black (and Latino) Americans and white Americans on virtually every socioeconomic
indicator, from incarceration and unemployment rates to home ownership and educational achievements. The optimism Americans felt on the
racial front after the election should have been tempered by (though it
may have been a salve for) the memory of the floods in New Orleans—
the first issue Obama spoke out on after arriving in the Senate. At the
dawn of the twenty-first century, Katrina's devastation and Obama's victory represented both the pain and the promise of race in America.

Notes

Prologue

1. R. J. M. Blackett, *Beating against the Barriers: Biographical Essays in Nineteenth-Century Afro-American History* (Baton Rouge, 1986), 325.

2. Martin Luther King, *A Call to Conscience: The Landmark Speeches of Dr. Martin Luther King, Jr,* ed. Clayborne Carson and Kris Shepard (London, 2001), 81–87; "The Story of the 'Planter,'" *Christian Union,* May 1, 1872, 377.

3. Beth T. Bates, "'Double V for Victory' Mobilizes Black Detroit, 1941–1946," in *Freedom North: Black Freedom Struggles Outside the South, 1940–1980,* ed. Jeanne Theoharis and Komozi Woodard, 17–39 (New York, 2002), 18.

4. James Forman, *The Making of Black Revolutionaries* (Washington, DC, 1985), 513.

5. Zora Neale Hurston, *Dust Tracks on a Road: An Autobiography* (Urbana, 1984), 268.

6. W. E. B. Du Bois, "Strivings of the Negro People," *Atlantic Monthly* 80 (August 1897): 194.

7. Herbert Aptheker, *A Documentary History of the Negro People in the United States,* vol. 2 (New York, 1969), 615.

8. *Congressional Record,* 56th Cong., 2nd sess., vol. XXXIV, part 2 (Washington, DC, 1901), 1636.

9. William Henry Chafe, *The Unfinished Journey: America since World War Two* (New York, 1986), 161.

10. Peter B. Levy, *Civil War on Race Street: The Civil Rights Movement in Cambridge, Maryland* (Gainesville, 2003).

11. Ralph Ellison, *Shadow and Act* (New York, 1964), 315.

12. Nell Irvin Painter, *Exodusters: Black Migration to Kansas after Reconstruction* (New York, 1976), 28.

13. J. Saunders Redding, "A Negro Looks at This War," *American Mercury* (November 1942), 426.

14. David L. Chappell, *A Stone of Hope: Prophetic Religion and the Death of Jim Crow* (Chapel Hill, 2004), 71.

15. D. Michael Cheers, "Nelson Mandela: A Special Message to Black Americans," *Ebony* 45 (May 1990): 179, 180.

16. "Survey of Intelligence Materials Supplement to Survey No. 25, Bureau of Intelligence," OWI, July 14, 1942, 10, RG208, E87, Box 582, National Archives, College Park.

17. Sterling Allen Brown, *Sterling A. Brown's A Negro Looks at the South,* ed. John Edgar Tidwell and Mark A. Sanders (New York, 2006), 322.

18. Thomas Sugrue, *The Origins of the Urban Crisis: Race and Inequality in Postwar Detroit* (Princeton, 2005).

19. Louis E. Martin, "Dope and Data," *Chicago Defender,* February 16, 1957, 10.

1. The Freedom War, 1861–1865

1. Tera W. Hunter, *To 'Joy My Freedom: Southern Black Women's Lives and Labors after the Civil War* (Cambridge, 1997), 107.

2. "Negro Loyalty: A Bold Feat," *Circular,* May 22, 1862, 11; *Crisis* 56 (April 1949): 106–107; "Course and Events," *New York Evangelist,* May 22, 1862, 25; "The Steamer 'Planter' and Her Captor," *Harper's Weekly,* June 16, 1862, 372.

3. Nell Irvin Painter, *Sojourner Truth: A Life, a Symbol* (New York, 1996), 179.

4. Ira Berlin, Barbara J. Fields, Thavolia Glymph, Joseph P. Reidy, and Leslie F. Rowland, eds., *The Destruction of Slavery,* vol. 1, *Freedom: A Documentary History of Emancipation, 1861–1867* (Cambridge, 1985), 384.

5. Herbert Aptheker, *A Documentary History of the Negro People in the United States,* vol. 1 (New York, 1951), 525.

6. "Rejoicings over the Proclamation," *Independent,* January 8, 1863; "Emancipation Day in Boston," January 16, 1863.

7. Henry McNeal Turner, *The Negro in Slavery, War and Peace, by Bishop H. M. Turner, Dr. Charles W. Eliot [and] Rev. W. Spencer Carpenter* (Philadelphia, 1913), 5–6.

8. Quintard Taylor, *In Search of the Racial Frontier: African Americans in the American West, 1528–1990* (New York, 1998), 93.

9. Mitchell A. Kachun, *Festivals of Freedom: Memory and Meaning in African American Emancipation Celebrations, 1808–1915* (Amherst, 2003), 104, 107, 108.

10. "Riot in New York," *Christian Advocate,* July 23, 1863, 236. "Horrible and Barbarous," *Liberator,* July 31, 1863, 33.

11. Larry E. Nelson, "Black Leaders and the Presidential Election of 1864," *Journal of Negro History* 63 (January 1978): 47.

12. Frederick Douglass, *My Bondage and My Freedom* (New York, 1855), 445.

13. "Massachusetts Anti-Slavery Society," *Liberator,* February 10, 1865, 1.

14. Anonymous black writer, January 9, 1864, in Michael Vorenberg, *Final Freedom: The Civil War, the Abolition of Slavery, and the Thirteenth Amendment* (Cambridge, 2001), 81.

15. Malcolm Edwards, "The War of Complexional Distinction: Blacks in Gold Rush California and British Columbia," *California Historical Quarterly* 56 (Spring 1977): 34–45.

16. "Refuge of Oppression," from the *Harrisburg Keystone,* reproduced in *Liberator,* November 17, 1837; "The Convention: Negro Voters," *Doylestown Democrat,* reproduced in *Liberator,* September 1, 1837.

17. "Appeal of Forty Thousand," *Liberator,* April 13, 1838, 1.

18. *Political Debates Between Hon. Abraham Lincoln and Hon. Stephen A. Douglas, in the Celebrated Campaign in 1858, in Illinois* (Columbus, 1860), 241; George M. Fredrickson, "A Man but Not a Brother: Abraham Lincoln and Racial Equality," *Journal of Southern History* 41 (February 1975): 55.

19. Ira Berlin, *Slaves No More: Three Essays on Emancipation and the Civil War* (Cambridge, 1992), 12.

20. "Letter from the Negro Robert Smalls," *Liberator,* September 12, 1862, 148.

21. Leon F. Litwack, *Been in the Storm So Long: The Aftermath of Slavery* (New York, 1979), 130.

22. "Notes on Military and Naval Affairs," *Scientific American,* May 31, 1862, 338; David S. Cecelski, *The Waterman's Song: Slavery and Freedom in Maritime North Carolina* (Chapel Hill, 2001), 186.

23. Edward L. Pierce, "The Contrabands at Fortress Monroe," *Atlantic Monthly,* November 1861, 626–640; Hunter, *To 'Joy My Freedom,* 16.

24. Ira Berlin, "Who Freed the Slaves? Emancipation and Its Meaning," in *Union & Emancipation: Essays on Politics and Race in the Civil War Era,* ed. David W. Blight and Brooks D. Simpson (Kent, OH, 1997), 112–113.

25. Edward A. Miller, *Gullah Statesman: Robert Smalls from Slavery to Congress, 1839–1915* (Columbia, SC, 1995), 9.

26. "The Steamer 'Planter' and Her Captor," *Harper's Weekly,* June 14, 1862, p. 372; "The Steamer Planter," *New York Times,* August 15, 1862, p. 2.

27. "The Civil War in America," *London Times,* June 23, 1862, 9.

28. Litwack, *Been in the Storm,* 51.

29. "Course of Events," *New York Evangelist,* May 22, 1862, 4. "The Slave—The Freeman," *The Independent,* August 20, 1863, 4.

30. "A Freedman's First Act," *Liberator,* May 16, 1862, 32; "Army Correspondence," *Maine Farmer,* June 5, 1862, 30.

31. "Congress," *New York Times,* 1862, 4.

32. Richard Carwardine, *Lincoln* (Harlow, England, 2003), 225.

33. Howard Jones, *Union in Peril: The Crisis over British Intervention in the Civil War* (Chapel Hill, 1992).

34. Aptheker, *Documentary History,* 1:511–513.

35. Frank A. Rollin, *Life and Public Services of Martin R. Delany* (Boston, 1883), 163–171.

36. Litwack, *Been in the Storm,* 80.

37. David S. Cecelski, "Abraham H. Galloway: Wilmington's Lost Prophet and the Rise of Black Radicalism in the American South," in *Democracy Betrayed: The Wilmington Race Riot of 1898 and Its Legacy,* ed. David S. Cecelski and Timothy B. Tyson, 43–72 (Chapel Hill, 1998), quotation from 44–46.

38. Dora Costa and Matthew Kahn, "Forging a New Identity: The Costs and Benefits of Diversity in Civil War Combat Units for Black Slaves and Freemen," *Journal of Economic History* 66, (December 2006), 936–962; George C. Wright, *Life Behind the Veil: Blacks in Louisville, Kentucky, 1865–1930* (Baton Rouge, 1985), 17.

39. Bruce C. Levine, *Confederate Emancipation: Southern Plans to Free and Arm Slaves during the Civil War* (New York, 2006), 82.

40. Ibid., 16.

41. Eric Foner, *Reconstruction: America's Unfinished Revolution, 1863–1877* (New York, 1988), 72.

42. Litwack, *Been in the Storm,* 96.

43. Vorenberg, *Final Freedom,* 80.

44. "Speech of Hon. Morrow B. Lowry, of Erie, Colored People in Passenger Cars," *Liberator,* February 3, 1865, 1. Miller, *Gullah Statesman,* 23.

45. Leslie A. Schwalm, "'Overrun with Free Negroes': Emancipation and Wartime Migration in the Upper Midwest," *Civil War History* 50 (June 2004): 160.

46. David A. Gerber, *Black Ohio and the Color Line, 1860–1915* (Urbana, 1976), 27–28. "The Riot in Buffalo," *New York Times,* July 10, 1863, 8; "The Riot in Detroit," *Christian Inquirer,* March 14, 1863, 2; "History of the Three Days riot in New York, hunting Negroes," *New York Evangelist,* July 23, 1863, 4.

47. "An Official Report from General Banks: Operations to May 30—The Valor of Negro Troops Indorsed," *New York Times,* June 11, 1863, 8; "Speech of Gen. Schenok," *Liberator,* September 1, 1865, 1.

48. George M. Fredrickson, *The Black Image in the White Mind: The Debate on Afro-American Character and Destiny, 1817–1914* (Middletown, CT, 1987), 169. "Senator Sherman on Suffrage," *Liberator,* June 23, 1865, 1.

49. See also Thomas Wentworth Higginson, *The Writings of Thomas Wentworth Higginson* (Cambridge, 1900), 39.

50. "Miscegenation," *American Monthly Knickerbocker,* April 1864, 63; "The Union of Races," *Independent,* February 25, 1864, 16.

51. Painter, *Sojourner Truth,* 211.

52. Taylor, *In Search,* 94.

53. "Letter from Sojourner Truth," *Liberator,* December 23, 1864, 206; Painter, *Sojourner Truth,* 205.

54. "Speech of Hon. Morrow B. Lowry," 1; "Suffrage in the Free States," *Lib-*

erator, August 25, 1865, 1. "The Freedmen of the Mississippi Valley," *Liberator,* December 11, 1863, 199; Painter, *Sojourner Truth,* 184–185.

55. Edward Magdol and Edward M. Stoeber, "Martin R. Delany Counsels Freedmen, July 23, 1865," *Journal of Negro History* 56 (October 1971): 308.

56. Painter, *Sojourner Truth,* 215.

57. Eric Foner, "The Meaning of Freedom in the Age of Emancipation," *Journal of American History* 81 (September 1994): 458.

58. "The Freedmen of South Carolina," *Friends' Review,* May 9, 1863, 570; Berlin, *Slaves No More,* 155.

59. "Freedmen in Savannah," *Christian Advocate and Journal,* February 23, 1865, 60; "Frederick Douglass on President Lincoln," *Liberator,* September 16, 1864, 151.

60. Berlin, *Slaves No More,* 138.

61. Cecelski, "Abraham H. Galloway," 54.

62. Hunter, *To 'Joy My Freedom,* 20.

63. Ibid., 5, 19.

64. William Edward Farrison, *William Wells Brown: Author and Reformer* (Chicago, 1969), 391–393.

65. Vorenberg, *Final Freedom,* 157.

66. Aptheker, *Documentary History,* 1:511–528.

67. "Letter from North Carolina," *Zion's Herald and Wesleyan Journal* 36 (January 11, 1865), 1.

68. Noralee Frankel, "Breaking the Chains: 1860–1880," in *To Make Our World Anew: A History of African Americans to 1880,* ed. Robin D. G. Kelley and Earl Lewis, 227–280 (New York, 2000), 234.

69. Frederick Douglass, *The Frederick Douglass Papers,* vol. 3: 1855–1863, ed. John W. Blassingame and John R. McKivigan (New Haven, 1979), 204.

70. Aptheker, *Documentary History,* 1:550.

71. "The Slave—The Freeman," *Independent,* August 20, 1863, 15.

72. Richard Paul Fuke, "Blacks, Whites, and Guns: Interracial Violence in Post-Emancipation Maryland," *Maryland Historical Magazine* 92 (Fall 1997): 328.

2. Freedom Is Not Enough, 1865–1877

1. "A Freedman to His Old Master," *Christian Advocate and Journal,* September 7, 1865, 286; *Liberator,* September 1, 1865, 140.

2. Sally Dixon, 1938, in *The American Slave: A Composite Autobiography: Supplement,* ed. George P. Rawick, Jan Hillegas, and Ken Lawrence, ser. 1, vol. 7 (Westport, CT, 1977), 629.

3. Richard Paul Fuke, "Blacks, Whites, and Guns: Interracial Violence in Post-Emancipation Maryland," *Maryland Historical Magazine* 92 (Fall 1997): 329.

4. "The Jubilee Singers in England," *New York Evangelist* 44 (August 7, 1873), 4.

5. "Mr. Garrison at Fort Sumter," *Liberator* 35 (April 14, 1865), 58; "The Cer-

emony at Fort Sumter," *New York Evangelist* 36 (April 20, 1865), 1; "Fort Sumter," *New York Observer and Chronicle* 43 (April 20, 1865), 127; "The Old Flag at Sumter," *Liberator* 35 (April 21, 1865), 62.

6. Douglas R. Egerton, *He Shall Go Out Free: The Lives of Denmark Vesey* (Madison, 1999), xxiii–xxiv.

7. Shane White and Graham J. White, *Stylin': African American Expressive Culture from Its Beginnings to the Zoot Suit* (Ithaca, NY, 1998), 127.

8. "The Cradle of Treason," *Independent*, May 4, 1865, 1.

9. "A Trip to Fort Sumter, and the Doomed City," *New York Evangelist* 36 (April 27, 1865), 1.

10. Alan Farmer, *Reconstruction and the Results of the American Civil War 1865–1877* (London, 1997), 29.

11. Philip Sheldon Foner, *History of Black Americans* (Westport, CT, 1975), 449.

12. Leon F. Litwack, *Been in the Storm So Long: The Aftermath of Slavery* (New York, 1979), 257.

13. George M. Fredrickson, *The Black Image in the White Mind: The Debate on Afro-American Character and Destiny, 1817–1914* (Middletown, CT, 1987), 178.

14. Leslie A. Schwalm, "'Sweet Dreams of Freedom': Freedwomen's Reconstruction of Life and Labor in Lowcountry South Carolina," *Journal of Women's History* 9 (Spring 1997): 9.

15. Henry Latham, *Black and White: A Journal of a Three Month's Tour in the United States* (London, 1867), 140. James Cobb, *The Most Southern Place on Earth: The Mississippi Delta and the Roots of Regional Identity* (New York, 1994), 42.

16. Hunter, *To 'Joy My Freedom*, 1.

17. Litwack, *Been in the Storm*, 39, 233.

18. Laura F. Edwards, "The Politics of Marriage and Households in North Carolina During Reconstruction," in *Jumpin' Jim Crow: Southern Politics from Civil War to Civil Rights,* ed. Jane Elizabeth Dailey, Glenda Elizabeth Gilmore, and Bryant Simon, 7–27 (Princeton, 2000), 14.

19. Sharon Ann Holt, "Making Freedom Pay: Freedpeople Working for Themselves, North Carolina, 1865–1900," *Journal of Southern History* 60 (May 1994): 252.

20. Adam Fairclough, *Teaching Equality: Black Schools in the Age of Jim Crow* (Athens, GA, 2001), 4.

21. Laura F. Edwards, *Gendered Strife & Confusion: The Political Culture of Reconstruction* (Urbana, 1997), 317n20.

22. "The Freedmen's Celebration in Richmond," *The Independent*, April 12, 1866, 4: Elsa Barkley Brown, "Mapping the Terrain of Black Richmond," *Journal of Urban History* 21 (March 1995): 296–346, 305.

23. Frederick Douglass, "What to the Slave Is the Fourth of July? An Address Delivered in Rochester, New York, on 5 July 1852," in *The Frederick Douglass Papers,* vol. 2, ed. John W. Blassingame and John R. McKivigan, 359–388 (New Haven, 1979), 368.

24. "The Revolt in Jamaica," *New York Times,* November 17, 1865, 5.

25. "About Negro Insurrections," *Liberator,* December 15, 1865, 1; Julie Saville, *The Work of Reconstruction: From Slave to Wage Laborer in South Carolina, 1860–1870* (Cambridge, 1994), 148–149.

26. Kenneth Goings and Gerald Smith, "'Unhidden Transcripts': Memphis and African American Agency, 1862–1920," *Journal of Urban History* 21 (March 1995), 372–394, 378.

27. Litwack, *Been in the Storm,* 224.

28. Michael W. Fitzgerald, *Urban Emancipation: Popular Politics in Reconstruction Mobile, 1860–1890* (Baton Rouge, 2002), 23.

29. Ira Berlin, *Slaves No More: Three Essays on Emancipation and the Civil War* (Cambridge, 1992), 143.

30. "Anti-Slavery Celebration at Framingham," *Liberator,* July 14, 1865, 112. LaWanda C. Fenlason Cox, *Lincoln and Black Freedom: A Study in Presidential Leadership* (Columbia, SC, 1981), 148–149.

31. "Interview with President Andrew Johnson," and "Reply of the Colored Delegation to the President," both in Frederick Douglass, *The Life and Writings of Frederick Douglass,* vol. 4, ed. Philip Sheldon Foner (New York, 1950), 182–191, 191–193.

32. "South Carolina and Her New Slave Code," *New York Evangelist,* November 16, 1865, 1; Michael W. Fitzgerald, *Splendid Failure: Postwar Reconstruction in the American South* (Chicago, 2007), 33. "Designs of the Democratic Party," *Liberator,* October 6, 1865, 158.

33. William Richter, "'Oh God, Let Us Have Revenge': Ben Griffith and His Family During the Civil War and Reconstruction," *Arkansas Historical Quarterly* 62 (Autumn 1998): 255–286.

34. Quintard Taylor, *In Search of the Racial Frontier: African Americans in the American West, 1528–1990* (New York, 1998), 111.

35. Foner, *Reconstruction,* 215.

36. Schwalm, "Sweet Dreams," 15–17.

37. Lee W. Formwalt, "The Origins of African-American Politics in Southwest Georgia: A Case Study of Black Political Organization during Presidential Reconstruction, 1865–1867," *Journal of Negro History* 77 (Autumn 1992): 215.

38. Eric Foner, "Reconstruction and the Crisis of Free Labor," in *Major Problems in the Civil War and Reconstruction,* ed. Michael Perman, 458–473 (Lexington, MA, 1991), 459. Donald Shaffer, *After the Glory: The Struggles of Black Civil War Veterans* (Lawrence, KS, 2004), 32; "Southern Opinion of the Negro," *Friends' Review,* September 2, 1865, 13.

39. Schwalm, "Sweet Dreams," 19.

40. Ibid., 21.

41. "The Memphis Massacre," *The Independent,* May 17, 1866, 4; "The Horrors of Memphis," *The Independent,* May 31, 1866, 2.

42. Hamilton W. Pierson, *A Letter to Hon. Charles Sumner: With "Statements" of Outrages Upon Freedmen in Georgia, and an Account of My Expulsion from Andersonville, Ga., by the Ku-Klux Klan* (Washington, DC, 1870).

43. "Inauguration of Douglass Institute," *Liberator,* October 13, 1865, 162.

44. Fuke, "Blacks, Whites, and Guns," 338, 340–341.

45. "The Late Isaac Myers," *African Methodist Episcopal Church Review* 7 (April 1891), 356.

46. Fuke, "Blacks, Whites, and Guns."

47. Ena Farley, *The Underside of Reconstruction New York: The Struggle over the Issue of Black Equality* (New York, 1993), 4.

48. David A. Gerber, *Black Ohio and the Color Line, 1860–1915* (Urbana, 1976), 37.

49. Leslie H. Fishel, Jr., "Northern Prejudice and Negro Suffrage 1865–1870," *Journal of Negro History* 39 (January 1954): 8–26.

50. Eugene H. Berwanger, "Reconstruction on the Frontier: The Equal Rights Struggle in Colorado," in *African Americans on the Western Frontier,* ed. Monroe Lee Billington and Roger D. Hardaway, 37–53 (Niwot, CO, 1998).

51. Paul Buhle and Mari Jo Buhle, eds., *The Concise History of Woman Suffrage: Selections from History of Woman Suffrage* (Urbana, 2005), 240.

52. Foner, *Reconstruction,* 314.

53. Herbert Aptheker, *A Documentary History of the Negro People in the United States,* vol. 2 (New York, 1969), 615.

54. "Button on the Black Man," *New York Times,* August 9, 1865, 4. Gerber, *Black Ohio,* 38–39.

55. "Current Events," *New York Evangelist,* January 28, 1869, 4; David M. Katzman, *Before the Ghetto: Black Detroit in the Nineteenth Century* (Urbana, 1973), 3–4.

56. Taylor, *In Search,* 114–117.

57. Farley, *Underside of Reconstruction,* 89n37.

58. Ibid., 73–74.

59. Leslie H. Fishel, Jr., "The Negro in Northern Politics, 1870–1900," *Mississippi Valley Historical Review* 42 (December 1955): 466–489.

60. David M. Katzman, *Before the Ghetto: Black Detroit in the Nineteenth Century* (Urbana, 1973), 87–90.

61. "Naked Labor Congress," *New York Observer and Chronicle,* August 16, 1869, 270. Philip Sheldon Foner, *Organized Labor and the Black Worker, 1619–1973* (New York, 1974), 25.

62. Foner, *Organized Labor,* 17; "The National Labor Convention of Colored Men," *The Independent,* December 16, 1869, 1.

63. Stephen Ward Angell, *Bishop Henry McNeal Turner and African-American Religion in the South* (Knoxville, 1992).

64. "Editorial Notes," *The Independent,* October 8, 1868, 4; Angell, *Turner,* 91; "Affairs in Georgia," *New York Times,* July 26, 1869, 5.

65. Michael W. Fitzgerald, *The Union League Movement in the Deep South: Politics and Agricultural Change During Reconstruction* (Baton Rouge, 1990), 492.

66. John Rodrigue, "Labor Militancy and Black Grassroots Political Mobilization in the Louisiana Sugar Region, 1865–1868," *Journal of Southern History* 67 (February 2001): 126.

67. Fitzgerald, *Union League,* 495.

68. Foner, *Reconstruction,* 426, 496.

69. "Editorial," *Christian Advocate,* March 26, 1874, 100; Steven Hahn, *A Nation under Our Feet: Black Political Struggles in the Rural South, from Slavery to the Great Migration* (Cambridge, 2003), 219.

70. Fitzgerald, *Splendid Failure,* 158.

71. Fitzgerald, *Urban Emancipation.*

72. "How the Colored Members of Congress Look," *Zion's Herald (1868–1910);* May 16, 1872, 235; Fitzgerald, *Splendid Failure,* 155.

73. "South Carolina," *Old and New,* May 1870, 5; Foner, *Reconstruction,* 404.

74. Holt, "Making Freedom Pay," 246.

75. Loren Schweninger, *Black Property Owners in the South, 1790–1915* (Urbana, 1990), 161.

76. Adam Fairclough, *A Class of Their Own: Black Teachers in the Segregated South* (Cambridge, 2006), 51.

77. Elsa Barkley Brown, "Negotiating and Transforming the Public Sphere: African American Political Life in the Transition from Slavery to Freedom," in *Jumpin' Jim Crow: Southern Politics from Civil War to Civil Rights,* ed. Jane Elizabeth Dailey, Glenda Elizabeth Gilmore, and Bryant Simon (Princeton, 2000), 37–39.

78. James Oliver Horton and Lois E. Horton, *Hard Road to Freedom: The Story of African America* (New Brunswick, NJ, 2001), 190.

79. Hahn, *A Nation,* 172.

80. Barry A. Crouch, "The 'Chords of Love': Legalizing Black Marital and Family Rights in Postwar Texas," *Journal of Negro History* 79 (Autumn 1994): 343.

81. Karin L. Zipf, *Labor of Innocents: Forced Apprenticeship in North Carolina, 1715–1919* (Baton Rouge, 2005).

82. "Art. vi: The Negro," *Methodist Quarterly Review* 27 (January 1875), 79.

83. Sven Beckert, "Democracy in the Age of Capital: Contesting Suffrage Rights in Gilded Age New York," in *The Democratic Experiment: New Directions in American Political History,* ed. Meg Jacobs, William J. Novak, and Julian E. Zelizer, 146–174 (Princeton, 2003), 163.

84. Farley, *Underside of Reconstruction,* 85.

85. Stephen D. Engle, "Mountaineer Reconstruction: Blacks in the Political Reconstruction of West Virginia," *Journal of Negro History* 78 (Summer 1993): 154.

86. "Liberty Strangled in the South," *New York Times,* October 3, 1876, 4; "The Rifle Clubs 'Dividing Time'," *New York Times,* October 20, 1876, 1; "South Carolina Chivalry," *New York Times,* January 16, 1877, 2; Brian Kelly, "Black Laborers, the Republican Party, and the Crisis of Reconstruction in Lowcountry South Carolina," *International Review of Social History* 51 (December 2006): 375–414.

87. David W. Blight, *Frederick Douglass' Civil War: Keeping Faith in Jubilee* (Baton Rouge, 1989), 197.

88. Kelly, "Black Laborers," 410, 411.

89. Foner, *Reconstruction,* 582.

90. Kelly, "Black Laborers," 412.

91. "Duties and Destiny of the Negro Race," *African Repository* 49 (September 1873), 282.

92. McFeely, *Frederick Douglass,* 295.

93. "The Jubilee Singers," *Christian Advocate,* January 11, 1872, 12. Andrew Ward, *Dark Midnight When I Rise: The Story of the Jubilee Singers, Who Introduced the World to the Music of Black America* (New York, 2000), 136.

94. "The Jubilee Singers," *London Times,* May 7, 1873, 5.

95. "Jubilee Songs," *New York Evangelist,* April 4, 1872, 43.

96. "Foreign," *Christian Union,* December 17, 1878, 8. "The Jubilee Singers in England," *Independent,* June 5, 1873, 709; "Mr. Gladstone and the Jubilee Singers," *Independent,* August 21, 1873, 1036.

3. Resisting the Juggernaut of White Supremacy, 1878–1906

1. Edward L. Ayers, *The Promise of the New South: Life after Reconstruction* (New York, 1992), 256.

2. Stephen Tuck and Desmond King, "De-Centring the South: America's Nationwide White Supremacist Order after Reconstruction," *Past and Present* 194 (February 2007): 227.

3. "The Anti-Lynching Committee," *London Times,* November 9, 1894, 15.

4. Alessandra Lorini, *Rituals of Race: American Public Culture and the Search for Racial Democracy* (Charlottesville, 1999), 79.

5. "Negroes Mutiny in Jail," *New York Times,* September 25, 1906, 1.

6. Letter from Shreveport, Louisiana, August 31, 1877, reproduced in "A Great Movement," *The African Repository* 53 (October 1877), 114.

7. *Charleston News,* April 16, 1878, reproduced in "The New Liberia Movement," *New York Times,* April 19, 1878, 2.

8. "The Negro Emigrants," *New York Observer and Chronicle* 56 (July 18, 1878), 229.

9. George B. Tindall, "The Liberian Exodus of 1878," *South Carolina Historical Magazine* 53 (July 1952): 144.

10. "Leaving Misery Behind," *New York Times,* April 7, 1879, 1.

11. Rebecca Basko, "The Exoduster Experience: During and after the Migration," *Journal of Mississippi History* 59 (Summer 1997): 143.

12. *Charleston News,* April 16, 1878, in "The New Liberia Movement."

13. Nell Irvin Painter, *Sojourner Truth: A Life, a Symbol* (New York, 1996), 247.

14. "An Exodus," *Friends' Intelligencer* 38 (January 21, 1882), 780.

15. William Cohen, *At Freedom's Edge: Black Mobility and the Southern White Quest for Racial Control, 1861–1915* (Baton Rouge, 1991), xvi; Jacqueline Jones, "Southern Diaspora: Origins of the Northern Underclass," in *The "Underclass" Debate: Views from History,* ed. Michael B. Katz, 27–54 (Princeton, 1993), 42.

16. Athens (Ga.) *Banner,* in "Why Negroes Flock to the Towns," *New York Times,* January 27, 1887, 3.

17. Charleston (S.C.) *News and Courier,* December 31, 1881.

18. "The South Carolina Exodus," *New York Times,* December 22, 1886, 3.

19. Nell Irvin Painter, *Exodusters: Black Migration to Kansas after Reconstruction* (New York, 1976), 180–182.

20. Tera W. Hunter, *To 'Joy My Freedom: Southern Black Women's Lives and Labors after the Civil War* (Cambridge, 1997), 77–79, 92.

21. Stephen Kantrowitz, *Ben Tillman & the Reconstruction of White Supremacy* (Chapel Hill, 2000), 96–97.

22. Natchez *Democrat,* December 21, 1886.

23. Daniel Letwin, "Interracial Unionism, Gender, and 'Social Equality' in the Alabama Coalfields, 1878–1908," *Journal of Southern History* 61 (August 1995): 519.

24. "Politics in Tennessee," *New York Times,* July 6, 1882, 3.

25. J. Morgan Kousser, *The Shaping of Southern Politics: Suffrage Restriction and the Establishment of the One-Party South, 1880–1910* (New Haven, 1974), 27.

26. Jane Elizabeth Dailey, *Before Jim Crow: The Politics of Race in Postemancipation Virginia* (Chapel Hill, 2000), 66–68, 76.

27. John C. Rodrigue, "Labor Militancy and Black Grassroots Political Mobilization in the Louisiana Sugar Region, 1865–1868," *Journal of Southern History* 67 (February 2001): 115–142, 140.

28. Dennis C. Rousey, "Yellow Fever and Black Policemen in Memphis: A Post-Reconstruction Anomaly," *Journal of Southern History* 51 (August 1985): 357–374.

29. Hunter, *To 'Joy My Freedom,* 92.

30. Theodore L. Cuyler, "Our Contributors: Meanings of the Negro Exodus," *New York Evangelist* 50 (April 24, 1879), 1.

31. "The Colour Conflict Again Threatens," *London Times,* May 19, 1879, 11.

32. James G. Blaine, et al., "Ought the Negro to Be Disfranchised? Ought He to Have Been Enfranchised?" *North American Review* 128 (January/June 1879): 225–283, 231.

33. Richard Franklin Bensel, *The Political Economy of American Industrialization, 1877–1900* (Cambridge, 2000), 171.

34. Richard Valelly, "National Parties and Racial Disfranchisement," in *Classifying by Race,* ed. Paul E. Peterson, 188–216 (Princeton, 1995), 200.

35. Kenneth O'Reilly, *Nixon's Piano: Presidents and Racial Politics from Washington to Clinton* (New York, 1995), 54–57.

36. *Civil Rights Cases* 109 U.S. 3 (1883).

37. Elizabeth Dale, "'Social Equality Does Not Exist among Themselves, nor among Us': *Baylies vs. Curry* and Civil Rights in Chicago, 1888," *American Historical Review* 102 (April 1997): 323.

38. Bess Beatty, *A Revolution Gone Backward: The Black Response to National Politics, 1876–1896* (New York, 1987), 57; John Dittmer, "The Education of Henry McNeal Turner," in *Black Leaders of the Nineteenth Century,* ed. Leon F. Litwack and August Meier, 253–274 (Urbana, 1988), 265.

39. Dailey, *Before Jim Crow,* 116.

40. Kousser, *Shaping of Southern Politics.*

41. Kevin Kelly Gaines, *Uplifting the Race: Black Leadership, Politics, and Culture in the Twentieth Century* (Chapel Hill, 1996), 23.

42. Mary Ellen Curtin, *Black Prisoners and Their World, Alabama, 1865–1900* (Charlottesville, 2000), 55.

43. George Campbell, *White and Black: The Outcome of a Visit to the United States* (London, 1879), 365; Cohen, *At Freedom's Edge*, 226–227.

44. Cohen, *At Freedom's Edge*, 206.

45. Michael Perman, *Struggle for Mastery: Disfranchisement in the South, 1888–1908* (Chapel Hill, 2001), 38.

46. Emma Lou Thornbrough, "The National Afro-American League, 1887–1908," *Journal of Southern History* 27 (November 1961): 495–496.

47. "Fortune's Speed: Founding Convention of Afro-American League, 1890," in *A Documentary History of the Negro People of the United States*, vol. 1, ed. Herbert Aptheker (New York, 1951), 704–705.

48. "Race Riot on West Side," *New York Times*, August 16, 1900, 1.

49. Michael L. Goldstein, "Preface to the Rise of Booker T. Washington: A View from New York City of the Demise of Independent Black Politics, 1889–1902," *Journal of Negro History* 62 (January 1977): 91.

50. Citizens' Protective League, *Story of the Riot* (New York, 1900), 2, 8, 70.

51. "Police in Control in Riotous District," *New York Times*, August 17, 1900, 2.

52. "Akron's riot," *Zion's Herald (1868–1910)*; August 29, 1900, 1091; William English Walling, "The Race War in the North," *The Independent*, September 3, 1908, 529; Roger Lane, *Roots of Violence in Black Philadelphia, 1860–1900* (Cambridge, 1986), 18.

53. Ida B. Wells-Barnett, "Lynch Law in America," *Arena* 23 (January–June 1900), 3; S. Laing Williams, "Frederick Douglass at Springfield, Mo.," *African Methodist Episcopal Church Review* 23 (1906), 9. The data on lynching are drawn from the NAACP's records, later published in NAACP, *Thirty Years of Lynching in the United States, 1889–1918* (New York, 1919). The data on populations are taken from the United States Bureau of the Census, *Historical Statistics of the United States: Colonial Times to 1970*, vol. 1 (Washington, DC, 1975). The relevant tables are Series A 23, "Annual Estimates of the Population by Sex and Race, 1900–1970," 9; Series A 172–94, "Population of Regions, by Sex, Race, Residence, Age, and Nativity," 22–37.

54. "Race in Education," *New York Times*, January 16, 1890, 4; W. E. B. Du Bois, "The Black North," published weekly in *New York Times*, November 17 to December 15, 1901.

55. Randy Roberts, *Papa Jack: Jack Johnson and the Era of White Hopes* (New York, 1983), 19; Tuck, "De-Centring the South."

56. Sarah-Jane (Saje) Mathieu, "North of the Colour Line: Sleeping Car Porters and the Battle against Jim Crow on Canadian Rails, 1880–1920," *Labour/Le Travail* 47 (Spring 2001): 9–42.

57. Mrs. Jefferson Davis, "The White Man's Problem: Why We Do Not Want the Philippines," *Arena* 23 (January–June 1900), 3; Eric Tyrone Lowery Love, *Race over Empire: Racism and U.S. Imperialism, 1865–1900* (Chapel Hill, 2004).

58. Lorini, *Rituals of Race*, 31; David W. Blight, *Race and Reunion: The Civil War in American Memory* (Cambridge, 2001).

59. "The Future of the Negro," *Congregationalist and Christian World*, February 21, 1903, 264. Kenneth Kiple and Virginia Kiple, "The African Connection: Slavery, Disease and Racism," *Phylon* 41 (3rd Quarter 1980), 211–222; George M. Fredrickson, *The Black Image in the White Mind: The Debate on Afro-American Character and Destiny, 1817–1914* (Middletown, CT, 1987).

60. James H. Dormon, "Shaping the Popular Image of Post-Reconstruction American Blacks: The 'Coon Song' Phenomenon of the Gilded Age," *American Quarterly* 40 (December 1988): 453, 458.

61. Alexander Keyssar, *The Right to Vote: The Contested History of Democracy in the United States* (New York, 2000), 120–122; Kousser, *Shaping of Southern Politics*, 57.

62. "The Strike at Omaha," *New York Times*, May 22, 1880, 2.

63. Albert S. Broussard, *African-American Odyssey: The Stewarts, 1853–1963* (Lawrence, KS, 1998), 52; Dale, "'Social Equality.'"

64. "Colored Pupils Made a Rush," *Washington Post*, October 12, 1897, 1.

65. Percy E. Murray, "Harry C. Smith–Joseph B. Foraker Alliance: Coalition Politics in Ohio," *Journal of Negro History* 68 (Spring 1983): 172; David M. Katzman, *Before the Ghetto: Black Detroit in the Nineteenth Century* (Urbana, 1973), 193–200.

66. David A. Gerber, *Black Ohio and the Color Line, 1860–1915* (Urbana, 1976), 228–229.

67. Ibid., 235–240.

68. Davison Douglass, *Jim Crow Moves North: The Battle over Northern School Segregation, 1865–1954* (New York, 2005), 117–122.

69. Emma Lou Thornbrough, *The Negro in Indiana: A Study of a Minority* (Indianapolis, 1957), 5.

70. Robert A. Campbell, "Blacks and the Coal Mines of Western Washington, 1888–1896," in *African Americans on the Western Frontier*, ed. Monroe Lee Billington and Roger D. Hardaway, 92–109 (Niwot, CO, 2001), 101.

71. Ronald L. Lewis, "Job Control and Race Relations in Coal Fields, 1870–1920," *Journal of Ethnic Studies* 12 (Winter 1985): 48.

72. Broussard, *African-American Odyssey*, 52; Dale, "'Social Equality.'"

73. Joe William Trotter, Jr., "Blacks in the Urban North: The 'Underclass Question' in Historical Perspective," in *The "Underclass" Debate: Views from History*, ed. Michael B. Katz, 55–84 (Princeton, 1993), 61.

74. Sundiata Keita Cha-Jua, *America's First Black Town: Brooklyn, Illinois, 1830–1915* (Urbana, 2000), 16.

75. Mark R. Schneider, *Boston Confronts Jim Crow, 1890–1920* (Boston, 1997), 32.

76. Canter Brown, *Florida's Black Public Officials, 1867–1924* (Tuscaloosa, 1998), 65.

77. *Southwestern Christian Advocate*, reproduced in *Independent* 39, December 8, 1887, 12.

78. "Patrolled by Vigilants," *New York Times*, November 21, 1887, 5.

79. John C. Rodrigue, *Reconstruction in the Cane Fields: From Slavery to*

Free Labor in Louisiana's Sugar Parishes, 1862–1880 (Baton Rouge, 2001), 183–188.

80. Fon Louise Gordon, *Caste and Class: The Black Experience in Arkansas, 1880–1920* (Athens, GA, 1995), 29; Kousser, *Shaping.*

81. Lewis, "Job Control," 248.

82. William F. Holmes, "The Demise of the Colored Farmers' Alliance," *Journal of Southern History* 41 (May 1975): 191.

83. Daniel Letwin, *The Challenge of Interracial Unionism: Alabama Coal Miners, 1878–1921* (Chapel Hill, 1998), 80.

84. Lewis, "Job Control," 246.

85. Steven Hahn, *A Nation under Our Feet: Black Political Struggles in the Rural South, from Slavery to the Great Migration* (Cambridge, 2003), 432; Curtin, *Black Prisoners,* 169.

86. Patrick Dickson, "A Brief History of the Colored Farmer's Alliance through 1891," www.kalamumagazine.com (accessed January 2006), 2, 8.

87. M. Langley Biegert, "Legacy of Resistance: Uncovering the History of Collective Action by Black Agricultural Workers in Central East Arkansas from the 1860s to the 1930s," *Journal of Social History* 32 (Autumn 1988): 73–99.

88. Lawrence C. Goodwyn, "Popular Dreams and Negro Rights: Fort Texas as a Case Study," *American Historical Review* 76 (December 1971): 1135–1171.

89. Edward A. Miller, *Gullah Statesman: Robert Smalls from Slavery to Congress, 1839–1915* (Columbia, SC, 1995), 229.

90. *Congressional Record,* 56th Cong., 2nd sess., vol. XXXIV, part 2 (Washington, DC, 1901), 1636.

91. Loren Schweninger, *Black Property Owners in the South, 1790–1915* (Urbana, 1990), 176.

92. *Congressional Record,* 1368. Allison Dorsey, *To Build Our Lives Together: Community Formation in Black Atlanta, 1875–1906* (Athens, GA, 2004), 1638.

93. William F. Holmes, "Whitecapping: Agrarian Violence in Mississippi, 1902–1906," *Journal of Southern History* 35 (May 1969): 168.

94. Dorsey, *To Build Our Lives,* 159.

95. Kantrowitz, *Ben Tillman.*

96. Glenda E. Gilmore, "Murder, Memory, and the Flight of the Incubus," in *Democracy Betrayed: The Wilmington Race Riot of 1898 and Its Legacy,* ed. David S. Cecelski and Timothy B. Tyson, 73–93 (Chapel Hill, 1998), 83.

97. Frederick Douglass, "Lynch Law in the South," *North American Review* 155 (July 1892): 17–24.

98. Gordon, *Caste and Class,* 18.

99. Joel Chandler Harris, *Life of Henry W. Grady: Including His Writings and Speeches* (New York, 1890), 100; William Dorsey Jelks, Ex-Governor of Alabama, "The Acuteness of the Negro Question: A Suggested Remedy," *The North American Review,* February 15, 1907, 389.

100. "John Temple Graves, Editor of the Daily Atlanta Georgian, Discusses Cause and Effects of Riot," *Washington Post,* September 24, 1906, 1; Dorsey, *To Build Our Lives,* 160.

101. "Atlanta and Its Warnings," *Life* 48 (November 8, 1906), 538.

102. A. J. McKelway, "The Atlanta Riots: A Southern White Point of View," *Outlook* 84 (November 3, 1906): 562.

103. "Whites and Negroes Killed at Atlanta," *New York Times,* September 25, 1906, 1.

104. W. Fitzhugh Brundage, *Lynching in the New South: Georgia and Virginia, 1880–1930* (Urbana, 1993), 133–135.

105. Albert C. Smith, "'Southern Violence' Reconsidered: Arson as Protest in Black-Belt Georgia, 1865–1910," *Journal of Southern History* 51 (November 1985): 546.

106. Catherine A. Barnes, *Journey from Jim Crow: The Desegregation of Southern Transit* (New York, 1983), 11.

107. J. Morgan Kousser, *Dead End: The Development of Nineteenth-Century Litigation on Racial Discrimination in Schools* (Oxford, 1986), 5; Perman, *Struggle for Mastery,* 249; Gordon, *Caste and Class,* 58.

108. Barnes, *Journey from Jim Crow,* 11.

109. Stephen Tuck, "Democratization and the Disfranchisement of African Americans in the U.S. South during the Late Nineteenth Century," *Democratization* 14 (August 2001): 580–602.

110. Miller, *Gullah Statesman,* 214.

111. McKelway, "Atlanta Riots," 558.

112. Paula Giddings, *When and Where I Enter: The Impact of Black Women on Race and Sex in America* (New York, 2001), 21, 24.

113. Gail Bederman, *Manliness & Civilization: A Cultural History of Gender and Race in the United States, 1880–1917* (Chicago, 1995), 59; Ralph Luker, *The Social Gospel in Black and White: American Racial Reform, 1885–1912* (Chapel Hill, 1991), 96–97.

114. "As to Ida B. Wells," *Washington Post,* August 2, 1894, 4.

115. "Lynching in America," *London Times,* October 6, 1897, 7, Vron Ware, *Beyond the Pale: White Women, Racism and History* (London, 1992), 208.

116. Ray Stannard Baker, *Following the Colour Line: An Account of Negro Citizenship in the American Democracy* (London, 1908), 18.

4. Black Leaders Reckon with Jim Crow, 1893–1916

1. William Edward Burghardt Du Bois and Isabel Eaton, *The Philadelphia Negro: A Social Study* (Philadelphia, 1899), 310.

2. Victoria W. Wolcott, "'Bible, Bath, and Broom': Nannie Helen Burroughs's National Training School and African-American Racial Uplift," *Journal of Women's History* 9 (Spring 1997): 88.

3. David Kenneth Wiggins and Patrick B. Miller, *The Unlevel Playing Field: A Documentary History of the African American Experience in Sport* (Urbana, 2003), 73.

4. Letter from Secretary McAdoo to F. I. Cobb, editor of the *World,* November 26, 1914, in Woodrow Wilson, *The Papers of Woodrow Wilson,* ed. Arthur Stanley Link, vol. 29 (Princeton, 1966), 261 (emphasis in original).

5. "Atlanta Exposition Address," Atlanta, Ga., September 18, 1895, in Booker

T. Washington, *The Booker T. Washington Papers,* ed. Louis R. Harlan and Raymond Smock, 14 vols. (Urbana, 1972), 3:583–587; "Quite as Profitable, Anyhow," *Boston Transcript,* quoted in *New York Times,* September 28, 1895, 7.

6. "South's New Epoch," *New York World,* September 18, 1895, in ibid., 4:9.

7. *Boston Transcript,* in ibid., 1:80.

8. Louis R. Harlan, *Booker T. Washington: The Making of a Black Leader, 1856–1901* (New York, 1972), 227.

9. Alessandra Lorini, *Rituals of Race: American Public Culture and the Search for Racial Democracy* (Charlottesville, 1999), 58.

10. "To the Editor of the *Montgomery Advertiser,*" Tuskegee, Ala., April 24, 1885, in Washington, *Washington Papers,* 2:273.

11. Washington, *Washington Papers,* 1:234.

12. *Daily News* (London), July 3, 1899.

13. Washington, *Washington Papers,* 1:260, 301.

14. Robert J. Norrell, "Understanding the Wizard: Another Look at the Age of Booker T. Washington," in *Booker T. Washington and Black Progress: Up from Slavery 100 Years Later,* ed. W. Fitzhugh Brundage, 58–80 (Gainesville, 2003).

15. H. F. Kletzing and W. H. Crogman, *Progress of a Race; The Remarkable Advancement of the Negro from the Bondage of Slavery, Ignorance and Poverty to the Freedom of Citizenship, Intelligence, Affluence, Honor and Trust* (Atlanta, 1897); Charles Alexander, *One Hundred Distinguished Leaders* (Atlanta, 1899). John N. Ingham, "Building Businesses, Creating Communities: Residential Segregation and the Growth of African American Business in Southern Cities, 1880–1915," *Business History Review* 77 (Winter 2003): 643.

16. Fon Louise Gordon, *Caste & Class: The Black Experience in Arkansas, 1880–1920* (Athens, GA, 1995), 108.

17. "An Article in *Gunton's Magazine,*" March 1901, in Washington, *Washington Papers,* 6:77.

18. Ibid., 1:250.

19. Loren Schweninger, *Black Property Owners in the South, 1790–1915* (Urbana, 1990), 184; Ingham, "Building Businesses," 643.

20. B. F. Lee, Jr., "Negro Organizations," *Annals of the American Academy of Political and Social Science* 49 (September 1913): 134.

21. Theda Skocpol and Jennifer Lynn Oser, "Organization Despite Adversity: The Origins and Development of African American Fraternal Associations," *Social Science History* 28 (Autumn 2004): 367–437.

22. W. H. Johnson, "The Case of the Negro," *Dial* 34 (May 1, 1903): 299–302.

23. "Tuskegee Receives Its Baldwin Fund," *New York Times,* April 6, 1906, 2.

24. Louis R. Harlan, "Booker T. Washington and the White Man's Burden," *American Historical Review* 71 (January 1966): 441–467.

25. Sven Beckert, "From Tuskegee to Togo: The Problem of Freedom in the Empire of Cotton," *Journal of American History* 92 (September 2005): 500.

26. "From Henry McNeal Turner," Atlanta, Ga., November 5, 1901, in Washington, *Washington Papers,* 6:287.

27. Gordon, *Caste and Class,* 39.

28. "To Charles William Anderson," Tuskegee, Ala., November 7, 1906, in Washington, *Washington Papers,* 9:118–119.

29. Norrell, "Understanding the Wizard," 71.

30. "Some Book Figures," *New York Times,* September 12, 1903, BR15.

31. Andrew Zimmerman, "A German Alabama in Africa: The Tuskegee Expedition to German Togo and the Transnational Origins of West African Cotton Growers," *American Historical Review* 110 (December 2005): 1362–1398.

32. Harlan, *Wizard,* 7.

33. Brian Kelly, "Sentinels for New South Industry: Booker T. Washington, Industrial Accommodation and Black Workers in the Jim Crow South," *Labor History* 44 (August 2003): 347.

34. Brian Kelly, *Race, Class, and Power in the Alabama Coalfields, 1908–21* (Urbana, 2001), 99.

35. Ibid., 106.

36. "Chapter XI: The Solidarity of Human Interests," in *The World's Congress of Representative Women,* ed. May Wright Sewall and Carrie Chapman Catt, 632–777 (Chicago, 1894).

37. Anna Julia Cooper, "The Intellectual Progress of the Colored Women in the United States since the Emancipation Proclamation: A Response to Fannie Barrier Williams," in *World's Congress,* ed. Sewall and Catt, 711–715; Anna Julia Cooper, "Do Two and Two Make Four?" *Independent,* July 26, 1894, 7.

38. Cooper, "Intellectual Progress," 717–718.

39. Vivian M. May, *Anna Julia Cooper, Visionary Black Feminist: A Critical Introduction* (New York, 2007), 21.

40. Evelyn Brooks Higginbotham, *Righteous Discontent: The Women's Movement in the Black Baptist Church, 1880–1920* (Cambridge, 1993), 10.

41. Anna J. Cooper, *The Voice of Anna Julia Cooper,* ed. Charles C. Lemert and Esme Bhan (Lanham, MD, 1998), 237, 251.

42. "Extracts from an Address before the Birmingham Lyceum," Birmingham, Ala., March 30, 1899, in Washington, *Washington Papers,* 5:66.

43. Higginbotham, *Righteous Discontent,* 207.

44. Anna J. Cooper, *A Voice from the South* (New York, 1988), 143.

45. Cooper, *Voice from the South,* 145.

46. "For the Negro," *Friends' Intelligencer,* January 17, 1903, 43. Glenda Elizabeth Gilmore, *Gender and Jim Crow: Women and the Politics of White Supremacy in North Carolina, 1896–1920* (Chapel Hill, 1996).

47. Cooper, *Voice from the South,* 96.

48. Ibid., 30–31.

49. Ibid., 79, 76, 75, 139–140.

50. May, *Visionary Black Feminist,* 18.

51. Cooper, *Voice from the South,* 99, 100, 104.

52. Hazel V. Carby, *Reconstructing Womanhood: The Emergence of the Afro-American Woman Novelist* (New York, 1987), 118.

53. Higginbotham, *Righteous Discontent,* 214.

54. Cooper, *Voice from the South,* 33, 32.

55. Ibid., 254.

56. Gordon, *Caste and Class,* 116.

57. Higginbotham, *Righteous Discontent,* 193.

58. Tera W. Hunter, *To 'Joy My Freedom: Southern Black Women's Lives and Labors after the Civil War* (Cambridge, 1997), 136–139.

59. May, *Visionary Black Feminist,* 72.

60. Deborah G. White, *Too Heavy a Load: Black Women in Defense of Themselves, 1894–1994* (New York, 1999), 80.

61. Higginbotham, *Righteous Discontent,* 200. Jeffrey Hess, "Black Settlement House, East Greenwich, 1902–1914," *Rhode Island History* 29 (Summer and Fall 1970): 127.

62. White, *Too Heavy,* 65.

63. "Negroes in a Riot," *The Washington Post,* July 31, 1903, 1. Elliott M. Rudwick, "Race Leadership Struggle: Background of the Boston Riot of 1903," *Journal of Negro Education* 31 (Winter 1962): 21.

64. Stephen R. Fox, *The Guardian of Boston: William Monroe Trotter* (New York, 1970), 29.

65. Louis R. Harlan, "Booker T. Washington and the Politics of Accommodation," in *Black Leaders of the Twentieth Century,* ed. John Hope Franklin and August Meier, 1–18 (Urbana, 1982), 6–7; "For a Black Man's Party," *New York Times,* November 8, 1903, 3.

66. "A Statement in the *Boston Globe,*" Boston, July 31, 1903, Washington, *Washington Papers,* 7:240.

67. "To Theodore Roosevelt," Tuskegee, Ala., September 15, 1903, Washington, *Washington Papers,* 7:284.

68. W. E. B. Du Bois, *Dusk of Dawn: An Essay toward an Autobiography of a Race Concept* (New York, 1940), 8.

69. Joel Williamson, *The Crucible of Race: Black-White Relations in the American South since Emancipation* (New York, 1984), 408.

70. W. E. B. Du Bois, "Strivings of the Negro People," *Atlantic Monthly* 80 (August 1897): 194–198.

71. "From William Edward Burghardt Du Bois," Atlanta, Ga., April 10, 1900, Washington, *Washington Papers,* 5:480.

72. W. E. B. Du Bois, "The Evolution of Negro Leadership," *Dial* 31 (July 16, 1901), 53–55.

73. W. E. B. Du Bois and Brent Hayes Edwards, *The Souls of Black Folk* (Oxford, 2007), 193, 44, 76.

74. W. E. B. Du Bois to Kelly Miller, Atlanta, Ga., February 25, 1903, in W. E. B. Du Bois, *The Correspondence of W. E. B. Du Bois,* ed. Herbert Aptheker, 3 vols. (Amherst, 1973), 1:53. Washington, "To William Edward Burghardt Du Bois," Tuskegee, Ala., November 8, 1903, Washington, *Washington Papers,* 7:339.

75. Fox, *Guardian of Boston,* 38.

76. Raymond Wolters, *Du Bois and His Rivals* (Columbia, MO, 2002), 68.

77. Du Bois, *Dusk of Dawn,* 75.

78. W. E. B. Du Bois to Oswald Garrison Villard, Atlanta, Ga., April 20, 1905, in Du Bois, of *Correspondence of Du Bois,* 1:104.

79. D. Wolf Kyle, "The Niagara Movement of 1905: A Look Back to a Century Ago," *Afro-Americans in New York Life and History* 32 (July 2008): 9–22.

80. Dominic J. Capeci, Jr., and Jack C. Knight, "Reckoning with Violence: W. E. B. Du Bois and the 1906 Atlanta Race Riot," *Journal of Southern History* 62 (November 1996): 727–766.

81. "From Oswald Garrison Villard," New York, May 26, 1909, in Washington, *Washington Papers,* 10:116–118.

82. Randy Roberts, *Papa Jack: Jack Johnson and the Era of White Hopes* (New York, 1983), 22.

83. "Johnson Wanted Wine," *Washington Post,* January 21, 1910, 8; "Jack Johnson Arrested," *New York Times,* February 9, 1910, 9; Roberts, *Papa Jack,* 72–74.

84. *Chicago Tribune,* April 4, 1909, 4.

85. "John L.'s Views on the Big Fight," *New York Times,* May 1, 1910.

86. "Johnson Rends Jeff to Pieces in 15 Rounds, *Washington Post,* July 5, 1910, A1.

87. "Crowd Is Subdued When Johnson Wins," *New York Times,* July 5, 1910, 3.

88. "Race Clashes in Many Cities," *Washington Post,* July 5, 1910, 1; *Daily Express,* July 6, 1910.

89. Geoffrey C. Ward, *Unforgivable Blackness: The Rise and Fall of Jack Johnson* (New York, 2006), 214–215, 264.

90. Russell Sylvester, "Jack Johnson in London," *Chicago Defender,* June 17, 1911, 1.

91. "Johnson Is After $60,000 Property," *Chicago Defender,* December 3, 1910.

92. Ward, *Unforgivable Blackness,* 246, 221.

93. Jack Johnson, *In the Ring and Out: The Classic Autobiography by the First Black Champion,* ed. Gilbert E. Odd (London, 1977), 168–169.

94. "Jack Johnson a Hero," *Chicago Defender,* April 23, 1910, 1; "Jack Johnson, Sunday School Teacher," *Chicago Defender,* August 6, 1910, 1.

95. "A Statement on Jack Johnson for the United Press Association," [Tuskegee, AL], October 23, 1912, Washington, *Washington Papers,* 12: 43–44.

96. Al-Tony Gilmore, *Bad Nigger! The National Impact of Jack Johnson* (Port Washington, NY, 1975), 53.

97. "Jack Johnson vs. the Ministers," *Chicago Defender,* February 3, 1912, 4.

98. Ward, *Unforgivable Blackness,* 301.

99. Thomas Cripps, *Slow Fade to Black: The Negro in American Film, 1900–1942* (New York, 1977), 59.

100. "The Black Man's Part in the Bible," *Chicago Defender,* April 29, 1916, 8.

101. "'Birth of a Nation' Barred from S. A.," *Chicago Defender,* June 3, 1916, 4.

102. Thomas Cripps, "The Birth of a Race Company: An Early Stride toward a Black Cinema," *Journal of Negro History* 59 (January 1974): 30.

103. Ibid., 36.

104. Herbert Aptheker, *A Documentary History of the Negro People in the United States*, vol. 2 (New York, 1951), 76.

105. Cripps, *Slow Fade*, 62.

106. Dittmer, *Black Georgia*, 111.

107. Hunter, *To 'Joy My Freedom*, 213.

5. Great War and Great Migration, 1917–1924

1. Harry Haywood, *Black Bolshevik: Autobiography of an Afro-American Communist* (Chicago, 1978), 5.

2. Robert Trent Vinson, "'Sea Kaffirs': 'American Negroes' and the Gospel of Garveyism in Early Twentieth-Century Cape Town," *Journal of African History* 47 (July 2006): 290.

3. Black combat fatalities from American Battle Monuments Commission, *American Armies and Battlefields in Europe* (Washington, DC, 1938), courtesy of Adrian Gregory and Lisa Budreau. "More than 1,000 African Americans" taken from mid-range estimates of the death tolls in major riots, Walter Rucker and James Nathaniel Upton, eds., *Encyclopedia of American Race Riots* (Westport, CT, 2006), and lynchings, www.law.umkc.edu (accessed May 15, 2009).

4. "Troops Quell Illinois Riots," *Chicago Defender*, July 7, 1917, 1.

5. Malcolm McLaughlin, "Reconsidering the East St Louis Race Riot of 1917," *International Review of Social History* 47 (August 2002): 187–212; Elliott M. Rudwick, *Race Riot at East St. Louis, July 2, 1917* (Carbondale, 1964).

6. "Negro Mutiny in Chicago Jail," *New York Times*, July 4, 1917, 5.

7. James Weldon Johnson, *Along This Way: The Autobiography of James Weldon Johnson* (New York, 1933), 308.

8. Ibid., 308–309.

9. William Jordan, "'The Damnable Dilemma': African-American Accommodation and Protest During World War I," *Journal of American History* 81 (March 1995): 1571.

10. Richard B. Sherman, *The Republican Party and Black America from McKinley to Hoover, 1896–1933* (Charlottesville, 1973), 123.

11. Adriane Danette Lentz-Smith, "The Great War for Civil Rights: African American Politics and World War I, 1916–1920," (Ph.D. diss., Yale University, 2005), forthcoming as Adriane Danette Lentz-Smith, *Freedom Struggles: African Americans and World War I* (Cambridge, 2009); "The Houston Mutiny," *Outlook*, September–December 1917, 10.

12. Lentz-Smith, "Great War," 80.

13. Neil R. McMillen, *Dark Journey: Black Mississippians in the Age of Jim Crow* (Urbana, 1989), 304. Lentz-Smith, "Great War," 39.

14. McMillen, *Dark Journey*, 303.

15. Mark Ellis, *Race, War, and Surveillance: African Americans and the United States Government during World War I* (Bloomington, 2001), 77.

16. Haywood, *Black Bolshevik*, 42, 49–50.

17. Bernadette Pruitt, "'For the Advancement of the Race,' the Great Migrations to Houston, Texas, 1914–1941," *Journal of Urban History* 31 (May 2005): 435–478.

18. Jennifer D. Keene, *Doughboys, the Great War, and the Remaking of America* (Baltimore, 2001), 40.

19. David L. Lewis, *W. E. B. Du Bois: Biography of a Race, 1868–1919* (New York, 1993), 543.

20. Addie W. Hunton and Kathryn M. Johnson, *Two Colored Women with the American Expeditionary Forces* (Brooklyn, NY, 1920), 157n47.

21. Susan Kerr Chandler, "'That Biting, Stinging Thing Which Ever Shadows Us': African-American Social Workers in France during World War I," *Social Service Review* 69 (September 1995): 498–514.

22. Ibid., 509.

23. Emmett Jay Scott, *Scott's Official History of the American Negro in the World War* (Chicago, 1919), wwi.lib.byu.edu (accessed May 5, 2009).

24. Lentz-Smith, "Great War," 151–152.

25. "Interview with W. E. B. Du Bois by Charles Mowbray White, August 22, 1920," Marcus Garvey and Universal Negro Improvement Association, *The Marcus Garvey and Universal Negro Improvement Association Papers*, ed. Robert A. Hill, vol. 2 (Berkeley, 1983), 620.

26. Dittmer, *Black Georgia*, 204.

27. Nancy MacLean, *Behind the Mask of Chivalry: The Making of the Second Ku Klux Klan* (New York, 1994), 27.

28. Judith Stein, *The World of Marcus Garvey: Race and Class in Modern Society* (Baton Rouge, 1986), 58.

29. Steven A. Reich, "Soldiers of Democracy: Black Texans and the Fight for Citizenship, 1917–1921," *Journal of American History* 82 (March 1996): 1494.

30. Greta De Jong, *A Different Day: African American Struggles for Justice in Rural Louisiana, 1900–1970* (Chapel Hill, 2002), 69.

31. Johnson, *Along This Way*, 315.

32. James R. Grossman, *Land of Hope: Chicago, Black Southerners, and the Great Migration* (Chicago, 1989), 60.

33. Nan Elizabeth Woodruff, *American Congo: The African American Freedom Struggle in the Delta* (Cambridge, 2003), 43, 44.

34. Ben Green, *Before His Time: The Untold Story of Harry T. Moore, America's First Civil Rights Martyr* (New York, 1999), 19, 21.

35. Dittmer, *Black Georgia*, 198.

36. NAACP Papers, Part 7: The Anti-Lynching Campaign, 1912–1955, Series B: Anti-Lynching Legislative and Publicity Files, 1916–1955, Library of Congress (Microfilm, Reel 3, Frames 570–573).

37. Lewis, *Biography of a Race*, 579.

38. Langston Hughes, *The Big Sea: An Autobiography* (New York, 1940), 33.

39. William J. Collins, "When the Tide Turned: Immigration and the Delay of the Great Black Migration," *Journal of Economic History* 57 (September 1997): 616.

40. Ellis, *Race, War and Surveillance*, 159.

41. William G. Jordan, *Black Newspapers and America's War for Democracy, 1914–1920* (Chapel Hill, 2001), 119, 113.

42. Ibid., 113.

43. W. E. B. Du Bois, *Writings*, ed. Nathan Irvin Huggins (New York, 1986), 740, 1293.

44. Mark Ellis, "'Closing Ranks' and 'Seeking Honors': W. E. B. Du Bois in World War I," *Journal of American History* 79 (June 1992): 96–124; Jordan, "Damnable Dilemma," *Journal of American History* 81 (March 1995): 1562–1583; Mark Ellis, "W. E. B. Du Bois and the Formation of Black Opinion in World War I: A Commentary on 'The Damnable Dilemma,'" *Journal of American History* 81 (March 1995): 1584–1590.

45. Jordan, *Black Newspapers*, 125.

46. Wilson Jeremiah Moses, *The Golden Age of Black Nationalism, 1850–1925* (Hamden, CT, 1978), 230–231.

47. Arvarh E. Strickland, *History of the Chicago Urban League* (Urbana, 1966), 51.

48. Jordan, *Black Newspapers*, 112, 104.

49. Reid Badger, *A Life in Ragtime: A Biography of James Reese Europe* (New York, 1995), 8, 5.

50. Eric Porter, *What Is This Thing Called Jazz? African American Musicians as Artists, Critics, and Activists* (Berkeley, 2002), 20, 19.

51. "Jazzing Away Prejudice," *The Chicago Defender*, May 10, 1919, 20.

52. Johnson, *Along This Way*, 334.

53. Matthew Pratt Guterl, *The Color of Race in America, 1900–1940* (Cambridge, 2001), 124.

54. Haywood, *Black Bolshevik*, 82.

55. Lee E. Williams, *Post-War Riots in America, 1919 and 1946: How the Pressures of War Exacerbated American Urban Tensions to the Breaking Point* (Lewiston, NY, 1991), 56, 77.

56. "If We Must Die," *Liberator* 2 (July 1919), 21.

57. Williams, *Post-War Riots*, 58.

58. Alain LeRoy Locke, *The Critical Temper of Alain Locke: A Selection of His Essays on Art and Culture*, ed. Jeffrey C. Stewart (New York, 1983), 5.

59. Jacqueline M. Moore, *Leading the Race: The Transformation of the Black Elite in the Nation's Capital, 1880–1920* (Charlottesville, 1999), 211–212.

60. Mark R. Schneider, *We Return Fighting: The Civil Rights Movement in the Jazz Age* (Boston, 2002), 17.

61. Du Bois, *Writings*, 1181.

62. Woodruff, *American Congo*, 91.

63. Lewis, *Biography of a Race*, 579.

64. Stephen H. Norwood, "Bogalusa Burning: The War against Biracial Unionism in the Deep South, 1919," *Journal of Southern History* 63 (August 1997): 591–628, quotation from 613.

65. Bruce Nelson, *Divided We Stand: American Workers and the Struggle for*

Black Equality (Princeton, 2001), 165; Michael K. Honey, *Southern Labor and Black Civil Rights: Organizing Memphis Workers* (Urbana, 1993), 19.

66. Johnson, *Along This Way,* 355.

67. Daniel Letwin, *The Challenge of Interracial Unionism: Alabama Coal Miners, 1878–1921* (Chapel Hill, 1998).

68. Brian Kelly, *Race, Class, and Power in the Alabama Coalfields, 1908–21* (Urbana, 2001), 188.

69. Lewis, *Biography of a Race,* 538.

70. Rick Halpern, *Down on the Killing Floor: Black and White Workers in Chicago's Packinghouses, 1904–54* (Urbana, 1997), 52.

71. Kelly, *Race,* 130.

72. Norwood, "Bogalusa Burning," 617.

73. Nelson, *Divided,* 167.

74. Glenda Elizabeth Gilmore, *Gender and Jim Crow: Women and the Politics of White Supremacy in North Carolina, 1896–1920* (Chapel Hill, 1996), 199.

75. Ibid., 200.

76. , W. E. B. Du Bois, "Editorial, Votes for Women," *The Crisis,* 4 (September 1912), 234.

77. Paula Giddings, *When and Where I Enter: The Impact of Black Women on Race and Sex in America* (New York, 2001), 123.

78. Rosalyn Terborg-Penn, *African American Women in the Struggle for the Vote, 1850–1920* (Bloomington, 1998), 132.

79. J. Douglas Smith, *Managing White Supremacy: Race, Politics, and Citizenship in Jim Crow Virginia* (Chapel Hill, 2002), 49–51, 68.

80. Lentz-Smith, "Great War," 147.

81. David L. Lewis, *W. E. B. Du Bois: The Fight for Equality and the American Century, 1919–1963* (New York, 2000), 59.

82. Jonathan Rosenberg, *How Far the Promised Land? World Affairs and the American Civil Rights Movement from the First World War to Vietnam* (Princeton, 2006), 4.

83. Theodore Kornweibel, *Seeing Red: Federal Campaigns against Black Militancy, 1919–1925* (Bloomington, 1998), xiv, 29.

84. Edmund David Cronon, *Black Moses: The Story of Marcus Garvey and the Universal Negro Improvement Association* (Madison, 1955), 63.

85. Reports of the Convention, August 3, 1920, printed in *Negro World Conference Bulletin,* August 7, 1920, in Garvey, *Garvey Papers,* 2:510.

86. Report of a Madison Square Garden Meeting, printed in *Negro World Convention Bulletin,* August 3, 1920, in Garvey, *Garvey Papers,* 2:498.

87. Report by Special Agent P-138, New York, August 21, 1920, in Garvey, *Garvey Papers,* 2:612.

88. Mary G. Rolinson, *Grassroots Garveyism: The Universal Negro Improvement Association in the Rural South, 1920–1927* (Chapel Hill, 2007), 23, 2.

89. Quintard Taylor, *In Search of the Racial Frontier: African Americans in the American West, 1528–1990* (New York, 1998), 241–243.

90. Kornweibel, *Seeing Red,* 106.

91. Vinson, "Sea Kaffirs," 281.

92. Opening of the UNIA Convention, Liberty Hall, New York, August 1, 1920, printed in *Negro World Conference Bulletin,* August 2, 1920, in Garvey, *Garvey Papers,* 2:479.

93. W. E. B. Du Bois, *On the Importance of African in World History* (Ann Arbor, 1978), 21.

94. Nelson, *Divided,* 33.

95. Schneider, *We Return,* 85.

96. Rolinson, *Grassroots Garveyism,* 124.

97. Kimberley L. Phillips, *Alabamanorth: African-American Migrants, Community, and Working-Class Activism in Cleveland, 1915–45* (Urbana, 1999), 187.

98. Report of the Convention, New York, August 31, 1920, printed in *Negro World,* September 11, 1920, in Garvey, *Garvey Papers,* 2:647.

99. Stein, *World of Marcus Garvey,* 165–166.

100. Interview with Frederick Moore by Charles Mowbray White, New York, August 23, 1920, in Garvey, *Garvey Papers,* 2:622.

101. Stein, *World of Marcus Garvey,* 130.

102. Ibid., 3, 243–244, 246.

103. Phillips, *Alabamanorth,* 165.

104. Ula Y. Taylor, *The Veiled Garvey: The Life & Times of Amy Jacques Garvey* (Chapel Hill, 2002).

105. "Harding Dedicates Lincoln Memorial; Blue and Gray Join," *New York Times,* May 31, 1922, 1.

106. "Address of Dr. Robert Russa Moton at the Dedication of the Lincoln Memorial, Washington, D.C., May 30, 1922," www.gloucesterinstitute.org (accessed May 5, 2009).

107. Ellis, *Race War,* 216, 219.

108. Gavin Wright, *Old South, New South: Revolutions in the Southern Economy since the Civil War* (New York, 1986), 195–197.

109. Joe William Trotter, *Black Milwaukee: The Making of an Industrial Proletariat, 1915–45* (Urbana, 1985), 47.

110. Nelson, *Divided,* 168, 169.

111. Klarman, *From Jim Crow,* 100.

112. Edwin R. Lewinson, *Black Politics in New York City* (New York, 1974), 55.

113. Johnson, *Along This Way,* 196.

114. Ibid., 307.

115. Sherman, *Republican Party,* 145.

116. Terborg-Penn, *African American Women,* 146.

6. Renaissance in Harlem, Dark Ages Elsewhere, 1924–1941

1. "1 Dead, 6 Shot in Alabama Riot," *Chicago Defender,* July 5, 1931, 1; "U.S. Acts to Curb 'Reds,'" *Chicago Defender,* August 8, 1931, 1.

2. Neil R. McMillen, *Dark Journey: Black Mississippians in the Age of Jim Crow* (Urbana, 1989), 26.

3. Michel Fabre and Isabel Barzun, *The Unfinished Quest of Richard Wright* (Urbana, 1993), 115.

4. David Levering Lewis, *When Harlem Was in Vogue* (New York, 1909).

5. Alain LeRoy Locke and W. E. B. Du Bois, "The Younger Literary Movement," *Crisis* 28 (February 1924): 161–163.

6. Patrick J. Gilpin, "Charles S. Johnson: Entrepreneur of the Harlem Renaissance," in *The Harlem Renaissance Remembered: Essays,* ed. Arna Wendell Bontemps (New York, 1972): 231.

7. James Weldon Johnson, *The Selected Writings of James Weldon Johnson,* ed. Sondra K. Wilson, vol. 2 (New York, 1995), 59, 398.

8. Lewis, *When Harlem Was in Vogue,* 125.

9. Alain LeRoy Locke, *The New Negro: An Interpretation* (New York, 1925), 13.

10. Langston Hughes, *The Big Sea, an Autobiography* (New York, 1940), 223.

11. Alain LeRoy Locke, *The Critical Temper of Alain Locke: A Selection of His Essays on Art and Culture,* ed. Jeffrey C. Stewart (New York, 1983), 6.

12. Rudolph Fisher, *The City of Refuge: The Collected Stories of Rudolph Fisher,* ed. John McCluskey (Columbia, MO, 1987), 3–4.

13. "The Negro in Art: How shall he be portrayed? A Symposium," *Crisis,* 31–33 (February–November 1926). Langston Hughes, "The Negro Artist and the Racial Mountain," *Nation* 122 (June 23, 1926): 694.

14. Maria Balshaw, "'Black Was White': Urbanity, Passing and the Spectacle of Harlem," *Journal of American Studies* 33 (September 2000): 313.

15. Hughes, *The Big Sea,* 334.

16. Alain Locke, "Harlem: Dark Weather-vane," *Survey Graphic,* 25, (August 1936), 457.

17. A. B. Christa Schwarz, *Gay Voices of the Harlem Renaissance* (Bloomington, 2003), 42.

18. Robert F. Worth, "Nigger Heaven and the Harlem Renaissance," *African American Review* 29 (Autumn 1995): 464.

19. Ibid., 468.

20. Lewis, *When Harlem,* 164.

21. James Weldon Johnson, *Writings* (New York, 2004), 787–789.

22. Hughes, *Big Sea,* 228.

23. Bessye Bearden, "Throngs Weep Over Bier of 'Flo' Mills," *Chicago Defender,* November 12, 1927, 1.

24. Cheryl Lynn Greenberg, *"Or Does It Explode?" Black Harlem in the Great Depression* (Oxford, 1991), 21.

25. Gilbert Osofsky, *Harlem; the Making of a Ghetto: Negro New York, 1890–1930* (New York, 1966), 136.

26. "It's the Blood That Counts," *Chicago Defender,* November 28, 1925, 22.

27. Kevin Boyle, *Arc of Justice: A Saga of Race, Civil Rights, and Murder in the Jazz Age* (New York, 2004), 257.

28. Walter White, "The Negro and the Flood," *Nation* 124 (June 22, 1927): 688–689; "The Flood, the Red Cross, and the National Guard," *Crisis* 35 (January 1928): 5–7, 26, 28. Minutes of the Board of Directors, 1909–1950, 9 May 1927, p. 3, part 1, NAACP Papers, part 1, reel 2, NAACP Papers on microfilm; Minutes of the Board of Directors, 13 June 1927, p. 2, NAACP Papers; Minutes of the Board of Directors, 12 September 1927, p. 4, NAACP Papers.

29. Charles S. Johnson, *Shadow of the Plantation* (Chicago, 1934), 99.

30. Charles S. Johnson, *Growing up in the Black Belt: Negro Youth in the Rural South* (Washington, DC, 1941), 296.

31. Hortense Powdermaker, *After Freedom: A Cultural Study in the Deep South* (New York, 1939), 191. William H. Chafe, "Presidential Address: 'The Gods Bring Threads to Webs Begun,'" *Journal of American History* 86 (March 2000): 1547.

32. John Dollard, *Caste and Class in a Southern Town* (New Haven, 1937), 287.

33. Charles S. Johnson, *Patterns of Negro Segregation* (New York, 1943), 267.

34. Bertram Doyle, *The Etiquette of Race Relations in the South: A Study in Social Control* (Chicago, 1937), 111. William Alexander Percy and Carl H. Pforzheimer, *Lanterns on the Levee: Recollections of a Planter's Son* (New York, 1941), 299.

35. Lois E. Myers and Rebecca Sharpless, "'Of the Least and the Most': The African American Rural Church," in *African American Life in the Rural South, 1900–1950,* ed. R. Douglas Hurt (Columbia, MO, 2003): 55.

36. Powdermaker, *After Freedom,* 300.

37. Johnson, *Growing Up,* 113.

38. Powdermaker, *After Freedom,* 341.

39. Johnson, *Patterns,* 265.

40. Langston Hughes, "Cowards from the Colleges," *Crisis* 41 (August 1934): 227.

41. McMillen, *Dark Journey,* 137.

42. Johnson, *Growing Up,* 307.

43. Studs Terkel, *Hard Times: An Oral History of the Great Depression* (New York, 1970), 82.

44. John B. Kirby, *Black Americans in the Roosevelt Era: Liberalism and Race* (Knoxville, 1980), 98.

45. Nell Irvin Painter, *Creating Black Americans: African-American History and Its Meanings, 1619 to the Present* (New York, 2006), 199.

46. "Topics of the Times," *New York Times,* May 9, 1933, 16.

47. "Conservation Army Has Fine Appetite," *Chicago Defender,* August 26, 1933, 4.

48. Thomas Patton, "'A Forest Camp Disgrace': The Rebellion of Civilian Conservation Corps Workers at Preston, New York, July 7, 1933," *New York History* 82 (Summer 2001): 231–258.

49. Raymond Wolters, "The New Deal and the Negro," in *The New Deal,* ed. John Braeman, Robert Hamlett Bremner, and David Brody, vol. 1, 170–217 (Columbus, 1975), 194.

50. Walter Francis White, *A Man Called White: The Autobiography of Walter White* (London, 1949), 169.

51. Lorena A. Hickok, *One Third of a Nation: Lorena Hickok Reports on the Great Depression,* ed. Richard Lowitt and Maurine Hoffman Beasley (Urbana, 1981), 151–152.

52. De Jong, *Different Day,* 106.

53. Mark I. Solomon, *The Cry Was Unity: Communists and African Americans, 1917–36* (Jackson, MS, 1998).

54. James E. Goodman, *Stories of Scottsboro* (New York, 1995).

55. Robin D. G. Kelley, *Hammer and Hoe: Alabama Communists during the Great Depression* (Chapel Hill, 1990), 39–53, 45, 53.

56. Ibid., 80.

57. Solomon, *Cry Was Unity,* 200.

58. Patricia Sullivan, *Days of Hope: Race and Democracy in the New Deal Era* (Chapel Hill, 1996), 58.

59. Richard Walter Thomas, *Life for Us Is What We Make It: Building Black Community in Detroit, 1915–1945* (Bloomington, 1992), 215, 219.

60. Kimberley L. Phillips, *Alabamanorth: African-American Migrants, Community, and Working-Class Activism in Cleveland, 1915–45* (Urbana, 1999), 199.

61. W. E. B. Du Bois, "The N.A.A.C.P. and Race Segregation," *Crisis* 41 (February 1934): 53.

62. W. E. B. Du Bois, "Segregation," *Crisis* 41 (January 1934): 20.

63. Walter White, "Segregation—A Symposium," *Crisis* 41 (February 1934): 80–81.

64. Solomon, *Cry Was Unity,* 158.

65. Jill Watts, *God, Harlem U.S.A.: The Father Divine Story* (Berkeley, 1992), 83.

66. "Harlem 'Messiah' Shies at Politics," *New York Times,* November 7, 1933, 18.

67. Watts, *God,* 173.

68. Mark D. Naison, "Communism and Black Nationalism in the Depression: The Case of Harlem," *Journal of Ethnic Studies* 2 (Summer 1974): 27.

69. Mark Naison, *Communists in Harlem during the Depression* (Urbana, 1983), 145.

70. Nancy J. Weiss, *Farewell to the Party of Lincoln: Black Politics in the Age of FDR* (Princeton, 1983), 211.

71. Nancy Grant, *TVA and Black Americans: Planning for the Status Quo* (Philadelphia, 1990), 112.

72. Rollins L. Winslow, "An Alley in the Valley," *Crisis* 44 (January 1937).

73. Genna Rae McNeil, *Groundwork: Charles Hamilton Houston and the Struggle for Civil Rights* (Philadelphia, 1983), 45.

74. McNeil, *Groundwork,* 116.

75. John P. Davis, "NRA Codifies Wage Slavery," *Crisis* 41 (October 1934): 298–299, 304.

76. Jonathan Scott Holloway, *Confronting the Veil: Abram Harris, Jr., E. Franklin Frazier, and Ralph Bunche, 1919–1941* (Chapel Hill, 2002), 74.

77. Kirby, *Black Americans,* 163–164.

78. For example, "Ethiopians Shout for War," *Chicago Defender,* October 5, 1935.

79. James Hunter Meriwether, *Proudly We Can Be Africans: Black Americans and Africa, 1935–1961* (Chapel Hill, 2002), 32.

80. Ibid., 43.

81. Beth Tompkins Bates, *Pullman Porters and the Rise of Protest Politics in Black America, 1925–1945* (Chapel Hill, 2001), 32.

82. "'Forward!' Exhortation of A. Phillip Randolph to Congress," *Chicago Defender,* February 22, 1936, 2.

83. Andrew Edmund Kersten, *A. Philip Randolph: A Life in the Vanguard* (Lanham, MD, 2007), 160.

84. Bates, *Pullman Porters,* 146.

85. Rackham Holt, *Mary McLeod Bethune: A Biography* (Garden City, NY, 1964), 216.

86. Anthony J. Badger, *The New Deal: The Depression Years, 1933–40* (Basingstoke, 1989), 208.

87. Price V. Fishback, Michael R. Haines, and Shawn Kantor, "The Impact of the New Deal on Black and White Infant Mortality in the South," *Explorations in Economic History* 38 (January 2001): 93–122.

88. De Jong, *Different Day,* 88.

89. Jarod Heath Roll, "Road to the Promised Land: Rural Rebellion in the New Cotton South, 1890–1945," (Ph.D. diss., Northwestern University, 2006), 228–288, 267.

90. Bates, *Pullman Porters,* 126.

91. Bruce Nelson, *Divided We Stand: American Workers and the Struggle for Black Equality* (Princeton, 2001), 199, 191.

92. Dan Burley, "Five Men Killed in Bloody Steel Strike," *Chicago Defender,* June 5, 1937, 1.

93. Deborah G. White, *Too Heavy a Load: Black Women in Defense of Themselves, 1894–1994* (New York, 1999), 160.

94. Elna Green, "Relief from Relief: The Tampa Sewing-Room Strike of 1937 and the Right to Welfare," *Journal of American History* 95 (March 2009): 1012–1037.

95. Karen Ferguson, *Black Politics in New Deal Atlanta* (Chapel Hill, 2002), 97.

96. John T. Appleby, "A Gifted Negro," *Washington Post,* April 24, 1938, B10.

97. Richard Wright, "How 'Bigger' Was Born," in *Works,* ed. Arnold Rampersad, vol. 1, 853–881 (New York, 1991), 874.

98. Lewis Gannett, "Books and Things," *Washington Post,* March 5, 1940, 13.

99. Arnold Rampersad, *Richard Wright: A Collection of Critical Essays* (Englewood Cliffs, NJ, 1995), 3.

100. Richard Wright, "The Ethics of Living Jim Crow," in *Works,* ed. Arnold Rampersad, vol. 1, 225–237 (New York, 1991), 235.

101. Richard Wright, "Black Boy (American Hunger)," in *Works,* ed. Arnold Rampersad, vol. 2, 5–365 (New York, 1991), 249.

102. Wright, *Early Works,* 854, 877, 880.

103. Hazel Rowley, *Richard Wright: The Life and Times* (Chicago, 2008), 142.

104. Richard Wright, "Native Son," in *Works,* ed. Arnold Rampersad, vol. 1, 447–850 (New York, 1991), 776.

105. Kirby, *Black Americans,* 117–118.

106. Michael J. Klarman, *From Jim Crow to Civil Rights: The Supreme Court and the Struggle for Racial Equality* (Oxford, 2004), 167.

107. Robert C. Weaver, *Negro Labor: A National Problem* (New York, 1946), 15.

108. Wolters, "New Deal," 175.

109. Lizabeth Cohen, *Making a New Deal: Industrial Workers in Chicago, 1919–1939* (Cambridge, 1990), 279.

110. McMillen, *Dark Journey,* 564.

111. Michael W. Fitzgerald, "'We Have Found a Moses': Theodore Bilbo, Black Nationalism, and the Greater Liberia Bill of 1939," *Journal of Southern History* 63 (May 1997): 305.

112. Kirby, *Black Americans,* 225.

7. World War II and Its Aftermath, 1941–1948

1. August Meier and Elliott Rudwick, *Along the Color Line* (Champaign, IL, 2002), 328.

2. Horace R. Cayton and St. Clair Drake, *Black Metropolis* (London, 1946), 745.

3. *Dayton News,* June 24, 1943.

4. Neil R. McMillen, "Fighting for What We Didn't Have: How Mississippi's Black Veterans Remember World War II," in *Remaking Dixie: The Impact of World War II on the American South,* ed. Neil R. McMillen, 93–110 (Jackson, MS, 1997), 97.

5. David Reynolds, *Rich Relations: The American Occupation of Britain, 1942–1945* (London, 1995), 303.

6. Charles S. Johnson, *A Monthly Summary of Events and Trends in Race Relations* 2 (November 1944), 95.

7. "Bestsellers of the Week," *New York Times,* September 6, 1943, 15.

8. Roi Ottley, *New World* (New York, 1943), 343, 347.

9. Maureen Honey, *Bitter Fruit: African American Women in World War Two* (Columbia, MO, 1999), 79.

10. "Ellington's Fans Applaud Concert," *New York Times,* December 12, 1943, 62.

11. "Survey of Intelligence Materials Supplement to Survey No. 25," 5, Bureau of Intelligence, OWI, July 14, 1942, RG208, E87, Box 582 File: Riots, National Archives, College Park.

12. John Modell, Marc Goulden, and Sigurdur Magnusson, "World War II in

the Lives of Black Americans: Some Findings and Interpretation," *Journal of American History* 76 (December 1989): 842–843.

13. Ottley, *New World,* 343.

14. Louis E. Martin, "Detroit," *Journal of Educational Sociology* 17 (January 1944): 287.

15. Truman K. Gibson and Steve Huntley, *Knocking Down Barriers: My Fight for Black America* (Evanston, IL, 2005), 116.

16. Wynn, *Afro-American,* 108.

17. "This Book Has Got People Thinking," *New York Times,* September 19, 1943, BR13.

18. Johnson, *A Monthly Summary of Events and Trends in Race Relations* 2 (August–September 1944), 11.

19. Ed Peterson, "The South Fears for the Future," *Chicago Defender,* September 26, 1942, 14.

20. Gunnar Myrdal, *An American Dilemma* (1944; New York, 1964); Alistair Cooke, *Alistair Cooke's American Journey: Life on the Home Front in the Second World War* (London, 2006), 261.

21. "Milton Starr (Consultant, OWI) to William B. Lewis (Chief, Radio Bureau), Oct 21, 1942," Folder—Race Relations, 1942–43, RG 208, Entry 1, Box 8, National Archives, College Park.

22. "Survey S-1, In the field 4–15–42 to 5–11–42," RG 208, Entry 3D, Box 6. Folder "Negro Morale, 1942," National Archives, College Park.

23. "Survey of Intelligence Materials No. 25, OFF, Bureau of Intelligence," May 27, 1942, RG 208, Entry 3D, Box 6, Folder "Negro Morale, 1942," National Archives, College Park.

24. "Race Riots: Sub-Committee Report to the Production Information Committee, Chair Charles Levitt," July 5, 1943, RG208, E87, Box 582, File: Riots, National Archives, College Park.

25. C. S. Johnson, *Into the Main Stream: A Survey of Best Practices in Race Relations in the South* (Chapel Hill, 1947), x.

26. Roi Ottley, *Inside Black America* (London, 1948), 244.

27. "Survey of Intelligence Materials Supplement to Survey No. 25, Bureau of Intelligence, OWI, July 14, 1942, 10, RG208, E87, Box 582, File: Riots, National Archives, College Park.

28. Robert C. Weaver, *Negro Labor: A National Problem* (New York, 1946), 15.

29. "The Negro's War," *Fortune* 25 (June 1942): 80.

30. William J. Collins, "Race, Roosevelt, and Wartime Production: Fair Employment in World War Two Labor Markets," *American Economic Review* 91 (March 2001): 274.

31. Weaver, *Negro Labor,* 23.

32. Michael K. Honey, *Southern Labor and Black Civil Rights: Organizing Memphis Workers* (Urbana, 1993), 192–193.

33. Dominic J. Capeci, *Race Relations in Wartime Detroit: The Sojourner Truth Housing Controversy of 1942* (Philadelphia, 1984), 53.

34. "Memo: Correspondence Panels Section to Philleo Nash," July 7, 1943, RG208, E87, Box 582, File: Riots, National Archives, College Park.

35. Kevin Boyle, "'There Are No Union Sorrows That the Union Can't Heal': The Struggle for Racial Equality in the United Automobile Workers, 1940–1960," *Labor History* 36 (Winter 1995): 9.

36. Bruce Nelson, "Organized Labor and the Struggle for Black Equality in Mobile during World War II," *Journal of American History* 80 (December 1993): 960.

37. Karen Tucker Anderson, "Last Hired, First Fired: Black Women Workers During World War II," *Journal of American History* 69 (June 1982): 86.

38. Taylor, *In Search*, 269.

39. Charles S. Johnson, *A Monthly Summary of Events and Trends in Race Relations* 1 (August 1943), 10.

40. Taylor, *In Search*, 265.

41. Roi Ottley, *Black Odyssey: The Story of the Negro in America* (London, 1949), 259.

42. "Negro's War," 162.

43. "Memo: Richard Deveall, OWI Labor Consultant, to Charles Levitt," OWI DC, no date, RG208, E87, Box 582, National Archives, College Park.

44. "Report No. D3," August 21, 1943, Domestic Information Service, OWI, RG208, E87, Box 582, National Archives, College Park.

45. C. M. Vandeburg (Office Emergency Management) to Mr. Elmer Davis, Sept. 19, 1942, Folder "Race Relations 1942–3," RG 208, Entry 1, Box 8, National Archives, College Park.

46. Charles S. Johnson, *A Monthly Summary of Events and Trends in Race Relations* 1 (August 1943): 3–5.

47. Ralph Ellison, *The Collected Essays of Ralph Ellison,* ed. John F. Callahan and Saul Bellow (New York, 1995), 150.

48. F. B. Ransom (Mme CJ Walker Manuf Co, Indiana) to Earl Peters, State Director FHA, RG 208, Entry 5, Box 3, OWI, Records of the Office of Facts and Figures, Decimal File of the Director, Folder: Special Groups: Negroes, National Archives, College Park.

49. Johnson, *A Monthly Summary* 1 (August 1943): 3–5.

50. Mary C. King, "Occupational Segregation by Race and Sex, 1940–88," *Monthly Labor Review* 115 (April 1992): 30–37.

51. Nan Elizabeth Woodruff, *American Congo: The African American Freedom Struggle in the Delta* (Cambridge, 2003), 212.

52. Weaver, *Negro Labor,* 78, 179.

53. A. Philip Randolph, "March on Washington Movement Presents Program for the Negro," in *What the Negro Wants,* ed. Rayford Whittingham Logan, 133–162 (Chapel Hill, 1944), 153.

54. "Report No. D3, August 21, 1943, Domestic Information Service," p. 1, OWI, RG208, E87, Box 582, File: Riots, National Archives, College Park.

55. Richard M. Dalfiume, *Desegregation of the U.S. Armed Forces: Fighting on Two Fronts, 1939–1953* (Columbia, MO, 1969), 26.

56. Daniel Kryder, *Divided Arsenal: Race and the American State During World War Two* (Cambridge, 2000), 166.

57. Charles S. Johnson, *A Monthly Summary of Events and Trends in Race Relations* 2 (February 1945), 184.

58. Fernand Auberjonois Capt PWS Rabat to Jay Allen—Chief PWS Morocco, January 25, 1943, RG208, E76, Box 237, File: Negro Activities, National Archives, College Park.

59. McMillen, "Fighting," 99.

60. H. C. Brearley, "The Negro's New Belligerency," *Phylon* 5 (Winter 1944): 339.

61. Charles S. Johnson, *A Monthly Summary of Events and Trends in Race Relations* 1 (August 1943), 9.

62. "Report of Investigation at Camp Stewart," June 4, 1943, Ralph Mark Gilbert, Personal Correspondence, King-Tisdell Cottage, Savannah; Reynolds, *Rich Relations,* 224, 232.

63. Gibson and Huntley, *Knocking,* 89, 78.

64. "Statement of Truman K. Gibson, Jr., Civilian Aide to the Secretary of War, At Press Conference, Monday, April 9, 1945, Washington DC," in Desegregation of Armed Forces Folder 1945, RG208, E87, Box 582, National Archives, College Park.

65. Gibson and Huntley, *Knocking,* 97.

66. Kenneth Robert Janken, *White: The Biography of Walter White, Mr. NAACP* (New York, 2003), 274–275.

67. Penny M. Von Eschen, *Race against Empire: Black Americans and Anticolonialism, 1937–1957* (Ithaca, NY, 1997), 40.

68. Richard Wright, "Introduction," in *Black Metropolis,* ed. Horace R. Cayton and St. Clair Drake, xvii—xxxiv (London, 1946), xxv.

69. *Common Ground,* Fall 1943, 104.

70. "Race Riots: Sub-Committee Report to the Production Information Committee." Chair Charles Levitt, July 5, 1943, RG208, E87, Box 582, File: Riots, National Archives, College Park.

71. Rayford W. Logan, "The Negro Wants First-Class Citizenship," in *What the Negro Wants,* ed. Rayford W. Logan, 1–30 (Chapel Hill, 1944), 29.

72. Guy B. Johnson, "The Stereotype of the American Negro," in *Characteristics of the American Negro,* ed. Otto Klineberg, 1–22 (New York, 1944), 3.

73. Wilton M. Krogman, "What We Do Not Know About Race," *Scientific Monthly* 57 (August 1942): 103.

74. "Speech by Walter White," p. 1, Writers Congress, LA, October 1, 1943, Series II, Box A, 277, Folder: Film: Hollywood Writers Mobilization Writers' Congress 1943, National Archives, College Park.

75. 1944, Press Release, sent as telegram, NAACP 1940–55, General Office File, Films: *The Negro Soldier,* 1944–45, NAACP Microfilm. See too *PM,* Friday, April 28, 1944.

76. *Friends Intelligencer* 101 (April 8, 1944): 226; "Press Release," March 16, 1944, NAACP 1940–55, General Office File, Films: *The Negro Soldier,* 1944–45, NAACP microfilm.

77. *PM,* Friday, April 28, 1944.

78. Barbara Dianne Savage, *Broadcasting Freedom: Radio, War, and the Politics of Race, 1938–1948* (Chapel Hill, 1999).

79. *Ladies Home Journal 59* (August 1962): 75–79.

80. *Life,* July 1944–December 1945.

81. "Current Surveys: Negro-White Attitudes toward the Negro's Role in the War," July 7, 1943, OWI Surveys Division, Re Chicago, Detroit, Oklahoma, Raleigh, Birmingham, File: Riots, RG208, E87, Box 582, National Archives, College Park.

82. R. Koppes Clayton and Gregory D. Black, "Blacks, Loyalty, and Motion-Picture Propaganda in World War Two," *Journal of American History* 73 (September 1986): 404.

83. Charles S. Johnson, *A Monthly Summary of Events and Trends in Race Relations* 2 (June 1945), 339.

84. Duke Ellington, *The Duke Ellington Reader,* ed. Mark Tucker (New York, 1993), 238; Harvey G. Cohen, "Duke Ellington and Black, Brown, and Beige: The Composer as Historian at Carnegie Hall," *American Quarterly* 56 (December 2004): 1003.

85. John Kieran, "The Big Punch Stirs Pugilism's Hopes," *New York Times,* September 22, 1935, SM6.

86. Howard Taubman, "The 'Duke' Invades Carnegie Hall," *New York Times,* January 17, 1943, SM10.

87. Dean B. Cromwell and Alfred F. Wesson, *Championship Technique in Track and Field; a Book for Athletes, Coaches, and Spectators* (New York, 1941), 6.

88. C. K. Doreski, "'Kin in Some Way': *The Chicago Defender* Reads the Japanese Internment, 1942–1945," in *The Black Press: New Literary and Historical Essays,* ed. Todd Vogel, 161–187 (New Brunswick, NJ, 2001), 181.

89. Wynn, *Afro-American,* 109.

90. Charles S. Johnson, *A Monthly Summary of Events and Trends in Race Relations* 1 (May 1944), 26.

91. Sterling Allen Brown, *Sterling A. Brown's A Negro Looks at the South,* ed. John Edgar Tidwell and Mark A. Sanders (New York, 2006), 322.

92. Eleanor Roosevelt, *Freedom: Promise or Fact,* ed. Allida M. Black (New York, 1999), 138.

93. Hazel Gaudet Erskine, "The Polls: Race Relations," *Public Opinion Quarterly* 26 (Spring 1962): 137–148.

94. Cooke, *American Journey,* 203.

95. "Report No. D3, August 21, 1943, Domestic Information Service," OWI, RG208, E87, Box 582, File: Riots, National Archives, College Park.

96. Otto Klineberg, ed., *Characteristics of the American Negro* (New York, 1944), 203.

97. Honey, *Bitter Fruit,* 79.

98. Lee Finkle, "The Conservative Aims of Militant Rhetoric: Black Protest during World War Two," *Journal of American History* 60 (December 1973): 703.

99. Ottley, *Inside,* 182.

100. Cayton and Drake, *Black Metropolis,* 721.

101. Berry to Ulrich Bell and Archibald MacLeish, May 20, 1942, Folder "Negro Morale, 1942," RG 208, Entry 3D, Box 6, National Archives, College Park.

102. Martha Biondi, *To Stand and Fight: The Struggle for Civil Rights in Postwar New York City* (Cambridge, 2003), 7.

103. Ella Baker to Roy Wilkins, March 11, 1942, II A 72, NAACP Microfilm.

104. Barbara Ransby, *Ella Baker & the Black Freedom Movement: A Radical Democratic Vision* (Chapel Hill, 2003), 118.

105. Charles S. Johnson, *A Monthly Summary of Events and Trends in Race Relations* 1 (October 1943): 7–8.

106. *Ebony* 1 (November 1945): 2.

107. "And a Child Shall Lead Them," *Ebony* 1 (December 1945): 28.

108. "Sixty Million Jobs or Else. This Again?" *Ebony* 1 (November 1945): 50.

109. Hughes, *Collected Works,* 2:261.

110. Mary L. Dudziak, *Cold War Civil Rights: Race and the Image of American Democracy* (Princeton, 2000), 62.

111. Robert Rogers Korstad, *Civil Rights Unionism: Tobacco Works and the Struggle for Democracy in the Mid-Twentieth-Century South* (Chapel Hill, 2003).

112. Weaver, *Negro Labor,* 267.

113. Charles S. Johnson, *A Monthly Summary of Events and Trends in Race Relations* 3 (January 1946): 165.

114. Korstad, *Civil Rights Unionism,* 257.

115. William J. Collins, "African-American Economic Mobility in the 1940s: A Portrait from the Palmer Survey," *Journal of Economic History* 60 (September 2000): 772.

116. Gibson and Huntley, *Knocking,* 219.

117. Charles S. Johnson, *A Monthly Summary of Events and Trends in Race Relations* 3 (October 1945): 93.

118. Suzanne Mettler, "'The Only Good Thing Was the G.I. Bill': Effects of the Education and Training Provisions on African-American Veterans' Political Participation," *Studies in American Political Development* 19 (April 2005): 43.

119. Ibid., 49.

120. Martin Luther King and Clayton Riley, *Daddy King: An Autobiography* (New York, 1980), 134.

121. Honey, *Bitter Fruit,* 75.

8. Three Steps Forward, Two Steps Back, 1949–1959

1. Martha Biondi, *To Stand and Fight: The Struggle for Civil Rights in Postwar New York City* (Cambridge, 2003), 252.

2. "White Faces Negro Mob," *Chicago Defender,* July 16, 1949, 1.

3. Biondi, *Stand and Fight,* 240.

4. Josh Sides, *L.A. City Limits: African American Los Angeles from the Great Depression to the Present* (Berkeley, 2003), 154.

5. Russ J. Cowans, "Freak Storm Skips Negro Section, Kills 52 Whites," *Chicago Defender,* January 15, 1949, 1.

6. Venice Spraggs, "Writer Shows Civil Rights Gains in Survey," *Chicago Defender,* January 1, 1949, 13.

7. "The Promise of '49," *Chicago Defender,* January 1, 1949, 6.

8. Henry Lee Moon, "What Chance for Civil Rights," *Crisis* 56 (February 1949): 42–45.

9. Roy Wilkins and Tom Mathews, *Standing Fast: The Autobiography of Roy Wilkins* (New York, 1982), 208.

10. Adam Clayton Powell, *Adam by Adam: The Autobiography of Adam Clayton Powell, Jr.* (New York, 1971), 91.

11. Wilkins and Mathews, *Standing Fast,* 222.

12. Michael J. Klarman, *From Jim Crow to Civil Rights: The Supreme Court and the Struggle for Racial Equality* (Oxford, 2004).

13. George S. Schuyler, "All Over the Country," *American Mercury* (June 1949), in Clayborne Carson, *Reporting Civil Rights,* vol. 1, 112–121 (New York, 2003), 121.

14. James Baldwin, *Notes of a Native Son* (New York, 1990), 94.

15. Davison Douglas, *Jim Crow Moves North: The Battle Over Northern School Segregation, 1864–1954* (Cambridge, 2005), 238.

16. Aaron Henry and Constance Curry, *Aaron Henry: The Fire Ever Burning* (Jackson, MS, 2000), 83.

17. Penny M. Von Eschen, *Race against Empire: Black Americans and Anticolonialism, 1937–1957* (Ithaca, NY, 1997), 120.

18. Jules Tygiel, *Baseball's Great Experiment: Jackie Robinson and His Legacy* (New York, 1983), 265–266.

19. Stephen G. N. Tuck, *Beyond Atlanta: The Struggle for Racial Equality in Georgia, 1940–1980* (Athens, GA, 2001), 85.

20. Thomas Cripps, *Making Movies Black: The Hollywood Message Movie from World War Two to the Civil Rights Era* (New York, 1993), 234.

21. Brian Ward, *Radio and the Struggle for Civil Rights in the South* (Gainesville, 2004), 49–50.

22. Tygiel, *Baseball's Great Experiment,* 295.

23. Ward, *Radio and the Struggle,* 6–7.

24. Brian Ward, *Just My Soul Responding: Rhythm and Blues, Black Consciousness and Race Relations* (London, 1998), 19–20, 124.

25. Ibid., 128.

26. Tygiel, *Baseball's Great Experiment,* 332.

27. Ibid., 306.

28. Ward, *Radio and the Struggle,* 84.

29. Joyce Kent, "Old Times," *Harlem Quarterly* 1 (Spring 1950): 23.

30. American Federation of Musicians, *Three Years of Free Music* (New York, 1950), 3.

31. Ward, *Just My Soul,* 95.

32. Nell Irvin Painter, *Creating Black Americans: African-American History and Its Meanings, 1619 to the Present* (New York, 2006), 251.

33. Jackie Robinson, *I Never Had It Made* (New York, 1972), 92.

34. Arnold R. Hirsch, *Making the Second Ghetto: Race and Housing in Chicago, 1940–1960* (Cambridge, 1983), 77.

35. L. F. Palmer, Jr., "Housing Riot Flares up Again in Chicago," *Chicago Defender,* September 5, 1953, 1.

36. "Family Target of Riot in Chicago Faces Ouster," *Chicago Defender,* December 12, 1953, 1.

37. Albert Barnett, "'Bedford-Stuyvesant' Community in Brooklyn and in Chicago," *Chicago Defender,* August 21, 1954, 5.

38. "1,500 in Protest of Housing Bias," *Chicago Defender,* March 27, 1954, 1.

39. "Let's Try Prayer," *Chicago Defender,* July 31, 1954, 11.

40. Christopher Robert Reed, *The Chicago NAACP and the Rise of Black Professional Leadership, 1910–1966* (Bloomington, IN, 1997), 170.

41. Stephen Grant Meyer, *As Long as They Don't Move Next Door: Segregation and Racial Conflict in American Neighborhoods* (Lanham, MD, 2000), 178.

42. Davison M. Douglas, *Jim Crow Moves North: The Battle over Northern School Desegregation, 1865–1954* (New York, 2005), 238.

43. James Ralph, *Northern Protest: Martin Luther King, Jr., Chicago, and the Civil Rights Movement* (Cambridge, 1993), 11.

44. Reed, *Chicago NAACP,* 139.

45. Matthew Countryman, *Up South: Civil Rights and Black Power in Philadelphia* (Philadelphia, 2006), 50; Sugrue, *Origins of the Urban Crisis.*

46. "Fisk Race Relations Institute," *Chicago Defender,* July 26, 1958, 11.

47. Countryman, *Up South,* 52.

48. Sides, *L.A. City Limits,* 95.

49. James Baldwin, *Nobody Knows My Name* (New York, 1993), 63.

50. Surveys by National Opinion Research Center, University of Chicago, during May 1944, May 1946, January 1956, April 21–30, 1956, and June 27–July 5, 1956; and by Gallup Organization, September 24–29, 1958. Retrieved February 1, 2008, from the iPOLL Databank, Roper Center for Public Opinion Research, University of Connecticut; Sugrue, *Origins of the Urban Crisis,* 216.

51. *Amsterdam News,* May 29, 1954.

52. "Housing: Up from the Potato Fields," *Time,* July 3, 1950, 67–72.

53. Biondi, *Stand and Fight,* 230.

54. Steven Conn, "Bold Experiment in Way We Live Is a Social Failure," *Philadelphia Inquirer,* August, 11, 2002.

55. Meyer, *As Long as They Don't,* 147.

56. *Life,* September 2, 1957.

57. David Brittan, "A Flaming Cross," *Look,* August 19, 1958, in Carson, *Reporting Civil Rights,* 2:406.

58. "Fight Proposed All-White Levittown for New Jersey," *Chicago Defender,* July 12, 1958, 9.

59. "Tennessee Gov. Says 'No Federal Troops!'" *Chicago Defender,* November 30, 1957.

60. Henry and Curry, *Aaron Henry,* 103.

61. Luther Jackson, "Voting Registration in Georgia," *Southern Regional Council Publications* 8 (January 1953).

62. Henry and Curry, *Aaron Henry*, 79.

63. Timothy J. Minchin, *The Color of Work: The Struggle for Civil Rights in the Southern Paper Industry, 1945–1980* (Chapel Hill, 2001), 44–45.

64. *Atlanta Daily World,* 31 October 1948.

65. Howard Schuman, *Racial Attitudes in America: Trends and Interpretations* (Cambridge, 1997), 125.

66. Luther Jackson, "Voting Registration in Georgia," January 1953, 8, Southern Regional Council Publications (on microfilm).

67. Southern Regional Council, *Changing Patterns in the New South: A Unique Record of the Growth of Democracy in the South in the Last Decade* (Atlanta, 1955), 25.

68. Tuck, *Beyond Atlanta,* 83, 85; *Southern School News* 2 (June 1956), 9.

69. Henry and Curry, *Aaron Henry,* 82.

70. James T. Patterson, *Brown v. Board of Education: A Civil Rights Milestone and Its Troubled Legacy* (New York, 2001), xiv.

71. "Oliver Hill," *London Times,* August 28, 2007.

72. Thurgood Marshall, *Crisis* 58 (June–July 1951), 399.

73. Patterson, *Brown v. Board,* 71, 88.

74. Dan Wakefield, "The Citizens Council Movement," *The Nation,* October 22, 1955, in Carson, *Reporting Civil Rights,* 2:266.

75. Patterson, *Brown v. Board,* 72.

76. Henry and Curry, *Aaron Henry,* 85.

77. John Bartlow Martin, *The Deep South Says "Never"* (London, 1958), 168–169, 156, 23–24.

78. Henry and Curry, *Aaron Henry,* 98.

79. Patterson, *Brown v. Board,* 87.

80. Pete Daniel, *Lost Revolutions: The South in the 1950s* (Chapel Hill, 2000), 185.

81. Martin, *Deep South,* 156.

82. Louis E. Lomax, *The Negro Revolt* (London, 1963), 84–85.

83. Henry and Curry, *Aaron Henry,* 100.

84. Patterson, *Brown v. Board,* 60, 81.

85. Lomax, *Negro Revolt,* 84–85.

86. Taylor Branch, *Parting the Waters: Martin Luther King and the Civil Rights Movement, 1954–63* (London, 1988), 180.

87. J. Mills Thornton, *Dividing Lines: Municipal Politics and the Struggle for Civil Rights in Montgomery, Birmingham, and Selma* (Tuscaloosa, 2002), 40, 20–40.

88. Rosa Parks and Gregory J. Reed, *Quiet Strength: The Faith, the Hope, and the Heart of a Woman Who Changed a Nation* (Grand Rapids, MI, 1994), 23.

89. Louis E. Martin, "Dope and Data," *Chicago Defender,* February 16, 1957, 10.

90. David J. Garrow, *Bearing the Cross: Martin Luther King, Jr., and the Southern Christian Leadership Conference* (New York, 1988), 77.

91. Elizabeth Jacoway, *Turn Away Thy Son: Little Rock, the Crisis That Shocked the Nation* (Fayetteville, 2008).

92. Klarman, *From Jim Crow,* 424.

93. Jacoway, *Turn Away,* 105.

94. "Negro Progress," *Ebony* 13 (January 1958): 82.

95. John A. Kirk, *Redefining the Color Line: Black Activism in Little Rock, Arkansas, 1940–1970* (Gainesville, 2002), 276.

96. Clive Webb, "A Continuity of Conservatism: The Limitations of *Brown v. Board of Education*," *Journal of Southern History* 70 (May 2004): 330; Michal R. Belknap, *Federal Law and Southern Order: Racial Violence and Constitutional Conflict in the Post-Brown South* (Athens, GA, 1987), 28–29.

97. Douglas S. Massey and Nancy A. Denton, *American Apartheid: Segregation and the Making of the Underclass* (Cambridge, 1993), 49.

98. Thornton, *Dividing Lines,* 112, 95.

99. "Roy Wilkins Says Faubus Is 'Valuable Enemy,'" *Jet,* November 13, 1958, 4.

100. Matthew D. Lassiter, *The Silent Majority: Suburban Politics in the Sunbelt South* (Princeton, 2006), 24.

101. Atlanta Committee on Cooperative Action, *A Second Look* (Atlanta, 1960).

102. Michael J. Klarman, "Brown, Racial Change, and the Civil Rights Movement," *Virginia Law Review* 80 (February 1994): 84, 78.

103. Thornton, *Dividing Lines,* 100.

104. Danielle L. McGuire, "'It Was Like All of Us Had Been Raped': Sexual Violence, Community Mobilization, and the African American Freedom Struggle," *Journal of American History* 91 (December 2004): 916.

105. James Smith, "Local Leadership, the Biloxi Beach Riot, and the Origins of the Civil Rights Movement on the Mississippi Gulf Coast, 1959–64," in *Sunbelt Revolution: The Historical Progression of the Civil Rights Struggle in the Gulf South, 1866–2000,* ed. Samuel C. Hyde, 210–223 (Gainesville, 2003).

106. Glenn T. Eskew, *But for Birmingham: The Local and National Movements in the Civil Rights Struggle* (Chapel Hill, 1997), 125, 124.

107. Timothy B. Tyson, *Radio Free Dixie: Robert F. Williams and the Roots of Black Power* (Chapel Hill, 1999), 149, 66, 149.

108. "The Great Debate," *Southern Patriot* 18 (January 1960): 3.

109. "The Black Supremacists," *Time* 74 (August 10, 1959): 21.

110. "Women in the National Picture," *Chicago Defender,* January 1, 1944, 14; "N.Y. Police Head to Probe Cop Slaying of Harlem Boy," *Chicago Defender,* January 5, 1946, 4; "Woman Makes 10 Trips to Escort War Brides," *Chicago Defender,* January 25, 1947, 12.

111. *New York Age,* September 13, 1958.

9. The Civil Rights Movement, 1960–1965

1. Interview with Will Davis Campbell, 1968, *Ralph J. Bunche Oral History Collection,* Howard University.

2. Kevin Kruse, *White Flight: Atlanta and the Making of Modern Conservatism* (Princeton, 2005), 4–5.

3. Louis E. Lomax, *The Negro Revolt* (London, 1963), 17.

4. Joshua Benjamin Freeman, *Working-Class New York: Life and Labor since World War Two* (New York, 2000), 191.

5. William Henry Chafe, *Civilities and Civil Rights: Greensboro, North Carolina, and the Black Struggle for Freedom* (Oxford, 1980), 115, 119.

6. L. F. Palmer, Jr., "New Face of Young Negro America," *Daily Defender,* March 21, 1960, 1.

7. Robert A. Goldberg, "Racial Change on the Southern Periphery: The Case of San Antonio, Texas, 1960–1965," *Journal of Southern History* 49 (August 1983): 356.

8. James Farmer, *Lay Bare the Heart: An Autobiography of the Civil Rights Movement* (New York, 1985), 199.

9. L. F. Palmer, Jr., "Uprising for Freedom," *Daily Defender,* March 22, 1960, 9; L. F. Palmer, Jr., "Will Student 'Sit-in' Movement Continue?" *Daily Defender,* March 28, 1960, 1.

10. Chafe, *Civilities,* 111.

11. James Baldwin, "A Negro Assays the Negro Mood," *New York Times,* March 12, 1961, SM25.

12. Howard Schuman, Lawrence Bobo, and Charlotte Steeh, *Racial Attitudes in America: Trends and Interpretations* (Cambridge, 1985).

13. Brian Ward, *Just My Soul Responding: Rhythm and Blues, Black Consciousness and Race Relations* (London, 1998), 228.

14. Gene Roberts and Hank Klibanoff, *The Race Beat: The Press, the Civil Rights Struggle, and the Awakening of a Nation* (New York, 2006), 271.

15. Thomas Noer, "Segregationists and the World: The Foreign Policy of the White Resistance," in *Window on Freedom: Race, Civil Rights, and Foreign Affairs, 1945–1988,* ed. Brenda Gayle Plummer, 141–162 (Chapel Hill, 2003), 143.

16. Bruce J. Schulman, *From Cotton Belt to Sunbelt: Federal Policy, Economic Development, and the Transformation of the South, 1938–1980* (Durham, NC, 1994), 220.

17. Hazel Gaudet Erskine, "The Polls: Race Relations," *Public Opinion Quarterly* 26 (Spring 1962): 137–148.

18. Stacy Kinlock Sewell, "The 'Not-Buying Power' of the Black Community: Urban Boycotts and Equal Employment Opportunity, 1960–1964," *Journal of African American History* 89 (Spring 2004): 138.

19. Chafe, *Civilities,* 136.

20. Richard H. King, *Civil Rights and the Idea of Freedom* (New York, 1992).

21. "Sees All Public Segregation Ending in Two or Three Years," *Chicago Defender,* June 3, 1963, 8.

22. Baldwin, "A Negro Assays."

23. Palmer, "New Face of Young Negro America."

24. Baldwin, "A Negro Assays."

25. Interview with Gloria Richardson Dandridge, October 11, 1967, in *Ralph J. Bunche Oral History Collection,* Howard University.

26. Peter B. Levy, *Civil War on Race Street: The Civil Rights Movement in Cambridge, Maryland* (Gainesville, 2003).

27. August Meier and Elliott Rudwick, *CORE: A Study in the Civil Rights Movement, 1942–1968* (New York, 1973), 182.

28. Sewell, "Not-Buying Power," 139.

29. Matthew Countryman, *Up South: Civil Rights and Black Power in Philadelphia* (Philadelphia, 2006), 105.

30. Thomas F. Jackson, *From Civil Rights to Human Rights: Martin Luther King, Jr., and the Struggle for Economic Justice* (Philadelphia, 2007), 136.

31. Thomas J. Sugrue, "Affirmative Action from Below: Civil Rights, the Building Trades, and the Politics of Racial Equality in the Urban North, 1945–1969," *Journal of American History* 91 (June 2004): 145–173.

32. Jackson, *From Civil Rights,* 137.

33. Countryman, *Up South,* 145.

34. Verity Harding, "Black Power on a Black Campus" (B.A. thesis, University of Oxford, 2007), 8.

35. *Chicago Defender,* March 24, 1960, 1.

36. Stephen G. N. Tuck, *Beyond Atlanta: The Struggle for Racial Equality in Georgia, 1940–1980* (Athens, GA, 2001), 142–143.

37. Farmer, *Lay Bare,* 220.

38. W. F. Minor, "Oxford, Mississippi," *New York Amsterdam News,* October 6, 1962, in Carson, *Reporting Civil Rights,* 2:661, 663.

39. Tuck, *Beyond Atlanta,* 147.

40. Robin D. G. Kelley, "The Black Poor and the Politics of Opposition in a New South City, 1929–1970," in *The "Underclass" Debate,* ed. Michael B. Katz, 293–333 (Princeton, 1993), 312.

41. Ibid., 317.

42. "Martin Luther King, Jr., Letter from Birmingham Jail, April 16, 1963," http://mlk-kpp01.stanford.edu (accessed May 10, 2009).

43. Glenn T. Eskew, *But for Birmingham: The Local and National Movements in the Civil Rights Struggle* (Chapel Hill, 1997), 265.

44. Ibid., 268.

45. Ibid., 288.

46. Jackson, *From Civil Rights,* 165.

47. Roberts and Klibanoff, *Race Beat,* 338.

48. Meier and Rudwick, *CORE,* 226.

49. *Chicago Defender,* April 27–August 20, 1963.

50. Ruth Feldstein, "'I Don't Trust You Anymore': Nina Simone, Culture, and Black Activism in the 1960s," *Journal of American History* 91 (March 2005): 1349–1350.

51. Thomas Borstelmann, *The Cold War and the Color Line: American Race Relations in the Global Arena* (Cambridge, 2001), 141.

52. Mary L. Dudziak, *Cold War Civil Rights: Race and the Image of American Democracy* (Princeton, 2000), 182.

53. "John F. Kennedy, Radio and Television Report to the American People on Civil Rights, June 11, 1963," www.presidency.ucsb.edu (accessed 10 May 2009).

54. Aaron Henry and Constance Curry, *Aaron Henry: The Fire Ever Burning* (Jackson, 2000), 149.

55. B. R. Brazeal to Harold Fleming, 27 May 1959, "Some Facts Involved

in the Political Studies of Negro Residents in Baker County, Georgia," 13–14, Southern Regional Council Papers, Atlanta.

56. "Do Not Despair," *Time* 84 (November 27, 1964): 23.

57. Charles Sherrod to Jack Minnis, 9 October 1962, Voter Education Project Files, Southern Regional Council Papers, Atlanta.

58. Chana Kai Lee, *For Freedom's Sake: The Life of Fannie Lou Hamer* (Urbana, 1999), 12–13, 25.

59. Jack Chatfield, "Field Report, 29 March 1963," VEP Files, SRC Papers.

60. *Southern Patriot* 20 (December 1962): 3.

61. John Dittmer, *Local People: The Struggle for Civil Rights in Mississippi* (Urbana, 1994), 125.

62. Tuck, *Beyond Atlanta*, 170.

63. Editorial, *Atlanta Constitution*, September 16, 1963.

64. Interview with Fannie Lou Hamer, August 8, 1968, in *Ralph J. Bunche Oral History Collection*, Howard University, 23–32.

65. Ibid., 9.

66. Jack Chatfield, "Field Report, 4 December 1962," VEP Files, Student Nonviolent Coordinating Committee Papers (on microfilm).

67. Lee, *For Freedom's Sake*, 40.

68. Interview with Fannie Lou Hamer, 9.

69. Tuck, *Beyond Atlanta*, 176; Affidavits: Roberta Freeman and Henrietta Fuller, September 13, 1963, Series XV, SNCC Papers.

70. Dittmer, *Local People*, 194.

71. Ibid., 302, 286, 302.

72. Ibid., 230.

73. Winston A. Grady-Willis, *Challenging U.S. Apartheid: Atlanta and Black Struggles for Human Rights, 1960–1977* (Durham, NC, 2006), 73.

74. John Churchville, "Field Report," February 11, 1963, SNCC Papers.

75. Countryman, *Up South*.

76. Dittmer, *Local People*, 254.

77. James Forman, *The Making of Black Revolutionaries* (Washington, DC, 1985), 405.

78. Lee, *For Freedom's Sake*, 100.

79. Jon Perdew, "Southwest Georgia Field Report," November 22, 1965, 6, SNCC Papers.

80. Lance E. Hill, *The Deacons for Defense: Armed Resistance and the Civil Rights Movement* (Chapel Hill, 2004), 144.

81. Ibid., 137, 161, 224.

82. Ibid., 159.

83. Charles M. Payne, *I've Got the Light of Freedom: The Organizing Tradition and the Mississippi Freedom Struggle* (Berkeley, 1995), 370.

84. Forman, *Making of Black Revolutionaries*, 437.

85. "125,000 Rally in Detroit," *New York Times*, June 24, 1963, 20; "King Leads Demonstration by 100,000 Detroit Marchers," *Washington Post*, June 24, 1963, 7. Peniel E. Joseph, *Waiting 'Til the Midnight Hour: A Narrative History of Black Power in America* (New York, 2006), 83.

86. "Racial Unrest Reaching Critical Point in Auto City," *Chicago Defender*,

June 3, 1963, 9; David A. Bobbitt, *The Rhetoric of Redemption: Kenneth Burke's Redemption Drama and Martin Luther King, Jr.'s "I Have a Dream" Speech* (Lanham, MD, 2004), 16.

87. Suzanne E. Smith, *Dancing in the Street: Motown and the Cultural Politics of Detroit* (Cambridge, 1999), 45.

88. Heather Ann Thompson, *Whose Detroit? Politics, Labor, and Race in a Modern American City* (Ithaca, 2004), 40, 41.

89. Joseph, *Waiting,* 84.

90. Quintard Taylor, "The Civil Rights Movement in the American West: Black Protest in Seattle, 1960–1970," *Journal of Negro History* 80 (Winter 1995): 4.

91. "Racial Unrest Reaching Critical Point in Auto City," *Chicago Defender,* June 3, 1963, 9.

92. Clarence Taylor, *Knocking At Our Own Door: Milton A. Galamison and the Struggle to Integrate New York City Schools* (New York, 1997), 141.

93. Josh Sides, *L.A. City Limits: African American Los Angeles from the Great Depression to the Present* (Berkeley, 2003), 162–166; Meier and Rudwick, *CORE,* 247.

94. Meier and Rudwick, *CORE,* 141.

95. Hugh Davis Graham, *The Civil Rights Era: Origins and Development of National Policy, 1960–1972* (New York, 1990), 149, 111.

96. Countryman, *Up South,* 165, 144.

97. "Dr. King Takes Walk in Atlanta," *Jet* 29 (February 17, 1966), 46; Vine City Council, "'The City Must Provide.' South Atlanta: The Forgotten Community," (no date) 1–2, Atlanta Project, SNCC Papers.

98. Interview with Gloria Richardson Dandridge.

99. "Commission on Racial Discrimination Impressed by Negro Student Protest," *Washington Post,* January 28, 1964, A2.

100. Freeman, *Working-Class New York,* 199.

101. Ronald Lawson and Mark Naison, *The Tenant Movement in New York City, 1904–1984* (New Brunswick, NJ, 1986), 180.

102. Taylor, *Knocking,* 151.

103. Surveys by Louis Harris and Associates during November 1963; and by Opinion Research Corporation, October 15–November 15, 1963; and by National Opinion Research Center, University of Chicago, during April and December, 1963. Retrieved February 1, 2008, from the iPOLL Databank, Roper Center for Public Opinion Research, University of Connecticut; Schuman, Bobo and Steeh, *Racial Attitudes.*

104. Quintard Taylor, *In Search of the Racial Frontier: African Americans in the American West, 1528–1990* (New York, 1998), 291.

105. "Atlanta Schools," *New South,* February 20, 1965, 9.

106. Schuman, Bobo, and Steeh, *Racial Attitudes,* 75.

107. Kruse, *White Flight,* 107, 248.

108. "Black Muslims Join New Militant Northern Negro Organization," *Chicago Defender,* November 21, 1963, 16.

109. John A. Williams, *This Is My Country Too* (New York, 1965), 167.

110. Thompson, *Whose Detroit?* 44, 137.

111. Robert Penn Warren, *Who Speaks for the Negro?* (New York, 1965), 197.

112. Malcolm X and Alex Haley, *The Autobiography of Malcolm X* (New York, 1965), 346.

113. Malcolm X, *Malcolm X Speaks: Selected Speeches and Statements,* ed. George Breitman (New York, 1965), 143, 240, 93.

114. Julius Lester, "The Angry Children of Malcolm X," *Sing Out!* 16 (October/November 1966): 24.

115. X, *Malcolm X Speaks,* 56.

116. Ibid., 228.

117. Cynthia Young, "Havana Up in Harlem: LeRoi Jones, Harold Cruse and the Making of a Cultural Revolution," *Science and Society* 65 (Spring 2001): 14.

118. X, *Malcolm X Speaks,* 53.

119. Tuck, *Beyond Atlanta,* 128.

120. "London Solidarity March," *West Indian Gazette and Afro-Asian-Caribbean News,* September 1960, 1; Martin Luther King, *A Call to Conscience: The Landmark Speeches of Dr. Martin Luther King, Jr.,* ed. Clayborne Carson and Kris Shepard (London, 2001), 81–87.

121. Interview with Ella Baker, June 19, 1968, in *Ralph Bunche Oral History Collection,* Howard University, 85–86. Keith D. Miller, *Voice of Deliverance: The Language of Martin Luther King, Jr., and Its Sources* (New York, 1992), 146.

122. Jackson, *From Civil Rights,* 3, 140, 24.

123. Andrew Young, *An Easy Burden: The Civil Rights Movement and the Transformation of America* (New York, 1996), 341.

124. United States Commission on Civil Rights, *Political Participation: A Study of the Participation by Negroes in the Electoral and Political Processes in 10 Southern States since Passage of the Voting Rights Act of 1965* (Washington, 1968), 224–225.

125. Ralph David Abernathy, *And the Walls Came Tumbling Down: An Autobiography* (New York, 1989), 317.

126. J. Mills Thornton, *Dividing Lines: Municipal Politics and the Struggle for Civil Rights in Montgomery, Birmingham, and Selma* (Tuscaloosa, 2002), 434.

127. Steven F. Lawson, *Running for Freedom: Civil Rights and Black Politics in America since 1941* (New York, 1997), 107.

128. Abernathy, *And the Walls,* 318.

129. "President Promises Dr. King Vote Move," *New York Times,* February 10, 1965, 1, 18.

130. Garrow, *Bearing the Cross,* 388.

131. Lyndon B. Johnson, *The Vantage Point: Perspectives of the Presidency, 1963–1969* (New York, 1971), 162.

132. Pat Watters and Reese Cleghorn, *Climbing Jacob's Ladder: The Arrival of Negroes in Southern Politics* (New York, 1967), 248.

133. Garrow, *Bearing the Cross,* 399, 145.

134. Lewis and D'Orso, *Walking with the Wind,* 334.

135. "Lyndon B. Johnson, Special Message to the Congress: The American Promise," www.presidency.ucsb.edu (accessed 10 May 2009).

136. Estes, *I Am a Man!* 103.

137. Robert Dallek, *Flawed Giant: Lyndon Johnson and His Times, 1961–1973* (Oxford, 1998), 217.

138. Doris Kearns Goodwin, *Lyndon Johnson and the American Dream* (London, 1976), vii–viii.

139. Rowland Evans and Robert D. Novak, *Lyndon B. Johnson: The Exercise of Power: A Political Biography* (New York, 1966), 497.

140. Steven F. Lawson, *Black Ballots: Voting Rights in the South, 1944–1969* (New York, 1976), 314.

141. Lawson, *Black Ballots,* 321.

142. Stephen G. N. Tuck, "Making the Voting Rights Act," in *The Voting Rights Act: Securing the Ballot,* ed. Richard M. Valelly, 95–112 (Washington, DC, 2006), 112.

10. Black Power and Grassroots Protest, 1966–1978

1. Interview with Ella Baker, June 19, 1968, in *Ralph J. Bunche Oral History Collection,* Howard University, 85–86.

2. Peter B. Levy, *Civil War on Race Street: The Civil Rights Movement in Cambridge, Maryland* (Gainesville, 2003), 163.

3. Interview with Ewart Brown, September 14, 1968, in *Ralph J. Bunche Oral History Collection,* Howard University, 56.

4. Annelise Orleck, *Storming Caesars Palace: How Black Mothers Fought Their Own War on Poverty* (Boston, 2005).

5. "Heat on Highway 51," *Time* 87 (June 17, 1966): 30–31.

6. "Meredith Has Voters March in Dixie," *Chicago Daily Defender,* June 6, 1966, 4.

7. Steven F. Lawson, *In Pursuit of Power: Southern Blacks and Electoral Politics, 1965–1982* (New York, 1985), 50.

8. "Meredith March Miffs NAACP," *Chicago Daily Defender,* June 2, 1966, 5.

9. *Chicago Defender,* June 1–5, 1966; Kevin L. Yuill, "The 1966 White House Conference on Civil Rights," *Historical Journal* 41 (January 1998): 267.

10. "Johnson Orders Full U.S. Inquiry," *New York Times,* June 7, 1966, 29; "Meredith Is Wounded by Shotgun Blasts; He Won't Die," *Chicago Defender,* June 7, 1966, 1.

11. Adolph J. Slaughter, "White Supremacy Must Go: Meredith," *Chicago Defender,* June 25, 1966, 2.

12. Henry Hampton, Steve Fayer, and Sarah Flynn, *Voices of Freedom: An Oral History of the Civil Rights Movement from the 1950s through the 1980s* (New York, 1990), 291; "The New Leadership," *Chicago Defender,* July 9, 1966, 10.

13. "Quit Conference Table, Seek Power: Rep. Powell," *Chicago Defender,* May 31, 1966, 6; "Watts, a District without Bootstraps; Watts Described as without Hope," *New York Times,* March 20, 1966, 1.

14. "Negro Nationalism a Black Power Key," *New York Times,* July 24, 1966, 1.

15. Jack V. Fox, "Ain't Nobody Ready to Start Revolution," *Chicago Defender,* February 26, 1968, 1.

16. Stephen Tuck, *Beyond Atlanta: The Struggle for Racial Equality in Georgia, 1940–1980* (Athens, GA, 2001), 201; Sondra K. Wilson, *In Search of Democracy: The NAACP Writings of James Weldon Johnson, Walter White, and Roy Wilkins (1920–1977)* (New York, 1999), 424; John Lewis and Michael D'Orso, *Walking with the Wind: A Memoir of the Movement* (New York, 1998), 368.

17. Julius Lester, *Look Out, Whitey! Black Power's Gon' Get Your Mama!* (London, 1970), 100.

18. Ibid., 97.

19. "Only in America," *Washington Post,* May 6, 1967, 12.

20. Lester, *Look Out, Whitey!* 101.

21. "Armed Negroes Protest Gun Bill," *New York Times,* May 3, 1967, 23.

22. Louis E. Lomax, *The Negro Revolt* (London, 1963), 18.

23. Stokely Carmichael and Charles V. Hamilton, *Black Power: The Politics of Liberation in America* (New York, 1967), 106, 52, 44, viii.

24. William L. Van Deburg, *New Day in Babylon: The Black Power Movement and American Culture, 1965–1975* (Chicago, 1992), 21.

25. Steve Estes, *I Am a Man! Race, Manhood, and the Civil Rights Movement* (Chapel Hill, 2005), 157.

26. Thomas Sugrue and Andrew Goodman, "Plainfield Burning: Black Rebellion in the Suburban North," *Journal of Urban History* 33, no. 4 (2007): 588.

27. Lawrence Stewart, *Militant,* July 24, 1967.

28. Interview with Anonymous "A," November 26, 1968, in *Ralph J. Bunche Oral History Collection,* Howard University.

29. Manfred Berg, *"The Ticket to Freedom": The NAACP and the Struggle for Black Political Integration* (Gainesville, 2005), 211–212.

30. Robert O. Self, *American Babylon: Race and the Struggle for Postwar Oakland* (Princeton, 2003), 222.

31. John Langston Gwaltney, *Drylongso: A Self-Portrait of Black America* (New York, 1980), 5, 8.

32. Simon Hall, *Peace and Freedom: The Civil Rights and Antiwar Movements of the 1960s* (Philadelphia, 2005).

33. Hugh Davis Graham, *The Civil Rights Era: Origins and Development of National Policy, 1960–1972* (New York, 1990), 334.

34. Lester, *Look Out, Whitey!* 53.

35. Self, *American Babylon,* 202.

36. Matthew Countryman, *Up South: Civil Rights and Black Power in Philadelphia* (Philadelphia, 2006); Heather Ann Thompson, *Whose Detroit? Politics, Labor, and Race in a Modern American City* (Ithaca, NY, 2004), 82.

37. Lester, *Look Out, Whitey!* 16.

38. Matthew D. Lassiter, *The Silent Majority: Suburban Politics in the Sunbelt South* (Princeton, 2006), 6.

39. Thomas Borstelmann, *The Cold War and the Color Line: American Race Relations in the Global Arena* (Cambridge, 2001), 226.

40. Self, *American Babylon*, 15.

41. United States National Advisory Commission on Civil Disorders, *Report*, 1.

42. Simon Hall, "The NAACP, Black Power, and the African American Freedom Struggle, 1966–1969," *Historian* 69 (Spring 2007): 73.

43. David Plank and Marcia Turner, "Changing Patterns in Black School Politics: Atlanta, 1872–1973," *American Journal of Education* 56 (August 1987): 601.

44. Douglas Robinson, "Dr. King Proposes a Boycott of War," *New York Times*, April 5, 1968, 1.

45. Andrew Young, *An Easy Burden: The Civil Rights Movement and the Transformation of America* (New York, 1996), 413.

46. "McKissick Says Nonviolence Has Become Dead Philosophy," *New York Times*, April 5, 1968, 26.

47. Hall, "The NAACP," 80.

48. "Action, Not Sympathy, Urged," *Chicago Defender*, April 9, 1968, 16.

49. Peniel E. Joseph, *Waiting 'Til the Midnight Hour: A Narrative History of Black Power in America* (New York, 2006), 194.

50. James Forman, *The Making of Black Revolutionaries* (Washington, DC, 1985), 483.

51. Frantz Fanon, *The Wretched of the Earth* (London, 1963), 73.

52. "U.S.A. Newsletter, Changes in Color," *West Indian Gazette* and *Afro-Asian Caribbean News*, September 1960, 2; Timothy B. Tyson, *Radio Free Dixie: Robert F. Williams and the Roots of Black Power* (Chapel Hill, 1999), 227.

53. Kevin Gaines, *African Americans in Ghana: Black Expatriates and the Civil Rights Era* (Chapel Hill, 2007); Komozi Woodard, *A Nation within a Nation: Amiri Baraka (LeRoi Jones) and Black Power Politics* (Chapel Hill, 1999), 32.

54. Maulana Karenga, "Us, Kawaida and the Black Liberation Movement in the 1960s: Culture, Knowledge and Struggle," in *Engines of the Black Power Movement: Essays on the Influence of Civil Rights Actions, Arts, and Islam*, ed. James L. Conyers, 95–133 (Jefferson, NC, 2007), 114.

55. "Church Council Hears Self-Abolition Plan," *Washington Post*, December 2, 1969, 6.

56. Van Deburg, *New Day*, 46.

57. LeRoi Jones, *Black Art*, ed. LeRoi Jones and Larry Neal (New York, 1969), 303.

58. "Tribute to the Queen," *Hilltop*, October 21, 1966, quoted in Harding, "Black Power," 23.

59. *Look*, February 18, 1969.

60. Ibid., 195.

61. Van Deburg, *New Day*, 253.

62. Ben Caldwell, "Prayer Meeting, or, the First Jubilant Minister," in *Black Fire: An Anthology of Afro-American Writing*, ed. LeRoi Jones and Larry Neal, 589–594 (New York, 1969), 592.

63. Larry Neal, "Afterword: And Shine Swam On," in *Black Fire*, ed. Jones and Neal, 656.

64. LeRoi Jones, "Black Art," in *Black Fire,* ed. Jones and Neal, 302.

65. Van Deburg, *New Day,* 65.

66. Woodard, *A Nation,* 35.

67. Interview with Anonymous "B," April 24, 1968, in *Ralph J. Bunche Oral History Collection,* Howard University, 18.

68. Lawson, *In Pursuit,* 87.

69. R. E. Weems, *Desegregating the Dollar: African American Consumerism in the Twentieth Century* (New York, 1998), 78–79.

70. "Announcing a Brief Course in American History," *Ebony* 25 (1970): 181.

71. Woodard, *A Nation,* 93.

72. Francis Njubi Nesbitt, *Race for Sanctions: African Americans against Apartheid, 1946–1994* (Bloomington, 2004), 79.

73. Hall, "The NAACP," 55.

74. Calvin C. Hernton, "Sex and Racism in Films," *White Papers for White Americans* (1966), in Clayborne Carson, *Reporting Civil Rights,* vol. 2 (New York, 2003), 469, 471.

75. Brian Ward, *Radio and the Struggle for Civil Rights in the South* (Gainesville, 2004), 284.

76. Phyl Garland, "Blacks Challenge the Airwaves," *Ebony* 26 (November 1970): 35–36.

77. Weems, *Desegregating the Dollar,* 95.

78. Van Deburg, *New Day,* 217.

79. Ward, *Just My Soul,* 412.

80. Simon Hall, "Protest Movements in the 1970s: The Long 1960s," *Journal of Contemporary History* 43 (October 2008): 655–672; Countryman, *Up South,* 252.

81. Emilye Crosby, *A Little Taste of Freedom: The Black Freedom Struggle in Claiborne County, Mississippi* (Chapel Hill, 2005), 91, 44.

82. Ibid., 132.

83. James L. Jones, "Troopers, Negroes in Comic Opera Campus Clash," *Chicago Defender,* April 6, 1966, 4.

84. Walter Rugaberjackson, "We Can't Cuss White People Any More. It's in Our Hands Now," *New York Times,* August 4, 1968, SM12.

85. A. S. Doc Young, "Evers Moves the Throng," *Chicago Defender,* July 1, 1967, 1.

86. Crosby, *A Little Taste of Freedom,* 108.

87. Ibid., 178.

88. Ibid., 112.

89. Tuck, *Beyond Atlanta,* 205.

90. *New South* 24 (Summer 1964): 96.

91. J. Todd Moye, *Let the People Decide: Black Freedom and White Resistance Movements in Sunflower County, Mississippi, 1945–1986* (Chapel Hill, 2004), 168.

92. "800 in Mississippi March on Capitol," *New York Times,* August 15, 1967, 35; "800 Poor Mississippians March on Capitol," *Chicago Defender,* August 15, 1967, 1.

93. "The 'Goods' on Claude Purcell," Constance Curry to Jean Fairfax, Mem-

orandum, 4 May 1965, American Friends Service Committee Files, Philadelphia; letter, Curtis Thomas to Vernon Jordan, 11 November 1966 (in possession of Curtis Thomas); Tuck, *Beyond Atlanta,* 215–216, 187–188.

94. Tuck, *Beyond Atlanta,* 188.

95. Author interviews with Joe Hendricks, John Goolsby, and Linda Mitchell; Campbell, *Forty Acres,* 243–248.

96. Gareth Davies, "Richard Nixon and the Desegregation of Southern Schools," *Journal of Policy History* 19 (4th Quarter 2007): 369.

97. "Closing the Gap," *Chicago Defender,* February 4, 1970, 15.

98. Berg, *Ticket to Freedom,* 270.

99. Lerone Benett, "Black Americans and the Energy Siege," *Ebony* 34 (October 1979): 31.

100. "Black Voices Speak Up," *Time* 112 (December 18, 1978): 31.

101. Graham, *Civil Rights Era,* 311.

102. Richard A. Pride, *The Political Use of Racial Narratives: School Desegregation in Mobile, Alabama, 1954–97* (Urbana, 2002), 107.

103. Dan T. Carter, *The Politics of Rage: George Wallace, the Origins of the New Conservatism, and the Transformation of American Politics* (New York, 1995), 45.

104. Davies, "Richard Nixon," 368–394.

105. Graham, *Civil Rights Era,* 448.

106. Gareth Davies, "The Great Society after Johnson: The Case of Bilingual Education," *Journal of American History* 88 (March 2002): 1405–1429.

107. Lance Jay Robbins, "Federal Remedies for Employment Discrimination in the Construction Industry," *California Law Review* 60 (June 1972): 1196–1234.

108. Kevin Michael Kruse, *White Flight: Atlanta and the Making of Modern Conservatism* (Princeton, 2005).

109. Robert O. Self, *American Babylon: Race and the Struggle for Postwar Oakland* (Princeton, 2003), 261.

110. Kruse, *White Flight.*

111. Lassiter, *Silent Majority,* 1.

112. Ibid., 194.

113. Phyl Garland, "FCC License Contests Provide New Pressure for More 'Soul' in TV, Radio," *Ebony* 26 (November 1970): 35.

114. Jeanne Theoharis, "'I'd Rather Go to School in the South': How Boston's School Desegregation Complicates the Civil Rights Paradigm," in *Freedom North: Black Freedom Struggles Outside the South, 1940–1980,* ed. Jeanne Theoharis and Komozi Woodard, 125–151 (New York, 2002), 139.

115. Nancy MacLean, *Freedom Is Not Enough: The Opening of the American Work Place* (New York, 2006); Timothy J. Minchin, *Hiring the Black Worker: The Racial Integration of the Southern Textile Industry, 1960–1980* (Chapel Hill, 1999); "Washington Coalition," *Chicago Defender,* February 2, 1970, 13.

116. MacLean, *Freedom Is Not Enough,* 87.

117. Nicholas Pedriana and Robin Stryker, "The Strength of a Weak Agency: Enforcement of Title VII of the 1964 Civil Rights Act and the Expansion of State

Capacity, 1965–1971," *American Journal of Sociology* 110 (November 2004): 709–760.

118. *United States v. Bethlehem Steel Corp.*, 446 F.2d 652, 659 (2d Cir. 1971).

119. *Griggs v. Duke Power Co.*, 401 U.S. 424, 431, 1971.

120. "$30 Million for Workers," *Chicago Defender*, April 16, 1974, 6.

121. Bruce Nelson, *Divided We Stand: American Workers and the Struggle for Black Equality* (Princeton, 2001), 281.

122. James P. Smith and Finis R. Welch, "Black Economic Progress after Myrdal," *Journal of Economic Literature* 27 (June 1989): 554; Gavin Wright, "The Civil Rights Revolution as Economic History," *Journal of Economic History* 59 (June 1999): 277; MacLean, *Freedom Is Not Enough*, 103.

123. Thomas J. Sugrue, *The Origins of the Urban Crisis: Race and Inequality in Postwar Detroit* (Princeton, 1996).

124. Jacqueline Trescott, "One of God's Angry Men," *Washington Post*, September 23, 1977, C1; "The 100 Most Influential Black Americans," *Ebony* 23 (May 1978): 70.

125. James Lane, "Black Political Power and Its Limits: Gary Mayor Richard G. Hatcher's Administration, 1968–87," in *African-American Mayors: Race, Politics, and the American City*, ed. David R. Colburn and Jeffrey S. Adler, 57–79 (Urbana, 2001), 63.

126. Cedric Herring, *African Americans and the Public Agenda: The Paradoxes of Public Policy* (Thousand Oaks, CA, 1997), 49.

127. Tuck, *Beyond Atlanta*, 237.

128. Deborah G. White, *Too Heavy a Load: Black Women in Defense of Themselves, 1894–1994* (New York, 1999), 215.

129. Johnnie Tillman, "Welfare Is a Women's Issue," *Ms.* 1 (Spring 1972).

130. Carolyn DuBose, "Champion of Welfare Rights," *Ebony* 25 (April 1970): 29.

131. "Mrs. Tillmon Heads NWRO," *Chicago Daily Defender*, January 23, 1973, 5.

132. James T. Patterson, *America's Struggle against Poverty in the Twentieth Century* (Cambridge, 2000), 189.

133. Marisa Chappell, "Rethinking Women's Politics in the 1970s: The League of Women Voters and the National Organization for Women Confront Poverty," *Journal of Women's History* 13 (Winter 2002): 163.

134. *Washington Daily News*, June 25, 1970; Ethel L. Payne, "So This Is Washington," *Chicago Defender*, August 29, 1970, 7.

135. Charles G. Hurst, Jr., "Black Focus," *Chicago Defender*, September 8, 1973, 20.

136. Steven Kest, "Acorn and Community-Labor Partnerships," *WorkingUSA* 6 (March 2003): 84; Steven Greenhouse, "Wages of Workfare," *New York Times*, July 7, 1997, B3.

137. Todd Shaw, "We Refused to Lay Down Our Spears: The Persistence of Welfare Rights Activism, 1966–1996," in *Black Political Organizations in the Post-Civil Rights Era*, ed. Ollie A. Johnson and Karin L. Stanford, 170–192 (New Brunswick, NJ, 2002), 183.

138. Susan M. Hartmann, "Pauli Murray and the 'Juncture of Women's Liberation and Black Liberation,'" *Journal of Women's History* 14 (Summer 2002): 74–77.

139. "Blacks Declare War on Dope," *Ebony* 25 (June 1970): 31.

140. Hartmann, "Pauli Murray."

141. Chappell, "Rethinking Women's Politics," 155.

142. Chana Kai Lee, *For Freedom's Sake: The Life of Fannie Lou Hamer* (Urbana, 1999), 171.

143. Elsa Barkley Brown, "'What Has Happened Here': The Politics of Difference in Women's History and Feminist Politics," *Feminist Studies* 18 (Summer 1992): 300.

144. White, *Too Heavy,* 245.

145. J. Christopher Schutz, "The Burning of America: Race, Radicalism, and the 'Charlotte Three' Trial in 1970s North Carolina," *North Carolina Historical Review* 76 (January 1999): 44, 53.

146. "Black Panther Panels," *Chicago Defender,* January 3, 1970, 6.

147. Faith C. Christmas, "It's Still a 'Plot,'" *Chicago Defender,* December 31, 1969, 1.

148. Manning Marable, *Race, Reform, and Rebellion* (Jackson, MS, 1991), 30.

149. Ginny Looney, "Segregation Order at Reidsville Prison," *Southern Changes* 1 (1979): 19–21.

150. Betty Norwood Chaney, "Tupelo, Hometown in Turmoil," *Southern Changes* 1 (1978): 16–19; Jim Alexander, "Confrontation—Tupelo, Mississippi, 1978," *Black Commentator* 198 (September 21, 2006), www.blackcommentator.com (accessed April 2007); Wayne King, "The Klan Has More Crosses to Bear Than Burn," *New York Times,* July 30, 1978, E5; Warren Brown, "Boycott; Black Protest in Tupelo Stirs Klan-Led Backlash," *Washington Post,* June 26, 1978, A1.

11. Reagan, Rap, and Resistance, 1979–2000

1. "University of New Hampshire Surrenders to Black Student Protests," *Journal of Blacks in Higher Education* 22 (Winter, 1998–1999): 33–34.

2. "Ronald Reagan, Remarks Announcing Candidacy for the Republican Presidential Nomination, November 13, 1979," www.presidency.ucsb.edu (accessed May 13, 2009).

3. "Ronald Reagan, Remarks at Neshoba County Fair, August 3, 1980," www.neshobademocrat.com (accessed May 13, 2009).

4. "Campaign Report: Reagan Wins Endorsement of a Major Klan Group," *New York Times,* July 31, 1980, B10.

5. Andrew Young, "Chilling Words in Neshoba County," *Washington Post,* August 11, 1980, A19.

6. Francis Njubi Nesbitt, *Race for Sanctions: African Americans against Apartheid, 1946–1994* (Bloomington, 2004), 113.

7. "Cabinet Aide Greeted by Reagan as 'Mayor,'" *New York Times,* June 19, 1981, A17.

8. *New Pittsburgh Courier,* January 15, 1994.

9. "William J. Clinton, Address Before a Joint Session of the Congress on the State of the Union, January 23, 1996," www.presidency.ucsb.edu (accessed May 13, 2009).

10. Allison Samuels, "Minstrels in Baggy Jeans?" *Newsweek,* May 5, 2003, 62.

11. "Blacks in Film," *Washington Post,* August 15, 1982, F1.

12. Bakari Kitwana, *Why White Kids Love Hip-Hop: Wankstas, Wiggers, Wannabes, and the New Reality of Race in America* (New York, 2005), 10.

13. Angela Ards, "Organizing the Hip-Hop Generation," in *That's the Joint: The Hip-Hop Studies Reader,* ed. Mark Anthony Neal and Murray Forman, 311–324 (London, 2004), 315.

14. Nelson George, "Hip-Hop's Founding Fathers Speak the Truth," in *That's the Joint,* ed. Neal and Forman, 45–56.

15. Jeff Chang, *Can't Stop Won't Stop: A History of the Hip-Hop Generation* (London, 2005), 276; Jeff Chang, "Who Will Be Our Leaders," *Colorlines Magazine: Race, Action, Culture* 8 (Fall 2005).

16. Chang, *Can't Stop,* 210.

17. Derrick P. Alridge, "From Civil Rights to Hip Hop: Toward a Nexus of Ideas," *Journal of African American History* 90 (Summer 2005): 232.

18. Thomas Edsall, "Clinton Stuns Rainbow Coalition," *Washington Post,* June 14, 1992, A1; Sheila Rule, "Rapper, Chided by Clinton, Calls Him a Hypocrite," *New York Times,* June 17, 1992, A1.

19. Nancy MacLean, *Freedom Is Not Enough: The Opening of the American Work Place* (New York, 2006), 291.

20. See, for example, W. Elliot Brownlee and Hugh Davis Graham, *The Reagan Presidency: Pragmatic Conservatism and Its Legacies* (Lawrence, KS, 2003).

21. Chang, *Can't Stop,* 247.

22. Ibid., 331.

23. Ibid., 397.

24. Margot Hornblower, "Miami Violence Abates, but Blacks Simmer," *Washington Post,* May 20, 1980, A1; Warren Brown, "Black Miami's Voices," *Washington Post,* May 23, 1980, A1; "Profile of a Rioter: Under 30, Male, Frustrated," *Washington Post,* June 22, 1980, A7.

25. David Samuels, "The Rap on Rap: The 'Black Music' That Isn't Either," in *That's the Joint,* ed. Neal and Forman, 147–154.

26. "Sister Souljah Statement," www.theroc.org (accessed May 13, 2009).

27. Juan Williams, "Black Leaders Find a Hot New Issue," *Washington Post,* December 12, 1984, A1.

28. Karlyn Barker, "Antiapartheid Movement to Mark Anniversary," *Washington Post,* November 27, 1985, B1; Evalyn Tennant, "Dismantling U.S.-Style Apartheid," *Colorlines* 7 (April 30, 2004): 10.

29. Williams, "Black Leaders."

30. "U.S. Manoeuvres in Southern Africa," *Sechaba,* April, 1984, 1–2.

31. Tennant, "Dismantling."

32. Glenn Frankel, "Botha Terms Moves Harmful; Tutu Calls Reagan a Racist," *Washington Post,* September 10, 1985, A1.

33. Karlyn Barker and Michel Marriott, "1960s Tactics Revived for Embassy Sit-Ins," *Washington Post,* November 29, 1984, A12.

34. Karlyn Barker, "D.C. Workers Protest at Embassy," *Washington Post,* April 5, 1985, A1.

35. Williams, "Black Leaders."

36. Barry Sussman, "Apartheid Protests Supported by Most Who Know of Them," *Washington Post,* January 27, 1985, A23.

37. Nesbitt, *Race for Sanctions,* 143.

38. D. Michael Cheers, "Nelson Mandela: A Special Message to Black Americans," *Ebony* 45 (May 1990): 179, 180.

39. *Tri-State Defender* 35 (June 18, 1986).

40. Lawrence Feinberg, "Arrests at British Embassy," *Washington Post,* December 23, 1984, A6.

41. Nicolas Alexander, "What Ever Happened to the Free South Africa Movement?" *Third Force* 1 (April 30, 1993): 9.

42. Ibid.

43. Dale Russakoff, "As in the '60s, Protesters Rally; But This Time the Foe Is PCB," *Washington Post,* October 11, 1982, A1.

44. Ibid.

45. Robert D. Bullard, "Environmental Justice in the Twenty-First Century," in *The Quest for Environmental Justice: Human Rights and the Politics of Pollution,* ed. Robert D. Bullard, 19–42 (San Francisco, 2005), 30.

46. Robert D. Bullard, *Confronting Environmental Racism: Voices from the Grassroots* (Boston, 1993), 22; Bullard, "Environmental Justice," 7.

47. Luke W. Cole and Sheila R. Foster, *From the Ground Up: Environmental Racism and the Rise of the Environmental Justice Movement* (New York, 2001), 21.

48. Robert D. Bullard and Damu Smith, "Women Warriors of Color on the Front Line," in *The Quest for Environmental Justice,* ed. Bullard, 102.

49. Ziba Zashef, "Saving Our Backyard," *Essence* 30 (September 1999): 164.

50. Cole and Foster, *From the Ground Up,* 162.

51. Ibid.

52. Christina Bledsoe, "Burke Country Today," *Georgia Poverty Journal* 1 (Fall 1986): 6–14.

53. "Changing Sides," *Time* 123 (March 19, 1984): 24.

54. MacLean, *Freedom Is Not Enough,* 302.

55. Copy of speech in possession of author, courtesy of Julian Bond.

56. "William J. Clinton, Satellite Remarks and a Question-and-Answer Session with the National Council of La Raza, July 19, 1995," www.presidency.ucsb.edu (accessed May 14, 2009).

57. MacLean, *Freedom Is Not Enough,* 313, 302.

58. Copy of speech in possession of author, courtesy of Julian Bond.

59. Ron Daniels, *Michigan Citizen,* January 27, 1990.

60. "Frontline: Henry Louis Gates, Jr., Interview with William Julius Wilson," www.pbs.org (accessed May 14, 2009).

61. Steven Greenhouse, "2 Well-Known Churches Say No to Workfare Jobs," *New York Times,* August 4, 1997, B3.

62. Steven Greenhouse, "City Labor Director Backs Effort to Organize Workfare Participants," *New York Times,* February 9, 1997, 40.

63. Vanessa Tait, "Workers Just Like Anyone Else," in *Still Lifting, Still Climbing: Contemporary African American Women's Activism,* ed. Kimberly Springer, 297–311 (New York, 1999).

64. Steven Greenhouse, "Wages of Workfare," *New York Times,* July 7, 1997, B3.

65. Lynette Holloway, "Plurality of Workfare Recipients Said to Vote in Favor of a Union," *New York Times,* October 24, 1997, B5.

66. *Third Force,* September 30, 2000.

67. Nina Bernstein, "City Fires 3,500 Former Welfare Recipients," *New York Times,* January 5, 2002, B3.

68. Diane Weathers, "Corporate Race Wars—Racism," *Essence* 28 (October 1997): 80–88.

69. Bari-Ellen Roberts and Jack E. White, *Roberts vs. Texaco: A True Story of Race and Corporate America* (New York, 1998).

70. "New Hope in Inner Cities: Banks Offering Mortgages," *New York Times,* March 14, 1992, 1; "Chemical and Hanover Reach Accord with Community Group," *New York Times,* November 21, 1991, D3.

71. William Harms, "Research Shows Pre-'90s Progress in Narrowing Achievement Gap Has Stalled," *University of Chicago Chronicle* 24 (May 12, 2005).

72. Michael B. Katz, Mark J. Stern, and Jamie J. Fader, "The New African American Inequality," *Journal of American History* 92 (June 2005): 83.

73. Ellis Cose, *The Rage of a Privileged Class: Why Do Prosperous Blacks Still Have the Blues?* (New York, 1993), 13.

74. Katz, Stern, and Fader, "New African American Inequality," 105.

75. "Racial Differences in Mortgage Lending," *New York Times,* July 19, 1992, 32; Thomas M. Shapiro, *The Hidden Cost of Being African American: How Wealth Perpetuates Inequality* (New York, 2004).

76. "Old Memories, New Marches," *Washington Post,* January 28, 1987, A20.

77. William Raspberry, "But Did the March Have a Purpose?" *Washington Post,* January 23, 1987, A19.

78. David Firestone, "Many See Their Future in County with a Past," *New York Times,* April 8, 1999, A18.

79. Kendra Hamilton, "Activists for the New Millennium," *Black Issues in Higher Education* 20 (April 24, 2003): 16.

80. Philip S. Gutis, "Town Houses to Emerge from South Bronx Rubble," *New York Times,* July 25, 1986, A13; Alexander Von Hoffman, *House by House, Block by Block: The Rebirth of America's Urban Neighborhoods* (New York, 2003), 31–32.

81. "William J. Clinton, Remarks to the Bronx Community in New York City, December 10, 1997," www.presidency.ucsb.edu (accessed May 14, 2009).

82. "May 10 in Riverside; For 46, a Good Day to Go to Jail," *Los Angeles Sentinel,* May 12, 1999, A1; "Tenants Assail Conditions but Fail to Get New Housing Chief's Ear," *New York Times,* February 26, 1992, B3.

83. Joyce Jones, "Filling a Void," *Black Enterprise* 26 (November 1995): 24; "Protest for Affordable Housing," *Washington Post,* July 26, 1990, D1.

84. Von Hoffman, *House by House,* 15, 16.

85. Robert Worth, "Guess Who Saved the South Bronx? Big Government," *Washington Monthly* 31 (April 1999): 26–32.

86. David Muhammad, "An Historical Perspective," www.millionsmore movement.com (accessed May 14, 2009).

87. Devon W. Carbado, *Black Men on Race, Gender, and Sexuality: A Critical Reader* (New York, 1999), 27.

88. "Million Man March, October 16, 1995," www.pbs.org (accessed May 14, 2009).

89. Kristal Brent Zook, "A Manifesto of Sorts for a Black Feminist Movement," *New York Times,* November 12, 1995, SM86.

90. "Thirteen Ways of Looking at a Black Man," *New Yorker,* October 23, 1995.

91. Houston A. Baker, Jr., "America's War on Decency and a Call to the Mall: Black Men, Symbolic Politics, and the Million Man March," www.blackcultural studies.org (accessed May 14, 2009).

92. Michael C. Dawson, *Black Visions: The Roots of Contemporary African-American Political Ideologies* (Chicago, 2001), xii.

93. Brian Cross, *It's Not About a Salary: Rap, Race, and Resistance in Los Angeles* (London, 1994), 206.

94. Chang, *Can't Stop,* 327.

95. Patricia Hill Collins, *Fighting Words: Black Women and the Search for Justice* (Minneapolis, 1998), 76.

96. John Howard, *Men Like That: A Southern Queer History* (Chicago, 1999).

97. Cathy J. Cohen, *The Boundaries of Blackness: AIDS and the Breakdown of Black Politics* (Chicago, 1999), 96.

98. *USA Today,* June 11, 2001.

99. *New Pittsburgh Courier,* August 9, 2000.

100. Cohen, *Boundaries of Blackness,* 262.

101. Larry Aubry, "Urban Perspective: The Black Radical Congress," *Sentinel* 64, A7.

102. *New York Amsterdam News,* June 22, 2000.

103. *New York Amsterdam News,* February 5, 1998.

104. Ron Walters, "The Black Radical Congress," *Washington Informer,* July 1, 1998.

105. *Los Angeles Sentinel,* August 5, 1998.

106. *Washington Informer,* October 8, 1998.

Epilogue

1. Treshea N. Wade, "Is There Still a Reason to March in the 21st Century?" *New Pittsburgh Courier,* January 15, 2000, C4.

2. "March Held for Freedom over Poverty," *Sacramento Observer,* July 6–12, 2006, A7.

3. "Black Leaders Arrested at Protest," *Oakland Post,* May 17–23, 2006, 3.

4. Blake Gopnik, "Coloring Perception: Kerry James Marshall Thinks the Old Masters Have Room for a New Face: His Own," *Washington Post,* February 15, 2009.

5. *Kerry James Marshall, Along This Way* (exhibition guide), (London, 2005), 17–21. "Many Mansions," interview with Kerry James Marshall, PBS, www.pbs.org /art21/artists/marshall/clip1.html (accessed August 15, 2009).

6. Nikki Burns, "Report: 9 in 10 Black Farmers Shut out of $2.3 Billion Settlement," *Mississippi Link,* July 29–August 4, 2004, A1. Darryl Fears, "Protesters Take Over USDA Office in Tennessee," *Washington Post,* July 2, 2002, A3.

7. Jason DeParle, "What Happens to a Race Deferred?" *New York Times,* September 4, 2005, sec. 4:4.

8. Oral history interview with Pamela Mahogany, June 4, 2006, Interview U-0243, Southern Oral History Program Collection, www.docsouth.unc.edu (accessed August 7, 2009).

9. Barack Obama, "Remarks to the National Conference of Black Mayors in Baton Rouge, Louisiana," May 5, 2007, www.presidency.ucsb.edu (accessed August 7, 2009).

10. "Obama Warns of 'Quiet Riot' Among Blacks," June 5, 2007, www .cbs2chicago.com (accessed August 7, 2009).

11. George W. Bush, "Address to the Nation on Hurricane Katrina Recovery from New Orleans, Louisiana," 15 September 2005, www.presidency.ucsb.edu (accessed August 7, 2009).

12. Michael Fletcher, "Bush's Poverty Talk Is Now All but Silent; Aiding Poor Was Brief Priority after Katrina," *Washington Post,* July 20, 2006.

13. "The State of New Orleans By Numbers," *Southern Exposure* 34 (February/March 2006): 2, www.southernstudies.org (accessed August 7, 2009).

14. Ibid., 5.

15. *Wall Street Journal,* September 9, 2005.

16. Oral history interview with Stephen Bradberry, June 9, 2006, Interview U-0225, Southern Oral History Program Collection, www.lib.unc.edu/dc/sohp/ (accessed August 7, 2009).

17. Common Ground Collective, "Make History: Join the 'Second Freedom Rides' to Rebuild New Orleans, February 15, 2006," www.cwsworkshop.org/ katrinareader (accessed August 7, 2009).

18. Rebecca Solnit, "Lower Ninth Battles Back," *Nation,* August 23, 2007.

19. Jennifer Bihm, *Los Angeles Sentinel,* April 6–12, 2006.

20. Elena Everett, "Stopping the Bulldozers of New Orleans," *Southern Exposure* 34 (2006): 16–17.

21. Matt Bai, "Is Obama the End of Black Politics?" August 6, 2008, www .nytimes.com (accessed August 7, 2009).

22. Charles Hirschman, "Race and Ethnic Population Projections," in *American Diversity,* ed. Nancy Denton and Stewart Tolnay (Albany, NY, 2002), 53. Earl Hutchinson, *San Francisco Sun Reporter,* April 20, 2006; Leroy Robinson, *Indianapolis Recorder,* April 14, 2006; Jasmyne Cannick, *Real Times,* May 31, 2006; James Clingman, *Tennessee Tribune,* May 25, 2006.

23. *New York Amsterdam News,* August 22, 2002; "Blacks Gather to Discuss Reparations at National Convention in Chicago," *Jet,* February 26, 2001; Walter

Olson, "Reparations, R.I.P.," *City Journal* 18 (Autumn 2008); Martha Biondi, "The Rise of the Reparations Movement," *Radical History Review* 87 (Fall 2003): 5–18.

24. Andrew Miga, "New Orleans Activist Wins RFK Award," November 16, 2005, www.washingtonpost.com (accessed August 7, 2009).

25. Speech at funeral of Rosa Parks, November 2, 2005.

26. Felicia Lee, "Grieving for Parks, Rights Leaders Ponder Future," *New York Times,* October 31, 2005, 17.

27. Ibid.

28. Barack Obama, *The Audacity of Hope: Thoughts on Reclaiming the American Dream* (New York, 2006), 230.

29. Ibid., 233.

30. Barack Obama, "Address at the National Constitution Center in Philadelphia: 'A More Perfect Union,'" March 18, 2008, www.presidency.ucsb.edu (accessed August 7, 2009).

31. Barack Obama, *Dreams from My Father: A Story of Race and Inheritance* (New York, 2004), 140.

32. Obama, *The Audacity of Hope,* 11.

33. Abdon Pallasch, "Obama Tells Fathers to Meet Their Responsibilities," *Chicago Sun Times,* June 16, 2008.

34. Obama, *Dreams,* xvi.

35. Ibid., 52, 51.

36. Ibid., 48, 82, 85, 4.

37. Ibid., 202, 111.

38. Ibid., 134, 135.

39. Barack Obama, "Why Organize? Problems and Promise in the Inner City," in *After Alinsky: Community Organizing in Illinois,* ed. Peg Knoepfle, 35–40 (Springfield, IL, 1990).

40. Obama, *Dreams,* 278.

41. "Full Transcript of Obama interview with Chicago Public Radio, 2001," www.foxnews.com (accessed August 7, 2009).

42. Obama, "Why Organize?" 35–40. "Transcript," www.foxnews.com (accessed August 7, 2009).

43. John B. Judis, "Creation Myth," *New Republic,* September 10, 2008.

44. David Moberg, "Obama's Community Roots," April 3, 2007, www.thenation.com (accessed August 7, 2009).

45. Obama, *Audacity,* 244, 248.

46. Barack Obama, "Inaugural Address, January 20, 2009," www.presidency.ucsb.edu (accessed August 7, 2009).

47. Author telephone interview with Mitchell Diggs, Associate Director of Media & P.R., Ole Miss, 15 October, 2009.

48. Frank Newport, "Obama's Race May Be as Much a Plus as a Minus," October 9, 2008, www.gallup.com (accessed August 7, 2009).

49. Michael S. Lewis-Beck and Charles Tien, "Race Blunts the Economic Effect? The 2008 Forecast," *PS: Political Science and Politics* 42, no. 1 (January 2009): 21.

50. "2008 Surge in Black Voters Nearly Erased Racial Gap," July 20, 2009, www.nytimes.com (accessed August 7, 2009).

51. "Doubts Remain about Florida Vote," January 20, 2001, www.bbcnews.com (accessed August 7, 2009).

52. "Black Mayor of Mississippi Town Brings 'Atomic Bomb of Change,'" June 1, 2009, www.cnn.com (accessed August 7, 2009).

53. "First Black Mayor in City Known for Klan Killings," May 21, 2009, www.nytimes.com (accessed August 7, 2009).

54. "Fannie Lee Chaney," June 5, 2007, www.timesonline.co.uk (accessed August 7, 2009).

55. New York Times/CBS News Poll, April 22–26, 2009.

56. Wanda Sykes, White House Correspondents' Association Dinner, May 9, 2009.

57. Patricia J. Williams, "Mrs. Obama Meets Mrs. Windsor," April 8, 2009, www.thenation.com (accessed August 7, 2009).

58. Obama, *Dreams*, xiii.

59. Fox Butterfield, "First Black Elected to Head Harvard's Law Review," February 6, 1990, www.nytimes.com (accessed August 7, 2009).

60. Barack Obama, "Address at the National Constitution Center in Philadelphia: 'A More Perfect Union,'" March 18, 2008, www.presidency.ucsb.edu (accessed August 7, 2009).

61. "Transcript: President Obama's News Conference," March 24, 2009, www.nytimes.com (accessed August 4, 2009).

Acknowledgments

Fortunate is the person who gets to write history for a living, especially when that history is as important and gripping and perplexing and inspiring as the African American freedom struggle. So, my thanks to Pembroke College and the Oxford University History Department for giving me a job, and the British Arts and Humanities Research Council for funding my leave to finish writing.

I am fortunate, too, to have had many helpful colleagues at every stage of this research—at Cambridge, then Brown, then Oxford, and more generally from the academic world in Europe and America. Very many people have read parts of the manuscript in draft, discussed aspects of the book, answered questions, or replied at length to out-of-the-blue emails. I cannot begin to name everybody, and I am reluctant to name anybody for fear of leaving out other valued friends. But I am especially grateful to the (fool)hardy souls who read all or most of the manuscript and offered advice: Robert Cook, Gareth Davies, Simon Hall, Joe Martin, and Jim Patterson.

It was my students who suggested a website to go along with the book, and four of them—Verity Harding, Elizabeth Lane, Will Hazell, and Eleanor Thompson—have put the website together: www.weaintwhatwe oughttobe.com. Nick Juravich, Will, and especially Eleanor have helped with the research in the later stages too, and I am grateful to the Andrew W. Mellon Foundation for funding them.

I owe a great debt to archivists in scores of institutions, from the humble to the grand. As often as not, they didn't just call up materials, they suggested useful primary sources that I hadn't known about. In particular, the staffs at the Moorland-Spingarn Research Center in Washington, D.C., the Auburn Avenue Research Library in Atlanta, the National Archives in Maryland, and the Vere Harmsworth Library in Oxford went far beyond the call of duty. I am grateful, too, to the very many people who participated in this history and shared their recollections (and sometimes their papers or photographs) with me along the way. A book like this also draws on the remarkable work by literally thousands of historians—from local enthusiasts to research graduates to professional academics—on all aspects of the freedom struggle. For the sake of space, I had to limit the number of endnote references, but I am acutely aware that behind many a paragraph lies the help of an archivist or two and the thoughts of an historian or three.

My thanks to my literary agent, David Godwin, and his team for first approaching me and then getting excited about the manuscript. My thanks also to Joyce Selzer and others at Harvard University Press for their expertise, energy, efficiency, and good humor at every turn.

Many of the people to whom I owe my biggest debt—friends and family—knew little of this book except that I was writing it, and most of them probably aren't planning to read much beyond these acknowledgments (until provoked by this sentence, perhaps). Thanks to all of you, especially my parents, George and Norah.

Above all, I would like to thank my wife, Katie, for being wonderful. I dedicate this book to our dear children—Molly, Anna, Sam, and Amy—who have distracted me at every turn. I wouldn't want it any other way.

Index